T0180758

Communications
in Computer and Information Science   **2046**

Rationale

The CCIS series is devoted to the publication of proceedings of computer science conferences. Its aim is to efficiently disseminate original research results in informatics in printed and electronic form. While the focus is on publication of peer-reviewed full papers presenting mature work, inclusion of reviewed short papers reporting on work in progress is welcome, too. Besides globally relevant meetings with internationally representative program committees guaranteeing a strict peer-reviewing and paper selection process, conferences run by societies or of high regional or national relevance are also considered for publication.

Topics

The topical scope of CCIS spans the entire spectrum of informatics ranging from foundational topics in the theory of computing to information and communications science and technology and a broad variety of interdisciplinary application fields.

Information for Volume Editors and Authors

Publication in CCIS is free of charge. No royalties are paid, however, we offer registered conference participants temporary free access to the online version of the conference proceedings on SpringerLink (http://link.springer.com) by means of an http referrer from the conference website and/or a number of complimentary printed copies, as specified in the official acceptance email of the event.

CCIS proceedings can be published in time for distribution at conferences or as post-proceedings, and delivered in the form of printed books and/or electronically as USBs and/or e-content licenses for accessing proceedings at SpringerLink. Furthermore, CCIS proceedings are included in the CCIS electronic book series hosted in the SpringerLink digital library at http://link.springer.com/bookseries/7899. Conferences publishing in CCIS are allowed to use Online Conference Service (OCS) for managing the whole proceedings lifecycle (from submission and reviewing to preparing for publication) free of charge.

Publication process

The language of publication is exclusively English. Authors publishing in CCIS have to sign the Springer CCIS copyright transfer form, however, they are free to use their material published in CCIS for substantially changed, more elaborate subsequent publications elsewhere. For the preparation of the camera-ready papers/files, authors have to strictly adhere to the Springer CCIS Authors' Instructions and are strongly encouraged to use the CCIS LaTeX style files or templates.

Abstracting/Indexing

CCIS is abstracted/indexed in DBLP, Google Scholar, EI-Compendex, Mathematical Reviews, SCImago, Scopus. CCIS volumes are also submitted for the inclusion in ISI Proceedings.

How to start

To start the evaluation of your proposal for inclusion in the CCIS series, please send an e-mail to ccis@springer.com.

Bharathi Raja Chakravarthi · Bharathi B ·
Miguel Ángel García Cumbreras ·
Salud María Jiménez Zafra ·
Malliga Subramanian ·
Kogilavani Shanmugavadivel · Preslav Nakov
Editors

Speech and Language Technologies for Low-Resource Languages

Second International Conference, SPELLL 2023
Perundurai, Erode, India, December 6–8, 2023
Revised Selected Papers

Springer

Editors
Bharathi Raja Chakravarthi 🆔
National University of Ireland
Galway, Ireland

Miguel Ángel García Cumbreras 🆔
University of Jaén
Jaén, Jaén, Spain

Malliga Subramanian 🆔
Kongu Engineering College
Erode, Tamil Nadu, India

Preslav Nakov
Mohamed Bin Zayed University
of Artificial Intelligence
Abu Dhabi, Abu Dhabi,
United Arab Emirates

Bharathi B 🆔
Sri Sivasubramaniya Nadar College
of Engineering
Kalavakkam, Tamil Nadu, India

Salud María Jiménez Zafra 🆔
University of Jaén
Jaén, Jaén, Spain

Kogilavani Shanmugavadivel 🆔
Kongu Engineering College
Erode, Tamil Nadu, India

ISSN 1865-0929   ISSN 1865-0937 (electronic)
Communications in Computer and Information Science
ISBN 978-3-031-58494-7   ISBN 978-3-031-58495-4 (eBook)
https://doi.org/10.1007/978-3-031-58495-4

This Springer imprint is published by the registered company Springer Nature Switzerland AG
The registered company address is: Gewerbestrasse 11, 6330 Cham, Switzerland

Paper in this product is recyclable.

Preface

We are excited to present the proceedings of the Second International Conference on SPEech and Language technologies for Low-resource Languages (SPELLL 2023), which was held at Kongu Engineering College, Tamil Nadu, India, during 6–8 December, 2023. The conference was organized by a research group consisting of people from various academic institutions and industries across the globe. In particular, general chairs of SPELLL 2023 Anand Kumar M., Bharathi Raja Chakravarthi, Durairaj Thenmozhi, B. Bharathi, Subalalitha C. N. and Malliga Subramanian meticulously worked on all the finer details towards the successful organization of this conference. Colm O'Riordan of University of Galway, Ireland, Preslav Nakov of Mohamed Bin Zayed University of Artificial Intelligence, UAE, Ivan Koychev of Sofia University St. Kliment Ohridski, Bulgaria, Thomas Mandl of Universität Hildesheim, Germany, and Rafael Valencia-Garcia of Universidad de Murcia, Spain constituted the scientific advisory committee who gave continuous support towards conducting this conference. The aim of this series of conferences is to provide an international platform to discuss, exchange, disseminate, and cross-fertilize innovative ideas that solicit experimental and theoretical work and methods in solving problems and applications of current issues of speech and language technologies for low-resourced languages.

The enthusiastic response received for this second edition of the conference was overwhelming. The papers presented at the conference were across a spectrum of areas such as language resources, language technologies, speech technologies, and other related topics including multi-modal analysis. We reached out to more than 100 experts in the field of natural language processing to review the papers received. Each submitted paper went through comprehensive double-blind reviews by at least 3 reviewers and their review comments were communicated to the authors before the conference. Out of 94 papers received through the EquinOCS submission management system, only 33 papers were accepted and those papers were presented by authors from India and abroad. Our volume editors Bharathi Raja Chakravarthi of University of Galway, B. Bharathi of Sri Sivasubramaniya Nadar College of Engineering, India, Miguel Ángel García Cumbreras and Salud María Jiménez Zafra of Universidad de Jaén, Spain, Malliga Subramanian and Kogilavani Shanmugavadivel of Kongu Engineering College, India, and Preslav Nakov from Mohamed Bin Zayad University of Artificial Intelligence, UAE played a significant role in selecting these papers. The final submissions were checked by the program committee to ensure that all the comments had been addressed.

The conference proceedings were inaugurated on December 6, 2023 with an inaugural talk by S. Jaya Nirmala of National Institute of Technology, Trichy. Seven keynote talks were delivered at the conference. K. Parameshwari of IIIT, Hyderabad delivered a talk on Domain Adaptation in building neural machine translation: A Linguistic Enquiry, Kaja Dobrovoljc of Univerza v Ljubljani, Slovenia spoke on the topic Advantages and challenges of cross-lingually harmonized approaches to spoken data annotation, and

Genta Indra Winata of Bloomberg LP, New York delivered the keynote on Benchmarking Language Models on Underrepresented Languages. A talk on Computational models for poetry generation and automatic analysis of poetry was delivered by Manex Aguirrezabal Zabaleta of University of Copenhagen, Denmark, Endang Wahyu Pamungkas of Universitas Muhammadiyah Surakarta, Indonesia gave a talk on Hate Speech Detection in Low-Resourced Indonesian: Challenges and Opportunities, and Radhika Mamidi of IIIT, Hyderabad gave a talk on Dialog System. The conference was concluded with a talk by Steffen Eger of Bielefeld University, Germany on the topic Low-resource Text Generation and Evaluation.

Three workshops, namely "Second Workshop on Multimodal Machine Learning in Low-Resource Languages (MMLow 2023)", "Second Workshop on Fake News Detection in Low-Resource Languages (RegionalFake 2023)" and "Low Resource Cross-Domain, Cross-Lingual and Cross-Modal Offensive Content Analysis (LC4) - Multimedia and Generative AI" were collocated with SPELL 2023. The MMLow workshop was conducted on December 7, 2023 in which a talk was given by P. Balasubramanian, IIIT Kottayam. The LC4 workshop was conducted on December 8, 2023. In this workshop, a keynote talk was given by Kingshuk Banerjee, Hitachi India Pvt. Ltd, Bengaluru, on the topic Helping Convergence between Content and Creativity: A Generative AI Perspective. Another keynote was given by Dhivya Chinnappa, JP Morgan Chase & Co., USA. A session talk was given by Senthilnathan Chidambaranathan of Virtusa, USA on the topic Identifying the Fake News from the Multimodal Data in Low Resource Languages in the RegionalFake workshop, which was conducted on December 7, 2023. Presentations of the accepted papers were organized as 9 tracks which included 6 tracks for SPELLL and 1 for each workshop: MMLoW, RegionalFake, and LC4.

This volume contains revised versions of all thirty-three papers presented at the conference. We sincerely hope that these papers provide significant research contributions and advancements in the fields of speech and language technologies for low-resourced languages. We thank the Kongu Engineering College for their support and encouragement to host the second edition of SPELLL 2023, and Springer for publishing these proceedings. We thank all the scientific advisory committee members, program committee members, reviewers, session chairs, organizing committee members, and participants for their contributions towards the success of the conference.

December 2023

Bharathi Raja Chakravarthi
Bharathi B
Miguel Ángel García Cumbreras
Salud María Jiménez Zafra
Malliga Subramanian
Kogilavani Shanmugavadivel
Preslav Nakov

Organization

Scientific Advisory Committee

Colm O'Riordan	University of Galway, Ireland
Preslav Nakov	Mohamed Bin Zayed University of Artificial Intelligence, UAE
Ivan Koychev	Sofia University St. Kliment Ohridski, Bulgaria
Thomas Mandl	Universität Hildesheim, Germany
Rafael Valencia-Garcia	Universidad de Murcia, Spain

General Chairs

Anand Kumar M.	National Institute of Technology Karnataka, India
Bharathi Raja Chakravarthi	University of Galway, Ireland
Durairaj Thenmozhi	Sri Sivasubramaniya Nadar College of Engineering, India
B. Bharathi	Sri Sivasubramaniya Nadar College of Engineering, India
Subalalitha C. N.	SRM Institute of Science and Technology, India
Malliga Subramanian	Kongu Engineering College, India

Program Committee Chairs

N. Shanthi	Kongu Engineering College, India
C. S. Kanimozhiselvi	Kongu Engineering College, India
Kogilavani Shanmugavadivel	Kongu Engineering College, India
Ratnavel Rajalakshmi	Vellore Institute of Technology, Chennai, India
Ratnasingam Sakuntharaj	Eastern University, Sri Lanka
R. R. Rajalaxmi	Kongu Engineering College, India
Khalil Mirini	Meta, USA
Shibani Antonette	University of Technology Sydney, Australia

Program Committee

Alexander Gelbukh	National Polytechnic Institute, Mexico
Aline Villavicencio	University of Sheffield, UK
Alla Rozovskaya	Queens College (CUNY), USA
Aytuğ Onan	İzmir Katip Çelebi Üniversitesi, Bilgisayar Mühendisliği Bölümü, Turkey
Bharathi Ganesh	Resiliance Business Grids LLP, India
Bianca Pereira	University of Galway, Ireland
Brian Davis	Dublin City University, Ireland
Christiane D. Fellbaum	Princeton University, USA
Deepak Padmanabhan	Queen's University Belfast, UK
Dhanalakshimi V.	Pondicherry University, India
Dhivya Chinnappa	Thomson Reuters, USA
Dinesh Kumar Vishwakarma	Delhi Technological University, India
Emily Prudhommeaux	Boston College, USA
Eswari Rajagopal	National Institute of Technology Tiruchirappalli, India
Eva Schaeffer-Lacroix	Université INSPE de l'académie de Paris
Fausto Giunchiglia	Università di Trento, Italy
Grigori Sidorov	Centro de Investigación en Computación, Mexico
Hamdy Mubarak	Qatar Computing Research Institute, Qatar
Hanmin Jung	Korea Institute of Science and Technology Information, South Korea
Hung-Yu Kao	National Cheng Kung University, Taiwan
Jamin Shin	Hong Kong University of Science and Technology, China
José Antonio García-Díaz	University of Murcia, Spain
Kalika Bali	Microsoft Research, India
Kathleen McKeown	Columbia University, USA
Kevin Patrick Scannell	Saint Louis University, USA
Krisana Chinnasarn	Burapha University, Thailand
Malvina Nissim	University of Groningen, The Netherlands
Marcos Zampieri	Rochester Institute of Technology, USA
Marissa Griesel	University of South Africa, South Africa
Mathieu d'Aquin	University of Galway, Ireland
Manikandan Ravikiran	Hitachi Research and Development, India
Marta R. Costajussa	Universitat Politècnica de Catalunya, Spain
Md. Rezaul Karim	Fraunhofer FIT and RWTH Aachen University, Germany
Md. Shajalal	Fraunhofer FIT and University of Siegen, Germany

Melvin Johnson	Google, USA
Menno Van Zaanen	North-West University, South Africa
Miguel Ángel García	Universidad de Jaén, Spain
Monojit Choudhury	Microsoft Research, India
Pascale Fung	Hong Kong University of Science Technology, China
Paul Buitelaar	University of Galway, Ireland
Prasanna Kumar Kumaresan	Indian Institute of Information Technology and Management Kerala, India
Priya Rani	Insight SFI Research Centre for Data Analytics, Galway
Rahul Ponnusamy	Indian Institute of Information Technology and Management Kerala, India
Rafael Valencia-Garcia	Universidad de Murcia, Spain
Ruba Priyadharshini	Gandhigram Rural Institute-Deemed to be University, India
Sajeetha Thavareesan	Eastern University, Sri Lanka
Salud María Jiménez-Zafra	Universidad de Jaén, Spain
Sinnathamby Mahesan	University of Jaffna, Sri Lanka
Shashirekha	Mangalore University, India
Subalalitha C. N.	SRM Institute of Science and Technology, India
Taraka Rama	University of Texas, USA
Thomas Mandl	Universität Hildesheim, Germany
Valerio Basile	University of Turin, Italy
Viktor Hangya	Ludwig Maximilian University of Munich, Germany
Viviana Patti	Università di Torino, Italy
Yuta Koreeda	Hitachi Ltd., USA

Workshop Chairs

S. Angel Deborah	Sri Sivasubramaniya Nadar College of Engineering, India
Sangeetha Sivanesan	National Institute of Technology, Tiruchirappalli, India (lead)
Abirami Murugappan	Anna University, India
B. Krishnakumar	Kongu Engineering College, India
Eswari Rajagopal	National Institute of Technology, Tiruchirappalli, India
Gyorgy Kovacs	Luleå University of Technology, Sweden
Dhivya Chinnappa	Thomson Reuters, USA
Momchil Hardalov	Amazon AWS AI Lab, Spain

Additional Reviewers

Shubhanker Banerjee
Malliga S.
Kogilavani Shanmugavadivel
Kavi Priya S.
Angel Deborah S.
Nandhini Kumaresh
Ratnavel Rajalakshmi
Soubrayalu Sivakumar
Kingsy Grace R.
Arjun Paramarthalingam
Abirami Murugappan
Ramesh Kannan
Betina Antony
C. Jerin Mahibha
Rajalakshmi Sivanaiah
Josephine Griffith

Kayalvizhi Sampath
Rajeswari Natarajan
Kingston Thamburaj
Miguel Ángel García Cumbreras
Sangeetha Sivanesan
Richard Saldanha
Hariharan R. L.
György Kovács
Sripriya N.
Lakshmi Kanthan Narayanan
Deepak P.
Briskilal J.
Hosahalli Shashirekha
Anushiya Rachel Gladston
Manikandan Ravikiran

Contents

Language Resources

PolitiKweli: A Swahili-English Code-Switched Twitter Political Misinformation Classification Dataset

Cynthia Amol$^{(\boxtimes)}$ ⓘ, Lilian Wanzare ⓘ, and James Obuhuma ⓘ

Maseno University, Maseno, Kenya
{cynthia,ldwanzare,jobuhuma}@maseno.ac.ke
https://www.maseno.ac.ke/

Abstract. In the age of freedom of speech, users of the various social media platforms post millions of unverified messages, resulting in misinformation. Despite these platforms' set policies against misinformation, there is an alarming rise in misleading news dissemination. On political matters, misinformation online can result in defamation and in extreme cases, violence offline. Misinformation classification involves classifying text as fake or fact. Most of the existing studies address misinformation classification for posts in a single language only. Among most bilingual or multilingual social media users, code-switching such as Swahili-English, is common practice. This poses a threat to code-switching being used to spread misinformation. There is need for more research in low-resource languages such as Swahili, especially their use to spread misinformation. This study curated the PolitiKweli (dataset: https://github.com/jayneamol/kweli) dataset, a Swahili-English code-switched misinformation classification dataset, containing 6,345 Swahili-English code-switched texts, 22,954 English texts and 211 Swahili texts. The texts are labeled as fake, fact or neutral as compared to fact-checked Twitter dataset also created as part of this study. The paper discusses the dataset curation process including data collection, data processing and data annotation. It also highlights the challenges during the annotation. The study develops a benchmark classification model based on pretrained language model BERT that achieves an F-score of 0.62. The results of the experiment show promising results on the usefulness of the Swahili-English code-switched misinformation classification models. When applied, the classification model can be able to flag instances of misinformation on social media platforms.

Keywords: code-switching · low-resource language · swahili · misinformation classification

1 Introduction

The increasing popularity of social media has shifted the preference of information dissemination channels from mainstream media to digital platforms. Social

B. R. Chakravarthi et al. (Eds.): SPELLL 2023, CCIS 2046, pp. 3–17, 2024.
https://doi.org/10.1007/978-3-031-58495-4_1

media platforms such as Twitter offer real-time, more interactive and less censored channels to follow and comment on current topics [2,27]. Previous studies [18,24,27,31,34] on misinformation and hate speech detection have used social media platforms such as Twitter, Reddit and Facebook as sources of high volume data. When online, social media users are often emboldened by the anonymity of an online persona [13] and take advantage of the lack of accountability to fuel the spread of misleading information. By posting fake messages, links or re-posting other users' misleading news, social media users can easily amplify one false post, causing it to trend and sometimes be picked up by mainstream news channels.

Various definitions of misinformation have been coined by previous studies. [12] defines misinformation as information that is unambiguously false, explaining that misinformation occurs when a person firmly holds wrong information. In [35], misinformation is considered circulating information that is false regardless of the intention of the spreader. In their review of definitions of misinformation, the study [3] concludes that the two most popular definitions of misinformation are 'false and misleading information' and 'false and misleading information spread unintentionally' depending on the methods (qualitative or quantitative) of respective experts questioned. Twitter defines misinformation as claims that have been confirmed to be false by external or subject-matter experts [39]. In this study, we adopted the definition by [34]: false and intentionally or unintentionally misleading news, hyper-partisan news and satirical news.

Since misinformation classification involves identifying and classifying text as either false or fact by comparing the text to fact-checked data, the accuracy of classification models are hugely dependant on the nature and quality of training data. Datasets form the basis for training, evaluating, and benchmarking machine learning models [28]. Classification models therefore need high volume, high quality training datasets to be able to classify text accurately. Most existing misinformation classification datasets are in a single language such as English. Low-resource languages such as Swahili are relatively unexplored [38] despite their rising number of speakers, especially in the creation of large datasets to train machine learning models that perform tasks such as misinformation classification. Some of the publicly available Swahili datasets [1,17,22,38] have been applied in named entity recognition, sentiment analysis and hate-speech detection. Africa and India host around 2000 low-resource languages [16]. So far, there is hardly any work involving East African languages in detecting misinformation on social media [24]. Currently, a Swahili-English code-switched misinformation classification dataset does not exist.

A more challenging aspect of misinformation detection is Code-switching, which is the mixing of words, phrases and sentences from distinct grammatical systems across sentence boundaries [7]. Code-switching introduces a degree of semantic complexity to phrases or sentences which negatively impacts the accuracy of models trained on a single language only when classifying code-switched text [27]. This makes it necessary to curate code-switched datasets to train these models on classification tasks involving code-switched data. Studies such as [24, 27, 31] address code-switching in Luganda-English, Swahili-English and Hindi-English respectively. The study by [37] argues that machines have to understand what is being said in varied registers to be able to partake in human conversations.

This study contributes to efforts in low-resource research and detection of misinformation in the context of code-switching by curating a novel dataset: PolitiKweli. This dataset is a Swahili-English misinformation classification dataset built from tweets relating to the highly contested 2022 General Elections in Kenya. The focus of this study were tweets relating to voter education, the polling process and results broadcasting voting posted pre, post and during the 2022 General Elections in Kenya. The study also curates a fact-checked dataset of tweets posted by Kenya's electoral commission, Independent Electoral and Boundaries Commission, verified Twitter handle.

PolitiKweli dataset can be used to train and test text classification models which can be applied to Twitter and other social media platforms to flag cases of misinformation on political issues in Swahili-English code-switched texts. Misinformation classification helps preserve the integrity of news posted on social media and curb any adverse effects that may result from misinformation.

The rest of the paper is structured as follows: Sect. 2 discusses code-switching on social media while Sect. 3.1 focuses on the context of misinformation on Twitter. In Sect. 4, related studies are discussed. Section 5 outlines the methodology used while Sect. 6 discusses results from experiments. We offer conclusions and recommendations for future work in Sect. 7.

2 Code-Switching on Social Media

Code-switching involves the mixing of words, phrases and sentences from distinct grammatical systems across sentence boundaries [7]. The occurrence of code-switching is frequent in conversations among people who are familiar with each other and have a shared educational, ethnic and socio-economic background [11]. Such switching is typically considered informal and is more likely to be found in speech and in casual text as now found in social media [37] among bilingual or multilingual communities.

There are different types of code-switching according to [11]; intra-sentential switching, inter-sentential switching, establishing continuity switches and emblematic switching. Intra-sentential switching occurs when more than one language is used within a phrase or sentence boundary while inter-sentential switching occurs when more than one language is used between phrase or sentence boundaries. When establishing continuity, switching occurs when a speaker continues the utterance of a previous speaker. For instance, when answering a question asked in Swahili, a speaker may switch from a previous English speech by using Swahili phases or sentences. Emblematic switching occurs in tags or exclamations where a word in one language is inserted into utterance in a different language. A study by [33] indicates that the extent and type of code-switching can vary across language pairs around and 3.5% of tweets were code-switched. Social media platforms such as Twitter are therefore major sources of code-switched data in this digital age.

Table 1 shows some of the variations in code-switched texts. In the first sentence, English and Swahili words are used successively. It reads, 'propaganda *imeganda* [is stuck] people *kama huna* [if you don't have] facts dont talk *na watu haujui* [people you don't know]'. The second sentence is an instance of two independent English and Swahili sentences used consecutively. It reads '*kwa hivyo kuibiwa ni shida* [is being stolen from a problem] why hurt them'. In the third sentence, one Swahili word in used in an English sentence. It reads: 'we will be voting through secret ballot *sindio* [right?]'.

Table 1. Variations in code-switched texts.

Language	Text	Type
|eng |swa |eng |swa |eng |swa	|propaganda |imeganda |people |kama huna |facts dont talk |na watu haujui	Intra-setential
|swa |eng	|kwa hivyo kuibiwa ni shida |why hurt them	Inter-setential
|eng |swa	|we will be voting through secret ballot |sindio	Emblematic

Use of Swahili-English Code-Switching on Social Media. Swahili (Kiswahili) is a language in the Bantu family [14] spoken by more than 100 million people in both Eastern and Central Africa. With the rapid development of social networks, Swahili is also spreading in online places that result in the growth of web data [17]. Swahili-English code-switching is mostly used in informal communication. In Kenya, both Swahili and English are considered national languages [14]. Aside from the use of standard Swahili or English and other native languages, an ever-evolving slang (sheng') is often developed among social media users[1].

3 Political Misinformation on Social Media

The power of using misinformation to shape public opinion, especially in politics, dates back to the world wars. According to Twitter, political content is content that references a candidate, political party, election or referendum. This includes regulation, and judicial outcome [39]. In the past, politicians and journalists in the mainstream media affected the themes and contents of the public debate,

---

[1] The aspect of slag is not discussed in this study and left for future work.

however, their capacity for social influence has weakened in the digital environment [8]. Twitter is a prominent stage where conversations and political communication takes place and in the current hybrid media system, discussions can have an impact on both the agenda of mainstream media and the offline political life [8]. Despite the platform's defined policies against misinformation dissemination, multiple posts relating to misleading news were flagged and labeled. Disinformation campaigns like these can fuel more chaos and distrust online and spiral into violence offline [21]. Twitter, used mostly by 26-35-year-old users [26] not only an avenue to share news and comment on current topics but also makes it convenient for users to post or repost information, to follow other users and get informed about them and their posts [18]. This has birthed the era of 'alternative journalism' [25] where any person with a smart phone and internet connection can create and disseminate news whether fact-checked or not.

3.1 Case of Kenyan Politics on Twitter

Kenya is a multicultural country with 42(+) tribes [5] each speaking non-mutually intelligible dialects and two national languages. According to [23], Kenya is one of the leading countries in terms of online blogging in Africa and Twitter is considered a platform for political engagement. Major political events such as general elections in Kenya are tweeted about widely. Despite policies against misinformation dissemination and Twitter's efforts to label or take down misleading content, multiple posts relating to fake polls, unverified electoral results, and unsubstantiated statements from individuals and political parties were flagged [21]. Misinformation, especially on political issues may result in polarisation of the country along political divides which in turn may cause violence offline. The social media platform Twitter is often used to mobilize Kenyans on the internet to stage protests in the streets [23]. On the Kenyan Twitter space, code-switching is often used to spread misinformation. With the number of social media users in Kenya steadily, there is a need to ensure that users have access to credible information especially on sensitive issues like politics.

4 Related Work

This section discusses related work on misinformation detection with specific focus on code-switching in low-resource settings.

There are several previous studies that have developed datasets and models for misinformation detection, particularly for English. 'FACTOID' [34] is an English language dataset designed for misinformation detection on Reddit. The dataset was built by classifying Reddit users as 'misinformation spreaders' versus 'real news spreaders' and assigning credibility scores to each user based on the factuality of the news sources. The datasets 'FakeNewsNet' by [36] and 'ISOT' used by [4] were built for fake news detection tasks. FakeNewsNet [36] is in English and contains instances of fake news campaigns by Twitter users and who they follow which can be used to create a social network of various spreaders of fake news [18]. The dataset 'ISOT' used by the study [4] on the other hand, contains English language news stories sourced from Reuters, Wikipedia, Politifact. The real articles were gathered from the Reuters website, while the fake or false ones were from different sites identified as fictitious by Wikipedia and Politifact.

When it comes to code-switching, the study by [24] curated a Luganda-English code-mixed COVID-19 misinformation classification dataset by comparing tweets and Facebook posts about COVID-19 against credible information posted by the Ugandan Ministry of Health. The posts were annotated as 'misinformation' or 'no-misinformation'. In the study by [27], a Swahili- English code-mixed dataset was created from tweets from the 2017 and 2012 general election in Kenya. The dataset focused on hate-speech rather than misinformation detection. A similar hate-speech detection dataset was created by [31] for Indian Political Memes (IPM). IPM [31] is a Hinglish (Hindi-English) code-switched dataset and contains memes - satirical image with text sourced from social media. The texts were then separated from the images before annotation as 'hate-inducing', 'satirical and benign' or 'non-offensive'.

Some of the publicly available datasets that focus on low-resource languages including Swahili are 'Afrisenti' [22] that looks at sentiment analysis based on Twitter data for several African languages including Swahili, 'Kencorpus' [38] that focuses on collection general texts for several Kenyan languages including Swahili, and 'MasakhaNER' [1] focused on Named Entity Recognition (NER) tasks for Swahili and other African languages. The process of creation of these datasets include data collection, data cleaning and data annotation or labeling.

During the creation of PolitiKweli, we took inspiration from the studies by [22,24,27,38] in dataset creation for code-switched texts and exploration of the low-resource language, Swahili.

5   Methodology

An exploratory research design was applied in order to curate the dataset. The process begun with data collection using the Twitter API, followed by a data processing step to remove any unusable characters or texts and lastly a data annotation step with a team of annotators as shown in Fig. 1. The output is PolitiKweli dataset, a Swahili-English code-switched dataset for misinformation detection.

5.1   Data Collection

Data on Twitter was collected using Twitter Academic API [39] which offers access to historical data as in [22]. The study collected approximately 50,000 tweets posted between 4th October, 2021 which was the first day of voter registration for 2022 elections in Kenya and 5th September, 2022 when the contested presidential election results were upheld by the Supreme Court of Kenya. The

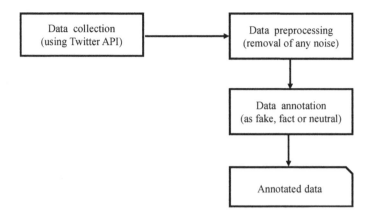

Fig. 1. Dataset curation process

collection was aimed at sampling tweets on the electoral process including voter registration, voter education, opinion polling, voting, results transmission and results declaration.

In order to get relevant tweets, the study experimented with several keywords based on hashtags, mentions, users and politically related keywords. In the end, the collection process involved sampling of tweets with hashtags relating to elections that trended during the election period and had the highest number of engagements such as *#ElectionsBilaNoma, #KenyaElections2022, #KURA 2022, #Uamuzi2022, #KenyaDecides2022* and *#GE2022*. For keywords, the study used some of the most frequent keywords during the election period such as *kura, elections, vote, general elections* and *tallying*. The study also used mentioned of the top contenders such as *@RailaOdinga* and *@WilliamsRuto*. In order to get factual information, the keyword *@IEBCKenya*, which is the verified, official Twitter handle of the Independent Electoral and Boundaries Commission (IEBCKenya), was used. Only tweets posted by this user or tweets retweeted by this user were considered as factual.

The data collection process resulted in two sets of tweets: general posts by various Twitter users about the 2022 General Elections in Kenya and the official tweets and retweets posted by the electoral body. The data collected from the official Twitter handle of the electoral body were regarded as the factual data.

5.2   Data Processing

Data processing involved manual language identification, data cleaning and normalisation, and data anonymization.

Language Identification. The data was sourced from a multilingual social media user group thus the presence of several other languages in one tweet was anticipated. The data collection process produced tweets in languages that were different from the target ones (Swahili-English) necessitating language detection, including code-switching between Swahili/English and other local Kenyan languages. For instance, a tweet such as '*@user itimo marach [you have done wrong] to reveal this about the commissioner*' is a code-switched Luo-English sentence while '*omogaka [my leader] i stand to be corrected, is this the candidate to beat in the ballot*' is a code-switched Kisii-English. Such Tweets were manually identified and removed from the dataset.[2]

We took inspiration on a similar manual language identification methodology as [22]. A manual language identification process was done due to semantic complexities of code-switched data and a lack of tools to automatically identify the local languages. A team of ten annotators labeled the data in four categories: 'Swahili-English', 'Swahili', 'English' or 'Other'. The output of the language identification process was four sets of data classified data according to language category.

Measure of Code-Switching: To measure the extent of code-switching in the collected data, we employed the Multilingual Index (M-index) [6] as a Measurement of code-switching. The M-Index calculated is a word-count-based measure that quantifies the inequality of the distribution of language tags in a corpus of at least two languages [10]. The M-index is 0 when the corpus is monolingual and 1 when there is equal distribution of tokens across all the languages. Our code-switched texts had an average M- index of 0.67 which indicated good level of code-switching.

Data Cleaning. Posts on Twitter are not limited to text-only. A single message could have texts, emojis, links, photo and video attachments which may make the text analysis process quite complex. This study focused on text-only messages thus the data cleaning and normalisation process resulted in removal of any advertisements, URLs, emojis, special characters such as hashtags (#) and stopwords such as 'the', 'of', 'and', 'to' [40]. Some other factors that resulted in removal of text from the raw corpus were usability and validity.

Usability: aside from regulation on the maximum number of characters per post, Twitter does not have restrictions on the type and quality of posts. During labeling, almost 40% of the text were unusable because of the nature of text. Some were single word only, contained links only or comprised of emojis only. Some of the texts also contained coarse language and derogatory terms and were therefore not considered usable.

Validity: since the key word 'elections' was used in data collection, some of the texts referred to other elections that were conducted in the country during the same period. The focus of the study was on the general elections in 2022 so the data had to be dropped.

---

[2] As part of the larger project, we plan to expand the dataset to include code-switched texts for other local languages.

Data Anonymization: The data anonymization process involved changing of any mentions to @user to protect identities of Twitter users mentioned in tweets. Despite most Twitter users not being aware that their posts are public and available for analysis [2], data anonymization was essential in line with ethical and data protection regulations. In addition to anonymization, the human annotators were bound by signed data privacy agreements to keep identities of data subjects and message contents confidential.

5.3   Data Annotation

Data annotation can be done in three ways: manually by using human annotators, semi-automatically or fully-automatically [30]. Semi-automatically or fully-automatically can be done using websites like mediabiasfactcheck.com as used in the annotation of the dataset, FACTOID [34]. While manual annotation is disadvantageous in that human annotators are susceptible to bias, automating annotation of a code-switched dataset may not be feasible due to the grammatically complex nature of code-switched texts. Most automated annotators like mediabiasfactcheck.com are built for single languages, especially English.

The study employed a team of ten annotators to label the processed data as fake, false or neutral. The team consisted of 6 undergraduate students and 4 post-graduate students. They used Google Sheets which allowed for collaborative editing both online and offline. All the annotators were fluent in both English and Swahili. The grammatical complexity of code-switched texts necessitated that the human annotators be conversant with both languages used. The ten annotators were divided in 5 teams meaning each tweet was annotated by at least two annotators. In case of annotator disagreement, the study lead assigned a third annotator drawn from the other groups to intervene and the majority rule would be applied to resolve conflict.

The study took inspiration from studies such as [22,27] that have conducted annotations in low-resource code-switched setting to develop the annotator guidelines. The study adopted the definition of misinformation as false, misleading, hyper-partisan and satirical news [34] and used this to guide the development of the annotation guidelines. The developed guidelines were communicated and discussed with the teams over several annotation meetings. The annotation guidelines, such as in such as [19], covered data privacy, data labeling rules including ways of labeling questions and sarcastic statements and conflict resolution procedure. In data privacy, the guidelines covered prohibition of both redistribution of the data to third parties and discussing data subjects or contents outside the annotation groups.

We broadly defined three labels: Fake, Fact and Neutral. Fake label was assigned to texts that could be proven as false compared to the fact-checked dataset, the Fact label was assigned to texts that could be proven as true compared to the fact- checked dataset while Neutral label was assigned to texts that were neither fact nor false, merely an opinion that could not be fact-checked.

Table 2 shows sample tweets and their labels. In Table 2, the tweet is the message posted by users of Twitter on the electoral process of the general election in Kenya in 2022. The messages can be in any language as Twitter, like all social media sites, allows users to post any message. The messages are restricted to 280 characters or less [29].

Table 2. Data labeling.

Text	Label
spoilt ballots haziingi kwa [*are not inserted in*] ballot box, hio ni [*that is*] rejected	Fact
kama [*if*] voter amepewa [*is given*] six ballot papers and he only vote one, he rest of the ballot papers are return to the clerks because he hasnt marked the papers	Fake
if everything aligns sisi tutakua kwa [*we will also be in*] ballot paper pia 2027	Neutral

Measure of Annotator Agreement. Annotator agreement was determined by calculating the Free-Marginal Multirater Kappa score. Unlike the Cohen's Kappa and Fleiss' Kappa which are fixed-marginal kappa and only allow a rater to select exactly one category for each subject [20], the Free-Marginal Multirater Kappa is recommended when raters select from more than one category - in the case of this study, three categories, and do not know a priori how cases are to be distributed in categories [22,32]. The Kappa scores were then interpreted according to the Kappa Interpretation Table [15].

During the pilot annotation session, all annotators including the lead annotators were divided in 3 teams of 3–4 people each. The teams' (Team 1, Team 2 and Team 3) grouping was done randomly. The annotation agreement scores were based on the initial 3 groups. The scores are as shown in Table 3.

A lower Kappa score was realized in certain teams during the pilot annotation session because of the individual interpretations of fake and factual news and the effect of sarcasm on the meaning of certain phrases. In order to ensure that all team members were on the same page during labeling, more joint training sessions were conducted and the fact-checked dataset expanded to cover more topics. This improved the quality of annotated data. After several rounds of discussions, 5 teams of 2 people each were created and each group was assigned a lead annotator to coordinate the process and resolve any conflicts.

Data Annotation Challenges. During the annotation process, the team encountered certain challenges. Some of these challenges including cost of the study, fundamental disagreements among team members and the complex nature of texts are discussed earlier in this section.

Table 3. Pilot Annotation Kappa Scores.

Team	Score
Team 1	0.48
Team 2	0.53
Team 3	0.40

Disagreements. During the pilot labeling sessions, there were concerns over definitions of 'fake' and 'false' especially when handling opinions or predictions of election results. For instance, a tweet like *'candidate x has won seat y'* before official gazettement by the electoral commission. In order to guide the annotators during the labeling process, timestamps were appended to each tweet. Anything posted before the official results were considered misinformation. This improved consensus among the various teams which in turn improved the quality of the annotated data.

Satire. Some of the texts in the raw corpus had elements of satire which is common in social media political commentary. This resulted in difference in opinion on labels to be used in annotation. Such cases were referred to the lead annotator who resolved the conflicts. An example of satirical text is the text *'wewe [you] @user umekuwa [are you] head ya [of] iebc'*. Which points to some user asking if he or she has become the head of IEBC. Such texts were considered neutral.

Cost. Dataset curation is an expensive process. Since the study did not have any external funding, the cost of research was shouldered by the researchers themselves. The research therefore relied heavily on volunteers whose adherence to schedules was constrained by other commitments. Despite these challenges, the volunteers were generous with available time and skills. The annotation period had to be extended to ensure that all the clean data was annotated correctly.

5.4 Data Analysis

We collected approximately 50,000 tweets using the parameters discussed in Sect. 5.1. The collected tweets comprised relevant posts about the electioneering process and some posts that were considered irrelevant by this study such as advertisements. These irrelevant posts and posts in any other language other than the target languages - Swahili and English were removed. During the cleaning process, we removed over 40% of the tweets resulting in a usable dataset containing 29,510 texts as summarized in Table 4: 6,345 Swahili-English texts, 22,954 English texts and 211 Swahili texts. Table 4 shows a summary of the total number of clean texts per language. The fact-checking dataset collected using *@IEBCKenya* user contained 1,817 tweets.

Table 4. Summary of the number of texts per language.

Language	Number of texts
swa-eng	6345
eng	22954
swa	211

The total number of labeled texts in the PolitiKweli dataset is 29,510 with most of the data being *Neutral*, followed by *Fact*. The *Fake* label had the fewest datapoints. A summary of the respective labels per language and per label is shown in Table 5. The fact-checked dataset was mostly in English as they were tweets from the official electoral commission's Twitter handle.

Table 5. Summary of the respective labels per language.

Data	eng-swa	eng	swa
Factual	1221	6065	8
Neutral	4094	13380	19
Fake	1030	3512	184

6   Experimentation and Results

For the experiments, we only focused on data that was code-switched. The Swahili-English code-switched dataset comprised of 6,345 labeled texts as shown in Table 4. The data was split into 80% training set and 20% test set. This resulted in 5,076 texts used in training and 1,269 text in testing.

We developed a benchmark misinformation detection classifier based on BERT pre-trained language model [9]. Previous comparable studies show that both monolingual and multilingual pre-trained language models perform averagely better with datasets in low-resource languages such as Swahili since these models are either trained with limited low-resource language data or not trained with data in these languages at all. With BERT, the Kencorpus [38] dataset containing Swahili and other African languages, for instance, achieved 60% accuracy while AfriSenti [22] achieved 61.5 accuracy for Swahili data with AfriBERTa.

For the benchmark model, we used the BERT [9] pretrained language model with one dense layer, 0.1 dropout, Adam's optimizer, categorical cross-entropy, trained in 5 epochs initially then 10 epochs. For evaluation, we used the standard metrics of precision, recall and f-score. Table 6 shows the results of the experiment.

The low performance can be attributed to the pre-trained model being trained on mono-lingual data. In the case of code-switching, texts are semantically complex.

Table 6. Results of experiment.

BERT	Scores
Precision	0.53
Recall	0.76
F-score	0.62

7   Conclusion and Future Work

This study set out to curate a Swahili-English code-switched misinformation classification dataset. Data was collected, cleaned and annotated. Our contribution is therefore two datasets. The first dataset named PolitiKweli, has three sets of texts: 6,345 Swahili-English texts, 22,954 English texts and 211 Swahili texts. The second dataset is a fact-checking dataset containing 1,817 tweets (texts and links) sourced from Kenya's official electoral body's Twitter posts.

The PolitiKweli dataset can be used to train models that perform classification tasks for both Swahili-English code-mixed texts, English only texts and Swahili only texts. Aside from text classification, the dataset can be tailored to train models that identify and map misinformation-spreading social media accounts. The fact-checking dataset can be used to annotate social media texts, especially in the context of Kenyan elections.

With constant advancements in technology and increased use of code-switching in the new generations of language speakers, there is need for more research in low-resource languages such as Swahili. This study paves way for more research in code-switching and ways that machine learning can be leveraged to provide solutions for constantly evolving problems such as misinformation detection on social media. As an extension to this study, further experimentation with fine-tuned, pre-trained multilingual language models trained on Swahili and English datasets is expected to result in better accuracy and precision. Additionally, further work involving use of text matching tools trained to match code-switched text would automate annotation and enable curation of larger datasets using less resources.

Acknowledgements. We acknowledge the contributions of Shamsuddeen Hassan who assisted with the data collection from Twitter, Martin Okech, Edwin Onkoba and the Maseno University School of Computing and Informatics staff and students. We thank Mary Gitaari, Ezekiel Maina, Nelson Odhiambo, Stephen Otieno, Monicah Odipo, Harrison Kioko, Elphas Otieno, Bowa Marita, Peter Gathuita and Samwel Okonda for their contribution in data annotation.

References

1. Adelani, D.I., et al.: Masakhaner: named entity recognition for African languages. Trans. Assoc. Comput. Linguist. **9**, 1116–1131 (2021)

2. Ahmed, W., Bath, P.A., Demartini, G.: Using twitter as a data source: an overview of ethical, legal, and methodological challenges. Ethics Online Res. **2**, 79–107 (2017)
3. Altay, S., Berriche, M., Heuer, H., Farkas, J., Rathje, S.: A survey of expert views on misinformation: definitions, determinants, solutions, and future of the field. Harvard Kennedy School Misinformation Rev. **4**(4), 1–34 (2023)
4. Amer, E., Kwak, K.S., El-Sappagh, S.: Context-based fake news detection model relying on deep learning models. Electronics **11**(8), 1255 (2022)
5. Balaton-Chrimes, S.: Who are Kenya's 42 (+) tribes? The census and the political utility of magical uncertainty. J. Eastern Afr. Stud. **15**(1), 43–62 (2021)
6. Barnett, R., et al.: The lides coding manual: a document for preparing and analyzing language interaction data version 1.1–july 1999. Int. J. Bilingualism **4**(2), 131–271 (2000)
7. Candra, L.K., Qodriani, L.U.: An analysis of code switching in leila s. chudori's for nadira. Teknosastik **16**(1), 9–14 (2019)
8. Casero-Ripollés, A.: Influencers in the political conversation on twitter: identifying digital authority with big data. Sustainability **13**(5), 2851 (2021)
9. Devlin, J., Chang, M.W., Lee, K., Toutanova, K.: Bert: pre-training of deep bidirectional transformers for language understanding. arXiv preprint arXiv:1810.04805 (2018)
10. Guzmán, G.A., Ricard, J., Serigos, J., Bullock, B.E., Toribio, A.J.: Metrics for modeling code-switching across corpora. In: Interspeech, pp. 67–71 (2017)
11. Hoffmann, C.: In introduction to bilingualism, ed. Logman, Newyork (1991)
12. Jerit, J., Zhao, Y.: Political misinformation. Annu. Rev. Polit. Sci. **23**, 77–94 (2020)
13. Köchler, H.: Idea and politics of communication in the global age. In: Digital Transformation in Journalism and News Media: Media Management, Media Convergence and Globalization, pp. 7–15 (2017)
14. Kresse, K., Vierke, C.: Swahili language and literature as resources for Indian ocean studies. Hist. Compass **20**(7), e12725 (2022)
15. Landis, J.R., Koch, G.G.: An application of hierarchical kappa-type statistics in the assessment of majority agreement among multiple observers. Biometrics 363–374 (1977)
16. Magueresse, A., Carles, V., Heetderks, E.: Low-resource languages: a review of past work and future challenges. arXiv preprint arXiv:2006.07264 (2020)
17. Martin, G., Mswahili, M.E., Jeong, Y.S., Woo, J.: Swahbert: language model of swahili. In: Proceedings of the 2022 Conference of the North American Chapter of the Association for Computational Linguistics: Human Language Technologies, pp. 303–313 (2022)
18. Michail, D., Kanakaris, N., Varlamis, I.: Detection of fake news campaigns using graph convolutional networks. Int. J. Inf. Manag. Data Insights **2**(2), 100104 (2022)
19. Mohammad, S.: A practical guide to sentiment annotation: challenges and solutions. In: Proceedings of the 7th Workshop on Computational Approaches to Subjectivity, Sentiment and Social Media Analysis, pp. 174–179 (2016)
20. Moons, F., Vandervieren, E.: Measuring agreement among several raters classifying subjects into one-or-more (hierarchical) nominal categories. a generalisation of fleiss' kappa. arXiv preprint arXiv:2303.12502 (2023)
21. Mozilla: New research: In Kenya, disinformation campaigns seek to discredit pandora papers (2021). https://foundation.mozilla.org/en/blog/new-research-in-kenya-disinformation-campaigns-seek-to-discredit-pandora-papers/
22. Muhammad, S.H., et al.: Afrisenti: a twitter sentiment analysis benchmark for African languages. arXiv preprint arXiv:2302.08956 (2023)

23. Mukhongo, L.L.: Participatory media cultures: virality, humour, and online political contestations in Kenya. Afr. Spectr. **55**(2), 148–169 (2020)
24. Nabende, P., Kabiito, D., Babirye, C., Tusiime, H., Nakatumba-Nabende, J.: Misinformation detection in luganda-english code-mixed social media text. arXiv preprint arXiv:2104.00124 (2021)
25. Ogola, G.: # whatwouldmagufulido? Kenya's digital "practices" and "individuation" as a (non) political act. J. East. Afr. Stud. **13**(1), 124–139 (2019)
26. Okoth, G.B.W.: How Kenyans on twitter use visuals as a form of political protest. J. Kommunikation. Medien 1–27 (2020)
27. Ombui, E., Muchemi, L., Wagacha, P.: Hate speech detection in code-switched text messages. In: 2019 3rd International Symposium on Multidisciplinary Studies and Innovative Technologies (ISMSIT), pp. 1–6. IEEE (2019)
28. Paullada, A., Raji, I.D., Bender, E.M., Denton, E., Hanna, A.: Data and its (dis) contents: a survey of dataset development and use in machine learning research. Patterns **2**(11) (2021)
29. X developer platform documentation (2023). https://developer.twitter.com/en/docs
30. Qureshi, M.A., et al.: A novel auto-annotation technique for aspect level sentiment analysis. Comput. Mater. Contin. **70**(3), 4987–5004 (2022)
31. Rajput, K., Kapoor, R., Rai, K., Kaur, P.: Hate me not: detecting hate inducing memes in code switched languages. arXiv preprint arXiv:2204.11356 (2022)
32. Randolph, J.J.: Free-marginal multirater kappa (multirater k [free]): an alternative to fleiss' fixed-marginal multirater kappa. Online submission (2005)
33. Rijhwani, S., Sequiera, R., Choudhury, M., Bali, K., Maddila, C.S.: Estimating code-switching on twitter with a novel generalized word-level language detection technique. In: Proceedings of the 55th Annual Meeting of the Association for Computational Linguistics (Volume 1: Long Papers), pp. 1971–1982 (2017)
34. Sakketou, F., Plepi, J., Cervero, R., Geiss, H.J., Rosso, P., Flek, L.: Factoid: a new dataset for identifying misinformation spreaders and political bias. arXiv preprint arXiv:2205.06181 (2022)
35. Shahi, G.K., Dirkson, A., Majchrzak, T.A.: An exploratory study of covid-19 misinformation on twitter. Online Soc. Netw. Media **22**, 100104 (2021)
36. Shu, K., Mahudeswaran, D., Wang, S., Lee, D., Liu, H.: Fakenewsnet: a data repository with news content, social context, and spatiotemporal information for studying fake news on social media. Big Data **8**(3), 171–188 (2020)
37. Sitaram, S., Chandu, K.R., Rallabandi, S.K., Black, A.W.: A survey of code-switched speech and language processing. arXiv preprint arXiv:1904.00784 (2019)
38. Wanjawa, B., Wanzare, L., Indede, F., McOnyango, O., Ombui, E., Muchemi, L.: Kencorpus: a Kenyan language corpus of swahili, dholuo and luhya for natural language processing tasks. arXiv preprint arXiv:2208.12081 (2022)
39. X: How we address misinformation on x (2023). https://help.twitter.com/en/resources/addressing-misleading-info
40. Zampieri, M., et al.: Semeval-2020 task 12: multilingual offensive language identification in social media (offenseval 2020). arXiv preprint arXiv:2006.07235 (2020)

Telugu Meme Dataset and Baseline System for Automatic Identification of Domain, and Troll in Memes

N. Lohith[1]([✉]), S. Adnan Raqeeb[1], Poreddy Sai Manoj Reddy[1],
Chekuri Venkata Sunil Kumar[1], M. Anand Kumar[1],
and Bharathi Raja Chakravarthi[2]

[1] Department of Information Technology, National Institute of Technology
Karnataka, Surathkal, India
{lohithn.201it133,adnan.201it162,saimanojporeddy.201it241,
chekurivenkatasunilkumar.201it215,m_anandkumar}@nitk.edu.in
[2] Insight SFI Research Centre for Data Analytics, Data Science Institute,
National University of Ireland Galway, Galway, Ireland
bharathi.raja@insight-centre.org

Abstract. Everyone now uses social media to communicate information
and ideas, which has become a requirement for everyone. Social media
posts can offend people or be helpful or educational for them. Memes
are one type of media that is disseminated in this way through direct
messages, videos, or photographs. A meme is an image or video that
captures the opinions and sentiments of a particular group of people.
Memes can be trolling or not, and they include an image and text that
express an emotion. Most memes are unique to a particular linguistic
group of people. The most frequent cause of this is different languages.
Memes must be categorized since studying them can help us understand
the interests of each user. As both are necessary for interpretation, the
meme cannot be considered acceptable if we only gaze at the text or the
image. In this article, we provided a method for categorizing memes in
Telugu that considers both the meme's text and visual features, classifies
trolling and non-trolling memes, attempt to determine the emotion the
meme conveys and categorizes the meme according to the domain it
belongs to.

1   Introduction

A meme is an idea, behaviour, or style that circulates through imitation from
person to person within a culture and carries symbolic meaning representing a
particular theme. A social network is a site where people can create or share
information, ideas, or other kinds of expression among people, and a Meme is
a form of media that spreads an idea or emotion across the internet, especially
through social networks. Memes can be great content to have a laugh or gain
information about the things happening around us. However, a piece of content one person finds humorous may be abhorrent to another. Some people may

purposefully make memes that spread hatred toward a group of people or an individual. Since the reach of content in social media is vast, reading memes is common for a college student. However, many people are spreading offensive memes and promoting their viewpoints on social media platforms. These memes aim to mock their intended subject. We must stop these memes' ideas and statements before it is too late. Many students see these memes and might believe that the idea is okay. Data analysts from various parts of the world are attempting to identify these memes. The challenge of dealing with memes is that they are linguistic to region, and their meaning is often obscured in humour or sarcasm. The meme analysis by a user is handled by considering both the linguistic and visual features, hence its classification should too.

Telugu is the official language of the Indian states of Andhra Pradesh and Telangana and is a Dravidian language spoken by the Telugu people. The language's first writings date back to 575 CE. The Calukya dynasty's writing from the sixth century served as the basis for the Telugu script, which is connected to the Kannada script. The first piece of Telugu literature dates back to the 11th century and retells the Hindu epic Mahabharata by the author Nannaya Bhatta. There are four distinct regional dialects in Telugu and three social dialects that have developed around education, class, and caste. The formal, literary language is distinct from the spoken dialects.

This paper aims to classify linguistic memes in the Telugu language. Mostly, the memes in the Telugu language on social media do not contain the Telugu script but are written using the Roman script. This trend may be because the usual meme creators find the meme to get more trending if they are written in the Roman script. The script is in English, but the context meaning is of the Telugu language, and to classify these memes on various aspects, we are proposing this paper. As we know, meme classification should contain both linguistic and visual features. In consideration, we have proposed both methods based on image and text and combined Multi-Modal too.

The remainder of the paper is organized as follows. Section 2 discusses the related work on meme classification. The dataset about the shared task is described in Sect. 3. Section 4 outlines the features and machine learning algorithms used for this task. Section 5 is about results, and Sect. 6 concludes the paper.

2   Literature Review

The widespread adoption of social media in various parts of the word enables communication faster and different ways of communicating with one another. Social media provides a sense of pseudo anonymity to its users making them feel less incentivised in keeping civil discourse. This leads to special kind of anti-social behaviour from its users called as trolling as defined by [10] on their work surveying the direction of research. We derive the definitions of 'trolling' form [11] to define what images may be considered as a trolling. The annonater's bias can't be mitigated reasonable efforts were put in to make sure they understand the definition correctly.

Memes are humorous images made using images of celebrities or images of peculiar persons relating to the situations of the present time. It contains images and text, so it is very much required to analyze both to predict the right emotion from it and classify them. However, there will be many cases where the emotion in the image varies from the emotion of the text, which will change the overall sentiment.

The study [7] showcases BERT's success in NLP and its potential for multimodal tasks like meme classification. The researchers target VL models for meme classification, but this demands linguistic meme data. Learning from [6], we grasped how to create such datasets. Consequently, we compiled a dataset of around 2000 meme images to support further research.

Further delving into the domain of text sentiment and emotion classification, particularly when coupled with visual content, has yielded an array of methodological approaches. In the referenced work [9], the author undertakes the task of generating meme descriptions through non-parametric estimation techniques. These techniques leverage features such as Part-of-Speech (Pos), named-entities, frame-semantics, dependency triples, and linguistic attributes. The intention behind referring to this work was to draw insights from its approach and apply relevant strategies within the current study.

In meme classification research, the common practice involves integrating both textual and visual attributes to enhance model performance. Referenced work [1] outlines meme categorization through image processing, OCR Tesseract, and the Naive Bayes Algorithm. Conclusions drawn from references [3,4], and [5] collectively endorse the superiority of pretrained Deep Learning models in image classification due to their elevated accuracy and efficiency, particularly with smaller datasets, as compared to traditional machine learning's bag of features methodology [5]. In contrast, insights derived from the approach described in [2] demonstrate that concentrating solely on textual aspects yielded favorable results, attaining a significant F1 score of 0.50. This context presents a pivotal question regarding the fundamental perspective to be adopted within this study.

The paper [8] talks about the classification of memes and the multimodal approach to detecting offensive memes. We followed its implementation on conflict resolution for memes and the definition of a troll or no troll were also adopted from this. Here authors talk about specific domains where memes hold a lot of meaning, which leads us to develop domain-wise classification.

In our research, we developed models for meme classification, employing a dual approach that distinguishes memes based on their textual and visual characteristics. Additionally, we implemented an advanced multimodal model that seamlessly integrates both textual and visual cues. These models served as a cornerstone for generating hypotheses, providing a sturdy basis to guide our subsequent investigations. In the following section, we present a comprehensive overview of our methodology, shedding light on the framework proposed in our study. We also found inspiration from the work of [12], particularly their insights on using multimodal approaches for troll classification. This insight significantly influenced our approach to addressing a similar problem. It is important to note that the classification of Internet troll behavior necessitates the incorporation of both textual and visual content for meaningful categorization.

Our Contributions: to the best of our knowledge there is no publicly available dataset for telugu memes. Telugu is considered as resource poor language, our research aims to build a labeled dataset of images in telugu (roman script) on troll, domain and emotion produce baseline results on the same. We aim to improve the resource availability specifically in the Telugu language.

3   Meme Data-Set Discussion

3.1   Dataset Creation

We have created this Telugu memes dataset from social media sites like Facebook, Instagram, Twitter, and Reddit. Text in most of the collected memes on the internet is in Roman script.

The Example of the collected memes is shown in Fig. 1.

Fig. 1. Sample memes in the Dataset

We opted to link transcripts to the data since we wanted to store it in a usable way. To do this, we constructed a backend server. We started labeling the data before it was even built and stored there. Three people worked on the data labeling procedure, as shown in Fig. 2.

- Person 1: The meme's collector assigned the label to it.
- Person 2: It was labeled by the person tasked with gathering memes from various domains.
- Person 3: The third person, a meme creator with a dedicated social media presence for memes, is responsible for this categorization. We hired two meme makers to assist us in this role.

Fig. 2. Labelling Procedure

We employed three annotators, all undergraduate students Native speakers of telugu and fluent in English. We used highest voting to get a consensus on the labels. Each annotator labeled images independently to avoid confirmation bias. We observe very strong agreement in the data with variation occurring in less that 10% of labels.

3.2   Backend Server for Dataset

We built a static frontend where the image is uploaded, and it uses an ajax library to send the API request to the backend server, which processes the file and saves it as a JPG file. The technologies utilized were Node runtime, Express JS Server as the backend server, MongoDB as the database, and Nginx as the frontend server. After that, the project was uploaded to AWS as an EC2 instance and shared with the team for labeling.

We first saved the labels in the database and then renamed the file using their id/number to keep a one-to-one correlation with files and database entries. After the initial labeling and uploading process, we retrieved the full folder, extracted the labels from MongoDB, and stored them in CSV (uploaded to a Google Spreadsheet). After combining the three CSV files, this process was repeated three times to choose the correct label.

We used Keras-OCR to extract the English text of the memes from the image to create the transcripts, and we then saved the transcripts in a JSON file with the file name as the key. Before turning it into a Pandas data frame, we combined all the JSON files from the various sites using Python (Fig. 3).

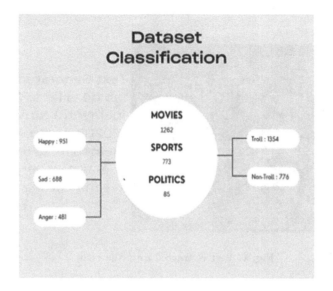

Fig. 3. Total Distribution of memes in each label and class

3.3 Data Cleaning

Later, three annotators (native speakers) reviewed all JSON files and cleaned the data, i.e., removed all incorrect labels in JSON files and all nan values from the CSV file (labels). Finally, all the data was combined using python script and made into a JSON array with images.

Fields in labels include

- Id: Positive Integer type and starts from 1.
- Image: Path to the image
- Trolling Label: It contains '0' for Trolling and '1' for non-trolling
- Text: Data generated by OCR,
- Emotion Label: [0,1,2], i.e., for happy/funny label is '0', Sad/Disappointment label is '1', and for anger is '2'

3.4 Dataset Analysis

Dataset is organized and contains the image file and transcriptions present in the image file. All the image files are in jpg format and have text embedded in them in the English language, but the meaning of the text is in Telugu.

The memes collected are primarily on sports, movies, and politics. These labels are also embedded with images. Further, the transcription of captions for each file is given in the data set. The text generated from the OCR is almost identical to the text in the image (Fig. 4).

Fig. 4. Text Extracted from the meme

If the meme does not contain any text in it, the text of the meme is an empty string (Fig. 5).

The data distribution of the train, test, and validation is shown below in the Table 1.

4   Meme Classification

4.1   Methodology

The core objective revolves around achieving three distinct classifications: binary categorization for "troll", and tertiary classifications for domains and emotional states. These primary goals are denoted as "classification objectives" throughout the paper. Raw dataset we have collected as shown in Table 1 is unbalanced and balancing it would be the ideal solution but could potentially lead to undertraining of specific features and necessitate tertiary classifications to adopt a binary format due to feature scarcity. Another critical aspect involves the management of pre-trained deep neural network weights—choosing between fine-tuning and freezing.

Thus, the two factors—pre-trained weights and data balancing—likewise offer dual possibilities for the three sub-models: exclusively image-based, exclusively text-based, and a multimodal approach for each classification objective. The optimization process for all three sub-models in each classification entails a brute-force methodology. Accordingly, we conducted comprehensive testing for each scenario, ultimately unveiling the most favourable outcomes. The ensuing

Text Generated is :
" "

Fig. 5. No-text meme

Table 1. Data distribution of Dataset for Train, Test, and Validation sets

Class Label	Train Set	Test set	validation set
Troll	850	262	262
Non-Troll	441	146	146
Total			2047
Movies	732	244	244
Sports	465	154	154
Politics	32	11	11
Total			2047
Happy	550	183	183
Sad	393	131	131
Anger	280	93	93
Total			2047

sections meticulously elaborate on the outcomes of these assessments, elucidating the distinctive attributes of the best results achieved for each configuration.

Image analysis is good with Convolutional neural networks, specifically in object detection or classification tasks and we have also used the same. DenseNet-169, pre-trained from ImageNet, was used to avoid the computational cost of training a CNN from the beginning. By training the last dense block and connecting it with three fully connected layers and other optimization techniques, the model had a validation accuracy of 97%. The reason for using DenseNet-169 rather than VGG, ResNet, DenseNet, and InceptionV3 in Keras API (Keras Applications) is that despite having a depth of 169 layers, it is relatively low in parameters compared to other models, and the architecture handles the vanishing gradient problem well.

4.2 Models and Their Features

Text Data Generation (OCR). To extract textual content from meme images, we employed the Keras OCR framework available at https://github.com/faustomorales/keras-ocr. Notably, all generated text was rendered in lowercase format. The OCR framework demonstrated commendable performance, particularly in the context of code-mixed English text. Despite this prowess, the arrangement of extracted text within memes yielded incoherence, prompting the necessity for a dedicated individual to meticulously review and revise the generated text. To ensure coherence and facilitate data management, the textual content was catalogued in JSON format, with corresponding file names serving as unique keys to uphold data correlation.

Exclusively Image-Based Model. The Image base model as discussed is desne169 [DenseNet] with image net weights and input shape as (224,224,3). We extended the image base model with a layer of GlobalAveragePooling2D and a dropout of 0.2, another Two dense layers with 'relu' activation functions, a dropout layer of 0.2 followed by a dense output layer with softmax activation layer model and was trained with binary cross entropy as loss function.

It was tested with both the possibilities of fine tuning and freezing the DenseNet. The results are displayed in the result section and include the accuracy score, precision score, recall score, f1 score, and classification report scores are of **fine tuning** because these performed well. We apply the same model with various hyperparameters (learning rate) to classify emotions. We introduced a softmax activation function at the output layer for emotion classification objective, with three output layers anticipated as [0,1,0], where 1 is the predicted class. We have used the unbalanced data and carefully adjusted the parameters to avoid overfitting the data; however, because the data classes had an uneven distribution, the model could not forecast lower frequency classes.

Exclusively Text Based Model. We employed the BERT model, specifically **BERT uncased L-6 H-768 A-12** exclusively for the text-based classification model. This lightweight BERT variant was fine-tuned through self-supervised tasks, predicting words within sentences based on contextual cues from vast text corpora like Wikipedia articles. This training, conducted without labelled data, empowers the model to develop a robust understanding of text semantics. Notably, this process demands substantial computation, requiring four days on 16 Tensor Processing Units (TPUs), as noted in the 2018 BERT paper. Leveraging the most effective preprocess layer, which transforms text into vector representations, was chosen due to BERT's strong performance in extracting text features across diverse datasets.

We have used the TensorFlow operators offered by the TF.text package to facilitate the seamless conversion of raw textual content into the numerical input tensors required by the encoder. These operations can be directly integrated into a TensorFlow model for efficient utilisation from textual inputs, eliminating the need for independent Python-based preprocessing. The preprocessing phase transforms raw text into fixed-length input sequences, aligning with the BERT encoder's expectations. Notably, TF Hub's preprocessing models come equipped with an embedded vocabulary and text normalisation mechanisms, negating the need for additional setup.

The preprocessing involves input mask use to distinguish tokens, paired with allocation of input type IDs. This yields a tensor with numeric identifiers for each tokenized input, covering initiation, conclusion, and padding tokens. Subsequently, a dedicated preprocessing layer is employed to encode text inputs of diverse lengths. The encoded information is subsequently subjected to BERT encoder processing, followed by traversal through a dropout layer characterised by a 0.2 dropout rate, and a dense layer comprising 500 neurons. This progression culminates in linkage with the output layer. The comprehensive text model materialises through the application of the softmax activation function, intertwined with the adoption of binary cross-entropy as the loss metric.

Multi-modal Approach Model. In this approach, the textual component presents substantial factual information, particularly pertinent for domain classification objective, leveraging keywords to great effect. Complementing this, the use of images furnishes a holistic perspective for emotion, troll classification objectives, encompassing both image and text layers through the application of the Keras concatenate API, these layers are seamlessly merged, culminating in a dense classification layer. To address potential overfitting concerns, ResNet50 with ImageNet classification weights is harnessed for image data, while BERT is judiciously selected for text classification.

Image Layers and Text Layers. In the case of image layers, a dense layer with an output dimension of 7x7x2028 is skillfully connected to the image base model. A pivotal global average pooling 2D layer efficiently reduces dimensions to 50, seamlessly followed by a dropout layer and the necessary flattening for the final output. Drawing inspiration from TensorFlow's documentation, our text model capitalises on the attributes of a small uncased BERT model (BERT uncased L-6 H-768 A-12). Encompassing L6 transformer layers of BERT model, it entails hidden embedding sizes of $H = 768$, strategically catered for classification tasks. The ensuing output dimension of 768 is coupled with a dropout layer, preluding a subsequent dense network with 256 neurons.

Concatenation. These distinct elements coalesce through the Keras concatenation layer, resulting in a unified output dimension of 306. Subsequently, a dedicated dense layer, bolstered by dropout, facilitates the classification task, leveraging the softmax activation function and binary cross-entropy loss. In scenarios necessitating multiclass classification, adaptations are introduced. For both domain and emotion classification, a dense(6) layer coupled with dropout(0.2) is employed, while the concluding output layer adopts a dense(3) configuration, featuring sigmoid activation and capitalising on categorical cross-entropy loss. Our model training regimen entails a well-calibrated batch size of 20, a learning rate of 1e-4, and the utilisation of the Adam optimizer.

5   Results

The construction of models was predicated upon three distinct classification objectives. Consequently, each of these classification objectives will be elaborated upon in the subsequent subsections. Additionally, for each of the three sub-models aligned with these objectives, the outcomes are meticulously presented within the context of the unbalanced dataset.

5.1   Troll and Non-troll Classification

In the assessment of classification performance, the image-based approach yielded a precision of 0.50 for the Troll class, while displaying a relatively higher recall of 0.76, signifying its ability to capture a substantial portion of actual troll instances. Conversely, precision for the Non-Troll class stood at 0.48, surpassing random guessing, yet with a recall of 0.40, indicating misclassification of non-troll memes as trolls. The resulting F1 scores for both classes were moderate, aligning with an overall accuracy of 0.48, implying a lack of balanced performance between troll and non-troll categories. The text-based approach, notably, encountered challenges in correctly classifying non-troll memes, resulting in a precision and recall of 0.00 for that class, while achieving an overall accuracy of 0.57 mainly due to its adeptness in identifying troll memes.

The introduced multimodal approach, with a trainable base model, demonstrated improved performance in identifying troll memes, as evidenced by balanced precision (0.57) and recall (0.54) for the Troll class, translating to an F1 score of 0.56. Moreover, the Non-Troll class displayed equilibrium in precision (0.55) and recall (0.58), contributing to an F1 score of 0.57, surpassing the image-based approach in recognizing non-troll instances. The multimodal approach, conducted without a base model yet remaining trainable, presented similar precision (0.57) for the Troll class and marginally improved recall (0.59), resulting in an F1 score of 0.58. Correspondingly, the Non-Troll class exhibited precision and recall of 0.57 and 0.54, respectively, yielding an F1 score of 0.55, akin to the multimodal approach with the base model. The consistent accuracy of 0.57 across these multimodal scenarios highlights the potential of this approach in achieving balanced troll and non-troll classifications (Table 2).

Table 2. Classification report on Troll and Non-Troll

Model Base	Class	Precision	Recall	F1 Score
Image Based	Troll	0.50	0.76	0.60
	Non-Troll	0.48	0.40	0.43
Accuracy				0.48
Text Based	Troll	0.57	1.00	0.73
	Non-Troll	0.00	0.00	0.00
Accuracy				0.57
Multimodal Approach With Base Model Trainable	Troll	0.57	0.54	0.56
	Non-Troll	0.55	0.58	0.57
Accuracy				0.56
Multimodal Approach Without Base Model Trainable	Troll	0.57	0.59	0.58
	Non-Troll	0.57	0.54	0.55
Accuracy				0.57

5.2   Domain Classification

The assessment of model performance across different domains (Movies, Sports, Politics) reveals varying trends. In the image-based approach, for the Movies domain, precision stood at 0.85, while recall was notably low at 0.03, resulting in an F1 score of 0.50. Similarly, in the Sports domain, precision was 0.86, recall was 0.51, and the F1 score reached 0.53. However, the Politics domain yielded negligible values across all metrics. The text-based approach presented improved results, with the Movies domain achieving precision of 0.71 and recall of 0.55, translating to an F1 score of 0.73. In the Sports domain, precision and recall were both 0.73, leading to an F1 score of 0.77. The Politics domain remained challenging for this approach as well.

The introduced multimodal approach, with a trainable base model, demonstrated notable enhancement across domains. In the Movies domain, precision reached 0.85, recall reached 0.97, and the F1 score stood at 0.90. However, in the Politics domain, precision reached 0.80, recall was 0.31, and the F1 score reached 0.47. The multimodal approach, conducted without a base model yet remaining trainable, yielded consistent precision of 0.75 for the Movies domain, with an improved recall of 0.589, culminating in an F1 score of 0.82. In the Sports domain, precision was 0.76, recall was 0.68, and the F1 score was 0.72. As with previous approaches, the Politics domain remained challenging. The overall accuracy for this approach was 0.76. These results underscore the complex interplay between model strategies and domain-specific nuances in achieving accurate classifications. The Politics Class F1 score of 0.00 is due to the data size differentiation. The politics Data size is very less compared to the Movies Class hence its F1 score is 0.00 (Table 3).

Table 3. Classification report on Various Domain Classes

Model	Class	Precision	Recall	F1 Score
Image Based	Movies	0.86	0.93	0.89
	Sports	0.86	0.81	0.83
	Politics	0.00	0.00	0.00
Accuracy				0.86
Text Based	Movies	0.71	0.75	0.73
	Sports	0.73	0.81	0.77
	Politics	0.00	0.00	0.00
Accuracy				0.73
Multimodal Approach With Base Model Trainable	Movies	0.85	0.97	0.90
	Sports	0.95	0.83	0.88
	Politics	0.80	0.31	0.44
Accuracy				0.88
Multimodal Approach Without Base Model Trainable	Movies	0.78	0.89	0.82
	Sports	0.76	0.68	0.72
	Politics	0.00	0.00	0.00
Accuracy				0.76

5.3   Emotion Classification

illustrates diverse outcomes. In the image-based approach, the Happy emotion achieved a precision of 0.50 and a relatively high recall of 0.76, resulting in an F1 score of 0.60. However, the Sad emotion showed minimal results, with precision of 0.05 and negligible recall and F1 score. The Anger emotion exhibited precision of 0.30, recall of 0.05, and an F1 score of 0.08. The overall accuracy for this approach was 0.48. Transitioning to the text-based approach, precision for the Happy emotion was 0.50, with a recall of 0.002 and an F1 score of 0.05. The Sad emotion displayed precision of 0.32, recall of 0.31, and an F1 score of 0.55. For the Anger emotion, precision reached 0.36, recall was 0.008, and the F1 score was 0.30. The overall accuracy for this approach was 0.37.

In the multimodal approach, utilizing a trainable base model led to an enhancement in emotion detection. In the Happy emotion, precision was 0.47, recall was 0.92, and the F1 score reached 0.62. For the Sad emotion, precision was 0.03, recall was 0.06, and the F1 score was 0.06. The Anger emotion yielded precision of 0.00, recall of 0.00, and an F1 score of 0.00. The accuracy for this approach was 0.15.

When considering the multimodal approach without a base model, the Happy emotion demonstrated precision of 0.51, recall of 0.89, and an F1 score of 0.52. The Sad emotion achieved precision of 0.31, recall of 0.68, and an F1 score of 0.72. Precision for the Anger emotion was 0.00, with recall also at 0.00. The accuracy for this scenario was not provided. These findings underline the intricate nature of classifying emotions, with varied success rates across different emotions and model strategies (Table 4).

Table 4. Classification report on Various Emotion Classes

Model	Class	Precision	Recall	F1 Score
Image Based	Happy	0.50	0.76	0.60
	Sad	0.48	0.40	0.43
	Anger	0.30	0.05	0.08
Accuracy				0.48
Text Based	Happy	0.48	0.42	0.45
	Sad	0.32	0.34	0.33
	Anger	0.36	0.08	0.13
Accuracy				0.37
Multimodal Approach With Base Model Trainable	Happy	0.47	0.92	0.62
	Sad	0.17	0.03	0.06
	Anger	0.00	0.00	0.00
Accuracy				0.45
Multimodal Approach Without Base Model Trainable	Happy	0.51	0.89	0.82
	Sad	0.31	0.68	0.72
	Anger	0.00	0.00	0.00
Accuracy				0.45

6   Conclusions and Future Trends

The analysis of memes predominantly composed of image content, devoid of substantial textual elements, reveals a noticeable pattern characterized by a fundamental concept portrayed through actions of individuals, often with comedic intent, coupled with accompanying text that delivers the punchline. Our investigation has illuminated a formulaic approach to meme construction, frequently reliant on widely recognized source material. This established framework significantly simplifies the evaluation of meme images, aiding in the identification of negative sentiments, particularly within the context of the troll classification objective. This pattern is consistently evident in our model's performance, demonstrating satisfactory proficiency in classifying troll-related content. Although the extracted textual data holds promise for classification, its efficacy is at times hindered by intricate troll meme nuances. These instances often avoid direct derogatory language, utilizing acronyms and rhymes to convey sentiments, posing challenges for accurate classification. Further research is needed to refine classification approaches for these elusive meme forms.

The domain-specific models display robust performance, where both text and image models achieve similar levels of accuracy, with images slightly surpassing. This phenomenon can be attributed to the inherent meme creation style within each specific classification objective and the prevalent use of common elements, such as sportswear in sports-related memes, alongside objective-specific keywords in the text. As a result, the models find it considerably easier to categorize memes according to their specific classification objectives due to these distinctive patterns.

Emotion analysis proves to be a nuanced undertaking, as it is subject to subtle complexities. Simplicity and complexity coexist, where a scenario evoking happiness in one context could induce sadness in another. Conducting a comprehensive perspective-based study seems more viable than a generalized approach. However, our endeavors remain dedicated to rendering this complexity manageable. Notably, we observe that classification, particularly between happiness and sadness, benefits from the tonality depicted in images. Conversely, interpreting anger remains a challenge.

Multimodal models emerge as notably effective in capturing nuanced situations. Furthermore, advancements in image and text processing have the potential to directly enhance these models. This improvement is particularly evident in scenarios where meme images may be absent. A thorough analysis of the results indicates that the multimodal approach consistently outperforms individual image and text models. This underscores the potential of integration and affirms the direction for refining emotion analysis within the meme domain.

References

1. Amalia, A., Sharif, A., Haisar, F., Gunawan, D., Nasution, B.B.: Meme opinion categorization by using optical character recognition (OCR) and Naïve Bayes algorithm. In: 2018 Third International Conference on Informatics and Computing (ICIC), Palembang, Indonesia, pp. 1–5 (2018). https://doi.org/10.1109/IAC.2018.8780410
2. Bharathi, B., Agnusimmaculate Silvia, A.: SSNCSE_NLP@DravidianLangTech-EACL2021: meme classification for Tamil using machine learning approach. In: Proceedings of the First Workshop on Speech and Language Technologies for Dravidian Languages, Kyiv, pp. 336–339. Association for Computational Linguistics (2021)
3. Boyd, A., Czajka, A., Bowyer, K.: Deep learning-based feature extraction in iris recognition: use existing models, fine-tune or train from scratch? In: 2019 IEEE 10th International Conference on Biometrics Theory, Applications and Systems (BTAS), pp. 1–9. IEEE Press (2019)
4. Kieffer, B., Babaie, M., Kalra, S., Tizhoosh, H.R.: Convolutional neural networks for histopathology image classification: training vs. using pre-trained networks. CoRR, abs/1710.05726 (2017)
5. Loussaief, S., Abdelkrim, A.: Deep learning vs. bag of features in machine learning for image classification. In: 2018 International Conference on Advanced Systems and Electric Technologies (IC_ASET), pp. 6–10 (2018)

6. Suryawanshi, S., Chakravarthi, B.R.: Findings of the shared task on troll meme classification in Tamil. In: Proceedings of the First Workshop on Speech and Language Technologies for Dravidian Languages, Kyiv, pp. 126–132. Association for Computational Linguistics (2021)
7. Suryawanshi, S., Chakravarthi, B.R., Verma, P., Arcan, M., McCrae, J.P., Buitelaar, P.: A dataset for troll classification of TamilMemes. In: Proceedings of the WILDRE5- 5th Workshop on Indian Language Data: Resources and Evaluation, Marseille, France, pp. 7–13. European Language Resources Association (ELRA) (2020)
8. Turc, I., Chang, M.-W., Lee, K., Toutanova, K.: Well-read students learn better: the impact of student initialization on knowledge distillation. CoRR, abs/1908.08962 (2019)
9. Wang, W.Y., Wen, M.: I can has cheezburger? A nonparanormal approach to combining textual and visual information for predicting and generating popular meme descriptions. In: Proceedings of the 2015 Conference of the North American Chapter of the Association for Computational Linguistics: Human Language Technologies, Denver, Colorado, pp. 355–365. Association for Computational Linguistics (2015)
10. Tomaiuolo, M., Lombardo, G., Mordonini, M., Cagnoni, S., Poggi, A.: A survey on troll detection. Future Internet **12**(2), 31 (2020). https://doi.org/10.3390/fi12020031
11. Hardaker, C.: Trolling in asynchronous computer-mediated communication: from user discussions to academic definitions. J. Politeness Res. Lang. Behav. Cult. **6**, 215–242 (2010). https://doi.org/10.1515/jplr.2010.011
12. Suryawanshi, S., et al.: TrollsWithOpinion: A Dataset for Predicting Domain-specific Opinion Manipulation in Troll Memes. arXiv preprint arXiv:2109.03571 (2021)

SamPar: A Marathi Hate Speech Dataset for Homophobia, Transphobia

Bhargav Chhaya[1]([✉])(iD), Prasanna Kumar Kumaresan[2](iD),
Rahul Ponnusamy[2](iD), and Bharathi Raja Chakravarthi[1](iD)

[1] School of Computer Science, University of Galway, Galway, Ireland
bhargavchhaya20@gmail.com, bharathi.raja@universityofgalway.ie
[2] College of Science and Engineering, University of Galway, Galway, Ireland

Abstract. Marathi-speaking communities, especially those experiencing a change of heart after Article 377 was repealed in India, have expressed their sentiments regarding the LGBTQ+ community on social media. Leveraging a meticulously curated dataset extracted from prominent social media platforms, YouTube and Facebook, the study unveils the social, cultural, and moral perspectives palpable across both urban and rural domains. The data, derived via a rigorous manual scraping methodology, was categorized into 'Homophobic', 'Non-LGBTQ+', and 'Transphobic' comments, attaining a commendable Cohen's Kappa score of 0.967, thus reflecting a high inter-annotator agreement. Our exploitative analysis unveiled a stark presence of homophobic (15.84%) and transphobic (10.52%) remarks within the digital discussions. Employing an array of machine learning and deep learning models, with a particular spotlight on Decision Trees and LSTM which achieved macro F1-scores of 0.45 and 0.53 respectively, the study not only elevates the understanding of the sociolinguistic intricacies prevalent in digital dialogues but also lays a substantive foundation for future research. It assists in understanding and potentially curtailing digital hate speech and discriminatory remarks against the LGBTQ+ community in the Marathi digital diaspora. Thus, the paper propels the conversation towards crafting a more inclusive, empathetic, and supportive digital environment, synchronizing technological prowess with socio-cultural cognizance.

Keywords: Hate Speech · Homophobia · Transphobia · Dataset development · Context-aware annotation

1 Introduction

Social media, while seamlessly integrating into our various daily activities and serving as a pivotal platform for expression and community-building, can also be a double-edged sword, particularly when it comes to the manifestation of hate speech. While global communities can engage in dialogue on these platforms, biases and negative sentiments towards certain communities, particularly the LGBTQ+ community, have led to a burgeoning problem of online hate speech

B. R. Chakravarthi et al. (Eds.): SPELLL 2023, CCIS 2046, pp. 34–51, 2024.
https://doi.org/10.1007/978-3-031-58495-4_3

[1]. There is a bias towards other communities or thoughts of a certain kind which can be perceived as a negative sentiment that can lead to the problem of hate speech. Detecting the problem of online hate speech is an important problem in making the online experience safe for members of every community. According to the seminal paper [2] hate speech and offensive speech are not identical, as hate speech can be differentiated with a targeted religion, race, or a community of people who identify with a particular thought. A very important aspect of the process of detecting hate speech is the creation of Hate speech-related datasets which comprise every instance possible and are as less biased as possible. This aspect is reflected in the paper by [3] where they create a dataset from a white supremacy forum to identify instances of hate speech across different platforms thus making it as diverse as possible so machine learning and deep learning models can be trained on such curated datasets. One of the most rampant forms of hate speech online is directed towards the LGBTQ+ community and they are most disproportionately affected by the hate speech online. The LGBTQ+ community faces a lot of hate speech and bullying via different forms on social media like direct messages, negative comments, etc. [4]. This type of bullying can lead to a hostile environment which can lead to several things like depression or other mental health issues. While primarily all the work has been done with respect to the English language, languages like The Marathi (ISO 639-2: mar) language belongs to the Indo-Aryan languages and is primarily spoken in Maharashtra, India, and by the Marathi diaspora worldwide. It holds official status in Maharashtra and Goa in India. Despite the burgeoning global discourse on online hate speech, the narrative surrounding Marathi, a language spoken by millions, remains markedly sparse. The journey towards crafting a safe digital haven for every individual necessitates a deeper understanding and mitigation of hate speech across a multitude of languages and cultural contexts. However, the road to achieving this in the Marathi digital discourse is fraught with challenges:

- *Data Scarcity:* The cornerstone of effective hate speech detection lies in the availability of robust and representative datasets. Unlike languages such as English, the reservoir of annotated datasets for Marathi is significantly limited. Recent endeavors like the L3Cube-MahaHate project have made preliminary strides towards creating Marathi-specific datasets for hate speech detection, but the landscape remains largely unexplored [5].
- *Linguistic Complexity:* Marathi's rich linguistic tapestry, characterized by a plethora of dialects and sociolects, presents a unique challenge in annotating and interpreting digital discourse. The linguistic nuances could harbor the potential for misinterpretation, thereby necessitating a nuanced approach to dataset annotation and hate speech detection.
- *Technological Limitations:* The nascent stage of technological advancements for Marathi language processing further exacerbates the challenge. While recent studies have begun employing deep learning architectures like BERT for Marathi hate speech detection, the journey towards achieving compara-

ble efficacy to models trained on languages with abundant resources is yet long [6].

– *Community Impact:* The vitriol of online hate speech has a profound impact on the well-being and mental health of individuals, especially marginalized communities. The LGBTQ+ community within the Marathi-speaking diaspora is among those significantly affected. By advancing the frontier of hate speech detection in Marathi, we inch closer to fostering a safer and more inclusive digital environment for all

The exigency for research in this domain is underscored by the aspiration to broaden the ambit of digital safety to encompass diverse linguistic and cultural communities. This study, poised at the nexus of linguistics, computer science, and social justice, endeavors to contribute to the burgeoning body of knowledge to combat online hate speech in Marathi, thereby rendering the digital sphere a safe harbor for discourse and dialogue for every individual.

Research Questions (RQ):

1. What are the challenges faced in creating a dataset for hate speech detection in a regional language, specifically focusing on Marathi and LGBTQ+ issues?
2. How do we ensure that annotations are both culturally and linguistically accurate for the Marathi language?
3. What are the best models for low-resource language tasks like this where data is very less and hard to find?

To make the online space safe for the Marathi LGBTQ+ community we propose a dataset that helps identify hate against LGBTQ+ people in Marathi. The dataset comprises:

– *Both Marathi and code-Mixed Language:* We've included both pure Marathi phrases and those mixed with English because that's how people often communicate online.
– *Collected from online comments:* We looked at comments from YouTube and Facebook to get a real picture of what people are saying.
– *Native and context-aware annotations:* Every comment was checked by two people who speak Marathi every day to make sure we understood it right.
– *Clear tags:* Each comment is labeled as either 'Homophobic', 'Transphobic', or 'Non-LGBTQ', so we know what kind of hate speech it is.

Thus by creating this dataset, we believe that this will result in a better and safer online space for the MARATHI LGBTQ community and also help us better understand the cultural attitudes and how to train effective models to detect hate speech.

2   Related Work

The domain of hate speech detection has seen remarkable advancements with monolingual and multilingual approaches at its core. Pioneering works like [2] laid down the groundwork in distinguishing hate speech from offensive language in English, which was furthered by [7] through employing BERT and Hate Speech Word Embedding. On the multilingual front, [8] explored hate speech recognition in Hinglish documents, highlighting the necessity and complexity of multilingual approaches. Meanwhile, generalizability and explainability in hate speech detection models have garnered attention, with a notable survey by [9] shedding light on generalizability issues and [10] proposing a rule-based approach for explainable hate speech detection.

Group-specific approaches and the development of comprehensive datasets are also pivotal in this domain. [11] proposed a group-specific approach to NLP for hate speech detection, emphasizing the importance of contextual understanding. The creation of linguistically diverse datasets, as seen in the works of [12] and [13], has been crucial for evaluating and enhancing the performance of hate speech detection models across different linguistic landscapes. Additionally, [14] explored machine learning models on the HASOC 2022 dataset, with [6] and [15] examining BERT-based models for Marathi offensive content detection. [16] focused on MuRIL for the HASOC 2022 dataset while [17] utilized XLM Roberta for tweet preprocessing, achieving a macro f1 score of 0.93. [18] introduced MUDES for span-level hate speech identification, outperforming the spaCy baseline. Zhang et al. developed a predictive model aiming to identify early signs of conversations derailing into antisocial behavior, which could be beneficial for social media platforms to prevent harassment and personal attacks before they escalate [19].

On the other hand, Jiang et al. proposed a novel method for text classification in low-resource scenarios by introducing a parameter-free classification method. They utilized compression algorithms, specifically a simple compressor like gzip, combined with a k-nearest-neighbor classifier for text classification. This paper has been recognized in the NLP community for its simple and efficient approach towards text classification in low-resource settings [20].

The related works underscore a multi-pronged approach towards hate speech detection, encompassing monolingual and multilingual models, generalizability, explainability, group-specific approaches, and dataset development. While significant strides have been made, challenges such as the scarcity of annotated data, the trade-off between explainability and performance, and the generalizability of models across diverse cultural and linguistic contexts persist, warranting further research and collaboration in the field.

3   Dataset Creation

The dataset is curated from comments on social media platforms, namely YouTube and Facebook, chosen due to their substantial Marathi user base. These platforms are prominent venues for discussions and reactions within the Marathi LGBTQ+ community, encompassing a wide demographic spectrum from rural to urban areas. The notable decision by the Supreme Court of India to repeal Article 377, legalizing same-sex relationships, stirred diverse reactions within the Marathi community. This historical change, extensively covered by Marathi news outlets, facilitated numerous discussions and thereby contributed to the dataset.

3.1   Search Criteria

A meticulous, strategic search approach was employed to ensure a comprehensive capture of sentiments from the Marathi-speaking community on LGBTQ+ issues.

Keyword Selection. The following keywords were identified based on their relevance and prevalence in LGBTQ+ discussions in Marathi:

- *Samlingi:* A term for homosexual individuals.
- *Parlingi:* Another term akin to "Samlingi".
- *Trutiya-panthi:* Translates to "third-gender", referring to transgender individuals.
- *Marathi LGBTQ:* A combination to ensure specificity to the Marathi-speaking community (Table 1).

Table 1. Glossary of Marathi LGBTQ Terms

Term	Description
Samlingi	A term for homosexual individuals
Parlingi	Another term akin to "Samlingi"
Trutiya-panthi	Translates to "third-gender", referring to transgender individuals
Marathi LGBTQ	A combination to ensure specificity to the Marathi-speaking community

Rationale for Keyword Selection. The selected keywords are pivotal in Marathi discussions about LGBTQ+ topics. They encapsulate the cultural nuances and specific terms used within the Marathi community, enabling the inclusion of a wide spectrum of discussions, ranging from formal debates to casual interactions.

Manual Scraping Process. Due to the sensitive nature of the topic and the imperative for high-quality data extraction, a manual scraping process was employed. Comments related to the chosen terms were individually reviewed and extracted from YouTube and Facebook, ensuring relevance and appropriateness while facilitating the immediate removal of any personal or identifiable information to uphold ethical standards.

3.2 Data Annotation

Comments were annotated into one of three categories:

Homophobic Comments: These remarks, directed at individuals based on their gay orientation, encompass negative feelings, stereotypes, slurs, or other derogatory expressions. They may manifest as explicit hate speech, implicit bias, or derogatory stereotypes about the gay and lesbian community.

Non-LGBTQ+ Comments: These comments, devoid of homophobic or transphobic remarks, may be objective, encouraging, or discuss LGBTQ+ issues without displaying bias or prejudice. It's notable that this category encapsulates both positive comments and remarks unrelated to LGBTQ+ issues.

Transphobic Comments: These comments exhibit prejudice, discrimination, or negative attitudes towards transgender individuals, manifesting as outright hate speech, denial or dismissal of gender identities, or harmful stereotypes about the transgender community.

Example Annotations. For instance, the Marathi comment *"Rajya adhi pan hota...jara hindu puran vach"* translated to "there was a kingdom before also read Hindu scriptures" is in response to negative claims about the LGBTQ+ community and can be considered LGBTQ+ affirming (Table 2).

Table 2. Examples and Annotations of Various Comments

Category	Example (Marathi)	Translation	Annotation/Explanation
Non-LGBTQ	Rajya adhi pan hota...jara hindu puran vach	There was a kingdom before also... read Hindu scriptures	Affirms LGBTQ+ by responding to negative claims
Transphobic	Sagale higade ahet	Everyone is confused	Directly derogatory towards trans individuals
Transphobic	Purvajanche shaap ahet tey	They are the curse of the ancestors	Negative and demeaning towards trans individuals
Homophobic	He khup chukiche aahe	This is very wrong	Moral judgment and denial of rights towards gay marriage

3.3 Annotation Process

The annotation process comprised three rounds to ensure the accuracy and appropriateness of labels assigned to each comment. Each comment was initially annotated by an independent reviewer fluent in Marathi, followed by a second annotation round by another fluent reviewer. A final review was conducted to allocate definitive labels to each comment. The process details are as follows:

Initial Annotation. Each comment was initially annotated by an independent reviewer fluent in Marathi. Comments were labeled as "homophobic," "non-lgbtq," or "transphobic," providing a preliminary insight into the sentiment and context of the discourse.

Second Annotation. Following the initial annotation, a second reviewer, also fluent in Marathi, independently reviewed the comments. The second annotator was not privy to the annotations made in the first round, ensuring an unbiased re-evaluation.

Final Annotation. Post the two rounds of independent annotations, a final label was allocated to each comment through a consensus discussion between the reviewers. This step ensured that the final categorization accurately reflected the sentiment, adhering to the linguistic nuances and contextual appropriateness within the Marathi community.

Inter-Annotator Agreement. The consistency between the annotations from the two rounds was quantified using the Cohen's Kappa score, computed via the Sci-kit-Learn library. A score of approximately 0.967 was achieved, indicating an exceptionally high level of agreement between the initial and secondary annotations, and thus, a reliable dataset.

Rationale for Labeling. During the annotation process, we acknowledged the complexities and potential ambiguities in categorizing comments as "homophobic" or "transphobic." To enhance transparency and provide clarity, reasons for each categorization, especially for comments labeled as "homophobic" or "transphobic," were documented. This elucidation aims to provide academics and practitioners with a clear understanding of the categorization criteria, minimizing any potential ambiguity and fostering informed utilization of the dataset.

3.4   Dataset Statistics

The dataset comprises 5,000 comments sourced from platforms such as YouTube and Facebook. Out of these, approximately 46.38% (or 2,319 comments) are classified as 'Pure Marathi', while the remaining 53.62% (or 2,681 comments) exhibit 'Code-Mixed' characteristics (Table 3).

Table 3. Dataset Composition from YouTube and Facebook

Classification	Number of Comments	Percentage
Total	5,000	100%
Pure Marathi	2,319	46.38%
Code-Mixed	2,681	53.62%

Non-LGBTQ Comments (3,659 - 73.18%): These make up the majority of the dataset. Most comments that don't deal with LGBTQ+ subjects directly fall under this category. They are based on a wide range of other subjects or congratulatory, irrelevant remarks. This shows that the majority of people are supportive of the community or remarks which are praising of the video maker.

Homophobic Comments (792–15.84%): This category is important and worrisome. These remarks, which make up over 16% of the dataset, express negative feelings toward the gay community. They serve as a sharp reminder of the bigotry that still exists and the difficulties the LGBTQ+ community experiences in online environments.

Transphobic Comments (526–10.52%): While fewer in number compared to homophobic remarks, the transphobic comments constitute an essential part of the dataset. They reflect the biases and misunderstandings surrounding the transgender community, a group often marginalized even within broader LGBTQ+ discussions. The length of comments in the dataset offers a window into the depth and style of user engagement. A closer look reveals intriguing patterns:

- *Average comment Length:* The average comment length is 94.94 characters which means that user engagement is moderate and that most users tend to express their thoughts in a concise manner. However, they do so and express meaning in doing so.
- *Median Comment Length:* The median length of the comments is 57 characters, which means comments are short, reinforcing the idea of succinct expressions being prevalent in the dataset.
- *Range of comment Engagement:* The dataset has a wide range of comment lengths. On one end, we have the briefest comments, which are in just 7 characters. These could be reactions, affirmations, or short remarks. On the other extreme, some comments can be in the range of 3,447 characters, suggesting in-depth discussions, stories, or detailed viewpoints (Table 4).

Table 4. Comment Length Statistics in the Dataset

Metric	Value
Average Comment Length	94.94 characters
Median Comment Length	57 characters
Shortest Comment	7 characters
Longest Comment	3,447 characters

We provide further visualizations of our dataset so there is a better understanding of the nuances of our dataset. In addition to the statistical story provided above, we seek to provide a more immediate and concrete understanding of the data through carefully chosen visualizations (Fig. 1).

The Pie Chart provides a clear visualization of the distribution of comments across different labels in the dataset. As evident the majority of comments are non-lgbtq followed by homophobic and transphobic. This distribution highlights the nature of user interactions on platforms such as YouTube and Facebook concerning LGBTQ+ topics.

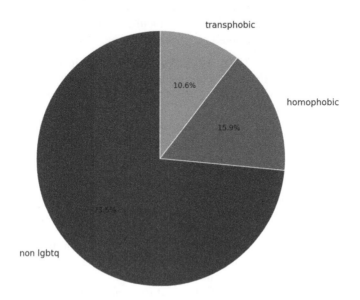

Fig. 1. Distribution of comments by label

The Density Plot in Fig. 2 illustrates the distribution of comment lengths in the dataset. The x-axis represents the length of comments, while the y-axis indicates the density or frequency of those lengths. Peaks in the plot signify the most common comment lengths, whereas valleys denote less frequent lengths.

From the Density Plot, several observations can be made:

- **Central Tendency**: A prominent peak on the left side of the plot indicates that the majority of comments are concise, suggesting users' preference for brevity in their feedback or reactions.
- **Spread**: Despite the dominance of shorter comments, there's a long tail extending toward the right. This reveals the presence of longer comments, hinting at a subset of users delving into more detailed discussions or viewpoints.
- **Variability**: The width of the plot at varying lengths demonstrates the variability in comment lengths. Narrower sections of the plot represent less frequent comment lengths, while broader sections signify a higher density of comments at that particular length.

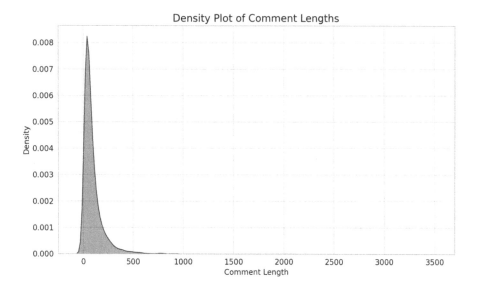

Fig. 2. Distribution of comment lengths in the dataset

Overall, the Density Plot offers a comprehensive view of comment lengths, underscoring the diverse range of user interactions.

3.5   Privacy Concerns

While collecting the comments we found a lot of different voices. Some were positive, offering support, praise, or constructive feedback. Others were full of biases, revealing deep-rooted prejudices that still exist in society. Each comment made us understand the digital landscape of discussions related to the LGBTQ+ community. However, in so many voices, we decided to respect user anonymity and privacy. We make a special effort to prevent the collection or storage of any personal identifiers, such as usernames or profile links. Without paying attention to any details that could identify a specific person, we concentrated only on the comments' actual substance. Our goal was to find a compromise between acquiring useful data and protecting the sanctity of individual privacy in an era of growing worries about digital privacy.

4   Experiments

4.1   TF-IDF and NLTK Baseline Experiment

The SAMPAR dataset was used to do the experimental analysis. The following preprocessing steps were undertaken to prepare the data for modeling:

1. *Text Vectorization:* The comments from the dataset were transformed using the Term Frequency-Inverse Document Frequency (TF-IDF) method. This

transformation was essential to convert textual data into a numerical format suitable for machine learning applications.

2. *Feature Selection:* To reduce the dimensionality of the dataset to prevent overfitting we limited the number of features to the top 5,000 terms based on their frequency using the TfidfVectorizer from the Scikit-learn library

3. *Dataset Split:* We split the dataset into training and testing subsets. Using the "train test split" function from the Sci-kit-learn library, 80% of the data was reserved for training, and the remaining 20% was set aside for testing

After this text preprocessing, we used sci-kit learn to create baseline classifiers like:

1. *Logistic Regression:* We trained a Logistic Regression model on our dataset with a maximum iteration of 1000 to ensure convergence.

2. *KNN classifier:*We trained a KNN model with 5 neighbors.

3. *Decision Tree:* We trained a Decision Tree classifier on our dataset

4. *Random Forest:* We trained Random Forest model was trained with 100 trees (estimators).

To address class imbalance in the dataset we used the Synthetic Minority Over-sampling Technique (SMOTE). SMOTE works by generating synthetic samples in the feature space to increase the minority classes. We used the Natural Language Toolkit (NLTK), a prominent library for natural language processing. Specifically, the "word-tokenize" function was employed for tokenization, and WordNetLemmatizer was used for lemmatization. After using NLTK we use Word2Vec to generate dense vector representations of words in large collections of texts. A Word2Vec model was trained using the tokenized comments. The model parameters were set as follows: Vector size=100: Each word is represented by a 100-dimensional vector. Window=5: The maximum distance between the current and predicted word within a sentence. "min-count=1": Words with a frequency less than this are ignored. Workers=4: Number of CPU cores to use during training.

We trained the following ensemble methods on the dataset.

1. *XGBoost:* We converted categorical labels in the dataset into a numerical format using a label encoder from scikit learn. XGBoost has its own data structure called DMatrix that it uses for efficient computation. The hyperparameters are defined for the model: max-depth=6: Maximum depth of the decision trees; eta = 0.3: Learning rate; objective: Specifies the learning task. Here, 'multi: softmax' is used for multi-class classification; num-class: Number of classes in the dataset.

2. *Adaboost:* We initialized an AdaBoost classifier with 100 weak learners (n-estimators = 100). random-state=42 was set for reproducibility.

3. *Random Forest:* We intialized (n-estimators = 100) were used for the ensemble. random-state=42 was set for reproducibility (Tables 5 and 6).

Table 5. Comparative Performance of Models Using Macro F1-score

Model	Macro F1-score
Logistic Regression	0.41
K-Nearest Neighbors	0.29
Decision Tree	0.45
Random Forest (TF-IDF)	0.42
XGBoost	0.36
Random Forest (Word2Vec)	0.32
AdaBoost	0.33
Support Vector Machine	0.33

Table 6. Hyperparameters Used for Each Model

Model	Hyperparameter	Value
Logistic Regression	Maximum Iterations	1000
KNN Classifier	Neighbors	5
Decision Tree	–	Default
Random Forest (TF-IDF)	Estimators	100
	Random State	42
Random Forest (Word2Vec)	Estimators	100
	Random State	42
XGBoost	max-depth	6
	eta	0.3
	objective	multi:softmax
AdaBoost	n-estimators	100
	Random State	42

4.2 Data Compression-Based Classifier Using Normalized Compression Distance (NCD)

We employed the Normalized Compression Distance (NCD) to gauge the similarity between text instances. NCD was computed for each pair of comments, encompassing both training and test sets, consequently generating distance matrices. Given two text strings x_1 and x_2, the NCD between them is determined as follows:

$$NCD(x_1, x_2) = \frac{C(x_1 x_2) - \min\left[C(x_1), C(x_2)\right]}{\max\left[C(x_1), C(x_2)\right]} \tag{1}$$

where $C(x)$ represents the size of the compressed string x. This measurement forms the foundation upon which we trained our classifiers, utilizing NCD as a pivotal feature (Table 7).

Table 7. Summary of Macro F1-Scores for Different Classifiers using NCD

Classifier	Macro F1-Score
KNN	0.49
Logistic Regression	0.44
Random Forest	0.34
AdaBoost	0.38
Decision Tree	0.41
SVM	0.27
Naive Bayes	0.22

From the results, the KNN classifier, with a k value of 5, achieved the highest macro F1-score of 0.49. This was closely followed by the Logistic Regression model with a score of 0.44. On the other end of the spectrum, the Naive Bayes classifier produced the lowest macro F1-score at 0.22, indicating potential challenges with this dataset when using the Naive Bayes algorithm. the SVM classifier had certain categories with no predicted samples, which resulted in a warning for ill-defined precision and f1-score.

4.3 Deep Learning Models

We try to test several cutting-edge deep learning models on our dataset by classifying comments into three distinct categories: homophobic, non-lgbtq, and transphobic.

1. *Long Short-Term Memory (LSTM)* networks are a type of recurrent neural network (RNN) architecture. Configuration: Data Preparation: Textual data from the dataset is tokenized and converted into sequences. We employed A fixed sequence length of 100 tokens and sequences are padded to ensure a uniform length. The Embedding Layer Maps each token in the sequence to a 128-dimensional vector. The LSTM Layer comprises 128 LSTM units. Dropout is applied to both input data and recurrent units with a rate of 0.2. This helps prevent overfitting by randomly setting a fraction of input units to 0 at each update during training. The Dense Layer is a fully connected layer with 3 output units (corresponding to 3 classes) and a softmax activation function. This provides the probability distribution over the classes. The model is compiled using the Adam optimizer and the categorical cross-entropy loss function, which is suitable for multi-class classification tasks. The model is trained for 5 epochs with a batch size of 32.
2. *Bidirectional Encoder Representations from Transformers (BERT):* We used BERT from the transformers library was used with the bert-base-uncased variant. Comments from both training and testing datasets were tokenized with a maximum length of 256 tokens. Configuration: We employed the 'bert-base-uncased' variant, undergoing ten epochs of training with a batch size of eight, evaluating the model after each epoch.

3. *ALBERT (a lighter BERT):* ALBERT is a more efficient and streamlined version of the original BERT model. Configuration: We employed the 'albert-base-v2' variant, which is a base version of ALBERT. The dataset is tokenized using the ALBERT tokenizer, with a maximum comment length set to 256 tokens. The model is trained for 10 epochs with a batch size of 8, and the best model is saved after each epoch.

4. *A Robustly Optimized BERT Pretraining Approach (RoBERTa):* RoBERTa, derived from "Robust BERT", is an optimized version of BERT that aims to improve its performance. Configuration: we employed the 'roberta-base' variant, which is a base version of RoBERTa. Comments from the dataset are tokenized using the RoBERTa tokenizer with a maximum length of 256 tokens. The model is trained for 10 epochs with a batch size of 8, and the best model is saved after each epoch.

5. *Hierarchical Attention Networks (HAN)* are designed to capture hierarchical structures in data, specifically for textual data where the hierarchy often comes from words forming sentences and sentences forming documents. The attention mechanism allows the model to focus on specific parts of the input when producing an output. The HAN model captures this hierarchical attention at both the word and sentence levels. Configuration: we employed Sentence Tokenization: Each comment is broken down into its constituent sentences. The tokenization is performed with a maximum vocabulary size of 5000 words, with "UNK" representing out-of-vocabulary words. Each comment is represented as a tensor. Each tensor has the shape of MAX-SENTENCES x MAX-WORDS, where each sentence is represented by a sequence of word tokens. We create an architecture such that the Embedding Layer Maps each word token to a 128-dimensional vector. The Bi-directional GRU Processes the word embeddings from both directions, capturing both past and future context. The Attention Layer Computes word-level attention scores and produces a sentence vector. Sentence Level Attention is applied after this process which includes a Time Distributed Layer which Applies the word-level attention mechanism to each sentence. The Bi-directional GRU Processes the sentence vectors. The Attention LayerComputes sentence-level attention scores and produces a document vector. Output Layer: A dense layer with 3 output units (corresponding to the 3 classes) and a softmax activation function. The model is compiled using the Adam optimizer and the categorical cross-entropy loss function. It is trained for 15 epochs with a batch size of 32.

6. *CharCNN* operates at the character level, leveraging convolutional neural networks. Configuration: The model utilized a 1D convolutional layer, followed by dense layers with dropout for regularization. It was trained for 50 epochs (Tables 8 and 9).

Table 8. Macro F1-Scores for Different Models

Model	Macro F1-Score
BERT	0.36
ALBERT	0.27
RoBERTa	0.27
LSTM	0.53
HAN	0.49
CharCNN	0.53

Table 9. Configuration of Deep Learning Models

Model	Epochs	Batch Size	Max Token Length	Additional Info
LSTM	5	32	100	Embedding: 128, LSTM units: 128, Dropout: 0.2
BERT	10	8	256	Variant: bert-base-uncased
ALBERT	10	8	256	Variant: albert-base-v2
RoBERTa	10	8	256	Variant: roberta-base
HAN	15	32	MAX-SENTENCES x MAX-WORDS	Bi-directional GRU
CharCNN	50	–	–	Conv Layers: 1D

4.4 Discussion

The experimental analysis carried out on the SAMPAR dataset presented a diverse range of performances across various machine learning and deep learning models. The primary metric for evaluating the performance of these models was the Macro F1-Score, which gives us a balanced measure of the models' precision and recall capabilities.

Baseline Classifiers and Ensemble Methods. Among the baseline classifiers and ensemble methods, Logistic Regression and Random Forest (TF-IDF) seemed to perform relatively better with Macro F1-Scores of 0.41 and 0.42 respectively. However, the performance of these models was not highly satisfying, potentially due to the inherent class imbalances in the dataset, which were partially mitigated using SMOTE. Even with class balancing, the traditional machine learning models struggled to capture the nuanced semantic relationships in the text data, which is essential for accurate sentiment classification.

Deep Learning Models. On the other hand, deep learning models, particularly LSTM, CharCNN, and HAN, exhibited a more robust performance with

Macro F1-Scores of 0.53, 0.53, and 0.49 respectively. This could be attributed to their ability to learn hierarchical representations of the text data, capturing both the sequential and contextual dependencies within the comments.

The transformer-based models like BERT, ALBERT, and RoBERTa didn't perform as well as expected, with Macro F1-Scores of 0.36, 0.27, and 0.27 respectively. This might be due to the limited amount of training data, which is often a bottleneck for training transformer models effectively. Additionally, the configuration and tuning of hyperparameters could play a significant role in the performance of these models, and a more extensive hyperparameter search might lead to improved results.

Normalized Compression Distance (NCD) Based Classifiers. Utilizing NCD as a pivotal feature for training classifiers showed promise, with the KNN classifier achieving the highest Macro F1-Score of 0.49 among the NCD-based models. This suggests that measuring textual similarity through compression-based distances could be a viable approach for sentiment analysis in Marathi text.

Challenges and Insights. The challenges encountered during this analysis highlight the complexity of sentiment analysis within the Marathi LGBTQ+ community discussions. The nuanced expressions of sentiments, dialectal variations, and the context-dependent nature of the text data might require more sophisticated models or ensemble techniques for improved performance.

Moreover, the differences in Macro F1-Scores among various models underscore the importance of selecting appropriate model architectures, preprocessing techniques, and feature representations for sentiment analysis tasks.

5   Conclusion and Future Work

In this paper, we introduce the pioneer Marathi dataset tailored for detecting hate speech against the LGBTQ+ community, with a particular emphasis on homophobia and transphobia. The dataset encompasses 5,000 comments meticulously curated from a diverse spectrum of data sources including YouTube and Facebook. One of the salient features of this dataset is its attempt to harmonize pure Marathi and code-mixed language, thereby encapsulating the authentic linguistic intricacies inherent in online Marathi dialogues.

The challenge of pinpointing hate speech is a multifaceted one, exacerbated by the lack of a standardized methodology even in the wake of advanced models like BERT and RoBERTa. The task's complexity often spirals owing to the intricate interplay of linguistic nuances and cultural contexts. Our study underscores the promising advancements epitomized by the KNN classifier, especially when empowered by the Normalized Compression Distance (NCD), demonstrating significant efficacy particularly in the realm of low-resource languages. The Hierarchical Attention Network (HAN), with its adeptness at delineating between word- and sentence-level attention, emerges as a pivotal asset in hate speech detection. This is attributed to the fact that a broader context can often be as revelatory as individual words in discerning hateful intent.

As we cast our gaze towards the future, the potential expansion of the "Sam-Par" dataset emerges as a crucial endeavor. This includes the integration of comments from a broader array of platforms and diverse Marathi-speaking regions to encapsulate a more extensive repertoire of hate speech instances. The inclusion of multimodal sources is imperative, given the frequent accompaniment of visual cues in memes or videos to textual hate speech. Moreover, we posit that forging collaborations with LGBTQ+ groups and activists can unfold invaluable insights into the evolving contours of hate speech. Such synergies not only enrich the dataset continually but also fine-tune the models to the dynamic nature of hate speech, thereby fostering a more nuanced and responsive framework for hate speech detection.

Acknowledgement. This work was conducted with the financial support of the Science Foundation Ireland Centre for Research Training in Artificial Intelligence under Grant No. 18/CRT/6223, supported in part by a research grant from the Science Foundation Ireland (SFI) under Grant Number SFI/12/RC/2289_P2(Insight_2).

References

1. Chakravarthi, B.R.: Detection of homophobia and transphobia in youtube comments. Int. J. Data Sci. Anal. 1–20 (2023)
2. Davidson, T., Warmsley, D., Macy, M., Weber, I.: Automated hate speech detection and the problem of offensive language. In: Proceedings of the International AAAI Conference on Web and Social Media, vol. 11, pp. 512–515 (2017)
3. ElSherief, M., Kulkarni, V., Nguyen, D., Wang, W.Y., Belding, E.: Hate lingo: a target-based linguistic analysis of hate speech in social media. In: Proceedings of the International AAAI Conference on Web and Social Media, vol. 12 (2018)
4. Garaigordobil, M., Larrain, E.: Bullying and cyberbullying in LGBT adolescents: prevalence and effects on mental health. Comunicar Media Educ. Res. J. **28**(1) (2020)
5. Joshi, R.: L3Cube-MahaCorpus and MahaBERT: Marathi monolingual corpus, Marathi BERT language models, and resources. In: Proceedings of the WILDRE-6 Workshop within the 13th Language Resources and Evaluation Conference, pp. 97–101, Marseille, France, June 2022. European Language Resources Association (2022)
6. Chavan, T., Patankar, S., Kane, A., Gokhale, O., Joshi, R.: A twitter BERT approach for offensive language detection in Marathi (2022). arXiv preprint arXiv:2212.10039
7. Saleh, H., Alhothali, A., Moria, K.: Detection of hate speech using BERT and hate speech word embedding with deep model. CoRR, abs/2111.01515 (2021)
8. Yadav, A.K., Kumar, M., Kumar, A., et al.: Hate speech recognition in multilingual text: hinglish documents. Int. J. Inf. Technol. **15**, 1319–1331 (2023)
9. Yin, W., Zubiaga, A.: Towards generalisable hate speech detection: a review on obstacles and solutions. PeerJ Comput. Sci. **7**, e598 (2021)

10. Clarke, C., et al.: Rule by example: harnessing logical rules for explainable hate speech detection. In: Proceedings of the 61st Annual Meeting of the Association for Computational Linguistics (Volume 1: Long Papers), pp. 364–376, Toronto, Canada, July 2023. Association for Computational Linguistics (2023)

11. Halevy, K.: A group-specific approach to NLP for hate speech detection, 2023

12. Gaikwad, S., Ranasinghe, T., Zampieri, M., Homan, C.M.: Cross-lingual offensive language identification for low resource languages: the case of Marathi. In: Proceedings of the International Conference on Recent Advances in Natural Language Processing (RANLP 2021), pp. 437–443, Held Online, September 2021. INCOMA Ltd. (2021)

13. Sharif, O., Hossain, E., Hoque, M.M.: M-BAD: a multilabel dataset for detecting aggressive texts and their targets. In: Proceedings of the Workshop on Combating Online Hostile Posts in Regional Languages during Emergency Situations, pp. 75–85, Dublin, Ireland, May 2022. Association for Computational Linguistics (2022)

14. Dikshitha Vani, V., Bharathi, B.: Hate speech and offensive content identification in multiple languages using machine learning algorithms. In: Forum for Information Retrieval Evaluation (Working Notes) (FIRE). CEUR-WS.org (2022)

15. Ripoll, M.L., Hassan, F., Attieh, J., Collell, G., Bouchekif, A.: Multi-lingual contextual hate speech detection using transformer-based ensembles. In: Forum for Information Retrieval Evaluation (Working Notes) (FIRE). CEUR-WS.org (2022)

16. Kalra, S., Maheshwari, K., Goel, S., Sharma, Y.: Hate speech detection in Marathi and code-mixed languages using TF-IDF and transformers-based BERT-variants (2022)

17. Chanda, S., Ujjwal, S., Das, S., Pal, S.: Fine-tuning pre-trained transformer based model for hate speech and offensive content identification in English, Indo-Aryan and code-mixed (English-Hindi) languages. In: Forum for Information Retrieval Evaluation (Working Notes) (FIRE), CEUR-WS.org (2021)

18. Zampieri, M., et al.: Predicting the type and target of offensive social media posts in Marathi. Soc. Netw. Anal. Min. **12**(1), 77 (2022)

19. Zhang, J., et al.: Conversations gone awry: detecting early signs of conversational failure. In: Proceedings of the 56th Annual Meeting of the Association for Computational Linguistics (Volume 1: Long Papers), pp. 1350–1361, Melbourne, Australia, July 2018. Association for Computational Linguistics (2018)

20. Jiang, Z., Yang, M., Tsirlin, M., Tang, R., Dai, Y., Lin, J.: Low-resource text classification: a parameter-free classification method with compressors. In: Findings of the Association for Computational Linguistics: ACL 2023, pp. 6810–6828, Toronto, Canada, July 2023. Association for Computational Linguistics (2023)

21. Qian, J., Bethke, A., Liu, Y., Belding, E., Wang, W.Y.: A benchmark dataset for learning to intervene in online hate speech. In: Proceedings of the 2019 Conference on Empirical Methods in Natural Language Processing and the 9th International Joint Conference on Natural Language Processing (EMNLP-IJCNLP), pp. 4755–4764, Hong Kong, China, November 2019. Association for Computational Linguistics (2019)

22. Chakravarthi, B.R.: HopeEDI: a multilingual hope speech detection dataset for equality, diversity, and inclusion. In: Proceedings of the Third Workshop on Computational Modeling of People's Opinions, Personality, and Emotion's in Social Media, pp. 41–53, Barcelona, Spain (Online), December 2020. Association for Computational Linguistics (2020)

L3Cube-MahaNews: News-Based Short Text and Long Document Classification Datasets in Marathi

Saloni Mittal[1,3], Vidula Magdum[1,3], Sharayu Hiwarkhedkar[1,3],
Omkar Dhekane[1,3], and Raviraj Joshi[2,3(✉)]

[1] Pune Institute of Computer Technology, Pune, Maharashtra, India
[2] Indian Institute of Technology Madras, Chennai, Tamil Nadu, India
ravirajoshi@gmail.com
[3] L3Cube, Pune, India

Abstract. The availability of text or topic classification datasets in the low-resource Marathi language is limited, typically consisting of fewer than 4 target labels, with some achieving nearly perfect accuracy. In this work, we introduce L3Cube-MahaNews, a Marathi text classification corpus that focuses on News headlines and articles. This corpus stands out as the largest supervised Marathi Corpus, containing over 1.05 lakh records classified into a diverse range of 12 categories. To accommodate different document lengths, MahaNews comprises three supervised datasets specifically designed for short text, long documents, and medium paragraphs. The consistent labeling across these datasets facilitates document length-based analysis. We provide detailed data statistics and baseline results on these datasets using state-of-the-art pre-trained BERT models. We conduct a comparative analysis between monolingual and multilingual BERT models, including MahaBERT, IndicBERT, and MuRIL. The monolingual MahaBERT model outperforms all others on every dataset. This work is a part of the L3Cube MahaNLP initiative, more information about it can be found at https://github.com/l3cube-pune/MarathiNLP.

Keywords: Marathi Text Classification · Marathi Topic Identification · Low Resource Language · Short Text Classification · Long Document Classification · News Article Datasets · BERT · Web Scraping

1 Introduction

Text Classification is a popular problem often discussed in machine learning and natural language processing (NLP) [1]. It deals with organizing, segregating, and appropriately assigning the textual sentence or a document into some predefined categories. It is a supervised learning task and has been solved using traditional machine learning approaches and more recent deep learning algorithms [15]. Text classification is important for applications like the automatic categorization of

B. R. Chakravarthi et al. (Eds.): SPELLL 2023, CCIS 2046, pp. 52–63, 2024.
https://doi.org/10.1007/978-3-031-58495-4_4

web articles or social media comments. While a lot of research has been done in the area of English text classification, low-resource languages like Marathi are still left behind. In this work, we focus on the classification of text in the Marathi language.

The Marathi language is one of the 22+ Indian languages[1] out of the 7000 languages spoken worldwide[2]. It is the third most spoken language of India, spoken by over 83 million people across the country. It ranks 11th in the list of popular languages across the globe[3]. Despite being a widely spoken language, Marathi-specific NLP monolingual resources are still limited in comparison to other natural languages [7]. As a result, sufficient data resources for machine learning tasks are less available for this language, making it challenging for researchers conducting studies in this widely used though low resource-based regional language. It can be noticed that the datasets available are largely in Mandarin Chinese, Spanish, English, Arabic, Hindi, and Bengali languages[4]. There are fewer datasets on regional languages like Marathi. The only four classification datasets publicly available are iNLTK headlines [2], IndicNLP articles [9], MahaHate [13], and MahaSent [12]. The paper [11] showed that the Indic-NLP News Article dataset achieves near-perfect accuracy (99%) thus limiting its usability. Therefore we need some complex datasets to evaluate the goodness of the models. Also, all of these datasets have at most four target labels. Thus, there is a significant need of datasets with exhaustive labels similar to that of BBC News[5] or AG News[6] for the language Marathi.

Datasets with varying sequence lengths are required as transformer-based classification models are sensitive towards the text length due to their self-attention operation [3]. Models like LongFormer [3] are specifically developed for datasets having longer sequences. In order to develop these models for Marathi we first need such target datasets. Thus, we present **L3Cube-MahaNews - A Marathi News Classification Dataset** in this paper.

The dataset we propose is available in three forms, viz. short, medium, and long text classification that is obtained from a renowned Marathi news website. This massive corpus of over 1 lakh records will serve as an excellent data source for the comparison of different machine-learning algorithms in low-resource settings. It contains information about 12 dynamic categories for diverse disciplines of study. We evaluate different monolingual and multilingual BERT [4] models like MahaBERT [7], indicBERT [9], and MuRil [10] and provide baseline results for future studies. The results are evaluated using the validation accuracy, testing Accuracy, F1 score (Macro), recall (Macro), and precision (Macro).

---

[1] https://en.wikipedia.org/w/index.php?title=Languages_of_India.

[2] https://en.wikipedia.org/w/index.php?title=Lists_of_languages.

[3] https://en.wikipedia.org/w/index.php?title=Marathi_language.

[4] https://en.wikipedia.org/w/index.php?title=List_of_datasets_for_machine-learning_research.

[5] https://www.kaggle.com/c/learn-ai-bbc.

[6] https://www.kaggle.com/datasets/amananandrai/ag-news-classification-dataset.

The main contributions of this work are as follows:

– We present L3Cube-MahaNews, the first extensive document classification dataset in Marathi with 12 target labels as shown in Table 1. The dataset will be released publicly.
– The corpus consists of three sub-datasets MahaNews-SHC, LPC, and LDC for short, medium, and long documents respectively. We provide three different datasets with varying sentence lengths and the same target labels.
– The datasets are benchmarked using state-of-the-art BERT models like MahaBERT, MuRIL, and IndicBERT with MahaBERT giving the best results. We thus present a comparative analysis of these monolingual and multilingual BERT models for Marathi text.

2   Related Work

Text classification is a very popular task in Natural Language Processing. Even though Marathi is a widely spoken language, the lack of proper Marathi datasets that can be used for text classification tasks has restricted the area of research for this language. In this section, we review a few of the publicly available Indian language datasets that are used for the objective task.

[9] curated large-scale sentence-level monolingual corpora- *IndicCorp* containing 11 major Indian languages. *IndicNLP News Article* dataset is part of the IndicNLPSuite[7] consists of news articles in Marathi categorized into 3 classes viz. sports, entertainment, and lifestyle. The datasets provided by IndicNLP are used to pre-train the word embedding and multilingual models.

[2] presented iNLTK[8] which is an open-source NLP library containing pre-trained language models and methods for data augmentation, textual similarity, tokenization, word embeddings, etc. The *iNLTK Headlines Corpus - Marathi*[9] is a Marathi News Classification Dataset provided by iNLTK, containing nearly 12000 news article headlines collected from a Marathi news website. The corpus contains 3 label classes viz. state (62%) entertainment (27%) sports (10%).

[5] presented a comparative study of Marathi text classification using monolingual and multilingual embeddings. For the experiment, they use *Marathi news headline dataset* sourced from Kaggle with 9K examples and three label classes - entertainment, state, and sport. The news article headlines were originally collected from a Marathi news website. Their study also showed that multilingual embeddings have 15% performance gain compared to traditional monolingual embeddings.

[6] evaluated and compared the performance of language models on text classification tasks over 3 Indian languages - Hindi, Bengali, and Telugu. For Hindi, they used *BBC Hindi News Articles* which contains annotated news articles classified into 14 different categories. While for Bengali and Telugu, they used classification datasets provided by Indic-NLP [9]. Their result demonstrated that

---

[7] https://github.com/anoopkunchukuttan/indic_nlp_library.
[8] https://github.com/goru001/inltk.
[9] https://www.kaggle.com/datasets/disisbig/marathi-news-dataset.

monolingual models perform better for some languages but the improvement attained is marginal at best.

[13] curated *MahaHate-* a tweet-based marathi hate speech detection dataset. The dataset is collected from Twitter and annotated manually. It consists of over 25000 distinct tweets labeled into 4 major classes i.e. hate, offensive, profane, and no. The deep learning models based on CNN, LSTM, and transformers that involved monolingual and multilingual variants of BERT were used for evaluation.

[12] offers first major publicly available Marathi Sentiment Analysis Dataset *L3CubeMahaSent*. The dataset is curated using tweets extracted from various Maharashtrian personalities' Twitter accounts. It consists of 16,000 distinct tweets classified into three classes - positive, negative, and neutral. The authors performed 2-class and 3-class sentiment analysis on their dataset and evaluated baseline classification results using deep learning models - CNN, LSTM, and ULMFiT.

[14] conducted a comparative study between monolingual and multilingual BERT models. The standard multilingual models such as mBERT, indicBERT, and xlm-RoBERTa along with monolingual models - MahaBERT, MahaAL-BERT, and MahaRoBERTa for Marathi [7] were used in this study.

Table 1. Categorical labels for MahaNews datasets

Labels	Description
Auto	Vehicle launches and their reviews
Bhakti	Horoscope, festivals, spirituality
Crime	Crimes and accidents in the country
Education	Educational institutes and their activities
Fashion	Fashion events, advertisements of fashion products
Health	Diseases, medicines, and health-related blogs
International	Happenings around the world
Manoranjan	Information related to movies, web series, and so on
Politics	Political incidents in the country
Sports	Various sports games, awards, sporting events and so on
Tech	Latest technologies, gadgets and their reviews
Travel	Travel tips, Top destinations recommendations, tourism information, et cetera

3   Curating the Dataset

We propose L3Cube-MahaNews which is a collection of datasets for short text and long document classification. The Short Headlines Classification (SHC), Long Document Classification (LDC), and Long Paragraph Classification (LPC) datasets are the three supervised datasets included in MahaNews.

Table 2. Category-wise distribution of SHC, LDC, LPC datasets into train, test and validation in ratio of 80:10:10.

Labels	SHC & LDC				LPC			
	Train	Test	Validation	Total	Train	Test	Validation	Total
Auto	1664	209	208	2081	3099	388	387	3874
Bhakti	1386	174	173	1733	3664	458	458	4580
Crime	2354	295	294	2943	4092	512	512	5116
Education	680	86	85	851	1438	180	180	1798
Fashion	1920	241	240	2401	874	110	109	1093
Health	1985	249	248	2482	6428	804	803	8035
International	2041	256	255	2552	4715	590	589	5894
Manoranjan	2986	374	373	3733	4825	604	603	6032
Politics	2250	282	281	2813	4379	548	547	5474
Sports	1882	236	235	2353	5337	668	667	6672
Tech	2111	264	264	2639	2049	257	256	2562
Travel	755	95	94	944	1970	247	246	2463
Total	22014	2761	2750	**27525**	42870	5366	5357	**53593**

- **Short Headlines Classification (SHC)**: This Short Document Classification dataset contains the headlines of news articles along with their corresponding categorical labels.
- **Long Paragraph Classification (LPC)**: This is a Long Document Classification dataset. The news articles are divided into paragraphs and each record in this dataset contains a paragraph each with its corresponding categorical label.
- **Long Document Classification (LDC)**: This Long Document Classification dataset contains records having an entire news article along with its corresponding categorical label.

The categorical labels in the supervised datasets are described in detail in Table 1.

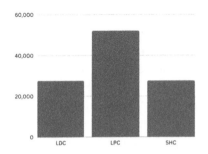

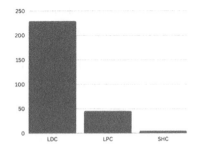

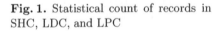

Fig. 1. Statistical count of records in SHC, LDC, and LPC

Fig. 2. Average count of words per record in SHC, LDC, and LPC

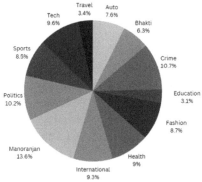

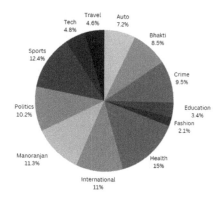

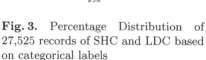

Fig. 3. Percentage Distribution of 27,525 records of SHC and LDC based on categorical labels

Fig. 4. Percentage Distribution of 53,593 records of LPC based on categorical labels

3.1 Data Collection

The datasets are compiled using scraped news data. The entirety of the information is taken from the Lokmat[10] website which houses news articles in the Marathi language. The data was scraped by using urllib package to handle URL requests and the BeautifulSoup package to extract data from the HTML of the requested URL.

Lokmat website had arranged the news articles under predefined categories like automobile, sports, travel, politics, etc. While scraping, this categorization was preserved and further used as target labels. The final curated datasets were shuffled, de-duplicated, and cleaned up.

3.2 Data Statistics

The L3Cube-MahaNews has a total of 1,08,643 records which are derived from 27,525 news articles scraped from Lokmat. SHC and LDC have a total of 27,525 rows with labels each and LPC has 53,593 labeled rows in it.

The statistical count of records in SHC, LDC, and LPC can be referred from Fig. 1 and the average count of words per record in each proposed dataset can be seen in Fig. 2.

The category-wise percentage distribution for the corpora can be referred from Fig. 3 and 4.

4   Evaluation

We fine-tune the monolingual and multilingual BERT models supporting the Marathi language on the curated L3Cube-MahaNews corpus for the text classification task. A dense layer is added on top of the BERT model which maps the [CLS] token embedding to the 12 target labels.

---

[10] https://www.lokmat.com/.

Table 3. Results for all the models trained on SHC, LDC, and LPC datasets in percentage (%)

		Validation Accuracy	Testing Accuracy	F1 Score (Macro)	Recall (Macro)	Precision (Macro)
SHC	MahaBERT	**91.418**	**91.163**	**90.230**	**89.700**	**91.047**
	indicBERT	90.073	89.388	88.303	87.953	88.758
	MuRIL	90.655	90.112	89.031	88.826	89.313
LDC	MahaBERT	**94.780**	**94.706**	**93.589**	**93.210**	**94.079**
	indicBERT	93.642	92.627	91.340	91.217	91.511
	MuRIL	93.564	93.020	92.337	92.213	92.501
LPC	MahaBERT	**88.754**	**86.731**	**84.915**	**83.455**	**87.138**
	indicBERT	86.298	85.222	86.688	81.697	84.249
	MuRIL	87.157	86.582	84.585	83.215	86.603

Table 4. Results for the MahaBERT models trained on SHC, LDC, and LPC datasets tested on the test set of other datasets in percentage (%)

MahaBERT model trained on	MahaBERT model tested on	Testing Accuracy	F1 Score (Macro)	Recall (Macro)	Precision (Macro)
SHC		**91.163**	**90.230**	**89.700**	**91.047**
LPC	SHC	73.234	73.001	75.669	77.353
LDC		74.171	79.570	76.599	79.570
SHC+LPC+LDC		86.780	85.484	86.195	87.689
SHC		73.234	73.001	75.669	77.353
LPC	LPC	86.731	84.915	83.455	87.138
LDC		72.201	75.741	72.530	70.521
SHC+LPC+LDC		**89.713**	**88.421**	**88.545**	**88.439**
SHC		80.314	79.042	84.109	81.521
LPC	LDC	87.294	86.511	88.559	86.424
LDC		**94.706**	**93.589**	**93.210**	**94.079**
SHC+LPC+LDC		87.758	86.686	87.869	91.918

4.1 Experiment Setup

Data Preparation. Each of the SHC, LDC, and LPC corpora are split into train, test, and validation datasets in a ratio of 80:10:10. We have ensured that the category-wise distribution ratio of data in SHC, LDC, and LPC remains constant in the split datasets.

The datasets are preprocessed to remove unwanted characters and words from it such as newline characters, hashtags, URLs, and so on. After preprocessing, only Devanagari, English, and numerical digits are retained.

Refer to Table 2 for the category-wise distribution of data into train, test, and validation datasets.

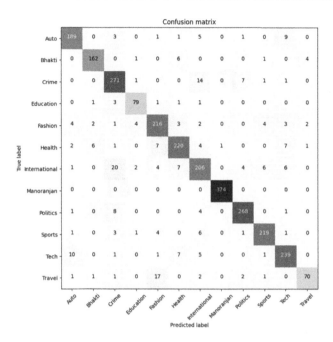

Fig. 5. Confusion matrix for SHC results

Models. The pre-trained BERT models that have been finetuned for text classification are as follows:

- **MahaBERT**[11]: MahaBERT is a 752 million token multilingual BERT model fine-tuned on L3Cube-MahaCorpus and other publicly available Marathi monolingual datasets.
- **indicBERT**[12,13]: IndicBERT is a multi-lingual AlBERT model exclusively pre-trained on 12 Indian languages. It is pre-trained on AI4Bharat IndicNLP Corpora consisting of 8.9 billion tokens.
- **MuRIL**[14]: MuRIL is a BERT model pre-trained in 17 Indian languages. It has been pre-trained on datasets from Wikipedia, Common Crawl, Dakshina, etc.

We chose mahaBERT and indicBERT as the models to finetune for text classification since we wanted to compare monolingual BERT models against multilingual BERT models. A study on this comparison [14] observes that the monolingual BERT models have better performance than the multilingual BERT variants for five different downstream fine-tuning tasks, so we finetune

---

[11] https://huggingface.co/l3cube-pune/marathi-bert-v2.
[12] https://indicnlp.ai4bharat.org/pages/indic-bert/#pretraining-details.
[13] https://huggingface.co/ai4bharat/indic-bert.
[14] https://huggingface.co/google/muril-base-cased.

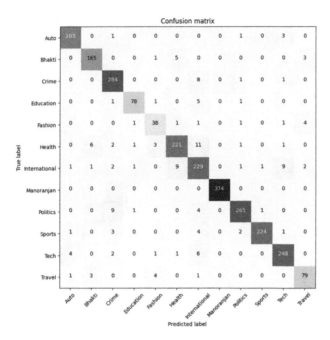

Fig. 6. Confusion matrix for LDC results

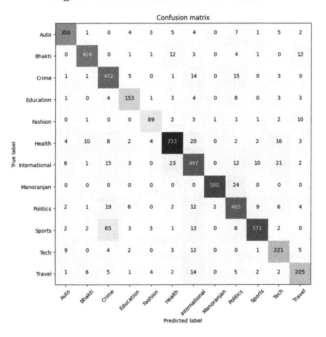

Fig. 7. Confusion matrix for LPC results

the mahaBERT and indicBERT models for the text classification downstream fine-tuning task to see how they compare.

It is evident from the results described in Table 3 that the monolingual model mahaBERT outperforms the multilingual model indicBERT for text classification task.

It was also observed that these models gave the best results when they were trained for 3 epochs on the training datasets at the default learning rate (1e-3). The MuRIL model, on the other hand, performed best during 5 training epochs for the SHC dataset.

The fine-tuned MahaBERT models were also tested against test sets of the other datasets like the pre-trained MahaBERT model fine-tuned on SHC dataset was tested against the test sets for LDC and LPC to compute the results of this cross-analysis.

4.2 Results

The results obtained from fine-tuning the models on our datasets are shown in Table 3 along with the confusion matrices in Fig. 5, 6 and 7. The results obtained on performing the cross-analysis by testing the MahaBERT model on test sets of different datasets can be referred from Table 4.

The key observations that were inferred are as follows:

– The monolingual MahaBERT model outperforms all other models in terms of the various scores depicted in the table for every corpus.
– Among SHC, LDC, and LPC, LDC gave the best results in fine-tuning for the text classification task. This is expected as the long document data contains more information as compared to the other two smaller-length datasets.
– LPC reports scores on the lower side for all the 3 models. A paragraph might at times contain more generic information and hence result in confusion for the models.

5   Conclusion

In this paper, we present L3Cube-MahaNews - a suite of 3 labeled datasets that consists of 1.08lakhs+ Marathi records for the Marathi Text Classification. The paper describes an extensive set of 12 categorical labels used to create the supervised datasets. We have performed fine-tuning on Marathi-based models to provide a benchmark for future studies and development. The models utilized were MahaBERT, IndicBERT, and MuRIL. We report the best accuracy using MahaBERT for the LDC dataset. We hope that our datasets will play an important role in the betterment of Marathi language support in the field of NLP.

Limitations

During data scrapping and preparation, it was seen that some news articles had scanned images, GIFs, banner ads, etc., as a part of web page content. Thus, additional tools (e.g. OCR-image-to-text converter) might be required to extract text from such web content and retain only the news-related textual data in a proper format. Moreover, since the LPC dataset was created by extracting random paragraphs from the parent articles, these might at times contain generic information not specific to the target label. In future, we can manually verify the dataset to filter such problematic entities.

Acknowledgment. This work was done under the L3Cube Pune mentorship program. We would like to express our gratitude towards our mentors at L3Cube for their continuous support and encouragement. This work is a part of the L3Cube-MahaNLP project [8].

References

1. Minaee, S., Kalchbrenner, N., Cambria, E., Nikzad, N., Chenaghlu, M., Gao, J.: Deep learning-based text classification: a comprehensive review. ACM Comput. Surv. (CSUR) **54**(3), 1–40 (2021)
2. Arora, G.: iNLTK : natural language toolkit for Indic languages (2020). arXiv preprint arXiv:2009.12534
3. Beltagy, I., Peters, M.E., Cohan, A.: Longformer: the long-document transformer (2020)
4. Devlin, J., Chang, M.W., Lee, K., Toutanova, K.: Bert: pretraining of deep bidirectional transformers for language understanding (2018). arXiv preprint arXiv:1810.04805
5. Eranpurwala, F., Ramane, P., Bolla, B.K.: Comparative study of Marathi text classification using monolingual and multilingual embeddings. In: Woungang, I., Dhurandher, S.K., Pattanaik, K.K., Verma, A., Verma, P. (eds.) Advanced Network Technologies and Intelligent Computing. ANTIC 2021. CCIS, vol. 1534, pp. 441–452. Springer, Cham (2022). https://doi.org/10.1007/978-3-030-96040-7_35
6. Jain, K., Deshpande, A., Shridhar, K., Laumann, F., Dash, A.: Indic- transformers: an analysis of transformer language models for Indian languages (2020). arXiv preprint arXiv:2011.02323
7. Joshi, R.: L3cube-mahacorpus and mahabert: Marathi monolingual corpus, Marathi Bert language models, and resources. In: LREC 2022 Workshop Language Resources and Evaluation Conference 20–25 June 2022, p. 97 (2022a)
8. Joshi, R.: L3cube-mahanlp: Marathi natural language processing datasets, models, and library (2022b). arXiv preprint arXiv:2205.14728
9. Kakwani, D., et al.: IndicNLPSuite: monolingual corpora, evaluation benchmarks and pre-trained multilingual language models for Indian languages. In: Findings of the Association for Computational Linguistics: EMNLP 2020, pp. 4948–4961 (2020)
10. Khanuja, S., et al.: MuRIL: multilingual representations for Indian languages (2021). arXiv preprint arXiv:2103.10730

11. Kulkarni, A., Mandhane, M., Likhitkar, M., Kshirsagar, G., Jagdale, J., Joshi, R.: Experimental evaluation of deep learning models for Marathi text classification. In: Gunjan, V.K., Zurada, J.M. (eds.) Proceedings of the 2nd International Conference on Recent Trends in Machine Learning, IoT, Smart Cities and Applications. LNNS, vol. 237, pp. 605–613. Springer, Singapore (2022). https://doi.org/10.1007/978-981-16-6407-6_53
12. Kulkarni, A., Mandhane, M., Likhitkar, M., Kshirsagar, G., Joshi, R.: L3cubemahasent: a Marathi tweet-based sentiment analysis dataset. In: Proceedings of the Eleventh Workshop on Computational Approaches to Subjectivity, Sentiment and Social Media Analysis, pp. 213–220 (2021)
13. Velankar, A., Patil, H., Gore, A., Salunke, S., Joshi, R.: L3cube-mahahate: a tweet-based Marathi hate speech detection dataset and Bert models. In: Proceedings of the Third Workshop on Threat, Aggression and Cyberbullying (TRAC 2022), pp. 1–9 (2022)
14. Velankar, A., Patil, H., Joshi, R.: Mono vs multilingual BERT for hate speech detection and text classification: a case study in Marathi. In: El Gayar, N., Trentin, E., Ravanelli, M., Abbas, H. (eds.) Artificial Neural Networks in Pattern Recognition. ANNPR 2022. LNCS, vol. 13739, pp. 121–128. Springer, Cham (2023). https://doi.org/10.1007/978-3-031-20650-4_10
15. Wagh, V., Khandve, S., Joshi, I., Wani, A., Kale, G., Joshi, R.: Comparative study of long document classification. In: TENCON 2021-2021 IEEE Region 10 Conference (TENCON), pp. 732–737. IEEE (2021)

Creation and Classification of Kannada Meme Dataset: Exploring Domain and Troll Categories

Sahana Y. Kundargi[1]([✉]), Lohith N[1], Anand Kumar M[1],
and Bharathi Raja Chakravarthi[2]

[1] Department of Information Technology, National Institute of Technology
Karnataka, Surathkal, India
{sahanaykundargi.201it253,lohithn.201it133,m_anandkumar}@nitk.edu.in
[2] Insight SFI Research Centre for Data Analytics, School of Computer Science,
University of Galway, Galway, Ireland
bharathi.raja@universityofgalway.ie

Abstract. In this pioneering research, the first-ever Kannada memes dataset is established, marking a groundbreaking contribution. This dataset encompasses 2002 memes, spanning various categories such as movies, politics, sports, trolls, and non-troll memes. The classification models have been meticulously fine-tuned for memes, incorporating image-based models using DenseNet169 and text-based models with BERT for text encoding. An innovative multimodal approach combines insights from images and text, acknowledging the comprehensive nature of meme content. Throughout the study, model strengths and weaknesses are assessed, emphasizing their reliance on cutting-edge technologies like Deep Learning and Natural Language Processing. Valuable improvements are recommended, such as the implementation of oversampling techniques and regular dataset updates to enhance relevance and accuracy. This work extends beyond immediate research, contributing to the development of adaptive meme classification systems, particularly for Kannada-speaking audiences within the evolving meme culture landscape. Notably, the results indicate that multimodal models achieved the best scores for domain classification, while image-based models excelled in troll meme classification, further highlighting the significance of this approach within the field.

Keywords: Meme Classification · Kannada Dataset · Multimodal · BERT · DenseNet169

1 Introduction

In the dynamic landscape of the internet, where ideas and expressions are constantly evolving, memes have emerged as a significant cultural phenomenon that transcends geographical boundaries. Notably, our research stands out due to

B. R. Chakravarthi et al. (Eds.): SPELLL 2023, CCIS 2046, pp. 64–78, 2024.
https://doi.org/10.1007/978-3-031-58495-4_5

its pioneering effort in creating the first-ever Kannada memes dataset. This endeavor is of utmost significance in the context of meme research, particularly for Kannada-speaking audiences.

As highlighted by Suryawanshi et al. [14], datasets play a crucial role in meme classification research, and Hande et al. [6] have shed light on language intricacies essential for comprehending Kannada memes. Memes are not mere fleeting images or humorous captions; they encapsulate ideas, behaviors, or styles propagating rapidly through imitation, carrying profound thematic meanings. Social media platforms act as catalysts for the swift dissemination of memes, providing a platform for users to post, share, and engage with a wide spectrum of content, ranging from profound reflections to lighthearted humor that resonates with a broad audience.

Consider the world of Kannada memes, flourishing within a vibrant community steeped in rich cultural history. In the realm of social media, Kannada memes exhibit a distinctive visual style, often incorporating the Roman alphabet rather than traditional Kannada script. This choice is driven by meme creators who believe that Roman letters enhance the popularity of their memes. Even when expressed in English, these memes continue to convey significant ideas deeply rooted in the Kannada culture.

However, memes are not solely conduits of amusement and jest; they also serve as powerful instruments for conveying emotions, ideas, and social commentary. Ghanghor et al. and Yasaswini et al. [5,16] have contributed to offensive language identification and meme classification in Dravidian languages, underlining the significance of understanding linguistic nuances and domain-specific characteristics when analyzing Kannada memes. Memes possess the unique ability to evoke laughter, contemplation, or inspiration, but they can also be wielded to disparage and insult others. Regrettably, some individuals create memes that propagate hatred targeting specific individuals or groups, thereby contributing to social discord.

In the realm of academia, memes have infiltrated college campuses, courtesy of the pervasive influence of social media. While these platforms offer a means for self-expression, they are not immune to the proliferation of derisive memes that mock and belittle others, often leading to hurtful consequences. The intricacy of meme interpretation arises from their use of diverse languages and the camouflage of their true intent behind humor and satire.

This paper endeavors to unravel the world of Kannada memes and decipher their underlying meanings. Building on insights from Afridi et al. [1], we aim to improve meme classification using approaches from deep learning and computer vision, recognizing that the collaborative nature of meme research showcases exciting opportunities and challenges ahead. To accomplish this, we propose an innovative approach that involves the analysis of both text and visual elements. We acknowledge that an effective meme comprehension system must consider both linguistic and visual cues. Thus, our study employs a multimodal approach that integrates these components to gain a comprehensive understanding of meme content.

Here is what you will find in this paper: In Sect. 2, an examination of existing research on meme comprehension is presented to assess prior efforts in this domain. In Sect. 3, an overview of the data employed in this study is provided. Section 4 offers an explication of the methodologies employed, encompassing the utilization of both textual and visual elements to enhance meme comprehension. Section 5 presents the outcomes achieved through our method and evaluates its effectiveness. Finally, in Sect. 6, this paper concludes by offering significant insights and suggestions for future research. It is worth noting that the task of comprehending and categorizing Kannada memes is continually evolving due to the dynamic nature of internet usage patterns.

Memes have emerged as influential tools for the dissemination of ideas and emotions. This study seeks to enhance our comprehension of their societal impact and promote more effective discourse around them.

2   Related Works

Memes, as visual and textual forms of communication, have become an integral part of modern Internet culture. Exploring the nuances of memes and their classification in regional languages like Kannada presents an intriguing research domain. This literature review delves into various studies and approaches that contribute to the creation and classification of Kannada meme datasets while exploring domain-specific aspects and troll categories.

Suryawanshi and Chakravarthi [14] have significantly contributed to the field of meme classification research, emphasizing the pivotal role of datasets in this domain, as exemplified in their dataset for Tamil memes. While their primary focus is on Tamil memes, their research emphasizes the fundamental importance of a quality dataset tailored to a specific language or region, forming the cornerstone for training and evaluating classification models. Moreover, in their paper presenting findings from the shared task on Troll Meme Classification in Tamil [13], they provide valuable insights into the challenges and methodologies relevant to meme classification in Dravidian languages. These insights hold significance for the domain of Kannada memes and can guide future research in this field. Their work collectively highlights the critical role of datasets and the applicability of research findings across different linguistic contexts.

Hande et al. [6] have introduced a dataset that addresses language intricacies, which are a crucial factor in meme understanding. The challenges and insights from this study can be adapted to create a comprehensive Kannada meme dataset.

Ghanghor et al. and Yasaswini et al. [5,16] contribute to offensive language identification and meme classification in Dravidian languages. Their research underscores the importance of comprehending domain-specific characteristics and linguistic nuances when classifying Kannada memes, especially those involving trolling. The workshop showcased papers that explored meme classification in various Dravidian languages. While some papers were not specifically focused on Kannada, they provide insights into adaptable and extensible classification techniques. Notably, the works of Huang and Bai, Hs et al. [7,8,11], and Li concentrate on text-image fusion, deep learning, and multimodal transformers.

Afridi et al. [1] present a comprehensive survey on multimodal meme classification. Their work highlights the evolving landscape of meme research and identifies outstanding research challenges. Adapting their insights can guide researchers in addressing challenges and identifying relevant troll categories.

Furthermore, meme classification draws inspiration from fields such as computer vision and natural language processing. Papers like Iandola et al., Devlin et al., Kieffer et al. [4,9,10,12], and Loussaief and Abdelkrim provide architectural and technical insights that can be applied.

Boyd et al. [3] explore deep learning-based feature extraction in iris recognition. Although not directly related to memes, their study highlights the relevance of feature extraction techniques, which can be adapted for capturing distinctive features within Kannada memes.

The work of Wang and Wen [15] introduces a nonparanormal approach to combining textual and visual information to predict and generate popular meme descriptions. While their focus is on popular meme descriptions, their fusion technique provides insights into combining textual and visual content.

Amalia et al. [2] propose meme opinion categorization using optical character recognition and the naïve Bayes algorithm. While their approach may not directly apply to Kannada memes, the integration of OCR and machine learning algorithms can inspire techniques for processing textual content.

The use of pre-trained models in meme classification is a recurring theme. Devlin et al. [4] present BERT, a pre-training technique for deep bidirectional transformers in language understanding. Similarly, Iandola et al. [9] introduce DenseNet, an efficient convolutional neural network architecture. These models can be fine-tuned and adapted to capture intricate patterns in both textual and visual elements.

In conclusion, this literature review explores various studies on creating and categorizing Kannada meme datasets. These studies cover areas like offensive language detection, combining text and images, and leveraging pre-trained models for better classification. By combining techniques from different fields like deep learning and natural language processing, meme analysis becomes more comprehensive. Our research draws from these studies to build a robust Kannada meme dataset, benefiting from insights into language nuances and humor. We also aim to improve meme classification using approaches from deep learning and computer vision. This review underscores the collaborative nature of meme research, presenting both exciting opportunities and forthcoming challenges.

3 Kannada Dataset

3.1 Data Gathering and Refinement

Our journey began by meticulously compiling a collection of Kannada memes sourced from well-known social media platforms like Facebook, Instagram, and

Twitter. Notably, a substantial portion of these memes featured text in the Roman script, showcasing the interplay between the Kannada language and its transliteration into English characters on the digital stage. Figure 1 offers a captivating glimpse into the diverse array of memes we gathered, illustrating the fascinating fusion of visual imagery with Kannada language expressions.

Diverse topics abound within our dataset, with sports, movies, and politics emerging as prominent themes. Furthermore, we've diligently organized the memes into categories: trolls and non-trolls, effectively capturing the wide spectrum of humor styles and content inherent in Kannada meme culture.

With the raw data in our possession, our next step was to refine it through a meticulous cleaning process. This involved purging duplicate files, ensuring only unique data remained. An interesting exception was made for memes that employed the same image while featuring distinct text - these were preserved for deeper analysis and exploration.

Fig. 1. Kannada Memes in the Data-set.

3.2 Dataset Annotation and Inter-Annotator Agreement

After acquiring the memes, we employed Google Forms to present the data to a diverse group of annotators. Each form tasked annotators with categorizing the memes as either troll or non-troll and assessing their relevance to sports, movies, or politics. To aid annotators in accurately understanding and applying these categories, we supplied a range of meme examples from different domains, including troll memes. This set of examples served as a guide to help annotators recognize meme characteristics. An expert annotator, proficient in Kannada and meme culture, conducted the annotations for these instances.

To ensure the reliability of the annotations, we assembled a diverse group of annotators. This group comprised native Kannada-speaking college students from Karnataka, India. Each meme underwent evaluation by three annotators, each with a distinct role. The first annotator, pivotal in the initial meme collection process, assigned the preliminary labels. The second annotator, a college student with a deep understanding of meme culture, contributed a youthful perspective, which was crucial for meme-related tasks. The third annotator, deeply immersed in meme culture and online trends, brought expertise that enhanced the accuracy and relevance of the annotations.

The dependability and consistency of annotations were assessed using Fleiss' kappa, suitable for multiple annotators. Fleiss' kappa considers individual annotators' tendencies and handles situations with more than two annotators. It's computed as:

$$\kappa = \frac{P\alpha - P\epsilon}{1 - P\epsilon} \tag{1}$$

Here, κ is Fleiss' kappa value, $P\alpha$ is proportion of observed agreement, and $P\epsilon$ is proportion of expected agreement by chance. Fleiss' kappa values of 0.85 for the Troll category and 0.71 for the Domain category were obtained from data analysis. These values surpass chance agreement, confirming annotation dependability and consistency across experiments.

3.3   Data Statistics and Analysis

To construct a comprehensive dataset, we painstakingly collected a total of 2002 memes from diverse sources. Specifically, we categorized 1132 memes under the umbrella of movies, while 139 were attributed to politics, and 731 were seamlessly woven into the vibrant fabric of sports. A graphical representation of the data distribution is depicted in Fig. 2.

DATA DISTRIBUTION

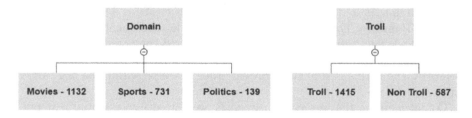

Fig. 2. Flowchart illustrating the distribution of memes across different labels.

Furthermore, a significant chunk of memes, precisely 1415, was classified as belonging to the intriguing realm of trolls, highlighting the extensive usage and

impact of humor, sarcasm, and satire in the online landscape. Equally noteworthy, 587 entries were designated as non-trolling, showcasing a diverse spectrum
of memes that aren't necessarily centered around comedic or provocative themes.

The distribution of data across the train, test, and validation subsets is presented in Table 1.

Table 1. Data split for Train, Test, and Validation sets

Class	Labels	Train	Test	Validation	Total
Domain	Movies	779	161	192	1132
	Sports	480	115	136	731
	Politics	101	25	13	139
Total		1360	301	341	2002
Troll	Troll	977	208	230	1415
	Non troll	383	93	111	587
Total		1360	301	341	2002

3.4 Text Extraction and Data Preprocessing

In the initial stages of our process, we employed Keras-OCR to extract English
text from the memes within the images, generating corresponding transcripts.
The extracted text appeared entirely in lowercase. Notably, the OCR exhibited
proficiency in dealing with code-mixed English text, which closely resembled
the content present in the images. One of the key reasons we opted for Keras-
OCR over pytesseract was its capability to effectively handle code-mixed text,
maintaining coherence even when the extracted text contained errors. This was
particularly crucial given that the arrangement of text within memes often led
to incoherence. Despite this, we chose to maintain the text in its original form
without making modifications. Illustrative examples can be seen in Fig. 3.

To ensure uniformity in our dataset, we initiated image preprocessing by
resizing all images to dimensions of 224 × 224 pixels, utilizing 3 channels to represent RGB images. This standardization step aids in subsequent processing and
analysis. Following resizing, each image is loaded and converted into a NumPy
array. To optimize model performance, we normalized the pixel values within
the array. The normalized image arrays are then collected within the img_array
list.

Complementing the image preprocessing, we delved into essential text preprocessing procedures. The goal of this step is to enhance the quality and efficacy
of our textual data. Our text data underwent a series of transformations to create
a refined and cohesive dataset for analysis. These transformations encompassed
key operations such as tokenization, converting all text to lowercase, removing
special characters and punctuation marks, eliminating stopwords, and applying
either stemming or lemmatization techniques. These measures are pivotal as

IMAGE	TEXT GENERATED USING OCR
	"nim madtane eegen heroh olle gal idavey jaatre maadtne uuta kannada kt trolls join agona naavu banni"
	"troll anthammas match paapa first irli abd alva d t nodkothare so after watching me mann playing test se va devru guru neenu abd troll anthammas after abd hit three six d even though knew I hell hit itroll anthammas"
	"geluvalla idu nanna t geluvu memers troll anthammas itrollanthammas f"

Fig. 3. Texts Extracted from the Kannada Meme.

they cultivate a foundation of accuracy and comprehension, serving as a basis for subsequent analysis and modeling tasks within the realm of natural language processing (NLP).

4 Kannada Meme Classification

4.1 Models and Their Features

The process of deliberating between images and text for classification has been a subject of substantial interest and discourse. Consequently, we embarked on developing discrete models to classify memes based on their textual and visual elements. This approach allowed us to formulate hypotheses from these individual models and subsequently integrate them into a comprehensive multimodal methodology.

Within the domain of our research endeavor, the meticulous selection of the bert_en_uncased_L-12_H-768_A-12 and DenseNet169 models was grounded in a thorough evaluation of the distinctive requisites inherent in meme classification. The strategic inclusion of the bert_en_uncased_L-12_H-768_A-12 model, acclaimed for its adeptness in multilingual comprehension, surfaced as an informed decision. This model's proficiency in processing text across diverse languages conferred a substantial advantage, particularly considering the multilingual character intrinsic to memes. By leveraging its pre-trained capabilities in self-supervised tasks like predicting sentence contexts, we harnessed its capacity to discern the intricate nuances of textual semantics—an essential attribute for deciphering the contextual cues woven into meme text.

Simultaneously, the incorporation of the DenseNet169 model, pre-trained on the ImageNet dataset, was a deliberate maneuver aimed at tapping into its latent potential for visual recognition tasks. Its inherent capability to identify fundamental visual patterns and attributes across a wide spectrum of images resonated with our objectives in meme classification. Additionally, the architecture's proficiency in circumventing the challenge of vanishing gradients attested to its robust training convergence—an indispensable factor for achieving precise classification. The model's efficient parameter utilization, despite its substantial depth, seamlessly aligned with our computational constraints, facilitating optimal memory utilization and training efficiency.

In essence, the strategic amalgamation of the bert_en_L-12_H-768_A-12 and DenseNet169 models was not a random choice, but rather an outcome of a discerning comprehension of our classification imperatives. By harnessing their unique strengths in multilingual text comprehension and visual pattern recognition, we constructed a unified framework poised to elevate the accuracy and effectiveness of meme classification.

4.2   Image Modality

In this study, the foundational image model employed is the **DenseNet169**, meticulously pre-trained on the ImageNet dataset with tailored weights. Building upon this base model, a series of additional layers are introduced to enhance its predictive prowess. Commencing this augmentation process, a GlobalAveragePooling2D layer takes center stage, adeptly reducing the spatial dimensions of feature maps. To counter the specter of overfitting, a strategically positioned dropout layer with a rate of 0.2 is inserted, meticulously ensuring model generalization. The integration of two dense layers follows suit, each adorned with the Rectified Linear Unit (ReLU) activation function. These layers are then thoughtfully accompanied by dropout layers, with rates of 0.2 and 0.5 respectively, serving as effective bulwarks against overfitting tendencies. Further enrichment unfolds with the addition of another dense layer featuring ReLU activation, seamlessly bridged by a subsequent dropout layer with a rate of 0.3. Culminating this orchestration is a dense output layer, characterized by the sigmoid activation function—a fitting choice for binary classification tasks.

To orchestrate the training and optimization dance, the model is compiled with the aid of the Adam optimizer—an esteemed stalwart in the deep learning optimization realm. The learning rate is judiciously set at 1e-4, harmonizing with the selection of the 'binary cross-entropy' loss function—an optimal match for our classification objectives. The model's performance evaluation is propelled by the accuracy metric, standing as a guiding beacon during the intricate dance of training. Notably, the trainability of the base model remains under our purview, adjustable through the strategic manipulation of the trainability flag. Stepping into the training phase, the model is honed over a stipulated number of epochs, the optimizer, loss function, and metrics symbiotically orchestrating the refinement process.

Foraying into the nuanced realm of domain classification, a softmax activation function graces the output layer. Here, the compilation saga continues with the tenacious partnership of the Adam optimizer, replete with a designated learning rate. The loss function seamlessly transforms to 'sparse categorical cross-entropy,' aligning harmoniously with the crux of domain classification intricacies. In tandem, a comprehensive classification report takes shape, meticulously synthesizing the model's performance nuances across diverse classes.

4.3 Text Modality

The text modality is harnessed using the **bert_en_uncased_L-12_H-768_A-12** model, which excels in self-supervised tasks. These tasks involve predicting words within a sentence by analyzing the context provided by a vast corpus of text, such as archives of Wikipedia articles.

The process begins with the model taking text input, which then undergoes preprocessing to make it suitable for BERT encoding. The BERT encoder generates a contextualized representation of the preprocessed text, capturing its intricate nuances. This representation undergoes additional refinement through a 1-dimensional convolutional layer with 128 filters and a kernel size of 5. The ReLU activation function is employed to infuse non-linearity.

Following the convolutional layer, a global max pooling operation extracts the most pertinent features from the evolved text representation. The output is reshaped to include a timestep dimension, preparing it for engagement with an LSTM layer. This LSTM layer, comprising 64 units, adeptly captures the sequential dependencies inherent in the text representation. Post LSTM, two fully connected dense layers are introduced. The initial dense layer comprises 64 units, utilizing the ReLU activation function. A dropout layer, with a rate of 0.5, is strategically inserted to mitigate overfitting risks. This comprehensive architectural approach, which includes the LSTM layer, allows the model to effectively recognize and interpret nuanced patterns crucial for accurate classification across various dimensions.

The full-text model emerges, characterized by specific configurations based on classification objectives. For troll and non-troll classification, the activation function used is sigmoid, and the loss function is binary cross-entropy. However, for domain classification, the activation function shifts to softmax, complemented by sparse categorical cross-entropy loss. This versatile model architecture embraces the complexity of textual information, adeptly extracting its subtleties and contextual significance to enable robust classification across different dimensions.

4.4 Multimodal Approach

The multimodal approach in meme classification capitalizes on the unique strengths of both text and image data. Textual content tends to offer more factual insights, such as keywords, making it particularly valuable for domain classification. On the other hand, images encapsulate the holistic context of a meme, lending themselves well to accurate classification. This approach involves merging the image-related aspects and text-based layers using the Keras concatenate API. The fusion culminates in a dense layer designed for classification.

In terms of image integration, a dense layer comprising 169 units is connected to the output of the image base model. This model's output boasts dimensions of $7 \times 7 \times 1664$, signifying a spatial resolution of 7×7 and 1664 channels. Enhancing the model for classification, a ReLU activation-powered dense layer is introduced, followed by a dropout layer to counter overfitting. Ultimately, a dense layer with softmax activation generates the probabilities required for classification.

The textual dimension of the multimodal approach draws inspiration from the approach detailed in a tensorfloworg-article. The chosen strategy involves leveraging small uncased L6 transformer layers (L) with a hidden embedding size of 768 for classification tasks. This yields an output dimension of 768. Prior to output, a dropout layer is applied to the tensor, which is then directed to a dense network consisting of 128 neurons, serving troll classification purposes. Additionally, a 1D convolutional layer featuring 16 filters and a ReLU activation, followed by global max pooling, captures essential features. After a reshaping step and another dropout layer, the tensor is fed into a dense layer featuring softmax activation, effectively fulfilling domain classification needs.

The amalgamation of image and text insights is accomplished through the utilization of the Keras concatenation layer. This process unifies the outputs from both the image and text pathways, resulting in a merged dimension of 306. Subsequently, a dense layer, supported by dropout regularization, takes on the responsibility of classification. In the context of domain classification, a dropout rate of 0.2 is implemented, and the output layer consists of a dense layer boasting softmax activation and categorical cross-entropy loss. Model training is undertaken with a batch size of 20, a learning rate of 1e-4, and the Adam optimizer.

This comprehensive approach effectively integrates text and image data, leading to enhanced performance in the realm of meme classification. By synergistically utilizing the strengths of both modalities and employing thoughtful model architectures, accurate classification outcomes are achieved for both trolling and domain categorization tasks.

5 Results

Our model design aligns closely with the input types—images or text—resulting in specialized models adept at categorizing these distinct data types. We've also explored how well these models manage both images and text together, known as multimodal results. In our upcoming discussion, we will delve into each categorization aspect and the models' performance when handling combined images and text. We'll break it down into different parts: examining how the models deal with images, how they handle text, and then how they manage both elements simultaneously.

5.1   Domain Classification

The Image-Based model showed promising performance with reasonably high precision and recall for the Movies and Sports classes, achieving an F1 score of 0.77 and 0.68, respectively. However, it struggled to classify the Politics class, as evidenced by its low precision (0.25) and F1 score (0.30). The overall accuracy of the Image-Based model was 0.71.

The Text-Based model demonstrated excellent precision and recall for the Movies class (0.75 and 0.94, respectively) and reasonable performance for the Sports class (precision = 0.87, recall = 0.75). However, it completely misclassified all instances of the Politics class, resulting in a precision, recall, and F1 score of 0.00 for this category. The overall accuracy of the Text-Based model was 0.79.

The Multimodal Approach exhibited the best overall performance among the three models, with high precision and recall for both the Movies and Sports classes, leading to F1 scores of 0.85 and 0.82, respectively. However, similar to the Text-Based model, it also misclassified all instances of the Politics class, resulting in a precision, recall, and F1 score of 0.00 for this category. The overall accuracy of the Multimodal Approach was 0.80. Table 2 provides a summary of the Domain Classification Results.

Table 2. Classification report on Various Domain Classes

Model	Class	Precision	Recall	F1 Score
Image-Based	Movies	0.76	0.79	0.77
	Sports	0.74	0.63	0.68
	Politics	0.25	0.38	0.30
Accuracy				0.71
Text-Based	Movies	0.75	0.94	0.84
	Sports	0.87	0.75	0.80
	Politics	1.00	0.00	0.00
Accuracy				0.79
Multimodal Approach	Movies	0.82	0.88	0.85
	Sports	0.78	0.86	0.82
	Politics	1.00	0.00	0.00
Accuracy				0.80

5.2   Troll Classification

The Image-Based model achieved the highest precision for the Non-Troll class (0.78) but had a relatively low recall for the Troll class (0.22), resulting in a moderate F1 score of 0.33. The Text-Based model had a higher recall for the Troll class (0.33) compared to the Image-Based model, but its precision (0.57) and F1 score (0.42) were lower. The Multimodal Approach showed a balanced performance with better precision (0.64) and recall (0.32) for the Troll class, leading to an improved F1 score of 0.43.

Considering accuracy as an overall measure, the Image-Based model performed the best with an accuracy of 0.77, followed by the Multimodal Approach with an accuracy of 0.73, and finally, the Text-Based model with an accuracy of 0.72. Table 3 provides a summary of the Troll Classification Results.

Table 3. Classification Report on Troll and Non-troll

Model	Class	Precision	Recall	F1 Score
Image-Based	Troll	0.63	0.22	0.33
	Non-Troll	0.78	0.96	0.86
Accuracy				0.77
Text-Based	Troll	0.57	0.33	0.42
	Non-Troll	0.75	0.89	0.81
Accuracy				0.72
Multimodal Approach	Troll	0.64	0.32	0.43
	Non-Troll	0.75	0.92	0.83
Accuracy				0.73

6   Conclusions and Future Trends

In conclusion, our study on multimodal models for troll classification revealed both promising outcomes and areas for improvement. While we had initially expected higher performance from multimodal models in classification tasks, the challenge of classifying political content proved to be particularly demanding. Each model demonstrated its strengths and weaknesses in detecting trolls, and the optimal model choice depends on the specific requirements and trade-offs between recall and precision. To achieve better performance in real-world applications, further testing and fine-tuning are necessary.

One notable finding is that the addition of multimodal techniques did not lead to a significant increase in classification accuracy. However, when compared to image-based methods, employing multimodal methodologies and fine-tuning the dataset resulted in improved domain detection. The use of deeper networks proved to be highly effective in capturing the nuanced emotional complexity inherent in the data.

As a potential future direction, oversampling techniques could be explored to address the challenge of classifying political content and enhance the model's overall performance. Oversampling involves generating synthetic samples for the minority class (e.g., political memes) to balance the class distribution, thus preventing the model from being biased towards the majority class. By artificially increasing the representation of political memes in the training data, we can potentially improve the model's ability to accurately classify them.

Moreover, as meme culture and trends evolve rapidly, continuous updates and refinements to the dataset and models are essential to maintain relevance and robustness. The inclusion of newer memes and the ongoing evaluation of model performance will be critical in ensuring the continued effectiveness of the classification system in real-world scenarios.

In summary, our study paves the way for further advancements in multimodal troll classification and opens up exciting possibilities for addressing the challenges of classifying diverse content on social media platforms. By embracing the dynamic nature of meme culture and incorporating cutting-edge techniques, we can build more reliable and adaptive systems capable of tackling the complexities of troll detection and content classification.

Acknowledgments. Bharathi Raja Chakravarthi was supported in part by a research grant from the Science Foundation Ireland (SFI) under Grant Number SFI/12/RC/ 2289_P2(Insight_2).

References

1. Afridi, T.H., Alam, A., Khan, M.N., Khan, J., Lee, Y.K.: A multimodal memes classification: a survey and open research issues. In: Ben Ahmed, M., Rakip Karas, I., Santos, D., Sergeyeva, O., Boudhir, A.A. (eds.) Innovations in Smart Cities Applications. Lecture Notes in Networks and Systems, vol. 183, pp. 1451–1466. Springer, Cham (2021). https://doi.org/10.1007/978-3-030-66840-2_109
2. Amalia, A., Sharif, A., Haisar, F., Gunawan, D., Nasution, B.B.: Meme opinion categorization by using optical character recognition (OCR) and naïve bayes algorithm. In: 2018 Third International Conference on Informatics and Computing (ICIC), pp. 1–5. IEEE (2018)
3. Boyd, A., Czajka, A., Bowyer, K.: Deep learning-based feature extraction in iris recognition: use existing models, fine-tune or train from scratch? In: 2019 IEEE 10th International Conference on Biometrics Theory, Applications and Systems (BTAS), pp. 1–9. IEEE (2019)
4. Devlin, J., Chang, M.W., Lee, K., Toutanova, K.: BERT: pre-training of deep bidirectional transformers for language understanding. arXiv preprint: arXiv:1810.04805 (2018)
5. Ghanghor, N., Krishnamurthy, P., Thavareesan, S., Priyadharshini, R., Chakravarthi, B.R.: Iiitk@ dravidianlangtech-eacl2021: offensive language identification and meme classification in tamil, malayalam and kannada. In: Proceedings of the First Workshop on Speech and Language Technologies For Dravidian Languages, pp. 222–229 (2021)
6. Hande, A., Priyadharshini, R., Chakravarthi, B.R.: KanCMD: Kannada codemixed dataset for sentiment analysis and offensive language detection. In: Proceedings of the Third Workshop on Computational Modeling of People's Opinions, Personality, and Emotion's in Social Media, pp. 54–63 (2020)
7. Hs, C., et al.: Trollmeta@ dravidianlangtech-eacl2021: meme classification using deep learning. In: Proceedings of the First Workshop on Speech and Language Technologies for Dravidian Languages, pp. 277–280 (2021)
8. Huang, B., Bai, Y.: Hub@ dravidianlangtech-eacl2021: meme classification for Tamil text-image fusion. In: Proceedings of the First Workshop on Speech and Language Technologies for Dravidian Languages, pp. 210–215 (2021)

9. Iandola, F., Moskewicz, M., Karayev, S., Girshick, R., Darrell, T., Keutzer, K.: DenseNet: implementing efficient convnet descriptor pyramids. arXiv preprint: arXiv:1404.1869 (2014)

10. Kieffer, B., Babaie, M., Kalra, S., Tizhoosh, H.R.: Convolutional neural networks for histopathology image classification: training vs. using pre-trained networks. In: 2017 Seventh International Conference on Image Processing Theory, Tools and Applications (IPTA), pp. 1–6. IEEE (2017)

11. Li, Z.: Codewithzichao@ dravidianlangtech-eacl2021: exploring multimodal transformers for meme classification in Tamil language. In: Proceedings of the First Workshop on Speech and Language Technologies for Dravidian Languages, pp. 352–356 (2021)

12. Loussaief, S., Abdelkrim, A.: Deep learning vs. bag of features in machine learning for image classification. In: 2018 International Conference on Advanced Systems and Electric Technologies (IC_ASET), pp. 6–10. IEEE (2018)

13. Suryawanshi, S., Chakravarthi, B.R.: Findings of the shared task on troll meme classification in Tamil. In: Proceedings of the First Workshop on Speech and Language Technologies for Dravidian Languages, pp. 126–132 (2021)

14. Suryawanshi, S., Chakravarthi, B.R., Verma, P., Arcan, M., McCrae, J.P., Buitelaar, P.: A dataset for troll classification of Tamilmemes. In: Proceedings of the WILDRE5–5th workshop on Indian language data: resources and evaluation, pp. 7–13 (2020)

15. Wang, W.Y., Wen, M.: I can has Cheezburger? A nonparanormal approach to combining textual and visual information for predicting and generating popular meme descriptions. In: Proceedings of the 2015 Conference of the North American Chapter of the Association for Computational Linguistics: Human Language Technologies, pp. 355–365 (2015)

16. Yasaswini, K., Puranik, K., Hande, A., Priyadharshini, R., Thavareesan, S., Chakravarthi, B.R.: Iiitt@ dravidianlangtech-eacl2021: transfer learning for offensive language detection in Dravidian languages. In: Proceedings of the First Workshop on Speech and Language Technologies for Dravidian Languages, pp. 187–194 (2021)

The Impact of Tamil Python Programming in Wikisource

A. Vinoth[1]([✉]) [iD], Sathiyaraj Thangasamy[1] [iD], R. Nithya[2] [iD], C. N. Subalalitha[3] [iD], P. D. Mahendhiran[4] [iD], and Info-Farmer[5] [iD]

[1] Sri Krishna Adithya College of Arts and Sciences, Coimbatore 641042, India
vino.asstprof@gmail.com
[2] Government Arts and Science College (Co-Ed), Avinashi 641654, India
[3] SRM College of Engineering and Technology, Kattankulathur, Chennai, India
[4] Sri Krishna College of Engineering and Technology, Coimbatore 641042, India
[5] Tamil Wikimedian, Attur, Salem 636102, India

Abstract. Wikipedia, Wiktionary, Wikisource, Wikinews, Wikiquote, Wikiversity, Wikitour, Meta-Wiki, and Wikimedia are all Wikimedia projects that provide copyright-free data. Among these, Wikisource stands out as an online library utilized by 72 languages. Tamil Wikisource specifically caters to Tamil-language content, converting image-based data into text format. While human resources and automated methods contribute to data improvement, this research paper proposes the implementation of a Python program in Tamil for automation to further enhance or operate the Tamil Wikisource project. Given that most volunteers working on Wikimedia projects in Indian languages may be more comfortable with their native language rather than English, this paper highlights the efforts made by Info Farmer in writing Python programs for Wikisource. This initiative is expected to open up more possibilities for scaling similar projects in other Indian languages, thereby assisting volunteers in Wikimedia projects. Additionally, the individual has developed over a hundred Python programs in Tamil, enhancing more than two lakh pages. This underscores a potential lack of awareness regarding the capability to create computer programming content in native languages, a phenomenon not exclusive to Tamil but applicable to other Indian languages as well. The primary aim of this article is to emphasize that when volunteers from various Indian languages recognize this potential, they can develop the necessary automation tools for their respective languages. Consequently, this research paper delves into topics such as wiki projects, the voluntary contributions of individuals involved, the noteworthy Tamil Python contributions of Info-farmer—a Tamil Wikimedian— the use of Python keywords written and executed in Tamil, an exploration of how Python functions, an overview of PAWS (Python Data Science environment for Jupyter notebooks), PyWikiBot, and outlines plans for future activities in detail.

Keywords: Wikimedia · Wikipedia · Wikisource · PAWS · PyWikiBot · Python · PyTamil

B. R. Chakravarthi et al. (Eds.): SPELL 2023, CCIS 2046, pp. 79–90, 2024.
https://doi.org/10.1007/978-3-031-58495-4_6

1   Introduction

Human resources can make a tremendous contribution. Many tasks that were traditionally handled by human resources can now be easily automated. This necessity arises from the need to digitize and utilize the vast amount of information generated by human efforts over time. Numerous books have been authored, and in the current era, computerizing the data from these books is crucial. Wikimedia serves as a repository for diverse data types, including audio, video, images, animations, articles, and books. Various projects such as Wikipedia, Wiktionary, Wikisource, Wikinews, Wikiquote, Wikiversity, Wikitour, Meta-Wiki, and Wikimedia work collectively to integrate and organize this data.

Each of these projects has the potential for technological advancements, with the continuous improvement of technologies associated with them. However, since these projects rely on volunteers, the process of data creation is not always rapid or straight-forward. Therefore, automation becomes a necessity to enhance the efficiency and speed of these projects.

For instance, Wikisource functions as a library repository. Utilizing the data within this repository, it is feasible to automatically generate a variety of articles. Python, a programming language, proves to be highly beneficial in this regard. Automation not only streamlines the workflow but also ensures that the wealth of information within these projects is harnessed effectively.

Hence, this research paper delineates Wikimedia projects, the contributions of Wiki-medians, the Tamil Python automation endeavors led by Info-farmer (a Tamil Wikimedian), the enhancements made to Wikisource through Tamil Python [12], and identifies areas requiring further improvement.

2   Wikisource and Tamil Wikisource

The books available on Wikisource can be studied at various levels, necessitating the implementation of automation. Through this automation, it becomes feasible to rapidly elevate the data not only for Tamil Wikisource but also for 72 other Wikisource languages, enhancing their creative activity levels. Despite efforts by the Wikimedia Foundation to increase volunteers through annual competitions involving 11 languages, the impact on language data improvement has been limited. Some languages see the competition concluded without any participation, highlighting the need for additional strategies. In light of these observations, the significance of automation becomes more apparent.

This paper highlights the invaluable contributions made by an individual Info-farmer (one line intro) to Wikisource through the implementation of Python programming in the Tamil language [12]. By leveraging the power of Python, the author has significantly enhanced the efficiency and functionality of Wikisource in the Tamil domain. Their contributions encompass a range of activities, including but not limited to, automating content creation, improving data organization, and streamlining editing processes. Through their dedicated efforts, the Wikisource community benefits from a more seamless and dynamic platform, empowering contributors to engage more effectively with Tamil content. This paper serves as a testament to the impactful fusion of linguistic expertise and programming proficiency, showcasing the positive influence of Tamil Python programming on the enrichment of Wikisource content.

Therefore, this research paper demonstrates that it is possible to write and execute Python programs in Tamil, and that it can be used to perform various automation tasks, and that it can be used to improve Tamil language data.

3 Contribution of Wikimedians

When examining a book, it can be segmented into three parts: the header part, the content part, and the footer part. Automation is also required for these divisions, underlining the inadequacy of relying solely on human resources. The process can sometimes be tedious, and to overcome these challenges, automation emerges as a viable and efficient solution. It not only addresses the limitations posed by human resources but also provides a more dynamic and effective approach to managing and enhancing the content on Wikisource.

3.1 Python Automation for Other Projects Using Wikisource Data

To automate tasks on Tamil Wikisource using Python, you can leverage the MediaWiki API provided by Wikimedia Foundation. Begin by installing the mwclient library, a Python client for the MediaWiki API. Next, authenticate and connect to Tamil Wikisource using the API endpoint. You can then use the API to search for pages, edit content, or perform other actions. For example, you might retrieve a page using its title, modify the content programmatically, and then save the changes. Ensure that your Python script adheres to Wikimedia's terms of service, respecting the wiki's policies and guidelines. Additionally, handle authentication securely and be mindful of rate limits to avoid disruptions. Regularly check the Wikimedia API documentation for any updates or changes in their endpoints or policies.

Moreover, Wikisource data has the potential to be seamlessly transferred to various other Wikimedia projects, including Wikipedia, Wiktionary, Wikinews, Wikiquote, Wikiversity, Wikitour, Meta-Wiki, and Wikipedia. As an illustration, the content of a book on Wikisource can be parsed into individual words and effortlessly integrated into Wiktionary, serving as a valuable addition to the dictionary. Furthermore, if the book incorporates image files, these visual assets can be efficiently transferred to Wikimedia Commons. It is essential to underscore that all of these processes can be automated with great ease, streamlining the integration of Wikisource data into multiple Wikimedia platforms.

Wikimedians engaged in the Wiki Project are dedicated volunteers who contribute their time, expertise, and passion to enhance the Tamil Wikimedia ecosystem. These individuals actively participate in creating, editing, and curating content on platforms like Tamil Wikisource. Introducing Python automation in Tamil significantly benefits Wikimedians by streamlining repetitive tasks, expediting content creation, and improving overall efficiency. Python programs can automate processes such as data extraction, formatting, and uploading, allowing Wikimedians to focus more on content quality and community collaboration. This automation not only enhances productivity but also empowers Wikimedians to make a more significant impact on the Wii Project, fostering a dynamic and thriving Tamil Wikimedia community.

3.2 Tamil Wikisource Contributor Info-Farmer

The individual in question is Info-Farmer, also recognized as R. Lokanathan. Born in Attur, Salem, he possesses expertise in fields such as law and librarianship. His unwavering dedication is directed towards the advancement of Tamil Wikimedia projects. Since September 16, 2008, he has been actively contributing [12] to Wikimedia projects, marking a remarkable 15-year journey. Remarkably, his sole occupation revolves around the full-time development of Tamil Wikimedia projects.

The extent of his substantial contribution is evident in the fact that he has amassed edits exceeding five digits. Engaging in diverse activities within the Wikimedia community, Info-farmer has taken on various responsibilities, as detailed in the following Table 1 [12].

Table 1. CrossActivity for Info-farmer

family	wiki	Local groups
wikipedia	ta.wikipedia.org	(sysop)
meta	meta.wikimedia.org	(autopatrolled)
wiktionary	ta.wiktionary.org	(bureaucrat, sysop)
commons	commons.wikimedia.org	(autopatrolled, filemover)
wikisource	ta.wikisource.org	(sysop)

This Wikimedia contributor engages in outreach activities by visiting various colleges in Tamil Nadu. Notably dedicated to fostering female participation, he actively recruits women as volunteers for Wikimedia projects. His journey has motivated him to acquire proficiency in Python, allowing him to write programs in Tamil and automate tasks effectively. Beyond his personal achievements, his inspiring journey resonates with other Tamil Wikimedia contributors. His confidence stems from the belief that the fundamentals of Python can be articulated and executed in Tamil, yielding tangible results [12].

3.3 Automation in Wikimedia

To achieve automation, it is essential to possess a foundational understanding of Python. Someone with a grasp of Python basics can author and execute Python programs in Tamil, enabling the automation of numerous tasks—a valuable gift in the realm of streamlining processes. It is upon this foundation that the Info-former has delivered various creative services, contributing to the advancement of Wikisource development [12].

In the modern era, technology plays a major role. Python, a computer language, remains fundamental to the subject and excels among various programming languages. In the future, it will continue to perform with language excellence.

When attempting to acquire knowledge of the Python language, which involves a mixture of technical activities, it is exemplified in such a manner. There is a programming language called EZHIL [16, 43] for writing programs in Tamil. However, Python still stands as the best computer programming language used by the majority of programmers. Henceforth, this paper explores, in particular, Python programming, as it can be written in Tamil and the ways in which it may be quite useful for Wikisource development.

4 Tamil Python Programming

4.1 Python Tags and PyTamil Tags

Python keywords [14] are familiar to Python programmers. The assumption that one must know English to write programs in Python has arisen due to the language utilizing the English alphabet. However, it's important to note that Python programming is not confined to English keywords alone. In fact, you can compose programs in Python using PyTamil keywords as well, as demonstrated in Table 2.

Table 2. Python tags & PyTamil tags

Python tags	PyTamil tags	Python tags	PyTamil tags
print	விளைவிடு	if	ஆனால்
break	நிறுத்து	elseif	இருப்பினும்
continue	ததாடர்	else	இல்லல
for	ஆக	input	உள்ளீடு
import	இறக்குமதி தெய்	def	விதிமுறை
return	பின்கொடு	while	வளர

Info-farmer has been consistently working to create Tamil keywords, establish a Python library infrastructure for them, and facilitate the writing of programs in Tamil for task automation. Currently, he is in the process of creating and implementing a project page to automatically generate various articles on Wikipedia [13]. If you have any doubts about the feasibility in Tamil, the following code serves as evidence. It distinctly illustrates the contrast between the format in English and the format in Tamil [22].

```
#!/usr/bin/python2
import pywikibot
aPage = 'page:அங்கும் இங்கும்.pdf/9'
site = pywikibot.Site('ta', 'wikisource')
page = pywikibot.Page(site, aPage)
print "page"
```

Output: ta:page:அங்கும் இங்கும்.pdf/9

This program contains English syllables. Before the code, Tamil syllables in the Python module are presented.

```
#!/usr/bin/python3
import பைவிக்கிமூலம்
எடுக்கும்பக்கம் = 'பக்கம்:அங்கும் இங்கும்.pdf/9'
உரலி = பைவிக்கிமூலம்.உரலியிடு (எடுக்கும்பக்கம்)
விளைவிடு (உரலி)
```

விளைவு : <u>ta:பக்கம்:அங்கும் இங்கும்.pdf/9</u>

4.2 Wikisource Development for Tamil Python Programming

Info-farmer, a dedicated Wikimedia contributor, has authored over 20 programs in Tamil, covering a diverse range of topics [12]. These programs encompass functionalities such as bolding dictionary words [23], filling table blocks [24], managing sections of tables [25], combining words split across two pages [26], only numbers in the middle of Keeladi [27], moving titles [28], handling pages of moving titles [29], creating book subpages [30], analyzing page numbering indexes [31], generating section indexes [32], extracting section pages [33], cleaning content [34], creating contentless subpages for books [35], merging split words [36], performing full page cleaning [37], containing only numbers in the middle of the footer [38], retrieving API/section pages [39], and CSV files in Python [40]. Info-farmer's programming initiatives have significantly enhanced the efficiency and functionality of Wikisource in Tamil [12].

For instance, the program designed to bold dictionary words facilitates the identification of dictionary entries, while the one merging words split on two pages contributes to enhanced text readability. Info-farmer's substantial contributions play a crucial role in the development of Tamil Wikipedia. His programs have simplified access and participation for Tamil speakers, making significant strides in improving the overall user experience on the platform [12].

It is noteworthy that, in addition to the mentioned initiatives, Info-farmer has authored more than hundreds of programs in Tamil to contribute to the development of Wikisource [12].

4.3 PAWS

Pywikibot is a Python library and a set of tools designed to automate tasks on wikis. Initially created for Wikipedia, Pywikibot has gained widespread usage across various projects within the Wikimedia Foundation and is now employed on numerous other MediaWiki wikis. This page aims to guide you in utilizing Pywikibot within the PAWS (Python Alpha WIKI Bot Shell) environment. Additionally, it includes a link to a notebook-based tutorial, enabling you to grasp the basics of performing tasks on wikis using Pywikibot [45].

According to Shrinivasan, PAWS [7] is illustrated as follows.

- It is an online browser-based programming IDE provided by wikimedia foundation
- It is based on Jupyter Notebook Software [5–7, 42].

(Shrini., கந.-0சோ-உ0உ.உ, உ.க: உ.ன) by San Gerald Tsai, who emerges as prominent in the Global Wiki, discusses Python as a web service. The information is presented in a step-by-step guide to enable Python programming languages in a wiki [5, 6]. As shown in Fig. 1, the following image will appear to enter the Jupyter notebook page.

Fig. 1. Notepad, Console, Other functions can be seen

Correspondingly, there are up to three options: Console, Notebook, and Other. Programming languages include Python3 (Python 3 (ipykernel)), Bash, Julia (Julia 1.6.3), OpenRefine [↗], R, RStudio [↗] and SPARQL. Let us create or run programs ourselves. Before that, it is better to familiarize ourselves with some basic terms for writing in the Python programming language. In particular, for effective communication in any language, letters, wording, sentences, and meaning provide support.

This platform can be utilized to automate various tasks. For instance, the process of adding a footer to a specific page within a book can be demonstrated here. The following Fig. 2, 3, 4, 5, and 6 illustrate the procedure and the resulting output.

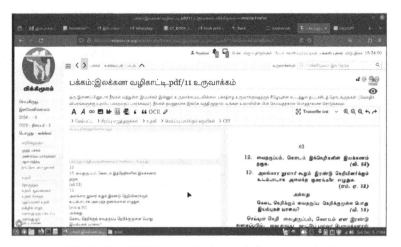

Fig. 2. Tamil Wikisource Book page before automation

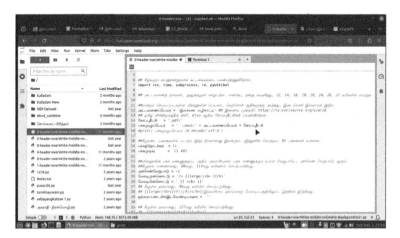

Fig. 3. PAWS and Tamil Python programming page

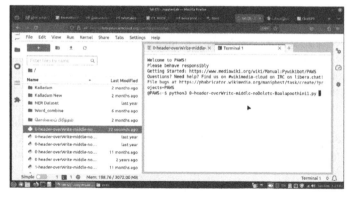

Fig. 4. PAWS terminal

Fig. 5. PAWS automation result

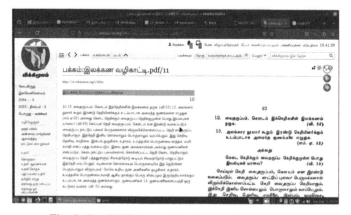

Fig. 6. Tamil Wikisource Book page after automation

5 Conclusion and Future Scope

At the commencement of this study, we provided an introduction to Wikimedia projects. Subsequently, we delved into an explanation of Wikisource, with a specific focus on Tamil Wikisource. We explored the general activities of volunteers contributing to Wikisource, discussed the nature of the Tamil language in the context of Python usage, highlighted the propensity for increased creations when employing Python programs in Tamil, and underscored the ongoing contributions of Info-Farmer. Furthermore, we reported on the automated functionality of PAWS. This elucidated that the creation of free educational resources can be facilitated with great ease through automation tools like Python.

The initiative of an info-farmer in championing Tamil Python programming is a commendable endeavor aimed at cultivating a fertile ground for knowledge dissemination and technological empowerment within the Tamil-speaking community. This visionary effort involves sowing the seeds of Python programming skills and expertise, nurturing a crop of individuals capable of harnessing the language for diverse applications. Through workshops, resources, and community engagement, the info farmer is fostering a vibrant ecosystem where the Tamil language converges with Python's versatility, empowering individuals to contribute meaningfully to technology and knowledge-sharing initiatives. This initiative not only bridges linguistic and technological gaps but also cultivates a community of learners and contributors, paving the way for a sustainable and thriving landscape of Tamil Python programming.

The potential usage of Tamil Python programming extends far beyond Wikisource, presenting a versatile tool for building applications catering to the Tamil medium and beyond. The scalability and adaptability of Python make it an ideal language for developing a wide array of applications, ranging from educational tools and content delivery platforms to business applications and community-driven projects. The success of implementing Python in the Tamil context serves as a blueprint that can be replicated for other languages, promoting inclusivity and cultural diversity in the tech landscape. By harnessing the power of Python, developers across different linguistic domains can create innovative solutions tailored to their specific needs, fostering a global collaborative ecosystem that embraces the richness of diverse languages and cultures.

Based on the information provided thus far, it is apparent that enhancing Wikisource can be achieved by developing programming language content in Tamil using Python3. This serves as a foundational step. For a deeper understanding of such programming languages, it is recommended to explore the 'Category: Python Programs' and acquire knowledge. Through the creation of scripts, Wikisource can be improved. Python stands out as a versatile programming language, suitable for the development of a wide array of applications without specialization in any particular problem domain.

References

1. Python Wikipedia. https://ta.wikipedia.org/s/112. Accessed 10 Nov 2023
2. Kaniyam. https://tinyurl.com/5bm5f67t. Accessed 10 Nov 2023
3. Kaapiyam. https://kaapiyam.com/tiruvalluvar-tirukkural-meaning-definition-tamil-english-daily-kural/ennenpa-enai-ezhuththenpa-ivvirantum-392/. Accessed 10 Nov 2023

4. Github. https://github.com/tshrinivasan/tools-for-wiki. Accessed 10 Nov 2023
5. Github. https://github.com/tshrinivasan/Python-Beginners-Guide. Accessed 10 Nov 2023
6. Wikimedia. https://tinyurl.com/yp5kruw8. Accessed 10 Nov 2023
7. Debian. https://www.debian.org/distrib/. Accessed 10 Nov 2023
8. Konsole. https://konsole.kde.org/. Accessed 10 Nov 2023
9. Pypi. https://pypi.org/project/pywikisource/. Accessed 10 Nov 2023
10. Projectmadurai   GUPope.   https://www.projectmadurai.org/pm_etexts/pdf/pm0153.pdf. Accessed 10 Nov 2023
11. Thirukkural GUPope. https://thirukkural.io/kural/392. Accessed 10 Nov 2023
12. Navaneethakrishnan, S.C., Thangasamy, S., Neechalkaran: Exploring the opportunities and challenges in contributing to Tamil Wikimedia. In: Anand Kumar, K., et al. (eds.) SPELLL 2022. CCIS, vol. 1802, pp. 253–262. Springer, Cham (2023). https://doi.org/10.1007/978-3-031-33231-9_18
13. Wikiproject Plants. https://ta.wikipedia.org/s/ca9f. Accessed 10 Nov 2023
14. Pywiki Automation Wikipedia. https://ta.wikipedia.org/s/5ety. Accessed 10 Nov 2023
15. Beginners   book.   https://beginnersbook.com/2019/06/python-user-defined-functions/. Accessed 10 Nov 2023
16. Ezhil Programming Language Wikipedia. https://ta.wikipedia.org/s/27xm. Accessed 10 Nov 2023
17. Swaram Programming Language Wikipedia. https://ta.wikipedia.org/s/27v2. Accessed 10 Nov 2023
18. Program Title content Wikipedia. https://ta.wikipedia.org/s/6x3. Accessed 10 Nov 2023
19. Kanini Tamil Wikipedia. https://ta.wikipedia.org/s/5v8. Accessed 10 Nov 2023
20. Thamizhkanimai Wikipedia. https://ta.wikipedia.org/s/3v8. Accessed 10 Nov 2023
21. Pywiki program Wikisource. https://ta.wikisource.org/s/9z0e. Accessed 10 Nov 2023
22. Pywikisource. https://ta.wikisource.org/s/9zcl. Accessed 10 Nov 2023
23. Bolding Dictionary words Wikisource. https://ta.wikisource.org/s/ag4m. Accessed 10 Nov 2023
24. Filling Table Blocks Wikisource. https://ta.wikisource.org/s/acm3. Accessed 10 Nov 2023
25. Managing sections of tables Wikisource. https://ta.wikisource.org/s/9zgp. Accessed 10 Nov 2023
26. Combining words split across two pages Wikisource. https://ta.wikisource.org/s/9z2k. Accessed 10 Nov 2023
27. Only numbers in the middle of footer Wikisource. https://ta.wikisource.org/s/9y3j. Accessed 10 Nov 2023
28. Moving titles Wikisource. https://ta.wikisource.org/s/9y3h. Accessed 10 Nov 2023
29. Handling pages of moving titles Wikisource. https://ta.wikisource.org/s/9zo8. Accessed 10 Nov 2023
30. Creating book subpages Wikisource. https://ta.wikisource.org/s/9zdc. Accessed 10 Nov 2023
31. Analyzing page numbering indexes Wikisource. https://ta.wikisource.org/s/9zf1. Accessed 10 Nov 2023
32. Generating section indexes Wikisource. https://ta.wikisource.org/s/9z0c. Accessed 10 Nov 2023
33. Extracting section pages Wikisource. https://ta.wikisource.org/s/9yki. Accessed 10 Nov 2023
34. Cleaning content Wikisource. https://ta.wikisource.org/s/9z2m. Accessed 10 Nov 2023
35. Creating contentless subpages for books Wikisource. https://ta.wikisource.org/s/aiha. Accessed 10 Nov 2023
36. Merging split words Wikisource. https://ta.wikisource.org/s/9zfn. Accessed 10 Nov 2023
37. Performing full page cleaning Wikisource. https://ta.wikisource.org/s/9zcw. Accessed 10 Nov 2023

38. Containing only numbers in the middle of the footer Wikisource. https://ta.wikisource.org/s/9y3i. Accessed 10 Nov 2023
39. Retrieving API/section pages Wikisource. https://ta.wikisource.org/s/9zdn. Accessed 10 Nov 2023
40. Wikisource. https://ta.wikisource.org/s/9zc6. Accessed 10 Nov 2023
41. Learn Tamil Online. https://ilearntamil.com/thirukural-with-english-meaning-athigaram-40/. Accessed 10 Nov 2023
42. Github. https://github.com/Ezhil-Language-Foundation/Ezhil-Lang. Accessed 25 Nov 2023
43. Wikipedia Projects. https://commons.wikimedia.org/wiki/File:Wikimedia_logo_family_few-Tamil-simple-explanations-ta.svg. Accessed 25 Nov 2023
44. Tamil readability terminal. https://upload.wikimedia.org/wikipedia/commons/8/83/KDE-konsole_terminal-clear_view_of_Tamil_language-October2012.png. Accessed 25 Nov 2023
45. PAWS and Pywikibot. https://wikitech.wikimedia.org/wiki/PAWS/PAWS_and_Pywikibot. Accessed 25 Nov 2023

Language Technologies

Natural Language Processing for Tulu: Challenges, Review and Future Scope

Poorvi Shetty[✉]

JSS Science and Technology University, Mysuru, India
pooorvishetty1202@gmail.com

Abstract. This paper provides a comprehensive analysis of publicly-available research done to date on Natural Language Processing (NLP) in Tulu while exploring its development, challenges, and future scope. Tulu is a low-resource Dravidian language with more than 2.5 million speakers. Work done in NLP for Tulu includes code-mixed corpus generation, optical character recognition of historical manuscripts, machine translation, sentiment analysis, speech recognition, and morphological analysis. However, due to data scarcity, morphological complexity, and code-mixing, challenges arise for NLP practitioners and more research and innovation are needed. Future work in NLP for Tulu involves expanding code-mixed corpora, improving machine translation and speech recognition, cross-lingual transfer learning, specialized named entity recognition, and interdisciplinary collaborations. Unlocking Tulu's potential as a language with a rich cultural heritage requires addressing these challenges and embracing future opportunities to enhance linguistic diversity and accessibility of NLP technologies.

Keywords: Natural Language Processing (NLP) · Tulu · low-resource language · Dravidian language · challenges · review

1 Introduction

1.1 Introduction to Tulu

Language Tulu, a Dravidian language, boasts rich oral traditions [1] and a diverse array of dialects [2]. Despite its linguistic richness, it remains a low-resource language. However, a few resources such as a Tulu-English dictionary [3] and linguistic research and experimental studies [4,5] are present. NLP applications in this domain are in their early stages of development, indicating the burgeoning potential for further advancements.

1.2 Importance of NLP Technologies for Low-Resource Languages

The significance that NLP plays in linguistic empowerment and the preservation of low-resource communities' rich cultural legacy makes it of utmost relevance for those languages. These languages frequently preserve and transmit

B. R. Chakravarthi et al. (Eds.): SPELLL 2023, CCIS 2046, pp. 93–109, 2024.
https://doi.org/10.1007/978-3-031-58495-4_7

ancient customs, oral histories, and specialised expertise [6]. By utilising NLP, we make it easier to digitise and preserve their cultural artefacts, historical records, and indigenous knowledge, making sure that their history is preserved and passed down to succeeding generations. NLP also makes it possible to produce language-specific tools and resources, which promotes the creation of literary works, instructional materials, and digital content [7]. By using NLP technology to revive and celebrate the linguistic variety of low-resource languages [8], we support the holistic preservation of their cultural identity and work to create a world where cultural legacy coexists with technological developments.

1.3 Scope and Objectives of the Paper

This review study intends to provide a thorough evaluation of the NLP development specifically for Tulu. The main goal of this study is to present an in-depth examination of the developments, difficulties, and future prospects in NLP for Tulu.

2 Present Challenges

2.1 Limited Data Availability

Tulu's low-resource nature hinders the availability of annotated data, significantly restricting the development of robust NLP models. Due to limited datasets, NLP models often encounter a high number of out-of-vocabulary words, complicating their handling during processing. Additionally, the data collected for NLP in Tulu is often skewed towards positive sentiments, as people are enthusiastic about engaging with Tulu media [9].

2.2 Lack of Digital Resources

There is an absence of resources for lexicons in the Tulu language [10]. Although non-typed, scanned dictionaries are available, they may not be sufficient to meet the demands of most NLP tasks, which typically require a comprehensive and rich dictionary.

Additionally, the lack of Tulu language detection libraries presents challenges during corpus creation and data filtering. Identifying and distinguishing Tulu language content from other languages in the corpus becomes problematic without suitable language detection tools, impacting the quality and accuracy of the data used for NLP tasks in Tulu.

2.3 Code-Mixing and Language Variation

Tulu's body of written literature is not as extensive as that of other literary Dravidian languages like Tamil [11]. Modern-day Tulu literature is written using the Kannada script. With limited use of the Tigalari alphabet, Tulu is primarily written in the Kannada and English scripts. However, the situation is evolving. The corpus of written Tulu without code-mixing is relatively small, making it challenging to find substantial data for NLP tasks. Tulu's oral traditions are invaluable for understanding the finer aspects of the language, but incorporating them into NLP is complex.

Additionally, the Kannada script does not fully accommodate Tulu's phonetic features, resulting in representation challenges.

2.4 Morphological Complexity

Tulu exhibits a highly agglutinative and morphologically rich structure, resulting in complex word formation with morphophonemic changes [12]. The ordering of suffixes attached to root words determines morpho-syntax, further adding to the linguistic intricacies. Tulu's distinct features present challenges for NLP tasks like Named Entity Recognition (NER) and Cross-Lingual Transfer.

2.5 Speech Recognition Challenges

High quality corpus is needed, especially since the corpus size is small. Amoolya et al. [13] have noted that errors can crop up if the audio is not recorded properly with a consistent speaker pace. Additionally, in a small corpus, not all features will be well-trained for audio and transcript. Tulu accents differ from location to place. Two words that have the same meaning and sound quite similar might be confusing. Such phrases might be perplexing to the computer system.

2.6 Machine Translation Challenges

Limited data availability also affects the development of Machine Translation systems for Tulu due to the lack of parallel corpora. Construction of parallel corpus from scratch is needed for most tasks. DL architectures are used for MT, but they need large amounts of data during train, making it unsuitable for low-resource language [14].

2.7 Character Recognition

Lack of benchmark datasets is one of the major problems encountered while addressing the issue of document analysis in Tulu [15,16].

The multifaceted challenges faced in NLP for Tulu underscore the need for innovative solutions and community engagement to unlock the language's potential for various NLP applications.

3 Existing Digital Resources

The domain of Tulu NLP currently faces a scarcity of digital resources, particularly concerning libraries and embeddings. Presently, the two primary digital resources available are BPEmb [17], offering pre-trained subword embeddings, and FastText [18], providing pre-trained word vectors [19]. Beyond these resources, the Tulu language lacks a comprehensive set of tools and data sets for advanced NLP tasks. This paucity of resources may pose challenges for researchers and practitioners seeking to explore and develop NLP applications specific to the Tulu language. Therefore, further efforts are warranted to bridge this gap and foster the development of Tulu NLP methodologies.

4   Morphological Analysis and Generation

One study has been conducted in the development of MAG model for Tulu by Antony et al. [12]. This study and its conclusion are discussed below.

4.1   Morphological Complexity of Tulu

The Morphological Analyzer and Generator (MAG) plays a pivotal role in various natural language processing applications such as Machine Translation, spell checking, and Information Retrieval. It serves as an indispensable tool for describing root words and organizing their various morphemes within the word forms.

However, when dealing with Tulu, a highly agglutinative and morphologically rich language, the development of a morphological analyzer becomes notably more intricate compared to other Dravidian languages. Careful analysis and identification of roots and morphemes, as well as the creation of well-structured rules to cover diverse inflections, are essential elements [20] in constructing an effective Tulu morphological analyzer.

Antony et al. provide a detailed and insightful analysis of Tulu morphology, offering a valuable understanding of the language's complex linguistic features.

4.2   Overview of the Rule-Based Approach

The rule-based approach in morphological analysis and generation relies on pre-defined rules and lexicon containing root words and morphemes [21]. However, this method's dependency on preceding rules and the absence of certain morphemes in the dictionary can lead to system failures. In this study, a rule-based system using the AT&T Finite State Machine was proposed, integrating lexicon, morphotactics, and orthographic rules from a two-level morphology. The system addressed various inflections and differences by employing morphotactic and Sandhi rules for all noun and verb forms through the Finite State Transducer (FST). The key components required for building the morphological analyzer and generator model were the lexicon, morphotactics, and orthographic rules.

4.3   Model Description

The module processes the input against the defined and compiled rules. The resulting output is obtained in Romanized form, which can later be converted back to Unicode. Romanizing Tulu presents challenges due to the discrepancy

between AT&T Finite State Machine's support [22] for only ASCII characters and Tulu's reliance on Unicode. To bridge this gap and facilitate mapping
between the two representations, mapping files were created. These files contain rules that associate each Kannada alphabet with its corresponding English
alphabet, enabling the Romanization of Tulu words. Regarding the Morphological Generator, if the input contains the root word and its morphemic information and is accepted by the system, the generator proceeds to produce the
corresponding root word and morpheme units in the first level.

4.4   System Performance

The system's performance was evaluated through two sets of 100 different words
each against a gold standard. The results indicated that the system achieved an
impressive accuracy of 99% for the recall words. For the second set of words,
which were out of the system's lexicon, the accuracy ranged between 70% to
80% for both word analysis and generation. The proposed Morphological Analyzer and Generator (MAG) demonstrated its effectiveness across various cases,
successfully handling nouns and verbs, including continuous and negative words.

5   Automatic Speech Recognition

There appears to be only one study done in the field of Automatic Speech Recognition in Tulu, by G, Amoolya et al. [13]. This study and its conclusion are
discussed below.

5.1   Existing Corpus

Tulu sentence lists for speech recognition have already been collected for a different study to check noise speech recognition threshold [23].

5.2   Corpus Creation and Analysis

The Tulu language consists of 50 fundamental phonetic units known as 'monophones' [3]. These monophones serve as the foundational linguistic elements.
When developing Automatic Speech Recognition (ASR) systems, different basic
units like phones, aksharas (syllables), or subwords derived from combinations of
monophones can be used. However, employing triphones, which include contextual information, has been found more effective for ASR systems due to speech's
context-dependent nature.

Audio data was collected from native Tulu speakers of various age groups (11
to 65) and processed to enhance feature extraction analysis. The study's script
was sourced from the online newspaper platform, 'Times of Kudla.'

5.3   Model Overview

The Kaldi toolkit was used, a versatile and robust platform utilized for the development of Automatic Speech Recognition (ASR) systems [24]. Kaldi's front-end processing for feature extraction contributes to the enhancement of the ASR pipeline. The toolkit also supports multiple classifiers, such as GMM-HMM (Gaussian Mixture Model-Hidden Markov Model) and DNN-HMM (Deep Neural Network-Hidden Markov Model) approaches.

The GMM-HMM approach utilizes a generative model to capture parameterized variability from features, making it more data-efficient. On the other hand, the DNN-HMM approach is discriminative and non-parametric, relying on larger datasets to effectively distinguish phonetic unit occurrences. Researchers can make informed choices based on data availability and system requirements while harnessing Kaldi's potential to develop cutting-edge ASR systems.

The experiment involved Grapheme-to-phoneme (G2P) conversion for the Kannada language using rule-based G2P with Bhashini services' grapheme-to-phoneme rules [25]. The language model was constructed using the SRILM toolkit, employing a 4-gram model to predict word probabilities within word sequences.

5.4   System Performance

The ASR models employed a GMM-HMM approach, with the tri1 model achieving a better Word Error Rate (WER). However, the DNN-HMM approach demonstrated superior performance for the tri2 and tri3 models in terms of WER. Notably, the tri3_2750_55000 model, trained with Linear Discriminant Analysis (LDA) and Maximum Likelihood Linear Transform (MLLT) alongside Speaker Adaptive Training (SAT), exhibited the highest WER at 4.05%, utilising 2750 Hidden Markov Model (HMM) states and 55000 Gaussians.

The ASR system's errors were found to be influenced by various factors, notably the speech rates of the speakers during audio recordings. These variations in speech speed—ranging from rapid to slow or consistent pacing—pose challenges and present research opportunities for developing ASR systems that effectively handle diverse speech speeds. The characteristics extracted from each triphone significantly contribute to determining the system's error rates and overall performance.

6   Sentiment Analysis

To the best of our knowledge, to date, all corpora developed for sentiment analysis in the Tulu language exhibit code-mixing, a prevalent linguistic phenomenon characterized by the fusion of two or more languages within a single communicative context. The baseline models have been developed for the same. There exist two such corpora, created by studies from Kannadaguli et al. [10] and Hedge et. al [9]. These studies and their conclusions are discussed below.

6.1 Nature of Corpus Created

In the realm of social media, individuals are afforded the freedom to express their thoughts, leading to the common practice of code-mixing, as technological constraints do not limit the use of multiple languages [26, 27].

The adoption of code-mixing is facilitated by the ease of inputting text in Latin script and the utilization of familiar English words. As a result, users often compose comments that blend the Latin script with native scripts or rely solely on the Latin script. Given the linguistic landscape, it is noteworthy that Tulu speakers possess fluency in both Tulu, their regional language, and Kannada, the official language of Karnataka. Moreover, English proficiency is prevalent among numerous Tulu speakers, particularly those actively engaged in social media interactions. Hedge et al. note that comments posted by Tulu users concerning Tulu programs on social media platforms commonly constitute a code-mixture of Tulu, Kannada, and English, resulting in a wealth of trilingual code-mixed data that remains underexplored in the realm of research.

6.2 Methods for Corpus Creation

Kannadaguli et al. generated a corpus by collecting comments from various social media platforms, including YouTube, Instagram, Facebook, LinkedIn, and Twitter. To streamline the data processing procedure, a constraint was imposed on the comment length, setting the upper limit to 12 words, and any comments exceeding this limit were excluded from the dataset. As a result, the final corpus comprised a total of 5,536 comments. For annotation purposes, four distinct classes were utilized, namely, Constructive, Destructive, Assorted, and Undecided.

In their study, Hedge et al. conducted the creation of a corpus scraping comments from Tulu-language YouTube videos. These comments exhibited linguistic diversity, being written either entirely in English, Kannada, Tulu, or in a combination of these languages using Kannada/Latin script or a combination of Kannada and Latin scripts. The data filtration process was carried out manually to remove purely English entries. Subsequently, the corpus was reduced to 7,171 comments. For annotation purposes, the comments were categorized into five distinct groups based on their sentiment: Positive, Negative, Neutral, Mixed-Feelings, and Not Tulu.

6.3 Corpus Annotation and Annotator Agreement

Both Kannadaguli et al. and Hedge et al. use 10 or more annotators, carefully chosen for their proficiency in both Tulu and English, as well as their diverse educational backgrounds. These annotators were tasked with assigning sentiment labels to the comments in the corpus.

To assess the inter-annotator agreement and the reliability of the annotations, the researchers calculated the Disagreement-Aware Krippendorff's Alpha value

(DAC) [28]. The DAC is a widely used metric to measure agreement among multiple annotators.

In Kannadaguli et al.'s study, the calculated alpha value was found to be 0.9, indicating a high level of agreement among the annotators in their sentiment label assignments. The metric agreement for the annotation for the code-mixed Tulu corpus obtained by Hedge et al. was 0.6832.

6.4   Baseline Models

Kannadaguli et al. explored both Machine Learning (ML) and Deep Learning (DL) models for sentiment analysis. They used ML algorithms such as Decision Tree (DT), K-Nearest Neighbors (KNN), Logistic Regression (LR), Naïve Bayes (Multimodal) (NB), Principal Component Analysis (PCA), Random Forest (RF), and Support Vector Machines (SVM), with Term Frequency Inverse Document Frequencies (TFIDF) [29] as feature vectors. DL models included Bi-LSTM [30], Bidirectional Encoder Representation Transformers (BERT) [31], and Contextualized Dynamic Meta Embeddings (CDME) [32].

The analysis indicated that DT, LR, and RF achieved notable precision, recall, and F1 scores, while KNN and NB showed higher precision but lower recall. The DL models, especially CDME, performed well in identifying all classes. Among the classifiers, Bi-LSTM stood out with superior performance.

In Hedge et al.'s study, traditional ML algorithms like MNB, LR, SVM, kNN, DT, RF, and MLP were employed on code-mixed Tulu text using TF-IDF representations. Overall, all classifiers achieved moderate performance, with SVM and MLP showing comparatively better results, both achieving a weighted average F1-score of 0.60. SVM's 5-fold cross-validation produced a weighted average F1-score of 0.62.

In conclusion, both studies highlight the effectiveness of ML and DL models for sentiment analysis in code-mixed languages, with specific classifiers exhibiting superior performance. However, further research is needed to better understand the intricacies of code-mixed datasets and enhance model performance in this context, especially the problem of class-imbalance.

7   Kannada-Tulu Machine Translation

Hegde et al. has already conducted a comprehensive investigation on the translation from Kannada to Tulu [33]. Additionally, a shared task was organized at the DravidianLangTech-2022 workshop, held in conjunction with ACL 2022. This shared task comprised five sub-tasks, one of which focused on the translation between Kannada and Tulu languages. Datasets were made available, and the translations were evaluated against gold-standard datasets. Further insights and outcomes derived from the shared task were subsequently documented and discussed in the work by Madasamy et al. [34]. This study and its conclusions are discussed below.

7.1   Corpus Creation

The dataset comprises 10,300 sentence pairs that were meticulously curated. Due to the unavailability of a parallel corpus for translating between Kannada-Tulu language pairs, constructing a parallel corpus poses challenges in this low-resource language combination. In order to address this issue, the researchers gathered monolingual Tulu texts from digitally accessible sources and conducted manual translations of the corresponding Kannada sentences to create the parallel corpus.

7.2   Model Description

Goyal et al. [35] achieved the most favourable outcomes in the domain of Kannada-Tulu translation. They addressed the task using the openNMT system [36]. Notably, their approach's exceptional performance is credited to the careful adjustment of hyperparameters within the openNMT system. Additionally, they adopted the indic tokenization scheme offered by IndicNLP [37], which led to noteworthy enhancements in the reported results.

7.3   System Performance

The primary conclusion that the authors drew from the participants' findings was that in order to attain improved performance in translating morphologically rich languages, such as Kannada-Tulu, it is essential to utilize not only baseline machine translation models but also efficient dataset preparation techniques like back-translation and subword tokenization.

Specifically, Goyal et al. achieved a BLEU score of 0.6149 in their translation experiment for the Kannada-Tulu language pair.

8   English-Tulu Machine Translation

A system proposed by Shenoy et al. [38] explores the translation process of a machine translation system from English to Tulu based on rule-based machine translation. The study and its conclusions are discussed below.

8.1   Overview of the Rule-Based Approach

Rule-based machine translation (RBMT) is a classical approach that uses linguistic information from dictionaries and grammars to translate between source and target languages while preserving their meanings [39]. It employs language and grammar rules along with dictionaries for common words. Specialized dictionaries can be made for specific industries or disciplines, resulting in word-by-word translations without strong semantic correlations.

RBMT involves morphological, syntactic, and semantic analysis of the source text. Triplets are extracted and translated based on prepositions, followed by reordering the sentence using the target language's semantic structure. If no prepositions are found, this step is skipped. The translation process entails identifying rules for English sentences, finding corresponding rules for Tulu, generating internal representations of Tulu sentences, and using contextual semantic and syntactic generation to determine the exact words or sentences in Tulu.

8.2   Model Description

The source language is inputted into the Morphological Analyzer, which utilizes a language dictionary to produce its output. Subsequently, the output undergoes parsing, followed by a lookup process in the bilingual translator's dictionary. The Target Language Generator is responsible for the translation into the target language and presenting the final result. However, the authors have not furnished specific information concerning the dictionaries employed in the process.

8.3   System Performance

The authors of the study did not reveal the performance of the system.

9   Character Recognition

The field of research related to Tulu script has seen significant development, with notable influence from the Grantha script and similarities with the Malayalam script. For processing a large number of documents available in Tulu, researchers have referred to offline Malayalam script recognition papers [40].

The common steps followed in this research domain include preprocessing, which involves noise elimination and binarisation, as well as segmentation, feature extraction, and classification [15]. Savitha C K and Anthony P J, along with different collaborators, have conducted extensive research in this area, contributing studies on binarisation, feature selection, and segmentation techniques [41–44].

Manimozhi et al. conducted a study on identifying Tulu characters by OCR and mapping it to Kannada. The mapping database was created manually [45]. In their study, Kumar et al. [46] presented Lipi Gnani, an OCR system specifically designed for recognizing documents printed in the Kannada script. Notably, they conducted tests to evaluate its performance on Tulu documents written in the same script.

In their work on character recognition framework study, Anthony PJ et al. have presented a novel framework for the recognition of handwritten Tulu characters. The proposed framework consists of five modules, covering image acquisition and preprocessing, feature extraction to vectors, system learning through models, classification and recognition, and mapping the recognized Tulu characters to their equivalent Kannada characters.

Additionally, Savitha et al. [16] and Bhat et al. have employed the DCNN model on their custom corpus for single character recognition.

9.1   Existing Corpus

There exists a dataset comprising scanned pages of Tulu books online [47].

9.2   Corpora Creation

Several corpora have been created for the purpose of OCR in Tulu. The absence of a benchmark dataset for Tulu script led the researchers to collect their own data for the system. The datasets can usually fall under two categories: 'Tulu characters from modern documents' and 'Tulu characters from palm leaf manuscripts'. For Savitha et al.'s ML study, they created both in their study. A dataset of 30,000 isolated handwritten Tulu characters was collected from 625 writers.

Anthony et al.'s Haar feature study conducted their research using a corpus of Tulu documents. To train their system, they utilized a set of scanned handwritten character samples sourced from students in different schools across coastal Karnataka. The dataset consisted of 13 vowels, 45 consonants, and vowel diacritics, summing up to a total of 598 characters.

Bhat et al. created a dataset comprises a total of 90,000 characters, encompassing both vowels and consonants. It consists of 45 Aksharas. The handwritten data was gathered from 40 native Tuluvas. Manual tagging and classification were performed to group the extracted characters into different classes. It is important to note that compound characters are not part of this dataset.

9.3   Pre-processing Approaches

Savitha et al.'s block detection study proposed a segmentation algorithm that utilized simple constructs like projection profiles to partition word blocks. These partitioned word blocks were then characterized into single and multiple-character blocks using an unsupervised technique based on partitioning and statistical features. The proposed technique achieved an efficiency of more than 90% for Tulu script.

In the experiments conducted in Anthony et al.'s binarisation study, a dataset comprising 48 images of the Tulu manuscript, specifically the Sundara Khanda episode of Ramayana, was utilized. The evaluation of the results was based on performance measures such as PSNR and MSE. The Adapt_Sobel combination exhibited the best performance with a PSNR of 63.360103 dB and an MSE of 0.0300.

Anthony et al.'s aegmentation study is centered on Tulu palm leaf manuscripts, with experimentation conducted on 25 randomly selected images from various episodes such as Anathavathara, Bhagavatha, Ramayana, and Durga Stuthi. The study involved the application and evaluation of different techniques, including binarisation, thresholding, and edge detection. To assess the effectiveness of the binarisation process, a ground truth image is usually required. However, due to the unavailability of a ground truth image for the Tulu dataset, the researchers used the AMADI_LONTARSET benchmark dataset [48] as an alternative for evaluating and measuring the performance of their algorithm for binarising palm leaf manuscripts. The combination of Otsu and Total Variation (Otsu_TV) yielded the best result, boasting a high PSNR value of 53.7676 and a low MSE value of 0.2731.

Savitha et al.'s ML study applied pre-processing in their study to reduce variations in writing styles. To improve recognition rates with minimal elements, a zoning technique is employed. The image is converted into a 3×3 grid, and features are extracted from each of the 9 zones. Contour following is utilized to extract 12 directional features from each zone, forming vectors for further analysis.

9.4   Feature Extraction

Anthony et al.'s Haar features study discuss the use of Haar features. Following preprocessing, character features are extracted to minimize storage needs. The Wavelet transform is employed to extract features in the spatio-frequency domain, presenting them in a compressed format. Viola and Jones [49] adopted Haar wavelets, the most straightforward wavelet, and introduced Haar features. Extracted Haar features are stored as feature vectors, preserving information in a lower-dimensional space.

9.5   Model Description

In Anthony et al.'s segmentation study, they utilized a finalized DCNN architecture with 500 neurons in the fully connected (FC) layer. However, they encountered challenges in handling segmented compound characters, leading them to focus solely on simple isolated characters. Additionally, they faced an issue with character class imbalance, which proved difficult to completely avoid.

In Savitha et al.'s ML study, ANN, SVM, AdaBoost and Deep CNN was used.

Anthony et al.'s Haar study used a Cascade trainer which utilises the AdaBoost machine learning algorithm for training and classification. Extracted Haar feature vectors from the earlier stage are the input. At each stage, Haar features are employed. Each stage is trained using the boosting technique with the AdaBoost algorithm.

Bhat et al., employed a 13-layer model inspired by VGGNet, consisting of sequential small-sized convolutional and fully connected (FC) layers. They introduced modifications to the network architecture. The paper provides a comprehensive description of the model architecture.

9.6   System Performance

Anthony et al.'s Segmentation study The study revealed that the DCNN model achieved a recognition rate of 79.92% for recognizing isolated handwritten Tulu palm leaf characters.

According to the comparative analysis in Savitha et al.'s ML study, Deep Convolutional Neural Networks achieve higher efficiency, reaching 98.49%, compared to shallow learning techniques for isolated Tulu characters from modern documents. Furthermore, for isolated characters from Tulu palm leaf manuscripts, Deep CNN still performs well with an efficiency of 80.49%.

After comparing different models, Bhat et al. found DCNN approach to be the best. Their VGGNet-based DCNN model achieved 92.41% recognition accuracy for the classification of 45 handwritten characters.

10   Future Scope

The scope for future work in NLP for this language is significant, considering the limited progress made in various areas. Here are some potential directions for future research and development:

One of the primary areas of focus lies in creating an expanded code-mixed corpus for Tulu. Code-mixing is prevalent in multilingual communities, and a diverse and comprehensive corpus will be invaluable in developing NLP models that can effectively handle code-mixed language scenarios, reflecting the language's dynamic usage patterns accurately.

Another vital avenue for future research is the advancement of machine translation capabilities for Tulu. Developing sophisticated machine translation systems will facilitate cross-lingual communication, breaking barriers between Tulu and other languages and promoting cultural exchange and collaboration.

Universal translation systems could potentially mitigate the requirement for extensive bilingual datasets in the context of under-resourced languages [50]. By leveraging such systems, the translation performance for these languages could be enhanced, even with limited available data.

Data augmentation techniques [51], offer another promising approach. This method involves utilizing a monolingual large-side dataset in conjunction with a monolingual target-side dataset and employing pivots that are grounded in a third high-resource language. By doing so, data augmentation can effectively supplement the available resources and improve the overall translation quality for low-resource languages.

Alongside machine translation, enhanced speech recognition systems for Tulu will empower voice-based interactions and facilitate transcription services, making audio content more accessible and engaging for Tuluvas.

To address the challenges of limited resources, cross-lingual transfer learning is a promising direction in NLP for Tulu. Leveraging knowledge from resource-rich languages and fine-tuning models for Tulu can yield significant improvements in various NLP tasks, even in the low-resource setting. Additionally, there is a need to develop specialized named entity recognition (NER) models for Tulu to accurately identify and categorize entities, supporting information extraction and knowledge discovery in the language.

Community involvement and crowdsourcing efforts play a vital role in the future development of NLP for Tulu. Engaging the linguistic community in data collection, annotation, and resource creation will foster a sense of ownership and ensure the authenticity of language-specific tools and datasets. Moreover, interdisciplinary collaborations between NLP researchers, linguists, and language experts will enrich the understanding of Tulu's linguistic characteristics, guiding the design of tailored NLP methodologies and applications.

11   Conclusion

This review paper examined the state of Tulu Natural Language Processing (NLP), highlighting its accomplishments, difficulties, and prospects for further study. NLP's journey in this low-resource environment has only just begun, and coordinated efforts in this direction hold the potential to advance the field and have a long-lasting effect on linguistic inclusion and diversity in the digital sphere. The advancement of NLP in Tulu necessitates collaborative efforts involving the linguistic community to address the challenges and promote the language's development.

References

1. Brückner, H.: Oral Traditions in South India: Essays on Tulu Oral Epics. Harrassowitz Verlag, Wiesbaden (2017). OCLC: ocn995845113
2. Padmanabha Kekunnaya, K.: A comparative study of Tulu dialects. https://cir.nii.ac.jp/crid/1130282273061170560
3. Männer, A.: Tulu-English dictionary. Basel Mission Press, Mangalore (1886). Google-Books-ID: FuAUAAAAYAAJ
4. Somashekar, S.: Developmental Trends in the Acquisition of Relative Clauses: Cross-linguistic Experimental Study of Tulu. Cornell University (1999)
5. Caldwell, R.: A Comparative Grammar of the Dravidian Or South-Indian Family of Languages. Trübner (1875). Google-Books-ID: rHUZAAAAIAAJ
6. Navare, N.: Conservation of Culture through Language. (2013)
7. Gruetzemacher, R.: The power of natural language processing. Harvard Bus. Rev. (2022). https://hbr.org/2022/04/the-power-of-natural-language-processing. ISSN 0017-8012
8. Zhang, S., Frey, B., Bansal, M.: How can NLP help revitalize endangered languages? A case study and roadmap for the Cherokee language. In: Proceedings Of The 60th Annual Meeting Of The Association For Computational Linguistics (Volume 1: Long Papers), pp. 1529-1541 (2022). https://aclanthology.org/2022.acl-long.108
9. Hegde, A., Anusha, M., Coelho, S., Shashirekha, H., Chakravarthi, B.: Corpus creation for sentiment analysis in code-mixed Tulu text. In: Proceedings Of The 1st Annual Meeting Of The ELRA/ISCA Special Interest Group On Under-Resourced Languages, pp. 33-40 (2022). https://aclanthology.org/2022.sigul-1.5
10. Kannadaguli, P.: A code-diverse Tulu-English dataset for NLP based sentiment analysis applications. In: 2021 Advanced Communication Technologies And Signal Processing (ACTS), pp. 1-6 (2021)
11. Kamila, R.: The Hindu: Karnataka/Mangalore News : 'Tulu is a highly developed language of the Dravidian family' (2009)

12. Antony, P., Raj, H., Sahana, B., Alvares, D., Raj, A.: Morphological analyzer and generator for Tulu language: a novel approach. In: Proceedings Of The International Conference On Advances in Computing, Communications and Informatics, pp. 828-834 (2012)
13. Amoolya, G., Hans, A., Lakkavalli, V., Durai, S.: Automatic speech recognition for Tulu Language using GMM-HMM and DNN-HMM techniques. In: 2022 International Conference on Advanced Computing Technologies and Applications (ICACTA), pp. 1-6 (2022)
14. Pan, X., Wang, M., Wu, L., Li, L.: Contrastive learning for many-to-many multilingual neural machine translation. In: Proceedings of the 59th Annual Meeting of the Association for Computational Linguistics and the 11th International Joint Conference on Natural Language Processing (Volume 1: Long Papers), pp. 244–258 (2021)
15. Bhat, S., Seshikala, G.: Character recognition of Tulu script using convolutional neural network. In: Advances in Artificial Intelligence and Data Engineering, pp. 121-131 (2021)
16. Savitha, C., Antony, P.: Machine learning approaches for recognition of offline Tulu handwritten scripts. In: Journal Of Physics: Conference Series, vol. 1142, p. 012005 (2018). https://doi.org/10.1088/1742-6596/1142/1/012005
17. BPEmb. https://bpemb.h-its.org/
18. Wiki word vectors . fastText. https://fasttext.cc/index.html
19. DravidianLangTech-2022. https://dravidianlangtech.github.io/2022/
20. Goyal, V., Lehal, G.: Hindi morphological analyzer and generator. In: Emerging Trends in Engineering Technology, International Conference On, pp. 1156-1159 (2008)
21. Kessikbayeva, G., Cicekli, I.: A rule based morphological analyzer and a morphological disambiguator for Kazakh Language. Linguis. Lit. Stud. **4**, 96–104 (2016)
22. Hetherington, L.: The MIT finite-state transducer toolkit for speech and language processing. In: Interspeech 2004, pp. 2609-2612 (2004)
23. Bhat, S., Kalaiah, M., Shastri, U.: Development and validation of Tulu sentence lists to test speech recognition threshold in noise. J. Indian Speech Lang. Hear. Assoc. **35**, 50 (2021)
24. Povey, D., et al.: The Kaldi Speech Recognition Toolkit
25. H R Kumar, S.: Tamil / Kannada G2P. (Bhashini AI Solutions Pvt Ltd,2023,1). https://github.com/bhashini-ai/g2p, original-date: 2017-11-15T01:48:43Z
26. Thara, S., Poornachandran, P.: Code-mixing: a brief survey. In: 2018 International Conference on Advances in Computing, Communications and Informatics (ICACCI), pp. 2382-2388 (2018)
27. Tay, M.: Code switching and code mixing as a communicative strategy in multilingual discourse. World Englishes **8**, 407–417 (2007)
28. Yannakakis, G., Martinez, H.: Grounding truth via ordinal annotation. In: 2015 International Conference on Affective Computing and Intelligent Interaction (ACII), pp. 574-580 (2015). http://ieeexplore.ieee.org/document/7344627/
29. Das, B., Chakraborty, S.: An improved text sentiment classification model using TF-IDF and next word negation (2018). http://arxiv.org/abs/1806.06407, arXiv:1806.06407 [cs]
30. Zhou, P., Qi, Z., Zheng, S., Xu, J.: Text classification improved by integrating bidirectional LSTM with two-dimensional max pooling
31. Batra, H., Punn, N., Sonbhadra, S., Agarwal, S.: BERT-based sentiment analysis: a software engineering perspective (2021). http://arxiv.org/abs/2106.02581, arXiv:2106.02581 [cs]

32. Kiela, D., Wang, C., Cho, K.: Dynamic meta-embeddings for improved sentence representations. In: Proceedings of The 2018 Conference on Empirical Methods in Natural Language Processing, pp. 1466-1477 (2018). https://aclanthology.org/D18-1176

33. Hegde, A., Shashirekha, H., Madasamy, A., Chakravarthi, B.: A study of machine translation models for Kannada-Tulu. In: Third Congress on Intelligent Systems, pp. 145-161 (2023)

34. Madasamy, A., et al.: Overview of the shared task on machine translation in Dravidian languages. In: Proceedings of the Second Workshop on Speech and Language Technologies for Dravidian Languages, pp. 271-278 (2022). https://aclanthology.org/2022.dravidianlangtech-1.41. Conference Name: Proceedings of the Second Workshop on Speech and Language Technologies for Dravidian Languages Place: Dublin, Ireland Publisher: Association for Computational Linguistics

35. Goyal, P., Supriya, M., Dinesh, U., Nayak, A.: Translation Techies@DravidianLangTech-ACL2022-machine translation in Dravidian languages. In: Proceedings of the Second Workshop on Speech and Language Technologies for Dravidian Languages (2022)

36. Klein, G., Kim, Y., Deng, Y., Senellart, J., Rush, A.: OpenNMT: open-source toolkit for neural machine translation (2017). http://arxiv.org/abs/1701.02810, arXiv:1701.02810 [cs]

37. Kakwani, D., et al.: IndicNLPSuite: monolingual corpora, evaluation benchmarks and pre-trained multilingual language models for Indian languages. In: Findings of the Association for Computational Linguistics: EMNLP 2020, pp. 4948-4961 (2020). https://www.aclweb.org/anthology/2020.findings-emnlp.445

38. Amrutha Shenoy, M.A., Rao, P., Shenoy, V., Kudva, V., Nayak, V.: English to Tulu Translator. IRJET (2020)

39. Sreelekha, S.: Statistical vs rule based machine translation; a case study on Indian language perspective. (2017). http://arxiv.org/abs/1708.04559, arXiv:1708.04559 [cs]

40. Antony, P., Savitha, C.: A framework for recognition of handwritten South Dravidian Tulu script. In: 2016 Conference on Advances in Signal Processing (CASP), pp. 7-12 (2016)

41. Antony, P., Savitha, C., Ujwal, U.: Efficient binarization technique for handwritten archive of south Dravidian Tulu script. In: Shetty, N., Patnaik, L., Prasad, N., Nalini, N. (eds. Emerging Research in Computing, Information, Communication and Applications. ERCICA 2016, pp. 651–666. Springer, Singapore (2018). https://doi.org/10.1007/978-981-10-4741-1_56

42. Savitha, C.K., Ujwal, U.J., Smitha, M.L.: Detection of single and multi-character Tulu text blocks. In: 2021 IEEE International Conference on Mobile Networks and Wireless Communications (ICMNWC), pp. 1-6 (2021)

43. Antony, P., Savitha, C.: Segmentation and recognition of characters on Tulu palm leaf manuscripts. Int. J. Comput. Vis. Robot. **9**, 438 (2019)

44. Antony, P., Savitha, C., Ujwal, U.: Haar features based handwritten character recognition system for Tulu script. In: 2016 IEEE International Conference on Recent Trends in Electronics, Information & Communication Technology (RTE-ICT), pp. 65-68 (2016)

45. Manimozhi, I., Challa, M.: An efficient translation of Tulu to Kannada south Indian scripts using optical character recognition. In: 2021 5th International Conference on Computing Methodologies and Communication (ICCMC), pp. 952-957 (2021)

46. Shiva Kumar, H.R., Ramakrishnan, A.G.: Lipi Gnani - A Versatile OCR for Documents in any Language Printed in Kannada Script. (2019). http://arxiv.org/abs/1901.00413, arXiv:1901.00413 [cs]

47. HR Kumar, S.: TuluDocuments. (MILE lab, IISc,2019,2), https://github.com/MILE-IISc/TuluDocuments, original-date: 2018-10-28T03:28:13Z

48. Kesiman, M., Burie, J., Wibawantara, G., Sunarya, I., Ogier, J.: AMADI LontarSet: the first handwritten Balinese palm leaf manuscripts dataset. In: 2016 15th International Conference on Frontiers in Handwriting Recognition (ICFHR), pp. 168-173 (2016). ISSN: 2167-6445

49. Viola, P., Jones, M.: Rapid object detection using a boosted cascade of simple features. In: Proceedings of the 2001 IEEE Computer Society Conference on Computer Vision and Pattern Recognition. CVPR 2001 (2001). https://doi.org/10.1109/CVPR.2001.990517

50. Gu, J., Hassan, H., Devlin, J., Li, V.: Universal neural machine translation for extremely low resource languages. (2018). http://arxiv.org/abs/1802.05368, arXiv:1802.05368 [cs]

51. Xia, M., Kong, X., Anastasopoulos, A., Neubig, G.: Generalized data augmentation for low-resource translation. In: Proceedings of the 57th Annual Meeting of the Association for Computational Linguistics, pp. 5786-5796 (2019)

DepBoost-TransNet: Boosted Transformer Network for Depression Classification

Pratik Anil Rahood[1(✉)] [ID], Prasanna Kumar Kumaresan[2] [ID],
and Bharathi Raja Chakravarthi[1] [ID]

[1] School of Computer Science, University of Galway, Galway, Ireland
pratikrahood@gmail.com
[2] Insight SFI Research Centre for Data Analytics, University of Galway,
Galway, Ireland

Abstract. Depression presents a significant global mental health challenge affecting countless individuals across the globe. Early detection is of paramount importance, yet conventional methods, such as self-reporting and professional evaluations, possess inherent limitations and subjectivity. With the proliferation of social media and the abundance of user-generated content, novel approaches employing transformer-based models and text-mining techniques hold the potential to reveal signs of depression within social media text. This study delves into the efficacy of transformer-based models and natural language processing techniques in recognizing depressive symptoms within social media text. Social media serves as a distinct window into mental well-being, and this investigation explores the utilization of advanced transformers to tackle this issue. Results indicate that transformers trained on imbalanced datasets outperform those employing data augmentation techniques, like SMOTE, due to their proficiency in discerning intricate patterns and sensitivity to synthetic data. Furthermore, the ensemble model, which amalgamates predictions from multiple transformer models, surpasses individual models, underscoring the potential of harnessing the diverse strengths of these models for enhanced depression classification. Despite certain limitations and privacy considerations, leveraging social media data for early depression detection shows promise in improving the well-being of affected individuals through timely intervention and treatment. Subsequent research endeavors should prioritize hyperparameter optimization and the acquisition of more balanced datasets to further enhance the accuracy and dependability of depression diagnosis via the analysis of social media text.

Keywords: Depression · NLP · Transformers · Machine Learning · SMOTE

1 Introduction

Depression stands as a significant global mental health concern, impacting the lives of millions across the world [1]. Its repercussions on individuals' health,

© The Author(s), under exclusive license to Springer Nature Switzerland AG 2024
B. R. Chakravarthi et al. (Eds.): SPELLL 2023, CCIS 2046, pp. 110–128, 2024.
https://doi.org/10.1007/978-3-031-58495-4_8

productivity, and overall well-being are severe, underscoring the critical need for early intervention. Current methods for depression detection primarily involve self-reporting and professional examinations, often combining both. Nonetheless, these methods possess limited and subjective scopes. However, in light of the rapid expansion of social media users and their prolific content generation, an opportunity arises to explore novel avenues for identifying depression from individuals' data. This paper endeavors to probe the potential of machine learning algorithms and text mining techniques in discerning signs of depression within social media text. The burgeoning realm of social media has prompted individuals to divulge nearly every facet of their lives through posts, updates, and messages. This profusion of user-generated content provides a unique opportunity not only to glean insights into individual behaviors and emotions but also into their mental well-being.

The primary objective of this paper is to investigate the feasibility of employing social media text analysis as a tool for diagnosing depression. The vast reservoir of user-generated content on platforms such as Twitter, Facebook, and Reddit presents an avenue for understanding people's emotional states, thoughts, and experiences. When coupled with advanced pre-trained Transformers and natural language processing techniques, this text-based data exhibits the potential to identify depressive symptoms and predict depression risk. These innovative approaches offer several advantages over conventional methodologies. First, they are cost-effective and practical. Machine learning algorithms and text mining techniques for depression diagnosis via social media text have demonstrated their efficiency and effectiveness in comparison to traditional methods. The capability to swiftly and comprehensively analyze substantial volumes of social media data facilitates effective and scalable depression identification. Second, these techniques can circumvent limitations and support clinical diagnosis in a more adaptable fashion. Traditional approaches to depression diagnosis, including professional assessments and self-reporting, suffer from subjectivity and scope constraints. For instance, the accurate reporting of symptoms and events is pivotal in professional evaluations and may be influenced by factors like memory bias or the desire to present oneself in the best possible light.

This study will commence by reviewing existing research on the detection of depression within social media language, laying the foundation for our investigation. Studies such as Guntuku et al. [1], Choudhury et al. [2], Kamite et al. [3], and Deng et al. [4] have explored the relationships between linguistic patterns and depressive symptoms in social media posts, revealing the potential for automated identification. Choudhury et al. [5] also conducted an in-depth analysis of data from online platforms, indicating the viability of using social media as a reliable source for mental health monitoring.

This paper will further delve into the techniques employed for social media text analysis. Methods such as sentiment analysis, linguistic feature extraction, topic modeling, and deep learning approaches have been employed to collect pertinent data and discern signs of depression. This paper will explore different methodologies, along with their advantages and drawbacks in capturing the nuances of depression within text-based data. The use of social media data for mental health detection hinges significantly on ethical considerations. To ensure the ethical and responsible utilization of individuals' personal information, it is imperative to address privacy concerns, data anonymization, and potential biases in analysis algorithms. These factors must be carefully considered to maintain the credibility of the research and ensure the long-term viability of depression diagnosis through the analysis of social media text.

2   Motivation

Numerous compelling factors underlie the emergence of social media text analysis as a promising avenue for depression detection. Firstly, the widespread utilization of social media platforms by billions of individuals worldwide furnishes an extensive and diverse dataset. This data serves as a valuable resource for training and assessing machine learning algorithms. The availability of such data has empowered researchers and programmers to construct robust models capable of precisely discerning patterns and indicators of depression within social media posts.

Secondly, social media posts often serve as a repository of highly personal information pertaining to individuals' lives, thoughts, emotions, and experiences. On social networking platforms, people tend to express themselves candidly, sharing their triumphs, setbacks, and challenges. This candid content yields invaluable insights into their mental well-being, insights that may not be as readily accessible through other means. Analyzing these textual expressions allows for the identification of linguistic cues, mood patterns, and semantic connections suggestive of depressive symptoms.

Previous studies, such as those conducted by Poswiata and Perelkiewicz et al. [6] and Kayalvizhi and Thenmozhi et al. [7], have explored the application of machine learning algorithms and transformers in the context of depression detection with imbalanced data. While Kayalvizhi and Thenmozhi et al. harnessed machine learning algorithms and noted enhanced accuracy by employing the data augmentation tool SMOTE, Poswiata and Perelkiewicz et al., who employed transformers for classification, did not investigate the potential benefit of using SMOTE to balance the dataset before applying transformers for the classification task. This gap in research leaves room for machine learning algorithms to potentially exhibit higher accuracy than transformers, as transformers are generally expected to perform optimally on balanced datasets. Consequently, this thesis endeavors to bridge the research gap between these two studies and furnish an explanatory framework for this phenomenon.

This thesis also examines the necessity for an architecture to seamlessly integrate data augmentation with transformers, considering that standard data augmentation primarily targets vectors while transformers predominantly handle textual input. A variety of strategies, encompassing sentiment analysis, linguistic feature extraction, topic modeling, and transformer-based approaches, have been employed in an attempt to identify signs of depression. This discourse entails a comprehensive examination of these diverse techniques, taking into account their respective advantages and limitations in accurately capturing the subtle nuances of depression within text-based data.

Research Question: How can the incorporation of data augmentation techniques, such as the Synthetic Minority Over-sampling Technique (SMOTE), enhance the effectiveness of transformer models in detecting depression within imbalanced datasets?

Moreover, the utilization of social media data for the identification of mental health issues raises profound ethical considerations. The preservation of privacy, data anonymization, and the mitigation of biases within analytic algorithms demand meticulous attention to ensure the ethical and responsible utilization of individuals' personal information. Addressing these concerns actively is pivotal not only for upholding the integrity of the research but also for ensuring the enduring viability of diagnostic approaches that leverage social media text in the pursuit of a legitimate and trustworthy method for diagnosing depression.

3   Literature Review

Numerous research studies have focused on the utilization of language analysis on online platforms, such as social media and online forums, for the identification of individuals at risk for depression and self-harm. These studies have explored the use of social media data to assess depression rates and risk factors in populations [2]. An analysis of twelve articles published between 2009 and 2016 revealed that social media data can serve the purpose of monitoring changes in depression rates over time, identifying risk factors, and fostering innovative treatments [2]. However, ethical considerations pertaining to the collection and use of social media data for research, as well as the necessity for further research into the accuracy of various methodologies, require attention [2].

In addition to social media data, studies have employed natural language processing (NLP) methods to enhance the understanding and detection of depression. A comprehensive overview, covering 102 articles published between 2009 and 2016, unveiled that text analysis, sentiment analysis, and social network analysis were frequently utilized techniques for the identification of depression on social media [1]. Social media data has displayed the potential to serve as a valuable tool for identifying depression and other mental illnesses, although challenges such as the absence of standardized datasets and the need for further research on the effectiveness of different techniques have been underscored [1].

Similarly, online forums have been explored as a resource for assessing the risk of depression and self-harm. A critical study witnessed the development of unique machine learning algorithms aimed at identifying linguistic patterns indicative of depression and self-harm risk [5]. The findings suggested that Internet discussion boards could offer valuable insights into the identification and evaluation of mental health issues, affording an opportunity for early intervention [5]. Incorporating emotional artificial intelligence (EAI), a dataset of emotionally labeled Twitter posts was employed to diagnose depression [8]. The EAI model achieved an 80% accuracy rate in predicting emotions expressed in tweets, while also capturing characteristics linked to depression [8]. Another avenue of research was dedicated to the utilization of deep learning methods for the identification of depression among Twitter users. A dataset containing Twitter users classified as "depressed" or "not depressed" was utilized to create a deep learning model that predicted users' depressive condition with 85% accuracy [9]. In alignment with earlier studies, this model identified various linguistic characteristics associated with depression [9].

Exploring the topic of self-stigmatized depression within constrained writing, researchers emphasized the importance of linguistic indicators in the detection of depression [4]. The paper by Deng et al. highlighted the potential of NLP techniques to unveil hidden signs of depression in textual data. The use of words with negative emotions, first-person singular pronouns, and terms with morbid or suicidal connotations can all serve as linguistic indications of depression. These linguistic markers can be identified and flagged as potential instances of depression through the application of NLP techniques like natural language processing and machine learning. The use of NLP approaches to identify depression may enhance early detection and treatment of this mental health concern [4]. Machine learning methods have also been deployed to identify depression in social media posts. In a specific study, a dataset of tweets classified as "depressed" or "not depressed" was utilized to train a classifier, which was then employed to categorize new tweets [3]. The researchers achieved an 80% accuracy rate in correctly categorizing tweets, with the classifier demonstrating the ability to recognize linguistic characteristics associated with depression, such as the use of pejorative language, expression of suicidal thoughts, and loss of interest in previously enjoyable activities [3]. This study underscored the potential of machine learning techniques in identifying textual signals related to depression.

Recent studies have also harnessed pre-trained language models, specifically Roberta, for the identification of depression in social media text [6]. These studies contribute to the growing body of knowledge on the identification of depression through linguistic analysis across various online platforms. They illustrate the potential of machine learning algorithms and NLP approaches in the identification of linguistic indicators of depression, providing insights into the development of effective tools for mental health screening and intervention [6].

4   Dataset

The dataset employed originates from the shared task titled "Detecting Signs of Depression from Social Media Text at LT-EDI@RANLP 2023"[1], which draws inspiration from the work of Kayalvizhi and Thenmozhi et al. [7]. This dataset has been tailored to facilitate the identification of indications of depression in individuals based on their social media posts, wherein they candidly express their emotions and sentiments. The DepSign-LT-EDI@RANLP-2023 shared task is aimed at confronting this challenge by developing systems capable of accurately categorizing signs of depression into three classifications: "not depressed," "moderately depressed," and "severely depressed."

---

[1] https://codalab.lisn.upsaclay.fr/competitions/11075.

The dataset furnished for this endeavor comprises an assortment of social media posts composed in English. These posts encompass a wide array of content, including personal reflections, emotions, and experiences shared by individuals. A panel of domain experts has meticulously annotated this dataset, assigning the appropriate depression label to each post to denote the level of depression conveyed by the author. In this study, the dataset is harnessed for the purpose of addressing the task of identifying signs of depression from social media text.

4.1   Dataset Analysis

The dataset consists of social media postings written in English, which have been annotated with labels indicating the severity of depression exhibited by the authors (Table 1).

Table 1. Number of comments in the Train, Dev, and Test datasets and their Classification

Labels	Train	Test	Dev	Total
Moderate	3,678	275	2169	**7201**
Not Depressed	2755	135	848	**3245**
Severe	768	89	228	**499**

- **Dataset Size and Structure:** The dataset encompasses 10,945 instances, with each instance representing a social media posting. It adopts a tabular format, with each instance featuring the following elements:
  Text: The content of the social media posting.
  Depression Label: The categorization of depression severity linked to the posting, classified into three categories: "not depressed," "moderately depressed," and "severely depressed."
- **Class Distribution:** Evaluating the distribution of instances among the various depression labels is crucial for comprehending the dataset's equilibrium and potential biases. This evaluation aids in appraising the intricacy of the classification task and uncovering any imbalances within the classes that could impact model performance. The dataset's class distribution is as follows:

  - "Not depressed": 3,245 instances - "Moderately depressed": 7,201 instances - "Severely depressed": 499 instances

  The distribution of classes exhibits an imbalance, making it challenging to ensure that the developed models encounter a substantial number of instances from each class.
- **Textual Analysis:** Conducting a comprehensive analysis of the textual content in the dataset offers valuable insights into the characteristics of social media posts pertaining to depression. This examination aids in the identification of patterns and linguistic traits associated with each depression label.

Key aspects to consider during this textual analysis encompass:

1. Lexical Diversity: Assessing the breadth and diversity of vocabulary employed throughout the dataset.
2. Emotion and Sentiment Analysis: Engaging in sentiment analysis to detect the prevalence of positive, negative, or neutral sentiments within the posts.

5 Methodology

5.1 Implemented Architecture

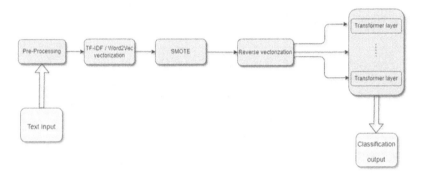

Fig. 1. Implemented Architecture

The implemented model as shown in the Fig. 1 has been tailored to address the complex challenge of identifying depression through textual inputs. Various strategies have been employed to enhance classification accuracy and tackle class imbalance within the dataset. In the initial stage, data preparation is carried out, involving the cleaning and normalization of textual inputs. Subsequently, the cleaned text is transformed into numerical representations using techniques such as Word2Vec or TF-IDF. This numerical conversion allows for the transformation of intricate verbal expressions into a format suitable for computational analysis.

To address the issue of unbalanced datasets, data augmentation techniques (SMOTE) are applied. This phase involves the manipulation of the dataset to ensure a balanced representation of distinct classes and mitigate the challenges posed by class imbalance. The model ensures that the learning process remains unbiased toward the more prevalent class, thereby yielding a more accurate and balanced classification outcome.

Following the data balancing process, the model reverses the numerical vectors back into textual representations. This intricate maneuver facilitates the seamless integration of these vectors with the transforming capabilities of Transformers. The core categorization model is built upon the foundation of the Transformer architecture, which excels in capturing complex contextual relationships within textual data.

The model cleverly incorporates ensemble methodologies to achieve optimal performance. By combining the predictive power of multiple models, the classification method excels in identifying subtle indicators of depression. Each individual model's strengths are harnessed within an ensemble technique, resulting in a comprehensive and dependable classification outcome.

The primary objective of the implemented architecture is to accurately classify depression severity based on textual inputs. The model aims to provide precise insights into the various levels of depression, utilizing a cascade of techniques that encompass data preparation, vectorization, data augmentation, transformer-based analysis, and ensemble methods.

Following are the Feature Extraction steps and Key Modules for the model:

5.2 Feature Extraction

Dataset Pre-processing: Machine learning methods find a prominent application in the realm of text analysis. However, these methods typically demand raw text documents with variable lengths as input, rather than pre-defined numerical feature vectors. As such, it is imperative to subject the raw data, represented as a sequence of symbols, to preprocessing[2] procedures before it becomes suitable for algorithmic analysis. These preprocessing steps commonly encompass the following:

- **Tokenization:** Splitting the text into individual tokens (words, punctuation marks, etc.) for further analysis.
- **Stop Word Removal:** Eliminating common words that do not carry significant meaning (e.g., "and," "the," "is").
- **Lemmatization or Stemming:** Reducing words to their base or root form to consolidate variations of the same word.
- **Handling Special Characters:** Addressing any issues related to special characters, emojis, or other non-standard textual elements.

Vectorizer: In natural language processing (NLP), the term "vectorizer"[3] is frequently used to describe a process or instrument that turns text data into numerical vectors. Since most machine learning algorithms operate on numerical input rather than raw text, vectorization is a crucial stage in NLP jobs.

In NLP, various vectorizers are employed, including:

- **TF-IDF:** A text document is represented as a vector by the TF-IDF (Term Frequency-Inverse Document Frequency) vectorizer, with each element representing the TF-IDF value of a particular word in the text. The TF-IDF

---

[2] https://scikit-learn.org/stable/modules/feature_extraction.html.

[3] https://scikit-learn.org/stable/modules/feature_extraction.html.

considers a word's frequency in a document as well as its rarity throughout the entire corpus.

- **Word2Vec:** Word2Vec, a program created by Mikolov et al. at Google, converts text input into numerical representations that effectively capture key semantic information, enabling NLP models to process it. The precise NLP task at hand as well as the features of the dataset will determine which vectorizer is best.

5.3   Key Modules

Data Augmentation Using Imbalance Learn (SMOTE): A significant issue in the field of imbalanced classification is the dearth of samples within the minority class. This constraint illustrates a common flaw in this case, preventing the model from accurately identifying the decision border. One popular strategy for addressing this problem is to oversample members of the minority class. By boosting the representation of the minority class in the training dataset, this technique seeks to address the imbalance in the distribution of the classes. Replicating examples from the minority class before model fitting is a simple oversampling method. Although this method produces a more balanced distribution, it falls short of providing the model with fresh data points to learn from[4] The production of synthetic samples for the minority class is a more sophisticated technique that is a major advancement above the simple duplication of examples. This type of data augmentation, which works especially well in cases involving tabular data, has a lot of potential. The Synthetic Minority Oversampling Technique (SMOTE), which is well-known and used for creating new samples, is a renowned technique in this area. SMOTE, which was first used by Nitesh Chawla et al. uses a creative approach to improve the representation of the minority class.

Identifying instances in the feature space that are close to one another is a key component of SMOTE's operation. These nearby instances are connected by a connecting line, on which a synthetic sample is produced at a particular place along the line. To further explain, the procedure starts by choosing a representative at random from the minority class. Then, for this selected instance, the k-nearest neighbors are identified (usually k = 5). Then it is randomly positioned between the original instance and one of its chosen neighbors to produce a synthetic sample.

SMOTE's effectiveness depends on its capacity to generate synthetic examples that closely mimic minority class instances that already exist in the feature space. The method avoids adding misleading examples by purposefully ignoring the majority class during the construction of the synthetic sample, which is critical when there is a lot of class overlap. In a larger sense, the term "data augmentation" refers to techniques that increase the quantity and diversity of a

---

[4] https://machinelearningmastery.com/smote-oversampling-for-imbalanced-classification/.

dataset, a practice that has significant implications for machine learning.[5] When the initial dataset is small or unbalanced, this augmentation helps the model perform better and be more robust. SMOTE emerges inside this framework as a powerful data augmentation strategy for dealing with imbalanced datasets.[6]

Transformers: A class of deep learning model architecture known as transformers[7] have revolutionized a number of NLP applications, including text classification, question answering, and machine translation. Using self-attention techniques, which were popularised by the movie Transformers, models can now recognise the contextual relationships between words in a phrase without the aid of recurrent neural networks (RNNs)[8] or convolutional neural networks (CNNs)[9].

Main Elements of a Transformer Model

- **Self-Attention:** It enables the model to capture long-range dependencies by weighing the significance of various terms in a phrase based on their links.
- **Encoder-Decoder Structure:** Transformers frequently have an encoder and a decoder in their design. While the decoder creates the output sequence, the encoder analyses the input sequence.
- **Multi-Head Attention:** This mechanism enables the model to simultaneously concentrate on several elements of the input sequence.
  Transformers use positional encoding to convey information about the word order in a phrase because self-attention by itself does not take word order into account. Transformers are frequently utilised in both research and business since they have attained cutting-edge performance on numerous NLP tasks. BERT (Bidirectional Encoder Representations from Transformers), GPT(Generative Pre-trained Transformer), Transformer-XL, and other well-known transformer-based models.

Evaluation: The accuracy, precision, recall, and F1-score will be used as relevant evaluation metrics to assess the performance of the implemented architecture. The model's performance may be fully understood by using the assessment metrics accuracy, precision, recall, and F1-score, which capture the model's aptitude to accurately categorise various levels of depression. With the help of these metrics, true positives, true negatives, false positives, and false negatives can all be evaluated fairly, allowing for a thorough assessment of the model's prediction skills. To verify the viability of the suggested strategy, comparative assessments will be made against other cutting-edge depression categorization models.

---

[5] https://imbalanced-learn.org/stable/references/generated/imblearn.over_sampling. SMOTE.html.

[6] https://machinelearningmastery.com/smote-oversampling-for-imbalanced-classification/.

[7] https://huggingface.co/models.

[8] https://en.wikipedia.org/wiki/Recurrent_neural_network.

[9] https://towardsdatascience.com/convolutional-neural-networks-explained-9cc5188c4939.

6   Experiments

Experiments were divided into two phases: one involving data augmentation and the other without. The aim was to investigate how the Synthetic Minority Oversampling Technique (SMOTE) influenced the performance of transformers trained on imbalanced datasets.

6.1   Without Data Augmentation

In this phase, a series of experiments employed various base models, including DistilBERT, RoBERTa, XLM RoBERTa, and DeBERTa. To enhance performance, an ensemble model combining DeBERTa, XLM RoBERTa, and RoBERTa was introduced. The methodology for these experiments can be summarized as follows:

Data Preprocessing: Before model training, the dataset underwent crucial preprocessing stages, which included tokenization, the removal of stop words, lemmatization or stemming, and addressing special characters. After preprocessing, models were trained using default hyperparameters, with subsequent hyperparameter tuning to evaluate its impact on accuracy.

Base Models: DistilBERT, a compact derivative of BERT, was fine-tuned using the dataset. Model performance was assessed with default hyperparameters and then compared against other base models. The transformer-based models, namely RoBERTa, XLM RoBERTa, and DeBERTa, underwent training with default hyperparameters. Subsequently, hyperparameter tuning was conducted, and their performance was evaluated using the same set of metrics.

Proposed Ensemble Model: An innovative ensemble model was introduced, combining predictions from DistilBERT, DeBERTa, XLM RoBERTa, and RoBERTa models. This ensemble model aggregated the predictions from each base model through a majority vote or weighted average mechanism, resulting in the final prediction. The ensemble model's performance was assessed and compared with that of the individual base models. This initial phase aimed to evaluate the performance of different models without data augmentation, with the ensemble model emerging as a strong contender for improved results. Hyperparameter tuning was also explored to identify optimal configurations. The subsequent section explores the second phase of experimentation, focusing on the incorporation of data augmentation techniques.

6.2   With Data Augmentation

In the second phase of experimentation, the model underwent comprehensive evaluation with the inclusion of data augmentation techniques, specifically SMOTE. The purpose of this phase was to assess how SMOTE impacted the classification outcomes of the transformer models, addressing the challenges posed by imbalanced datasets. The experimentation involved the following key steps:

Base Models and Ensemble Approach: Similar to the first phase, a suite of base models was utilized, including DistilBERT, RoBERTa, XLM RoBERTa, and DeBERTa. Once again, the ensemble model was augmented with DeBERTa, XLM RoBERTa, and RoBERTa to harness their predictive synergy for improved outcomes.

Data Preprocessing: The foundation of this phase was solid data preprocessing. It encompassed preparatory steps such as tokenization, stop word removal, lemmatization or stemming, and effective handling of special characters. These measures ensured the refinement and harmonization of input data for subsequent analysis.

Feature Extraction and Reverse Vectorization: In conjunction with model augmentation, various vectorization techniques were used to transform textual data into numerical representations. This encompassed methods like count vectorization, TF-IDF, word embeddings (Word2Vec and GloVe), BERT embeddings, Doc2Vec, and Word2Vec. The transformation was then reversed, converting numerical vectors back into textual representations, enabling seamless integration with transformer capabilities.

Augmentation with SMOTE: Central to this phase was the strategic application of data augmentation through SMOTE. This technique addressed the challenge of class imbalance within the dataset by enhancing the representation of underrepresented classes. This mitigated biases and promoted a more balanced learning process, resulting in improved classification precision.

Ensemble Model with Augmentation: The proposed ensemble model, strengthened by augmentation techniques, harnessed the collective predictive strength of DistilBERT, DeBERTa, XLM RoBERTa, and RoBERTa models. This approach aggregated predictions from each base model through techniques such as majority voting or weighted averaging, resulting in a refined final prediction. The ensemble model's performance was rigorously assessed and compared to that of the individual base models, shedding light on the impact of augmentation.

In summary, the second phase of experimentation involved fortifying the model with data augmentation (SMOTE) and elucidating its mechanisms. Through meticulous data preprocessing, diverse feature extraction methods, and ensemble approaches, the model demonstrated its ability to address the intricacies of depression classification within text-based inputs.

7   Results

The results indicate that adjusting hyperparameters significantly enhanced the performance of DistilBERT, resulting in improved accuracy, F1-score, precision, and recall. However, the synergy between hyperparameter adjustment and SMOTE (Synthetic Minority Over-sampling Technique) seemed less effective for this model. RoBERTa's performance saw substantial improvement

Table 2. Model Performance Metrics for Different Configurations

Model	Accuracy	F1-score	Precision	Recall
DistilBERT	0.45	0.39	0.46	0.40
DistilBERT(with hp tunning)	**0.61**	**0.57**	**0.59**	**0.56**
DistilBERT(with hp tunning and SMOTE)	0.49	0.42	0.47	0.43
RoBERTa	0.48	0.41	0.50	0.43
RoBERTa(with hp tunning)	**0.61**	**0.58**	**0.58**	**0.57**
RoBERTa(with hp tunning and SMOTE)	0.38	0.29	0.50	0.36
XLM-RoBERTa	0.51	0.34	0.31	0.34
XLM-RoBERTa(with hp tunning)	**0.60**	**0.57**	**0.58**	**0.57**
XLM-RoBERTa(with hp tunning and SMOTE)	0.49	0.40	0.53	0.41
DeBERTa	0.46	0.40	0.44	0.42
DeBERTa(with hp tunning)	**0.61**	**0.58**	**0.59**	**0.58**
DeBERTa(with hp tunning and SMOTE)	0.37	0.29	0.37	0.36
Ensemble	0.49	0.42	0.51	0.43
Ensemble(with hp tunning)	**0.63**	**0.60**	**0.62**	**0.59**
Ensemble(with hp tunning and SMOTE)	0.47	0.39	0.50	0.42

across all metrics following hyperparameter adjustment, showcasing the model's untapped potential. However, incorporating SMOTE appeared counterproductive for RoBERTa, as performance, particularly in recall and F1-score, deteriorated (Table 2).

XLM-RoBERTa also experienced performance gains after hyperparameter adjustment, aligning with trends observed in earlier models. Unlike several other models, this one consistently improved across all metrics with the addition of hyperparameter tuning and SMOTE. This suggests that the synthetic data generated by SMOTE offered some value for this model. DeBERTa exhibited a similar pattern of significant improvement with hyperparameter adjustment, akin to RoBERTa. Nonetheless, the introduction of SMOTE led to performance decline across most metrics, highlighting the variable impact of SMOTE depending on the model.

Ensemble models consistently demonstrated improvement with hyperparameter adjustment. However, the results of combining hyperparameter tuning with SMOTE were inconsistent, signifying that while SMOTE may benefit specific ensemble configurations, it does not guarantee universal enhancements (Table 3).

Table 3. Best Performing Parameter Values for Different Transformer Models in Hyperparameter Tuning

Parameter	DistilBERT	RoBERTa	XLM-RoBERTa	DeBERTa
Batch size	16	16	16	16
Epochs	10	10	15	10
Optimizer	AdamW	AdamW	AdamW	AdamW
Learning rate	5e−5	1e−5	2e−5	5e−6
Validation steps	100	100	200	100

The ensemble model surpasses DistilBERT, DeBERTa, and RoBERTa when using default hyperparameters, while it achieves comparable results to XLM-RoBERTa. This underscores the ensemble's ability to aggregate outcomes from diverse models, leading to overall performance improvement. Even after adjusting hyperparameters, the ensemble model consistently outperforms individual models, showcasing steady enhancements across all metrics. This emphasizes the value of integrating fine-tuned models to enhance performance. Furthermore, the ensemble model retains its competitive edge over the majority of individual models, even with hyperparameter adjustments and the inclusion of SMOTE. Despite the varying impacts of SMOTE on different models, the ensemble model consistently draws unique insights from multiple models, even when synthetic data is introduced.

In the study, several language models experienced improvements through the application of SMOTE and hyperparameter optimization. With the exception of DistilBERT, most models showed enhancements following hyperparameter tuning. DeBERTa improved with tuning but exhibited a decline with the introduction of SMOTE. Conversely, RoBERTa and XLM-RoBERTa demonstrated performance gains, although SMOTE had a detrimental effect on RoBERTa. Despite these variations, ensemble models consistently outperformed individual models, even after making revisions. The influence of SMOTE on model performance varied, but ensemble models effectively assimilated knowledge from other models, even in the presence of synthetic data.

The finding that transformers trained on imbalanced data outperform transformers trained on augmented data with SMOTE, while machine learning algorithms exhibit improved performance after applying SMOTE [7], can be attributed to the specific characteristics of transformers and traditional machine learning algorithms and their interaction with data augmentation techniques such as SMOTE. Similar conclusions were drawn by studies like Xia et al. [10] in the context of text generation tasks using BERT.

Let's break down the possible reasons for this phenomenon:

– **Model Complexity and Capacity:**

Transformers are deep learning models that excel at identifying intricate data patterns. They are made to handle sequences and are especially good with text-based sequential data. They can learn the connections between dispersed pieces in a sequence thanks to mechanisms in their design like self-attention [11]. They may be well adapted to directly learn from uneven data without largely relying on augmentation thanks to this innate ability. Traditional machine learning algorithms, on the other hand, might be less naturally able to capture complex interactions. As a result, data augmentation techniques like SMOTE may be more advantageous for them. SMOTE contributes to the dataset's diversity and balance, potentially facilitating the generalisation of these techniques across classes.

– Model Sensitivity to Synthetic Data:

Transformers can be susceptible to the introduction of artificial data points that don't adequately represent genuine data distribution because of their ability to capture complicated patterns. These artificial data points could not have the same contextual or semantic relevance as actual data points. The transformer may perform worse when trained on supplemented data using SMOTE due to this sensitivity. Due to the fact that they frequently use simpler feature representations, traditional machine learning algorithms may be less sensitive to synthetic data. By boosting the representation of minority class instances, SMOTE can assist them in achieving greater performance and decision-making.

– Data Augmentation Impact:

Due to their ability to address the class imbalance issue that standard machine learning algorithms frequently face, data augmentation techniques like SMOTE are more frequently used in this context. A more balanced dataset may be advantageous for traditional algorithms like decision trees, random forests, and support vector machines because they may rely on certain data distribution assumptions. Transformers, as was previously established, possess processes that allow them to concentrate on relevant instances even in data that is unbalanced. As a result, transformer models might not benefit as much from the synthetic instances generated by SMOTE, and it's possible that doing so will prevent them from discovering useful patterns.

– Attention Mechanisms and Imbalance Handling:

Transformers can weigh the relative value of various items in a sequence in an adaptive manner thanks to their attention processes. This makes it possible for them to concentrate on underrepresented classes, easing some of the difficulties caused by class inequality. Transformers can naturally identify relationships across the entire dataset thanks to the self-attention mechanism, regardless of how classes are distributed. Traditional machine learning algorithms, on the other hand, could find it difficult to balance their attention between classes, especially if one class is disproportionately large. By producing synthetic examples that can assist the algorithm in learning stronger decision bounds for the minority class, SMOTE aids conventional algorithms.

The observed behaviour may be caused by transformers' inherent ability to recognise complicated patterns, along with their sensitivity to synthetic input and capacity to manage imbalanced data because of attention mechanisms. Due to their limitations in managing complicated relationships, traditional machine learning algorithms can gain from SMOTE's capacity to balance the dataset and provide more representative instances for underrepresented classes. Transformers may therefore outperform traditional algorithms when trained on unbalanced data, while traditional algorithms may profit from data augmentation methods like SMOTE.

8   Conclusion

In conclusion, this paper explored the utility of social media content on various social media platforms for analyzing transformer-based models in the context of depression classification. This investigation introduced an innovative ensemble model that amalgamated predictions from DistilBERT, DeBERTa, XLM-RoBERTa, and RoBERTa, while also examining foundational models such as DistilBERT, RoBERTa, XLM-RoBERTa, and DeBERTa. The experimental outcomes underscored the superior performance of the ensemble model over individual base models, particularly evident in substantial improvements in F1 scores and accuracy.

These findings show that transformer-based computer programs are really good at understanding the deeper meanings and context in conversations on social media. These programs are especially good at spotting signs of depression and telling how severe it is just by reading what people write. Importantly, when we used a combination of these programs, they worked even better together in classifying depression.

To summarize, this research delves into the application of transformer-based models for depression classification using social media content. The newly introduced ensemble model vividly illustrates the advantages of amalgamating multiple models, culminating in improved performance. By employing natural language processing techniques, these findings make a substantial contribution to the evolving field of mental health analysis, shedding light on the development of effective tools for depression diagnosis and treatment planning.

The findings unequivocally demonstrate that hyperparameter tuning yielded improved results in transformers dealing with imbalanced datasets. Following hyperparameter adjustment, the ensemble model, encompassing DeBERTa, XLM-RoBERTa, and RoBERTa, exhibited higher accuracy and F1-score compared to the default hyperparameters. The tests revealed that transformers trained on unbalanced data without data augmentation (using default settings) outperformed transformers trained on augmented data with SMOTE. This underscores the notion that the adoption of data augmentation methods like SMOTE may not consistently enhance transformers' capacity to detect depression. The results imply that transformers inherently excel at managing imbalanced datasets and deciphering intricate patterns. Consequently, the amalgamation of SMOTE with transformers may not be as essential as it is for traditional machine learning methods. In contrast, traditional algorithms benefit from SMOTE's ability to enhance their performance by introducing synthetic instances to balance the dataset.

8.1 Limitations

One issue that restricted the research was a lack of access to big-size GPUs. Additionally, relying solely on participants' self-reported emotions can skew the findings. The degree to which the findings are generalizable to other contexts may depend on how the data was gathered. It's challenging to identify subtle indications of sadness in text, and other difficulties like overfitting, the dynamic nature of social media, and the intricacy of language may alter how well the results perform in various contexts.

8.2 Future Scope

Further research could focus on the subtleties of hyperparameter tweaking, maximizing the performance of the model by optimizing its architecture, learning rates, and batch sizes. The model's robustness and generalizability would also be improved by collecting a more balanced dataset, either through partnerships with mental health specialists or access to more varied sources. Overcoming difficulties with data collection and privacy issues would be necessary for this. Such developments would support the development of a depression classification system that is more precise and trustworthy.

Acknowledgement. This work was conducted with the financial support of the Science Foundation Ireland Centre for Research Training in Artificial Intelligence under Grant No. 18/CRT/6223, supported in part by a research grant from the Science Foundation Ireland (SFI) under Grant Number SFI/12/RC/2289_P2(Insight_2).

References

1. Guntuku, S.C., Yaden, D.B., Kern, M.L., Ungar, L.H., Eichstaedt, J.C.: Detecting depression and mental illness on social media: an integrative review. Curr. Opin. Behav. Sci. **18**, 43–49 (2017)
2. De Choudhury, M., Counts, S., Horvitz, E.: Social media as a measurement tool of depression in populations. In: Proceedings of the 5th Annual ACM Web Science Conference, pp. 47–56 (2013)
3. Kamite, S.R., Kamble, V.B.: Detection of depression in social media via Twitter using machine learning approach. In: 2020 International Conference on Smart Innovations in Design, Environment, Management, Planning and Computing (ICSIDEMPC), pp. 122–125. IEEE (2020)
4. Wolohan, J.T., Hiraga, M., Mukherjee, A., Sayyed, Z.A., Millard, M.: Detecting linguistic traces of depression in topic-restricted text: attending to self-stigmatized depression with NLP. In: Proceedings of the First International Workshop on Language Cognition and Computational Models, pp. 11–21 (2018)

5. De Choudhury, M., Kiciman, E.: The language of social support in social media and its effect on suicidal ideation risk. In: Proceedings of the International AAAI Conference on Web and Social Media, vol. 11, pp. 32–41 (2017)
6. Poświata, R., Perełkiewicz, M.: OPI@ LT-EDI-ACL2022: detecting signs of depression from social media text using RoBERTa pre-trained language models. In: Proceedings of the Second Workshop on Language Technology for Equality, Diversity and Inclusion, pp. 276–282 (2022)
7. Sampath, K., Durairaj, T.: Data set creation and empirical analysis for detecting signs of depression from social media postings. In: Kalinathan, L., Priyadharsini, R., Kanmani, M., Manisha, S. (eds.) ICCIDS 2022. IFIPAICT, vol. 654, pp. 136–151. Springer, Cham (2022). https://doi.org/10.1007/978-3-031-16364-7_11
8. Deshpande, M., Rao, V.: Depression detection using emotion artificial intelligence. In: 2017 International Conference on Intelligent Sustainable Systems (ICISS), pp. 858–862. IEEE (2017)
9. Orabi, A.H., Buddhitha, P., Orabi, M.H., Inkpen, D.: Deep learning for depression detection of twitter users. In: Proceedings of the Fifth Workshop on Computational Linguistics and Clinical Psychology: from Keyboard to Clinic, pp. 88–97 (2018)
10. Hu, L.: Performance evaluation of text augmentation methods with BERT on imbalanced datasets. Ph.D. thesis, University of Missouri–Columbia (2022)
11. Ren, H., et al.: Combiner: full attention transformer with sparse computation cost. In: Advances in Neural Information Processing Systems, vol. 34, pp. 22470–22482 (2021)
12. Deng, F.-L., et al.: Metabonomics reveals peripheral and central short-chain fatty acid and amino acid dysfunction in a naturally occurring depressive model of macaques. Neuropsychiatric Dis. Treat. **15**, 1077–1088 (2019)
13. Dewey, C.: A stunning map of depression rates around the world. The Washington Post (2013)
14. Arora, P., Arora, P.: Mining Twitter data for depression detection. In: 2019 International Conference on Signal Processing and Communication (ICSC), pp. 186–189. IEEE (2019)
15. Aswathy, K.S., Rafeeque, P.C., Murali, R.: Deep learning approach for the detection of depression in Twitter. In: Proceedings of the International Conference on Systems, Energy Environment (ICSEE) (2019)
16. Coppersmith, G., Dredze, M., Harman, C., Hollingshead, K., Mitchell, M.: CLPsych 2015 shared task: depression and PTSD on Twitter. In: Proceedings of the 2nd Workshop on Computational Linguistics and Clinical Psychology: From Linguistic Signal to Clinical Reality, pp. 31–39 (2015)
17. Devlin, J., Chang, M.-W., Lee, K., Toutanova, K.: BERT: pre-training of deep bidirectional transformers for language understanding. In: Proceedings of NAACL-HLT, vol. 1, p. 2 (2019)
18. Haque, A., Reddi, V., Giallanza, T.: Deep learning for suicide and depression identification with unsupervised label correction. In: Farkaš, I., Masulli, P., Otte, S., Wermter, S. (eds.) ICANN 2021. LNCS, vol. 12895, pp. 436–447. Springer, Cham (2021). https://doi.org/10.1007/978-3-030-86383-8_35
19. Pirina, I., Çöltekin, Ç.: Identifying depression on reddit: the effect of training data. In: Proceedings of the 2018 EMNLP Workshop SMM4H: The 3rd Social Media Mining for Health Applications Workshop & Shared Task, pp. 9–12 (2018)
20. Tadesse, M.M., Lin, H., Xu, B., Yang, L.: Detection of depression-related posts in reddit social media forum. IEEE Access **7**, 44883–44893 (2019)
21. William, D., Suhartono, D.: Text-based depression detection on social media posts: a systematic literature review. Procedia Comput. Sci. **179**, 582–589 (2021)

22. Yang, Z., Dai, Z., Yang, Y., Carbonell, J., Salakhutdinov, R.R., Le, Q.V.: XLNet: generalized autoregressive pretraining for language understanding. In: Advances in Neural Information Processing Systems, vol. 32 (2019)
23. Zogan, H., Razzak, I., Jameel, S., Xu, G.: DepressionNet: learning multi-modalities with user post summarization for depression detection on social media. In: Proceedings of the 44th International ACM SIGIR Conference on Research and Development in Information Retrieval, pp. 133–142 (2021)
24. Bhathiya, H.S., Thayasivam, U.: Meta learning for few-shot joint intent detection and slot-filling. In: Proceedings of the 2020 5th International Conference on Machine Learning Technologies, pp. 86–92 (2020)
25. Hu, L., Li, C., Wang, W., Pang, B., Shang, Y.: Performance evaluation of text augmentation methods with BERT on small-sized, imbalanced datasets. In: 2022 IEEE 4th International Conference on Cognitive Machine Intelligence (CogMI), pp. 125–133 (2022)

Optimized BERT Model for Question Answering System on Mobile Platform

Priyadarshini Patil[✉], Chandan Rao, and S. M. Meena

School of Computer Science and Engineering, KLE Technological University, Hubballi 580031, Karnataka, India
priyadarshini.patil@kletech.ac.in

Abstract. In Natural Language Processing (NLP), question-answering systems are a classic problem, yet they pose several open challenges. After the pandemic situation of COVID-19, online learning has become crucial, in which question-answering systems are also beneficial to students in searching for answers to subject-related questions. The paper aims to address the challenge of providing a lightweight and efficient question-answering system, especially for students with limited resources, particularly those using low-cost mobile devices. The strategy involves post-training quantization to reduce the size of the BERT model while maintaining high accuracy. Quantization is a technique that reduces the memory footprint of deep learning models, making them more suitable for deployment on mobile devices and low-cost hardware. The reduction in the BERT model size from 438 MB to 181 MB with negligible accuracy degradation is a significant achievement. The resulting mobile application works offline, making educational content accessible in areas with limited internet connectivity. The system achieved an F1 score of 0.87 with negligible degradation compared to the accuracy of the BERT model F1 score: 0.90. Key considerations include user experience, maintenance and memory optimization. This paper offers a practical and cost-effective solution to enhance educational access on mobiles while addressing resource constraints.

Keywords: Bidirectional Encoder Representation from Transformers (BERT) · Natural Language Processing (NLP) · Question-Answering · Quantization

1 Introduction

Question answering systems are intended to provide automated responses in natural language to questions posed by humans [1]. Information retrieval is the main task of this system. It deals with giving the correct short answer to the question rather than giving multiple possible answers. A question answering system helps find answers to a question posed within the document. It can be applied in various applications like chatbots and virtual assistants. A chatbot gives answers to the question asked by the user by learning all the documents in the database. Instead of the user going through all the software documentation, the user can ask questions to the chatbot and get the answers needed. Also, it saves human resources like customer support since humans do not have to chat with customers, and the answering process is automated. Virtual assistants like Siri, Alexa, and Google Assistant [2] give answers to the customers by voice since the questions are asked in audio format. Virtual assistants listen to the commands of customers. They can perform typical tasks like scheduling appointments, making phone calls, and controlling items in our homes such as lights, thermostats, and many more. The main application of question answering systems is the search engines [3]. It evaluates the semantic interpretations of a search query and ranks all the possible answers or articles, and displays accordingly by highlighting them.

Ever since the Covid-19 pandemic situation has impacted the teaching and learning process and changed the way of learning, there has been a significant transformation towards online-based learning [4]. As a result, there has been an increase in e-learning, in which teaching and learning are done remotely on digital platforms, and many exams are conducted online. Most of the students use mobiles for online learning. Students tend to search for answers concerning their syllabus on mobile phones. We have a high priority to have efficient question-answering systems, which must also work efficiently for students, despite resource constraints of memory on devices like mobile. Since students use mobiles that are typically low-cost to the medium-cost range with normally 2 GB–4 GB RAM and storage of 16 GB to 32 GB, it becomes difficult for them to use an app that requires more computational power and memory storage. Hence, there is a need to build a question-answering application that is lightweight and requires low computational power. Also, students in remote areas do not get adequate internet facilities. They require an app that can answer their questions without internet connectivity sometimes. Hence, we propose to develop a lightweight question-answering system that can work efficiently on mobile devices. Further, our proposed system works offline whenever there is no internet connection.

Instead of manually searching the answers in a context or document using keywords or reading the whole document, the question answering system can be used to find the appropriate answers needed by posing questions related to the context. The difference between searching answers on the internet using Google and using the question answering system is that: in Google search, the answer will be searched throughout the internet and not precisely some document. Google is used to find answers in a general context throughout the internet. Also, the Google search engine has recently started providing direct answers to the questions by the user. Earlier it used to rank the list of documents to find the answers [5]. Then the user had to go through the document to find answers. In our question answering system, we can search for the answers we need in a specific document without the internet. Sometimes if the document is long, searching for answers in that specific document, our question answering system will be beneficial to retrieve the answer quickly and correctly. Our proposed system is designed to retrieve small snippets of texts that contain the answers in the document.

Question answering systems till the last decade, focused on information retrieval and query processing. With the recent breakthrough performance of deep learning models in natural language processing applications, the popular methods like the MIT START system, recurrent neural networks, bi-directional LSTM and BERT are used to build question answering systems. Question answering system can be open domain or close domain. Open-domain question answering systems received more significant attention in the 90s. They returned the most relevant answers to the questions using a combination of NLP and information retrieval techniques. Boris Katz's MIT START system is one of the most well-known approaches. It comprehends and generates language, and it responds to questions in natural language. As a question answering system, START parses incoming questions and is used to create queries from the parse trees against its knowledge base and present information to the user by providing just the correct answers. Then deep learning techniques like recurrent convolutional neural networks (RCN) were applied for question answering systems. It recorded both the semantic correlations implicit in the sequence of answers as well as the semantic matching between question and answer [6]. Then sequence to sequence attention-reading comprehension model was implemented [7]. The basic structure was bi-directional LSTM encodings with attention mechanisms. Then, to solve sequence to sequence problems while dealing with long-range dependencies, transformers were introduced. The transformer is a deep learning model that uses the attention mechanism to weigh the influence of different parts of the input data. It was first introduced in 2017. Then the most recent BERT (Bi-directional encoder representations from transformers) was used. It is a pre-trained deep learning model that can be fine-tuned for our question-answering task. By applying this transfer learning model [7], there is a significant increase in results. Based on transformer models like XLNet, RoBERTa, GPT-3, GPT-4, LLM's produced state-of-the-art results for all NLP tasks. They are huge models trained on a massive dataset of 160 GB (16 GB BERT data+ 144 GB additional data) are significantly larger than BERT [8].

Although the models XLNet, RoBERTa, GPT-3, GPT-4, and LLM perform with high accuracy, their drawbacks are huge model size (1.5 GB average) and compute-intensive at inference time [9]. All these big neural language models need high computational resources 512 TPU v3 chips * 2.5 to 3 days to train/fine-tune and make inferences [10]. These models contain 24 layers transformer blocks, 1024 hidden layers, 16 attention heads, and 340m parameters [11]. State of art models like GPT-3 with 175 billion parameters, GPT-4 with 1.76 trillion parameters and LLM's with 70 billion parameters are heavily parameterized. These models are not suitable to run on low computational power devices like mobiles. This leads to a considerable memory constraint on device. Therefore, there is a need to optimize these models to run on less computational resources and not be expensive at production levels.

The main aim of our project is to build an optimized model for question answering system to reduce various costs like memory, computational power, and inference time so that it can be deployed on devices using embedded platforms, since most applications today go on mobile devices with an average of 2 GB RAM and 32 GB storage. The model size should be less and perform with a good F1 score comparable to original state of art models and then to be deployed on edge devices. The reduced model should work in the limited amount of CPU computational power and produce faster inference times with less latency, along with retaining accuracy of the original model.

The proposed work is carried in phases. In phase 1, in the initial phase of the project, an evaluation of various question-answering models was conducted, ultimately selecting BERT as the base model due to its competitive F1 scores. While models like XLNet, RoBERTa, GPT-4 and LLM show promise in improving F1 scores, they come with large model sizes due to extensive training on substantial datasets. The primary project objective is to significantly reduce the model size for deployment on edge devices, with a target size range of 150–200 MB to cater to mobile devices. Given the challenge of achieving substantial size reduction while maintaining F1 scores, BERT, with a 438 MB size, was chosen as the starting point for further size reduction and deployment on mobile devices.

In phase 2, we work on optimizing the model. The aim is to reduce the model size and then deploy on edge devices. Towards optimization approaches, there are several ways through which the model size can be reduced, like weight pruning, knowledge distillation, and quantization. Weight pruning is done by making the network sparse, lowering the parameters, and removing the nodes [12]. But removing neurons and weights sometimes will significantly affect its performance, so we don't use this method. Knowledge distillation is a technique through which compress the model by teaching a smaller network [13, 14]. BERT can be considered as a teacher model, and we distill it to a student model called DistilBERT, which will be smaller in size. Quantization is the process of converting the weights from float32 to int8.We applies quantization and deploys the quantized model as an app on device with Tensor flow Lite [15]. We choose the quantization technique for the BERT model for our task of question answering system, since it has performed with 0.6% lower F1 score on GLUE dataset for MRPC NLP task [16].

In phase 3, we perform testing of the optimized BERT model on SQUAD dataset and our proprietary academic dataset of computer science. Question Answering is a mobile-based application that gives the output, answering the specified context with questions provided to the model. The input can be a text with 2000 words, and the output will be the answer based on the question provided by the user. This action is provided within a short time (5–6 s). Question answering intends to express the content of a document in a condensed form that meets the user's needs. Much information that can realistically be digested is available on the internet and in other electronic forms. It is impossible to read everything one wants to read or search for answers using keywords. Full-text documents, or the web, are a sea of knowledge that is constantly being produced. Typically, we are more concerned with getting the answer to our query than with really reading the paper [16]. QA systems assist in locating relevant information on the web and offer insights. Quantized BERT would be an effective and precise method of answering questions to meet the issues raised. We are flooded with massive amounts of information in full-text documents i.e., web. Usually, we are interested in knowing the answer to our question rather than looking at the document [17]. QA systems help retrieve needed information from the web and providing insights. Question answering technique through quantized BERT would be an efficient and accurate solution for the problems addressed.

The most significant advantage of the proposed question answering system is that it is memory optimized and it decreases the searching time of the answer by a considerable time. Reading an article of 600–2000 words can take at least 6 min, but in the proposed question-answer model format, the user can get the required answer within 5–6 s Also, it makes the user read less but still receive the essential information and arrive at conclusions. The added advantage is its ability to work in offline mode also.

2   Related Works

Choosing a right model to get accuracy greater than 0.85(F1 score) for our task of question answering is very crucial. This section gives a brief overview of all the models that gives state of the art results so that we can arrive at a model for optimization and deploy it on edge devices while maintaining the accuracy.

The architecture of LSTM and memory networks for closed domain question answering is presented in G. Rohit et al. "approaches to Question Answering Using Long Short Term Memory (LSTM) and Memory Networks" [18]. JacobDevlin, et al.'s "BERT's Pre-training of Deep Bi-directional Transformers" [11] proposes to pre-train deep bi-directional representations from unlabeled text by jointly conditioning on both left and right in all layers. As a result, it may be adjusted with just one additional output layer to provide cutting-edge models for a variety of jobs. By maximizing anticipated likeli-hood, Zhillin Yang, et al. "XLNET:'s Generalized Autoregressive Pretraining" presents approaches that permit learning bi-directional contexts and get beyond BERT's con-straints brought on by autoregressive formulation [19]. Additionally, XLNET incorpo-rates concepts from Transformer-XL. Its size is five times that of BERT. In "RoBERTa: A robustly optimized BERT," by Yinhan Liu et al. BERT was considerably undertrained, according to the pre-training approach, but it can perform on par with or better than every model published after it [20]. BERT's next-sentence pre-training objective is removed, its hyper parameters are modified, and RoBERTa trains with substantially bigger mini-batches and learning rates. As opposed to BERT's 16 GB of training data, RoBERTa's 160 GB of datasets are used, 5 times as big as BERT is RoBERTa [21]. According to Olasile Babatunde et al., "Covid-19 pandemic and online learning: the challenges and opportunities", the paper shows that Covid-19 pandemic has disrupted instruction in a number of institutions, and electronic learning (e-learning) has taken the place of traditional classroom instruction as the primary way to impart knowledge [22]. Online courses may not be accessible to teachers or students with poor internet connections because they are fully dependent on technology and an internet connection. We propose to use the quantized BERT model for our task of question answering since it already gives state-of-the-art results for squad dataset (F1 score: 0.90) and the size of the model is less (440 Mb), where we can further optimize the model under constraints of memory, computational power and inference.

3   Optimized BERT Based Question-Answering System

3.1   Post-training Quantization

Our objective is to optimize the BERT model. Optimization has a significant role in designing a system. Optimization can be both hardware optimization and software opti-mization. The critical parameters for a system optimization are execution time, memory requirements, power consumption, and resource allocation. In this effort, we transformed the well-known, cutting-edge NLP model BERT into a quantized BERT. Quantization has limited implications for accuracy but can minimize the model's size. Quantization uses lower-bit values to mimic floating-point numbers, which saves memory and boosts performance. Since quantization reduces the number of bits available, the precision and range of values may suffer. We can show that weights and activations can be expressed using 8-bit integers (INT 8) without a large accuracy loss. We can reduce data storage and bandwidth by 75% when quantizing FP32 to INT8, lowering energy use and computational expense. Additionally, we must guarantee that the quantized BERT produces accurate results. The format (FP32, FP16, INT8, INT4, and INT1) allows us to specify the inference and level of precision we desire while lowering the size of the model by $2\times$, $4\times$, $8\times$, or $32\times$, depending on the number of weights (parameters) a network model employs to complete the calculations required for inference jobs. Post-training quantization refers to this. By simulating inference time quantization during training, later tools will use a model to generate quantized models. The weights during the process were quantized.

If we convert our model to int8 then the parameters and activations are quantized to integers. Model executes with integer operations only. Post-training quantization in its most basic form statically quantizes simply the weight, converting it from floating-point to an integer with an accuracy of 8 bits. Firstly we have to generate a Tensor flow model. Then we can convert the trained model to Tensorflow Lite format using the TFLite Converter inbuilt function and apply the degree of quantization we need. Sometimes this version of quantization leaves some of the data in float format. So, with increasing amounts of quantization, we either get int8 or uint8. This type of quantization achieves a $4\times$ reduction in model size.

Additionally, TFLite supports mixing floating-point kernels for various areas of the graph and on-the-fly quantization and dequantization of activations to employ quantized kernels for quicker implementation when available. The activations are quantized to an 8-bit precision before processing and de-quantized to float precision after processing. They are stored in floating-point. In quantized BERT, the activations are dynamically quantized at inference, and the weights are quantized post-training. As a result, the model weights need to be retrained to account for mistakes brought on by quantization. We must determine whether the quantized model's precision is sufficient. Using the following formula as in Eq. (1), 8-bit quantization approximates floating-point values:

$$Real\_value = (Int\ 8\_value - zero\_point) \times Scale \qquad (1)$$

In Conv ops, per-axis (also known as per-channel) or per-tensor weights are represented by int8 two's complement numbers with a zero-point value of 0. Int8 two's complement values with a zero-point in the range $[-128, 127]$ are used to represent per-tensor activations and inputs. Asymmetric activations have a signed int8 range of $[-128, 127]$ for their zero-point, which can be located anywhere. Zero-point precision can be effectively increased up to an additional binary bit at a reasonably low cost. Since weights are symmetric, their zero-point must be equal to 0. An inherent runtime penalty is associated with multiplying zero-point values since weight values are multiplied by dynamic input and activation values. The expenditure can be avoided by mandating that the zero-point is 0. A is a m $\times$ n matrix of quantized activations B is a n $\times$ p matrix of quantized weights. Consider multiplying the jth row of A, aj by the kth column of B, bk, both of length n. The quantized integer values and zero-point values are qa, za and qb, zb respectively as shown in Eq. (2) [19].

$$aj.bk = \sum_{i=0}^{n} q^{(i)} a \, q^{(i)} b - \sum_{i=0}^{n} q^{(i)} {}_{a} a_b - \sum_{i=0}^{n} q^{(i)} {}_{b} z_a + \sum_{i=0}^{n} z_a z_b \qquad (2)$$

Here, because it is performing the dot product of the input value and the weight value, term cannot be avoided. The and terms can be estimated in advance because they are made up of constants that do not change for each inference invocation Since the activation varies with each inference, the term must be calculated for each inference. We can eliminate the cost of this term by mandating that weights to be symmetric.

4   Results and Discussion

We evaluate the precision of our model on the dataset using the F1 score [2]. The F1 score combines the model's precision and recall, and it is the harmonic mean of these two metrics. Precision is the percentage of recovered instances that are relevant as in Eq. 3.

$$precision = (true\ positive)/(true\ positive + false\ positive) \qquad (3)$$

True positive is an outcome where the model correctly predicts the positive class. True negative is an outcome where the model correctly predicts the negative class. A false positive is an outcome where the model incorrectly predicts the positive class. Moreover, a false negative is an outcome where the model incorrectly predicts the negative class. Recall is the fraction of relevant instances that were retrieved as in Eq. (4).

$$recall = (true\ positive)/(true\ positive + false\ negative) \qquad (4)$$

The F1 score is calculated as in Eq. (5) below:

$$F1\ score = 2 * \left[(precision * recall)/(precision + recall) \right] \qquad (5)$$

Stanford Question Answering Dataset (SQUAD) is a dataset that contains comprehension consisting of questions that is asked by the users on Wikipedia articles and also contains the answers to it. It contains 1.5 lakh questions asked with answers provided with respect to the context. It not only tests the system's capability to answer the questions but also checks if the system abstains from answering the question if the answers are not in the comprehension.

4.1 Accuracy Score, Model Size and Inference Time

The Table 1 below shows the comparison of F1 score, model size and inference time scores before and after quantization on SQUAD data.

Table 1. Comparison of F1 score, model size and inference time scores before and after quantization on SQUAD data

Precision	F1 score	Model size	Inference time of 1 thread	Inference time of 4 threads
FP32 BERT	0.90	438 MB	160 s	85 s
INT8 Quantized BERT	0.87	181 MB	90 s	46 s

The original BERT model after evaluating the squad dataset that is with floating point 32 (FP32) we got a F1 score of about 0.9019 with about 110 million parameters amounting to the model size of 438 MB with an inference of about 160 s for a single thread for 408 examples of squad dataset. Then we applied post-training quantization technique to convert the original BERT FP32 to quantized BERT INT8 which reduced the model size by 60%, and gave an impressive F1 score of 0.8753 which is a little degradation to the original BERT and a good inference of about 90 s for a single thread. For our proprietary data of computer science course question answers, the results are as in Table 2:

Table 2. F1 score for Proprietary dataset

Course Name	F1 score
Operating system	0.86
Database Management System	0.84

4.2 Question Answering Results and Mobile App

(See Figs. 1, 2 and 3).

An Operating System (OS) is an interface between a computer user and computer hardware. An operating system is a software which performs all the basic tasks like file management, memory management, process management, handling input and output, and controlling peripheral devices such as disk drives and printers.Some popular Operating Systems include Linux Operating System, Windows Operating System, VMS, OS/400, AIX, z/OS, etc

```
question = "What tasks does OS do?"
answer_question(question, bert_abstract)

Query has 91 tokens.

Answer: "file management , memory management , process management , handling input and output , and controlling peripheral devices"

question = "Name some OS?"
answer_question(question, bert_abstract)

Query has 89 tokens.

Answer: "linux operating system , windows operating system , vms , os / 400 , aix , z / os"

question = "What is OS?"
answer_question(question, bert_abstract)

Query has 89 tokens.

Answer: "an interface between a computer user and computer hardware"
```

Fig. 1. Answers given by question answering systems for questions on Operating System course

A database is a collection of related data which represents some aspect of the real world. A database system is designed to be built and populated with data for a certain task.Database Management System (DBMS) is a software for storing and retrieving users' data while considering appropriate security measures. It consists of a group of programs which manipulate the database. The DBMS accepts the request for data from an application and instructs the operating system to provide the specific data. In large systems, a DBMS helps users and other third-party software to store and retrieve data.DBMS allows users to create their own databases as per their requirement. The term "DBMS" includes the user of the database and other application programs. It provides an interface between the data and the software application.

```
question = "What does DBMS consists of?"
answer_question(question, bert_abstract)

Query has 169 tokens.

Answer: "a group of programs which manipulate the database"

question = "How does DBMS work?"
answer_question(question, bert_abstract)

Query has 168 tokens.

Answer: "storing and retrieving users ' data while considering appropriate security measures"

question = "How does DBMS work with an application and an OS?"
answer_question(question, bert_abstract)

Query has 174 tokens.

Answer: "accepts the request for data from an application and instructs the operating system to provide the specific data"
```

Fig. 2. Answers given our question answering systems for questions on Database Management System course.

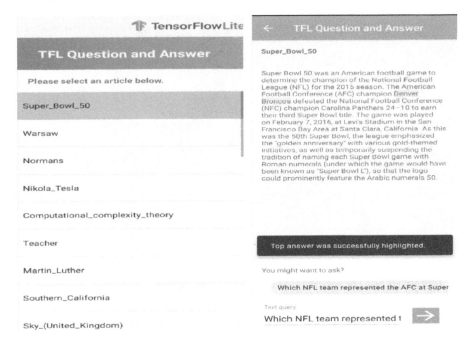

Fig. 3. The TFLite mobile app of our question-answering system

5   Conclusion

By applying quantization techniques on the BERT model, we have converted the weights from float32 (original BERT-base) to int8 (quantized BERT) which reduced the model size and were able to deploy the quantized BERT to TFLite android application which requires low computational powers, less memory footprint, works without internet and gives results in faster inference times with good UI/UX interface for users. The user of the app can easily find the answers that he is looking for in the documents. The model works very well with the proprietary academic dataset (F1 score: 0.85). The performance of quantized BERT is F1 score: 0.8753, while that of BERT is F1 score: 0.9019, along with a reduction of 60% in model size from 438 MB (BERT-small) to 181 MB (quantized BERT). Inference time is also reduced by 44% of quantized BERT compared to that of single thread and four threads of BERT model. This work can be extended by providing more features to the app, like asking questions through the user's voice and getting answers. Presently we have deployed our quantized model on android platform; it can be deployed even on iOS.

References

1. Satapathy, R.: Question answering in natural language processing. LingvoMasino (2018)
2. Ramos, D.: Virtual assistants changing our daily lives. Smarsheet blog (2021)

3. Zadeh, L.A.: From search engines to question-answering systems—the need for new tools. In: Menasalvas, E., Segovia, J., Szczepaniak, P.S. (eds.) AWIC 2003. LNCS, vol. 2663, pp. 15–17. Springer, Heidelberg (2003). https://doi.org/10.1007/3-540-44831-4_2
4. Impact of covid-19 on education system. https://www.weforum.org/agenda/2020/04/Corona virus-education-global-covid19-online-digital-learning/
5. How to Use Google's Question and Answer Feature (2023). https://www.hillwebcreations. com/google-answer-engine/
6. Fundamentals of recurrent neural network (RNN) and long short-term memory (LSTM) network. Physica D: Nonlinear Phenomena **404**, 132306 (2020). ISSN 0167-2789
7. Staudemeyer, R.C., Morris, E.R.: Understanding LSTM–a tutorial into long short-term memory recurrent neural networks. arXiv preprint arXiv:1909.09586 (2019)
8. Devlin, J., Chang, M.-W., Lee, K., Toutanova, K.: BERT: pre-training of deep bidirectional transformers for language understanding. CoRR, abs/1810.04805 (2018)
9. Andurkar, U., Marathe, S., Ambekar, M.: Decoding deep learning approach to question answering. Int. J. Eng. Res. Tech. (IJERT) **10**(03) (2021)
10. Transfer learning for deep learning models. https://machinelearningmastery.com/transfer-lea rning-for-deep-learning/
11. Robustly optimized BERT, Vikas Bhandary. https://towardsdatascience.com/robustly-optimi zed-bert-pretraining-approaches-537dc66522dd
12. Study of comparison of XLNet and BERT with large models
13. Deep learning models cost to compute. https://analyticsindiamag.com/deep-learning-costs-cloud-compute/
14. Desai, S.D., et al.: Advanced computing and communication technologies, pp. 133–144 (2019)
15. Vaswani, A., et al.: Attention is all you need. In: Advances in Neural Information Processing Systems, vol. 30 (2017)
16. Wang, C., Grosse, R., Fidler, S., Zhang, G.: EigenDamage: structured pruning in the kronecker-factored eigenbasis. In: Proceedings of the 36th International Conference on Machine Learning, vol. 97, pp. 6566–6575. PMLR (2019)
17. Prasad Ganta, D., Das Gupta, H., Sheng, V.S.: Knowledge distillation via weighted ensemble of teaching assistants. arXiv e-prints, arXiv-2206 (2022)
18. Quantization techniques to quantize the weights from floating point to integer. https://www.tensorflow.org/lite/performance/post_training_quantization
19. Rohit, G., Dharamshi, E.G., Subramanyam, N.: Approaches to question answering using LSTM and memory networks. In: Bansal, J.C., Das, K.N., Nagar, A., Deep, K., Ojha, A.K. (eds.) SocProS 2017. AISC, vol. 816, pp. 199–209. Springer, Singapore (2019). https://doi. org/10.1007/978-981-13-1592-3_15
20. Yang, Z., Dai, Z., Yang, Y., Carbonell, J.G., Salakhutdinov, R., Le, Q.V.: XLNet: generalized autoregressive pretraining for language understanding. CoRR, abs/1906.08237, pp. 199–209 (2019)
21. Liu, Y., et al.: RoBERTa: a robustly optimized BERT pretraining approach. arXiv preprint arXiv:1907.11692 (2019)
22. Adedoyin, O.B., Soykan, E.: Covid-19 pandemic and online learning: the challenges and opportunities. Interactive Learn. Environ. 1–13 (2020)

A Comparative Analysis of Pretrained Models for Sentiment Analysis on Restaurant Customer Reviews (CAPM-SARCR)

S. Santhiya[1]([✉])(iD), C. Sharmila[2](iD), P. Jayadharshini[1](iD), M. N. Dharshini[1], B. Dinesh Kumar[1], and K. Sandeep[1]

[1] Department of Artificial Intelligence, Kongu Engineering College, Perundurai 638060, India
santhiya.cse@kongu.edu
[2] Department of Computer Science, Kongu Engineering College, Perundurai 638060, India

Abstract. Sentiment analysis plays a crucial role in understanding customer opinions and attitudes towards various products and services. In this study, proposed work is based on comparative analysis of five pretrained models, namely BERT Tokenizer, RoBERTa, MBERT, DeBERTa, and XLNet, for sentiment analysis on restaurant customer reviews. The dataset used for evaluation contains customer reviews labeled as positive or negative, indicating the sentiment associated with the restaurant experience. The main objective is to identify the most effective pretrained model for sentiment classification in the context of restaurant customer reviews. The models are evaluated based on testing accuracy and loss to determine their performance on the unseen test dataset. Among these models, RoBERTa and DeBERTa emerged as the most promising ones, achieving remarkable testing accuracies. These models demonstrated their exceptional capability to effectively capture and comprehend sentiment patterns in the feedback provided by restaurant customers. The outcomes of this study can provide useful insights into the use of pretrained models for sentiment analysis in the restaurant sector, as well as contribute to the advancement of natural language processing.

Keywords: Sentiment Analysis · Pretrained Models · BERT Tokenizer · RoBERTa · m-BERT · DeBERTa · XLNet · Restaurant Customer Reviews · Comparative Analysis

1 Introduction

Sentiment analysis, also referred to as opinion mining, involves the process of recognizing and categorizing the sentiment expressed in textual data using techniques from natural language processing. Understanding customer sentiments is

B. R. Chakravarthi et al. (Eds.): SPELLL 2023, CCIS 2046, pp. 140–147, 2024.
https://doi.org/10.1007/978-3-031-58495-4_10

essential for businesses, particularly in the restaurant industry, where customer feedback directly impacts reputation and customer satisfaction. With the advent of pretrained language models, such as BERT Tokenizer, RoBERTa, MBERT, DeBERTa, and XLNet, the accuracy and efficiency of sentiment analysis have significantly improved. The proposed work aims to compare the performance of these pretrained models on a restaurant customer review dataset to identify the most suitable model for sentiment classification.

2   Related Work

Sentiment analysis, a significant field within natural language processing (NLP), is dedicated to the comprehension and categorization of sentiments conveyed in text data, often referred to as opinion mining. Over the years, various techniques and models have been proposed to perform sentiment analysis on different types of text, including social media posts, product reviews, and customer feedback. In recent times, the rise of pretrained language models has brought substantial advancements to the field of sentiment analysis, delivering exceptional outcomes across diverse NLP tasks.

Bidirectional Encoder Representations from Transformers has been introduced [1] a groundbreaking pretrained language model that leverages bidirectional attention mechanisms to learn contextual word representations. BERT has been extensively employed in numerous NLP tasks due to its ability to capture context-aware embeddings, making it a popular choice for sentiment analysis tasks. RoBERTa further improved [2] the performance by optimizing the model on more training data and using larger batch sizes. Its pretraining approach involved removing the next sentence prediction task and focusing on the masked language model, leading to better contextual representations.

Multilingual BERT (m-BERT) was designed [3] to handle multiple languages. It demonstrated the ability to perform sentiment analysis across different languages, enabling cross-lingual applications. m-BERT utilizes shared parameters for various languages, leveraging transfer learning to achieve competitive results on sentiment analysis tasks. DeBERTa is a decoder-enhanced BERT variant that incorporates [4] additional self-attention mechanisms. DeBERTa utilizes disentangled attention mechanisms and outperforms BERT on various NLP benchmarks, making it a strong candidate for sentiment analysis on customer reviews.

XLNet is a generalized autoregressive pretraining model [4] that outperformed BERT on several NLP tasks. Given its novel permutation-based training, XLNet has the potential to excel in sentiment analysis and deserves consideration in the comparative analysis. A transfer learning approach, Universal Language Model optimization has been presented [5] for text classification. The method achieved competitive results on various datasets, including sentiment analysis tasks, making it relevant for comparing with pretrained models on restaurant reviews.

The original Transformer model introduced [6] the attention mechanism, which revolutionized NLP tasks, including sentiment analysis. This seminal work serves as a foundation for many pretrained models used in the comparative analysis. mBERT, a multilingual version of BERT that learns [7] cross-lingual representations. Given the multilingual nature of customer reviews, mBERT could be a relevant pretrained model for sentiment analysis in diverse languages.

Enriching pre-trained language representations has been explored [8] with external knowledge for Chinese text comprehension. While focusing on machine comprehension, their approach may offer insights into adapting pretrained models for sentiment analysis on Chinese restaurant reviews [9]. The Hugging Face's Transformers library, which uses various pretrained models [10] and it discusses the strengths and limitations of different models, making it valuable for selecting suitable models for sentiment analysis.

CTRL, a conditional transformer model [11] that enables controlled generation of text. While not directly tailored for sentiment analysis, CTRL's controllability may offer advantages for fine-tuning on specific sentiment targets in restaurant reviews [12]. SciBERT is a domain-specific BERT model fine-tuned [13] on scientific literature. Although restaurant reviews differ from scientific texts, SciBERT's domain adaptation approach could be relevant when analyzing specialized restaurant reviews or specific aspects of food and beverages. Sentiment classification has been explored [14] for restaurant reviews using ELMo and an attention mechanism. Their study contributes to the diversity of models considered for sentiment analysis and highlights the effectiveness of attention-based methods.

3   Data Description

The dataset used in the proposed work is "Restaurant Customer Reviews." It is sourced from Kaggle and consists of customer reviews and sentiment labels for various restaurants. The dataset is designed for sentiment analysis tasks consists of 5 columns and 5000 rows, where the objective is to predict the sentiment (positive or negative) expressed in each review. Review Text column contains the textual content of the customer reviews. It includes the comments, feedback, and opinions expressed by customers regarding their dining experience at the respective restaurants. Sentiment Label column contains the sentiment label for each review, representing the sentiment expressed by the customer. It is a binary class label with two possible values: "1" indicates a positive sentiment, implying that the customer had a satisfactory or pleasant experience at the restaurant. "0" indicates a negative sentiment, implying that the customer had an unsatisfactory or unpleasant experience at the restaurant.

4   Proposed System

The methodology for conducting the comparative analysis of pretrained models for sentiment analysis on restaurant customer reviews involves several key steps which is depicted in Fig. 1

4.1   Data Preprocessing

The textual data is preprocessed by converting text to lowercase, removing special characters, and tokenizing the text using the corresponding pretrained model tokenizer. Sequences are padded or truncated to ensure uniform input size. The dataset is partitioned into three subsets: training, validation, and test sets. The training set is used for model training, the validation set is employed for hyperparameter optimization, and the test set serves for the final evaluation of the model's performance.

4.2   BERT Tokenizer

BERT (Bidirectional Encoder Representations from Transformers) pretrained language model developed by Google. It transformed the processing of natural language tasks by giving deep contextualized representations for words. BERT Tokenizer is the tokenizer associated with the BERT model, and it is responsible for converting raw text into a format suitable for input to the BERT model. In the context of sentiment analysis on restaurant customer reviews, the BERT Tokenizer is employed to preprocess the textual data. Each review is passed through the tokenizer, resulting in a sequence of numerical indices representing the words and sub words in the review. These tokenized patterns are then given into the BERT model for sentiment classification.

4.3   RoBERTa

RoBERTa, developed by Facebook AI, is an optimized variant of the BERT model. It builds on the BERT achievements and aims to improve its performance by introducing modifications in the pretraining process. RoBERTa is employed in sentiment analysis on restaurant customer reviews by optimizing the pretrained model on the specific sentiment analysis task. The RoBERTa model and tokenizer are tailored to the binary sentiment classification issue, which seeks to predict whether a review is good or negative.

4.4   mBERT

Multilingual BERT (mBERT) is a BERT model version developed by Google AI Research that can handle many languages in a single model. It is pre-trained on a vast corpus of literature from several languages, enabling it to understand and generate language representations for various languages. mBERT may be fine-tuned on the specific sentiment classification task in the overall setting of sentiment analysis on restaurant customer reviews. By providing the model with reviews in different languages, it can predict the sentiment (positive or negative) regardless of the review's language.

Fig. 1. Proposed System Workflow.

4.5   DeBERTa

Microsoft Research Asia created DeBERTa (Decoding-enhanced BERT with Disentangled Attention), an advanced language model which builds upon the BERT architecture with enhancements in attention mechanisms and decoding strategies. DeBERTa can be utilized in sentiment analysis tasks for restaurant customer reviews by optimizing the model on sentiment analysis tasks. Its advanced attention mechanisms and disentangled self-attention may enable it to capture more nuanced contextual information from reviews, leading to improved sentiment predictions.

4.6   XLNet

XLNet model extends the Transformer-XL architecture by Google Research. It introduces permutation-based training and removes the autoregressive property, addressing the limitations of traditional language models. XLNet can be applied to sentiment analysis on restaurant customer reviews by fine-tuning the model on the specific task. Its permutation-based training and autoregressive-free nature may enable it to capture bidirectional dependencies in reviews, leading to more accurate sentiment predictions.

5   Experimental Results and Discussion

The Table 1 outlines the outcome of sentiment analysis on restaurant customer reviews using five pretrained models: BERT Tokenizer, RoBERTa, MBERT, DeBERTa, and XLNet. Precision, recall, and F1-score are evaluation measures that are calculated individually for the "Negative" and "Positive" sentiment classes.

RoBERTa and DeBERTa emerged as the top-performing models for both the "Negative" and "Positive" sentiment classes. Their disentangled attention (DeBERTa) and permutation-based training (RoBERTa) likely contributed to their superior performance in capturing diverse and bidirectional contextual information. BERT Tokenizer and XLNet also delivered strong results, demonstrating the effectiveness of transformer-based architectures in sentiment analysis. MBERT achieved high recall for the "Negative" class but relatively lower precision and recall for the "Positive" class, suggesting room for improvement in handling positive sentiments. The differences in model performance highlight

Table 1. Performance measure of BERT Tokenizer, RoBERTa, MBERT, DeBERTa, and XLNet.

Algorithms	Class	Precision	Recall	F1-Score
BERT Tokenizer	Negative	94.73	91.13	92.9
	Positive	90.54	94.36	92.41
RoBERTa	Negative	97.46	96.34	95.46
	Positive	97.18	95.18	97.28
MBERT	Negative	78.12	94.93	85.71
	Positive	92.59	70.42	79.99
DeBERTa	Negative	98.7	96.2	97.43
	Positive	95.89	98.59	97.22
XLNet	Negative	95.06	97.46	96.25
	Positive	97.1	94.36	95.71

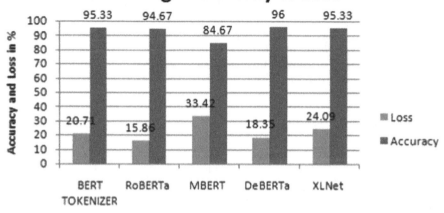

Fig. 2. Training Accuracy and Loss of Pre-Trained Models.

the importance of selecting appropriate pretrained models for specific tasks. In this case, DeBERTa and RoBERTa excelled in sentiment analysis on restaurant customer reviews, showing their potential for real-world applications. The comparative analysis of pretrained models presented in this study provides valuable insights into their performance variations. It highlights the strengths and areas for improvement of these models in the domain of restaurant customer reviews, thereby guiding the selection of appropriate models for similar real-world applications.

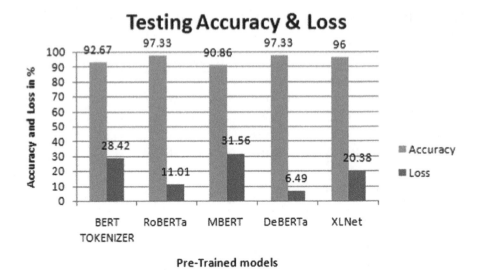

Fig. 3. Testing Accuracy and Loss of Pre-Trained Models.

Figures 2 and 3 show the training and testing accuracy and loss for five pretrained models used in sentiment analysis on restaurant customer reviews: BERT Tokenizer, RoBERTa, MBERT, DeBERTa, and XLNet.

6   Conclusion

RoBERTa and DeBERTa are the most promising pretrained models for sentiment analysis on restaurant customer reviews. They exhibited superior testing accuracies of 97.33%, showcasing their ability to effectively capture and understand sentiment patterns in customer feedback. XLNet also proved to be a strong contender with a testing accuracy of 96%. BERT Tokenizer and MBERT achieved reasonable testing accuracies but may benefit from further optimization. The choice of pretrained model plays a crucial role in sentiment analysis tasks, and selecting models like RoBERTa, DeBERTa, or XLNet can lead to highly accurate and valuable insights into customer sentiment for restaurant businesses. These models have the potential to be deployed in real-world applications, providing valuable insights into customer feedback and sentiment for restaurant businesses. However, further experimentation and fine-tuning may be necessary to optimize the models' performance for specific use cases and domains.

References

1. Devlin, J., Chang, M.-W., Lee, K., Toutanova, K.: BERT: pre-training of deep bidirectional transformers for language understanding. arXiv preprint arXiv:1810.04805 (2018)
2. Radford, A., Wu, J., Child, R., Luan, D., Amodei, D., Sutskever, I.: Language models are unsupervised multitask learners. OpenAI Blog **1**(8), 9 (2019)
3. Yang, Z., Dai, Z., Yang, Y., Carbonell, J., Salakhutdinov, R.R., Le, Q.V.: XLNet: generalized autoregressive pretraining for language understanding. In: Advances in Neural Information Processing Systems, vol. 32 (2019)
4. He, P., Liu, X., Gao, J., Chen, W.: DeBERTa: decoding-enhanced BERT with disentangled attention. arXiv preprint arXiv:2006.03654 (2020)
5. Howard, J., Ruder, S.: Universal language model fine-tuning for text classification. arXiv preprint arXiv:1801.06146 (2018)
6. Vaswani, A., et al.: Attention is all you need. In: Advances in Neural Information Processing Systems, vol. 30 (2017)
7. Luo, X., Yin, S., Lin, P.: A survey of cross-lingual sentiment analysis based on pre-trained models (2021)
8. Yang, A., et al.: Enhancing pre-trained language representations with rich knowledge for machine reading comprehension. In: Proceedings of the 57th Annual Meeting of the Association for Computational Linguistics, pp. 2346–2357 (2019)
9. Wolf, T., et al.: HuggingFace's transformers: state-of-the-art natural language processing. arXiv preprint arXiv:1910.03771 (2019)
10. Keskar, N.S., McCann, B., Varshney, L.R., Xiong, C., Socher, R.: CTRL: a conditional transformer language model for controllable generation. arXiv preprint arXiv:1909.05858 (2019)
11. Beltagy, I., Lo, K., Cohan, A.: SciBERT: a pretrained language model for scientific text. arXiv preprint arXiv:1903.10676 (2019)
12. Gao, Z., Feng, A., Song, X., Wu, X.: Target-dependent sentiment classification with BERT. IEEE Access **7**, 154290–154299 (2019)
13. Rita, P., Vong, C., Pinheiro, F., Mimoso, J.: A sentiment analysis of Michelin-starred restaurants. Eur. J. Manag. Bus. Econ. **32**(3), 276–295 (2023)
14. Li, H., Bruce, X.B., Li, G., Gao, H.: Restaurant survival prediction using customer-generated content: an aspect-based sentiment analysis of online reviews. Tour. Manag. **96**, 104707 (2023)

Lightweight Language Agnostic Data Sanitization Pipeline for Dealing with Homoglyphs in Code-Mixed Languages

Mohammad Yusuf Jamal Aziz Azmi[1]([✉])
and Subalalitha Chinnaudayar Navaneethakrishnan[2]

[1] Department of Computer Engineering, Faculty of Engineering and Technology, Aligarh
Muslim University, Aligarh 202002, Uttar Pradesh, India
`yusufjamal2773@gmail.com`
[2] Department of Computing Technologies, Faculty of Engineering and Technology, SRM
Institute of Science and Technology, Kattankulathur 603203, Tamil Nadu, India

Abstract. With the rise in hate speech on social media, numerous Natural Language Processing (NLP) techniques like text classification have been employed for detecting hate speech to make social media less toxic. However, hate speech users have started employing homoglyphs, which are characters that look identical to each other but have a different encoding or structure, to evade detection since most NLP models are trained on commonly recognized Unicode characters. In this paper we propose a novel lightweight language agnostic data sanitization pipeline which constitutes of a CNN for character level OCR followed by Symspell algorithm for candidate word generation and n-grams for word retrieval with the aim of retrieving dehomoglyphed sentences from homoglyphed sentences. We also introduce HEMNIST, an extended version of EMNIST that includes images of homoglyphs. We achieve a cosine similarity of 0.922, 0.845, 0.671, 0.508 and 0.231 between original and retrieved text at 5%, 10%, 20%, 30% and 50% masking respectively.

Keywords: homoglyphs · HEMNIST · hate speech detection · homographs · code-mixed

1 Introduction

Hate speech users often use different techniques to avoid getting banned, censored or detected by automated hate detection models which often use numerous text-based Natural Language Processing (NLP) techniques like text classification. One such technique is incorporating homoglyphs into their sentences to make sentences unfit for model consumption [1]. These characters can also be used to evade text-based NLP models assigned to perform spam detection or plagiarism detection.

Homoglyphs are characters that render to the same glyph or to a visually similar glyph, i.e., these characters may look similar but might have a different encoding or

B. R. Chakravarthi et al. (Eds.): SPELLL 2023, CCIS 2046, pp. 148–160, 2024.
https://doi.org/10.1007/978-3-031-58495-4_11

underlying structure. They can have a different encoding via having a different Unicode, for example, the character 'W'(U+0077) can be represented with 'ẅ'(U+1E85) or 'w'(U+FF57), these are single character homoglyphs. They can have a different structure by being multi-character, for example, the character 'W' can be written as 'VV' using 2 V's or 'VV' using '\' and '/' or 'I∧I' using 'I', '/' and '\'. Homoglyphs are often called homographs although in the conventional linguistic context, homographs refer to words that are spelled the same but have a different meaning.

Text-based NLP models are trained on datasets that mostly contain regular Unicode characters, hence, when they are fed with homoglyphed sentences they fail at their given task.

Code-mixed languages are informal languages where writing script is borrowed from one language and vocabulary is borrowed from two language. Code-mixed language users employ transliteration, it is the process of writing a word or phrase in another script. For example, " دل " (the word for heart in Urdu) or " दिल" (the word for heart in Hindi) can be transliterated as "dil" using the Latin script. Since these languages aren't formal, performing NLP on them is difficult. A comparison of code-mixed and homoglyphed code-mixed sentences can be seen in Table 1.

Previous works on homoglyph detection [2–4] have been limited to being applied in cyber-security spaces. Previous works on homoglyphs in NLP [1, 5] demonstrate how homoglyphs affect the performance of text-based NLP models but don't propose methods to counter them.

Homoglyphed sentence retrieval can be performed via a dictionary-based or rule-based method where a known homoglyphs can be mapped to corresponding characters but since code-mixed languages aren't formal, a dictionary-based approach becomes difficult. Direct OCR approaches aren't enough due to multi-character homoglyphs.

Table 1. Original code-mixed sentences (left) vs homoglyphed code-mixed sentences (right). Characters are visually same, hence are the same while reading

Original	Homoglyphed
BaH Guruji Kya style hai apka duni-yako hila ke chhore hain.	BaH Guruji Kya style hai apka dunɩyako hila ke chhore hain.
India me student pe atyachaar karra hai result nahi dikhaijara hai aur yaha ye inke aankho me dhul jhokra hai	Ⅱndia me student pe atyachaar karra hai result nahi dikhaijαrci hai aur yaha ye inke aankho me dhʋl jℏokra hai

In this paper our main contributions are:

1. We introduce a Language Agnostic Data Sanitization pipeline for code-mixed languages which constitutes of a CNN for performing character level OCR, followed by this we generate potential candidate words, which are words that could potentially be the corresponding dehomoglyphed word, using Symspell algorithm. We then select the most suitable candidate word using n-grams for word retrieval with the aim of retrieving dehomoglyphed sentences from homoglyphed sentences.

2. We introduce an extended version of EMNIST by adding homoglyph characters to it, we call it HEMNIST. We demonstrate that this increases the performance of the CNN to perform OCR on homoglyphs.

The rest of the paper is organized as follows, in Sect. 2 we discuss previous works, Sect. 3 discusses the methodology, Sect. 4 discusses the experiments performed, Sect. 5 discusses the results followed by Sect. 6 which discusses Limitations and then we finally conclude with Sect. 7.

2 Related Works

For our literature survey, we focused on papers and techniques regarding homoglyphs in NLP, homoglyph detection, code-mixed NLP, candidate word recommendation and word retrieval techniques.

2.1 Homoglyphs in NLP

Boucher et al. [1] discussed how homoglyphs can be used as an imperceptible encoding-specific perturbation to manipulate the outputs of text-based NLP models. They demonstrate that homoglyphs are font-specific and that even if the underlying linguistic system denotes two characters in the same way, fonts are not required to respect this. They provide an example of an attack using homoglyphs and recommend input sanitization should be performed on all inputs to NLP models to remove any characters that are not part of the expected character set as a defense against these attacks.

Li et al. [5] discusses hidden backdoors through two state-of-the-art trigger embedding methods. One of these uses homographs as triggers for hidden textual backdoor attacks in modern NLP models. They use homograph replacement to embed triggers into deep neural networks. They demonstrate that the proposed hidden backdoors can be effective across three downstream security-critical NLP tasks, including toxic comment detection, neural machine translation (NMT), and question answering (QA).

We couldn't find any studies on homoglyphs in text-based code-mixed NLP.

2.2 Homoglyph Detection

Majumder et al. [2] proposes a method to identify homoglyphs using shallow Convolutional Neural Networks. The ensembled model achieves 99.72% accuracy on the independent test dataset. The dataset used in the study consists of character image pairs that look similar or dissimilar. Private Use Area (PUA) characters were omitted from the list of confusable character pairs provided by the Unicode consortium, and character pairs that were dependent on certain fonts were also omitted. The dataset was based on then available list of homoglyphs and is one of its limitations since it may not be comprehensive. They also do not explore the performance of the proposed method on detecting homoglyphs in languages other than English.

Deng et al. [3] proposes a deep learning model that uses embedding learning, transfer learning, and data augmentation to identify homoglyphs. The paper also presents a clustering method to group homoglyphs into sets of equivalence classes. The paper does not address the issue of homoglyphs in non-Latin scripts. The model's performance may also be affected by the font used to display the characters. The clustering method may not be effective for large datasets with a high number of homoglyphs.

Tolstosheyev et al. [4] proposes a solution that uses the Levenshtein edit distance algorithm (that is commonly used in misspelled words detection) and dividing dictionary databases into users with their being allowed to extend them with own terminologies and words to detect homoglyphs and replace them with correct words.

2.3 Code-Mixed Language Models

MuRIL [6] is a BERT model designed to understand and process text in 17 Indian languages. It is pre-trained on a large corpus of text from various sources, including Wikipedia, news articles, and books. The authors also explicitly enhance monolingual text corpora by incorporating both translated and transliterated document pairs. This approach is utilized as supervised cross-lingual signals, which enables the model to learn and associate similar meanings across different languages. The model is fine-tuned on several downstream tasks, including part-of-speech tagging, named entity recognition, and machine translation. The final vocabulary size is 197,285. It outperforms mBERT on most of the downstream tasks, achieving state-of-the-art results on several benchmarks.

2.4 Candidate Word Generation

Symspell [7] - Symmetric Delete spelling correction algorithm is a language agnostic spelling correction algorithm that works by reducing the complexity of edit candidate generation and dictionary lookup for a given Damerau Levenshtein distance by using deletes only instead of traditional methods of deletes, transposes, replaces, and inserts. It creates a prefix index to keep its memory requirement in check. First it generates terms with an edit distance from each dictionary term and adds them together with the original term to the dictionary. This is done only once during a pre-calculation step. The algorithm generates a list of suggested corrections for a given input string by generating all possible terms with an edit distance from the input term and searching them in the dictionary. It then ranks the suggested corrections based on their frequency in the dictionary and returns the top suggestions.

2.5 N-grams for Information Retrieval

N-gram is a statistical and language-independent method, making it suitable for the multilingual Indian context. Majumder et al. [8] discusses the use of N-grams for developing basic tools in the area of Information Retrieval and Natural Language Processing in the multilingual Indian context. They discuss various language processing tasks such as statistical stemming, spelling correction, and indexing for retrieval.

The main gaps that we identified via our literature survey was the lack of methods to dehomoglyphise sentences and lack of studies on homoglyphs in text-based code-mixed NLP.

3 Proposed Methodology

3.1 Datasets

Homoglyphs Collection: 1,012 Single character homoglyphs (an example of which is shown in Fig. 1) were collected from homoglyphs [9] Python package. Additionally, some multi-character homoglyphs were created by combining characters an example of which is demonstrated in Fig. 2. We collected a total of 3,156 homoglyphs.

A A A

Fig. 1. Homoglyphs of the letter A: 1) A(U+0041) 2) A (U+FF21) 3) **A**(U+1D400)

Cι

Fig. 2. Multi-character homoglyph of letter 'a' generated by combing letter 'c' and letter 'i': here c(U+0063) + ι(U+0269)

Masked Homoglyphed Code-Mixed Dataset: [10] introduced IIITH, a Hind-English codemixed dataset for which they collected user comments from popular public Facebook pages in India, manually pre-processed the data, and annotated it for sentiment polarity. The dataset contains 15% negative, 50% neutral and 35% positive comments owing to the nature of conversations in the selected pages. The dataset has 3,879 sentences in total. Number of sentences per sentiment can be seen in Table 3.

We generate five distinct datasets from this source dataset, wherein specific characters in each sentence are substituted with their corresponding homoglyphs. The sentences are obfuscated through the masking of characters by their length, with a masking threshold that is determined by the datasets. Through this methodology, we generate a range of datasets that are masked at rates of 5%, 10%, 20%, 30%, and 50% as shown in Table 2.

We use these datasets in order to effectively illustrate the manner in which homoglyphs can significantly hamper and undermine the performance and efficacy of various NLP models. We demonstrate that the presence of homoglyphs can significantly diminish MuRIL's text classification capabilities, thereby rendering it much less effective in achieving its intended objectives.

Fonts: The fonts used to convert homoglyph characters to images are mentioned in the Table 4.

Homoglyphed Extended MNIST-HEMNIST: EMNIST [11] By_Class is a subset of the EMNIST dataset that contains handwritten digits and letters. It consists of 62 balanced classes, where each class represents a combination of a digit and a letter. We only select the letters subset which has 52 classes.

Table 2. Masked sentences

Mask-ing	Sentence
Original	Wah! Jitni sundar geet ke bhao hain utnihi sundar aur sureeli aawaz hai .
5%	Wah! J*i*tni sundar geet ke bhao hain utnihi sunc|ar aur sureeli aawaz hai .
10%	Wah! J*i*tni sundar geet *t*e bhao hain ʋtnihi sunc*l*ar aur sureeli aawaz hai .
20%	Wah! Jitni sunc1ar *geet* ke bhao hain ut*n*ihi sund*ci*r aur sureeli aaw c *iz* hai .
30%	W*ci*ḥ! *J*itn*i* sund*a*r geet k*e* b*l*ḥao hc*ii*n utn*i*hi sundar au*r* sʋreel*i* aawaz hc*u* .
50%	Wc*u*h! Jit*n*i su*n*clar geet k*e* bhc i *o* hain utnihi *s*un*c* I cir aur sur*œ*eli aa*ʋ* v c*ι*z hci*i* .

Table 3. IIITH script and sentiment distribution

Dataset	Scripts Available	Positive	Neutral	Negative
IIITH	COMMON, LATIN	1352	1957	570

Table 4. Fonts and the number of single character homoglyphs that used them.

Font	Number of characters
Unifont-Upper	803
Unifont	147
Coptic Eyes Latin	63

While making HEMNIST, we save both original and augmented (dilated with a kernel size of 2×2) image, which ends up doubling the images to 6,312 which are split in 90:10 ratio and added to EMNIST By_Class. Table 5 shows number of images in train-test split. The images being added were visually verified by the authors. A sample of the images being added to EMNIST By_Class to create HEMNIST is shown in Fig. 3.

Code-Mixed Sentences for Training N-grams and Symspell: To train n-grams and Symspell models we extend the sentences in IIITH [10] with 10,000 randomly selected sentences from the CC-100 [12] corpus's Hindi Romanized and Urdu Romanized subsets. We then dropped sentences with less than 3 words (because we use trigrams) which resulted in total 13,531 sentences.

Table 5. Number of images in train and test in EMNIST and HEMNIST by_class letters

Dataset	Train	Test	Classes
EMNIST by class letters	352897	58405	52
H-EMNIST by class letters	358611	59003	52

Fig. 3. HEMNIST-Homoglyphed EMNIST

3.2 Pipeline

To retrieve dehomoglyphed sentences we have to generate sentences as similar as possible. We first train a CNN on HEMNIST with which we perform OCR, then we train our Symspell and n-grams model on the 13,531 sentences. The algorithm for sentence retrieval is discussed in Algorithm 1 and shown in Fig. 4.

ALGORITHM 1: Retrieving dehomoglyphed sentences from homoglyph sentences

	Input:
	x: Sentence that has homoglyph characters
	Output:
	Dehomoglyphed sentence
1.	**DH** ← ""
2.	**K** ← string.ascii_letters //Acceptable characters
3.	**H** ← x.split() //Split the sentence into an array of its words
4.	**for** word ∈ H **do**
5.	**dh_word** ← "" //For saving dehomoglyphed word
6.	**h_counter** ← 0 //To check if there are any homoglyphs in the word
7.	**for** character ∈ word **do**
8.	**if** character ∉ K **do**
9.	//perform OCR and append character to dh_word
10	dh_word += **OCR**(character)
11	h_counter ++
12	**else**
13	dh_word += character //Just append character to word
14	**end if**
15	**end for**
16	**if** h_counter == 0 **OR** len(DH) == 0 **do**
17	//Append dh_word to DH if dh_word has no homoglyphs or no previous words
18	DH += dh_word
19	**continue**
20	**end if**
21	**candidate_words** ← Symspell(dh_word) //Get an array of candidate words
22	//Get the candidate word using n-grams with max log-score
23	dh_word = retrieve_word(candidate_words, DH)
24	DH += dh_word
25	**end for**
26	**return** DH

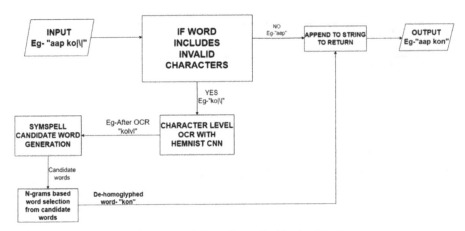

Fig. 4. System design of Data Sanitization Pipeline

4 Experiment

In the first Sect. 4.1, we demonstrate how homoglyphs deteriorate the performance of text-based code-mixed NLP model like MuRIL using masked datasets discussed in Sect. 3.1, in Sect. 4.2 we demonstrate the character level OCR capabilities of a CNN trained on HEMNIST and in Sect. 4.3 we discuss how n-grams and Symspell were trained.

4.1 Effects of Homoglyphs on MuRIL

We fine-tuned MuRIL BERT on IIITH and its masked variants for 10 epochs at a learning rate of $2e-5$ with weight decay of 0.01, warmup steps of 500 and batch size of 8 on one NVIDIA T4 GPU on Google Colab.

Table 6 shows that MuRIL's performance deteriorates as more homoglyphs are introduced.

Table 6. Performance of MuRIL on masked-IIITH; MF - micro F1-score; WF - weighted F1-score; MP - micro Precision; WP - weighted Precision; MR - micro Recall; WR - weighted Recall; MCC-Matthew's correlation coefficient

Masked	MP	MR	MF	WP	WR	WF	MCC
Original	0.693	0.693	0.693	0.695	0.693	0.693	0.492
5%	0.650	0.650	0.650	0.650	0.650	0.647	0.416
10%	0.643	0.643	0.643	0.649	0.643	0.637	0.408
20%	0.574	0.574	0.574	0.565	0.574	0.567	0.278
30%	0.530	0.530	0.530	0.471	0.530	0.436	0.131
50%	0.514	0.514	0.514	0.429	0.514	0.463	0.100

4.2 OCR

We tested single homoglyph character retrieval accuracy on Tesseract OCR engine [13] and an EMNIST-CNN [14] implementation that we retrained on HEMNIST and EMNIST by class letters only.

The optimal performance of Tesseract OCR was observed when images were rendered at a resolution of 100×100, subsequently subjected to dilation using a 2×2 kernel and finally a 3×3 median blur.

EMNIST CNN (CNN trained on EMNIST by class) and HEMNIST CNN (CNN trained on HEMNIST) were trained for 7 epochs using Stochastic Gradient Descent (SGD) with a learning rate of 0.001 and momentum value of 0.9. The loss function utilized was Categorical Cross Entropy. For both the CNNs, the best results were obtained when the images were rendered at a resolution of $28 \times 28 \times 1$ followed by dilation via a 2×2 kernel.

EMNIST by class letters achieved a training accuracy of 83.25% and test accuracy of 85.36%. HEMNIST by class letters CNN achieved a training accuracy of 83.11% and test accuracy of 85.32%.

Table 7 summarizes the performance of the models discussed above for single character homoglyph retrieval.

Table 7. Performance of different models on mapping homoglyphs to their correct ASCII equivalent

Model	Size	Accuracy	Correct	Total
Tesseract OCR(cased)	100×100	13.814	436	3156
Tesseract OCR(uncased)	100×100	15.145	478	3156
Tesseract OCR(cased)	28×28	10.67	337	3156
Tesseract OCR(uncased)	28×28	11.78	372	3156
EMNIST CNN(cased)	28×28	15.52	490	3156
EMNIST CNN(uncased)	28×28	33.079	1044	3156
HEMNIST CNN(cased)	28×28	61.596	1944	3156
HEMNIST CNN(uncased)	28×28	63.149	1993	3156

HEMNIST CNN with uncased letters achieved the best single character homoglyph retrieval accuracy of 63.149%.

4.3 N-grams and Symspell Training

We use n-grams with $n = 3$ (trigrams) and use Laplace smoothing to deal with unseen combinations.

We extract n-gram frequencies and word frequencies for Symspell from our extended IIITH dataset with 13,531 sentences.

5 Results

For validating the retrieval accuracy of our pipeline we calculate word-based cosine similarity of retrieved sentences with original sentences. Table 8 shows the effectiveness of our proposed pipeline.

Table 8. Performance of Data Sanitization Pipeline in recovering homoglyphed sentences.

HEMNIST by class (uncased) CNN [OCR] + Symspell [Candidate Words] + Trigrams model [Word retrieval]	Masked	Similarity of Masked with Original (avg. cosine similarity)	Similarity of Retrieved with Original (avg. cosine similarity)	Max Edit Distance Required
	5%	0.866	0.922	30
	10%	0.700	0.845	30
	20%	0.460	0.671	30
	30%	0.317	0.508	40
	50%	0.161	0.231	40

The retrieval similarity at 50% masking is low because at that level of masking a lot of context is lost, hence context based word retrieval doesn't work.

Table 9. Performancec of MuRIL on Retrieved IIITH

Masked	MP	MR	MF	WP	WR	WF	MCC
Original	0.693	0.693	0.693	0.695	0.693	0.693	0.492
5%	0.682	0.682	0.682	0.680	0.682	0.679	0.465
10%	0.652	0.652	0.652	0.651	0.652	0.651	0.412
20%	0.643	0.643	0.643	0.637	0.643	0.637	0.388
30%	0.636	0.636	0.636	0.644	0.636	0.630	0.379
50%	0.515	0.515	0.515	0.478	0.515	0.468	0.130

Table 9 shows MuRIL's performance on retrieved sentences. Up to 30% masking the performance sees significant improvements. Since the retrieval at 50% masking is low, the performance is similar to the 50% masked sentences and doesn't see any improvement in performance.

6   Limitations

To pass the sentence through the pipeline we first detect if it has any homoglyphs with different encodings, if the sentence has multi-character homoglyphs and no encoding-based homoglyphs, we end up skipping that sentence since we do not have a way to detect multi-character homoglyphs.

Since the pipeline uses OCR, it may be affected by the font used to display the characters. We use trigrams, hence sentences with less than 3 words won't do well.

Excess homoglyphic masking results in context loss, which makes retrieval difficult. One way to tackle loss of context due to homoglyphic masking, like masking at 50% could be to include homoglyphed data while pre-training transformer models so that non-ascii characters aren't unknown.

We only experimented with alphabet characters, further studies can focus on numbers and punctuations.

There is a lack of studies on homoglyphed code-mixed languages.

7   Conclusion

In this paper we demonstrated that homoglyphs deteriorate the performance of text-based NLP models and discussed a novel light-weight data sanitization pipeline for retrieving code-mixed homoglyphed sentences.We introduced an extension of EMNIST by_class letters dataset by adding homoglyph character images, we call it HEMIST. We used a CNN trained on HEMNIST for character level OCR, followed by Symspell for candidate word generation and retrieved the dehomoglyphed word via trigrams. We hope other researchers will explore and improve ways of dealing with homoglyphs in texts.

References

1. Boucher, N., Shumailov, I., Anderson, R., Papernot, N.: Bad characters: imperceptible NLP attacks; bad characters: imperceptible NLP attacks. In: 2022 IEEE Symposium on Security and Privacy (SP) (2022). https://doi.org/10.1109/SP46214.2022.00045
2. Majumder, M., Rahman, M., Iqbal, A., Rahman, M.S.: Convolutional neural network based ensemble approach for homoglyph recognition. Math. Comput. Appl. **25**, 71 (2020). https://doi.org/10.3390/mca25040071
3. Deng, P., Linsky, C., Wright, M.: Weaponizing Unicodes with Deep Learning – Identifying Homoglyphs with Weakly Labeled Data (2020). https://doi.org/10.1109/ISI49825.2020.9280538
4. Tolstosheyev, R., Sadykhzadeh, A.: Methods of detecting and recovering after homoglyph attacks. Research Gate (2021). https://doi.org/10.13140/RG.2.2.31410.27846
5. Li, S., et al.: Hidden backdoors in human-centric language models. In: Proceedings of the ACM Conference on Computer and Communications Security, pp. 3123–3140 (2021). https://doi.org/10.1145/3460120.3484576
6. Khanuja, S., et al.: MuRIL: Multilingual Representations for Indian Languages (2021)
7. Wolf Garbe: SymSpell vs. BK-tree: 100x faster fuzzy string search & spell checking. https://towardsdatascience.com/symspell-vs-bk-tree-100x-faster-fuzzy-string-search-spell-checking-c4f10d80a078. Accessed 07 May 2023

8. Majumder, P., Mitra, M., Chaudhuri, B.B.: N-gram: a language independent approach to IR and NLP (2002)

9. Gram: life4/homoglyphs: Homoglyphs: get similar letters, convert to ASCII, detect possible languages and UTF-8 group. https://github.com/life4/homoglyphs. Accessed 14 May 2023

10. Prabhu, A., Joshi, A., Shrivastava, M., Varma, V.: Towards Sub-Word Level Compositions for Sentiment Analysis of Hindi-English Code Mixed Text (2016)

11. Cohen, G., Afshar, S., Tapson, J., van Schaik, A.: EMNIST: an extension of MNIST to handwritten letters (2017)

12. Conneau, A., et al.: Unsupervised cross-lingual representation learning at scale. In: Proceedings of the Annual Meeting of the Association for Computational Linguistics, pp. 8440–8451 (2020). https://doi.org/10.18653/V1/2020.ACL-MAIN.747

13. Tesseract: Tesseract documentation | Tesseract OCR, https://tesseract-ocr.github.io/. Accessed 28 May 2023

14. austin-hill/EMNIST-CNN: austin-hill/EMNIST-CNN: Convolutional neural network implemented in pytorch achieving a 99.71% test accuracy on the EMNIST dataset. https://github.com/austin-hill/EMNIST-CNN. Accessed 28 May 2023

TextGram: Towards a Better Domain-Adaptive Pretraining

Sharayu Hiwarkhedkar[1,3], Saloni Mittal[1,3], Vidula Magdum[1,3],
Omkar Dhekane[1,3], Raviraj Joshi[2,3(✉)], Geetanjali Kale[1], and Arnav Ladkat[1,3]

[1] Pune Institute of Computer Technology, Pune, Maharashtra, India
[2] Indian Institute of Technology Madras, Chennai, Tamil Nadu, India
ravirajoshi@gmail.com
[3] L3Cube, Pune, India

Abstract. For green AI, it is crucial to measure and reduce the carbon footprint emitted during the training of large language models. In NLP, performing pre-training on Transformer models requires significant computational resources. This pre-training involves using a large amount of text data to gain prior knowledge for performing downstream tasks. Thus, it is important that we select the correct data in the form of domain-specific data from this vast corpus to achieve optimum results aligned with our domain-specific tasks. While training on large unsupervised data is expensive, it can be optimized by performing a data selection step before pretraining. Selecting important data reduces the space overhead and the substantial amount of time required to pre-train the model while maintaining constant accuracy. We investigate the existing selection strategies and propose our own domain-adaptive data selection method - *TextGram* - that effectively selects essential data from large corpora. We compare and evaluate the results of finetuned models for text classification task *with* and *without* data selection. We show that the proposed strategy works better compared to other selection methods.

Keywords: Data Selection · Domain Adaption · Pretraining · Fine-tuning · In-Domain · Out-Domain · Domain-Specific · Contextual embedding · Downstream Tasks · Text Classification

1 Introduction

The pervasive adoption of the internet, interconnected devices, social media networks, and cloud-based services has led to the generation of an enormous volume of data on a global scale. The development of state-of-the-art NLP models hinges on the effective usage of this large-scale data to train transformer-based language models termed as PLMs (pre-trained language models). To meet the demands of training PLMs, data scientists and engineers often rely on high-end hardware in production environments, entailing significant time and computational resources. Consequently, a critical aspect of the preprocessing phase involves judiciously selecting and utilizing high-quality data to optimize the training time and compute requirements of these models.

© The Author(s), under exclusive license to Springer Nature Switzerland AG 2024
B. R. Chakravarthi et al. (Eds.): SPELLL 2023, CCIS 2046, pp. 161–173, 2024.
https://doi.org/10.1007/978-3-031-58495-4_12

Our proposed work aims to enhance the training efficiency of pretraining models by employing improved data selection techniques with various data metrics. We have explored and compared the most recent data selection training methods used for the optimal pretraining and finetuning tasks.

A pre-trained model is a deep neural network that has previously been trained on a large dataset and can be reused for a variety of downstream applications. Choosing how much data and which data samples to use to train a machine learning model is an important step in the field of Artificial Intelligence. If the data is insufficient, it may result in either overfitting (the model has low training errors but high test errors) or underfitting (the model is incapable of capturing the relationship in the data) situations. If the data is too large, it may entail a significant amount of computational time and resources. It could also result in negative transfer, which refers to a large amount of data having a negative impact on the model.

Moreover, we employ a 12-layered Bidirectional Encoder Representations from Transformers (BERT) model as the base model [4]. BERT is trained on the complete English Wikipedia and Book corpus using Masked Language Modeling (MLM) as one of the pretraining strategies. In MLM, a portion of the input text is masked, and the model is trained to predict the masked words. This aids the model in comprehending word context and their relationships. Conducting adaptive pre-training with transformer models like BERT on out-of-domain corpus is a time and resource-intensive process.

A continuous pretraining of the BERT-based model with a large amount of general corpus data may take 3–4 days with a good GPU system and up to a week without GPU support. To shorten this duration, efficient data selection is necessary, wherein the dataset can be reduced while maintaining model accuracy. Data selection involves choosing the most relevant data from the vast corpus so that pretraining on the selected data can be accomplished in a shorter amount of time without compromising on results. Selecting the right data is thus a critical step. By implementing data selection before applying the pretraining task on huge datasets, we reduce the time and computational resources required. Through the exploration of available data selection techniques, we propose and implement a data selection strategy that enhances the pretraining task.

2   Motivation

Pre-training from scratch is a costly process with significant environmental impacts. Reducing the carbon footprint is a crucial factor to consider. A study at the University of Massachusetts reveals that the electricity consumed during transformer training can emit over 6,26,000 pounds of CO_2, which is five times more than a car's emissions [12]. By 2030, data centres might consume more than 6% of the world's energy. Utilizing intelligent data selection techniques not only saves computational time and resources but also protects the environment by avoiding negative transfer and eliminating data with adverse impacts on the output.

In various survey papers, methods like N-Grams, IF-IDF, and Perplexity-based selections have been considered. However, some of these methods are computationally expensive, making them less suitable for production-level use. Developing a data selection method that improves pretraining efficiency with reduced computational cost will benefit NLP researchers in building more effective systems.

Our goal is to perform better research and provide superior solutions by developing efficient data selection techniques for pretraining.

3   Related Work

The previous work done, which focuses on data selection strategies, is discussed in this Section. A few techniques that are majorly used in machine translation are context-dependent and independent-based functions. They include N-Grams, TF-IDF, Perplexity-based selection, Cross-entropy, etc. Generally, the subsets of data are varied for training. NMT iterates over the training corpus in several epochs, using a different subset in every iteration. Another method mentioned is gradual fine-tuning, where the training data is reduced in a few iterations [14].

Matthias et al. suggest a weighting scheme which allows us to sort sentences based on the frequency of unseen n-grams [5]. The technique is applied to the BREC corpus with relatively simple sentences from the travel domain for the translation task. Marlies et al. use ngrams LMs to determine the domain relevance of sentence pairs and provide a comparative analysis with LSTM-based selection [14]. The authors also introduce dynamic data selection - a method in which the selected subset of training data varies between different training epochs. Additionally, Prafulla et al. use a TF-IDF-based approach for a clustering problem [2]. Another paper by Catarina et al. also proposes a variant of the TF-IDF data selection method [3].

To compute the TF-IDF measure in their experiments, the authors first pre-process the corpus and consider every sentence in the domain corpus as a query sentence, and every sentence in the generic corpus as a document. Then, the authors obtain, for each query, a ranking of the documents computed with cosine similarity. This ranking is stored for every query sentence and used to retrieve the K-nearest neighbors (KNN) necessary to obtain different data selection sizes.

The work [1] investigates efficient domain adaptation for the task of statistical machine translation by retrieving the most pertinent sentences from a large general-domain parallel corpus. An assumption in domain adaptation, as described in this paper, is that a general-domain corpus of a sizable length will likely contain some sentences that are relevant to the target domain and should thus be used for training. The paper also highlights that the general-domain corpus is expected to contain sentences that are so dissimilar to the domain that using them to train our model will be more harmful than beneficial. It presents a method that applies language modeling techniques to Machine Translation, called the *perplexity-based selection* method, which has been done by Gao et al. [7], as well as by Moore and Lewis [11]. The ranking of the sentences in a general-domain corpus based on the in-domain's perplexity score has also been applied to machine translation by both Yasuda et al. [15] and Foster et al. [6].

Another perplexity-based method proposed by Moore and Lewis is *cross entropy* and *cross-entropy difference* [11]. A low perplexity sentence corresponds to a low cross-entropy sentence under the in-domain language model. The author used a language model trained on the Chinese side of the IWSLT corpus.

There are a few more complex techniques that are based on CNNs. Various algorithms are implemented under the data selection techniques like Recurrent Neural Network, EM-Clustering, Nearest Neighbor Selection, CNNs, a 5-parameter variation of FDA - FDA5, classification, etc.

4   Experimentation Setup

We discuss the experimental settings that we followed to obtain and evaluate efficient pre-training by data selection.

4.1   Datasets

For our experiment, we mainly use two kinds of data. One is *out-domain*, which acts as a general domain corpus, and another is *in-domain*, which is a domain-specific corpus. The in-domain data is smaller compared to the out-domain data. The summary of datasets used is shown in Table 1.

Table 1. Datasets used in the experiments

Dataset	Description	Corpus Size	Data Columns
RealNews	This is a large corpus of news articles	1 M news	Text, Score
IMDb	Movie review dataset	50,000 reviews	Review sentiments

The *RealNews* Dataset is a large corpus of news articles scraped from Common Crawl [16]. It consists of 5000 news domains that are indexed by Google news. *IMDb Movie Reviews* is a binary sentiment analysis dataset made up of 50,000 reviews from IMDb that have been classified as positive or negative [9]. The IMDb Reviews dataset is widely used in many NLP subdomains. Here, we use the RealNews dataset as an out-domain dataset while IMDb Movie Reviews as an in-domain corpus. We evaluate our model on entertainment-specific domains.

4.2   Model Architecture

As shown in Fig. 1, we collect and preprocess data and apply a selection strategy to obtain the best data. The selected data is then used for the second pretraining phase, with the objective of Masked Language Modeling (MLM). Finally, using the IMDb dataset [8], we perform the classification task and analyze the results.

In the experiments, we utilize the Bidirectional Encoder Representations from Transformers (BERT) model for the MLM task and fine-tune it for text classification on the target dataset, IMDb dataset [8]. The BERT model comprises 12 layers of bidirectional transformer-based encoder blocks, where each layer consists of 12 self-attention heads. The BERT base cased model is pre-trained on a large English corpus using a self-supervised approach with the objective of Masked Language Modeling (MLM).

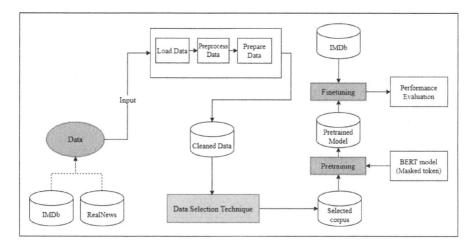

Fig. 1. High-Level System Architecture Diagram - The corpus (both in-domain and out-domain) is first fed into pre-processing pipeline which will prepare the data for selection. Then, the selection strategy will be applied that will select data from out-domain based on in-domain training set. Further, selected corpus is used for continuous pre-training of BERT model. After pre-training, we perform fine-tuning to adapt the model on in-domain corpus.

4.3   Data Selection Techniques

This section explains the data selection techniques used for experimentation.

N-Grams Coverage. N-grams define the sequence of 'n' contiguous elements from text or speech data. N-gram-based models are very popular in computational linguistics (for instance, statistical natural language processing). Many researchers have found this technique intuitive for exploring and implementing the variations of data selection techniques.

The notion is to select top_k sentences from the general domain corpus based on the top n-grams from the target domain corpus. This is also called the adaptive approach as we consider the target domain for the selection method. A

non-adaptive approach, on the other hand, only considers the general domain corpus and selects sentences based on the same notion of n-grams.
Selection Criteria (S):

$$S = \left[frequency(n - gram) \right] \tag{1}$$

for n = 1,2,3...
Another selection approach based upon the n-gram model includes weighing each sentence in the corpus as a sum over the frequency of unseen n-grams, ranking the sentences based on the sentence weight, and then selecting top_k sentences from the ranked list.

TF-IDF Based Selection. This approach leverages the TF-IDF weighing scheme. TF-IDF measure is widely used in information retrieval. The term frequency (TF) defines the frequency of a term (t) in a document (d). The inverse document frequency (IDF) measures how much information a word can provide. Together, they are used to find the importance of a given word in a document.

The main idea of this approach is to represent each document D as a TF-IDF vector $(w_1, w_2, w_3, ...w_m)$ where m is the size of the vocabulary. The TF-IDF weight (w_k) for the kth term in the term vector is calculated as,

$$w_k = TF_k * IDF_k \tag{2}$$

where,

$$TF_k = \frac{\text{count of } k \text{ in } document(D)}{\text{no. of terms in } document(D)} \tag{3}$$

and,

$$IDF_k = \frac{\text{count of } documents \text{ in collection}}{\text{count of } documents \text{ containing } k \text{ -th term}} \tag{4}$$

The similarity between two documents is calculated using cosine similarity and finally, documents are selected based upon the similarity score.

Perplexity Based Data Selection. In this method, the main idea is that the sentences in the general-domain corpus are scored by their perplexity score using an in-domain language model, and only the lowest ones are kept.

Perplexity is an intrinsic evaluation metric for language models. It entails determining some metric to evaluate the language model as a whole, without regard for the particular tasks it will be used for.

There are several approaches to perplexity-based data selection, the one used in this work is described below.

Perplexity as the Normalized Inverse Probability of the Test Set. Unigram-Normalized Perplexity as a Language Model Performance Measure with Different Vocabulary Sizes [13] explains the perplexity as the inverse probability of the test set, normalized by the number of words in the sequence.

Models which assign probabilities to sequences of words $(w_1, w_2, w_3...w_n)$ are called language models.

For a test set,

$$W = w_1 w_2 w_3 ... w_n \tag{5}$$

By Chain Rule of Probability,

$$P(W) = P(w_1)P(w_2|w_1)P(w_3|w_{1:2})...P(w_n|w_{1:n-1}) \tag{6}$$

$$P(W) = \Pi_{k=1}^{n} P(w_k|w_{1:k-1}) \tag{7}$$

An n-gram language model looks at the previous (n-1) words to estimate the next word in the sequence. For example, a bigram model will look at the previous 1 word, so:

$$P(W) = P(w_{1:n}) = \Pi_{k=1}^{n} P(w_k|w_{k-1}) \tag{8}$$

As per the definition of perplexity in this approach, the paper thus defines the formula for perplexity (PPL) for a Bigram model as,

$$PPL(W) = \sqrt[n]{P(w_{1:n})} = \sqrt[n]{\Pi_{k=1}^{n} P(w_k|w_{k-1})} \tag{9}$$

Therefore, as we're using the inverse probability, a lower perplexity indicates a better model. This method is dependent on the size of the sequence, and it also implies that adding more sentences to the dataset will introduce more uncertainty, thus reducing the probability and increasing the perplexity. To make the metric independent of the dataset size, normalization of the probability is done by dividing it by the total number of tokens to obtain a per-word measure. This is why we take the n-th root (where n is the length of the sequence) of the inverse probability of the sequence.

Cross Entropy. Cross-entropy is a popular loss function in machine learning. It is used to compute the overall entropy between distributions. The loss function helps determine how effectively your program models the dataset.

In this method, we train a model on the entire dataset using cross entropy as the loss function. Next, we evaluate the model on the same dataset and calculate the cross entropy for each data point. The data points with low entropy scores are selected.

The cross-entropy score (CE) is calculated as follows:

$$CE(S, p, q) = -\sum_{i=1}^{n} p(x_i) \log q(x_i) \tag{10}$$

Here, x_i are the information units collected from a dataset and p and q are the probability distribution over them; p from the training dataset and q from the testing dataset.

TextRank. TextRank is a graph-based language processing technique that is utilized for keyword and sentence extraction [10]. It is grounded on the PageRank algorithm, commonly used for ranking web pages. The input text is tokenized into text units (words or sentences) that represent the vertices/nodes of a graph. Two nodes are connected using the co-occurrence relation, meaning that nodes having N co-occurring units are connected with an edge. The score of a vertex is calculated using the following formula:

$$WS(V_i) = (1 - d) + d \sum_{V_j \in In(V_i)} \frac{w_{j,i}}{\sum_{V_k \in Out(V_j)} w_{j,k}} WS(V_i) \tag{11}$$

Here, $WS(V_i)$ represents the score of a vertex V_i. Set In represents the set of vertices pointing to the vertex, and set Out represents the set of vertices the vertex points to. d is the damping factor, which describes the probability of visiting a vertex from the given vertex.

In the case of sentence extraction, similarity scores between sentences are calculated. Finally, the final vertex scores are sorted, and the top n vertices are selected. TextRank is an unsupervised technique that does not require training on domain-specific corpora and can be effectively used for extractive summarization.

Random Selection. Subsets of data (d) are collected at random from the huge dataset. The features or the type of data selected could not be promised in this case of data selection.

5   Proposed Technique - TextGram

The existing TextRank technique has a few shortcomings, such as its non-adaptive nature, meaning it does not consider in-domain datasets during data selection. This lack of adaptiveness hampers the performance of the model when fine-tuned for downstream tasks. To address this limitation, we have introduced an n-gram technique in the initial processing phase of TextRank.

In our proposed approach, we start by selecting the top k in-domain sentences based on the highest frequencies of n-grams calculated from the in-domain corpus. These selected in-domain sentences are then combined with the out-domain corpus. Subsequently, we perform paraphrase mining on this combined set of sentences to determine similarity scores for various pairs of sentences.

To construct a graph representation, we create a sparse matrix using the similarity scores, where the nodes represent sentences and the edges indicate the scores between the sentences. This graph is then fed into the PageRank algorithm, which computes the scores of each sentence based on the node weights. The obtained scores are then sorted in descending order, and we select the top N sentences.

Next, we separate the in-domain sentences from the selected sentences, resulting in the final selected out-domain dataset. As a result of incorporating n-grams, our technique yields better results compared to the original TextRank approach. Refer to Fig. 2 for the TextGram architecture.

Algorithm 1: TextGram

Input: IMDb dataset (50K), Realnews (1M)
Output: selectedRealnews dataset (0.25M)
   IMDb ← IMDb dataset;
   bigrams ← {};
   for sentence in IMDb **do**
       tokens ← wordTokenize(sentence);
       for i in range (len(tokens)) **do**
           bigram ← tokens[i] + tokens[i+1];
           bigrams[bigram] ← bigrams[bigram]+1;
       end for
   end for
   Sort *bigrams* dictionary in descending order based on frequency values.
   TopBiGrams ← *bigrams*[0...100]
   selectedIMDb ← []
   for sentence in IMDb **do**
       for bigram in TopBiGrams **do**
           if bigram in sentence **then**
               selectedIMDb ← sentence;
           end if
       end for
   end for
   realnews ← Realnews;
   collatedDataset ← [];
   for sentence in realnews **do**
       collatedDataset.append(sentence,'Realnews')
   end for
   for sentence in selectedIMDb **do**
       collatedDataset.append(sentence,'IMDb')
   end for
   SimilarityScores ← paraphraseMining(collatedDataset);   // Similarity score is a list of 3-tuple element: //(score,sentence1Index,sentence2Index)
   similarityMatrix ← [][]
   for i in range(len(SimilarityScores) **do**
       sentence1Index = SimilarityScores[i][1]
       sentence2Index = [SimilarityScores[i][2]

similarityMatrix[sentence1Index][sentence2Index] ← SimilarityScores[i][0]
similarityMatrix[sentence2Index][sentence1Index] ← SimilarityScores[i][0]
end for
sentencesGraph ← Graph(similarityMatrix)
rankings ← = Pagerank(sentencesGraph)
Sort *rankings* list of tuples in descending order based on rank of sentences.
selectedRealnews ← []
for i in range(2500000) **do**
    tupleSentence ← collatedDataset[ranking[i][0]]
    if tupleSentence[1] = 'Realnews' **then**
        selectedRealnews ← tupleSentence[0] ;
    end if
end for

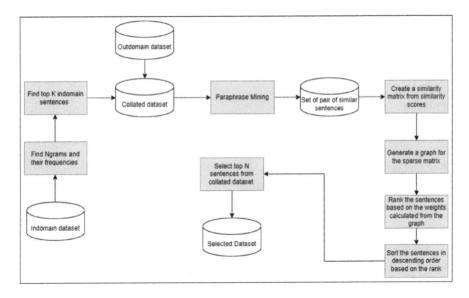

Fig. 2. Architecture diagram: TextGram based ranking

6 Evaluation Results

6.1 Fine-Tuning Without Data Selection

Below we discuss the results of our classification experiments using *with selection* and *without selection* strategy and measure the classification quality using performance metrics such as Accuracy, Precision, Recall, and F1-score.

Table 2 shows evaluation scores for our classification task. We got the following results after performing the pre-training step on *RealNews* examples **Without Data Selection** and then performing the downstream task with the IMDb dataset.

Table 2. Fine-tuning results without data selection

Accuracy (%)	Recall (%)	Precision (%)	F1 Score (%)
90.40	89.91	90.80	90.36

The above table shows that, When we directly fine-tune our RealNews pretrained model using the IMDb review dataset with no selection strategy applied, we see a very small change in F1-score value compared to F1-scores using *with-selection* (see Table 3).

6.2   Fine-Tuning with Data Selection

Table 3. The classification results after fine-tuning of bert-base model on IMDb dataset. Before fine-tuning, the bert-base is first pretrained on the out-domain selected data. Above table shows the effect of various data selection strategies on the performance of the model.

Data Selection Technique	Accuracy (%)	Recall (%)	Precision (%)	F1 Score (%)
Random Selection	90.77	90.32	91.14	90.73
N-Grams	91.03	90.44	91.52	90.97
Perplexity	90.99	90.96	91.02	90.99
Cross-Entropy	90.81	90.42	91.14	90.77
TextRank	90.60	89.23	91.75	90.47
TextGram	**91.02**	**91.02**	**91.02**	**91.02**

The Table 3 shows a comparative analysis of fine-tuning results on the IMDb dataset, using various data selection strategies which are discussed in Sect. 4. Our evaluation shows that the TextGram-based ranking strategy outperforms the other selection strategies.

7   Conclusion and Future Work

An extensive literature review of the most widely used methods for effective data selection tasks was conducted for pretraining. We implemented these techniques and developed a suitable and optimum technique from the same. The scores say that N-Grams gave the highest accuracy. Also, TextRank is studied to have better impacts when combined with N-Grams because of its graph-based complex but deep implementations and research. TextRank is mostly used for sentence similarity and keyword extraction, but by studying the Page Rank algorithm, we developed this technique to work on domain adaptive data selection tasks. The techniques implemented give a score of around 1% similar to or higher than the baseline numbers computed without data selection.

Acknowledgments. This work was done under the L3Cube Pune mentorship program. We would like to express our gratitude towards our mentors at L3Cube for their continuous support and encouragement.

References

1. Axelrod, A., He, X., Gao, J.: Domain adaptation via pseudo in-domain data selection. In: Proceedings of the 2011 Conference on Empirical Methods in Natural Language Processing, pp. 355–362 (2011)
2. Bafna, P., Pramod, D., Vaidya, A.: Document clustering: TF-IDF approach. In: 2016 International Conference on Electrical, Electronics, and Optimization Techniques (ICEEOT), pp. 61–66. IEEE (2016)
3. Cruz Silva, C., Liu, C.H., Poncelas, A., Way, A.: Extracting in-domain training corpora for neural machine translation using data selection methods. Association for Computational Linguistics (2018)
4. Devlin, J., Chang, M.W., Lee, K., Toutanova, K.: BERT: pre-training of deep bidirectional transformers for language understanding. arXiv preprint: arXiv:1810.04805 (2018)
5. Eck, M., Vogel, S., Waibel, A.: Low cost portability for statistical machine translation based on N-gram frequency and TF-IDF. In: Proceedings of the Second International Workshop on Spoken Language Translation (2005)
6. Foster, G., Goutte, C., Kuhn, R.: Discriminative instance weighting for domain adaptation in statistical machine translation. In: Proceedings of the 2010 Conference on Empirical Methods in Natural Language Processing, pp. 451–459 (2010)
7. Gao, J., Goodman, J., Li, M., Lee, K.F.: Toward a unified approach to statistical language modeling for Chinese. ACM Trans. Asian Lang. Inf. Process. (TALIP) **1**(1), 3–33 (2002)
8. Ladkat, A., Miyajiwala, A., Jagadale, S., Kulkarni, R., Joshi, R.: Towards simple and efficient task-adaptive pre-training for text classification. arXiv preprint: arXiv:2209.12943 (2022)
9. Maas, A.L., Daly, R.E., Pham, P.T., Huang, D., Ng, A.Y., Potts, C.: Learning word vectors for sentiment analysis. In: Proceedings of the 49th Annual Meeting of the Association for Computational Linguistics: Human Language Technologies, pp. 142–150. Association for Computational Linguistics, Portland (2011). https://aclanthology.org/P11-1015
10. Mihalcea, R., Tarau, P.: TextRank: bringing order into text. In: Proceedings of the 2004 Conference on Empirical Methods in Natural Language Processing, pp. 404–411 (2004)
11. Moore, R.C., Lewis, W.: Intelligent selection of language model training data. In: Proceedings of the ACL 2010 Conference Short Papers, pp. 220–224 (2010)
12. Parcollet, T., Ravanelli, M.: The energy and carbon footprint of training end-to-end speech recognizers (2021)

13. Roh, J., Oh, S.H., Lee, S.Y.: Unigram-normalized perplexity as a language model performance measure with different vocabulary sizes. arXiv preprint: arXiv:2011.13220 (2020)
14. Van Der Wees, M., Bisazza, A., Monz, C.: Dynamic data selection for neural machine translation. arXiv preprint: arXiv:1708.00712 (2017)
15. Yasuda, K., Zhang, R., Yamamoto, H., Sumita, E.: Method of selecting training data to build a compact and efficient translation model. In: Proceedings of the Third International Joint Conference on Natural Language Processing: Volume-II (2008)
16. Zellers, R., Holtzman, A., Rashkin, H., Bisk, Y., Farhadi, A., Roesner, F., Choi, Y.: Defending against neural fake news (2020)

Abusive Social Media Comments Detection for Tamil and Telugu

Mani Vegupatti[1]([✉])[iD], Prasanna Kumar Kumaresan[2][iD], Swetha Valli[3][iD],
Kishore Kumar Ponnusamy[4][iD], Ruba Priyadharshini[5][iD],
and Sajeetha Thavaresan[6][iD]

[1] University of Galway, Galway, Ireland
mani.vegupatti@gmail.com
[2] College of Science and Engineering, University of Galway, Galway, Ireland
[3] Thiagarajar College of Engineering, Madurai, Tamil Nadu, India
[4] Digital University of Kerala, Veiloor, India
[5] Gandhigram Rural Institute-Deemed to be University, Dindigul, Tamil Nadu, India
[6] Eastern University Srilanka, Chenkalady, Sri Lanka
sajeethas@esn.ac.lk

Abstract. Multilingualism has added a new dimension to the issue of abusive language detection despite the increasing number of efforts to prevent abusive content from being shared on social media. When it comes to low-resource languages such as Tamil and Telugu, the difficulty is further increased by the lack of available resources. YouTube functions as both a video-sharing platform and a social media network. YouTube allows users to establish profiles and upload videos for their followers to view, like, and comment on. Users may find it offensive and detrimental to their mental health when other users post abusive comments on videos or in response to the comments of other users. It has been observed that the language used in these comments is frequently informal and multilingual, does not always correspond to the language's formal syntactic and lexical structure, and involves code-switching. To deal with the above issues we propose to use the multilingual pre-trained embeddings and to be more specific, our strategy can be divided into selecting suitable pre-trained models and post which adapting the models using various fine-tuning techniques to the abusive comments detection task. We use the Bidirectional Encoder Representation from Transformers (BERT) as an Encoder to generate phrase representations so that we can accurately capture the precise contextual characteristics of posts. We conduct experiments on the YouTube comments data set using various multilingual models and several fine-tuning techniques. We compared and analyzed results across the above models along with multiple classical machine learning models and found that IndicBERT and MuRIL large-cased models perform well in Tamil-English and Telugu comments data sets respectively.

Keywords: Abusive detection · Transformer · Fine-tuning · Machine learning

B. R. Chakravarthi et al. (Eds.): SPELLL 2023, CCIS 2046, pp. 174–187, 2024.
https://doi.org/10.1007/978-3-031-58495-4_13

1   Introduction

In order to facilitate interaction and cultivate a sense of community, social media platforms commonly extend the opportunity for readers to offer their feedback, share thoughts on posts, and engage using multimedia content [1]. This open avenue of user comments, while often fostering positive engagement, does come with certain challenges such as instances of abusive behavior, ranging from cyber-bullying and profanity to abusive and hate speech, which can cast a negative shadow over the reputation of news portals that host such content. This not only exposes these platforms to potential legal consequences, as seen in cases where comments incite unlawful actions but also has the unfortunate effect of discouraging genuine readership and customer loyalty [2,3].

In recognition of these issues, major social media corporations have sought solutions through the employment of human moderators. These moderators, however, frequently find themselves overwhelmed by the sheer volume and toxicity of the comments they have to review [4]. The resulting delays in the moderation process can lead to dissatisfaction among readers when their non-abusive comments do not promptly appear online [5]. Smaller news-focused social media entities, lacking the resources to maintain a moderation team, sometimes resort to the drastic measure of disabling user comments altogether [6].

In certain scenarios, an automated software-based system might appear to be an attractive option for comment moderation. This could be particularly relevant for platforms facing financial constraints that hinder the hiring of human moderators. However, it's essential to approach this solution with a dose of realism [7]. Counting on an entirely automated moderation process to be foolproof is a challenging expectation to hold. The inherent complexities of language and communication mean that abusive comments can often be veiled in irony, sarcasm, or subtle forms of harassment devoid of explicit profanity. These nuances pose considerable challenges for machine-based systems to effectively tackle [8].

A more pragmatic approach involves the development of semi-automatic systems that work in tandem with human moderators, rather than aiming to replace them outright. This perspective, perhaps previously under-explored, acknowledges the value of human judgment and the limitations of purely automated processes [9]. By assisting moderators during their availability, these semi-automatic systems can help alleviate the burden of moderation and enhance the overall quality of user interactions. In this way, a balanced and thoughtful approach to comment moderation can be established, promoting healthy engagement while curtailing abusive behavior.

In this paper, we collected the data set from the shared task Abusive Comment Detection in Tamil and Telugu-DravidianLangTech 2023[1]. We implemented various transformer models with different methods and five machine-learning models. We begin by describing the corpora and the related work for this task, analyze the data sets, explain the methodology, and discuss the results & evaluation, and conclude.

---

[1] https://codalab.lisn.upsaclay.fr/competitions/11096.

2   Related Work

The recognition and detection of abusive language in natural language have garnered significant attention within the research community. Nonetheless, the landscape of abusive language is intricate and exhibits its own nuances. In 2017, [10] proposed a classification of abusive language that divides it into two primary categories: "Directed" (aimed at specific individuals or entities) and "Generalized" (targeting broader groups). Further granularity exists within this classification through the separation into "Explicit" and "Implicit" subcategories, which characterize the level of explicitness in the abusive content.

[11] introduced a data set that labeled thousands of tweets as "hate", "offensive", or "neither". Their focus was on developing a classifier capable of identifying hate/offensive speech within tweets. Utilizing this data set, they investigated the impact of linguistic features such as character and word n-grams on classifier performance. Their classification approach incorporated additional features like binary and count indicators for hashtags, mentions, retweets, and URLs, along with metrics related to tweet length in terms of characters, words, and syllables. It was noted, however, that their most successful models struggled to differentiate between hate and offensive posts.

In 2018, [12] employed recurrent neural networks (RNNs) to detect offensive language in English text. They achieved substantial success in this task, obtaining a 0.9320 F1-score through ensemble methods. RNNs, with their capacity to retain the output from each step of the model, enable the capture of contextual nuances within the text-critical for accurate detection. While RNNs have demonstrated their aptitude for language models, other neural network architectures like Convolutional Neural Networks (CNNs) and Long Short-Term Memory (LSTM) networks have also shown prowess in identifying hate/offensive speech [13,14]. More recently, Transformer-based [15] language models such as BERT and m-BERT [16] have gained prominence across various downstream tasks, including classification and spam detection. Transformer models have proven their superiority over several traditional deep learning models [17] such as CNN-GRU and LSTM.

Given the remarkable performance exhibited by Transformer-based models, we focus on the development of these models to address our classification challenge. Now, there is an ever-increasing need for the detection of abusive comments on social media with more and more people progressively start using multiple social platforms. This task can broadly fit into sentiment classification in the General Language Understanding Evaluation (GLUE) tasks [18]. In the Natural Language Understanding (NLU) paradigm, the pre-trained Language Model Bidirectional Encoder Representations from Transformers (BERT) [16] exhibited state-of-the-art performance in the GLUE benchmarks. This architecture uses pre-training of Masked Language Modelling (MLM) with a large amount of unlabelled data and fine-tuning for specific tasks like Named Entity Recognition and classification with a small amount of labeled data.

3   Dataset Description

The total number of comments from various languages is listed in Table 1. This data set includes Tamil-English and Telugu language comments taken from YouTube. The comments are labelled as hope speech, homophobia, misandry, counter speech, transphobic, xenophobia misogyny, and none of the above for Tamil-English and for Telugu labeled as hate and non-hate as shown in Table 2. Further, The given data set is sorted as training, development, and testing.

- **Hope-speech:** A hope speech is a type of communication or expression that tries to give the audience or the recipients a sense of optimism, inspiration, or motivation. It entails spreading messages of optimism, opportunity, and hope frequently amid obstacles, hardships, or challenging situations. *EXAMPLE:* Super movie Ida pathu neriya per thiruthu vanga nu numburan. Love is love.
- **Homophobia:** Homophobia is the use of disparaging or discriminating rhetoric towards someone based on their sexual orientation. It entails the use of epithets, insults, or disparaging statements that are explicitly directed at LGBT (lesbian, gay, bisexual, or transgender) people. *EXAMPLE:* Yes we're so gay and we're always gay.
- **Misandry:** A strong or excessive hate, bias, or discrimination towards men is referred to as misandry. It refers to the occurrence of offensive or discriminatory language that targets men in the context of abusive language detection. *EXAMPLE:* veera vaanjinatha priyan veera tamil singam dai naye unne seruppala adikkanu naye paradesi naye.
- **Counter-speech:** Refers to a tactic or method intended to counteract hurtful or abusive talk with constructive and positive speech. It entails rebuking or combating abusive words by encouraging empathy, respect, and understanding. *EXAMPLE:* oru naaal aana feel panuvaanga bro avunga enda itha panonu... Unma theriya varumbothu.
- **Transphobic:** Transphobia is the term used to describe hostility, prejudice, or aversion towards transgender people or those whose gender identity differs from the sex they were assigned at birth. Transphobia, as used in the context of abusive language detection, refers to the use of disparaging or discriminating language that targets transgender people. *EXAMPLE:* ithu pombalaya aambalaya mental mari pesuthu Romba.
- **Xenophobia:** In terms of nationality, race, or culture, xenophobia is the fear, prejudice, or discrimination against people or groups who are seen as being foreign or different. Xenophobia refers to the existence of disparaging or discriminatory language that targets people based on their perceived foreignness or cultural origin in the context of abusive language detection. *EXAMPLE:* Chappa mookanunga appadi enna thaan thimbanungalo. Nammala saavadikranunga.
- **Misogyny:** The term "misogyny" describes a pervasive bias, dislike, or disdain for women or girls. Misogyny is the use of offensive or discriminatory language that targets women in particular or expresses sexist ideas and beliefs. *EXAMPLE:* Gotha neethandi Indha naatin sabakedu gommalakka ungala

mothala kollanumdi thevadiyalugala chai. **HATE:** In the context of abusive language detection, "hate" refers to the presence of language that expresses intense hostility, animosity, or prejudice towards individuals or groups based on certain characteristics like race, ethnicity, religion, gender, sexual orientation, or other protected attributes. *EXAMPLE:* Prajala samasyala gurinchi okaru kuda matladaru kadha ..nice.

- **NON-HATE:** When discussing abusive language detection, the term "non-hate"s refers to language that does not reflect hatred, enmity, or prejudice towards specific people or groups based on factors like their race, ethnicity, religion, gender, sexual orientation, or other protected traits. *EXAMPLE:* Mata tadabada kunda clear ga ktr sir matalu super.

Out of 17,292 comments taken from YouTube, we found 3,499 Tamil comments, 9,293 Tamil-English comments, and 4,500 Telugu comments.

Table 1. Dataset Description

Langauges	No. of Comments
Tamil-English	9293
Telugu	4500

Table 2. No. of comments in each set with each class for Tamil-English and Telugu

Languages	Lables	Training	Development	Testing
Tamil-English	None-of-the-above	3720	919	1141
	Hope-Speech	213	53	70
	Homophobia	172	43	56
	Misandry	830	218	292
	Counter-speech	348	95	88
	Transphobic	157	40	58
	Xenophobia	297	70	95
	Misogyny	211	50	57
Total		**5948**	**1488**	**1857**
Telugu	Hate	250	-	2061
	Non-hate	250	-	1939
Total		**500**	**-**	**4000**

4 Methodology

We formulate this task as a multi-class classification, where the abusive comment is a set of words that belongs to one of the categories in the given set of categories. This is shown by the below Formula 1.

$$P(s_i \mid [w_1 \ w_2 \ w_3 \ ... \ w_n]) \tag{1}$$

$$where,$$
$$s_i = abusive \ comment \ category_i \in S$$
$$S = set \ of \ abusive \ comment \ categories : \ \{s_1 \ s_2 \ s_3 \ ... \ s_n\}$$
$$[w_1 \ w_2 \ w_3 \ ... \ w_n] = Abusive \ comment : \ A \ sequence \ of \ words$$

In our methodology, we adopt a strategic approach that sidesteps the need to build a language model from scratch. Thus we employ the transfer learning paradigm, capitalizing on the capabilities of the pre-trained language model which is then fine-tuned to cater specifically to the task of detecting abusive comments. For this purpose, we opt for a BERT-based architecture, a versatile choice renowned for its effectiveness in handling language understanding tasks. Our focal point lies in addressing the challenge of abusive comment detection within code-mixed text originating from Tamil-English or Telugu social media contexts.

Among the array of techniques available for fine-tuning BERT, we navigate the landscape with discernment. These methods encompass feature extraction, selective fine-tuning of certain model layers, complete fine-tuning of all layers, and retaining the language model in a fixed state while fine-tuning solely the classification or last layer a strategy adeptly demonstrated in previous research [19,20]. In light of our objectives, we make a deliberate choice: we harness the potential of a fully fine-tuned BERT model, enabling comprehensive adaptation to our abusive comment detection task. Additionally, we explore the alternative avenue of fine-tuning solely the last layer while keeping the BERT backbone frozen. This multifaceted approach allows us to evaluate the trade-offs and performance variations associated with these distinct fine-tuning strategies.

Central to our methodology is the recognition of the nuances embedded in code-mixed text from Tamil or Telugu social media spheres. By selecting the fully fine-tuned BERT model, we capitalize on its capacity to grasp intricate linguistic patterns specific to the target languages and the task at hand. Simultaneously, the fine-tuned last layer with a frozen BERT model augments our exploratory toolkit, potentially uncovering a balance between nuanced understanding and leveraging the pre-trained model's inherent language versatility. Our methodology, thus grounded in strategic choices, seeks to extract the utmost potential from the transfer learning paradigm within the context of abusive comment detection in code-mixed social media text.

After a thorough analysis of the available BERT-based pre-trained models, we have determined that MuRIL and IndicBERT are the most suitable choices for our designated tasks. Our decision is founded on a series of factors elucidated in previous research [21–23]. Moreover, we intend to conduct a performance comparison involving these selected models alongside mBERT and classical machine learning models.

- Multilingual models like mBERT were trained on common word piece vocabulary which leads to the skewed representation of Indian languages.
- In these Multilingual models, The major grammar representation of a sentence is from English and related languages. Hence, these models perform poorly in those languages that differ in grammatical ordering.
- It is proven many times, often those models additionally pre-trained on the same language of downstream task perform better than the models only fine-tuned for the downstream task.

MuRIL stands out as a distinctive Indian Language Model, forged through extensive training on diverse Indian language corpora. However, its uniqueness doesn't end there. Beyond these foundational corpora, MuRIL's prowess is amplified through the integration of supplementary vocabulary via translation and transliteration techniques. This innovative augmentation serves a dual purpose: fostering parallel learning across languages and enabling effective handling of code-switching scenarios. As elucidated by [22], this sophisticated approach empowers MuRIL to navigate the complexities of multilingual contexts with unparalleled finesse.

IndicBERT, another prominent Indian Language Model, distinguishes itself through its exclusive training on a rich tapestry of Indian language corpora, specifically the expansive IndicCorp v2 dataset. This comprehensive compilation spans an impressive collection of 22 Indic Languages, embodying the diversity and intricacies inherent to the Indian linguistic landscape. Crafted upon the foundation of ALBERT architecture, IndicBERT's compactness, relative to MuRIL, is a hallmark attribute, boasting a significantly reduced parameter count. This insightful perspective, as articulated by [23], underscores IndicBERT's strategic design and its potential to excel in a variety of language-oriented tasks.

Our approach incorporates pre-trained transformer models sourced from the Hugging Face transformers model hub[2]. This hub serves as a centralized platform, offering a cohesive interface for both fine-tuning these models and constructing versatile pipelines. Beyond their proficiency in Masked Language Modeling, the hub encompasses a gamut of models tailored for various specialized downstream tasks, including but not limited to Named Entity Recognition and sentence classification. This comprehensive resource empowers us to harness state-of-the-art language models with ease and efficiency, streamlining our efforts toward effective abusive comment detection within code-mixed text.

We use the below models from the Hugging Face transformers model hub.

---

[2] https://huggingface.co/docs/transformers/index.

- bert-base-multilingual-cased[3]
- muril-base-cased[4]
- muril-large-cased[5]
- indic-bert[6]

Leveraging the aforementioned BERT models, we employed both the fully fine-tuned and frozen BERT techniques, with the additional refinement of fine-tuning the classification layer. Within the scope of fully fine-tuned models, we implemented gradient clipping to mitigate potential issues stemming from gradient explosion during back-propagation. Consequently, our suite of fine-tuned models encompassed each of the BERT variants mentioned above, strategically tailored to optimize performance in the context of detecting abusive comments within code-mixed social media text.

- Fully fine-tuned (mBERT base case, MuRIL base case, MuRIL Large case, IndicBERT)
- Fully fine-tuned with gradient clipping (mBERT base case, MuRIL base case, MuRIL Large case, IndicBERT)
- frozen BERT with classification layer fine-tuned (mBERT base case, MuRIL base case, MuRIL Large case, IndicBERT)

In addition to our exploration of various models, our testing repertoire encompasses conventional machine learning approaches such as Naive Bayes, Support Vector Machines (SVM), Logistic Regression, Decision Tree, and Random Forest. To facilitate the transformation of textual data into numerical vectors for these models, we harnessed the utility of the CountVectorizer module from the renowned sci-kit-learn library[7]. This methodological divergence serves as a comprehensive strategy, enabling us to juxtapose the performance of traditional machine learning techniques against the cutting-edge transformer models. Through this comparative analysis, we aim to glean insights into the most effective avenues for detecting abusive comments within code-mixed social media text, while appreciating both established and contemporary methodologies.

5 Results and Discussion

5.1 Results

We evaluate the performance of the models using the macro average results of precision, recall, and F1-score. The scores achieved by each of the models are shown in the below Tables 3 and 4.

---

[3] https://huggingface.co/bert-base-multilingual-cased.
[4] https://huggingface.co/google/muril-base-cased.
[5] https://huggingface.co/google/muril-large-cased.
[6] https://huggingface.co/ai4bharat/indic-bert.
[7] https://scikit-learn.org.

Table 3. Results for Tamil-English languages in percentage

Model	Precision	Recall	F1-Score
Fully Fine-tuned model			
mBERT base cased	47%	40%	41%
MuRIL base cased	14%	18%	16%
MuRIL large cased	64%	50%	55%
IndicBERT	61%	**70%**	**64%**
Fully Fine-tuned with gradient clipped model			
mBERT base cased	44%	37%	38%
MuRIL base cased	13%	16%	14%
MuRIL large cased	57%	47%	50%
IndicBERT	55%	66%	60%
Frozen BERT with classification layer fine-tuned			
mBERT base cased	11%	13%	10%
MuRIL base cased	8%	12%	10%
MuRIL large cased	14%	12%	10%
IndicBERT	38%	61%	47%
Conventional Machine Learning models			
Naive Bayes	62%	27%	30%
SVM	59%	25%	28%
Logistic Regression	66%	38%	45%
Decision Tree	43%	33%	36%
Random Forest	**80%**	25%	28%

5.2 Discussions

In this section, We will analyze and discuss the size of models in terms of the number of parameters and compare the performance of models with one another and shared task leader models.

Size

mBERT: Fully fine-tuned mBERT base-cased model has 177 million parameters and the frozen BERT with classification layer only fine-tuned model has 1500 parameters only.

MuRIL: Fully fine-tuned models of the MuRIL base case and large case have 237 and 505 million parameters respectively. Whereas the model frozen BERT with a classification layer only fine-tuned has merely 6000(base) and 8000(large) parameters.

IndicBERT: Compared to mBERT and MuRIL, the fully fine-tuned Indic-NLP model is much smaller and has only 33 million parameters. The IndicNLP

Table 4. Results for Telugu languages in percentage

Model	Precision	Recall	F1-Score
Fully Fine-tuned model			
mBERT base cased	69%	69%	69%
MuRIL base cased	71%	71%	71%
MuRIL large cased	55%	54%	51%
IndicBERT	66%	66%	65%
Fully Fine-tuned with gradient clipped model			
mBERT base cased	69%	69%	69%
MuRIL base cased	67%	66%	65%
MuRIL large cased	**79%**	**79%**	**79%**
IndicBERT	71%	71%	71%
Frozen BERT with classification layer fine-tuned			
mBERT base cased	37%	43%	36%
MuRIL base cased	25%	50%	33%
MuRIL large cased	42%	42%	41%
IndicBERT	66%	66%	65%
Conventional Machine Learning models			
Naive Bayes	52%	51%	48%
SVM	64%	64%	64%
Logistic Regression	65%	65%	65%
Decision Tree	53%	53%	51%
Random Forest	54%	54%	53%

model frozen BERT with classification layer only fine-tuned has 6000 parameters same as MuRil base-cased.

Performance Evaluation

On evaluation, we found that IndicBert's fully-fine-tuned model leads the board in Tamil-English comments and MuRIL's fully-fine-tuned with gradient clipping is the topper in Telugu comments.

In Tamil-English, IndicBERT outperforms all the MuRIL-based models. In Telugu, MuRIL both base cased and large cased models outperform the IndicBERT.

Overall, in all the tasks the models with Frozen BERT layers and only classification last layer fine-tuned performs poorly irrespective of any chosen base model.

We also compared the performance of these models with top-scoring models of the shared task and the evaluation as follows.

Three models were submitted by team MUCS [24] for the Telugu comments data set. These models were constructed by the re-sampling approach and changing the feature extraction methods. The feature extractions used were TF-IDF, Language-specific-BERT, and multilingual BERT respectively for the three models. The third model achieved the highest F1 score of 75%. Our MuRIL large-cased models outperform this model with the F1 Score of 79%. Since MuRIL was pre-trained using translation and transliteration, it could outperform mBERT with better code-switching ability.

The team DeepBlueAI [25] reached first place in the Tamil-English comments data set with an F1 score of 55%. The model was built by mixing multiple language data sets of varying proportions on the XLM-RoBERTa base model. Later cross-validation was used to generalise the model. The IndicBERT model built by us outdoes this model with an F1 score of 64%. This was possible because of the focused pre-training of IndicBERT on Indian regional languages.

6   Conclusion

The data set Telugu contains the Telugu language comments written in Telugu and Latin scripts. In this scenario, the performance of mBERT and IndicBERT comes slightly closer to each other. Since MuRIL does parallel learning using translation and transliteration, MuRIL handles the code-switching efficiently while evaluating comments and outperforms both IndicBERT and mBERT.

The data set Tamil-English contains the Tamil language comments written in Latin script. IndicBERT performs better in this case since it has been trained predominantly in Indic languages and no code-switching is involved.

Both IndicBERT and MuRIL outperform the mBERT models. Though the IndicBERT model is much smaller than MuRIL, it is able to outperform or come closer to MuRIL. MuRIL large-cased model performs mostly better than the base-cased model.

In all the datasets, it is evident that the LMs pre-trained exclusively in the Indian language outperform the mBERT which is trained using a shared vocabulary base of multi-languages. Another factor that might be useful is translation and transliteration helps in handling code-switching efficiently.

Acknowledgement. This work was conducted with the financial support of the Science Foundation Ireland Centre for Research Training in Artificial Intelligence under Grant No. 18/CRT/6223, supported in part by a research grant from the Science Foundation Ireland (SFI) under Grant Number SFI/12/RC/2289_P2(Insight_2).

References

1. Hossain, A., Bishal, M., Hossain, E., Sharif, O., Hoque, M.M.: Combatant@ tamilnlp-acl2022: fine-grained categorization of abusive comments using logistic regression. In: Proceedings of the Second Workshop on Speech and Language Technologies for Dravidian Languages, pp. 221–228 (2022)

2. Chakravarthi, B.R.: Detection of homophobia and transphobia in Youtube comments. Int. J. Data Sci. Anal. 1–20 (2023)
3. Chakravarthi, B.R., et al.: Detecting abusive comments at a fine-grained level in a low-resource language. Nat. Lang. Process. J. **3**, 100006 (2023)
4. Chakravarthi, B.R., Jagadeeshan, M.B., Palanikumar, V., Priyadharshini, R.: Offensive language identification in dravidian languages using mpnet and cnn. Int. J. Inf. Manage. Data Insights **3**(1), 100151 (2023). Offensive language identification in dravidian languages using mpnet and cnn. textitInternat@inproceedingswiegand2019detection, title=Detection of abusive language: the problem of biased datasets, author=Wiegand, Michael and Ruppenhofer, Josef and Kleinbauer, Thomas, booktitle=Proceedings of the 2019 conference of the North American Chapter of the Association for Computational Linguistics: human language technologies, volume 1 (long and short papers), pages=602–608, year=2019 ional Journal of Information Management Data Insights **3**(1):100151, 2023
5. Navaneethakrishnan, S.C., et al.: Findings of shared task on sentiment analysis and homophobia detection of Youtube comments in code-mixed dravidian languages. In: Proceedings of the 14th Annual Meeting of the Forum for Information Retrieval Evaluation, pp. 18–21 (2022)
6. Prasad, G., Prasad, J., Gunavathi, C.: Gjg@ tamilnlp-acl2022: using transformers for abusive comment classification in Tamil. In: Proceedings of the Second Workshop on Speech and Language Technologies for Dravidian Languages, pp. 93–99 (2022)
7. Pavlopoulos, J., Malakasiotis, P., Androutsopoulos, I.: Deeper attention to abusive user content moderation. In: Proceedings of the 2017 Conference on Empirical Methods in Natural Language Processing, pp. 1125–1135 (2017)
8. Karim, M.R., Dey, S.K., Islam, T., Shajalal, M., Chakravarthi, B.R.: Multimodal hate speech detection from Bengali memes and texts. In: M, A.K., (ed.) Speech and Language Technologies for Low-Resource Languages. SPELL 2022. CCIS, vol. 1802, pp. 293–308. Springer, Cham (2022). https://doi.org/10.1007/978-3-031-33231-9_21
9. Subramanian, M., et al.: Offensive language detection in Tamil Youtube comments by adapters and cross-domain knowledge transfer. Comput. Speech Lang. **76**, 101404 (2022)
10. Wiegand, M., Ruppenhofer, J., Kleinbauer, T.: Detection of abusive language: the problem of biased datasets. In: Proceedings of the 2019 Conference of the North American Chapter of the Association for Computational Linguistics: Human Language Technologies, vol. 1, pp. 602–608 (2019)
11. Davidson, T., Warmsley, D., Macy, M., Weber, I.: Automated hate speech detection and the problem of offensive language. In: Proceedings of the International AAAI Conference on Web and Social Media, vol. 11, pp. 512–515 (2017)
12. Pitsilis, G.K., Ramampiaro, H., Langseth, H.: Effective hate-speech detection in twitter data using recurrent neural networks. Appl. Intell. **48**, 4730–4742 (2018)
13. Goldberg, Y.: A primer on neural network models for natural language processing. J. Artif. Intell. Res. **57**, 345–420 (2016)
14. De la Pena Sarracén, G.L., Pons, R.G., Cuza, C.E.M., Rosso, P.: Hate speech detection using attention-based LSTM. EVALITA Eval. NLP Speech Tools Italian, **12**, 235 (2018)
15. Vaswani, A., et al.: Attention is all you need. In: Advances in Neural Information Processing Systems, vol. 30 (2017)

16. Devlin, J., Chang, M.W., Lee, K., Toutanova, K.: Bert: pre-training of deep bidirectional transformers for language understanding. In: Proceedings of naacL-HLT, vol. 1, pp. 2 (2019)

17. Mathew, B., Saha, P., Yimam, S.M., Biemann, C., Goyal, P., Mukherjee, A.: Hatexplain: a benchmark dataset for explainable hate speech detection. In: Proceedings of the AAAI Conference on Artificial Intelligence, vol. 35, pp. 14867–14875 (2021)

18. Worsham, J., Kalita, J.: Multi-task learning for natural language processing in the 2020s: where are we going? Pattern Recogn. Lett. **136**, 120–126 (2020)

19. Reiss, T., Cohen, N., Bergman, L., Hoshen, Y.: Panda: adapting pretrained features for anomaly detection and segmentation. In: Proceedings of the IEEE/CVF Conference on Computer Vision and Pattern Recognition, pp. 2806–2814 (2021)

20. Zheng, J., Cai, F., Chen, H., de Rijke, M.: Pre-train, interact, fine-tune: a novel interaction representation for text classification. Inf. Process. Manage. **57**(6), 102215 (2020)

21. Devlin, J., Chang, M.W., Lee, K., Toutanova, K.: BERT: pre-training of deep bidirectional transformers for language understanding. *CoRR*,abs/1810.04805 (2018)

22. Khanuja, S., et al.: Muril: multilingual representations for Indian languages (2021)

23. Doddapaneni, S., et al.: Towards leaving no Indic language behind: building monolingual corpora, benchmark and models for Indic languages. In: Proceedings of the 61st Annual Meeting of the Association for Computational Linguistics, vol. 1, pp. 12402–12426 (2023)

24. Hegde, A., Kavya, G., Coelho, S., Shashirekha, H.L.: Mucs@dravidianlangtech-2023: leveraging learning models to identify abusive comments in code-mixed dravidian languages. In: Proceedings of the Third Workshop on Speech and Language Technologies for Dravidian Languages, Varna, Bulgaria, September 2023. Recent Advances in Natural Language Processing (2023)

25. Luo, Z., Wang, J.: Deepblueai@dravidianlangtech. In: Proceedings of the Third Workshop on Speech and Language Technologies for Dravidian Languages, Varna, Bulgaria, September 2023. Recent Advances in Natural Language Processing (2023)

26. Chakravarthi, B.R.: Hope speech detection in Youtube comments. Soc. Netw. Anal. Min. **12**(1), 75 (2022)

27. Kumaresan, P.K., Ponnusamy, R., Sherly, E., Sivanesan, S., Chakravarthi, B.R.: Transformer based hope speech comment classification in code-mixed text. In: M, A.K., et al (eds.) Speech and Language Technologies for Low-resource Languages. SPELL 2022. CCIS, vol. 1802, pp. 120–137. Springer, Cham (2022). https://doi.org/10.1007/978-3-031-33231-9_8

28. Vasantharajan, C., et al.: Fine-grained emotion detection dataset for tamil. In: M, A.K., (eds.) et al. Speech and Language Technologies for Low-resource Languages. SPELL 2022, vol. 1802, pp 35–50. Springer, Cham (2022). https://doi.org/10.1007/978-3-031-33231-9_3

29. Chakravarthi, B.R., Hande, A., Ponnusamy, R., Kumaresan, P.K., Priyadharshini, R.: How can we detect homophobia and transphobia? experiments in a multilingual code-mixed setting for social media governance. Int. J. Inf. Manage. Data Insights **2**(2), 100119 (2022)

30. Bharathi Raja Chakravarthi: Multilingual hope speech detection in English and dravidian languages. Int. J. Data Sci. Anal. **14**(4), 389–406 (2022)

31. Bharathi, B., Chakravarthi, B.R., Subalalitha, C.N, Sripriya, N., Pandian, A., Valli, S.: Findings of the shared task on speech recognition for vulnerable individuals in Tamil. In: Proceedings of the Second Workshop on Language Technology for Equality, Diversity and Inclusion, pp. 339–345 (2022)
32. Chakravarthi, B.R., et al.: Overview of the shared task on homophobia and transphobia detection in social media comments. In: Proceedings of the Second Workshop on Language Technology for Equality, Diversity and Inclusion, pp. 369–377 (2022)

Sales Forecasting from Group Conversation Using Natural Language Processing

R. S. Shudapreyaa[1], P. Santhiya[1(✉)], S. Kavitha[1], and P. Prakash[2]

[1] Department of Computer Science and Engineering, Kongu Engineering College, Perundurai, Erode, Tamilnadu, India
{shudhapreyaa.cse,psanthiya.cse,kavitha.cse}@kongu.edu
[2] Department of Medical Electronics, Velalar College of Engineering and Technology, Thindal, Erode, Tamilnadu, India

Abstract. Natural Language Processing (NLP) refers to a computer program's ability to understand spoken and written human language. It is utilized to do large-scale research, receive a more objective and accurate analysis, increase customer satisfaction, develop a better understanding of the industry, and empower employees. Forecasting future sales by projecting the number of products or services a sales unit sell is known as sales forecasting. The system anticipates revenue projections from group conversations in WhatsApp using NLP. In recent years, WhatsApp has become the most popular and effective way of communication. WhatsApp chats feature a wide range of talks amongst various groups of people. Several new machine-learning technologies are found advantageous. In this project, the data was fetched from WhatsApp to analyze the chat. By applying sentiment analysis, it provides positive, negative, and neutral parts of the chat which helps identify people's mindset about a particular product which can be further helpful in sales forecasting. The main objective of this project is to analyze the chat data using the NLP analyzer and extract valuable statistical insights. These insights will be used to enhance sales strategies and product development. By understanding the data obtained from the analyzer, we aim to make data-driven decisions that will lead to improved sales performance and customer engagement. This project analyzed the most active customer, the most active day in the group, the most active hour, the status of each customer who have messaged in the group, the customer who sent more text, media, links to the group, total messages sent per month, total messages sent per day, message count of each customer, top 10 customers who sent a letter to the group and are plotted in the form of a graph for the benefit of the admin. Through this, they can easily get information about the customer who are liking their products and who interacted with them the most.

Keywords: Text Blob · Vader · Sentiment Analysis · WhatsApp-Chat-Analyzer · Sales Forecasting · Natural Language Processing

1 Introduction

NLP refers to the ability of computer software to understand both spoken and written natural language, just like humans do. It utilizes Artificial Intelligence to process real-world data and make it comprehensible for computers, regardless of the language

B. R. Chakravarthi et al. (Eds.): SPELLL 2023, CCIS 2046, pp. 188–209, 2024.
https://doi.org/10.1007/978-3-031-58495-4_14

format. Similar to how humans use ears to hear and eyes to see, computers employ programs to read and microphones to gather audio data. The primary objective is to create a computer system capable of comprehending the content of documents, including the intricacies of language, and extract accurate information, insights, and organize them effectively. Sentiment classification algorithms are used to classify user input effectively. They have trouble with sentences, but not with pages or paragraphs. Many sentiment analysis approaches, such as lexical analyzer and machine learning are ineffective when used in online chatting. The majority of the extensive consideration is required in this scenario. NLP is divided into two stages: data pre-processing and algorithm development. NLP employs two basic techniques: syntax and semantic analysis. Social media platforms are used to communicate with customers to establish sales brand and website drive traffic which is also known as social media marketing. It is used to creating a compelling material to our social profile for listening and engaging with our followers, assessing our outcome and social media conduct advertisements. The whatsapp chat is extracted and pre-processed to get a clear dataset as shown in Fig. 1.

The primary social media sites are Whatsapp, Twitter, Facebook, LinkedIn, YouTube, and others. WhatsApp-Chat-Analyzer, an application, is used to analyze WhatsApp discussions. It generates numerous charts based on conversation files which were exported from the WhatsApp. The term sentiment analysis refers to process of determining a text evaluative nature. Traditional sentiment analysis studies mainly try to determine if a sentence is favourable, negative, or neutral. These findings demonstrate that suggested computation technique is efficient and effective at track chatting users' emotion. To further analyse the quantitative experimental data, additional analyses and discussions were conducted. All of the findings backed up the utility and viability of the proposed method. With the important exception of chat messages, pre-processing the messages is identical to pre-processing of ordinary texts by using the techniques but other than notable exceptions of mixed words which is needed to be resolved by phonetic of mapping. For sentiment analysis, general programming approaches such as analyzing text using Application Programming Interface (API) used for extracting information and classifications have been employed. Because of the enormous number of active users, Instant Messaging has become one of the greatest platforms for conducting mobile commerce.

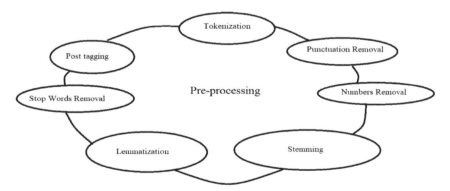

Fig. 1. Pre-processing

In a synchronous communication context, most salesperson performance indicators are available, whereas instant messaging is primarily asynchronous. Any text between a salesman and his or her consumer is ambiguous in terms of emotion interpretation. Although emoticons or strong sentences can be used to indicate emotion, the precise sentiment is impossible to predict because no movements, voice, or facial expression are transmitted.

2 Literature Survey

WhatsApp Chat Analyser [1]: Analyzes conversations and plots graphs based on parameters. The data was extracted from a WhatsApp chat and pre-processed [8]. The use and impact of WhatsApp has been the subject of numerous studies and analyses. Some of these studies are based on the general population in a particular location, while others are based on the impact of WhatsApp on students [9]. Group chats from WhatsApp dataset used for analyzing an one year old and contains 55563 records. It includes characteristics that defines how many people uses WhatsApp groups such as duration of usage in one day, response level, types of message and years of usages posted by each person [1]. Data pre-processing is the first step in the project, and it is used to learn how to construct and use various Python modules. Rather than implementing those functions, this technique helps us understand why different modules are useful. These diverse modules help to improve code representation and user comprehension. Numpy, pandas, csv, sklearn, matplotlib, emoji, and seaborn are among the libraries utilised. To employ a sentiment analysis method that delivers the good, negative, and neutral parts of the discussion and plots parameters which is based on pie charts.ST is used to plots the line graph which shows message and author count, media sent by the authors and their counts, message and author of each date, Display the message which do not have authors, plotting the graph of hour vs count of message, ordered graph of date vs count of message. It also shows some activities on which specific date, which is specified by the system at given period of time.

Tracking and Recognizing Text Message from Online Message Services [2]: To monitor and analyze emotions expressed in internet chat communications [10]. The term sentiment analysis is used refer the process of determining text evaluative nature. Traditional sentiment analysis studies mainly try to determine if a sentence is favourable, negative, or neutral [11]. A LSTM model which is used to generate levels of document representation for each texts and attention mechanisms used to employs to captures the informative words from the context which resulting inattention network model for predicting emotions [2]. It is divided into two parts. The proposed computational approach was evaluated in the first phase for its effectiveness in analysing chatting sentences. For a pre-planned discourse, the participants are asked to focus on tagging emotion to each of the sentence. The second phase has two internet users communicating in real time. Other types of studies exist that recognise numerous emotions in texts such as joy, rage, and fear, as well as phrases containing compound emotions and the uses of language in conveying complex feelings.

Text Segregation on Asynchronous Group Chat [3]: It is used to separate text in asynchronous group chat [12]. Extracts a summary from an online debate using a Hierarchical

Attention Network. To keep context at both levels, they used a sentence and thread level hierarchy [13]. From the contexts of teacher-student learning process, the asynchronous and synchronous interaction in learning was investigated. From Asynchronous online discussion or chats feature the time delay in communication and have been found to provide more educational and learning value. Asynchronous conversations, on the other hand, are more in-depth, have a wider range of responses, and cover a wider range of topics due to the additional thinking time provided to chat participants [14]. A domain-independent extractive summarising technique is presented, which makes use of length data, structural, participant, length data and lexical. They approach the summarising challenge as a machine learning classification task [3]. Multiple talks among various members of group taking place at same time are common in group conversations. These discussions could cover a wide range of themes, including sports, food, and academics. Automation activities might be muddled and complicated by this interleaving sequence of potentially unrelated messages. For multi-party asynchronous chats, this leads in text separation, as well as separation of the speaker, text, date, and time of the communication.

Developing Salesperson Performance Indicator on Instant Messaging Platform [4]: Because it is simple to set up and allows for great customer customization, instant messaging is popular sales channel for today's online stores [15]. Performance evaluations for salespeople are divided into three categories: There are three types of behavioral criteria: a) quantitative behavioral criteria b) qualitative behavioral criteria and c) quantitative outcome criterion. The number of sold products each transaction is referred to as the sales product quantity. It shows the product's sales volume per unit [16]. Product variants are the several options available for a product. The goal of product diversity is to meet a wide range of client product expectations, allowing the company to retain existing customers while also attracting new ones [4]. There are three parts to the methodology: evaluating mobile chat transcripts, finding important factors, and defining appropriate measurement.The transcripts used in this study are specific to sales person to customer conversations. A communication between a salesman and a customer is represented by a single transcript. From the retrieved key features, we determine meaningful variables by key performance indicator after examining a transcripts. Then we build the measurement for each performance indicator. Finally, we utilise the case study which is used to demonstrate how to calculate performance of salesperson using our identified factors and their metrics. Sales Closure Rate, Sales Amount, Sales Product Quantity, Product Variances and Response Time from the, group chat are identified using Key Performance Indicators (KPIs).

Effective Emoticon Extractor for Analyzing Behavior [5]: Based on words and emoticons, it is used to produce opinions about products or people [17]. Using a basic scoring scheme, we can classify the positive and negative post/comment by using opinion vocabulary and the final post of sentiment score is calculated from subtracting the positive from the negative values [18]. Furthermore, emoticons such as happy and sad emoticons are used in posts, comments, and tweets, making it easier to comprehend the online reputation of the item under investigation. There are several reputation management techniques that use a variety of techniques to neutralize unfavorable exposure on the internet, including Twitter, in this approach [5]. Positive or negative feelings have a huge impact on online purchase intent, so it makes sense to monitor market opinion in order to objectively classify and analyze user behaviour. Positive or negative feelings regarding a product, a brand, or a person are reflected in the opinions. To obtain the desired results, R techniques, functions and packages were used. This research is proven to be important by emoticon clusters and mapping text, analyzing sentiment and producing opinions by using R.

Application of Social Media Types [6]: is to determine how well salespeople have incorporated with social media platforms such as LinkedIn, Twitter and others into various stages of the personal selling or sales process [19]. The relationship between sales people uses of social media and that of retailer and hence of retailing customers. From that they discovered the more supplier's salesperson uses social media, the more the retailer uses social media and the relationship impact was carried on to consumers' use of social media. The reputation of the brand and/or retailer, as well as the supplier's and retailer's customer-orientation, has an impact on these connections [20]. Outlined a five-step process for developing a strong social customer service strategy. Understanding your consumer, defining internal ownership, selecting the most relevant tools, categorising, routing, and responding to enquiries, and linking social media with traditional channels were all part of this [6]. A survey was conducted, and the URL was put on Google as well as emailed to the formal students who are instructed to transmit it to the other salesperson they know resulting in the snowballs sample. The first question were asked participant to specify which one of the social media they was professionally associated with weekly basis, as well as how long they had worked in sales. There were a total of 57 questionnaires completed. The purpose of this exploratory study is to determine the use of social media in small geographic area.

The Impact of Social Media in Small and Medium Enterprises [7]: Through a Systematic Literature Review (SLR), is undertaken to determine the impacts of social media use on sales process in SME [21]. SME's (Small and Medium Enterprises) play an essential role in various countries throughout the world. It is due to their role in providing job and supporting regional developmental and innovations in all of which contribute to the country's economic well-being [22]. Identity, dialogues, reputation, presence, sharing, relationships and group are the seven categories of social medias functionality identified in this study. When it comes to SMEs, each type of social media have a different influence depending on its usefulness. As a result, a thorough examination of how SMEs use social media and how it affects them is required [7]. It enables gathering existing research literature as a source for obtaining research results. SLR stands for systematic literature review, and it is used to review many journals that will discuss relevant researches issues. Findings of this studies found that social media use in SMEs has similar effects in different nations. These types of social media utilised on accordance with SME business objective which depends on the type of industries and the type of social media usage. The initial step in the SLR is to gather existing research literature to use a source for obtaining a research outcomes. Two database sources, Emerald Insight and Science Direct, were used to conduct the literature search from Table 1, we analyze that the details like time, date of the text and message and the messenger of the chat both in the group chat and also in individual chats can also be known by extracting the asynchronous chat. Media, link that is shared in the group and also the most of the active user in the group, the active status of the group, positive negative and neutral part of the chat can be calculated to know whether the messenger is positive, negative or neutral person and also people opinion about the product they have purchased can also be generated. The five performance indicator like the sales product quantity, response time, sales closure rate, product variant and the sales amount can be predicted. The behaviour of the salesperson can also be determined by analyzing how they are active in the social media. The emotions like anger, happy, sad, frustrated etc., can be identified by tracking the emotions of the messenger of the chat. The impact of the social media on the sales process in small and medium enterprises can be identified through the Systematic Literature Review across various countries who are involved in marketing. All this information can be determined from exporting the data from various social media like whatsapp, Facebook, LinkedIn, Twitter.

Table 1. Methodologies

Title of the paper	Input	Algorithm/Methology	Output	Advantage	Dataset	Proposed method	Drawback
WhatsApp Chat Analyzer [1]	Exported data from whatsapp chat	Sentiment Analysis	Positive, negative and neutral part of chat	Consuming less resource algorithm	Whatsapp chat	Pre-processing the data and applying sentiment analysis to get positive, negative and neutral part of the chart	It cannot be over emphasized for large WhatsApp application
Tracking and recognizing of short text message from online message services [2]	Online chat message	Sentiment Analysis	Emotion analysis	Efficient and effective of tracking the emotions of users	PHP and Plurk API	First, to evaluate effectiveness of sentences from chat In second phase, message was analyzed and the results are sent to users	Difficult in persuade large participants to chat to analysis emotions
Text segregation on asynchronous group chat [3]	Asynchronous whatsapp chat	Pipeline and heuristics	Text segregation	Segregate speaker, text, date, time	Whatsapp chat	pipeline based heuristics was designed for segregating text	Lack of annotated dataset
Developing sales performance indicator on instant messaging platform [4]	Whatsapp chat	Whatsapp transcripts	Five performance indicator	To ease the statistical analysis process by using categorization	forbento.com	Three steps: 1) analysis mobile chat 2) identify relevant variables 3) defining suitable indicator	Do not pertain automatically define indicators from text

(continued)

Table 1. (*continued*)

Title of the paper	Input	Algorithm/Methology	Output	Advantage	Dataset	Proposed method	Drawback
Effective emoticons extractor for behaviour analysis from social media [5]	Text from social media	R Package and R Methods	To generate opinion on product or people based on text emoticons	Calculate positive and negative words	Transaction File	R programming technique is used to generate emotions from text	It calculated only the emotions from the chat
Application of social media type in the sales process [6]	Questionnaires from Facebook, LinkedIn, Twitter	Mean, SD, MD,MO	determine the amount to which salesmen have incorporated social media kinds	Using this process we get to know the salesperson behavior like how they are active in social media	Chats from Facebook, LinkedIn, Twitter	Questions are taken from the table developed by [23]. For analysis, three variables are taken to perform Mean. SD, MD, MO	Limitations based on length of questions, size of sample and geographic region.
The impact of social media usage on the sales process in small and medium enterprises [7]	24 previous research literatures from emerald insight, science direct	Systematic Literature Review	Identify similar impact on the use of social media SME across different countries	It is used to identify the impact of social media on the sales process in sme through SLR	Journals of science direct and emerald insight	First to collect literature from previous research. And next, assess each literature by OR operation. An last synthesis the values and impact on social media usage was identified	Focus only on impact of social media usage. Only less literatures were synthesized

3 Existing System

Because they are not well-structured, they are limited in length usually one or only a few sentences and they often reflect spoken language with grammatical and spelling mistakes, internet slang, and shortened forms of words, short and informal chatting messages pose new challenges to sentiment analysis and increase the difficulty of analysis. It uses sentiment analysis to analyse the Whatsapp discussion and detect negative and positive comments. It's also utilised to separate texts, dates, times, and speakers from text messages for easier comprehension. Emotion analytics may gather text data from a variety of sources in order to assess subjective data and comprehend the emotions underlying it. Authors of these communications may also use a range of oblique covert communication tactics, such as emoticons to mimic human expressions in text messages. Furthermore, the meanings of words used in a chat session may differ from what they signify in regular life. Text summarization has been intensively researched for various sorts of text corpus. Summarization works successfully if the text can be nicely separated into independent pieces with a well defined purpose. As a result, text summarization resembles text segregation based on a set of criteria. Sentiment analysis has been treated as a natural language processing task at various levels of granularity. It started with document classification and moved to sentence and higher-level classification. Twitter messages, on the other hand, do not follow an NLP paradigm due to the inherent restrictions of the Twitter messaging system. The simplest solution to the sentiment analysis problem is to employ bag of words models instead of words, with phrases in a specific order. Individual phrases emoticons are analysed separately, which is a common assumption in information retrieval and text mining. Instant messaging (IM) is a popular means to conduct mobile business, with millions of active users. IM is a sort of online chat that allows users to send and receive text in real time over the internet. Many people believe that instant messaging is a more cost-effective alternative to text messaging. Furthermore, some IM companies offer more features than message providers such as chat of group, video, image and audio sharing, and colourful emoticons.

3.1 Drawbacks

In the previous iteration, there were no features for displaying status, sharing documents, or sharing location. And also couldn't send photos through the doc format in previous versions. The difficulty of assessing salesperson performance is what limits the use of instant messaging for mobile commerce. The WhatsApp online application, which may be connected by QR code, can be used to access WhatsApp in Windows. Another function is exporting chat, which allows users to communicate, share, or obtain chat details for data analysis via email, Facebook, or another messenger application. And also in oldest iteration the chat of whatsapp cannot be extracted for analysis. This lead to difficulty in analyzing the sales on online whatsapp business.

4 Proposed System

Data pre-processing was the first step in this project is to learn how to use and implement several Python built-in modules. Rather than implementing such functions, the below mentioned process helps to understand why certain modules are useful. These different modules improve code representation and user comprehension. Numpy, pandas, csv, sklearn, matplotlib, sys, re, emoji, seaborn, and other libraries are utilised. The initial stage in exploratory data analysis is to employ a sentiment analysis algorithm, which offers positive, negative, and neutral parts of the conversation and it is used to build a pie based chart depending on those criteria. Plot a line graph showing author and message count for each date, plot a line graph showing author and message count for each author, ordered graph of date vs message count, media sent by authors and their count, plot graph of hour vs message count, monthly sales, suitable hour to send message, status of customer and sales analysis are implemented. By using a sentiment analysis method that gives good, negative, and neutral parts of the chat, you may detect people's attitudes toward a certain product, which can help with sales predictions. To evaluate the chat and provide statistical data for further sales development using the information obtained from the analysis.

5 Algorithm

In this proposed system there are two algorithms are used to analyze the chat and give the results better than existing system. By using these algorithm, the positive, negative and neutral part of the chat are obtained. The two algorithms used here are:

- Text Blob
- Vader

5.1 Text Blob

Text Blob is a sentiment analyzer based on lexicon. It contains some predetermined rules, or a word and weight dictionary, with some scores that help calculate the polarity of a statement. Lexicon-based sentiment analyzers are also known as Rule-based sentiment analyzers for this reason. It offers a straightforward API for delving into common NLP tasks like speech tagging, noun phrase extraction, sentiment analysis, classification, translation, and more. Text Blob returns a sentence's polarity and subjectivity. Polarity is defined as $[-1, 1]$, where -1 represents a negative sentiment and 1 represents a positive sentiment. Negative words flip the polarity. Semantic labels in Text Blob aid in fine-grained analysis. The library used to import this algorithm is text blob. By importing this library all the features of text blob is obtained. The Text Blob package's approach to sentiment analysis differs in that it is rule-based, requiring a pre-defined set of categorized words. These words could be imported from the NLTK database. Furthermore, sentiments are defined based on semantic relations and the frequency of each word in an input sentence, resulting in a more precise output. Text Blob uses the averaging technique to calculate a polarity score for a single word when computing sentiment for a single word, and thus a similar procedure applies to every single word, resulting in a combined polarity for larger texts. The steps involved in Text blob is shown in the Fig. 2.

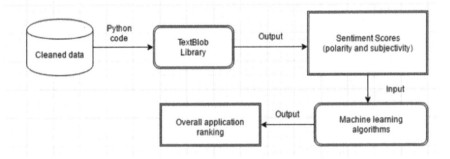

Fig. 2. Text Blob

5.2 Vader

VADER (Valence Aware Dictionary and Entiment Reasoner) is a lexicon and rule-based sentiment analysis tool that is customised to social media sentiments but also works on texts from other domains. It's a text sentiment analysis model that's sensitive to both emotion polarity positive or negative and intensity. It's included in the NLTK package and may be used on unlabelled text data right away. Vader sentimental analysis uses a dictionary to map lexical information to emotion intensities, which are referred to as sentiment scores. A text's sentiment score is calculated by adding the intensity of each word in the text. Vader is knowledgeable enough to recognise the underlying meaning of certain terms, such as did not like having a negative connotation. It also recognises the importance of capitalization and punctuation in words. The amazing aspect of Vader is that it can also predict an emoji's emotions. Vader is built for social media data and can produce impressive results when combined with data from Twitter, Facebook, and other sources. The fundamental disadvantage of the rule-based approach to sentiment analysis is that it is concerned only with individual words and ignores the context in which they are used. It employs a variety of lexical that are primarily distinguished by their semantic direction as positive or negative. The sentiment score is calculated by Vader as positive, negative, and neutral scores, which are then adjusted between −1 means most severe negative and +1 means most extreme positive.

6 Module Description

The five modules in this project are listed below:

1. Data retrieval and Pre-processing
2. Sentiment analysis
3. Exploratory data analysis
4. Data visualization
5. Sales analysis

Figure 3 shows the modules included in this of project. In this project, the overall project is divided into five modules for easy implementation.

6.1 Data Retrieval and Pre-processing

The data is retrieved from the whatsapp by exporting the whatsapp group chat shown in the Fig. 4 which contains date, time, messager and message. After pre-processing the data, the data frame contains 7 columns like date, time, messager, message, date_time, month, day as shown in the Fig. 5 for easy evaluation. These data are used for further implementation and getting results.

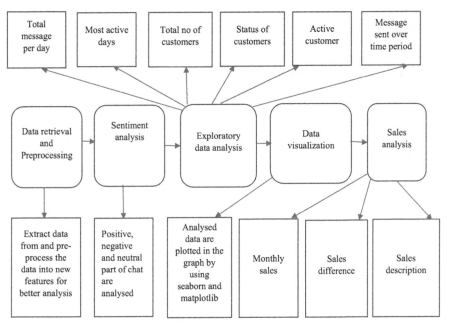

Fig. 3. Block Diagram

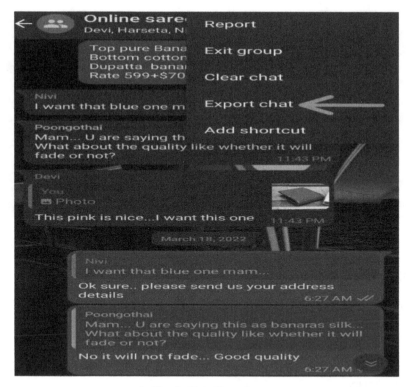

Fig. 4. Data Exporting

	Date	Time	Messager	Message	date_time	day	month	date
0	01-05-2021	9:16 PM	Mythili	<Media omitted>	2021-01-05 21:16:00	Tue	Jan	2021-01-05
1	01-05-2021	9:17 PM	Mythili	Available colours red black	2021-01-05 21:17:00	Tue	Jan	2021-01-05
2	01-05-2021	9:44 PM	Mythili	<Media omitted>	2021-01-05 21:44:00	Tue	Jan	2021-01-05
3	01-05-2021	9:44 PM	Mythili	<Media omitted>	2021-01-05 21:44:00	Tue	Jan	2021-01-05
4	01-05-2021	9:44 PM	Mythili	<Media omitted>	2021-01-05 21:44:00	Tue	Jan	2021-01-05
...	...	...	...	...	...	...	...	...
2016	10-05-2022	11:48 AM	poongothai	I receiver order ka	2022-10-05 11:48:00	Wed	Oct	2022-10-05
2017	10-05-2022	11:48 AM	poongothai	thanks for deleivering soon ka	2022-10-05 11:48:00	Wed	Oct	2022-10-05
2018	10-05-2022	11:48 AM	Mythili	ok da	2022-10-05 11:48:00	Wed	Oct	2022-10-05
2019	10-05-2022	11:48 AM	nivetha	enakum vandhuruchu ka	2022-10-05 11:48:00	Wed	Oct	2022-10-05
2020	10-05-2022	11:48 AM	Mythili	ok da	2022-10-05 11:48:00	Wed	Oct	2022-10-05

Fig. 5. Dataset

6.2 Sentiment Analysis

By applying a sentiment analysis algorithm which provides positive, negative and neutral part of the chat which is shown in the Fig. 6, helps in identifying the mind set of people about a particular product which can be further useful in sales forecasting.

```
x = sum(data["Positive"])
y = sum(data["Negative"])
z = sum(data["Neutral"])

def sentiment_score(a, b, c):
    if (a>b) and (a>c):
        print("Positive 😊 ")
    elif (b>a) and (b>c):
        print("Negative 😠 ")
    else:
        print("Neutral 😐 ")
sentiment_score(x, y, z)

Neutral 😐
```

Fig. 6. Chat Analyzing

6.3 Exploratory Data Analysis

i) **Total message per day**: The number of messages sent on each day will be counted and it will display the total number of messages sent per day as shown in Fig. 7.

ii) **Most active days**: Analyzing the frequency of messages sent on each day, most active days in the group can be found as shown in Fig. 8.

iii) **Total number of customers:** To find the total number of customers who are available in the group.

iv) **Status of customer**: The status of each customer can be found here. Total text messages sent by each customer and total number of multimedia messages sent by each customer will be displayed shown in the Fig. 9.

v) **Active customer**: This is used to find the most active customer in the group. This help to give some special offers, discounts to active members in the group. The total messages sent by each customer was calculated and from that, the active customers will be identified as shown in Fig. 10.

vi) **Message sent per day over a time period**: A graph will be plotted to for the message sent per day over a time period. This will be used to analysis the message sent over a particular time period as shown in Fig. 11.

	Date	message_count
0	01-01-2022	5
1	01-02-2022	15
2	01-03-2022	13
3	01-04-2022	9
4	01-05-2021	10
...	...	...
173	31-03-2022	14
174	31-05-2021	10
175	31-10-2021	10
176	31-11-2021	16
177	31-12-2021	10

Fig. 7. Total Messages per day

Top 10 Active days

	Date	message_count
0	28-11-2021	35
1	30-04-2022	26
2	01-06-2021	24
3	01-05-2022	21
4	25-02-2022	20
5	14-06-2021	20
6	28-05-2021	19
7	09-06-2021	19
8	26-05-2021	19
9	30-04-2021	19

Fig. 8. Most active days

```
--> Stats of +91 95007 60906 <--
Total Message Sent :  263
Total Media Message Sent :  197
-------------------------------------------------n
--> Stats of hems <--
Total Message Sent :  3
Total Media Message Sent :  0
-------------------------------------------------n
--> Stats of poongothai <--
Total Message Sent :  34
Total Media Message Sent :  0
-------------------------------------------------n
--> Stats of hari <--
Total Message Sent :  2
Total Media Message Sent :  0
-------------------------------------------------n
--> Stats of priyanka <--
Total Message Sent :  11
Total Media Message Sent :  0
-------------------------------------------------n
--> Stats of hem <--
Total Message Sent :  1
Total Media Message Sent :  0
-------------------------------------------------n
--> Stats of 91 95007 60906 <--
Total Message Sent :  1
Total Media Message Sent :  0
-------------------------------------------------n
--> Stats of neha <--
Total Message Sent :  405
```

Fig. 9. Status of customer

Most Active Customers			
	Messager	Message	✐
1	neha	405	
2	+91 95007 60906	263	
3	Devi	75	
4	hema	42	
5	poongothai	34	
6	Dharani	31	
7	nivetha	29	
8	Harseta	26	
9	+91 90920 46185	23	
10	+91 94981 09579	19	

Fig. 10. Most active customer

6.4 Data Visualization

All the results are analyzed and plotted in the graph for easy evaluation and visualization, by using seaborn and matplotlib libraries. By using the graph, the most active customer, suitable hour in a day, trendy products are analyzed. At that time when the customers are free, it is easy to see the products and purchase them. So, it is used to save time for both customer and admin. The system also analyzes the most active day of week, most active hour in a day, most suitable month and are plotted in a graph. And also, analyzing the time at which group is highly active is used to post the product at good time. The Fig. 11 shows, the graph of message sent on each date over a time period. This will help to improve the business and also it indicates the busiest time of the group where we can launch many products. The message sent on each date will be calculated and it is used to find the most active days in a group and also the graph will be plotted which is shown in the Fig. 12. From this, it is used to analyze on which day one could make more profit. Figure 13 shows the graph of most active customers in the group. The message count of each users in the group is calculated and from that the most active member of the group is identified. This helps to give some special offers, discounts to active members in the group. Figure 14 shows the graph which have most suitable time to send message on the group where all are mostly active during that time. At that time the admin will post the sales and get more attracted by the customers. The total number of messages sent on each day and month is calculated and it is plotted in the graph which is shown in the Fig. 15 and Fig. 16. Heatmap for the message sent on month and day is plotted in the graph which is shown in the Fig. 17.

Fig. 11. Message sent per day over a time period

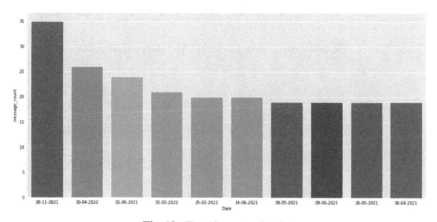

Fig. 12. Top 10 most active date

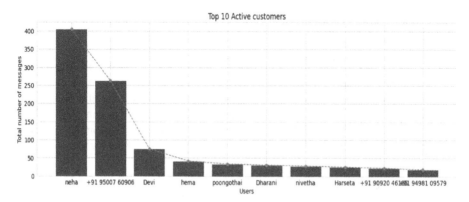

Fig. 13. Top 10 most active customer

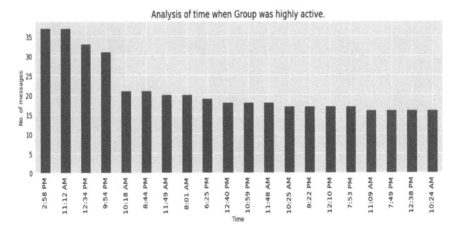

Fig. 14. Analysis of time when group is highly active

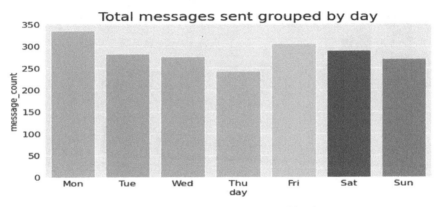

Fig. 15. Total messages sent grouped by day

6.5 Sales Analysis

In this module, analysis of the chat for predicting the sales for future is performed. From this, the monthly sales are found and to be used for further predicting purpose. Figure 18 shows the graph of the total sales amount on each month which is calculated and plotted in the graph. From this, it is to analyze the total sales for each month and also able to know in which month the sales is high and low. And also it is used to compare profit or loss on each month.

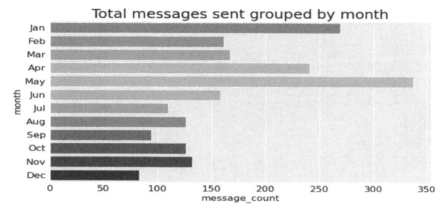

Fig. 16. Total messages sent grouped by month

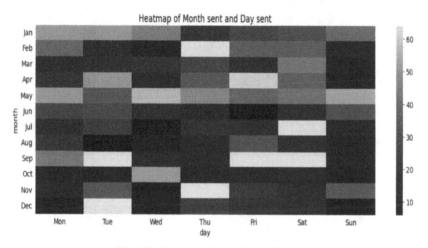

Fig. 17. Heatmap of month and day sent

The difference of amount which has sold between the months are also identified which is shown in the Fig. 19. And, total sales, maximum and minimum sales amount are also calculated which is shown in the Fig. 20.

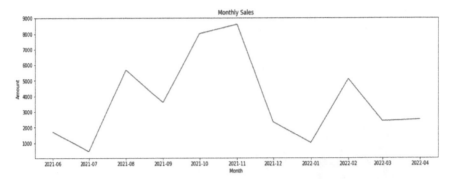

Fig. 18. Monthly sales

Month	Sales	Sales First Difference
2021-06-01	1700.0	NaN
2021-07-01	450.0	-1250.0
2021-08-01	5670.0	5220.0
2021-09-01	3600.0	-2070.0
2021-10-01	8000.0	4400.0
2021-11-01	8600.0	600.0
2021-12-01	2340.0	-6260.0
2022-01-01	1000.0	-1340.0
2022-02-01	5100.0	4100.0
2022-03-01	2400.0	-2700.0
2022-04-01	2500.0	100.0
2022-05-01	1600.0	-900.0

Fig. 19. Sales Difference

	Sales
count	12.000000
mean	3580.000000
std	2687.009152
min	450.000000
25%	1675.000000
50%	2450.000000
75%	5242.500000
max	8600.000000

Fig. 20. Sales Description

7 Results and Discussion

Using Whatsapp group chat dataset, we have analyzed a lot about the online sales which is useful for the admin to continue their online business. We can extract the data from various social media, but, as maximum of people are active in whatsapp, we have chosen this platform for data fetching. The dataset contains date, time, message, messager, day and month at which the message is delivered, shown in the Fig. 21. From this, we can get to know about the customers who liked our product the most. The reviews given by the customers for the products they had purchased motivates and helps to the growth of the business. The admin can also look for at which time the group is more active, as many customers have many works during the day time they will just relax with their phone during eve and night time so if the admin posts the products during that time they can catch more customers and many customers will react to their products. Therefore, there is high probability of profit for the admin. Thus, by using this kind of strategies, the admin and the small scale industry, new start-up business workers can get an idea to develop their business. In this technological world, this kind of online business also comforts the customer as they need not go to the shop directly and buy the product offline. They can able to view the product and get to know the product quality, description etc., and if they found any damage, they can exchange it. Figure 6.9, shows, sentiment analysis of chat using Text Blob and Vader algorithm. The blue color bar represents Text Blob algorithm and orange color bar represents Vader algorithm. By applying Text Blob algorithm to the dataset, it removes all the duplicate values from the chat and predicts the output. It removes all the duplicate values of message and gives 426 values as neutral part, 327 values as positive part and 61 values as negative part which is plotted in the above graph. And, by applying Vader algorithm to the dataset, it takes all the values from message and predicts the output. It predicts 1544 values as neutral, 416 vales as positive and 61 values as negative. From this, it shows that the neutral values are high in both the algorithm. So considering these results helps to improve the business with more positive range and also to improve the comments as more positive in future.

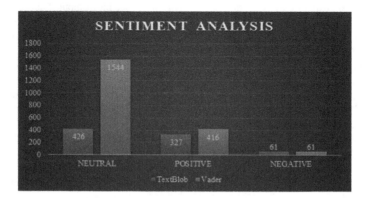

Fig. 21. Text Blob and Vader analysis

8 Conclusion and Future Work

This project analyzes the details like time, date of the text and message and the messenger of the chat both in the group chat and also in individual chats by extracting the chat. Through the media link that is shared in the group, we can also find the most of the active user in the group, the active status of the group, positive, negative and neutral part of the chat. This helps to define the people' opinion about the product they have purchased. The key performance indicators like response time, sales difference, and sales amount can be predicted. The behaviour of the salesperson can also be determined by analyzing how they are active in the social media. This project concludes that, analyzing the chat from Whatsapp or any other social media details like most active user in the group will be useful for the admin to catch more customers and also helps the admin to get know about the reviews from the customer about their product as different people have different opinion. The admin used the social media as a tool for their business and it helps them a lot to get succeed in their job. The other key performance indicators like number of sales product, sales closure rate and product variant are to be considered as key factors and are to be implemented in the future work. As such, in this technological world and also in the growth of social media this kind of online business really helps in increasing the growth of such small scale industrial people and bring their business to very great extent.

References

1. Ravishankara, K., Dhanush, V., Srajan, I.S.: Whatsapp chat analyzer. Int. J. Eng. Res. Technol. **9**(5), 897–900 (2020)
2. Chen, C.H., Lee, W.P., Huang, J.Y.: Tracking and recognizing emotions in short text messages from online chatting services. Inf. Process. Manage. **54**(6), 1325–1344 (2018)
3. Sinha, A., TK, M.M., Subramanian, S., Das, B.: Text segregation on asynchronous group chat. Procedia Comput. Sci. **171**, 1371–1380 (2020)
4. Nisafani, A.S., Wibisono, A., Imandani, S.K., Wibowo, R.P.: Developing salesperson performance indicators on instant messaging platform. Procedia Comput. Sci. **124**, 239–246 (2017)
5. Mahajan, C., Mulay, P.: E3: effective emoticon extractor for behavior analysis from social media. Procedia Comput. Sci. **50**, 610–616 (2015)
6. Schuldt, B.A., Totten, J.W.: Application of social media types in the sales process. Acad. Mark. Stud. J. **19**(3), R230 (2015)
7. Wardati, N.K., Mahendrawathi, E.R.: The impact of social media usage on the sales process in small and medium enterprises (SMEs): a systematic literature review. Procedia Comput. Sci. **161**, 976–983 (2019)
8. Kumar, N., Sharma, S.: Survey Analysis on the usage and Impact of Whatsapp Messenger. Glob. J. Enterp. Inf. Syst. **8**(3), 52–57 (2016)
9. Joshi, S.: Sentiment analysis on WhatsApp group chat using R. Data Eng. Appl. 47–55 (2019)
10. Pang, B., Lee, L.: Opinion mining and sentiment analysis. Found. Trends Inf. Retrieval **2**(1–2), 1–135 (2008)
11. Wang, Z., Zhang, Y., Lee, S., Li, S., Zhou, G.: A bilingual attention network for code-switched emotion prediction. In: Proceedings of COLING 2016, The 26th International Conference on Computational Linguistics: Technical Papers, pp. 1624–1634 (2016)

12. Tarnpradab, S., Liu, F., Hua, K.A.: Toward extractive summarization of online forum discussions via hierarchical attention networks. In: The Thirtieth International Flairs Conference (2017)
13. Johnson, G.M.: Synchronous and asynchronous text-based CMC in educational contexts: a review of recent research. TechTrends **50**(4), 46–53 (2006)
14. Murray, G., Carenini, G.: Summarizing spoken and written conversations. In: Proceedings of the 2008 Conference on Empirical Methods in Natural Language Processing, pp. 773–782 (2008)
15. Cavale, K.K.H.V.M.: Sales and Distribution Management: Text and Cases. Tata McGraw-Hill Education (2006)
16. Kale, V.: Agile Network Businesses: Collaboration, Coordination, and Competitive Advantage. Auerbach Publications (2017)
17. Ding, X., Liu, B., Yu, P.S.: A holistic lexicon-based approach to opinion mining. In: Proceedings of the 2008 International Conference on Web Search and Data Mining, pp. 231–240 (2008)
18. Lima, A.C.E., De Castro, L.N.: A multi-label, semi-supervised classification approach applied to personality prediction in social media. Neural Netw. **58**, 122–130 (2014)
19. Rapp, A., Beitelspacner, L.S., Grewal, D., Hughes, D.E.: Understanding social media effects across seller, retailer, and consumer interactions. J. Acad. Mark. Sci. **41**(5), 547–566 (2013)
20. Brinsmead, A.: Create a successful social customer service strategy. CRM Mag. **17**(5), 11 (2013)
21. Shemi, A.P., Procter, C.: E-commerce and entrepreneurship in SMEs: cases of myBot. J. Small Bus. Enterp. Dev. (2018)
22. Kietzmann, J.H., Hermkens, K., McCarthy, I.P., Silverstre, B.S.: Social media? Get serious! Understanding the functional building blocks of social media. Bus. Horiz. **54**(3), 241–251 (2011)
23. Andzulis, J.M., Panagopoulus, N.G., Rapp, A.: A review of social media and implications for the sales process. J. Pers. Sell. Sales Manag. **32**(3), 305–316 (2012)
24. Kiritchenko, S., Zhu, X., Mohammad, S.M.: Sentiment analysis of short informal texts. J. Artif. Intell. Res. **50**, 723–762 (2014)
25. Appel, O., Chiclana, F., Carter, J., Fujita, H.: A hybrid approach to the sentiment analysis problem at the sentence level. Knowl.-Based Syst.-Based Syst. **108**, 110–124 (2016)

Hands in Harmony: Empowering Communication Through Translation

C. Manikandan⬤, B. Keerthana(⊠)⬤, N. Raju⬤, Sunkavalli Supriya,
Pentyala Bhavani, and Grandhi Sirisha

School of EEE, SASTRA Deemed to be University, Thanjavur 613401, Tamil Nadu, India
keerthibalayadhav@gmail.com, raju@ece.sastra.ac.in

Abstract. Over the years, sign language has developed to be a remarkable advancement. Unfortunately, there are specific effects associated with this language. When speaking with speech disabilities or hard-of-hearing people, not everyone knows how to decode this sign language. This study investigates the notion of voice-to-Telugu text, sign language conversion systems, and sign language-to-Tamil text conversion systems to facilitate seamless communication between hearing and hard-of-hearing people. Using automated speech recognition (ASR) algorithms, it transcribes spoken words into text and produces sign language animations or gifs using computer vision methods. Similarly, sign language conversion systems use BiLSTM neural networks and media pipe holistic to understand sign language motions in real-time and translate them into Tamil. The proposed work stores the weights and uses the confusion matrix accuracy to assess the model. By overcoming different communication challenges, this well-designed architecture offers a practical and comprehensive solution for deaf and hard-of-hearing society.

Keywords: Voice-to-Telugu text · Sign language-to-Tamil text · Automatic speech recognition · Computer vision · Media pipe holistic · BiLSTM · Automatic speech recognition

1 Introduction

The World Health Organization estimates that the number of people worldwide with impaired hearing exceeds 466 million, and it is expected to rise due to population growth, an aging population, exposure to noise pollution and lack of access to healthcare services in certain regions. So, it's about developing a system to bridge the communication gap for those with hearing difficulties and others within society. Sign Language is a nonverbal, gestural language that deaf or hard-of-hearing people use to communicate with one another and others who understand sign language. It has grammar, words, and syntax, making it a comprehensive and distinct language. There is significant variability between countries and regions in using sign languages. Examples of widely recognized sign languages include American Sign Language (ASL), British Sign Language (BSL), Australian Sign Language (Auslan), and French Sign Language (FSL) [1, 2]. Recent

B. R. Chakravarthi et al. (Eds.): SPELLL 2023, CCIS 2046, pp. 210–224, 2024.
https://doi.org/10.1007/978-3-031-58495-4_15

research emphasizes the distinction between Indian Sign Language [3], American Sign Language and British Sign Language, but it is not an active issue in complex systems. These sign languages have unique signs, grammar rules, and cultural nuances. Sign language conveys meaning through hand position, facial expressions, body movements, and spatial references. They translate spoken language into sign language so that it can be understood by those with hearing impairments or those experiencing hearing loss.

Translation to sign language necessitates a deep comprehension of both the source and destination sign languages and an appreciation of cultural variations and context. Depending on the situation, interpreters may employ various approaches and strategies, such as simultaneous or consecutive interpretation. Sign language interpreters are trained professionals facilitating communication between deaf individuals and hearing individuals who do not understand sign language. They listen to spoken language and interpret it into sign language, or vice versa, allowing both understanding and communicating with each other effectively. Sign language is used in various settings, including educational institutions, workplaces, healthcare facilities, public events, and media[4]. It ensures deaf individuals access information, services, and opportunities equally. With technological advancements in research, sign language translation continues to evolve for the development of a system aimed at facilitating communication for deaf and hard-of-hearing individuals. Sign language serves as their primary mode of communication, but they encounter challenges in their daily lives. We aim to create a system that will make communication easier and more accessible for them.

To facilitate various processes, we incorporated multiple dependencies and pipelines, including media pipe [5], matplotlib, scikit-learn [6], NumPy, and OpenCV [7–9]. Media pipe was utilized to extract essential regions of the hand, torso, and face, which were then employed for training and testing [10]. Furthermore, we devised an action recognition algorithm that accurately predicts real-time gestures based on multiple frames [10, 11]. This algorithm plays a crucial role in promoting equitable communication access and inclusivity and ensuring the rights of deaf individuals to participate in society fully.

The significant contributions of the proposed research work.

The module enables bidirectional communication, making it easier for individuals in need to interact with the general public.

It allows users to deliver more signs when compared to the existing system,

Flexible and simple to interface,

A more accurate model can be achieved with less data requirement.

Training is quicker and detections are faster.

2 Related Work

In [2], the authors thoroughly assessed and analyzed machine learning techniques used for sign language recognition. This review provides an in-depth overview of artificial intelligence methods applied in sign language recognition systems and a brief summary of feature extraction and segmentation methods. Prior endeavors have been made to construct models for sign language identification, predict and achieve the most accurate model [12], and subsequently explore avenues for commercialization. Still, they have dealt mainly with static photos as their dataset[13] and not in their native language.

We want to forecast action in real-time and display the result in the native language, especially in Tamil [14].

Several noteworthy papers have been published in sign language recognition systems. The strengths and weaknesses of those works are outlined. In [15], remarkable training and validation accuracies of 99.17% and 98.80% are achieved, respectively. However, they need additional datasets to enhance their recognition method. In [16], the signed sentences yielded an average accuracy of 72.3%, while the isolated sign words achieved an average of 89.5%. Further improvement can be done by augmenting the training data with more samples. In [17], CNN architecture exhibits lower training and validation loss, indicating its effectiveness in the task, but their database was not publicly accessible. The work [18] achieved impressive training, testing and validation accuracies. Still, it did not address facial expression and context analysis. In [19], the authors introduced an economical solution using a mobile camera, which enhances user-friendliness. However, this approach may need to perform better in cluttered backgrounds and varying illumination conditions. [19] reveals comprehensive frameworks for sign language recognition, spanning image dataset handling, and classification strategies. This holistic approach aids in better understanding and advancing sign language recognition systems. However, developing and implementing this comprehensive framework can be technically challenging and resource-intensive, demanding significant hardware, software, and expertise. In [20–22], the authors conducted a study focusing on various aspects of sign language, including recording, recognition, translation, and representation. However, their research is limited to applying artificial intelligence techniques in sign language recognition. In [23], the authors delved into recognizing Portuguese Sign Language. They employed several classifiers such as Deep Neural Network (DNN), Multilayer Perceptron (MLP), Support Vector Machines (SVM), Hidden Markov Models (HMM), and Subspace Gaussian Mixture Model (SGMM) to classify Portuguese Sign Language between 2021 and 2018, thereby establishing its reliability. In [24], A model for identifying American sign language alphabets was developed. The study made use of ImageNet's deep CNN and the MNIST dataset. 97.62% of the model was accurate.

Apart from this, some methods are adopted for sign language recognition.

1. The Glove-based method entails the utilization of a hardware glove that the signer wears while their hand movements are being captured.
2. The Vision-based method can be further classified into static and dynamic recognition techniques. The static recognition approach focuses on detecting static gestures, typically represented as 2D images. On the other hand, emotional recognition involves the real-time capture of gestures, where the movements are captured and processed in real time. This method involves utilizing a camera to capture and record the continuous movements and gestures of the signer
3. Rule-based approach: The methods used are based on the standard language and grammar rules to translate speech into sign language.

Some of the limitations of the existing system.

1. It only supports a limited number of voice commands, which may lower the product's capacity.

2. One of the system's most significant flaws is that a dumb person must always carry the necessary hardware.
3. The controller may believe that the user is giving a command if the sensors are not put straight, which could lead to undesirable effects and a shorter hardware lifespan.
4. The user cannot perform other tasks while wearing flex sensors on their fingers.

3   Proposed Methodology

Those previously existing works are not available in Telugu and Tamil languages (Native languages) and are also designed for one-way communication. Despite its accuracy of over 90%, the Glove-based method is uncomfortable to use. The vision-based approach mainly discusses dynamic recognition. But no such systems are available for Telugu and Tamil Sign Languages. For the rules to be written, they usually require significant hand coding and linguistic expertise. However, they cannot reflect the subtleties of sign language and may be limited when interpreting complicated sentences.

In Fig. 1, we introduced a system where Speech-to-Sign Language and Telugu Text Translation take place, enabling individuals without hearing impairments to effectively communicate with those who are deaf or hard of hearing in their native language. Additionally, Fig. 2 illustrates the Sign Language to Text Conversion module, which facilitates communication between deaf or hard-of-hearing individuals and those without hearing impairments.

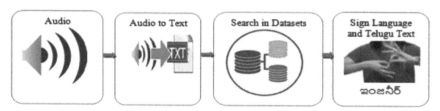

Fig. 1. Audio-to-sign language & Text translation

Fig. 2. Sign language to Text conversion

3.1 Module I: Speech-to-Sign Language & Telugu Text Translation

Translating spoken languages to sign language shall be its primary objective, facilitating adequate understanding and communication for individuals with hearing impairments. The conversion of speech into sign language is usually carried out in three main steps: speech recognition, natural language processing, and matching the generated text with stored filenames in the database. The files stored contain corresponding sign language gestures for the text fetched and displayed. In the initial stage, the technology employs automatic speech recognition (ASR) algorithms to convert spoken words into written text. Subsequently, the textual input undergoes analysis, considering factors such as grammar, context, and semantics, utilizing natural language processing (NLP) techniques. The system refers to the collected database at the sign language generation step. Sign language gestures match the processed text to the corresponding file, which contains the corresponding sign language representations for the spoken words and displays it.

Steps Involved in Speech-to-Sign Language Translation

Step 1: Audio-To-Text Conversion
This system utilizes a microphone to capture the speech of an ordinary individual. However, to ensure high-quality voice signals, the captured audio undergoes a process of noise elimination. Due to the potential lack of clarity in the sound captured by the microphone, an advanced noise removal system is employed to filter out undesired noise or signals from the input data. After the noise removal process, a speech-to-text conversion algorithm converts the audio signal into written English text. The resulting English Text is then passed to a Python translation module, which facilitates the translation of the Text into Telugu. Suppose the audio is not adequately detected or recognized. In that case, the user is prompted to speak again, and this iterative process continues until the audio is successfully detected and accurately converted into text. This iterative approach ensures the system effectively captures the user's speech, provides precise translations into Telugu & regenerates response.

Step 2: Sign Language Generation
When working with Indian sign language datasets, each file is saved in the.gif format and named in lowercase. This naming convention facilitates comparing the extracted English text and the file names. The extracted English text is converted to lowercase to ensure consistency with the file names. The lowercase text is then compared with all the file names in the collected datasets using the string manipulation capabilities provided by the Python string package. If a match between the text and a file name is found, the corresponding file is opened using image extraction and graphing algorithms for further processing. Figure 1 shows the design of our system model.

However, if there is a discrepancy between the file name and the extracted text, the text is divided into individual alphabets. For each alphabet, the system displays the corresponding image file associated with that specific alphabet. This visual representation of each alphabet assists in identifying and interpreting the sign language gesture (Fig. 3).

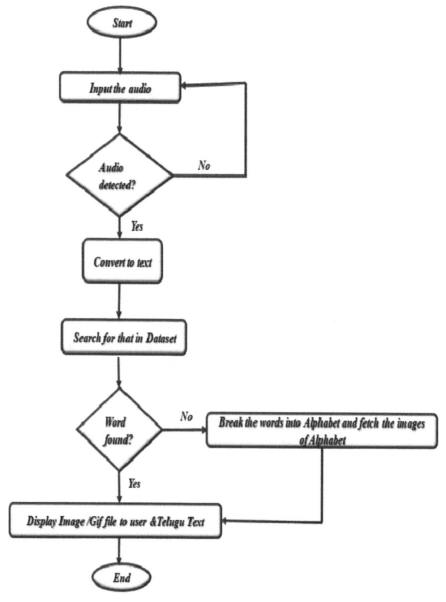

Fig. 3. Design of Proposed Model for speech-to-sign Language & Telugu Text Translation

3.2   Module II: Translation of Sign Language to Text

Translation of sign language into text involves recognizing and interpreting the gestures and movements of sign language and converting them into textual representations. Implementation of sign language conversion systems can apply more sophisticated techniques, including deep learning architectures and recurrent neural networks (RNN), depending on the complexity and requirements of the task.

In sign language-to-text conversion, a BiLSTM [16] can be employed to recognize and interpret the sequential patterns of sign language gestures and convert them into corresponding textual representations.

Bidirectional Long Short-Term Memory (BiLSTM) is a modification of the Long Short-Term Memory (LSTM) architecture, an example of a recurrent neural network (RNN) that integrates information from both past and future contexts when handling sequential data. BiLSTMs are widely used in tasks that require understanding and modeling temporal dependencies in both directions, hence used in converting sign language into text. The fundamental component is the LSTM unit, comprising a cell state (Ct), an input gate (i), a forget gate (f), an output gate (o) and cell state activation (tanh). These components work together to process sequential data. The input gate manages the extent to which new information is integrated, the forget gate decides what information to remove from the cell state, and the output gate controls the amount of data to be passed to the next hidden state and the output of the LSTM unit. The cell state acts as the memory, allowing information to flow through time while retaining long-term dependencies. In a standard LSTM, information flows only in one direction, from the past to the future. However, in a BiLSTM, two LSTMs are utilized. One LSTM processes the input sequence in a forward manner, while the other processes it in reverse. The forward LSTM handles the sequence from the start to the end, whereas the backward LSTM processes it from the end to the beginning.

At each time step, the outputs of both LSTMs are combined to capture the dependencies in both directions. This enables the model to incorporate future information while making predictions, resulting in a more robust representation of the input sequence. Building an accurate and reliable sign language-to-text conversion system using a BiLSTM model requires careful data preprocessing, model architecture design, and training. To create and sketch the sign language identification type, the key points are extracted(face, hands and body), BiLSTM is trained, and the OpenCV for real-time prediction is utilized. Figure 4 shows the proposed model's design for translating sign language to text. This type depends on the pipeline and involves extracting key points from the input data, training a BiLSTM model using sci-kit and NumPy, and using OpenCV for real-time prediction.MediaPipe Holistic is crucial in extracting the key points, while sci-kit and NumPy aid in training and evaluating the model.

After training and testing the BiLSTM model for sign language recognition, action prediction can be performed on new or unseen data. The model's weights, which capture the learned patterns and representations, are typically saved for future use or deployment.

Steps Involved in Sign Language to Text Translation

Step 1: Data Collection
A dataset of sign language videos with corresponding text translations is done in the data collection process. The dataset comprises videos representing three classes of phrases/signs that the system interprets. Video preprocessing steps were applied to the sign language videos. This could involve resizing the video frames to a standardized resolution and normalizing the video frames to enhance consistency and comparability. MediaPipe Holistic extracted face, hand, and body key points from the preprocessed sign language videos. These key points are important features that capture the significant areas and movements within the gestures. Folders or directories were created to organize the collected and preprocessed data. This step likely involves setting up an appropriate file structure to manage the dataset effectively. The dataset consists of three classes, each representing a specific phrase or sign. Each class comprises 50 videos, resulting in 150 videos in the input dataset for training the model. The input data for the machine learning model is represented as a sequence of NumPy arrays. Each array contains 1662 values, likely the landmark values obtained from the face, hand, and body key points.

Step 2: Model Architecture
Here, the architecture of the BiLSTM model is designed, and the corresponding model summary is depicted in Fig. 5.The architecture typically consists of input, BiLSTM, and output layers.

Encoder
Pass the preprocessed video frames through the BiLSTM layers. BiLSTM units process the input sequences in two directions, allowing the model to capture dependencies in both temporal directions. The output of the BiLSTM layers contains contextual information from the entire video sequence.

Decoder
Initialize the decoder using the output of the BiLSTM layers. At each time step, the decoder inputs the previously generated word/token and its previous hidden state. It generates the following word/token based on this information. This process is reiterated until an end-of-sentence token is generated or a predetermined maximum length is achieved.

Step 3: Training and Evaluation
TensorFlow and Sci-kit algorithms separated the labels and built features from the preprocessed dataset. This step involves preparing the input features and target labels for the training process. The dataset was split into training and testing sets. This separation aids in assessing the model's performance on unfamiliar data and mitigating issues of overfitting or underfitting. This ensures that the model generalizes well to new sign language gestures. Data processing includes various operations to modify and transform the data into a format suitable for training a BiLSTM model. This may include dimension conversions, datatype conversions, and output changes. Here the data is transformed into a valuable format used by machine translation models.

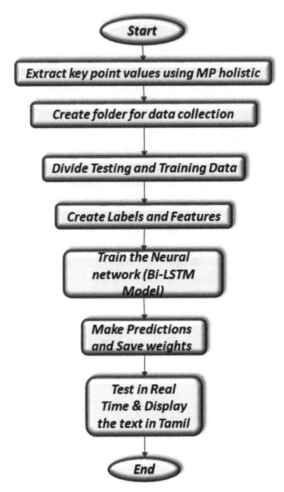

Fig. 4. Design of Proposed Model for Sign Language to Telugu Text Translation

The BiLSTM model is trained with a preprocessed dataset, and its architecture is implemented using libraries like TensorFlow. To predict the activity seen at a given point in time, the input data consists of a series of frames with 1662 values per frame are used by optimizing the model parameters and minimizing the loss function through propagation iterations. The trained BiLSTM model is evaluated against a different set of test datasets to measure performance, such as accuracy. This Evaluation helps assess how well the model distinguishes invisible sign language gestures and provides insight into its effectiveness in sign language-to-text translation.

4   Results and Discussion

The detection of sign language is a complex problem. This is due to the complexity and variety of expressions available in sign language. However, recent developments in deep learning have made it possible to detect sign language with high accuracy rates.

Layer (type)	Output Shape	Param #
lstm_6 (LSTM)	(None, 30, 64)	442112
lstm_7 (LSTM)	(None, 30, 128)	98816
lstm_8 (LSTM)	(None, 64)	49408
dense_6 (Dense)	(None, 64)	4160
dense_7 (Dense)	(None, 32)	2080
dense_8 (Dense)	(None, 3)	99

Total params: 596,675
Trainable params: 596,675
Non-trainable params: 0

Fig. 5. Model Summary

4.1   Speech-to-Sign Language & Text Translation

Although it takes some time, the proposed model uses an artificial voice recognition method to turn it into text and display the appropriate sign language and Telugu text. Figure 6 and 7 depict some of the findings.

Fig. 6. Sign language & Telugu text translation for the audio "Teacher"

Fig. 7. Sign language & Telugu text translation for the audio "Engineer"

4.2 Sign Language to Text Translation

The proposed model using OpenCV, MediaPipe Holistic, and Long Short-Term Memory (LSTM) approaches has shown promising results in sign language-to-text translation, achieving high accuracy on the testing dataset. Achieving 99.999% accuracy is impressive and indicates the model's effectiveness in accurately capturing the patterns and translating sign language gestures.

Observing Figs. 9 and 10, immediately highlighting the requested phrase with its corresponding color when the system detects the action in real time can enrich the user experience and deliver prompt feedback. The sign language-to-text translation system becomes more interactive and responsive, enhancing the application's overall user experience and usability (Fig. 8).

Fig. 8. Training Phase

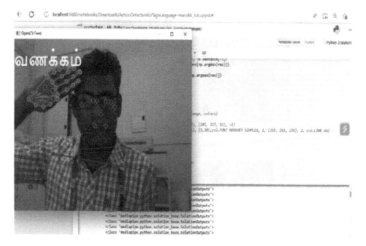

Fig. 9. Tamil Text for sign language "Hello"

We employed a multilabel confusion matrix shown in Fig. 11; the scikit-learn metrics package to assess the model's accuracy is a good practice. The confusion matrix, in particular, is a valuable tool for evaluating the model's performance and can provide insights into both correct and incorrect predictions, allowing for a better interpretation of the model's accuracy and potential areas of improvement.

Additionally, Fig. 9 and 10, showing the model predicting the dynamic sign created and highlighting the predicted phrase or word, further enhance the visualization and

Fig. 10. Tamil Text for sign language "Thanks"

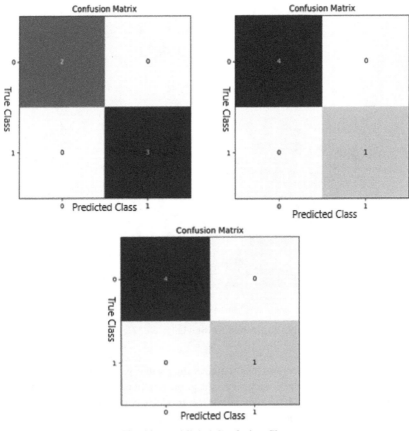

Fig. 11. Multilabel Confusion Chart

feedback for the user. This visual representation provides a clear indication of the model's output and can help users understand and verify the accuracy of the translation.

5 Conclusion

The Proposed Model for sign language recognition in the native languages (Telugu and Tamil) with two-way communication, a combination of media pipe holistic and LSTM, is an interesting approach. Leveraging these technologies can offer several advantages and lead to a model with exceptionally high accuracy. The benefits, particularly in addressing the challenges posed by limited data and achieving high precision in sign language recognition.

The proposed combination model is described as being faster in training and detection. This implies that the training process and real-time prediction or detection of sign language gestures can be performed efficiently, which is crucial for practical applications. Enhancing the model's performance is possible by utilizing larger datasets recorded with high-quality cameras. This can enhance detecting and extracting critical locations, leading to better representation and understanding of sign language gestures. Additionally, increased processing capability can allow for larger dataset sizes, leading to more robust model training and improved accuracy.

References

1. Min, Y., Hao, A., Chai, X., Chen, X.: Visual alignment constraint for continuous sign language recognition (2021)
2. Koller, O.: Quantitative survey of the state of the art in sign language recognition (2020)
3. ISL Dictionary Launch | ISLRTC. https://www.islrtc.nic.in/isl-dictionary-launch. Accessed 04 Jul 2023
4. R., Zuo, B., Mak.: Local Context-aware Self-attention for Continuous Sign Language Recognition 2022
5. Indriani, M., Harris, A., Agoes, S.: Applying hand gesture recognition for user guide application using MediaPipe. In: Proceedings of the 2nd International Seminar of Science and Applied Technology (ISSAT 2021), vol. 207, pp. 101–108 (2021)
6. Bisong, E.: Building Machine Learning and Deep Learning Models On Google Cloud Platform: A Comprehensive Guide For Beginners (2019)
7. Chandan, G., Jain, A., Jain, H., Mohana: Real time object detection and tracking using deep learning and OpenCV. In: Proceedings of the International Conference on Inventive Research in Computing Applications, ICIRCA 2018, pp. 1305–1308 (2018)
8. Zelinsky, A.: Learning OpenCV—computer vision with the OpenCV library. IEEE Robot. Autom. Mag. **16**(3), 100 (2009)
9. Čuljak, I., Abram, D., Pribanić, T., Džapo, H., Cifrek, M.: A brief introduction to OpenCV. In: 2012 Proceedings of the 35th International Convention MIPRO (2012)
10. Poppe, R.: A survey on vision-based human action recognition. Image Vis. Comput. **28**(6), 976–990 (2010)
11. Jhuang, H., Gall, J., Zuffi, S., Schmid, C., Black, M.J.: Towards understanding action recognition (2013)
12. Wang, H., Schmid, C.: Action recognition with improved trajectories. In: Proceedings of the IEEE International Conference on Computer Vision, pp. 3551–3558 (2013)

13. Patel, S., Dhar, U., Gangwani, S., Lad, R., Ahire, P.: Hand-gesture recognition for automated speech generation. In: 2016 IEEE International Conference on Recent Trends in Electronics, Information & Communication Technology, RTEICT 2016 - Proceedings, pp. 226–231 (2017)
14. Prakash, U.M., Thamaraiselvi, V.G.: Detecting and tracking of multiple moving objects for intelligent video surveillance systems. In: 2nd International Conference on Current Trends in Engineering and Technology, ICCTET 2014, pp. 253–257 (2014)
15. Wadhawan, A., Kumar, P.: Deep learning-based sign language recognition system for static signs. Neural Comput. Appl. 32(12), 7957–7968 (2020)
16. Mittal, A., Kumar, P., Roy, P.P., Balasubramanian, R., Chaudhuri, B.B.: A modified LSTM model for continuous sign language recognition using leap motion. IEEE Sens. J. 19(16), 7056–7063 (2019)
17. Rao, G.A., Syamala, K., Kishore, P.V.V., Sastry, A.S.C.S.: Deep convolutional neural networks for sign language recognition. In: 2018 Conference on Signal Processing and Communication Engineering Systems, SPACES 2018, vol. 2018-January, pp. 194–197 (2018)
18. Sruthi, C.J., Lijiya, A.: A deep learning based Indian sign language recognition system. In: Proceedings of the 2019 IEEE International Conference on communication and signal processing, ICCSP 2019, pp. 596–600 (2019)
19. Athira, P.K., Sruthi, C.J., Lijiya, A.: A signer independent sign language recognition with co-articulation elimination from live videos an Indian scenario. J. King Saud Univ. - Comput. Inf. Sci. 34(3), 771–781 (2022)
20. Moryossef, A., et al.: Evaluating the immediate applicability of pose estimation for sign language recognition (2021)
21. Amrutha, K., Prabu, P., Paulose, J.: Human Body pose estimation and applications. 2021 Innovations in Power and Advanced Computing Technologies (2021)
22. Papastratis, I., Chatzikonstantinou, C., Konstantinidis, D., Dimitropou-los, K., Daras, P.: Artificial intelligence technologies for sign language. Sensors 21(17), 5843 (2021)
23. Aguiar de Lima, T., Da Costa-Abreu, M.: A survey on automatic speech recognition systems for Portuguese language and its variations. Comput. Speech Lang. 62 (2020)
24. Hasan, M.M.; Srizon, A.Y., Sayeed, A., Hasan, M.A.M.: Classification of American sign language by applying a transfer learned deep convolutional neural network. In: 2020 23rd International Conference on Computer and Information Technology (ICCIT), pp. 1–6. IEEE (2020)

Offensive Text Detection for Tamil Language

R. Srishti Gulecha$^{(\boxtimes)}$, Sourav Kumar Neelamegam Rajaram Subramanian, and S. Abirami

Department of Information Science and Technology, College of Engineering Guindy, Anna University, Chennai, Tamil Nadu, India
srishtigulecha02@gmail.com

Abstract. In recent years, the Internet and social media have sparked a revolution in the way information is exchanged. The growth of social media and micro-blogging sites not only provides platforms for empowering freedom of expression and individual voices but has also led to a rise in anti-social behavior like online harassment, cyberbullying and hate speech. In multilingual social networks, users often engage in code-mixed communication, blending multiple languages in their posts and comments. There has been significant amounts of work in offensive text detection for the English language. However, the lack of adequate data makes it challenging to detect offensive text, particularly in Indian languages like Tamil, Hindi, and Marathi. This work presents a deep learning model for offensive text detection in Tamil and Tanglish. A CNN-BiGRU-based approach using fastText embeddings is proposed which aims to improve the detection of offensive content in Tamil code-mixed social media. The model was found to have an accuracy of 73.5%. Additional real-time testing was also done with the Twitter data.

Keywords: NLP · Offensive text detection · Tamil · Deep learning · CNN · BiGRU · Social media

1 Introduction

Day by day, online content including hate speech and offensive comments is rising rapidly. Based on the study conducted in 2021 the total number of online posts containing hate speech in the seven-day rolling average trended upward, it increased by 67% from 60,000 to 100,000 daily posts [13]. Generally, real-world events like elections and protests often lead to spikes in online offensive comments on various social media platforms due to which a large amount of online hate crimes are being reported. This poses significant problems in society. It can escalate to threats, harassment, and violence, compromising the safety and well-being of its victims. Additionally, hate speech facilitates online harassment and cyberbullying, causing distress and reputational damage.

Social media platforms are a place where users exchange views on different topics. Twitter was launched in 2006 and is one of the most actively used social networking sites. With 100 million daily active users and 500 million tweets sent daily, it is one of the most popular social media platforms used across the world [14]. According to reports [15], there has been a significant rise in hateful and offensive content on Twitter. Thus, it is very crucial to address this issue to foster inclusive and respectful environments.

Currently, there are relatively few offensive text-detecting models available for low-resource languages such as Tamil. The absence of a highly accurate offensive content-detecting model for the Tamil and code-mixed Tamil language poses significant challenges and concerns. It also highlights the gap in addressing their specific needs and nuances for Tamil texts. This work aims to address the above issues by building a model that classifies the given Tamil or Tanglish text as offensive or not offensive.

We propose a CNN-BiGRU-based deep learning model to effectively detect Tamil and Tanglish offensive texts/tweets. First, preprocessing is done which includes steps like transliteration, stemming and lemmatization. This step removes any form of noise present in the data. The next step is feature extraction which involves the usage of word embeddings for the Tamil language. The input text is transformed into vector representations. The deep learning model which is made up of multiple layers is trained to understand the data. Training and testing is done with the help of dataset. Finally, the model additional testing using the data scraped from Twitter. The Twitter data is scraped from Twitter based on keyword chosen by the external evaluator. This data is different from the dataset used for training and testing the model.

The significant contributions of this paper are

- Development of a deep learning model to classify offensive Tamil and Tanglish texts.
- Development of a web interface to analyze offensive tweets on Twitter.
- Evaluation of the model using real-time tweets and other performance metrics.

The rest of the paper is structured as follows: Sect. 2 explores the background and related work. Section 3 describes the system architecture, and Sect. 4 elucidates the methodology of the proposed system. Section 5 analyses the discussion and results, and Sect. 6 concludes the work by presenting relevant future works.

2   Background and Related Work

There has been a significant amount of research done on hate speech and offensive text detection. But offensive text detection for under-resourced languages such as Tamil, Marathi and Bengali face challenges due to lack of sufficient data for the Natural Language Processing tasks.

The research work by Md. Rezaul Karim et al. [1] proposes a Multichannel Convolutional-LSTM-based model for predicting different types of hate speech, document classification, and sentiment analysis. A new word embedding model called BengFastText was built and used. It is based on fastText which is a computationally efficient predictive model for learning word embeddings from raw Bengali texts. Among the predictions made by the classifier, 93% of predictions belonged to true positive predictions.

Pradeep Kumar Roy et al. [2] propose a Deep Convolutional Neural Network (DCNN) system. The system makes use of the tweet text with GloVe embedding vector to capture the tweet's semantics with the help of convolution operation and achieved the precision, recall and F1-score values as 0.97, 0.88, and 0.92 respectively.

Muhammad Bilal et al. [3] present a Context-Aware Deep Learning Model for the detection of Roman Urdu hate speech on social media platforms. The model was developed based on Bi-LSTM with an attention layer and custom word2vec was used for word embeddings. Experimental results showed that Bi-LSTM with attention had provided better results than traditional machine learning models and other deep learning models with an accuracy score of 0.875 and an F-Score of 0.885.

The system proposed by Abhishek Velankar et al. [4] detects hate speech in Hindi and Marathi texts. A variety of deep learning architectures are investigated, including CNN, LSTM, and BERT variants including multilingual BERT, IndicBERT, and monolingual RoBERTa. The research shows that transformer-based models perform the best and the basic models along with fastText embeddings give a competitive performance. Moreover, on the fine-grained Hindi dataset, the basic models perform better than BERT-based models along with normal hyper-parameter tuning was performed.

Malliga Subramanian et al. [5] propose a study that performs multiple tests to detect offensive texts in YouTube comments. Machine learning techniques, namely Bernoulli Naive Bayes, Support Vector Machine, Logistic Regression, and KNearest Neighbor, were tested to detect offensive comments. In addition, pre-trained multilingual transformer-based NLP models such as mBERT, MuRIL, and XLM-RoBERTa were also used. The research work shows that XLM-RoBERTa (Large) was found to have the highest accuracy of 88.5%.

The research work by Sreelakshmi K et al. [6] proposes a system to detect hate speech in Hindi-English Code-mixed Data. Pre-trained models such as fastText and bilingual embedding were used as features to perform the classification. The fastText features along SVM- RBF as the classifier gave the highest accuracy of 85.81%.

Shakir Khan e al. [7] propose a deep learning model based on Convolutional and Bi-Directional Gated Recurrent Unit With Capsule Network to detect hate speech in English texts. The capsule network considers the part-whole spatial/local relationship of hate speech-related words. The proposed model shows a performance of 0.90, 0.80, and 0.84 respectively considering precision, recall, and f-score. The proposed model has training and validation accuracy of 0.93 and 0.90 respectively.

The research work by Asif Hasan et al. [8] analyses hate speech against migrants and women through tweets Using an Ensembled deep learning model. The word embedding is implemented using a combination of deep learning models such as BiLSTM, CNN and MLP. These models are integrated with word embedding methods such as inverse GloVe, TF-IDF and transformer-based embedding.

Fatima Shannaq et al. [9] propose a model for the automatic detection of offensive tweets in the Arabic language. Word embedding models were fine-tuned using a dataset to extract the word features of the ArCybC corpus. The suggested method yielded better results, with the SVM algorithm and the Aravec SkipGram word embedding model achieving 88.2% accuracy and 87.8% F1-score rate, respectively.

Rahul et al. [10] present an approach that classifies Hingish texts as hate speech, abusive or non-offensive. The work makes use of character-level embeddings for Hinglish language. Among the various deep learning models that were trained, it was found that GRU with Attention Model performed best among all models.

From the above research works it can be inferred that embeddings are used to provide better results. Deep learning models are majorly used to detect hate speech and offensive texts. The main challenge is due to the lack of data for under-resourced languages. Our work is thus based on embeddings and deep learning model with a large dataset.

3   System Architecture

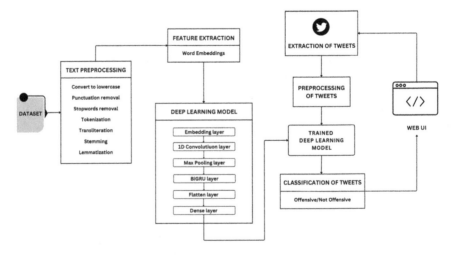

Fig. 1. Proposed architecture for offensive text detection for Tamil language

The proposed system detects offensive tweets in Tamil and Tanglish tweets across Twitter with the help of a deep learning model. The system architecture as shown in Fig. 1 describes the various steps involved in building a CNN-BiGRU-based deep learning model and using it for detection. The proposed system consists of four phases - data preprocessing, feature extraction, building the deep learning model and model evaluation.

The first phase is data preprocessing which consists of various steps like tokenization, removal of stopwords and punctuation, lemmatization and stemming. Another major process involved in preprocessing is transliteration. This is done to enable the detection of offensive texts in Tanglish. The second phase is feature extraction which involves extracting the important features of the text. This is later converted to vector sequences which are used for embedding. The word embeddings are obtained using fastText which transforms the text into dense vectors to be given as input to the model. The third phase of the system is where the deep learning model is built. The dataset is split for training and testing. The deep learning model is primarily based on CNN-BiGRU. It has various other layers like a dense layer, pooling layer and flatten layer. This model classifies the tweets as offensive or not offensive. The final phase involves scrapping tweets from Twitter, where additional testing is done with the help of the Tweepy module and using a streamlit-based web dashboard to present the results. Additional steps like removal links and user mentions need to be performed in preprocessing of tweets. Using the web UI tweets can be fetched based on the input text from the user. Preprocessed tweets can be analyzed for offensive tweets with the help of the trained model.

4 Methodology

4.1 Dataset

The dataset contains 43919 code-mixed Tamil YouTube comments which are labeled as Offensive, Not Offensive and Not Tamil as shown in Table 1. It consists of 31808 texts classified as offensive. and 10325 texts classified as not offensive. The remaining 1786 texts which were not in Tamil were omitted. The dataset contains a wide range of hate speech instances including offensive, derogatory and discriminatory content specific to Tamil Language. The dataset contains a lot of content available both in pure Tamil format and Tanglish format.

Table 1. Dataset Information

Text type	Count
Offensive	31808
Not Offensive	10325
Not Tamil	1786
Total	43919

As in the real-world data, the dataset contained Tanglish words that had to be dealt with in a specific way in order to gain better accuracy. This data is used to train and test the deep learning model to detect offensive texts. In addition, in order to test the ability of the model to adapt to heterogeneous sources, data was scraped from Twitter.

4.2   Data Preprocessing

Data preprocessing is a major task in all NLP tasks. It involves various steps as shown in Fig. 1 The text is first converted to lowercase characters to ensure uniformity. Non-alphanumeric characters, such as punctuation marks, are removed from the text. This step helps eliminate unnecessary noise and focuses on the essential words and context. The text might contain unnecessary words also known as stopwords. The stopwords are removed from both Tamil and English languages, ensuring that irrelevant words in either language are excluded. Transliteration is performed on the text to convert words or phrases from one script to another. In the context of detecting offensive tweets in code-mixed Tamil tweets, i.e., Tanglish tweets, this step involves transliterating English script to Tamil words. This is done with the help of indic_transliteration module that can be used for Tamil language as well. Stemming and lemmatization are techniques used to reduce words to their root forms. Stemming reduces words to their base or stem form, while lemmatization considers the context and morphological analysis to determine the word's lemma or base form. Thus, these two steps are performed as a part of preprocessing.

4.3   Feature Extraction and Word Embeddings

This module involves extracting features from text and converting text to a vector representation. The tokenized text is transformed into sequences of fixed length, typically 300. This step ensures a consistent shape and size for subsequent computations and modeling. Each word is assigned a particular value. This is used for embeddings. Algorithm 1 explains the procedure for feature extraction and embedding.

fastText provides word embeddings for the Tamil language. fastText word embeddings are a type of word representation model that captures semantic and syntactic information by representing words as continuous dense vectors. fastText takes into account the internal structure of words by considering subword units called character n-grams. This enables better understanding. The word embeddings obtained from fastText are used to construct an embedding matrix. This matrix maps each word in the vocabulary to its corresponding vector representation. This ensures that similar words with the same meaning get equal weightage. By utilizing fastText word embeddings, the module effectively transforms the input text into dense vector representations.

Algorithm 1. Feature extraction and embedding

Input: Preprocessed text/tweets
Output: Embedding matrix for features
1: Start
2: Get the preprocessed texts
3: Create a tokenizer and convert the texts to sequences
4: Pad the sequences to the length of 300
5: Load the fastText embeddings
6: *for* each word, i in wordindex.items *do*
7:    Set embedding_vector = fastText embedding of that word
8:    Set embedding_matrix[i] = embedding_vector
9: *end for*
10: End

4.4   Building the Model

The system presents a deep learning model for offensive text detection. The given dataset is split for training and testing. 80% of the data is used for training and 20% of the data is used for testing. The vector representation of texts is given as input to the first layer which is the embedding layer. The embedding matrix formed from the previous module is also used as weights. The proposed model has one 1D convolution layer whose output goes to the Max pooling layer. Max pooling operation is done to select the maximum element from the region of the feature map covered by the filter. A pool size of 2 is used in the proposed work.

The next layer used is the BiGRU layer. BiGRU is a type of RNN generally used in sequential modeling problems extracting the sequences from the forward and backward directions. A forward GRU and backward GRU are integrated to retrieve the succeeding and preceding feature sequences respectively. This module helps the model to retrieve forward and backward sequences having contextual information by applying the BiGRU layer on the convolutional layer output. Finally, the output is flattened using a flattening layer and fed to the dense layer. The sigmoid-activated dense layer is used.

4.5   Detection of Offensive in Tweets

Additionally, real-time testing is done with the help of real-world data from Twitter scraped using TweePy, a Python library capable of extracting tweets. The scraped tweets are then converted into a data frame, which organizes the tweet data into a tabular structure. The next phase is the preprocessing phase, where the text data is cleaned and prepared for analysis. It involves tasks such as eliminating special characters, converting text to lowercase, removal of stopwords, links and mentions and performing tokenization. Finally, the preprocessed tweets is passed to the trained model to classify tweets as offensive or not offensive. The results were evaluated manually.

A simple Web App is made using streamlit so that user input is taken for scraping the Twitter data and producing the desired output. The model applies its learned patterns and features to make predictions on the classification of each tweet, ultimately providing an output indicating whether a tweet is offensive or not offensive. This process enables the automated analysis of large volumes of tweets and helps in identifying and categorizing offensive content on Twitter.

5   Discussion and Results

A user interface is developed to provide an intuitive and user-friendly platform for detecting offensive content on Twitter in Tamil and Tanglish tweets with the help of streamlit library. The dashboard can be used to fetch tweets that contain our desired keyword. Once the tweets are fetched, the proposed model classifies each of them as offensive or not offensive. This helps us to test the model with real-time data. Figure 2 shows the dashboard of the web application developed for analyzing offensive tweets on the Twitter platform.

Fig. 2. Streamlit dashboard

Figure 3 shows the tweets that are scrapped from Twitter based on user's input. The input can be given in both Tamil and Tanglish. Figure 4 shows the result for each Tamil tweet classifying it as offensive or not offensive.

The dashboard can be used to predict offensive texts for Tanglish as well. Figure 5 shows the result for a few Tanglish tweets classifying them as offensive or not offensive.

A deep learning model that uses fastText word embeddings with the CNN-BiGRU model was used to detect offensive texts. The performance analysis is done with the help of the metrics - Accuracy, Recall, Precision and loss. The data is trained for 10 epochs and for each epoch accuracy and loss are saved. Loss is calculated with the help of binary_crossentropy loss function. This function computes the cross-entropy loss between true labels and predicted labels.

$$\text{Accuracy} = \frac{\text{True Positive} + \text{True Negative}}{\text{Total number of predictions}} \tag{1}$$

	User	Date Created	Num	Source of Tweet	Tweet
0	Vignesh	2023-05-28T15:15:44+00:00	0	Twitter Web App	RT @mkstalin: ஒய்வுநாளிலும் கூட அரசு நிகழ்ச்சிகளும் அரசியல் நிகழ்ச்சிகளும் ம
1	Chithu_twts	2023-05-28T15:15:36+00:00	0	Twitter for Android	RT @kmani2011: இந்திய அரசியல் வரலாற்றில் முதன் முறையாக இப்படி ஒரு வேண்
2	✦ மிthu ✦	2023-05-28T15:15:10+00:00	0	Twitter for Android	@UmaBalachandren @RVikraman அப்பழுக்கில்லா பால்முகம் காணும் போதும்.. அரசிய
3	௭ அசி஑ராய நம:	2023-05-28T15:15:09+00:00	0	Twitter Web App	RT @ArujunaArul: இந்தியாவிலேயே இதை எதிர்க்கும் ஒரே மாநில அரசியல்வாதிகள்
4	நா.தேன்நிலவன்	2023-05-28T15:14:43+00:00	0	Twitter for Android	RT @mkstalin: ஒய்வுநாளிலும் கூட அரசு நிகழ்ச்சிகளும் அரசியல் நிகழ்ச்சிகளும் ம
5	கலைக்காரன் பந்திரவள்ளி	2023-05-28T15:14:42+00:00	0	Twitter for Android	RT @KariKalankiru: இந்தியா இனி இந்துராஷ்ட்ரா! 2024ல் தேர்தல் நடக்கும்? - தமிழ்நா
6	Prof. Dr. Darwin Joseph	2023-05-28T15:14:33+00:00	0	Twitter for iPhone	RT @SankarRayan: ஏந்திய கணத்திலேயே வளைந்த செங்கோல். அரசியல் பிழைத்தே
7	Gounderrocks	2023-05-28T15:14:00+00:00	0	Twitter for Android	RT @DolphinSrithar: வரும் கால தலைமுறைக்காக பிரதமர் மோடி நிறைவேற்றிய புதி
8	செ.கதிரவன். தமிழ் நாடு	2023-05-28T15:13:55+00:00	0	Twitter for Android	RT @KariKalankiru: இந்தியா இனி இந்துராஷ்ட்ரா! 2024ல் தேர்தல் நடக்கும்? - தமிழ்நா
9	Pranesh	2023-05-28T15:13:43+00:00	0	Twitter for Android	RT @chandrukrus: மிக சரியான பார்வை இது போன்ற தொலைவு நோக்கு பார்வைவை
10	selvaraj	2023-05-28T15:13:41+00:00	0	Twitter for iPhone	RT @kmani2011: இந்திய அரசியல் வரலாற்றில் முதன் முறையாக இப்படி ஒரு வேண்
11	EswaranSu	2023-05-28T15:13:18+00:00	0	Twitter for Android	RT @mkstalin: ஒய்வுநாளிலும் கூட அரசு நிகழ்ச்சிகளும் அரசியல் நிகழ்ச்சிகளும் ம
12	durgairajaa	2023-05-28T15:12:55+00:00	0	Twitter for Android	RT @jothims: ஏந்திய கணத்திலேயே வளைந்த செங்கோல். அரசியல் பிழைத்தோர்ச
13	Mani Maran	2023-05-28T15:12:53+00:00	0	Twitter for Android	RT @roots_tamil: இந்தியா இனி இந்துராஷ்ட்ரா! 2024ல் தேர்தல் நடக்கும்? - தமிழ்நா

Fig. 3. Scrapping of tweets

	tweets	Offensive/Not Offensive
0	தமிழ்நாட்டு அரசியல் ஒழுங்கா தெரியாத ஆளுநர் கூட வம்பிழுத்து கலாய்க்கும்	Offensive
1	RT: இவ்ளோ கீழ்த்தர அரசியல் தேவையா த்து #12thResults	Not Offensive
2	ஏண்டா வந்தேறி புளுத்தி..... கவர்னர் அரசியல் பேசலாமாடா	Offensive
3	RT : தேர்தல் கமிஷனுக்கு தேவையான கமிஷனை கொடுத்து விட்டார்கள் போலிருக்கிறது மற்றவர்கள் புகார் செய்தால் உடனடியாக இந்த நாய்கள் நடவடி...	Offensive

Fig. 4. Prediction for Tamil tweets

	tweets	Offensive/Not Offensive
0	Seriymda sunni maara unaku enna kottai valikuuthuu	Offensive
1	RT : semma movie...jolly ah irunchu	Not Offensive
2	Avan getup dhan da sonna...ungoopan pola va sappa vanthan thevidiya paiya	Offensive

Fig. 5. Prediction for Tanglish tweets

$$\text{Mean accuracy} = \frac{\sum_{i=1}^{i=n} \text{Accuracy for i}^{\text{th}} \text{ epoch}}{\text{Total number of epochs (n)}} \qquad (2)$$

$$\text{Recall} = \frac{\text{True Positives}}{(\text{True Positives} + \text{False Negatives})} \qquad (3)$$

$$\text{Mean Recall} = \frac{\sum_{i=1}^{i=n} \text{Recall for i}^{\text{th}} \text{ epoch}}{\text{Total number of epochs (n)}} \qquad (4)$$

$$\text{Precision} = \frac{\text{True Positives}}{(\text{True Positives} + \text{False Positives})} \qquad (5)$$

$$\text{Mean Precision} = \frac{\sum_{i=1}^{i=n} \text{Average Precision for } i^{\text{th}} \text{ epoch}}{\text{Total number of epochs (n)}} \tag{6}$$

Accuracy is the calculated ratio between the number of correct predictions to the total number of predictions as shown in Eq. 1. The mean accuracy for 10 epochs is calculated with the help of the Eq. 2. Recall is calculated as the number of true positives divided by the total number of true positives and false negatives as shown in Eq. 3. The mean recall is the sum of recall for all the epochs divided by the number of epochs is calculated with the help of Eq. 4. Equation 5 calculates the precision which is calculated as the number of true positives divided by the total number of true positives and false positives. The mean precision is the sum of precision for all the epochs divided by the number of epochs as shown in Eq. 6.

Table 2. Performance analysis

Metric	Training	Testing
Mean accuracy	0.9254	0.7350
Mean loss	0.0651	0.3752
Mean recall	0.9093	0.7128
Mean precision	0.9521	0.7808

Table 2 shows the mean training and testing accuracy and loss obtained. It can be inferred that the mean accuracy is 0.9254 and 0.7350 for training and testing respectively. It can be observed that the mean recall is 0.9093 and 0.7128 and the mean precision is 0.9521 and 0.7808 for training and testing respectively. The mean training and testing loss is 0.0651 and 0.3752 respectively.

6   Conclusion and Future Works

In conclusion, offensive texts on social media platforms is detected by a CNN-BiGRU-based model and the results are demonstrated by scrapping data from Twitter and displaying it in a streamlit based dashboard. In the near future, the model's performance can be continuously improved by incorporating larger and more diverse datasets. This could be an additional annotated dataset specifically focused on different dialects of the Tamil language making the model perform perfectly well for texts from different areas of Tamil Nadu. The model can be extended in such a way that it can handle the stream of data and remove hate that is spread through them so that platforms such as the comment section of YouTube live videos can be kept clean. The model can also be made into a web extension that can automatically detect and clean the hate that is being spread through a webpage.

References

1. Karim, M.R., Chakravarthi, B.R., McCrae, J.P., Cochez, M.: Classification benchmarks for under-resourced Bengali language based on multichannel convolutional-LSTM network, pp. 390–399 (2020). https://doi.org/10.1109/DSAA49011.2020.00053

2. Roy, P.K., Tripathy, A.K., Das, T.K., Gao, X.-Z.: A framework for hate speech detection using deep convolutional neural network. IEEE Access 8, 204951–204962 (2020). https://doi.org/10.1109/ACCESS.2020.3037073

3. Bilal, M., Khan, A., Jan, S., Musa, S.: Context-aware deep learning model for detection of Roman Urdu hate speech on social media platform. IEEE Access 10, 121133–121151 (2022). https://doi.org/10.1109/ACCESS.2022.3216375

4. Velankar, A., Patil, H., Gore, A., Salunke, S., Joshi, R.: Hate and offensive speech detection in Hindi and Marathi (2021)

5. Subramanian, M., et al.: Offensive language detection in Tamil YouTube comments by adapters and cross-domain knowledge transfer, Comput. Speech Lang. 76, 101404 (2022). ISSN 0885-2308, https://doi.org/10.1016/j.csl.2022.101404

6. Sreelakshmi, K., Premjith, B., Soman, K.P.: Detection of hate speech text in Hindi-English code-mixed data. Procedia Comput. Sci. 171, 737–744 (2020). ISSN 1877-0509, https://doi.org/10.1016/j.procs.2020.04.080

7. Khan, S., et al.: HCovBi-Caps: hate speech detection using convolutional and bidirectional gated recurrent unit with capsule network. IEEE Access 10, 7881–7894 (2022). https://doi.org/10.1109/ACCESS.2022.3143799

8. Hasan, A., Sharma, T., Khan, A., Hasan Ali Al-Abyadh, M.: Analysing hate speech against migrants and women through tweets using ensembled deep learning model. Comput. Intell. Neurosci. (2022). https://doi.org/10.1155/2022/8153791

9. Shannaq, F., Hammo, B., Faris, H., Castillo-Valdivieso, P.A.: Offensive language detection in Arabic social networks using evolutionary-based classifiers learned from fine-tuned embeddings. IEEE Access 10, 75018–75039 (2022). https://doi.org/10.1109/ACCESS.2022.3190960

10. Gupta, R.V., Sehra, V., Vardhan, Y.R.: Hindi-English code mixed hate speech detection using character level embeddings. In: 2021 5th International Conference on Computing Methodologies and Communication (ICCMC), Erode, India, pp. 1112-1118 (2021). https://doi.org/10.1109/ICCMC51019.2021.9418261.

11. Watanabe, H., Bouazizi, M., Ohtsuki, T.: Hate speech on twitter: a pragmatic approach to collect hateful and offensive expressions and perform hate speech detection. IEEE Access 6, 13825–13835 (2018). https://doi.org/10.1109/ACCESS.2018.2806394

12. Ahmed, I., Abbas, M., Hatem, R., Ihab, A., Fahkr, M.W.: Fine-tuning Arabic Pre-trained transformer models for egyptian-arabic dialect offensive language and hate speech detection and classification. In: 2022 20th International Conference on Language Engineering (ESOLEC), pp. 170–174. Cairo, Egypt (2022). https://doi.org/10.1109/ESOLEC54569.2022.10009167.

13. Faguy.: Real-World Events Drive Increases In Online Hate Speech, Study Finds. https://www.forbes.com/sites/anafaguy/2023/01/25/real-world-events-drive-increases-in-online-hate-speech-study-finds/?sh=3d1d77273d6d

14. Forsey.: What Is Twitter and How Does It Work?. https://blog.hubspot.com/marketing/what-is-twitter

15. Cohen.: Analysis finds hate speech has significantly increased on Twitter. https://phys.org/news/2023-04-analysis-speech-significantly-twitter.html

Telugu-English Abusive Comment Detection Using XLMRoBERTa and mBERT

Pingala Revanth Reddy[✉] (ID), K. V. Munawwar(ID), and K. Nandhini(ID)

Central University of Tamil Nadu, Thiruvarur 610005, Tamil Nadu, India
pingalarevanthreddy144@gmail.com, nandhinikumaresh@cutn.ac.in

Abstract. The proliferation of social media platforms has enabled users to express their thoughts and opinions freely, but it has also given rise to the rampant spread of abusive and offensive content. The detection and moderation of such abusive comments have become crucial for maintaining a healthy online environment. Detecting abusive comments in multilingual settings is a challenging task due to the presence of diverse languages, writing scripts, and code-mixing. This paper presents a comprehensive approach for abusive comment detection in the Telugu-English language pair, fine-tuning the state-of-the-art models for native Telugu script, Telugu sentences written in English script, and code-mixing or a combination of Telugu and English script. We leverage the power of two state-of-the-art pre-trained language models, XLMRoBERTa and mBERT, to effectively tackle this task. Our results demonstrate the efficacy of XLMRoBERTa and mBERT models in addressing these challenges in the detection of abusive language in the multilingual context in terms of accuracy, precision, recall, and F1 score. The fine-tuned mBERT gave an Accuracy of 66.21% and fine-tuned XLMRoBERTa gave an Accuracy of 70.51%.

Keywords: XLMRoBERTa · mBERT · Telugu-English Data · Abusive Comment Detection · Code-Mixed Data

1 Introduction

With the rapid growth of online communication platforms, the prevalence of abusive language and hate speech has become a pressing concern. Detecting and mitigating such abusive comments is crucial for fostering a healthy and inclusive online environment. However, addressing this challenge becomes even more complex in multilingual settings, where diverse languages, writing scripts, and code-mixing are prevalent. In this paper, we focus on the task of detecting abusive comments in the Telugu-English language pair, which encompasses text written in both native Telugu script and Telugu written in English script, as well as instances of code-mixing between Telugu and English.

The Telugu-English language pair poses unique challenges due to the intricacies of its linguistic characteristics. Telugu, a Dravidian language predominantly spoken in the Indian states of Andhra Pradesh and Telangana, has its distinct script. On the other hand, English, being a widely used global language, introduces a different writing script and

B. R. Chakravarthi et al. (Eds.): SPELLL 2023, CCIS 2046, pp. 236–245, 2024.
https://doi.org/10.1007/978-3-031-58495-4_17

linguistic features. Furthermore, the phenomenon of code-mixing, where individuals mix Telugu and English within the same sentence or conversation, is common in online discussions, making it essential to account for such mixed-language patterns during abusive comment detection.

To effectively address the complexities of the Telugu-English language pair, we leverage the capabilities of two state-of-the-art pre-trained language models: XLMRoBERTa and mBERT. These models have demonstrated remarkable performance in various natural language processing tasks, including sentiment analysis, named entity recognition, and language understanding. By fine-tuning these models on the annotated dataset of Telugu-English abusive comments, we aim to train them to accurately identify instances of abusive language within this language combination.

2 Related Work

Several studies have been conducted on abusive comment detection and hate speech classification in various languages, including English, but limited research has focused specifically on the Telugu-English language paired with its unique challenges of native Telugu script, Telugu written in English script, and code-mixing. However, we draw inspiration from relevant studies in the broader context of multilingual abusive content detection, as well as studies that explore abusive comment detection in other language pairs.

Detecting abusive comments at a fine-grained level in a low-resource language by Patankar et al. (2023) [1] proposed an adaptive ensemble method for detecting abusive comments in a low-resource language. The method combines a variety of machine learning approaches, including traditional classifiers, deep learning models, and state-of-the-art language modelling. Multilingual Abusive Comment Detection at Scale for Indic Languages by Gupta et al. (2021) [2] presented a dataset of abusive comments in 10 Indic languages, along with a multilingual model for abusive comment detection. Their model AbuseXLMR is trained on a combination of monolingual and multilingual data and achieves state-of-the-art results on the Indic languages in the dataset. Abusive Comment Detection in Tamil by Patankar et al. (2022) [3] presented an approach for detecting abusive comments in Tamil. The approach uses a combination of ensemble models, recurrent neural networks, and transformers. Cross-lingual Abusive Comment Detection with Multilingual Transfer Learning (2021) [4] proposed a method for cross-lingual abusive comment detection using multilingual transfer learning. The method is evaluated on a dataset of English and Spanish comments.

Sentiment analysis of code-mixed text in Dravidian languages (2021) [5] presented an approach for sentiment analysis of code-mixed text in Dravidian languages. The approach uses a combination of transliteration and translation techniques. Code-Mixed Sentiment Analysis using Transformers (2020) [6] presents a system for code-mixed sentiment analysis using transformers for monolingual Spanish and English data and Spanish-English code-mixed data. Sentiment Analysis For Bengali Using Transformer-Based Models (2021) [7] presented a study on the applicability of transformer-based models for sentiment analysis in Bengali. The authors investigate pre-trained transformer models, for two-class and three-class sentiment classification tasks. They evaluate the models on three Bengali sentiment datasets and achieve state-of-the-art results.

Understanding Emojis for Sentiment Analysis (2021) [11] described how emojis affected the overall sentiment of the tweet and introduced a method for improving accuracy in the pre-processing steps. Effect of emojis in classifying Telugu code mixed movie reviews (2023) [12] described the significance of emojis and how they affect the polarity of a sentence in code-mixed Telugu text. Pre-Processing and Emoji Classification of WhatsApp Chats for Sentiment Analysis (2020) [13] described converting unstructured data to structured data for various data mining techniques and to deal with different emojis and emotions they depict, code mixed text and perform basic analysis.

Most of the related works in the Telugu language using transformer models are done on text data that is written in pure native Telugu script. Some works are done on code mixed but are limited to the text written in English/Latin Script. The dataset [8] that we used contains not only text written in pure native Telugu script but also code-mixed text written in English script and a combination of both native Telugu script and code-mixed script. More details are given in the Dataset Description. The models XLM RoBERTa and mBERT are fine-tuned for this dataset.

3   Dataset Description

The dataset used in this study comprises a diverse collection of Telugu-English comments from Abusive Comment Detection in Tamil and Telugu-DravidianLangTech 2023 [8]. The comments in the dataset are written in a combination of different forms, including text written in native Telugu script, Telugu written in English script, and instances of code-mixing between Telugu and English.

The dataset consists of comments written entirely in the native Telugu script. These comments reflect the authentic linguistic expressions used by Telugu speakers. They cover a wide range of topics and encompass various linguistic styles, including formal and informal language usage. The sample is as follows:

"యాంకర్ గారు అసలు మీకు దండం పెట్టా లండి బాబు మీ ఓపిక ఏంటండీ"

In addition to comments written in the native Telugu script, the dataset also includes comments where Telugu words are transliterated into the English script. This form of writing is commonly used in online communication platforms, allowing users to express themselves using the English alphabet. These comments introduce additional complexities due to the variations in transliteration schemes and potential ambiguities in the representation of Telugu phonetics. The sample is as follows:

"Meeru cheppindi nijam chesaru Raju garu"

Code mixing refers to instances where Telugu and English languages are mixed within the same comment. This phenomenon is prevalent in multilingual online conversations and reflects the linguistic practices of bilingual or multilingual users. Code-mixed comments can range from simple word-level mixing to more complex sentence-level mixing. They pose challenges in terms of understanding and interpreting the linguistic cues, context, and sentiment present within the mixed-language expressions. Samples are as follows:

"nag sir said about natraj master is absolutely correct ఆడియన్స్ మాస్టర్ గురించి ఏమనుకుంటున్నారో అదే చెప్పారు... super nag sir"

"MLA garu has very clarity in his thoughts... Chaala manchi ga express chesaru"

"Ayana nilabadithe chalu memu chusathsam bayya super dailogue"

The dataset is manually annotated by domain experts, classifying each comment as either hate or non-hate. The hate comments encompass a wide range of offensive, derogatory, and harmful content, while the non-hate comments include general conversations, opinions, and statements that do not exhibit abusive language. Some more samples of the dataset are given in Table 1.

Table 1. Dataset Samples

Comments	Label
Okkokkadiki 9 months pregnancy vundhi police'laki	hate
Acting chaalabaagundi mi timing kanivandi performance kanivandi dialogue delivery gaani nice kipet up all the best you have a great future as an artist	non-hate
Anna nuvvu chavaku యిది చాలా అన్యయం suspense అదిరిపోయింది next episode వేగంగా pettanna.	hate
Ee movie kosam Wait చేసేవాళ్ళు ... like vesukondiii....	non-hate
ఈ పాట కన్న .. మీ మాశే బాగుంది.....	non-hate
Character of the episode award goes to- "1A master" అంతే కధమ్మ రేయ్	non-hate
Hope that there is no ending in madhu character.. waiting for next episode in telugu with madhu again..... మధు పోకూడదమ్మారేయ్	non-hate
దేవి అడిగే ప్రశ్నలకు గట్టిగా దింపావూ గా (సమాధానాలు) విజయ్...	hate
జఫ్నా తిమింగలం 420 గాడికి RiP ఎప్పుడు చెపుతారు	hate
Pilichi pettinchukuntaru ga....TV9 ki eemadhya sarada ayindi...	hate
E tv 9 ki burra poyandhi	hate
నాగబాబు సెలక్షన్ సూపర్, గల్లీ బాయ్స్ అదుర్స్	non-hate
Ñeela oka 1hr kuda undalem sir jai rgv	non-hate
నీ judgement కరెక్ట్ గా ఉంటాది బ్రో	non-hate

The count of dataset samples are given in Table 2 below. The Validation dataset has 600 random samples that are generated from the Train dataset.

Table 2. Dataset Information

	hate	non-hate	Total
Train dataset	1,939	2,061	4,000
Test dataset	250	250	500

4 Proposed Approach

To address the task of Telugu-English abusive comment detection, we propose an approach that involves fine-tuning the XLMRoBERTa [9] and mBERT [10] models on the labelled dataset containing Telugu, English and code-mixed Telugu English comments [8]. The objective is to adapt these pre-trained language models to accurately identify instances of abusive language in the Telugu-English language pair, accounting for the nuances of writing scripts and code-mixing.

mBERT and XLMRoBERTa are based on the Transformer [14] architecture. Transformers are a type of deep learning model that has received a lot of interest in the natural language processing (NLP) and machine learning fields. They have transformed the way sequential data is processed by employing attention processes to record nuanced links between various items in a sequence. Transformers, unlike traditional models such as recurrent neural networks (RNNs), allow for concurrent data processing, making them highly efficient and effective for a variety of tasks such as language translation, text production, and sequence-to-sequence learning challenges. Transformers, with their capacity to capture complex patterns and relationships within data, have become an essential component of modern NLP models, providing enhanced performance and scalability (Fig. 1).

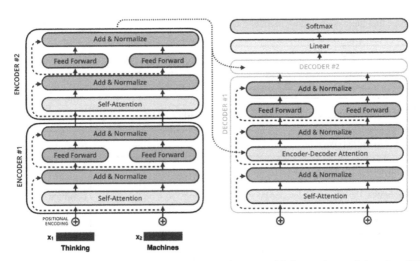

Fig. 1. Visual representation of Transformer architecture with 2 encoders and decoders [15]

mBERT or Multilingual BERT (Bidirectional Encoder Representations from Transformers) is a pre-trained language model method. The BERT architecture is made up of only Transformer encoders. Each Transformer encoder is made up of two layers: a self-attention layer and a feed-forward layer. BERT is trained largely on large amounts of monolingual text data from a single language, typically English, allowing it to grasp nuanced language characteristics unique to that language.

While mBERT is trained on a larger, more diversified dataset that contains text in many languages. This extensive training enables mBERT to understand numerous languages including low-resource languages like Telugu and their unique linguistic peculiarities. The model trains the artificial neural network using a corpus of plain text. In the pre-training stage, the multilingual BERT makes use of a corpus made up of more than 104 different languages including Telugu. The multilingual BERT base which we used consists of a multi-head attention mechanism with 12 transformer encoder levels, 110 million parameters, 768 hidden states and a total of 12 heads in the model design.

Robustly Optimized BERT Pre Training Approach, or RoBERTa [16], is a BERT clone created by Facebook with the following changes: dynamically adjusts the masking patterns, such as by taking care of masking whole multiword units, training the model longer with bigger batches as well as more and cleaner data and discarding the Next Sentence Prediction aim, training on longer sequences.

XLM [9] is modified BERT tailored to specifically address two tasks, namely, cross-lingual classification and machine translation. XLM uses Byte-Pair Encoding (BPE) instead of word or character encoding, to increase the shared vocabulary between languages. It trains BERT with dual-language input to learn cross-language contexts. It further initializes pre-trained BERT together with a translation of model embeddings to improve Back-Translation. The outperformance of XLM is due to pretraining over 100 languages, models were pre-trained on extraordinarily large corpora, such as those containing over 3 billion words for BERT.

A cross-lingual or multilingual version of RoBERTa called XLM-RoBERTa (XLM-R) demonstrates the ability to train a single model for several languages while maintaining per-language performance. It was trained in 100 languages using 2.5 TB of CommonCrawl data including support for Telugu and Telugu Romanized text (Fig. 2).

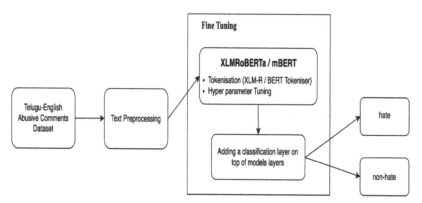

Fig. 2. Proposed Approach for Telugu-English Abusive Comment Detection

The steps involved in the proposed approach are explained. Before fine-tuning the models, we perform preprocessing steps on the Telugu-English dataset. This includes converting the labels hate and non-hate to 0 and 1 respectively for binary classification, cleaning the text by removing irrelevant characters, converting all the comments in English script to lowercase letters, and tokenising the comments into subword units compatible with the language models. Then, initialising instances of XLMRoBERTa or mBERT model, which is pre-trained on large-scale monolingual and multilingual corpora, approximately 100 &104 languages respectively. These models capture rich linguistic representations and have been trained on a wide range of natural language understanding tasks, providing a strong foundation for fine-tuning.

The fine-tuning process involves several steps to adapt the models to the task of abusive comment detection in the Telugu-English language pair. Modifying the classification head of the XLMRoBERTa and mBERT models to accommodate the binary classification task of identifying hate and non-hate comments. This entails adding a softmax layer on top of the model's final hidden states to generate probability scores for the two classes. The next step involves mapping the preprocessed tokenised comments to their corresponding embeddings as input to the models. This ensures that the models capture the semantic and syntactic information present in the Telugu-English text.

In the training procedure, the dataset is divided into training, validation, and test sets. During training, a binary cross-entropy loss function is used to optimise the models, comparing the predicted probabilities against the ground truth labels. Then hyper-parameter tuning to find the optimal configuration for the models. This includes adjusting learning rates, batch sizes, and the number of training epochs. Used the validation set to monitor the models' performance during training and select the best hyper-parameter settings. Once the fine-tuning process is complete, the performance of the XLMRoBERTa and mBERT models is evaluated on the test set. Then various evaluation metrics, including accuracy, precision, recall, and F1 score, to assess the models' effectiveness in detecting abusive comments in the Telugu-English dataset.

By fine-tuning the XLMRoBERTa and mBERT models on our annotated Telugu-English dataset, the aim is to leverage their pre-trained knowledge and adapt them to effectively detect abusive language, accounting for the complexities of different writing scripts and code-mixing. This proposed approach allows us to harness the power of these state-of-the-art language models in addressing the task of Telugu-English abusive comment detection.

5 Results

In this section, the results of the experiments on Telugu-English abusive comment detection using the fine-tuned XLMRoBERTa and mBERT models are given in the tables. The model type used for XLMRoBERTa is "xlm-roberta-base" and the model type used for mBERT is "bert-base-multilingual-cased" from Huggingface transformers library in python. The experimental setup for executing the code is Google Colab's Tesla T4 GPU. For hyper-parameter tuning the learning rate of $2e-5$, AdamW optimiser, batch size of 16, and 4 training epochs are used. Both models use the same hyper parameter tunings for experiments.

The evaluation metrics used are Precision, Recall, F1-score, Macro average F1-score and Accuracy. Precision is defined as the percentage of real positive predictions to total anticipated positives, emphasising positive prediction accuracy. Recall measures the ratio of true positive predictions to total actual positives, and it demonstrates the model's capacity to recognise all relevant cases.

The harmonic mean of precision and recall, or F1 score, establishes a balance between these two metrics, which is especially valuable in circumstances of uneven class distribution. In multiclass classification, the macro-average F1 score computes the average of the F1 scores for each class, treating all classes equally and disregarding class imbalance. Meanwhile, accuracy evaluates the ratio of successfully predicted cases to total instances to provide an overall assessment of a model's correctness. These indicators work together to provide a thorough assessment of model performance, providing insights into the model's suitability for real-world applications.

The performance of mBERT (bert-base-multilingual-cased) based on the evaluation metrics precision, recall and f1-score of both hate and non-hate classes are shown in Table 3. The macro f1-score average for mBERT (bert-base-multilingual-cased) is 0.6540 and the Test Accuracy is 66.21%.

Table 3. Performance of mBERT (bert-base-multilingual-cased)

	Precision	Recall	F1-score
hate	0.65	0.66	0.65
non-hate	0.66	0.65	0.66

The performance of XLMRoBERTa (base) based on the evaluation metrics precision, recall and f1-score are shown in Table 4. The macro f1-score average for XLMRoBERTa (base) is 0.6977 and Test Accuracy is 70.51%..

Table 4. Performance of XLMRoBERTa (base)

	Precision	Recall	F1-score
hate	*0.73*	*0.69*	*0.71*
non-hate	0.664	*0.71*	*0.69*

From the above observations, we can see that fine-tuned XLMRoBERTa has a higher score for Precision for hate class, Recall and F1-score for both classes. The Precision score was similar for the non-hate class in both fine-tuned modes. The macro average f1-score and Accuracy are higher for fine-tuned XLMRoBERTa than fine-tuned mBERT.

The experimental results highlight that the fine-tuned XLMRoBERTa performs better than mBERT in detecting abusive comments in the Telugu-English language pair. As XLMRoBERTa was pre-trained on Telugu and Telugu Romanized text, maintaining per language performance and architecture differences, gives better performance than mBERT.

6 Conclusion

Based on the experimental results of XLMRoBERTa and mBERT models, we can conclude that XLMRoBERTa (base) outperforms mBERT (bert-base-multilingual-cased) in the task of Telugu-English abusive comment detection with a test accuracy of 70.51% and 66.21% respectively. This indicates that the XLMRoBERTa model exhibits a better balance between precision and recall, resulting in improved overall performance in identifying abusive comments. The higher macro F1-score average of 0.6977 suggests that XLMRoBERTa is more effective in capturing the abusive language patterns present in the Telugu-English dataset.

Both models outperformed the baseline machine learning approaches, demonstrating the superiority of pre-trained language models in abusive comment detection. The XLM-RoBERTa and mBERT models excel in capturing linguistic patterns, contextual information, and code-mixing phenomena, enabling them to effectively handle the nuances of different writing scripts and code-mixing prevalent in Telugu-English abusive comments.

The findings from this study contribute to the development of more accurate and robust techniques for detecting abusive language in multilingual settings. It is important to note that despite the strong performance of these models, there are still areas for improvement. Further analysis of misclassified instances can provide insights into the models' limitations and guide future research efforts. Additionally, exploring techniques to handle specific challenges related to code-mixing and cultural nuances will contribute to enhancing the models' performance in detecting abusive language in the Telugu-English language pair.

In conclusion, the experimental results demonstrate the effectiveness of both XLM-RoBERTa and mBERT models in identifying abusive comments in the Telugu-English dataset. These models offer promising avenues for developing advanced systems to mitigate the spread of abusive language and foster inclusive online communities. The insights gained from this research contribute towards building safer and more respectful online platforms in the Telugu-English multilingual context.

References

1. Chakravarthi, B.R., et al.: Detecting abusive comments at a fine-grained level in a low-resource language. Nat. Lang. Process. J. 100006 (2023)
2. Gupta, V., et al.: Multilingual abusive comment detection at scale for Indic languages. In: Advances in Neural Information Processing Systems, vol. 35, pp. 26176–26191 (2022)
3. Patankar, S., Gokhale, O., Litake, O., Mandke, A., Kadam, D.: Optimize_Prime@ DravidianLangTech-ACL2022: abusive comment detection in Tamil. arXiv preprint arXiv: 2204.09675 (2022)
4. Bigoulaeva, I., Hangya, V., Fraser, A.: Cross-lingual transfer learning for hate speech detection. In: Proceedings of the First Workshop on Language Technology for Equality, Diversity and Inclusion, pp. 15–25 (2021)

5. Puranik, K.: IIITT@ Dravidian-CodeMix-FIRE2021: transliterate or translate? Sentiment analysis of code-mixed text in Dravidian languages. arXiv preprint arXiv:2111.07906 (2021)

6. Sultan, A., Salim, M., Gaber, A., El Hosary, I.: WESSA at SemEval-2020 task 9: code-mixed sentiment analysis using transformers. arXiv preprint arXiv:2009.09879 (2020)

7. Bhowmick, A., Jana, A.: Sentiment analysis for Bengali using transformer based models. In: Proceedings of the 18th International Conference on Natural Language Processing (ICON), pp. 481–486 (2021)

8. Priyadharshini, R., et al.: Overview of shared-task on abusive comment detection in Tamil and Telugu. In: Proceedings of the Third Workshop on Speech and Language Technologies for Dravidian Languages, Varna, Bulgaria. Recent Advances in Natural Language Processing (2023)

9. Conneau, A., et al.: Unsupervised cross-lingual representation learning at scale. arXiv preprint arXiv:1911.02116 (2019)

10. Devlin, J., Chang, M.-W., Lee, K., Toutanova, K.: BERT: pre-training of deep bidirectional transformers for language understanding. arXiv preprint arXiv:1810.04805 (2018)

11. Yoo, B., Rayz, J.T.: Understanding emojis for sentiment analysis. In: The International FLAIRS Conference Proceedings, vol. 34 (2021)

12. Effect of emojis in classifying Telugu code mixed movie reviews. 3rd International Conference on Mathematical Modeling & Computational Science ICMMCS 2023

13. Mohta, A., Jain, A., Saluja, A., Dahiya, S.: Pre-processing and emoji classification of whatsapp chats for sentiment analysis. In: 2020 Fourth International Conference on I-SMAC (IoT in Social, Mobile, Analytics and Cloud) (I-SMAC), pp. 514–519. IEEE (2020)

14. Vaswani, A., et al.: Attention is all you need. In: Advances in Neural Information Processing Systems, vol. 30 (2017)

15. Alammar, J.: The Illustrated Transformer [Blog post] (2018). https://jalammar.github.io/illustrated-transformer/

16. Liu, Y., et al.: RoBERTa: a robustly optimized bert pretraining approach. arXiv preprint arXiv:1907.11692 (2019)

A Knowledge Engineering Framework Addressing High Incidence of Farmer Suicides

Vivek Bokinala[1,2], Santosh Tirunagari[3], and Senthilkumar Mohan[4(✉)]

[1] Department of Computer Science, University of Surrey, Guildford, UK
[2] Rishi M.S. Institute of Engineering and Technology for Women, Hyderabad, India
drvivekraj@rishimsengg.ac.in
[3] Department of Computer Science, Middlesex University, London, UK
s.tirunagari@mdx.ac.uk
[4] School of Information Technology and Engineering, Vellore Institute of Technology, Vellore, India
senthilkumar.mohan@vit.ac.in

Abstract. This study addresses the pressing issue of farmer suicides in India, a problem that has escalated significantly since 1995, with over 0.3 million recorded cases. While scholars and activists have proposed various factors contributing to these suicides, quantitative insights into the influence and probabilistic significance of these factors remain elusive. Consequently, we introduce a pioneering two-tier knowledge engineering framework to tackle this challenge. In the first tier, we employ natural language processing to gather a comprehensive array of suicide-causing factors from news articles and blog posts on the World Wide Web. In the second tier, we undertake a meticulous analysis of the causal factors by calculating probabilities and categorising the identified causal factors into distinct groups: social, economic, socio-economic, nature-related, health-related, and governmental policies. Our analysis reveals that health-related causal factors account for over 50% of farmer suicides, while economic, social, and socio-economic factors contribute to 26%. By meticulously investigating these causal elements, our approach has the potential to substantially mitigate future instances of farmer suicides.

Keywords: Farmers · Suicide · Causal factors

1 Introduction

Emerging approximately 12,000 years ago, agriculture sparked a profound societal shift from traditional nomadic lifestyles to settled communities, engendering human development and fostering civilisations. This transition facilitated the growth of cities and populations, expanding from five million individuals 10,000 years ago to around 400–500 million by 1 AD. Through the 20th century's rapid globalisation, the global population burgeoned to over seven billion today. Despite increased urbanisation, agriculture continues to employ a substantial workforce of 1.3 billion people globally, constituting nearly 40% of the global labour force [3].

B. R. Chakravarthi et al. (Eds.): SPELLL 2023, CCIS 2046, pp. 246–254, 2024.
https://doi.org/10.1007/978-3-031-58495-4_18

Within India, agriculture assumes a pivotal role in its economy, contributing significantly to the Gross Domestic Product (GDP). Over 58% of rural households depend primarily on agriculture for sustenance. While the sector's share in the GDP has decreased, it remains a vital contributor to food security, employment, and poverty alleviation. Nevertheless, shifts in policies between 1980/1981 and 2009/2010 have impacted agricultural growth patterns and sources in India[1].

Since 1995, farmer suicides have emerged as a pressing concern in India, with over 0.3 million recorded cases and an escalating trend[2]. Activists and scholars have proposed a plethora of conflicting factors such as monsoon failures, mounting debt, genetically modified crops, governmental policies, mental health, personal problems, and familial issues as potential drivers for these suicides. However, a comprehensive statistical analysis regarding the influence or contributions of these factors remains absent [2]. Despite significant research and policy interventions, farmer suicide rates continue to rise, emphasizing the complexity of the issue.

While technology has evolved notably [7], incorporating Natural Language Processing (NLP) and machine learning [1,8], their potential in modelling the multifaceted causes of farmer suicides within the agricultural sector remains underutilised. NLP could amplify awareness of farmers' concerns, harnessing the information scattered across online articles and blogs. However, discerning trustworthy sources is challenging, advocating for a more holistic approach. The machine learning paradigm, especially in this domain remains an unexplored avenue to model farmer suicides, despite the availability of the vast repository of online textual data.

The novelty of our approach lies in its two-tier framework of using text mining and machine learning to unravel the complexities of causality. Our knowledge engineering framework is aimed at proactively identifying potential factors underlying farmer suicides. Examining these patterns, not only offers the prospect of enhancing farmer safety and policy-making recommendations but also envisions a path toward a more secure agricultural landscape.

2   Methodology

In this section, we outline the structure of our two-tier framework each playing a pivotal role in comprehending the intricate causes behind farmer suicides and furnishing valuable insights.

1. Causal Factor Extraction: In Tier 1, we leverage the power of text mining to unearth the latent causes of suicides embedded within an array of articles available on the Internet.
2. Probabilistic Analysis and Causal Factor Categorization: In Tier 2, we calculate the probabilities associated with the extracted causes and systematically categorize these causal factors.

---

[1] http://timesofindia.indiatimes.com/india/NDA-UPA-failed-to-curb-farmer-suicides/articleshow/39501676.cms.

[2] https://yourstory.com/2016/10/farmer-suicides/.

By adopting this approach, we aim to understand the intricate connections among the identified causal factors.

2.1 Cause-and-Effect Sentences

Identifying causal relations in the text has profound implications. Such relations not only help in understanding the underlying factors behind a phenomenon but also assist in predicting future occurrences.

To illustrate, consider a hypothetical article excerpt: "In the rural regions of India, the unpredictable monsoon has led to poor crop yields. *Consequently*, farmers find themselves trapped in a cycle of debt". In this example, our methodology (Tier 1) would identify the cause (unpredictable monsoon) and its effect (farmers in debt) using the connector "Consequently".

We address these linguistic elements that facilitate the linkage between cause-and-effect sentences, which we term "connecting words" (e.g., Table 1 [9]). These connecting words encompass a curated collection of around 200 frequently employed English language elements. These elements introduce alteration, contrast, emphasis, agreement, purpose, consequence, or conclusion, within the discourse of different sentences [4,5].

Table 1. Connective words used in our experiments

Connective Words			
consequently	Thus	for the reason	For this reason
as a result	because	caused	For all these reasons
Therefore	since	attributed	on account of
as a consequence	because of	so	due to

The connectives approach hinges on the extraction of causal sentences through the utilisation of these connecting words [11]. These connecting words often manifest as transitions, conjunctions, or verb phrases. Transitional phrases play a crucial role in connecting how the main idea relates to the supporting information. Different types of transitions serve various functions, such as being "Additive", "Adversative", "Causal", or "Sequential". However, this study reinterprets transition words as temporal indicators, illustrating instances when a specific time period led to the emergence of certain outcomes due to an influence. Transitions provide contextual cues within a causal sentence, establishing a coherent narrative. For example, consider the following instance:

"Farming stress entailed a confluence of physical and mental health implications. Consequently, it yielded distinct measurable effects". In this example, the term "Consequently" functions as a transition, facilitating the smooth transition from one sentence to the next.

Conjunctions are connective words that are often used to combine two complete sentences. The conjunctions used to link cause and effect sentences include 'because', 'as', 'since', 'so', and others. The words 'Because', 'as', and 'since' introduce a cause, while 'so' introduces an effect. For example, 'because/as/since' in "Farmers" families resort to suicide because/as/since they had no other alternative."

Verb phrases encompass the verb and an object in a sentence. They serve as connectors, linking two noun phrases: <Noun Phrase 1><Verb Phrase><Noun Phrase 2>. This structure establishes causal relations, with the verb phrase acting as a causal verb or indicating a result [6]. Both "cause" and "result" verbs are used actively. For instance, in the sentence "The failure of monsoons over the years causes/results-in rural employment", "Cause" can be passive with a "by phrase", while "result" is followed by "from"., e.g., "Illiteracy results-from/is-resulted-by poor childhood education".

3   Data, Experiments and Results

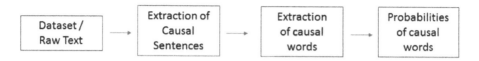

Fig. 1. Pipeline showing the dataset and experiment procedure.

Our data and experimental implementation pipeline details are shown in Fig. 1. The dataset employed in our experiments comprises "Research Articles on Farmer Suicides in India". A total of 150 articles were downloaded from Google Scholar and PubMed, utilising the search keyword "Farmer Suicides in India". Subsequently, meticulous scrutiny led to the selection of 87 PDF articles. The collected documents underwent conversion from .pdf to .txt format. Each PDF document was accessed via Foxit PDF reader software and then saved in .txt format. The extracted causal sentences of these 87 .txt files constitute the dataset for this study. The dataset is available for download at FigShare [10][3].

3.1   Extraction of Causal Sentences

To extract causal sentences, we employed the Linux command "grep"[4]. This allowed us to collect sentences from the .txt files that contain the transitions, conjunctions, and verb phrases listed in Table 1. The obtained causal sentences are provided as examples in Table 2.

The quantity of causal sentences, along with the total count of words and characters within the extracted sentences employing the connective words, is showcased in Table 3.

---

[3] https://figshare.com/account/articles/24316948.
[4] http://linux.die.net/man/1/grep.

Table 2. The example causal sentences that were extracted with our methodological procedure

Cause	Connective	Effect
Food insecurity was addressed with the rice-wheat technology but in the process inflicted neglect on coarse and	**Consequently,**	the farmers growing these crops also suffered.
Every 30 min an Indian farmer commits suicide.	**As a result**	of Monsanto's GM crops.
In the last decade, more than 250,000 Indian farmers have killed themselves	**because of**	costly seeds and pesticides

3.2   Extraction of Causal Words

Once the causal sentences were extracted, we read each sentence to manually select the causal words. A total of 41 causal words were thoughtfully chosen and are documented in Table 4. To provide a quantitative perspective, we proceeded to calculate the frequency of occurrences of these manually selected causal words within the dataset. This count is referred to as Evidence Retrieved (ER). The relative occurrence of a specific causal word is termed the Strength of Evidence (SE). The Strength of Evidence for a Causal Word (CW) is represented as SE_{CW} and is calculated using Eq. 1.

$$SE_{CW} = \frac{ER_{CW}}{\sum ER_{CWs}} \tag{1}$$

The collection of causal sentences from the 87 articles yielded a total of approximately 8,451 words. Among these sentences, stress was the most prevalent causal factor with 1,994 occurrences, accounting for 23.5% of the extracted content.

3.3   Probabilities and Grouping

The analysis on the strength of evidence from Table 4, revealed the interconnected factors contributing to farmer suicides. While some factors were expected such as debt, the strength and frequency of others were surprising. It is apparent that socio-economic factors, such as social changes and low income, exhibit a lower percentage of the occurrence. On the other hand, health-related issues, including stress, depression, labour, and distress, collectively contribute to 50% of the total occurrences in the reports.

While our analysis indicated a higher occurrence of health-related factors, we observed lower frequencies for other health-related elements such as psychological problems and suicidal behaviour. To determine the strength of evidence for the most significant contributing factors, we proceeded to categorise the causal

Table 3. Number of causal sentences and a total of words and characters present in the sentences extracted using the connective words.

Connective Word	Characters	Words	Sentences
consequently	23388	3535	61
as a result	28438	4349	72
Therefore	107633	16103	310
as a consequence	2353	378	9
For this reason	1644	246	5
For all these reasons	0	0	0
Thus	1077280	16189	297
because	180953	28330	473
since	71999	10966	200
because of	65208	10127	184
on account of	4044	651	17
due to	182488	26465	531
for the reason	439	64	1
caused	37415	5403	221
attributed	8580	1326	27
so	3007629	408044	7163

Fig. 2. Grouping of causal words into 6 major types.

words into six major groups. These groupings are presented in Fig. 2, and the corresponding strength of evidence is visualised in Fig. 3. Health-related causal factors collectively account for over 50% of farmer suicides, while economic, social, and socio-economic factors contribute approximately 26%.

The overwhelming evidence pointing towards health-related factors underscores the deep-rooted mental and psychological issues faced by the farmers. From an economic perspective, while factors such as low income and increasing debt are direct indicators, they are also reflective of deeper systemic issues in the agricultural sector, such as lack of access to modern farming techniques, proper storage facilities, and fair market prices. Furthermore, the strength of evidence associated with social and socio-economic factors paints a picture of the societal pressures and the changing dynamics of rural communities.

Table 4. Example causal words and their percentage of occurrence in the reports.

Causal Factor (CF)	(ER)	(SE)	Occured in X/87.
Stress	1994	23.59%	76
Distress	752	8.90%	55
Depression	607	7.18%	46
labour	483	5.72%	42
Loans	462	5.47%	47
Illness	453	5.36%	52
Drought	444	5.25%	54
Lenders	392	4.64%	45
Poverty	387	4.58%	44
Irrigation	336	3.98%	50
Disorder	333	3.94%	32
Isolation	235	2.78%	37
Marginal farm	232	2.75%	31
Debts	208	2.46%	45
Monsoon	157	1.86%	33
Socio-Economic	137	1.62%	25
family problems	93	1.10%	23
alcoholism	87	1.03%	25
Unemployment	85	1.01%	29
Finances	53	0.63%	16
Economic Crisis	46	0.54%	20
GM seeds	46	0.54%	11
Debt trap	36	0.43%	12
Health issues	36	0.43%	9
suicidal behaviour	18	0.21%	6
Family Disputes	16	0.19%	8
Poor rainfalls	16	0.19%	7
Low Income	13	0.15%	8
Natural calamities	12	0.14%	10
Social Issues	10	0.12%	4
lack of policies	9	0.11%	5
Marginal landholdings	9	0.11%	6

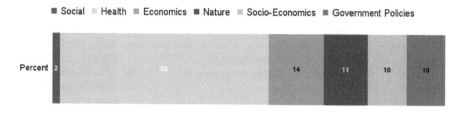

Fig. 3. Strength of Evidence in the 6 major groups

4   Conclusion

This study sheds light on the landscape of farmer suicides by employing a two-tier framework of text-mining/machine-learning techniques to extract and analyse causal keywords from text sources. Through meticulous data collection and analysis, we have identified key factors, with health-related issues like stress, depression, and distress emerging as prominent contributors. While economic, social, and socio-economic factors were second dominant. Our results emphasise the need for multi-faceted interventions. Addressing the economic concerns alone will not be sufficient; there's a dire need for mental health support and societal reforms in these communities. We anticipate that this research will serve as a foundational point for the development of robust tools and methodologies aimed at discerning human and organisational factors intrinsic to reports on farmer suicides.

References

1. Bengio, Y., Ducharme, R., Vincent, P., Jauvin, C.: A neural probabilistic language model. J. Mach. Learn. Res. **3**((Feb)), 1137–1155 (2003)
2. Bokinala, V.R.: Investigation into the causes and potential mitigation of the high incidence of farmers suicide (2022)
3. Calicioglu, O., Flammini, A., Bracco, S., Bellù, L., Sims, R.: The future challenges of food and agriculture: an integrated analysis of trends and solutions. Sustainability **11**(1), 222 (2019)
4. Girju, R.: Automatic detection of causal relations for question answering. In: Proceedings of the ACL 2003 Workshop on Multilingual Summarization and Question Answering, pp. 76–83 (2003)
5. Girju, R., Moldovan, D.I., et al.: Text mining for causal relations. In: FLAIRS Conference, pp. 360–364 (2002)
6. Grech, M.R., Horberry, T., Smith, A.: Human error in maritime operations: analyses of accident reports using the leximancer tool. In: Proceedings of the Human Factors and Ergonomics Society Annual Meeting, vol. 46, pp. 1718–1721. Sage Publications Sage CA: Los Angeles, CA (2002)
7. Hänninen, M., Sladojevic, M., Tirunagari, S., Kujala, P.: Feasibility of collision and grounding data for probabilistic accident modelling. Collision and grounding of ships and offshore structures, pp. 1–8. CRC Press/Taylor and Francis Group, London (2013)

8. Sahoo, J.: Modified TF-IDF term weighting strategies for text categorization (2018). https://doi.org/10.1109/INDICON.2017.8487593
9. Tirunagari, S.: Data mining of causal relations from text: analysing maritime accident investigation reports. arXiv preprint arXiv:1507.02447 (2015)
10. Tirunagari, S., Bokinala, V.: Dataset: investigation into the causes and potential mitigation of the high incidence of farmers' suicide. figshare (2023). https://doi.org/10.6084/m9.figshare.24316948
11. Tirunagari, S., Hanninen, M., Stanhlberg, K., Kujala, P.: Mining causal relations and concepts in maritime accidents investigation reports. Int. J. Innovative Res. Dev. 1(10), 548–566 (2012)

Event Categorization from News Articles Using Machine Learning Techniques

Kogilavani Shanmugavadivel[1]([✉]), Malliga Subramanian[2], K. Vasantharan[1],
G. A. Prethish[1], and S. Sankar[1]

[1] Department of Artificial Intelligence, Kongu Engineering College, Erode, India
kogilavani.sv@gmail.com
[2] Department of CSE, Kongu Engineering College, Erode, India

Abstract. Event detection from news articles using machine learning techniques is a crucial task which seeks to automatically identify and extract noteworthy events reported in a collection of news articles. This process involves the application of machine learning algorithms to analyze the textual content and discover relevant events. In this context, two common feature extraction methods - Count Vectorizer and TF-IDF (Term Frequency-Inverse Document Frequency) - play essential roles in transforming the raw text data into numerical representations that can be utilized by machine learning models. These feature vectors are then used as input to train a machine learning model, such as Logistic Regression, Gaussian Naïve Bayes, Random Forest, Multinomial Naïve Bayes, K-NN, Decision Tree, and Support Vector Classifier. Among all the models, Random Forest provides best accuracy of.

Keywords: Event Detection · Machine Learning · Feature Extraction · Random Forest · TF-IDF · Count Vectorizer

1 Introduction

A newspaper is a periodic publication that often has a white or grey backdrop and is typed in black ink. It contains written information about current occurrences. Newspapers frequently provide articles like opinion columns, weather predictions, and other similar content. They might talk about a range of topics, including politics, business, sports, and the arts. Newspapers have traditionally been printed (often on inexpensive, subpar paper known as newsprint). The majority of newspapers now publish online as well, and some have even stopped printing print editions altogether. News-related articles are only regarded as encyclopaedic if they can be proven to have a major, long-lasting, and historical significance and influence. As technology advances, news items and articles from newspapers are now available online in digital form. The topics and events covered in news stories are those that affect us daily across the world. These publications constitute the basis for several studies. Every topic, from economics to entertainment, politics to business, sports to social issues, has been written about as a news piece to assist the public in staying informed. Every person has a different interest in the news;

B. R. Chakravarthi et al. (Eds.): SPELLL 2023, CCIS 2046, pp. 255–267, 2024.
https://doi.org/10.1007/978-3-031-58495-4_19

some may be more interested in sports, while others may be more interested in politics. It all depends on how they think. Events that take place at a specific time and location make up the news. Manually classifying such events will be difficult and monotonous.

An event detection system from news articles is a powerful tool that can automatically identify and categorize events from a large corpus of news articles. The system works by training a machine learning model on a labelled dataset of news articles, which includes examples of different types of events and their corresponding features. These features can include the headline, text, date, and location of the article, as well as various linguistic and semantic attributes extracted from the text, such as named entities, sentiment, and part-ofspeech tags. By applying machine learning techniques for event detection from articles include their scalability, adaptability, and flexibility. Machine learning models can process large amounts of data quickly and efficiently, and can learn from new examples to improve their performance over time. They are valuable in a variety of fields, including politics, finance, sports, and health. They can also handle various event types, languages, and news article sources.

During the training phase, the machine learning algorithm learns from the patterns in the labeled dataset and builds a classification model that can predict the type of event for new, unseen news articles. The accuracy and generalization performance of the algorithm can be enhanced by using a variety of supervised learning approaches, such as decision trees, support vector machines, or deep neural networks. In the testing phase, the model's performance is assessed using a different, held-out dataset of news stories. Accuracy, precision, recall, and F1-score are measured for each type of event. Once the model is trained and tested, it can be deployed to detect events in real-time. As new news articles are published, the system processes them and applies the model to predict their type of event. This enables the system to monitor and analyse current events, anticipate future trends, and provide timely and accurate information to various stakeholders, such as decision-makers, journalists, or the public. A machine learning-based event detection system based on news articles has certain difficulties and has some limits. As well as the requirement for human monitoring and involvement to guarantee the accuracy and validity of the predictions, these might include problems with data quality, bias, ambiguity, and interpretation. Determining the trade-offs between various models, features, and evaluation metrics based on the unique requirements and restrictions of the application is therefore crucial when designing and evaluating the system.

The importance given to the word occurrences, disregarding the word order or context. For instance, if the input text contains the words "event", "detection", and "news", the Count Vectorizer will count the occurrences of each word and produce a corresponding numerical vector. TF-IDF, on the other hand, is a more sophisticated technique that assesses the significance of each word in a document in relation to the corpus as a whole. The sum of the Term Frequency (TF) and Inverse Document Frequency (IDF) is computed. The Inverse Document Frequency measures how uncommon or unique a word is over the entire document collection, whereas the Term Frequency indicates how frequently a word appears in a specific document. The TF-IDF score highlights terms that are common in a document but uncommon over the entire corpus by combining these two criteria, underscoring their importance.

To begin the process of event detection, a dataset of news articles is collected and preprocessed to standardize the text and remove irrelevant information. Next, the Count Vectorizer or TFIDF is applied to transform the pre-processed text data into numerical feature vectors. These feature vectors are then used as input to train a machine learning model, such as Logistic Regression, Gaussian Naïve Bayes, Random Forest, Multinomial Naïve Bayes, K-NN, Decision Tree, and Support Vector Classifier. Event detection from news articles using machine learning techniques and the mentioned feature extraction methods provides a scalable and efficient solution to process a vast amount of textual data and identify essential events that could otherwise be challenging and time-consuming for humans to handle. By leveraging the power of machine learning, this approach enables organizations, researchers, and analysts to stay up-to-date with current events and extract valuable insights from the ever-growing pool of news articles.

The rest of the paper is organized as follows. Section 2 provides literature review on various event detection systems. Section 3 discusses about proposed system methodology with various machine learning techniques. Section 4 provides performance evaluation metrics and Sect. 5 concludes the research work and provides future directions in event detection process.

2 Literature Review

[1] proposes a system that uses a combination of supervised and unsupervised machine learning techniques to detect and track events from a real-time stream of news articles. The system employs features such as text, date, and location, as well as semantic and contextual information to improve the accuracy and speed of the event detection. Deep neural networks are used to detect and classify events from social media streams in [2]. This system leverages the contextual and temporal features of social media data, as well as the power of deep learning models to improve the accuracy and scalability of the event detection. The work represented in [3] that provides a comprehensive survey of various approaches and techniques for automatic event detection from news articles. The authors discuss the challenges and opportunities of using machine learning models, including feature engineering, model selection, and evaluation metrics, and provide a taxonomy of event detection systems based on their features and methods.

In [4], the authors proposes a system that uses deep learning models with word embeddings to detect and classify events from online news sources. The system uses unsupervised feature learning to extract the semantic and syntactic relationships between words, and employs a convolutional neural network to learn the event classification. The research work mentioned in [5] uses machine learning techniques, including decision trees, Naive Bayes, and SVM, to detect and classify events from Twitter data. The system employs various features, such as hashtags, mentions, and sentiment, to improve the accuracy and coverage of the event detection. These studies present the promise and difficulties of event identification from news stories using machine learning algorithms. They draw attention to the significance of feature engineering, model choice, and assessment metrics as well as the requirement for scalable, flexible, and understandable event detection systems that can cope with the complexity and variety of news data. The following Table 1 represents review of existing methodology, limitations and accuracy details.

Table 1. Review of Existing Methodology, Limitations and Accuracy

Proposed System	Pros	Cons	Limitation	Performance
Global connectivity of news sources and news articles [6]	1. Natural language processing 2. Computer scientists with limited programming experience who would benefit from ready-touse main event extraction techniques are	1. The evaluation data sets of earlier articles are no longer accessible to the general public, which presents another difficulty for the evaluation of news event extraction	It requires a device like mobile phone with network connectivity to run or execute the model which is created	ACCURA CY: 87.2%
	welcome to modify or build on any of the modular components of our system and use our test collection and results as a benchmark for their implementations	Second, various quality metrics, including recall and precision or error rates, were utilized in each of the prior articles		
Using n-grams, suffixes, and prefix characteristics, Linear SVC is used to recognize text fragments that indicate events and categorize them into specified categories [7]	It serves as a preprocessing stage for several natural language processing applications, including relational extraction, topic modelling, and decision-making	This model's performance is poor, and it has to be enhanced to achieve accuracy	Standard new articles should only match terms found in the training dataset, which is used to train the machine	ACCURA CY: 87.8%
Utilizing an assessment strategy based on user studies and manually classifying information into relevant and irrelevant groups [8]	Quickly recognizing the question and classifying it appropriately	It is not accurate to detect an event 100% based on this analysis	For the data model to produce the desired results, a typical news story is required	ACCUAR CY: 85% to 90%
Employing hierarchical methods like singlelink, complete-link, and group wise average to find the clusters at the sentence level [9]	Categorizing the events through clusters and aligning them as categorical data	The proposed model does not provide a cent percent accurate detection based on the analysis	The model requires a greater number of articles to determine the same event	ACCUAR CY: 88.2%

(*continued*)

Table 1. (*continued*)

Proposed System	Pros	Cons	Limitation	Performance
By doing wavelet analysis on the frequency-based raw signals of the words, EDCoW creates signals for specific words. Then, by examining the matching signal autocorrelations of the words, it eliminates the unimportant words. A graph partitioning approach based on modularity then groups the remaining words into events. The EDCoW's experimental findings are encouraging [10]	1. In EDCoW, wavelet analysis is used to create a signal for each word, and it performs rather well 2. The mining may be applied in a variety of NLP scenarios. 3. The accuracy is over 25%	1. To constitute an event, words must be semantically near enough together to form a cluster 2. Only a tiny scale of the performance of EDCoW with the dataset is being studied	EDCoW still needs more improvement and it has been only tested for smaller dataset of one day report	ACCUAR CY: 69.7%
To use the Coreference relation to identify one central event in the news article [11]	1. Several NLP applications, including as text summarization, narrative development, and text segmentation, can be employed with the mining	Coreference relations Prediction failed to identify the central event	It finds more than one central event	ACCUAR CY: 58%

Natural language processing has seen a lot of study on event identification from news stories using machine learning approaches. Popular feature extraction techniques used to convert text data into numerical representations include Count Vectorizer and TF-IDF. [12] explored event detection using Convolutional Neural Networks, while [13] proposed a MultiGranularity Convolutional Attention Network for the same task. [14] utilized Matrix Factorization, and [15] incorporated Self-Attention Mechanism for event detection from news articles. [16] focused on Support Vector Machines with TF-IDF and Word2Vec features, while [17] introduced a BERTBased Hierarchical Attention Network for the task. [18, 19] extended the study by utilizing BERT with Contextualized Word Embeddings. These research efforts demonstrate the diverse and evolving approaches in the domain of event detection, showcasing the potential of combining machine learning techniques with Count Vectorizer and TF-IDF feature extraction for efficient and accurate event identification from news articles.

3 Proposed System

Event detection from news articles is a process that involves analyzing a large corpus of news articles to detect and classify different types of events. This task can be accomplished using machine learning techniques such as Logistic Regression, Random Forest, Multinomial Naive Bayes, Support Vector Classifier, Decision Tree Classifier, K Nearest Neighbor, and Gaussian Naive Bayes. The following Fig. 1 represents the proposed system workflow.

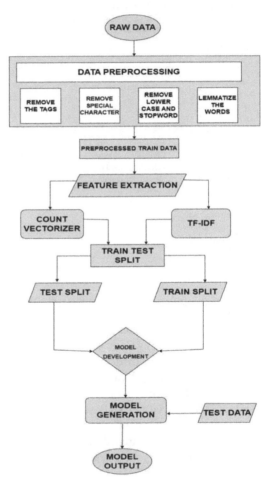

Fig. 1. Proposed System Workflow

3.1 Pre-processing

The words associated with the categories are now expected to be visualized. The same is shown using the Word Cloud module. The magnitude of each word in a word cloud, a data visualization approach for expressing text data, shows its frequency or relevance. Using a word cloud, significant textual data points may be emphasized. Word clouds are frequently employed for social network data analysis. The terms in the news items that are business-related are shown in Fig. 2. And the Figs. 2, 3, 4, 5 and 6 depict, respectively, terms relating to technology, politics, sports, and entertainment. Following the visualization of the categories' associated words, the tags, special characters, and stop words were deleted, the words were changed to lower case, and the words were lemmatized. Lemmatization is the process of combining a word's several inflected forms into a single unit for analysis. Like stemming, lemmatization adds context to the words. As a result, it ties words with related meanings together. Because lemmatization performs morphological analysis on the words, it is preferred over stemming. We have specified the dependent and independent values required for the categorization after cleaning the data. The bag of words is something we made and included into the model. The text is first preprocessed using the Bag of Words model, which creates a bag of terms from it and keeps track of how many times the most popular words appear overall. To extract the features for the bag of words, we utilized the TF-IDF feature extractor. Term Frequency - Inverse Document Frequency (TF-IDF) is a numerical statistic used to measure how significant a term is to a document inside a corpus or collection. In information retrieval, text mining, and user modeling searches, it is frequently employed as a weighting factor. The method of dividing the dataset into a Train set and a Test set for the model development followed. Using the train test split library imported from the Sklearn package, the dataset was divided into four sets: x test, x train, y test, and y train. We used seven ML models in order to obtain the best model. We made predictions using all seven models, and the top model was selected.

Fig. 2. Business Related Words

Fig. 3. Tech Related Words

Fig. 4. Politics Related Words

Fig. 5. Sport Related Words

Fig. 6. Entertainment Related Words

3.2 Machine Learning Techniques

Logistic Regression is a simple yet effective classification algorithm that is widely used in event detection systems. It works by estimating the probability of each event class based on a set of input features, such as the article headline, text, date, and location. The algorithm then uses a decision boundary to classify the article into one of the event classes. Random Forest is another popular machine learning algorithm that can be used for event detection. It is an ensemble method that combines multiple decision trees to improve the accuracy and robustness of the event classification. Each decision tree is trained on a random subset of the input features and samples, and the final prediction is based on the average or majority vote of the individual tree predictions.

Multinomial Naive Bayes is a probabilistic classification algorithm that is well-suited for text classification tasks such as event detection from news articles. It works by modeling the conditional probability of each event class given the article features, assuming that the features are conditionally independent. This simplifying assumption allows the algorithm to estimate the class probabilities efficiently and accurately, even with high-dimensional and sparse feature spaces. Support Vector Classifier is a discriminative algorithm that aims to find a hyperplane that separates the input feature space into different regions corresponding to each event class. It works by maximizing the margin between the hyperplane and the closest training samples, while minimizing the classification error. The algorithm can handle nonlinearly separable data by using kernel functions to map the input features into a higherdimensional space.

Decision Tree Classifier is a tree-based algorithm that recursively splits the input feature space based on the most informative feature, according to some splitting criterion, such as entropy or Gini impurity. The resulting tree can be used to classify new articles by following the decision path from the root to the leaf node that corresponds to the predicted event class. K Nearest Neighbor is a lazy, instance-based algorithm that classifies new articles based on the similarity of their feature vectors to the training samples. It works by finding the K nearest training samples to the query article, based on some distance metric, and using their majority vote to predict the event class. The algorithm can handle noisy and imbalanced data, but requires a large amount of memory and computation for large datasets.

Gaussian Naive Bayes is a variant of the Naive Bayes algorithm that assumes that the input features are continuous and normally distributed. It works by modeling the conditional probability of each event class given the article features using a Gaussian distribution for each feature. This allows the algorithm to estimate the class probabilities and the mean and variance of the feature distributions efficiently and accurately.

4 Performance Evaluation

4.1 Dataset Description

The BBC News Event Detection Dataset is a large and structured collection of news articles derived from the BBC News website. This unique dataset is designed specifically for event detection tasks, providing researchers and data scientists with a comprehensive source of realworld data to develop, evaluate, and compare their event detection models. The dataset contains hundreds of thousands of news articles from various categories such as Politics, Business, Sport, Environment, and Technology, among others. Each article is tagged with the date of publication, news category, and associated tags that could help identify key events.

The proposed system is experimented with seven machine learning models from the sklearn machine learning package in order to avoid the issue of sub-optimal model error. To choose the most effective optimal model, we used Logistic regression, Random forest, Multinomial Naive Bayes, Support vector classifier, Decision Tree classifier, K Nearest Neighbor, and Gaussian Naive Bayes models. And in order to extract the features, the system utilized CountVectorizer and TF-IDF feature extractor, of which we discovered that TF-IDF is superior. The metrics sklearn library is used to assess the performance of the ML models. And from among them, the finest model is picked. Among the models that are assessed, the Random Forest model is the best one. The performance of each model using count vectorizer feature extraction method is displayed in Table 2.

Table 2. Performance Evaluation of ML models using Count Vectorizer

Algorithm	Precision	Recall	F1-Score
Logistic Regression	0.97	0.97	0.97
Gaussian Navie Bayes	0.76	0.76	0.76
Random Forest	0.98	0.98	0.98
Multinomial Navie Bayse	0.97	0.97	0.97
K Nn	0.73	0.73	0.73
Decision Tree	0.82	0.82	0.82
Support Vector Classifer	0.97	0.97	0.97

From Table 2, it is clear that random forest machine learning model produces best precision, recall and f1-score values for the taken training dataset. The performance of each model using TF_IDF feature extraction method is displayed in Table 3.

Table 3. Performance Evaluation of ML models using TF-IDF

Algorithm	Precision	Recall	F1-Score
Logistic Regression	0.98	0.98	0.98
Gaussian Navie Bayes	0.74	0.74	0.74
Random Forest	0.98	0.98	0.98
Multinomial Navie Bayse	0.97	0.97	0.97
K Nn	0.86	0.86	0.86
Decision Tree	0.79	0.79	0.79
Support Vector Classifer	0.97	0.97	0.97

From Table 3, it is obvious that for the chosen training dataset, the logistic regression and random forest machine learning models offer the best precision, recall, and f1-score values. The classification report shown in Fig. 7 below includes test data's accuracy, precision, recall, and F1-Score.

	Model	Test Accuracy	Precision	Recall	F1
0	Logistic Regression	97.99	0.98	0.98	0.98
1	Random Forest	98.43	0.98	0.98	0.98
2	Multinomial Naive Bayes	97.54	0.98	0.98	0.98
3	Support Vector Classifer	97.54	0.98	0.98	0.98
4	Decision Tree Classifier	78.52	0.79	0.79	0.79
5	K Nearest Neighbour	86.13	0.86	0.86	0.86
6	Gaussian Naive Bayes	74.27	0.74	0.74	0.74

Fig. 7. Classification report of Machine Learning Models

The confusion matrix is another technique for summarizing the performance of a classification algorithm. With two dimensions (actual and predicted), identical sets of "classes," and two dimensions (any combination of dimension and class represents a variable in the contingency table), it is a special kind of contingency table. In the field of machine learning, and more specifically, the problem of statistical classification, the performance of an algorithm can be visualized using a special table structure called a confusion matrix, also known as an error matrix (in unsupervised learning, it is typically referred to as a matching matrix). The confusion matrices for the seven distinct ML models are shown in Figs. 8, 9, 10, 11, 12, 13 and 14.

```
[[101  1  0  1  0]
 [  0 76  0  1  0]
 [  3  0 76  2  0]
 [  0  0  0 97  0]
 [  0  0  1  0 88]]
```

Fig. 8. Logistic Regression

```
[[103  0  0  0  0]
 [  0 75  0  0  2]
 [  2  0 77  2  0]
 [  0  0  0 97  0]
 [  0  0  1  0 88]]
```

Fig. 9. Random Forest

```
[[100  2  0  1  0]
 [  0 74  1  0  2]
 [  2  0 77  2  0]
 [  0  0  0 97  0]
 [  0  0  1  0 88]]
```

Fig. 10. Multinomial Naive Bayes

```
[[98  2  1  2  0]
 [ 0 76  0  1  0]
 [ 1  0 76  3  1]
 [ 0  0  0 97  0]
 [ 0  0  0  0 89]]
```

Fig. 11. Support Vector Classifier

```
[[59  3 14  2 25]
 [ 1 57  2  6 11]
 [ 1  0 69  3  8]
 [ 1  0  1 87  8]
 [ 2  1  1  0 85]]
```

Fig. 12. Decision Tree Classifier

```
[[77  3 16  5  2]
 [ 1 64  9  1  2]
 [ 7  0 70  2  2]
 [ 0  0  1 95  1]
 [ 2  0  4  4 79]]
```

Fig. 13. K Nearest Neighbor

$$\begin{bmatrix} [56 & 4 & 2 & 2 & 39] \\ [\ 0 & 57 & 2 & 0 & 18] \\ [\ 1 & 0 & 45 & 0 & 35] \\ [\ 0 & 0 & 0 & 86 & 11] \\ [\ 0 & 1 & 0 & 0 & 88] \end{bmatrix}$$

Fig. 14. Gaussian Naive Bayes

5 Conclusion

In conclusion, event detection from news articles using machine learning techniques with Count Vectorizer and TF-IDF feature extraction is a powerful and scalable approach for automatically identifying and extracting significant events mentioned in a collection of news articles. Count Vectorizer provides a simple yet effective method to convert text into numerical representations based on word frequencies, while TF-IDF evaluates word importance relative to the entire corpus, emphasizing rare but significant terms. By leveraging machine learning algorithms such as Logistic Regression, Random Forest, Multinomial Naive Bayes, Support Vector Classifier, Decision Tree Classifier, K Nearest Neighbor, and Gaussian Naive Bayes enables efficient processing of vast amounts of textual data, aiding researchers, analysts, and organizations in staying up-to-date with current events and extracting valuable insights. From the results, it is clear that random forest machine learning model with TF_IDF feature extraction technique works better for both training and test data. In future, deep learning and transfer learning models may be applied for event detection from news articles.

References

1. Hamborg F., Breitinger C., Gipp B.: Giveme5w1h: a universal system for extracting main events from news articles. arXiv preprint arXiv:1909.02766 (2019)
2. Balouchzahi, F., Shashirekha, H.L.: An approach for event detection from news in indian languages using linear SVC. In: FIRE (Working Notes), pp. 829–834 (2020)
3. Khan, S.U.R., Islam, M.A.: Event-dataset: temporal information retrieval and text classification dataset. Data Brief **25**, 104048 (2019)
4. Toda, H., Kataoka, R.: A search result clustering method using informatively named entities. In: Proceedings of the 7th Annual ACM International Workshop on Web Information and Data Management, pp. 81–86 (2005)
5. Hu, L., Zhang, B., Hou, L., Li, J.: Adaptive online event detection in news streams. Knowl.-Based Syst. **138**, 105–112 (2017)
6. Weng, J., Lee, B.-S.: Event detection in twitter. In: Icwsm, vol. 11, pp. 401–408 (2011)
7. Khodra, M.L.: Event extraction on Indonesian news article using multiclass categorization. In: ICAICTA 2015 - 2015 International Conference on Advanced Informatics: Concepts, Theory and Applications (2015)
8. Lejeune, G., et al.: Multilingual event extraction for epidemic detection. Artif. Intell. Med. **65**, 131–143 (2015)
9. Campos, R., Dias, G., Jorge, A.M., Jatowt, A.: Survey of temporal information retrieval and related applications. ACM Comput. Surv. **47**(2), 15 (2014)

10. Choubey, P.K., Raju, K., Huang, R.: Identifying the most dominant event in a news article by mining event coreference relations. In: Proceedings of the 2018 Conference of the North American Chapter of the Association for Computational Linguistics: Human Language Technologies, vol. 2, pp. 340–345 (2018). Short Papers

11. Upadhyay, S., Christodoulopoulos, C., Roth, D.: Making the news': identifying noteworthy events in news articles. In: Proceedings of the Fourth Workshop on Events, pp. 1–7 (2016)

12. Jatowt, C., Man, A., Yeung, K.: Tanaka, Generic method for detecting focus time of documents. Inf. Process. Manag. **51**(6), 851–868 (2015)

13. Yang, B., Sun, L.: event detection from news articles using convolutional neural networks. In: Proceedings of the 2018 IEEE/ACM International Conference on Advances in Social Networks Analysis and Mining (ASONAM) (2018)

14. Huang, R., Zhang, W., Wang, T., Li, H.: A multi-granularity convolutional attention network for event detection from news articles. In: Proceedings of the 2019 Conference on Empirical Methods in Natural Language Processing and the 9th International Joint Conference on Natural Language Processing (EMNLP-IJCNLP) (2019)

15. Pera, M.S., Steyvers, M., Navarro, D.J.: Event detection from news articles with matrix factorization. In: Proceedings of the 43rd International ACM SIGIR Conference on Research and Development in Information Retrieval (2020)

16. Wu, X., Zhang, X.: Event detection in news articles using self-attention mechanism. In: Proceedings of the 2021 International Joint Conference on Neural Networks (IJCNN) (2021)

17. Adhikary, N., Dey, K.C., Ghosh, S., Chakraborty, S.: Event detection from news corpus using support vector machines with TF-IDF and Word2Vec features. In: Proceedings of the 2021 IEEE International Conference on Acoustics, Speech, and Signal Processing (ICASSP) (2021)

18. Zhang, Y., Yang, H.: A BERT-based hierarchical attention network for event detection from news articles. In: Proceedings of the 2021 Conference on Empirical Methods in Natural Language Processing (EMNLP) (2021)

19. Liu, Q., Jia, H., Huang, J.: Event detection from news articles using BERT with contextualized word embeddings. In: Proceedings of the 2021 IEEE International Conference on Big Data (Big Data) (2021)

From Words to Emotions: Identifying Depression Through Social Media Insights

Malliga Subramanian[(✉)], Gokulkrishna Raju, Arunaa Sureshkumar,
Chandramukhii Anbarasu, Kogilavani Shanmuga Vadivel, and P. S. Nandhini

Kongu Engineering College, Perundurai, Erode, Tamil Nadu, India
`mallisenthil.cse@kongu.edu`

Abstract. The rise of social media has led to a drastic surge in the dissemination of hostile and toxic content, fostering an alarming proliferation of hate speech, inflammatory remarks, and abusive language. The exponential growth of social media has facilitated the widespread circulation of hostile and toxic content, giving rise to an unprecedented influx of hate speech, incendiary language, and abusive rhetoric. The study utilized text representation and word embedding techniques such as bi-gram, tri-gram and FastText that aim to capture the semantic and syntactic information of the text data. Machine learning and deep learning techniques such as CNN, BERT, and SVM have been utilized to classify social media posts into depression and non-depression categories. To assess the effectiveness of the suggested approaches, this work employed performance metrics, including accuracy, precision, recall, and F1-score. The outcomes of the investigation indicate that the SVM can identify symptoms of depression with an average accuracy rate of 80.

Keywords: Bi-gram · Tri-gram · FastText · SVM · CNN · BERT

1 Introduction

In recent years, the exponential growth of social media platforms has transformed the way people interact and share their thoughts and emotions [1]. Social media platforms, such as Twitter, Facebook, and Instagram [2], have become a window into the daily lives of individuals, providing a rich source of information for researchers and healthcare professionals to better understand mental health patterns on a large scale. Among various mental health conditions, depression stands as a significant global challenge, affecting millions of individuals worldwide.

The early detection and intervention of depression are crucial for preventing severe outcomes and improving the overall quality of life for those affected [3]. Traditional methods of diagnosing depression often rely on self-reported assessments, questionnaires, or clinical evaluations, which may have limitations such as subjectivity, cost, and the reluctance of individuals to disclose their emotional struggles. As a result, researchers have increasingly turned to computational approaches, leveraging the vast amount of

B. R. Chakravarthi et al. (Eds.): SPELLL 2023, CCIS 2046, pp. 268–282, 2024.
https://doi.org/10.1007/978-3-031-58495-4_20

user-generated content available on social media platforms, to identify potential signs of depression more efficiently and in real-time.

This research article presents a comprehensive analysis of detecting and classifying signs of depression from social media texts. Leveraging machine learning and deep learning algorithms, our study aims to develop a robust framework for the early detection and classification of depression-related sentiments expressed in social media posts.

The primary objectives of this study are as follows:

- Explore the semantic features indicative of depression to create a meaningful feature set for machine learning models.
- Implement and fine-tune state-of-the-art machine learning and deep learning algorithms to classify social media texts into categories related to depression severity.
- Evaluate the performance and effectiveness of the proposed framework

The following sections of this document are structured as follows: Sect. 2 provides a comprehensive review of existing research on the identification of signs of depression through analysis of social media text. Section 3 provides a detailed explanation of the task at hand, including a description of the dataset employed in this study. Our proposed machine learning and deep learning models for detecting signs of depression are also presented in Sect. 3. Subsequently, Sect. 4 outlines the conducted experiments and presents the corresponding results. A thorough discussion of these results is provided within the same section. Finally, in Sect. 5, we present our concluding remarks based on the findings and suggest potential avenues for future research in this field.

2 Literature Survey

Due to its numerous benefits, including high temporal resolution, sensitivity, cost-effectiveness, ease of recording, and non-invasiveness, Electroencephalography (EEG) has been extensively studied and utilized in clinical diagnosis [3–6]. Li et. al [7] suggested an innovative approach for identifying depression through Electroencephalography (EEG), introducing an ensemble model that combines deep forest and Support Vector Machine (SVM). The study incorporated spatial information from EEG caps through image conversion techniques and conducted processing and analysis of EEG signals across various frequency bands.

In the research by Wang et al. [2], the authors introduced a novel approach to identify signs of depression. The framework leverages pre-trained language models, which capitalize on rich information rather than starting from scratch. The experimental results demonstrate the efficacy and resilience of this approach, as indicated by a macro F1-score of 0.552. Shah et al. [8] presented a novel hybrid model designed to detect depression through the analysis of user-generated textual posts. The researchers employed deep learning algorithms, training them with the provided training data, and subsequently evaluated their model's performance using the test data from the reddit dataset. This approach approach featured the utilization of BiLSTM with various word embedding techniques and metadata features. In their study, Lin et al. [9] developed a system called "SenseMood" to effectively detect and analyze users with depression.

They introduced a novel multimodal learning strategy that combines deep visual and textual elements, with the goal of revealing the psychological state of users on social networks. For depression detection, the researchers employed a CNN-based classifier to extract deep features from the pictures posted by users. Additionally, they utilized BERT, a powerful natural language processing model, to extract deep features from the textual content of the tweets. By leveraging this multimodal approach, the study demonstrated promising results in detecting users with depression more efficiently.

In their work, Burdisso et. al. [10] presented SS3 (Smoothness, Significance, and Sanction), an innovative supervised learning approach for text classification. SS3 has been specifically crafted as a versatile framework to address early risk detection challenges. To validate its performance, the authors conducted an assessment using the CLEF's eRisk2017 pilot task focusing on early depression detection. Chiong et al. [11] conducted an investigation into various text preprocessing and textual-based feature methods, along with machine learning classifiers, including both single and ensemble models. The study employed two publicly available, labeled Twitter datasets for training and testing the machine learning models. Additionally, three non-Twitter datasets containing depression-related content from sources like Facebook, Reddit, and an electronic diary were used to assess the models' performance across diverse social media platforms. The experimental findings revealed that the proposed approach effectively detects depression through social media texts, even in scenarios where the training datasets lack specific keywords such as 'depression' and 'diagnose'.

Zogan et al. [12] presented a novel approach called Hierarchical Attention Network (MDHAN) for explainable Multi-Aspect Depression Detection. The primary aim was to automatically identify depressed users on social media while offering insight into the model's predictions. The study involved incorporating additional features from Twitter to enhance user posts. The experimental results showed the superior performance of MDHAN compared to various widely used and robust baseline methods. Sharom and Rajalakshmi [3] utilized various machine learning approaches, including Support Vector Machine, Random Forest, and XGBoost classifier, to categorize indicators of depression. The findings from our experiments demonstrated that the XGBoost model outperformed the other methods, achieving the highest classification accuracy of 0.61% and a Macro F1 score of 0.54. Further, an attempt to present the overview of all the methods presented by various researchers for the shared task LT-EDI 2022 was carried out by Sampath et al. [13].

To summarize, social media material can reveal mental health issues like depression, according to research. However, detection systems need further research and improvement to be effective and ethical.

3   Methods and Materials

3.1   Dataset Description

The data set used to identify the signs of depression has been obtained from the Shared task released on Detecting Signs of Depression from Social Media Text at LT-EDI@RANLP 2023 [14]. The dataset includes training, development and testing datasets. And all of them are in English and comprise social media comments. The training dataset includes 3678 comments classified moderately depressed, 2755 not depressed comments, and 768 severely depressed comments. Sample texts for each class in shown in Table 1.

Table 1. Sample Training Texts

Documents	Texts	Label
Document [14]	Happy new year: Fuck 2019…2020 will be bettexaxaxaxaxaxa why do i even have to be happy because earth did a whole circle around sun nothing ….	moderate
Document [1664]	Has anyone used SAM-E?: I heard it helps with depression?Any personal experiences? Thanks greatly	Not depression
Document [2320]	I'm really struggling: So I don't know how to start things like this, So I'll start with basics. I'm 16yo, diagnosed depression at 14yo. Since then, my life is total mess. …	severe

The dataset is imbalanced, with varying numbers of instances across depression severity labels. To address this, the Synthetic Minority Over-sampling Technique (SMOTE) technique was used to generate synthetic samples of the minority class (severely depressed) and balance the dataset. By employing SMOTE, potential biases caused by the initial imbalance were alleviated, enhancing the reliability and robustness of the subsequent models. After applying SMOTE, the dataset underwent a significant transformation, becoming regular and balanced across all classes. With the application of SMOTE, the number of samples in the depressed class was artificially increased to match the count of 4,000 samples, aligning it with the majority class, resulting in a uniform distribution of 4,000 samples for each class. This synthetic augmentation of the minority class allowed for a more equitable representation of data and mitigated the issues caused by class imbalance. Figure 1 shows the size of the dataset before and after augmentation.

3.2 Preprocessing

Preprocessing the text is an essential step in any NLP task, including detecting signs of depression from social media comments. The goal is to clean and transform the raw text into a more structured and standardized format, making it easier for machine and deep learning models to understand and process the data. The following preprocessing steps have been performed in this work:

Text Lowercasing: We have converted all text to lowercase to ensure that the model treats words with the same spelling but different cases as the same word. This avoids duplicating features and helps with generalization.

Tokenization: Next, we split the text into individual words or tokens. This is crucial for analyzing word frequencies, building n-grams, and creating word embeddings.

Removing Special Characters and Punctuation: Then, we removed the special characters, symbols, and punctuation marks from the text. These characters are not usually helpful in understanding the sentiment or meaning of the text and can be safely discarded.

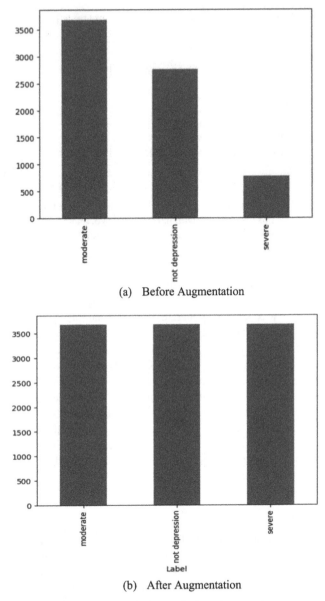

(a)   Before Augmentation

(b)   After Augmentation

Fig. 1. Datasets before and after augmentation

Removing URLs and User Handles: In social media comments, URLs and user handles (e.g., @username) are common but do not contribute much to sentiment analysis. So, we removed them too.

Removing Stop Words: Stop words are common words (e.g., "and", "the", "in") that occur frequently but do not carry significant meaning in the context of sentiment analysis.

Removing them can reduce noise in the data and speed up processing, so we removed them also.

Handling Emojis and Emoticons: Emojis and emoticons are prevalent in social media comments. They can carry valuable sentiment information and should be handled appropriately. We have converted them to text descriptions.

Handling Imbalanced Data: In real-world scenarios, the dataset may be imbalanced, with a higher number of non-depressive comments compared to depressive ones. Techniques like oversampling, undersampling, or using class weights can be applied to address this issue.

After preprocessing, the data is in more suitable form for various NLP tasks, such as sentiment analysis or detecting signs of depression in social media comments.

3.3 Feature Extraction and Word Embedding Technique

Bi-gram, trigram, and n-gram are the methods of representing text data, capturing local word dependencies and context, and are often used as part of feature extraction or word representation processes. Feature extraction techniques in NLP involve transforming raw text data into a set of numerical features that can be used as input for machine learning models. In this work, we use bi-gram and tri-for capturing local context from the dataset. Tables 2 and 3 show samples for bi-gram and tri-gram extraction.

Table 2. Tri-gram extraction

DOCUMENTS	LABEL	3 GRAM
Document [11]	moderate	['consistent tomorrow drastically', 'tomorrow drastically may', 'drastically may view', 'may view hopeless', 'addictive disappointed satisfaction'…..]
Document [615]	no depression	['psychiatrist physician uncomfortable', 'physician uncomfortable psychiatrist', 'uncomfortable psychiatrist medicated', 'psychologist soon based'….]
Document [641]	severe	['argue bpd aspergers', 'bpd aspergers ocd', 'aspergers ocd suspected', 'ocd suspected 2018', 'suspected 2018 22', '2018 22 crap', '22 crap partner', 'crap partner seriously', 'partner seriously alcoholic'……]

Table 3. Bi-gram Extraction

DOCUMENTS	LABEL	N GRAM
Document [11]	moderate	['consistent tomorrow', 'tomorrow drastically', 'drastically may', 'may view', 'view hopeless', 'hopeless hesitation', 'hesitation hand', 'hand escape', 'escape habit', language', etc....]
Document [629]	Not depression	['ya obviously', 'obviously throw', 'throw fucking', 'fucking stranger', 'stranger internet', 'internet give', 'give bunch', 'bunch die' etc.]
Document [2399]	severe	['gues unhealthily', 'unhealthily 30mg', '30mg 90mg', '90mg cymbalta', 'cymbalta sleepy', 'sleepy discussed', 'discussed 60', '60 boat', 'boat suppose', 'suppose psychiatrist' etc..]

Further, we have used word embedding techniques that aim to learn continuous vector representations for words in a way that captures semantic relationships and contextual similarities between words. Unlike feature extraction, word embedding methods are learned automatically from large amounts of data, such as word co-occurrence patterns or language model predictions. One of popular word embedding techniques, FastText, is used in this work. Here's how FastText is used:

1. Create a FastText model object.
2. Train the model on a large corpus of text to learn word representations.
3. Use the trained model to convert words into dense vectors.
4. Transform documents by averaging the vectors of the words they contain.

The result is a dense vector representation for each word or document, capturing the meaning and context of the text. These vectors are dense, meaning they do not contain many zeros. This enables efficient calculations and modeling using the learned representations. FastText is a valuable tool for various natural language processing tasks, including text classification, sentiment analysis, and language generation.

3.4 Proposed Classifiers

Having described the text to feature transformation, we present the classification algorithms used for detecting signs of depression from social media text. The scikit-learn and deep learning libraries have been used to implement the proposed models.

For feature extraction, we utilized FastText, 2-g, and 3-g techniques. FastText captures semantic and syntactic information by representing words as dense vectors. 2-g and 3-g extract contiguous sequences of 2 and 3 words respectively, capturing local word order and context information. In order to classify the extracted features, we propose to use three classifiers: SVM, CNN, and BERT. A brief introduction of these classifiers is given below:

Support Vector Machines (SVM): It is a supervised classification algorithm that constructs an optimal hyperplane to separate categories. SVM can be a suitable choice for classifying the signs of depression into different categories (moderately depressed, severely depressed, and not depressed) for the following reasons:

- Non-Linear Decision Boundaries: SVM can handle non-linear decision boundaries, which are essential for complex classification tasks like identifying different levels of depression. The signs of depression may not always follow linear separability, and SVM can effectively learn non-linear decision boundaries to distinguish between different categories.
- Robustness to High-Dimensional Data: In many NLP tasks, the feature space can be high-dimensional due to the large vocabulary of words. SVM is robust to high-dimensional data and can effectively handle large feature spaces, making it suitable for text classification tasks.

Hence, in this work, we propose to use SVM as one of the classifiers.

Convolutional Neural Networks (CNN): CNNs are deep learning models that are effective in capturing local patterns in text data. Even though, CNNS have traditionally been associated with computer vision tasks, such as image recognition, due to their ability to capture local patterns and spatial features effectively, CNNs have also proven to be suitable for NLP, including capturing long-term dependencies in text data. Here are some reasons why CNNs is used in the present study.

- Local Context Learning: CNNs use convolutional filters (kernels) to detect local patterns in the input data which contains the signs of depression. In NLP, this corresponds to learning meaningful representations from short contiguous sequences of words, which can be crucial for capturing local dependencies within phrases and clauses.
- Hierarchical Feature Extraction: By stacking multiple convolutional layers, CNNs can capture hierarchical patterns in the data. Lower layers detect basic features such as word-level patterns, while higher layers learn more complex patterns and relationships such as sentence-level pattern). This hierarchy allows CNNs to capture dependencies at different scales, including long-term dependencies.

Bidirectional Encoder Representations from Transformers (BERT): BERT is a powerful pre-trained language model that captures contextual information from text. It has been widely adopted for various NLP tasks, including text classification. The benefits of using BERT include:

- Contextual Word Embeddings: BERT generates contextual word embeddings, which means that the representation of each word is influenced by its surrounding words in the sentence. This allows BERT to capture complex semantic relationships and contextual information, which can be crucial for understanding the signs of depression in social media texts.
- Pretrained on Large Corpora: BERT is pretrained on a large amount of text data, making it capable of learning rich language representations. This pretrained model can be fine-tuned on specific tasks with smaller datasets, such as classifying depression signs, which can lead to better performance.

- Transformer Attention Mechanism: The Transformer architecture, which underlies BERT, uses a self-attention mechanism to weigh the importance of different words in a sentence. This attention mechanism allows BERT to focus on relevant parts of the text, helping it to identify important signals related to depression signs.
- Bidirectional Context: Unlike traditional language models that are unidirectional (e.g., LSTM), BERT is bidirectional. It can consider both left and right contexts of each word during training, enabling it to better understand long-range dependencies in the text.

Each classifier takes the respective feature vectors as input and outputs the classification for each social media text. These classifiers have different specialties, and their performance metrics may vary. By utilizing FastText, 2-g, and 3-g along with SVM, CNN, and BERT classifiers, we aim to effectively detect signs of depression from social media text, providing valuable insights for mental health analysis.

4   Results and Discussion

The models were implemented using scikit-learn and Python, and the training and testing were performed on the Google Collaboratory platform. Collaboratory provides a cloud-based Jupyter notebook environment, eliminating the need for local setup. For our study, we utilized the LT-EDI@RANLP 2023 dataset, which is designed for the task of detecting signs of depression from social media texts. Using the extracted features from the training set, we trained various classifiers, including SVM, CNN, and BERT. These classifiers were then evaluated using the test dataset. By leveraging scikit-learn, Python, and the LT-EDI@RANLP 2023 dataset, we aimed to detect signs of depression from social media text, contributing to the understanding and analysis of mental health indicators in online communication.

4.1   Performance Metrics

The performance of the classifiers used for classifying the signs of depression has been evaluated using the metrics such as Accuracy, Precision, Recall and F1-Score. These metrics are defined as follows.

Accuracy is defined as the number of texts correctly classified as belonging to a specific class divided by the total number of texts in that class and is calculated by Eq. (1).

$$\text{Accuracy} = (TP + TN)/(TP + TN + FP + FN) \tag{1}$$

The number of texts correctly categorized as a certain class out of the total number of actual texts in that class is defined as recall (also known as Sensitivity or True Positive Rate) and is computed using Eq. (2).

$$\text{Recall} = TP/(TP + FN) \tag{2}$$

Precision (Positive Predictive Value) is defined as the number of texts accurately categorized as a specific class out of the total number of texts categorized as that class, and is given by Eq. (3).

$$Precision = TP/(TP + FP) \qquad (3)$$

F1-Score is defined as the harmonic average of the Precision and Recall, that is, the weighted average of Precision and Recall. It is calculated as in Eq. (4).

$$F1\text{-}Score = (2 * Precision * recall)/(precision + recall) \qquad (4)$$

These metrics are calculated using indices such as True Positive (TP), True Negative (TN), False Positive (FP) and False Negative (FN). The number of correctly classified texts for each class is defined as TP. The number of texts misclassified in other class except the right class is denoted by FP. The number of texts misclassified in the relevant class is defined as FN. TN is the number of texts correctly classified in other class except the correct class.

Table 4 presents the values of the performance metrics obtained from each of the classifiers with augmented dataset. The confusion matrices are depicted in Fig. 2.

Table 4. Performance of the proposed classifiers

CLASSIFIERS	CLASS LABELS	ACCURACY	PRECISION	RECALL	F1-SCORE
SVM with FASTTEXT	moderate	0.43	0.65	0.53	0.58
	not depression		0.21	0.15	0.17
	severe		0.15	0.57	0.24
SVM with 2 g	moderate	0.27	0.35	0.75	0.48
	not depression		0.75	0.33	0.46
	severe		0.40	0.33	0.37
SVM with 3 g	moderate	0.80	0.55	0.75	0.63
	not depression		0.56	0.39	0.46
	severe		0.55	0.27	0.37
CNN with FASTTEXT	moderate	0.43	0.65	0.53	0.58
	not depression		0.21	0.15	0.17
	severe		0.15	0.57	0.24
CNN with 2 g	moderate	0.50	0.66	0.65	0.66
	not depression		0.20	0.11	0.14
	severe		0.19	0.52	0.28
CNN with 3 g	moderate	0.47	0.67	0.65	0.66

(continued)

Table 4. (*continued*)

CLASSIFIERS	CLASS LABELS	ACCURACY	PRECISION	RECALL	F1-SCORE
	not depression		0.20	0.11	0.15
	severe		0.18	0.50	0.26
BERT with FASTTEXT	moderate	0.42	0.65	0.52	0.58
	not depression		0.20	0.13	0.16
	severe		0.14	0.59	0.23
BERT with 2 g	moderate	0.50	0.67	0.66	0.66
	not depression		0.20	0.12	0.15
	severe		0.19	0.50	0.28
BERT with 3 g	moderate	0.49	0.66	0.64	0.65
	not depression		0.20	0.12	0.15
	severe		0.18	0.49	0.26

Of all the proposed models, we find SVM with 3-g outperformed with highest accuracy. With proper regularization parameters, SVMs tend to generalize well to new, unknown data. Deep learning models, on the other hand, are prone to overfitting, particularly when the dataset is limited or lacks diversity. When working with little data, SVMs' capacity to withstand overfitting can be advantageous. The findings of this research hold the potential to revolutionize the field of mental health assessment by providing a non-intrusive and scalable approach to identifying and supporting individuals who may be at risk of depression. Furthermore, the insights gleaned from the large-scale social media data could inform policymakers and healthcare providers about population-level mental health trends and aid in developing targeted interventions. The confusion matrix of various models has been generated and is presented, providing a comprehensive overview of their performance and predictive accuracy.

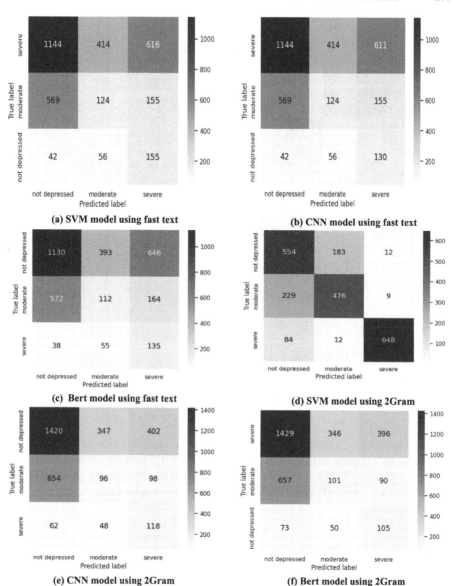

Fig. 2. Confusion Matrices

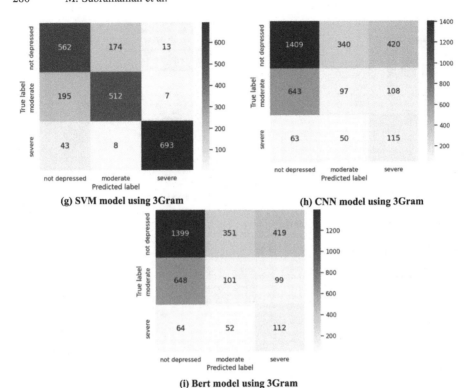

(g) SVM model using 3Gram   **(h) CNN model using 3Gram**

(i) Bert model using 3Gram

Fig. 2. (*continued*)

In addition, we conducted a comparison between our developed models and other existing models that aimed to classify the same dataset [14] The results of this comparison are shown in Table 5. The findings from Table 5 demonstrate that our proposed SVM with 3-g feature representation achieved higher accuracy than the other models discussed in the literature.

Table 5. Comparison with other models

References	Models	Accuracy
[15]	DistilBERT	0.342
	RoBERTa	0.510
	ALBERT	0.408
[16]	DistlBERT	0.526
	RoBERTa	0.563
	BERT	0.521
	autoBOT	0.641
	Knowledge Graph	0.602
[17]	Bidirectional LSTM	0.610
	Fine-tuned BERT	0.636
[18]	Logistic Regression	0.443
[2]	Gradient boosting models	0.571
	Pre-trained models	0.635
	Contrastive pre-trained models	0.597
	Ensemble model	0.633
[3]	XGBoost	0.643
	Random Forest	0.564
	SVM	0.567
Our model	**SVM with 3-g**	**0.80**

5 Conclusion and Future Work

This study presents the experimental work and corresponding results for the task of detecting signs of depression from social media text using the provided dataset. We employed feature extraction techniques such as FastText, 2-g, and 3-g to capture the textual information effectively. In our experiments, we compared different classifiers, including SVM, CNN, and BERT, to classify the extracted features and identify signs of depression. Among these models, Logistic Regression achieved the highest accuracy, indicating its effectiveness in this task. To further enhance our work, future extensions could explore alternative numerical or vectorial representations of the text, such as TF-IDF, to potentially improve classification performance. Additionally, it would be beneficial to explore new classifiers based on neural networks, leveraging their advanced linguistic features. By leveraging these techniques and classifiers, we aimed to contribute to the detection of signs of depression in social media text, facilitating a deeper understanding of mental health indicators in online communication.

References

1. Kayalvizhi, S., Thenmozhi, D.: Data set creation and empirical analysis for detecting signs of depression from social media postings. arXiv preprint arXiv:2202.03047 (2022)
2. Wang, W.-Y., Tang, Y.-C., Du, W.-W., Peng, W.-C.: NYCU_TWD@ LT-EDI-ACL2022: ensemble models with VADER and contrastive learning for detecting signs of depression from social media. In: Proceedings of the Second Workshop on Language Technology for Equality, Diversity and Inclusion, pp. 136–139 (2022)
3. Sharen, H., Rajalakshmi, R.: DLRG@ LT-EDI-ACL2022: detecting signs of depression from social media using XGBoost method. In: Proceedings of the Second Workshop on Language Technology for Equality, Diversity and Inclusion, pp. 346–349 (2022)
4. Parvinnia, E., Sabeti, M., Jahromi, M.Z., Boostani, R.: Classification of EEG signals using adaptive weighted distance nearest neighbor algorithm. J. King Saud Univ.-Comput. Inf. Sci. **26**(1), 1–6 (2014)
5. Acharya, U.R., Sudarshan, V.K., Adeli, H., Santhosh, J., Koh, J.E., Adeli, A.: Computer-aided diagnosis of depression using EEG signals. Eur. Neurol. **73**(5–6), 329–336 (2015)
6. Sudarshan, V.K., Santhosh, J., Koh, J.E.: Computer-aided diagnosis of depression using EEG signals. Eur. Neurol. **73** (2015)
7. Li, X., et al.: Depression recognition using machine learning methods with different feature generation strategies. Artif. Intell. Med. **99**, 101696 (2019)
8. Shah, F.M., et al.: Early depression detection from social network using deep learning techniques. In: 2020 IEEE Region 10 Symposium (TENSYMP), pp. 823–826. IEEE (2020)
9. Lin, C., et al.: Sensemood: depression detection on social media. In: Proceedings of the 2020 International Conference on Multimedia Retrieval, pp. 407–411 (2020)
10. Burdisso, S.G., Errecalde, M., Montes-y-Gómez, M.: A text classification framework for simple and effective early depression detection over social media streams. Expert Syst. Appl. **133**, 182–197 (2019)
11. Chiong, R., Budhi, G.S., Dhakal, S., Chiong, F.: A textual-based featuring approach for depression detection using machine learning classifiers and social media texts. Comput. Biol. Med. **135**, 104499 (2021)
12. Zogan, H., Razzak, I., Wang, X., Jameel, S., Xu, G.: Explainable depression detection with multi-aspect features using a hybrid deep learning model on social media. World Wide Web **25**(1), 281–304 (2022)
13. Kayalvizhi, S., Durairaj, T., Chakravarthi, B.R.: Findings of the shared task on detecting signs of depression from social media. In: Proceedings of the Second Workshop on Language Technology for Equality, Diversity and Inclusion, pp. 331–338 (2022)
14. (2022). https://codalab.lisn.upsaclay.fr/competitions/11075
15. Sivamanikandan, S., Santhosh, V., Sanjaykumar, N., Durairaj, T.: scubeMSEC@ LT-EDI-ACL2022: detection of depression using transformer models. In: Proceedings of the Second Workshop on Language Technology for Equality, Diversity and Inclusion, pp. 212–217 (2022)
16. Tavchioski, I., Koloski, B., Škrlj, B., Pollak, S.: E8-IJS@ LT-EDI-ACL2022-BERT, AutoML and knowledge-graph backed detection of depression. In: Proceedings of the Second Workshop on Language Technology for Equality, Diversity and Inclusion, pp. 251–257 (2022)
17. Adarsh, S., Antony, B.: SSN@ LT-EDI-ACL2022: transfer learning using bert for detecting signs of depression from social media texts. In: Proceedings of the Second Workshop on Language Technology for Equality, Diversity and Inclusion, pp. 326–330 (2022)
18. Agirrezabal, M., Amann, J.: KUCST@ LT-EDI-ACL2022: detecting signs of depression from social media text. arXiv preprint arXiv:2204.04481 (2022)

Text Summarisation for Low-Resourced Languages, A Review

Gareth Reeve Edwards$^{(\boxtimes)}$ (ORCID) and Tshephisho Joseph Sefara (ORCID)

Council for Scientific and Industrial Research, Pretoria, South Africa
{gedwards,tsefara}@csir.co.za

Abstract. Text summarisation is becoming increasingly important for humans to more quickly understand and analyse documents with large amounts of text. In this paper, we review and discuss approaches and methods used in the development of text summarisation models for low-resourced languages, specifically South African languages. We compare approaches and results to give guidance on what may be the best approach to building a sophisticated text summarisation model for South African languages. The results showed that there is one text summarisation model created for isiXhosa out of 11 South African languages, and only a few studies were done for African languages.

We recommend future work to focus on developing necessary datasets for South African languages, developing language-specific preprocessing tools such as stemmers and stop-word lists, and finally, using the developed data to build or use more sophisticated language models.

Keywords: Text summarisation · Low-resource languages · Natural language processing

1 Introduction

Text summarisation is the task of condensing a body of text to a shorter and more concise body of text that carries the same meaning and conveys the same message as the original text [20]. Natural language processing (NLP) coupled with various machine learning algorithms has been used to perform this task computationally, with varying degrees of success [24]. There are two main approaches to text summarisation using machine learning, namely, extractive approaches [20] and abstractive approaches [19].

Extractive text summarisation refers to the methodology that summarises text by identifying important words, sentences, or paragraphs in a text using various statistical and linguistic features. These important portions of the text are then extracted from the larger body and concatenated to create the resulting summary [11]. The importance of text in an extractive summary is based on positional or frequency factors such as word/phrase frequency and location in the text. This makes extractive summarisation a simpler method compared to

© The Author(s), under exclusive license to Springer Nature Switzerland AG 2024
B. R. Chakravarthi et al. (Eds.): SPELLL 2023, CCIS 2046, pp. 283–296, 2024.
https://doi.org/10.1007/978-3-031-58495-4_21

abstractive summarisation in terms of both computation and conceptual understanding [10]. Extractive text summarisation techniques, unfortunately, suffer
from a few drawbacks. The concatenation process of the extractive approach
sometimes negatively affects the coherence of the summarised output [11]. Furthermore, important information is usually spread across sentences, and extractive summary techniques are not able to identify these dispersed points of information [10].

Abstractive text summarisation approaches attempt to gain an understanding of concepts in a body of text and then paraphrases those concepts in a
clear and concise natural language [10]. Abstractive summarisation follows, more
accurately, the way a human would summarise a text. Abstractive approaches
are beneficial in that they produce sophisticated summaries and include additional content that enriches the resulting summary [11]. Compared to extractive
approaches, abstractive summarisation approaches are more coherent and well
structured.

Within each subsection (extractive and abstractive) of text summarisation,
there are further, more nuanced methods that can be used within each context.
Figure 1 shows a comprehensive plot of the various text summarisation methods
and preprocessing methods used in the text summarisation process.

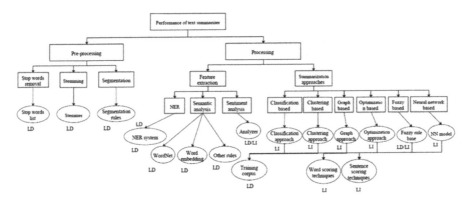

Fig. 1. Spider plot showing the various steps one can take when applying automated
text summarisation where LD represents language dependent and LI represents language independent.

Both extractive and abstractive text summarisation approaches using
machine learning have been extensively applied to popular world languages such
as English, French, Spanish, and others. Almost all text summarisation packages
today cater for these more prominent languages. Unfortunately, South African
and other low-resourced languages are not well represented in the context of
automatic text summarisation, as data for these languages are scarce [13].

This paper investigates current text summarisation models used in low-resourced languages and compares the approaches and results to give guidance to what may be the best approach to building a sophisticated text summarisation model for South African languages.

The remainder of the paper is outlined as follows. Section 2 discusses current available datasets for low-resource languages. Section 2 also discusses the generation and curation of datasets. Section 3 discusses various techniques applied in text summarisation for low-resource African languages. Section 4 explains the current methods of text summarisation. In Sect. 5, we discuss different evaluations of text summarisation models. Section 6 concludes the paper with future work and recommendations.

2   Datasets Generation and Curation

It is common knowledge that data is essential for any task related to machine learning or artificial intelligence (AI). NLP tasks are no different. Extensive research concerning automated text summarisation shows that the more sophisticated models are those trained with large datasets. Unfortunately, when it comes to low-resourced languages, there are no large datasets available to form such sophisticated models. This has come to the attention of researchers when developing text summarisation models for low-resourced languages. As a result, data creation or data curation is a highlighted task within this research context.

Data curation is essential to overcome the low-resource status of a language. One of the more notable efforts in this regard is the XL-Sum project [12]. XL-Sum is a diverse and comprehensive dataset of article-summary pairs obtained from the BBC news site. The XL-Sum dataset covers 44 different languages, ranging from low-resource to high-resource languages. XL-Sum is one of the largest abstractive datasets available. This means that abstractive text summarisers can be effectively trained on this dataset. Often low-resourced languages can only make use of rudimentary extractive techniques to summarise the text [5,20]. The creation of large datasets for low-resourced languages allows flexibility in the text summarisation approaches one could use. XL-Sum was curated using a web scraping tool that scraped article-summary pairs from the BBC news website. The effectiveness of the dataset was tested by using an abstractive summarisation model and evaluating its performance. If the model could be trained on the data and generate effective abstractive summaries, then there is proof that the data set is of good quality for abstractive summarisation tasks. The very popular and high-performing transformer model was applied to the low-resourced languages represented in the XL-Sum dataset (e.g., Bengali, Swahili, and others.) [28]. The transformer model produced promising results in generating abstractive summaries from low-resourced languages. The Recall-Oriented Understudy for Gisting Evaluation (ROUGE) scores of abstractive summaries for low-resourced languages are shown in Table 1. ROUGE is an objective text summarisation metric to evaluate the output of an automated text summary.

The study notes that a multilingual model (mT5) performed slightly better in low-resourced languages compared to the monolingual transformer model used [29]. The benefit of multilingual models is that, if similar languages are grouped together, there is a positive transfer effect between them during the model training phase [14]. The performance of the multilingual models compared to the monolingual transformer model is shown in Table 1.

Table 1. Performance comparison between a monolingual transformer model and a multilingual transformer model applied to low-resourced languages represented in the XL-Sum dataset. The values represent rouge scores (ROUGE-1, ROUGE-2 and ROUGE-L).

Language	Monolingual			Multilingual		
	R-1	R-2	R-L	R-1	R-2	R-L
Amharic	15.33	5.12	13.85	17.49	6.34	15.76
Azerbaijani	16.79	6.94	15.36	19.29	8.20	17.62
Bengali	25.33	9.50	22.02	28.32	11.43	24.02
Japanese	44.55	21.35	34.43	47.17	23.34	36.20
Swahili	34.29	15.97	28.21	38.18	18.16	30.98

A very similar low-resourced language dataset creation/curation project called LR-Sum is ongoing [22]. LR-Sum is a multilingual data set focused on low-resourced languages. It consists of article-summary pairs for 40 different low-resourced languages. There are other similar studies completed or ongoing on the creation of multilingual data sets, namely, MILSUM [25], MultiLing [9], MassiveSumm [27], and MultiSumm [4].

A similar approach has been taken with the Indonesian language [13]. The IndoSum dataset contains roughly 20 000 Indonesian articles and their corresponding abstractive summary created by an Indonesian native speaker. The data set was tested using extractive approaches and produced promising results. However, abstractive summarisation approaches have not yet been tested on the data set.

An Igbo (a Nigerian dialect) data set was also created for use in text summarisation models [17]. Researchers found that creating a text summarisation model for Igbo is difficult given the limited online text data. They went on to create an Igbo dataset by curating article and summary pairs in English and translating them into Igbo using the Google Translate API. Unfortunately, the translations were not always accurate, so native Igbo speakers were used to rectify the translations as a preprocessing step before applying the extractive summarisation technique used in the study (TexRank and LexRank). The Igbo data set consisted of 1500 Igbo articles and their corresponding summaries.

3   Summarisation Techniques for African Languages

There are very limited resources when it comes to text summarisation for African languages and even less when it comes to native South African languages. In the section below we present research and text summarisation models used on African languages such as Xhosa, Igbo, Hausa and Afan Oromo.

3.1   Xhosa

Based on current research, it seems that research on text summarisation for South African languages is extremely scarce. A study was found that develops an extractive summariser for Xhosa, one of the most spoken languages in South Africa [20]. The extractive summarisation approach in their study was based on fairly rudimentary statistical methods developed by H. P. Edmundson in 1969. The sentence extraction technique used was based on sentence weighting. Sentences that have more document-relevant terms are weighted higher than sentences with comparatively less document-relevant words [7]. The authors curated a data set of 200 Xhosa news articles from online sources. Fifteen of the 200 articles were used to create manual summaries for model evaluation purposes. These manual summaries were created by Xhosa experts. Before any model could be applied to the data, data preprocessing was performed. The preprocessing step focused mainly on tokenization, stop-word removal, and word stemming. A stop-word list had to be created specifically for the Xhosa language, shedding further light on the low-resource nature of Xhosa (and other South African languages). A custom stemmer was also required [21].

The study used a subjective and objective approach for model evaluation. The subjective approach was carried out by handing the fifteen manual summaries and fifteen corresponding automated summaries to native Xhosa speakers and each participant was to choose the "best" summary based on three criteria:

1. Informativeness
2. Linguistic quality
3. Coherence and structure

The objective evaluation approach used the common precision, recall and f1 score metrics. Their study produced promising results, with both subjective and objective evaluations showing that the automated summary was better than the manual summary written by the Xhosa experts.

3.2   Igbo

Igbo is a popular language spoken in Nigeria and is spoken by approximately 30 million people [6]. A study has been conducted to develop an automated text summarisation model for the Igbo language. However, due to the low-resource nature of the Igbo language, the authors quickly realised that more emphasis is needed on the first step, which is creating a data set [17]. The Igbo data set was created by obtaining English articles and summaries, then translating the texts and their corresponding summaries from English to Igbo using Google translate API. As a result, a data set of 1500 Igbo article-summary pairs was created. These summaries were used as reference summaries for later model evaluation.

The TextRank and LexRank extractive summarisation algorithms were applied to the 1500 Igbo article dataset (IgboSum1500). TextRank is a graph-based model that ranks sentences based on scores. Sentences with higher scores are considered more relevant to the document topic. These high scoring sentences would be more likely to be added to the summary [18]. These scores are based on the amount of topic-relevant words in a sentence and the positioning of the sentences in the document. LexRank is also a graph-based method. LexRank computes the importance of sentences based on the concept of centrality of the eigenvector in a graph representation of sentences [8].

The results of these extractive approaches were fairly promising, as it outperformed the base summary (which was just the title of the text) by a considerable amount. With an increase in ROUGE scores (ROUGE-1, ROUGE-2, ROUGE-L and ROUGE-S) between the base summary and the TextRank and LexRank summaries increasing by more than 50%.

3.3 Hausa

The Hausa language is another common African language. Hausa is a Chadic language widely spoken in West Africa with approximately 150 million people using it as a first or second language [3]. Hausa is also a low-resourced language as text data for Hausa is limited.

A study has been conducted to identify the best model that one can use to summarise the Hausa text [3]. The focus of the study was on a modified PageRank model that they proposed would perform better than other extractive methods. The other methods used for comparison were TextRank, LexRank, a centroid-based method, and the BM25-TextRank method (a modified TextRank method). Centroid-based methods for text summarisation are an unsupervised summarisation approach that uses word embedding techniques that help capture the semantic meaning of words [24]. The BM25-TextRank method is an alteration of TextRank that uses a probabilistic model to rank sentence importance [1]. PageRank is a graph-based model that views each sentence in a document as the vertices of an undirected weighted graph [2]. The edges of the graph were determined using word overlap between sentences. Thus, sentences with higher degree of word overlap contain higher scores and are extracted and used for the summary.

The models were applied to a Hausa dataset containing 113 Hausa news articles. In their study, it is proposed that a modified PageRank algorithm would perform better than the other models used. Their results supported this claim, as the PageRank summaries had significantly high ROUGE scores compared to their counterparts.

3.4   Afan Oromo

Afran Oromo is one of the popular languages in Africa, spoken mainly in Ethiopia, but also in Kenya and Somalia. There are approximately 37.4 million native Afan Oromo speakers in Africa [6]. A study has been conducted to automatically summarise the Afan Oromo text using an extractive text summarisation approach [5]. The extractive method used was based on rudimentary sentence weighting methods developed by Edmundson [7]. Sentences were weighted according to term frequency and sentence positioning. Sentences with more topic relevant words were weighted higher in comparison with other sentences and sentences that were positioned closer to the beginning of the document were weighted higher than sentences toward the end of the document.

Their study used only eight Afan Oromo news articles with at least more than 200 words each. The reference summary was created by four native Afan Oromo speakers. The Afan Oromo speaking participants were to extract sentences from the original document that they thought contained the most salient information. Reference summaries of 10%, 20%, 30%, and 40% of the original text length were created for each of the eight Afan Oromo news articles. The study used three different summarisers, a summariser based only on term frequency (S1), a summariser based on term frequency and sentence positioning (S2), and a summariser based on term frequency and an improved sentence position method (S3).

Each text summarisation method was applied to each of the eight articles after text preprocessing was completed for each article. The preprocessing step consisted of tokenization, stop-word removal, and stemming. The stemmer used was a lightweight custom made stemmer specific for the Afan Oromo language [26].

Each of the three summarisers was evaluated based on an objective and subjective approach. The objective approach used the common evaluation metric of precision, recall, and F-1 score based on the ROUGE-N metric. The subjective approach was done using four native Afan Oromo speakers. Each participant would receive a reference summary and an automated summary, and were asked to choose the best. If two of the four participants selected the automated summary, then the automated summary would have an informativeness score of 50%. The results show that S3 performed the best of the three approaches based on objective and subjective evaluations.

4   Model Training Methods

This section discusses different approaches to text summarisation that were applied to the above-mentioned low-resourced languages. These approaches include extractive and abstractive text summarisation. Extractive summarisation approaches work by choosing the most significant sentences from the original document. On the other hand, abstractive summarisation approaches generate a new summary from scratch, based on the main ideas of the original document.

4.1 Extractive Method

(i) **Edmundson Heuristic Summarisation**: automated text summarisation has been a topic of research for a longer time than one might think. Edmundson, in 1969, expanded on an automated text summarisation algorithm created by H. P. Luhn. Luhn proposed that sentence importance in a text is based on the relevant frequency of words and the positioning of words in a sentence. Sentences with more topic-relevant words would be considered more informative than their stop-word heavy counterparts. Furthermore, words found closer to the front of a text would also be weighted higher than words farther away, since Luhn proposed that more topic-relevant words are likely to feature early on in a text [16].

Edmundson built on Luhn's initial idea and proposed that cue words (words like "important" or "significant"), title words, headings and subheadings were also beneficial for text summarisation [7]. Edmundson's method took all these factors into account and developed a scoring method to determine which sentences should be added to a text's summary. Simply put, the score would be calculated as a linear combination of weights and the proposed summarisation factors. The equation would be as follows:

$$Score = (w_1 \times P) + (w_2 \times F) + (w_3 \times C) + (w_4 \times S) \tag{1}$$

where P refers to word position, F refers to topic-relevant word frequency, C refers to cue words and S refers to stop-words (where less stop words will mean a more informative sentence). The highest scoring sentences are then used in the summary.

(ii) **TextRank**: a text summarisation algorithm that was used to apply automated summarisation for both the Igbo and Hausa language. TextRank is based on the PageRank algorithm. PageRank is a graph-based algorithm created by Google to rank web pages in order of importance. The nodes of the graph would be the web pages and the edges would be links from one page to another. The idea is that nodes with more connected links would be considered more important as they contain higher levels of network traffic [2].

The TextRank algorithm is applied in a similar way. However, instead of web pages for nodes, there are sentences with links between the sentences representing similarity scores. These similarity scores could be cosine similarity, topic-relevant word overlap or any other scoring method that calculates sentence similarity [18]. The idea is that the vertices (or sentences) with higher scores are extracted and placed in the summary. The vertex scoring equation is as follows:

$$S(V_i) = (1 - d) + d \times \sum_{j \in In(V_i)} \frac{1}{|Out(V_j)|} S(V_j) \tag{2}$$

where V_i is the ith vertex of the graph, $In(V_i)$ represents the vertices pointing toward V_i, $Out(V_i)$ represents the vertices pointing out from V_i and d

is a dampening factor which integrates into the model the probability of jumping from one vertex to a random vertex.

(iii) **LexRank**: is another extractive summarisation method that was developed by Erkan et al. [8] in 2004. It works by ranking sentences in a text based on their importance, which is measured by their similarity to other sentences in the text. The highest-ranked sentences are then selected to form the summary. LexRank is a more sophisticated method than the Edmundson Heuristic, and it is generally considered to be more effective. It is less susceptible to noise and is able to generate summaries that are more coherent and informative.

(iv) **Centroid-based text summarisation**: is a type of extractive summarisation method that works by selecting the sentences that are most similar to the centroid of the text [23]. The centroid of a text is a vector that represents the average meaning of all sentences in the text. To generate summaries using centroid-based text summarisation, the following steps are taken:

- The centroid of the text is calculated
- Each sentence in the text is represented as a vector
- The similarity between each sentence vector and the centroid vector is calculated
- The sentences with the highest similarity scores are selected to form the summary.

Centroid-based text summarisation is a simple and effective method for text summarisation. It is able to generate summaries that are informative and concise. However, it can be susceptible to noise, such as irrelevant or redundant sentences.

4.2   Abstractive Method

(i) **Transformer model**: was developed in 2017, and since, has been the building blocks for many of the advanced large language models in use today (GPT-4, BERT, DistilBERT, BARD, T5, and others). Transformers, introduced by Vashwani et al. [28] have revolutionised how researchers view language-related tasks. This includes text summarisation. The transformer model is an improvement on the previously used sequence-to-sequence models, such as RNNs and LSTMs. The transformer method is an improvement on these models as it contains a self-attention mechanism. This means that transformers are able to capture dependencies and relationships between words in a more comprehensive and parallelised way [28].

The transformer model has shown state-of-the-art results when performing language-related tasks like language translation, text summarisation, question-answering, text generation, and others. Furthermore, due to the self-attention mechanism there is no longer need for convolutions or recurrences in the model thus significantly improving it's training time compared to sequence-to-sequence models [28].

(ii) **mT5 model**: is a large multilingual pre-trained text-to-text transformer created by Google. It is the multilingual version of the T5 model. mT5 extends its capabilities to a wide array of languages, making it a versatile and invaluable resource for summarisation tasks in linguistically diverse and low-resource contexts. One of the key strengths of mT5 lies in its ability to perform various text-to-text tasks, allowing it to generate effective abstractive summaries. mT5 outperforms previous models in terms of linguistic fluency and content retention, crucial aspects in summarisation tasks for languages with limited data and resources [29]. mT5's remarkable zero-shot and few-shot capabilities, combined with its extensive multilingual coverage, set itself up as a state-of-the-art tool for summarisation in low-resourced languages, where data scarcity and linguistic complexity pose significant challenges.

These are just a few of the many text summarisation methods that have been developed. Each method has its own strengths and weaknesses, and the best method to use will depend on the specific task at hand.

5   Model Evaluation Methods

The text summarisation models applied to the African languages, discussed in the previous section, resulted in varying degrees of success. Some studies evaluated their models using a subjective and objective approach [5,17,20], while others used an objective evaluation only [3].

All the African language text summarisation models discussed generated summaries that were subjectively better, on average, compared to the human created reference summary. However, the more common metric to use to evaluate text summarisation models is the objective ROUGE-N metric [15]. ROUGE evaluates summarisation by comparing machine-generated summarisation with other (ideal) summaries created by humans [15]. The ROUGE convention consists of four different evaluation types, namely ROUGE-N, ROUGE-L, ROUGE-W, and ROUGE-S. ROUGE-N compares the number of common n-grams between the generated summary and the ideal summary. The summary with a higher number of overlapping n-grams with the ideal summary is considered better than the generated summaries with fewer overlapping n-grams. ROUGE-L measures the longest common sub-sequence (LCS). Generated summaries with LCSs (when compared to the ideal summary) will be judged as better than summaries with shorter common sub-sequences. ROUGE-W uses an LCS metric also; the only difference is that it weights consecutive word sequences higher than nonconsecutive word sequences. ROUGE-S is a skip-bigram measurement that is similar to the ROUGE-N score; however, ROUGE-S allows for nonconsecutive bigrams. For example, in the sentence, "Hi my name is Fred", an example of a bigram would be "is Fred". An example of a skip bigram would be "name Fred" or "Hi Fred".

Table 2 shows the objective results for each text summarisation model applied to African languages (Xhosa, Igbo, Hausa, and Afan Oromo). All studies used the precision, recall, and F1 score based on overlapping n-grams to objectively evaluate model performance.

The one pitfall is that not all articles explicitly defined the size of n-grams in their evaluation calculations. Table 2 shows the evaluation of each model where ROUGE-1 and ROUGE-2 were used, an average was taken and presented in the table.

Table 2. Objective evaluation outcomes of the text summarisation models applied to the African languages; Xhosa, Igbo, Afan Oromo and Hausa.

Language	Algorithm	Avg Recall	Avg Precision	Avg F1 Score
isiXhosa	Edmundson sentence weighting	39	35	40
igboSum	TextRank	17.5	8	10
	LexRank	17.5	8	5
Afan Oromo	S1	34	34	34
	S2	47	47	47
	S3	81	81	81
Hausa	Modified PageRank	53.4	53.3	53.3

6 Conclusion

A common theme has been found in automated text summarisation for low-resourced languages, all facing the problem of lack of article-summary type data. As a result, the text summarisation models currently applied to African languages are mostly extractive approaches that use sentence extraction techniques like document-relevant word frequencies or sentences positioning. These extractive approaches do not require a training process and follow a more algorithmic way of summarising a text as opposed to a machine learning type algorithm.

Despite using only extractive summarisation techniques, the articles discussed still produce promising results. However, more sophisticated machine learning approaches are currently not available for use in most African languages, as there are not enough summary articles available. South African languages are no exception.

Abstractive text summarisation techniques using transformers [28] are currently the best performing text summarisation models around today; however, fine-tuning these models to work for South African languages becomes difficult as there are currently no datasets available for such a task.

Research needs to be implemented to form large article-summary data sets for the various low-resourced South African languages. This is the first and most important step in overcoming the "low-resource" status for most South African languages. Various approaches can be taken to develop data sets such as web scraping of news articles [12], translating current article-summary datasets from English to the required target language with the help of native speakers and

Google Translate API [17], or extracting target language articles and formulating human summaries for each article [3]. This is not an easy step as data set creation could take a lot of hours if manual summaries are being formed. However, the result is large datasets that can be used by sophisticated abstractive text summarisation models that could help further develop the native South African languages.

After the datasets have been created for a low-resourced language, the next important step is to create language-specific text preprocessing software such as stemmers for lemmatisation and stop-word lists for stop-word removal. This is a considerably easier task than dataset creation, as one would typically only need one native speaker to implement the stemming rules or give a list of the language-specific stop-words. All the articles that we discussed applied automated text summarisation to African languages, making use of a custom stemmer and stop-word list [3,5,17,21].

South African languages are especially low-resourced as there is only one known study in which text summarisation is applied to a South African language [20]. Due to the limited data (only 200 Xhosa articles), the summarisation approach used was an extractive one. The further development of the Xhosa article summary data sets, together with other South African language article-summary datasets, will help to build sophisticated abstractive text summarisation models, fine-tune existing advanced language models (T5, GPT-3, BertSum, and others) or build multilingual models like the one presented by the XL-Sum project [12].

We recommend future work to focus on developing these datasets for South African languages, developing language-specific preprocessing tools such as stemmers and stop-word lists, and finally, using the developed data to build or use more sophisticated language models. Once the datasets and preprocessing tools are created, further work can go into using more sophisticated language models for text summarisation and testing the various models to identify which works best for the given language.

References

1. Barrios, F., López, F., Argerich, L., Wachenchauzer, R.: Variations of the Similarity Function of TextRank for Automated Summarization (2016). https://doi.org/10.48550/arXiv.1602.03606. http://arxiv.org/abs/1602.03606. arXiv:1602.03606
2. Bianchini, M., Gori, M., Scarselli, F.: Inside PageRank. ACM Trans. Internet Technol. **5**(1), 92–128 (2005). https://doi.org/10.1145/1052934.1052938
3. Bichi, A.A., Samsudin, R., Hassan, R., Hasan, L.R.A., Rogo, A.A.: Graph-based extractive text summarization method for Hausa text. PLoS ONE **18**(5), e0285376 (2023). https://doi.org/10.1371/journal.pone.0285376376
4. Cao, Y., Wan, X., Yao, J., Yu, D.: MultiSumm: towards a unified model for multilingual abstractive summarization. In: Proceedings of the AAAI Conference on Artificial Intelligence, vol. 34, no. 01, pp. 11–18 (2020). https://doi.org/10.1609/aaai.v34i01.5328
5. DebeleDinegde, G., Yifiru Tachbelie, M.: Afan oromo news text summarizer. Int. J. Comput. Appl. **103**(4), 1–6 (2014). https://doi.org/10.5120/18059-8990

6. Eberhard, D., Simons, G., Fennig, C.: Ethnologue: Languages of the World, 22nd edn. SIL International (2019)
7. Edmundson, H.P.: New methods in automatic extracting. J. ACM **16**(2), 264–285 (1969). https://doi.org/10.1145/321510.321519
8. Erkan, G., Radev, D.R.: LexRank: graph-based lexical centrality as salience in text summarization. J. Artif. Intell. Res. **22**, 457–479 (2004). https://doi.org/10.1613/jair.1523. https://www.jair.org/index.php/jair/article/view/10396
9. Giannakopoulos, G., et al.: MultiLing 2015: multilingual summarization of single and multi-documents, on-line Fora, and call-center conversations. In: Proceedings of the 16th Annual Meeting of the Special Interest Group on Discourse and Dialogue, Prague, Czech Republic, pp. 270–274. Association for Computational Linguistics (2015). https://doi.org/10.18653/v1/W15-4638. https://aclanthology.org/W15-4638
10. Gupta, V., Lehal, G.: A survey of text summarization extractive techniques. J. Emerg. Technol. Web Intell. **2** (2010). https://doi.org/10.4304/jetwi.2.3.258-268
11. Hahn, U., Mani, I.: The challenges of automatic summarization. Computer **33**(11), 29–36 (2000). https://doi.org/10.1109/2.881692
12. Hasan, T., et al.: XL-Sum: Large-Scale Multilingual Abstractive Summarization for 44 Languages (2021). http://arxiv.org/abs/2106.13822. arXiv:2106.13822
13. Kurniawan, K., Louvan, S.: Indosum: a new benchmark dataset for indonesian text summarization. In: 2018 International Conference on Asian Language Processing (IALP), pp. 215–220 (2018). https://doi.org/10.1109/IALP.2018.8629109
14. Lample, G., Conneau, A.: Cross-lingual Language Model Pretraining (2019). https://doi.org/10.48550/arXiv.1901.07291. http://arxiv.org/abs/1901.07291. arXiv:1901.07291
15. Lin, C.Y.: ROUGE: a package for automatic evaluation of summaries. In: Text Summarization Branches Out, Barcelona, Spain, pp. 74–81. Association for Computational Linguistics (2004). https://aclanthology.org/W04-1013
16. Luhn, H.P.: The automatic creation of literature abstracts. IBM J. Res. Dev. **2**(2), 159–165 (1958). https://doi.org/10.1147/rd.22.0159. https://ieeexplore.ieee.org/abstract/document/5392672
17. MBONU, C.E., Chukwuneke, C.I., Paul, R.U., Ezeani, I., Onyenwe, I.: Igbosum1500-introducing the igbo text summarization dataset. In: 3rd Workshop on African Natural Language Processing (2022)
18. Mihalcea, R., Tarau, P.: TextRank: bringing order into text. In: Proceedings of the 2004 Conference on Empirical Methods in Natural Language Processing, Barcelona, Spain, pp. 404–411. Association for Computational Linguistics (2004). https://aclanthology.org/W04-3252
19. Moratanch, N., Chitrakala, S.: A survey on abstractive text summarization. In: 2016 International Conference on Circuit, Power and Computing Technologies (ICCPCT), pp. 1–7 (2016). https://doi.org/10.1109/ICCPCT.2016.7530193
20. Ndyalivana, Z., Shibeshi, Z., Botha, C.: IsiXhoSum: an extractive based automatic text summarizer for xhosa news items. In: Southern Africa Telecommunication Networks and Applications (2016)
21. Nogwina, M., Shibeshi, Z., Mali, Z.: Towards developing a stemmer for the isixhosa language. In: Southern Africa Telecommunication Networks and Applications, Boardwalk, Port Elizabeth (2014)
22. Palen-Michel, C., Lignos, C.: LR-Sum: Summarization for Less-Resourced Languages (2022). https://doi.org/10.48550/arXiv.2212.09674. http://arxiv.org/abs/2212.09674. arXiv:2212.09674

23. Radev, D.R., Jing, H., Styś, M., Tam, D.: Centroid-based summarization of multiple documents. Inf. Process. Manag. **40**(6), 919–938 (2004)
24. Rossiello, G., Basile, P., Semeraro, G.: Centroid-based text summarization through compositionality of word embeddings. In: Proceedings of the MultiLing 2017 Workshop on Summarization and Summary Evaluation Across Source Types and Genres, Valencia, Spain, pp. 12–21. Association for Computational Linguistics (2017). https://doi.org/10.18653/v1/W17-1003. https://aclanthology.org/W17-1003
25. Scialom, T., Dray, P.A., Lamprier, S., Piwowarski, B., Staiano, J.: MLSUM: The Multilingual Summarization Corpus (2020). https://doi.org/10.48550/arXiv.2004.14900. http://arxiv.org/abs/2004.14900. arXiv:2004.14900
26. Tesfaye, D.: Designing a Stemmer for Afaan Oromo Text: A Hybrid Approach. Master's thesis, Addis Ababa University (2010). http://thesisbank.jhia.ac.ke/5785/
27. Varab, D., Schluter, N.: MassiveSumm: a very large-scale, very multilingual, news summarisation dataset. In: Proceedings of the 2021 Conference on Empirical Methods in Natural Language Processing, Online and Punta Cana, Dominican Republic, pp. 10150–10161. Association for Computational Linguistics (2021). https://doi.org/10.18653/v1/2021.emnlp-main.797. https://aclanthology.org/2021.emnlp-main.797
28. Vaswani, A., et al.: Attention is all you need. In: Advances in Neural Information Processing Systems, vol. 30. Curran Associates, Inc. (2017)
29. Xue, L., et al.: mT5: a massively multilingual pre-trained text-to-text transformer (2021). https://doi.org/10.48550/arXiv.2010.11934. http://arxiv.org/abs/2010.11934. arXiv:2010.11934

Speech Technologies

Multi Speaker Activity Detection Using Spectral Centroids

K. V. Aljinu Khadar[1]([⊠]), R. K. Sunil Kumar[1], P. K. Neeraj Krishnan[2],
and V. V. Sameer[3]

[1] Department of Information Technology, Kannur University, Kannur, Kerala, India
{aljinu,sunilkumarrk}@kannuruniv.ac.in
[2] Department of Computer Science, University of Calicut, Malappuram, Kerala, India
[3] Department of Computer Science, Farook College, Kozhikode, Kerala, India
sameer@farookcollege.ac.in

Abstract. In recent years, there has been a notable increase in the demand for reliable and effective methods in the domain of audio processing, specifically for the purpose of analysing complex acoustic surroundings. Multi-Speaker Activity Detection (MSAD) is a fundamental task in this domain that entails the detection and classification of multiple speakers in an audio recording. In this work, we propose a novel approach for MSAD based on the concept of Spectral Centroids. Spectral Centroids provide valuable insights into the spectral characteristics of audio signals and have been widely used for tasks such as music genre classification and instrument recognition. In our work, we utilise spectral centroid data to create an efficient MSAD system. The performance of our proposed multi-speaker auditory Detection (MSAD) system is assessed using a broad dataset that encompasses a range of auditory situations and speaker configurations. The utilisation of gender-specific threshold values and the inclusion of the spectral centroid characteristic in the process of multi-speaker activity detection exhibit potential in effectively ascertaining the number of speakers in simultaneous voice recordings. The results obtained for male and female test sets indicate the effectiveness of this approach in differentiating between speakers of different genders. Continued research and refinement of the spectral centroid-based method could lead to advancements in multi-speaker activity detection systems, enabling applications such as speaker diarization and speech separation in complex audio environments.

Keywords: Spectral centroid · Speaker Diarization · speaker activity detection

1 Introduction

The spectral centroid is a significant metric in the field of digital signal processing and audio analysis since it offers vital insights into the typical frequency composition or tonal luminosity of a given sound. It is determined by considering the frequencies and amplitudes of spectral components obtained through Fourier transforms or spectrograms. The spectral centroid represents the center of mass of the sound's frequency distribution and can be interpreted as the average or dominant frequency of a sound. A higher centroid value indicates higher average frequency content, often associated with brighter or sharper sounds, while a lower centroid value suggests lower average frequency content, typically found in duller or darker sounds with more low-frequency components.

Since the frequencies of human voices are different from one another, the averages of frequencies over some short interval of time of the speech of multiple concurrent speakers, it would show different averages for each frame depending on which speaker's voice proved more significant in that particular frame. This would help in identifying the number of speakers.

The spectral centroid feature finds applications in various audio processing tasks. In music analysis, it helps classify different genres or identify specific instruments based on their tonal characteristics. For example, instruments like flutes or piccolos typically have higher spectral centroids compared to instruments like bass guitars or cellos, which exhibit lower centroid values. This information can be leveraged in music information retrieval systems, instrument recognition, or genre classification algorithms.

Moreover, the spectral centroid is valuable in audio effect processing and sound synthesis. Through the manipulation of the centroid, it becomes feasible to generate effects that have the capacity to alter the luminosity or darkness of a sound. For instance, increasing the centroid is able to simulate the perception of a sound becoming sharper while decreasing the centroid can result in a duller or bass-heavy sound. This control over spectral brightness offers creative possibilities in audio production, equalization, and sound design.

In summary, the spectral centroid is a powerful measure in digital signal processing and audio analysis, providing insights into the average frequency content or tonal brightness of sounds. It has applications in music analysis, instrument recognition, genre classification, audio effect processing, and sound synthesis. By leveraging the spectral centroid, researchers and practitioners are able to extract valuable information and manipulate the tonal characteristics of sounds for various applications in the audio domain.

While other contemporary techniques take cues from context or non-auditory information like visuals for the act of distinguishing between the categories of the number of speakers, this technique tries to isolate this one feature and use so as to make it more versatile and applicable in more or less any situation in which speech signals can be obtained, and still give good results.

In the context of multi-speaker activity detection, the spectral centroid feature proves as a useful tool for discriminating between speech and non-speech, speaker discrimination, and managing background noise. Analyzing the spectral centroids of different segments enables the identification and tracking of individual speakers in multi-speaker speech data.

2 Review of Related Works

Multi-speaker activity detection, also known as multi-speaker diarization or overlapping speech detection is a field of research within audio signal processing and speech recognition that focuses on the identification and segmentation of different speakers in an audio recording where multiple speakers are speaking simultaneously. It aims to determine the two objectives, understanding "who spoke when" and "who spoke together" in a given audio signal.

The origins of multi-speaker activity detection can be traced back to the initial stages of speaker diarization technology. During the 1990s, the predominant focus within this particular realm of study revolved around the augmentation of automated speech recognition (ASR) systems. This was achieved through the segregation of speech segments originating from distinct speakers, hence facilitating the implementation of speaker-adaptive training for acoustic models [1]. This aspect held significant importance in various applications, such as air traffic control talks and broadcast news recordings. During this period, several fundamental approaches for measuring the distance between speech segments and detecting speaker changes were developed. Notable methods include the generalized likelihood ratio (GLR) and Bayesian information criterion (BIC), which quickly became standard techniques for speaker change detection and clustering [2].

The advancements in multi-speaker activity detection led to the establishment of research consortia and challenges in the early 2000s, such as the Augmented Multiparty Interaction (AMI) Consortium and the RT Evaluation hosted by the National Institute of Standards and Technology (NIST). These collaborative efforts fostered further progress in speaker diarization technologies across various domains, including broadcast news, conversational telephone speech, and meeting conversations.

New approaches emerged from these advancements, such as beamforming, information bottleneck clustering (IBC), variation Bayesian (VB) approaches, and joint factor analysis (JFA). One influential development during this time was the introduction of i-vectors, which were speaker-specific representations derived from simplified JFA. I-vectors have demonstrated significant efficacy in the domain of speaker recognition, leading to their integration into speaker diarization systems as feature representations for brief speech segments [3].

Various challenges for the diarization and speaker detection process are being tackled in a number of ways ranging from the use of fisheye lens cameras to significantly increase the accuracy of speaker detection when it comes to video data to using a camera to detect the location of the speakers and a microphone array to capture the speech signals of the speakers while suppressing noise and interference from other sources to energy-based approach for multi-speaker voice activity detection using an ad hoc microphone array. Methods using independent component analysis and beam pattern analysis as well as methods of targeted voice activity detection using speaker embedding like i-vectors have been done in recent years to more custom scenario-dependent solutions [4, 5].

Malayalam is a prominent language in South India and there is indeed a need for developing solutions for speech analysis in regional languages. Previous studies have used features like MFCC, ΔMFCC and $\Delta\Delta$MFCC to have much success using much larger speech segments and datasets using single state Hidden Markov Models, but for speaker recognition rather than multi speaker activity detection over the last decade.

3 Methodology

3.1 Dataset

For this study on multi-speaker activity detection, a dataset comprising speech data from multiple individuals was collected. All of the speech was recorded on mobile phones in a silent atmosphere in uncompressed.wav format. Given the requirement of analyzing concurrent speech, the dataset consisted of recordings where speakers spoke the same text simultaneously. Specifically, the recordings included up to 10 speakers of the same gender simultaneously speaking the same sentence.

The recordings were all between 5 and 10 s in length. These recordings were stored as uncompressed waveform files, resulting in a dataset containing 138 recordings, with 66 involving male speakers and 72 involving female speakers. The dataset was split approximately 80–20 between training and test sets, with the sets based on gender.

The recordings on the male set were 12 clips of individual speakers, 12 of a duo, and the remaining 42 were recordings of more than two speakers speaking concurrently. The female set contains 15 recordings of individual speakers, 15 recordings of pairs of speakers, and 42 recordings of numerous concurrent speakers. The experiments were conducted disjoint from each other and there was no overlap in the training and test data of the male and female datasets (Figs. 1 and 2).

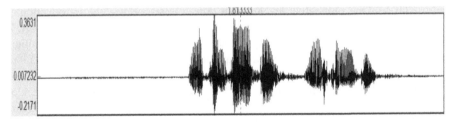

Fig. 1. Recording of Single-speaker speech

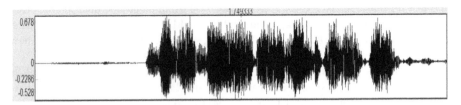

Fig. 2. Recording of four-speaker speech

3.2 Noise Removal of Speech Data Using Spectral Centroid

The spectral subtraction method is a widely employed technique in the field of audio signal processing for the purpose of noise reduction. It is known for its effectiveness in enhancing the quality of audio signals by mitigating the presence of undesirable noise. The approach employed in this methodology involves the utilisation of spectral analysis principles to effectively distinguish the noise component from the target signal. The initial step involves the examination of the power spectrum of the signal that contains noise, followed by the estimation of the power spectrum of the noise. After that, the noise spectrum is taken away from the original data spectrum. This makes a new spectrum with less noise. Finally, the changed spectrum is transformed back into the time domain to get a better copy of the original signal. The spectral subtraction method is a commonly employed technique in audio processing applications due to its practicality and computing efficiency. It provides an effective solution for reducing noise. Figure 3 shows the block diagram of noise removal of speech data using spectral centroid.

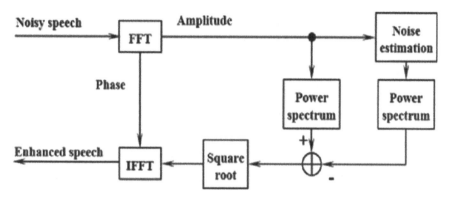

Fig. 3. Block Diagram -Noise removal using Spectral Centroid

3.3 Spectral Centroid

Spectral centroid is a measure used in audio analysis to characterize the center of mass, or average frequency, of a sound spectrum. It provides valuable information about the distribution of frequencies in a signal and is commonly used in music, speech, and acoustics. To calculate the spectral centroid, we first obtain the spectrum of a signal by applying a Fourier transform, typically using the Fast Fourier Transform (FFT) algorithm. The spectrum represents the amplitudes of different frequency components present in the signal. Once we have the spectrum, the spectral centroid is computed by taking the weighted mean of the frequencies and their corresponding magnitudes. Each frequency is multiplied by its magnitude and divided by the total magnitude of the spectrum. This calculation can be expressed using the following formula:

$$Spectral\ Centroid = \frac{\sum_{n=0}^{N-1} f(n)x(n)}{\sum_{n=0}^{N-1} x(n)} \tag{1}$$

F(n) represents the frequency bins in the spectrum and x(n) represents the corresponding magnitudes or amplitudes of the frequency bins [6, 7].

To extract spectral centroid features for multi-speaker activity detection, the process begins with preprocessing the audio samples. Prior to feature extraction, various pre-processing techniques are applied to enhance the quality and clarity of the signals. This includes pre-emphasis on boosting high-frequency components and denoising methods to reduce background noise interference.

Once the preprocessing stage is complete, the spectral centroid feature extraction process begins. The audio signal is sampled at a specific rate and converted into a digital format. The signal is then divided into frames or windows of short durations, typically ranging from 10 to 50 ms, with the option of using overlapping frames for improved temporal resolution.

Next, a fast Fourier transform (FFT) is performed on each windowed frame to convert the signal from the time domain to the frequency domain. The resulting complex spectrum is transformed into a magnitude spectrum by taking the absolute values. The frequency values corresponding to each bin in the magnitude spectrum are determined by dividing the sample rate by the FFT size and multiplying it by the bin index (Fig. 4).

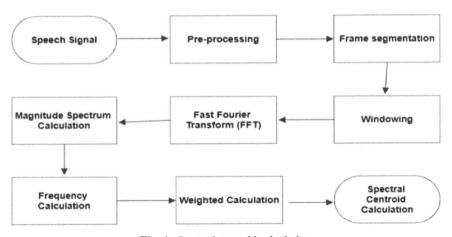

Fig. 4. Spectral centroid calculation

To obtain a weighted spectrum, each frequency value is multiplied by its corresponding magnitude. This step assigns greater importance to frequencies with higher magnitudes, capturing the spectral characteristics of the audio signal. The spectral centroid, which represents the weighted average of the frequencies, is then computed by dividing the sum of the products of frequency and magnitude by the sum of the magnitudes across all frequencies in the frame.

These spectral centroid features can be further analyzed for multi-speaker activity detection. Statistical measures such as mean, standard deviation, or temporal variation can be computed over a sequence of frames to capture dynamic changes in the audio signal. These extracted features provide valuable information for identifying different speakers and analyzing their activities within the audio recordings (Fig. 5).

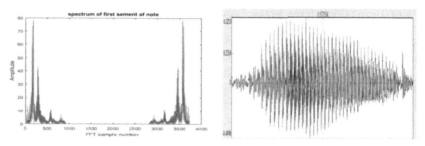

Fig. 5. Spectrum and speech signal of the Malayalam vowel signal /a/

Malayalam vowel /a/, a spectral centroid value got using the equation mentioned above is 1.7551e+03 which indicates that the average frequency of the vowel is around 1755.1 Hz.

To determine the number of speakers, present in the audio, a threshold value is set based on the difference in the frequency between adjacent spectral centroids. The choice of the threshold value is a very crucial step and it involves a manual process of trial and error. Multiple combinations of threshold values, frame sizes, and hop sizes are explored in order to find the values that yield the highest accuracy on the training dataset.

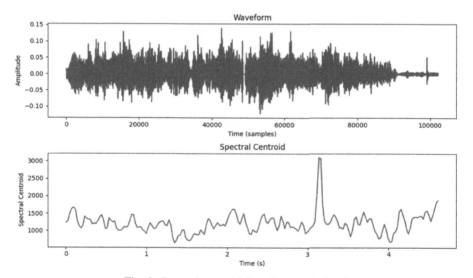

Fig. 6. Spectral centroid plot of a speech signal

Figure 6 displays the speech signal along with its corresponding spectral frame-based centroid. This visualization effectively demonstrates the varying spectral centroid values across the speech signal. Each frame in the plot represents a computed spectral centroid value.

3.4 Key Terms Considered in the Experiment

Sample rate is a fundamental concept in speech processing and audio engineering. It refers to the number of samples taken per second to represent an analog audio signal in a digital format. The sample rate is characteristically measured in Hertz (Hz) and determines the quality and fidelity of the digitized audio. In speech processing, the sample rate plays a crucial role in accurately capturing and reproducing the speech signal. The Nyquist-Shannon sampling theorem states that in order to faithfully reconstruct a signal, the sample rate must be at least twice the highest frequency component present in the signal. Since human speech typically contains frequencies up to around 8 kHz, a commonly used sample rate for speech processing applications is 16 kHz. This sample rate ensures that the essential information within the speech signal is accurately captured without aliasing or distortion. Higher sample rates like 44.1 kHz or 48 kHz, are used in professional audio applications where hi-fi audio reproduction is desired. These higher sample rates can capture a wider range of audio frequencies and provide a more accurate representation of the original analog signal.

Frame length, also known as window length or analysis window size, refers to the duration of each individual audio frame or segment in audio signal processing and analysis. It governs the length of the time window used to capture a portion of the audio signal for analysis or processing.

In speech processing and other audio applications, the audio signal is divided into consecutive frames or segments to analyze its spectral or temporal properties. The frame length determines the duration of each frame and it affects the trade-off between frequency resolution and temporal resolution in the analysis. It is usually represented as a percentage of the full sample rate in that context. The frame length is also specified in terms of the number of samples or the duration in seconds. The choice of frame length depends on various factors, including the characteristics of the audio signal and the specific analysis or processing task.

A greater frame length offers improved frequency resolution, enabling the analysis to record more precise spectral data. It is less suited for catching rapid shifts in the audio stream since it has a lower temporal resolution. In contrast, a shorter frame length offers a higher temporal resolution, enabling the analysis to record quick changes in the audio signal. It becomes less effective for recording precise spectral data, though, as the frequency resolution is reduced.

The optimal frame length depends on the specific application and the characteristics of the audio signal. Common frame lengths used in speech processing applications range from 10 to 30 ms, but that is not taken as a hard limit. However, it's crucial to note that the frame length is often times chosen in conjunction with the hop length, which determines the overlap between frames and affects the overall analysis characteristics, the combination of which results in better resolution of the signal.

Hop length, also known as frameshift or frame increment, is a term used in audio signal processing and analysis. It refers to the time interval between the starting points of consecutive audio frames or segments.

In speech processing and other audio applications, the audio signal is typically divided into frames or windows for analysis, processing, or feature extraction. The hop length defines how much the starting point of each consecutive frame shifts forward in time. The hop length is specified as a fraction of the sample rate. If the sample rate is the typical 16 kHz and the hop length is set to 0.01 or 1% of the sample rate, then the hop length would be 0.01/16000 kHz or 6.25 ms. In that case, each consecutive frame would start 6.25 ms after the previous one. The hop length determines the overlap between adjacent frames, and it can significantly affect the characteristics of the analysis or processing performed on the audio signal. A smaller hop length means more overlap and provides finer temporal resolution but increases the computational requirements. On the other hand, a larger hop length implies less overlap. It reduces the temporal resolution but requires fewer computational resources. The choice of hop length depends on the specific application and the trade-off between temporal resolution, computational complexity, and the desired analysis or processing goals. It is often determined empirically or based on the requirements of the particular speech or audio-processing task at hand.

This iterative process involves testing various threshold values and assessing their impact on the accuracy of speaker count predictions. The goal is to identify the threshold value that effectively discriminates between different speakers. This value is critical in determining whether the number of speakers exceeds a certain limit, such as two speakers.

During the experimentation process, the threshold value is attuned while keeping track of the corresponding accuracy. Hundreds of combinations are tested to find the optimal threshold value within an acceptable range. Additionally, the frame size and hop size, which determine the temporal resolution of the analysis, are also fine-tuned in order to improve accuracy. For instance, in the male training dataset, a threshold value of 1910 was chosen, along with a frame size of 4% of the sample rate and a hop size of 1% of the sample rate. In the female training dataset, a threshold value of 2045 was selected, along with a frame size of 2.5% of the sample rate and a hop size of 1.25% of the sample rate. These specific values were determined to provide optimal predictions and achieve accurate identification of the number of speakers in the given dataset.

The presence of frequencies that exhibit multiples higher than a designated threshold between consecutive frames serves as an indicative signal for the presence of multiple speakers within the audio. Specifically, when employing a threshold value of 2045, as selected for male audio samples, the occurrence of frequency differences surpassing 2045 Hz between adjacent spectral centroid values of frames signifies the involvement of additional speakers. Notably, a greater disparity in spectral centroid values corresponds to a higher likelihood of the presence of multiple speakers. This approach is mirrored in the case of female audio samples, albeit with a distinct threshold.

Spectral centroids for multi-speaker activity detection involves preprocessing the audio samples, extracting spectral centroids as features, and determining the threshold value to distinguish between different speakers. The selection of the threshold value is a manual process that requires experimenting with various combinations of values and evaluating their impact on accuracy. By fine-tuning the threshold value, along with the frame size and hop size, the system can effectively predict the number of speakers present in the audio data.

4   Results and Discussion

The observed variations in the threshold values for male and female speech can be attributed to the inherent differences in the frequency characteristics of speech between genders. The selection of these gender-specific threshold values helps to optimize the accuracy of multi-speaker activity detection systems, as it considers the unique spectral properties of male and female voices.

By applying the spectral centroid-based approach with the identified threshold values from the training data, promising accuracies were achieved for both male and female test sets. For the set of speech samples from multiple male speakers speaking concurrently, an accuracy of 71.42% was attained. Similarly, for the female test set, an accuracy of 73.3% was obtained. These results highlight the effectiveness of utilizing the spectral centroid feature in distinguishing between different numbers of speakers in gender-specific scenarios.

The achieved accuracies demonstrate the potential of the spectral centroid-based method for multi-speaker activity detection. However, it is important to note that the accuracy obtained may vary depending on the specific dataset, recording conditions, and the number and gender distribution of speakers. Further experimentation and evaluation on larger and more diverse datasets would be beneficial to assess the generalizability of the approach and to explore its performance in real-world scenarios. Increasing the temporal or frequency resolution to get clearer characteristics did not prove to be useful when it comes to improving multi-speaker activity detection accuracy (Figs. 7 and 8).

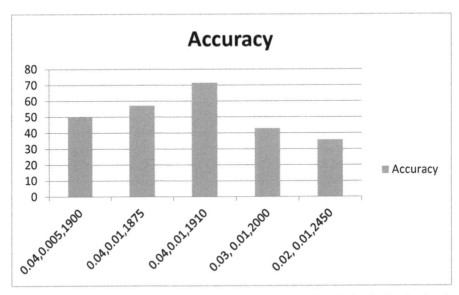

Fig. 7. Accuracy for different iterations of frame size, hop length, and threshold value for the male speaker set.

In conclusion, the use of gender-specific threshold values and the spectral centroid feature in multi-speaker activity detection show promise in accurately determining the

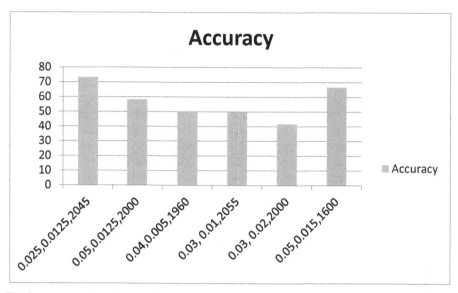

Fig. 8. Accuracy for different iterations of frame size, hop length, and threshold value for the female speaker set

number of speakers in concurrent speech recordings. The findings derived from the test sets comprising both male and female speakers demonstrate the efficacy of this methodology in discerning gender distinctions among speakers. Further investigation and improvement of the spectral centroid-based approach may result in progress in the development of systems for detecting multiple speakers' activities. This, in turn, could facilitate the implementation of many applications, including speaker diarization and speech separation, particularly in challenging audio situations (Table 1).

Table 1. The optimal arrangement for male and female vocal samples

Speaker	Sample rate (%), hop length (%), threshold(Hz)	Accuracy
Male	4%, 1%, 1910	71.42%
Female	2.5%, 1.25%, 2045	73.3%

The spectral centroid method has demonstrated its accuracy in detecting the presence of two or more speakers within the same speech clip. This approach holds promise for multi-speaker activity detection tasks, offering valuable insights into the number of speakers involved. However, it is important to note that the method is sensitive to noise interference, and therefore, a denoising step is crucial during the preprocessing stage. Noise in the audio signal can negatively impact the accuracy of the spectral centroid-based detection. Unwanted background noise can introduce additional frequency components that can obscure or distort the spectral characteristics of the speech segments.

This interference can lead to inaccurate estimation of the spectral centroids, affecting the reliability of the speaker count predictions.

To mitigate the adverse effects of noise, denoising techniques are employed during the preprocessing stage. Spectral subtraction denoising techniques are employed for denoising. These techniques aim to reduce or eliminate unwanted noise while preserving essential speech information. Common denoising approaches include spectral subtraction, wavelet denoising, or statistical modeling methods such as minimum mean square error estimation. By applying appropriate denoising techniques, the impact of noise can be minimized, improving the robustness and accuracy of the spectral centroid-based method for multi-speaker activity detection. Denoising ensures that the spectral centroids are computed from clean and representative speech signals, enhancing the discrimination between different speakers and facilitating more accurate speaker count predictions.

5   Conclusion

The present study on "Multi Speaker Activity Detection Using Spectral Centroids" has introduced a highly promising methodology for addressing the complex task of identifying multiple speakers in audio recordings. The authors have come up with a way to use the idea of spectral centroids to successfully look at the spectral features of audio signals in order to tell the difference between speakers. This shows that spectral centroids are a useful tool for multi-speaker activity detection, and could indeed help with speaker recognition in the future. It is a better alternative to some of the modern techniques owing to its simplicity and versatility when it comes to applications.

The study has highlighted the significance of spectral centroids as a feature in distinguishing between speakers, considering the variations in their vocal characteristics. The experiments conducted on diverse datasets have demonstrated the effectiveness of the proposed approach, showcasing its ability to accurately detect and classify multiple speakers in various scenarios. However, there are still avenues for further exploration and enhancement. Future research could focus on refining the proposed method by incorporating additional acoustic features, exploring more advanced machine-learning techniques, or considering the temporal dynamics of speaker activities. Furthermore, evaluating the approach on larger and more diverse datasets would help assess its robustness and generalizability.

References

1. Gish, H., Siu, M., Rohlicek, R.: Segregation of speakers for speech recognition and speaker identification. In: Proceedings of IEEE International Conference on Acoustics, Speech and Signal Processing, pp. 873–876 (1991)
2. Chen, S.S., Gopalakrishnan, P.S.: Speaker, environment and channel change detection and clustering via the Bayesian information criterion, pp. 127–132. Technical report, IBM T. J. Watson Research Center (1998)
3. Dehak, N., Kenny, P., Dehak, R., Dumouchel, P., Ouellet, P.: Front-end factor analysis for speaker verification. IEEE Trans. Audio Speech Lang. Process. **19**, 788–798 (2011)

4. Yoshioka, T., et al.: Advances in online audio-visual meeting transcription. In: Proceedings of IEEE Workshop on Automatic Speech Recognition and Understanding, pp. 276–283 (2019)
5. Ito, N., Araki, S., Yoshioka, T., Nakatani, T.: Relaxed disjointness based clustering for joint blind source separation and dereverberation. In: Proceedings of International Workshop on Acoustic Echo and Noise Control, pp. 268–272 (2014)
6. Grey, J.M., Gordon, J.W.: Perceptual effects of spectral modifications on musical timbres. J. Acoust. Soc. Am. **63**(5), 1493–1500 (1978)
7. Schubert, E., Wolfe, J., Tarnopolsky, A.: Spectral centroid and timbre in complex, multiple instrumental textures. In: Proceedings of the International Conference on Music Perception and Cognition. North Western University, Illinois (2004)

Spoken Language Identification System Using Convolutional Neural Networks

B. Bharathi[1(✉)] [iD] and A. Meenakshi[2]

[1] Sri Sivasubramania Nadar College of Engineering, Kalavakkam, Tamil Nadu, India
bharathib@ssn.edu.in
[2] SRM Institute of Science and Technology, Kattankulathur, Tamil Nadu, India
meenaksa@srmist.edu.in

Abstract. Spoken language identification has gained a lot of importance in the last decade with the advent of text-to-speech systems and intelligent assistants. Language Identification (LID) task revolves around the automated recognition of the language spoken in a given speech utterance. The traditionally used systems in this scenario are GMMs and SVMs. However, these systems also carry disadvantages like limitations in speed and size, discrete data handling, high algorithmic complexity and extensive memory requirements in large scale tasks. Deep Learning, a subset of machine learning, is pushing the boundaries of technological advancements in areas such as spoken language identification. It has already been proven that deep neural networks can be used to efficiently train the speech recognition system. A convolutional neural network refers to a feedforward artificial neural network containing multiple layers of hidden units positioned between its inputs and outputs. In this research work, we have generated melspectrogram images from a collection of speech utterances obtained from the open source website Voxforge. These melspectrograms are used to train the Convolutional Neural Network. The performance of the proposed spoken language identification using three languages namely French, English and Spanish are significantly better than the traditional machine learning approach.

Keywords: Deep learning · Mel spectrogram · Convolutional Neural Network · Spoken language identification system

1 Introduction

Language entails the capacity to grasp and employ intricate communication systems, primarily referring to the human aptitude for this, while a language encompasses any distinct instance of such a system. The count of languages globally fluctuates between 5,000 and 7,000. Human language possesses attributes like productivity and displacement, and it is entirely dependent on social norms and education. Its intricate framework allows for a significantly broader array of expressions than any recognized system. Despite having the potential to learn any language, individuals only acquire it when exposed to an environment where language is present and utilized by others. Consequently, language relies on speaker communities. Languages serve as tools for communication and addressing a multitude of social functions for their speakers. It becomes fairly imperative that there needs to be a system to identify languages which are foreign to indigenous speakers.

Automated Spoken Language Identification (LID) is the process of recognizing the language spoken in a particular speech utterance. LID systems find utility across various domains, including multilingual language translation, routing emergency or consumer calls, as well as surveillance and security applications. Notably, LID has garnered significant focus, largely owing to events like the NIST Language Recognition Evaluations (LRE) [6,8] and initiatives such as the DARPA Robust Automatic Transcription of Speech (RATS) program. Numerous strategies for Language Identification (LID) have emerged, utilizing techniques based on Gaussian Mixture Models (GMMs) as mentioned in [1], and approaches grounded in Support Vector Machines as outlined in [3]. More recently, techniques rooted in melspectrograms have emerged as the cutting-edge methods in LID, closely paralleling advancements seen in Speaker Identification (SID) practices. The state-of-the-art system in Spoken Language Identification consists of Deep Bottleneck Feature based i-vector representation for each utterance [2]. In more recent times, approaches for Language Identification (LID) that rely on Deep Neural Networks (DNNs) and Convolutional Neural Networks (CNNs) as highlighted in references [4,5,12] have gained growing prominence. These methods have demonstrated comparable, and often superior, performance when contrasted with i-Vector based LID techniques. In this research work, it is proposed to develop an automatic spoken language identification system using convolutional neural network. Convolution neural network is used to recognise the spoken language [11] for the speech corpus given in kaggle dataset.

The structure of the paper is outlined as follows: Sect. 2 provides a detailed explanation of the functioning of the proposed system. The performance of the proposed system is examined in Sect. 3. Finally, Sect. 4 concludes the paper.

2 Proposed Work

In the proposed spoken language identification task uses the speech utterances from three languages namely, English, French and Spanish as the input. Then the melspectrogram corresponds to the input speech utterances are generated. This melspectrograms are given as input to train the convolutional neural network. Trained CNN model is used to classify the test speech utterance. The proposed system architecture is depicted in the Fig. 1. The proposed CNN based spoken language identification primarily consists of four steps

- Data Collection
- Mel spectrogram generation
- CNN model training
- Testing

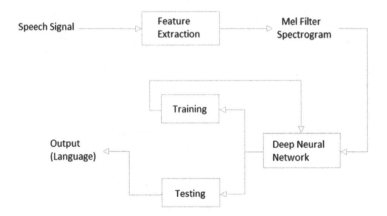

Fig. 1. Proposed system architecture

2.1   Data Collection

The data being is used in this research has been extracted from http://voxforge.org [7]. In this proposed work, we have considered only three languages namely, English, French and Spanish. VoxForge was set up to collect transcribed speech and is the largest opensource repository of speech data (Fig. 2).

Language	Number of Samples
English	6000
French	6000
Spanish	6000

Fig. 2. Details of speech corpus

2.2   Mel Spectrogram Generation

The mel frequency spectrum, as described in [9], depicts the power spectrum of a sound's short-term characteristics. This depiction is derived from a linear cosine transform applied to a logarithmic power spectrum, with the frequencies positioned on a non-linear mel scale. Frequency warping can enable an improved depiction of sound. These features are given a visual representation in the form of Mel Filter Spectrogram. The steps for generating melspectrogram is explained in the following section (Fig. 3).

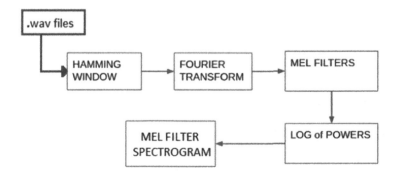

Fig. 3. Steps for extracting mel spectrogram

Windowing. The windowing block processes individual speech sample frames, mitigating signal discontinuities by gradually reducing the amplitude at the frame's start and end. The window's design ensures it becomes entirely zero at the frame's boundaries while adopting a specific pattern within. This function is then combined with the time-domain data block, inducing periodicity in the signal. This technique effectively mitigates leakage, enhancing the process of windowing.

Fourier Transform. One prevalent method of analyzing a speech signal involves the utilization of the power spectrum. This spectrum outlines the frequency distribution of the signal across time. To achieve this, the Discrete Fourier Transform (DFT) is executed, transforming a finite set of evenly spaced function samples into coefficients representing a finite amalgamation of complex sinusoids. These sinusoids are arranged by frequency, maintaining the original sample values. The calculation of spectral energy is accomplished using a 512-point DFT, facilitating the transition of the sampled function from its initial domain (typically time or position along a line) to the frequency domain. The sequence of N complex numbers $x_1, x_2, .., x_n$ is transformed into an N periodic sequence of complex numbers $X_0, X_1, .., X_N$ according to the DFT.

Mel Filter Bank Processing. The speech signal encompasses both high and low-frequency components. Since human ears are more attuned to frequencies below 1 KHz, the low-frequency components bear greater significance and carry more valuable information compared to the high-frequency counterparts. To accentuate the importance of the low-frequency elements, mel scaling is implemented. To achieve this, additional filters are positioned in the lower frequency range on the frequency axis, while fewer are allocated to the higher frequency region.

Logarithm. In the last phase to obtain the mel spectrogram images, the mel spectrum has to be converted back to time domain. As the final step the mel spectrogram is produced from these processed signals.

- A spark pipeline is deployed to convert the wav files present in the extracted data.
- These images are all directed to be stored at a single location with the language name being the name of the folder
- Precautionary step is to take care that there is enough space in the hard disk to accommodate the data.

2.3 Convolutional Neural Network Configuration

A Convolutional Neural Network (CNN) is an artificial neural network designed in a feed-forward manner, featuring multiple layers of hidden units situated between its input and output layers. Usually, every hidden unit, denoted as 'j', employs a logistic function to transform its cumulative input from the lower layer, represented as x_j, into the singular state value, y_j, which is then transmitted to the higher layer.

$$x_j = b_j + \sum_i w_{ij} y_i \tag{1}$$

where b_j is the bias of unit j, i is an index over units in the layer below, w_{ij} is a the weight on a connection to unit from unit i in the layer below and y_i is a logistic function of x. For multiclass classification, output unit j converts its total input, x_j, into a class probability, p_j, by using the softmax non-linearity:

$$p_j = exp(y_j) / \sum_l exp(y_l) \tag{2}$$

Convolutional Neural Networks (CNNs) can undergo discriminative training through the process of backpropagation, where derivatives of a cost function are propagated backward. This cost function gauges the disparity between the desired target outputs and the actual outputs generated for each training instance. When the softmax output function is utilized, the inherent cost function 'C' corresponds to the cross-entropy calculated between the desired probabilities 'd' and the softmax-generated outputs.

$$C = - \sum_j t_j log p_j \tag{3}$$

Here, the target probabilities, often represented as either one or zero, serve as the supervised information utilized to train the CNN classifier (Fig. 4).

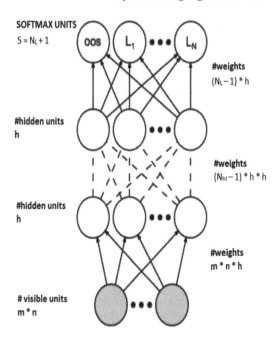

Fig. 4. Convolutional neural network

2.4 Convolutional Neural Network Model Training

The steps involved in training the CNN are:

1. Data collection and normalization
2. Deciding the configuration of the Convolutional neural network.
   - Shallow
   - Deep
3. Deciding the parameters of the training
   - Learning rate
   - Batch size
   - Training iterations
   - Input Shape
   - Output shape
4. Initializing training.

Data Collection and Normalization

The data that was processed, extracted, reduced to a specific time frame and stored as mel spectrogram images need to be converted into a csv file specifying the location of the file and the label of the corresponding language. Two sets of these csv files need to be prepared. One for training and the other for testing.

Depending on the hardware available and the amount to data to be processed, the configuration can be adjusted. There are basically two configurations of neural networks. They are:

- Shallow architecture network
- Deep architecture network

Shallow Architecture

In addition to the input and output layers, a neural network comprises intermediate layers, often referred to as hidden layers or encoders. A neural network with fewer hidden layers is commonly termed a shallow network. Although research suggests that a shallow network has the capacity to approximate any function, it would require a substantial width. Consequently, this leads to a substantial increase in the number of parameters (Fig. 5).

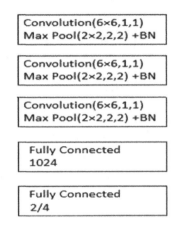

Fig. 5. Shallow convolutional neural network

Deep Architecture

Deep neural networks have a more number of hidden layers when compared to that of shallow networks. The primary rationale behind this phenomenon is that deep models possess the capability to extract and construct more effective features compared to shallow models, accomplished through their utilization of intermediate hidden layers. Empirical evidence strongly indicates that deep networks can outperform shallow networks in function approximation while employing fewer parameters. The proposed system uses deep convolutional neural network depicted in Fig. 6.

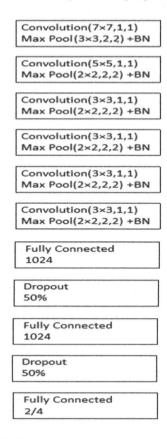

Fig. 6. Deep convolutional neural network

Convolutional Layers

Convolutional layers, as detailed in [8], employ a designated quantity of convolution filters on the image. Within each subregion, these layers execute a series of mathematical operations to generate a singular value within the output feature map. Subsequently, a ReLU activation function is commonly applied to the output of convolutional layers, introducing nonlinearities to the model.

Pooling Layers

Pooling layers play a role in diminishing the dimensionality of the feature map by downsampling the image data derived from convolutional layers. This reduction aids in decreasing processing time. A prevalent technique for pooling is max pooling, which involves selecting subregions from the feature map (for instance, 2×2-pixel tiles), retaining their maximum value, and discarding the rest of the values.

Dense (Fully Connected) Layers

Dense fully connected layers engage in classifying the features derived from convolutional layers and downsampled through pooling layers. Within a dense layer, each node establishes connections with every node present in the preceding layer.

Dropout Layers

Dropout stands as a regularization method within neural networks, curbing overfitting by deterring intricate co-adaptations in training data. It provides a highly effective approach for executing model averaging with neural networks, as elucidated in reference [10]. The concept of "dropout" pertains to the exclusion of units—both hidden and visible—within a neural network.

In a typical configuration, a CNN comprises a sequence of convolutional modules responsible for feature extraction. Each module is comprised of a convolutional layer succeeded by a pooling layer. Subsequent to the last convolutional module, one or more dense layers execute classification tasks. The ultimate dense layer within a CNN contains a node for every target class within the model (encompassing all possible predicted classes). This layer incorporates a softmax activation function, generating values between 0 and 1 for each node (summing up to 1). These softmax values for a given image can be understood as comparative indicators of the image's likelihood of belonging to each target class.

Learning Rate

The learning rate functions as a parameter dictating the degree of impact an updating step has on the existing weights. Concurrently, weight decay introduces an extra component in the weight update equation, causing the weights to progressively diminish towards zero in an exponential manner when no other updates are scheduled.

Batch Size

The batch size represents the amount of training data that is used to train the network at a time.

3   Performance Analysis

The performance of the CNN based Spoken language identification system is based on identification accuracy. Identification accuracy is defines as the ratio of the total number of test utterances correctly classified to the total number of test utterances.

Classification of different groups and their corresponding languages are given in Table 1.

Table 2 depicts the performance of the system and presents the accuracy of identification of each language that has been tested. It is observed that identification of Spanish language achieves the highest accuracy of 97% whereas identification of English language achieved the lowest accuracy of 91%.

Table 1. Class labels of languages

Class	Language
0	English
1	French
2	Spanish

Table 2. Performance of Spoken Language Identification system

S. No.	Language	Number of test utterances	Identification accuracy (%)
1	English	200	91
2	French	200	94.5
3	Spanish	200	97

Table 3. Confusion matrix

	English	French	Spanish
English	182	7	11
French	3	189	9
Spanish	2	4	194

Table 3 depicts the confusion matrix with respect to the identification of the languages. Identification of English language achieves an accuracy of 91%. English might be erroneously perceived to be Spanish or French with approximately a 1:1 ratio. It is clear that the highest accuracy is for Spanish with 194 utterances identified correctly out of 200. Identification of French language has the second best accuracy and Spanish might be wrongly identified as English or Spanish with approximately 1:3 ratio.

4 Conclusion

The premise of Spoken Language Identification has been implemented by extracting mel spectrogram from the speech utterances. These melspectrograms are then used to train a convolutional neural network. A separate set of melspectrogram is then used to test the CNN and identify the language of utterance. The entire system has been tested for three languages, namely; English, French and Spanish. The accuracy obtained is 91%, 94.5% and 97% respectively.

References

1. Reynolds, D.A., Campbell, W.M., Shen, W., Singer, E.: Automatic language recognition via spectral and token based approaches. In: Benesty, J., Sondhi, M.M., Huang, Y.A. (eds.) Springer Handbook of Speech Processing, pp. 811–824. Springer, Heidelberg (2008). https://doi.org/10.1007/978-3-540-49127-9_41

2. Martnez, D., Plchot, O., Burget, L., Glembek, O., Matjka , P.: Language recognition in iVectors space. In: Tweleveth Annual Conference of the International Speech Communication Association (2011)
3. Dehak, N., Kenny, P.J., Dehak, R., Dumouchel, P., Ouellet, P.: Front-end factor analysis for speaker verification. IEEE Trans. Audio Speech Lang. Process. **19**(4), 788–798 (2011)
4. Gelly, G., Gauvain, J.L., Lamel, L., Laurent, A., Le, V.B., Messaoudi, A.: Language recognition for dialects and closely related languages. Odyssey, Bilbao, Spain (2016)
5. Gonzalez-Dominguez, J., Lopez-Moreno, I., Moreno, P.J., Gonzalez-Rodriguez, J.: Frame-by-frame language identification in short utterances using deep neural networks. Neural Netw. **64**, 49–58 (2015)
6. The 2003 NIST language recognition evaluation plan (2003). http://www.nist.gov/speech/tests/lang/index.htm
7. VoxForge. http://www.voxforge.org/
8. Chollet, F.: Keras, Deep learning library for python. Runs on tensorflow, theano or CNTK (2017)
9. Bartz, C., Herold, T., Yang, H., Meinel, C.: Language Identification Using Deep Convolutional Recurrent Neural Networks (2017)
10. Sathe-Pathak, B.V., Panat, A.R.: Extraction of pitch and formants and its analysis to identify 3 different emotional states of a person. Int. J. Comput. Sci. **9**(4), 296 (2012)
11. Singh, G., Sharma, S., Kumar, V., Kaur, M., Baz, M., Masud, M.: Spoken language identification using deep learning. Comput. Intell. Neurosci. **2021**, 12, Article ID 5123671 (2021). https://doi.org/10.1155/2021/5123671
12. Kang, W., Alam, Md.J., Fathan, A.: Deep learning-based end-to-end spoken language identification system for domain-mismatched scenario. In: Proceedings of the Thirteenth Language Resources and Evaluation Conference, Marseille, France, pp. 7339–7343. European Language Resources Association (2022)

Exploring the Role of Entropy in Music Classification

J. Bryan Ronnie$^{(\boxtimes)}$, V. Harish Sharma, R. Aravind Angappan, and R. Srinivasan

Sri Sivasubramaniya Nadar College of Engineering, Chennai, India
{bryanronniej18023,harishsharmav18031,
aravindangappanr18014}@it.ssn.edu.in, srinivasanr@ssn.edu.in

Abstract. Music classification and analysis has been a very active area of study for quite a long time. While most of the research revolves around Convolutional Neural Networks (CNNs), we have employed information theoretic metrics to classify the songs. Abrupt amplitude changes in the music from time to time allow us to classify the music. We have used Shannon's entropy and Kullback-Leibler divergence to capture and quantify the changes in amplitude and based on this we have classified the songs into three categories, (1) melody (2) neutral, and (3) rock. To classify a song, we divide the music/song into small frames and apply the statistical and information theoretical methods to each frame. These results are then combined to obtain a single value representing the entire song, which is used for decision-making. Regardless of the language and instruments used, melody songs generally exhibit lower entropy values compared to rock songs. Our study includes songs from various languages such as English, French, Hindi, Japanese, Malayalam, Spanish, Tamil, and Telugu. Using the entropy values on the random forest model, we achieved a maximum accuracy of 82% in song classification. This study can enable a new way of classifying music without too much reliance on computational capacity.

Keywords: Music classification · Songs · Shannon's Entropy · Kullback-Leibler Divergence

1 Introduction

Music plays an important role in all our lives, and the choice of music varies from person to person, and from time to time. This necessitates music classification [3] like melody, rock, etc. The retrieved information can be further utilized in many applications including music recommendation, curation, playlist generation, and semantic search [6]. Many techniques have been explored in the literature to classify the songs. For example, CNN, KNN, and random forest are applied in the music classification [15]. Signal processing approaches are followed in [11,16].

The main theme of this work is to use the entropy of a song for classification [20]. On average, a melody encounters fewer changes in amplitude compared

B. R. Chakravarthi et al. (Eds.): SPELLL 2023, CCIS 2046, pp. 323–343, 2024.
https://doi.org/10.1007/978-3-031-58495-4_24

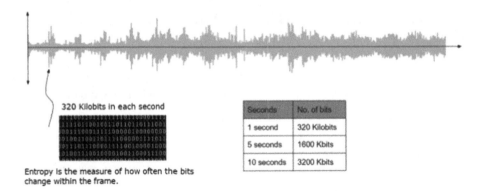

320 Kilobits in each second

Entropy is the measure of how often the bits
change within the frame.

Seconds	No. of bits
1 second	320 Kilobits
5 seconds	1600 Kbits
10 seconds	3200 Kbits

Fig. 1. A figure illustrating a song

to the rock type. The given music/song is split into small frames as shown in
Fig. 1, and the histograms of the amplitude samples are computed which upon
normalization gives us the probability mass function (PMF). This is followed
by the entropy computation of frames. The frame entropies are further used to
arrive at the song/music entropy. Though there are various entropies available in
the literature [19], Shannon's entropy is used in this work. Based on the entropy
values, a song is classified into

1. High entropy songs (rock type)
2. Moderate entropy songs (neutral)
3. Low entropy songs (melody)

Though the songs can be classified into various types, we currently restrict
ourselves to classifying songs as high energy, low energy, or mid-energy. To find
the entropy of a song, we split the song into frames, and for each frame, we
calculate the entropy from the amplitude values of each frame. Then we apply
the same method to various songs of different types and have an estimate of
a threshold entropy. This threshold entropy is later used to classify songs by
comparing it with the song's entropy. To increase the accuracy of the result of
the project, we could also study the frequency spectrum of the song [7]. We then
assign weights to the result produced in those two processes and then combine
them to get a very good classification of the song.

On a separate note, we also use cross entropy with Kullback-Leibler Divergence between a set of benchmark songs (consists of all three classes) and a target
song (song of a random class). The lesser the value, higher are the chances that
the target song class will be synonymous with the class of the benchmark song.
This also works well for comparison of songs with the same background music
and different vocals/languages/instrumentals.

Current Machine learning algorithms suffer from outliers. Thus, it is essential
to remove them before passing the data set into the machine algorithm. But
removing outliers is no easy task. With the help of entropy, we could bypass

this process of removing outliers as their contributions are severely reduced in the calculation. This would help us save significant time and provide us with a clearer picture.

Note that this could also be achieved with the help of the mode statistic formula, but the underlying problem is that the mode is not optimizable hence there is no scope for improvement. It is here where entropy helps as it is optimizable hence increasing its potential in the future.

We summarize the paper's contributions as follows:

- We explore various innate music properties that can be taken into consideration in the field of music analysis.
- We demonstrate that based on entropy, i.e., rate of change of amplitude in this case, the song's energy changes.
- We show that KL divergence is an effective measure to show how well two songs are similar/dissimilar.

This paper is organized as follows. In Sect. 2, we give an outlook where our way of music classification is relatable. In Sect. 3, we review the literature relevant to the paper. In Sect. 4, we present our proposed theoretical framework of entropy-based music analysis. In Sect. 5, we describe our approach including the experimental hypotheses. In Sect. 6, we show the results of our various methods. In Sect. 7, we provide a review of our work and comment on our contributions. We additionally discuss future extensions to the obtained results.

2   Motivation

This method of classification is useful in sorting songs for DJ playlists, dance floors, and events where the energy of the song is enough rather than sorted by genre. When the energy of the crowd goes down, a high-energy song can be played. When the crowd is exhausted, a series of low-medium energy songs can be played to give them a rest. This method is called Harmonic Mixing. By classifying based on the energy of the song rather than the genre, we can create customized playlists.

When you are going on a tour with your friends, or going on an adventure, most of them quickly think about high-energy songs rather than thinking of complex genres like pop/rock/fast beat and when you are driving alone for a long distance, you prefer low-energy songs [9].

The idea here is to analyze and classify music based on energy using minimal computational resources without having to keep in mind numerous genres of music.

3   Related Work

Wei Jiang et al. [1] aimed to analyze the overall characteristics of music by focusing on the smallest unit of music. They used a filtering process to extract important parameters and computed the Mel-frequency cepstral coefficients (MFCC).

Here, they used mathematical inversion algorithms to identify the characteristics of each music unit, and note recognition is the output of this step and made use of an improved version of the Dynamic Time Warping (DTW) algorithm for matching information. The researchers also introduced the energy-entropy ratio, which measures the ratio between short-time energy values and entropy. Lastly, they employed additive synthesis techniques for music modeling for the synthesis of standard piano notes and utilized a two-stage modeling approach to find the characteristics of music.

The final findings of the study are:

- Three mathematical models are used mathematical equation inverse recognition model, mathematical equation inverse recognition model, mathematical equation inverse recognition model, and adaptive Mathematical equation inverse recognition model.
- The adaptive mathematical equation inversion recognition model achieves excellent results in terms of accuracy and mean square error.
- As the characteristics of music increase, the grading mechanism will also be changed because they are classifying music-based frequency components.

Another study by Wenlong Zhang [2], titled "Music Genre Classification Based on Deep Learning" focused on the classification of music genres. The researchers considered three main characteristics of music, including time domain characteristics, frequency domain characteristics, and spectrum domain characteristics. They performed signal preprocessing, involving techniques such as pre-emphasis, framing, and windowing. Feature extraction was carried out using Fast Fourier Transform (FFT) to extract Mel-frequency Power Cepstral Coefficients (MPCC) characteristics. A standard neural network was trained using the extracted features, and an activation mechanism was employed for fine-tuning the classification process. The classification of genres was accomplished by calculating the cross-entropy loss and utilizing the SoftMax function for final classification. The study emphasized the importance of effective preprocessing and activation mechanisms in achieving greater accuracy and indicated future steps for further improvement in training.

Final findings of the study are:

- Accuracy of this classification is high
- For better classification better preprocessing should be used
- For classifying more genres training should be improved

Gregory Edward Cox [18] conducted research analyzing Meyer's hypothesis of meaning in music using Recurrent Neural Networks (RNN). The study encompassed the analysis of both monophonic and polyphonic music. For monophonic music analysis, an RNN combined with a hidden Markov model was employed. The music was divided into discrete time steps of equal length, with each step containing the musical information. The input layer represented several vectors for each part, where the dimensions of each part were pitch and rhythm. The current state served as input, and the next expected place was the output. A hidden layer with a logistic activation function was incorporated to enhance the output. The study involved calculating entropy for the overall probability distribution of pitches and the probability distribution of rhythms. To analyze polyphonic music, two models were trained based on the time span of knowledge: the Long-term model (LTM) and the Short-term model (STM). The research utilized Haydn's String Quartet First Movement as an example of polyphonic music. Like the analysis of monophonic music, both the LTM and STM models were trained, and the entropies of pitch and rhythm for both models were obtained. The entropies of the two models were combined, resulting in pitch entropy and rhythm entropy.

The findings of the study are as follows:

- An increase in tension was reflected by an increase in pitch and rhythmic entropy, with pitch entropy reaching a local maximum on the second beat of mm 24.
- The second theme group (mm 27–40) maintained consistent pitch entropy, while rhythmic entropy built up until the cello's eighth-note pulse disappeared in mm 34. This left only a high we melody with the other instruments holding chords in long rhythmic values.
- Rhythmic entropy continued to build until a resting point was reached at mm 70, characterized by an unclear tonality.
- Rhythmic entropy reached a local maximum at mm 90.
- In both cases, the rhythmic surface remained the same, but the pitches were different and assigned to different instruments. Consequently, it is logical that there would be more uncertainty about pitch than rhythm at the end of the exposition.
- Overall, these research studies shed light on various approaches for analyzing music characteristics, genre classification, and the relationship between entropy and musical elements.

4   Proposed Theoretical Model

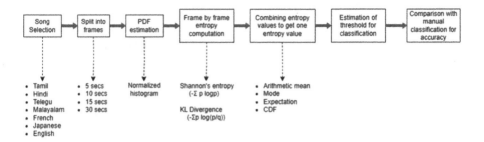

Fig. 2. A figure listing out the flow of the experiments

We follow all these steps listed above in Fig. 2 for each song one by one for our study.

4.1   Data Acquisition and Preprocessing

Obtain a decent-sized dataset of music signals, preferably in a digital audio format such as MP3. Preprocess the audio signals, including decoding the audio files and converting them to a suitable digital representation. Apply any necessary preprocessing steps such as resampling, normalization, or noise reduction. Down sampling is a necessary step for doing signal calculations in lower end machines. We use the envelope of the amplitude signal for further calculations.

4.2   Frame Separation

Divide the audio signals into frames of fixed durations like 5, 10, 15 and 30 s. Determine the number of frames based on the total length of the audio signals and the frame duration [13].

4.3   Histogram Computation

Compute histograms with a fixed number of bins equal to the duration of the selected frame. The reason behind this division is to split the audio data into equal-sized frames, where each frame represents a portion of the total time. By dividing the total time by the number of bins, the code aims to create roughly equally spaced frames, ensuring that the analysis covers the entire duration of the audio [8].

The choice of dividing by the number of bins is not a strict requirement but rather a design decision based on the desired granularity of analysis. It allows for the creation of a specific number of frames/bins to capture the variation in the audio signal adequately.

Use the histogram function to calculate the distribution of amplitude values within each frame. Normalize the histogram counts to obtain probability distributions for each frame.

4.4   Entropy Calculation

For each frame, calculate the entropy as a measure of the average information content or uncertainty in the frame's probability distribution. Use the formula:

$$Entropy = -\sum p(x) * log_2(p(x)) \tag{1}$$

where p(x) represents the probability distribution.

The below Fig. 3 shows the plot of entropies of different songs calculated from 5-s frames.

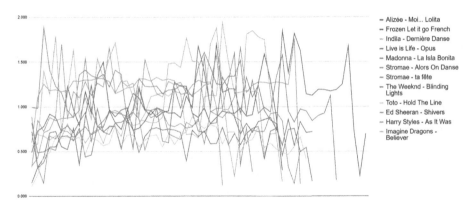

Fig. 3. Frame-by-frame Entropy line plot

4.5 Kullback-Leibler Divergence Calculation

We use cross entropy to say how far two signals are dissimilar. However, it will be more effective if we can obtain a relative scale to measure the dissimilarity [14] between the music signals. So, we are using Kullback-Leibler Divergence to measure the dissimilarity. Evaluate the KL divergence as a measure of the difference between two probability distributions.

$$KLDivergence = \sum p(x) * log_2\left(\frac{p(x)}{q(x)}\right) \qquad (2)$$

where p(x) and q(x) represent the probability distributions of two different signals or frames.

4.6 Earth Mover's Distance

Earth Mover's distance is another similarity metric [10] that can be used to rate the dissimilarity between the target song and the representational song.

Earth Mover's Distance between distributions A and B,

$$EMD(A, B) = \sum |x - y| * f(x, y) \qquad (3)$$

where,

$|x - y|$ is the distance between point x in distribution A and point y in distribution B

f(x, y) is the amount of mass that needs to be moved from x to y to transform distribution A into distribution B

4.7   Beats per Minute (BPM)

Beats per minute is a unit of measurement that describes the tempo or speed of a piece of music, particularly its rhythmic pace. It indicates the number of beats that occur in one minute of time. BPM is a fundamental element in music [12], helping musicians and composers convey the tempo at which a piece should be performed or the pace at which a listener should perceive the music.

BPM values can usually range from very slow, such as 40 BPM for a slow ballad, to very fast, like 200 BPM for a rapid dance track. The BPM of a piece of music can significantly influence its mood and style [17]. Slower tempos often create a more relaxed and gentle atmosphere, while faster tempos may convey energy and excitement. Musicians and DJs may adjust BPM to suit the genre, mood, or intended audience of a musical piece.

4.8   Analysis and Interpretation

Analyze the computed entropy and KL divergence values. Compare the results across different signal pairs, frames, or music compositions. Interpret the findings to gain insights into the similarity or dissimilarity between signals, music genres, or specific musical features [5]. We use statistical and information theoretical methods on top of the obtained frame-by-frame entropy values:-

a) Mean
b) Mode
c) Cumulative Distribution Function (CDF)
d) Expectation

4.8.1   Mean Mean, in mathematics, is a quantity that has a value intermediate between those of the extreme members of some set. Several kinds of means exist, and the method of calculating an arithmetic mean depends upon the relationship known or assumed to govern the other members. The arithmetic mean, denoted $\hat{x}$, of a set of n numbers x_1, x_2, ..., x_n is defined as the sum of the numbers divided by n. The mean of the frame-by-frame entropy of the song is a single value.

$$Arithmetic\,mean\,\hat{x} = \frac{x_1 + x_2 + ... + x_n}{n} \qquad (4)$$

where $\{x_1, x_2, ..., x_n\}$ is a set of numbers

4.8.2   Mode A mode, in statistics, is defined as the value that has a higher frequency in a given set of values. It is the value that appears the greatest number of times. This method has a slight limitation in that no mode value can be found sometimes if there are a smaller number of frames.

4.8.3   Expectation In probability theory, the expected value (also called expectation, expectancy, mathematical expectation, mean, average, or first moment) is a generalization of the weighted average. Informally, the expected value is the arithmetic mean of a large number of independently selected outcomes of a random variable. The expected value of a random variable with a finite number of outcomes is a weighted average of all possible outcomes. In the case of a continuum of possible outcomes, the expectation is defined by integration. In the axiomatic foundation for probability provided by measure theory, the expectation is given by Lebesgue integration.

$$Expectation\ E(X) = \sum_{i}^{n} x_i P(x_i) \tag{5}$$

where,

x is the value of the continuous random variable X
P(x) is the probability mass function of X

4.8.4   Cumulative Distribution Function (CDF) The Cumulative Distribution Function (CDF), of a real-valued random variable X, evaluated at x, is the probability function that X will take a value less than or equal to x. It is used to describe the probability distribution of random variables in a table. And with the help of these data, we can easily create a CDF plot in an excel sheet.

In other words, CDF finds the cumulative probability for the given value. To determine the probability of a random variable, it is used and also to compare the probability between values under certain conditions. For discrete distribution functions, CDF gives the probability values till what we specify and for continuous distribution functions, it gives the area under the probability density function up to the given value specified. The CDF is defined for a discrete random variable and is given as,

$$F(x) = P(X \le x) \tag{6}$$

where X is the probability that takes a value less than or equal to x that lies in the semi-closed interval (a, b], where a < b. Therefore, the probability within the interval is written as

$$P(a < X \le b) = F_x(b) - F_x(a) \tag{7}$$

We arrive at a calculated value for each song at the end and by using ML models like Random Forest and Decision trees, we find the threshold values to separate high entropy, low entropy and medium entropy songs. We repeat these steps for each of the statistical methods mentioned above.

4.9   Model Evaluation and Validation

Assess the performance of the proposed model by conducting experiments on various datasets and comparing the results against ground truth or human annotations. Validate the model's ability to capture meaningful patterns, identify similarities or differences, and provide accurate assessments of music signal comparison [4].

5   Experiments

With the proposed theoretical model as a base, we conduct various calculations as per the order mentioned in the flow diagram Fig. 2.

5.1   Calculating Entropy

As mentioned, the focus is to use entropy to classify the song. For that, we need to calculate the entropy as shown in Fig. 4. First, we sampled the song. Then we split the given song into frames with each frame having sizes of 5 s, 10 s, 15 s or 30 s. After splitting, we plot a PDF estimation for the song. With PDF, we calculate the entropy of each frame of the song using the formula $E = -\Sigma(p)*\log(p)$, where E is entropy and p is probability. The output here is an array of entropy values (See Table 1) since we are splitting the song into multiple frames.

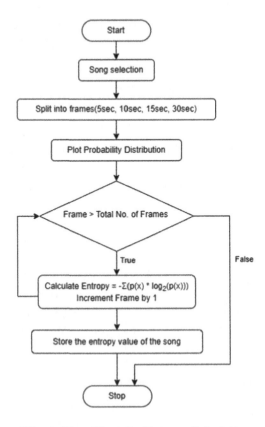

Fig. 4. Flow Chart for Entropy Calculation

Table 1. Table showing frame-by-frame entropy values of songs

Song Name	Frame by frame entropy values $-- \rightarrow$
Alizée - J'en ai marre!	0.532 0.474 0.671 0.917 0.933 0.922 ... ...
Alizée - Moi... Lolita	0.148 0.325 0.430 0.710 0.725 0.554 ... ...
Frozen Let it go French	0.490 0.730 0.778 0.920 0.881 0.721 ... ...
Indila - Dernière Danse	0.679 0.690 0.672 0.629 0.677 0.664 ... ...
Live is Life - Opus	0.722 0.317 0.377 0.550 0.553 0.670 ... ...
Madonna - La Isla Bonita	0.820 0.486 0.499 0.537 0.515 0.741 ... ...
Ricky Martin - Vente Pa' Ca	0.624 0.820 0.765 0.680 0.665 0.695 ... ...
Stromae - Alors On Danse	0.890 0.326 0.149 0.673 0.642 0.735 ... ...
Stromae - Santé	0.842 0.422 0.645 0.879 1.130 1.470 ... ...
Stromae - ta fête	0.325 0.849 0.725 0.883 0.847 0.872 ... ...
The Weeknd - Blinding Lights	0.995 0.984 1.890 1.410 1.230 1.155 ... ...
Toto - Hold The Line	0.111 0.240 0.452 0.485 0.663 0.648 ... ...

5.2 Estimation of Threshold for Classification

After finding the entropy values of the songs, it is essential we need a way to classify the songs. One such way is finding the threshold of each genre of the songs. To find the threshold, we need to convert the list of entropy values into a single entropy value [19]. For this, we make use of 4 statistical and information theoretical values namely,

- Mean
- Mode
- Expectation
- Cumulative Distributive Function (CDF)

The training data set consists of 310 songs of different languages and different types while the test data set consists of 50 different songs.

5.2.1 Calculating Mean of the Entropy After storing the entropy values of all the songs, we can calculate the mean of the songs(See Table 2), we can calculate the mean of the songs by the formula,

$$\mu = \frac{\sum_{i=1}^{n} E_i}{N} \tag{8}$$

where,

E is the Entropy of each frame
N is the total number of frames

This is done to all songs with various intervals like 5 s, 10 s, 15 s, and 30 s.

Sample Output

Table 2. Output for Mean Entropy

Song Name	Language	Mean Entropy .5	Mean Entropy .10	Mean Entropy .15	Mean Entropy .30
Alizée - J'en ai marre!	French	1.174	1.574	1.975	2.679
Alizée - Moi... Lolita	French	0.972	1.437	1.781	2.436
Frozen Let it go French	French	0.964	1.505	1.873	2.553
Indila - Dernière Danse	French	0.901	1.442	1.765	2.430
Live is Life - Opus	English	0.659	1.320	1.603	2.277
Madonna - La Isla Bonita	French	0.828	1.383	1.726	2.390
Ricky Martin - Vente Pa' Ca	English	0.805	1.526	1.913	2.564
Stromae - Alors On Danse	French	0.748	1.293	1.579	2.236
Stromae - Santé	French	1.117	1.510	1.892	2.578
Stromae - ta fête	French	0.897	1.442	1.674	2.314
The Weeknd - Blinding Lights	English	1.174	1.731	2.082	2.688
Toto - Hold The Line	English	0.611	1.232	1.471	2.076

5.2.2 Calculating Mode of the Entropy The mode is the value that appears most often in a set of data. The mode of a discrete probability distribution is the value x at which its probability mass function takes its maximum value. In other words, it is the value that is most likely to be sampled. After storing the entropy values of all the songs, we can calculate the mode of the songs. This is done to all songs with various intervals like 5 s, 10 s, 15 s, and 30 s.

5.2.3 Calculating Expectation of Entropy Expectation is an information theoretical concept that is used to find the weighted average of a random variable. In our project, the random variable is entropy. First, we need to plot the histogram of the entropy values of the song.

For plotting the histogram, we need to first find the range of the entropy i.e., minimum value and maximum value of the entropy values of the song. Then we split the range into 10 bins, each bin containing a fixed range. Then we note the frequency(f) of each bin. This is done to find the probability of each bin. Then, we calculate the expectation of the entropy (Fig. 5) of the song using the formula,

$$E = \sum_{i=1}^{n} x_i * P(x_i) \tag{9}$$

where,

$x_i = (low_i + high_i)/2$
low_i = lowest value of a bin
$high_i$ = highest value of a bin
$P(x_i) = frequency_i/$(total number of frames)

This is done to all songs with various intervals like 5 s, 10 s,15 s and 30 s (see Table 3).

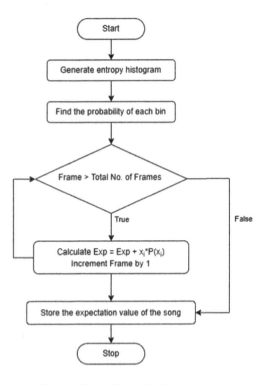

Fig. 5. Flow Chart for Expectation

Sample Output

Table 3. Output for Expectation

Songs	Expectation .5	Expectation .10	Expectation .15	Expectation .30
Adchithooku - Viswasam	1.748	1.757	1.779	1.771
Arabic Kuthu - Beast	1.648	1.624	1.673	1.703
Coldplay - Hymn For The Weekend	1.494	1.482	1.507	1.542
Ed Sheeran - Photograph	1.582	1.597	1.556	1.479
Eminem - So far	1.503	1.669	1.255	1.567
In The End - Linkin Park	1.564	1.519	1.322	1.600
James Arthur - Say You Won't Let Go	1.474	1.483	1.267	1.509
Jolly O Gymkhana - Beast	1.370	1.339	1.268	1.514
Linkin Park - In The End	1.683	1.685	1.482	1.687
Master - Kutti Story	1.752	1.817	1.572	1.800
One Direction - Night Changes	1.607	1.640	1.522	1.693

5.2.4 Calculating CDF of Entropy CDF is an information theoretical concept that is used to value that gives us the cumulative probability of 0.5. In this project, we aim to find the entropy value that gives the cumulative probability of either 0.5 or just crosses it. Like Expectation, we need to plot the histogram of the entropy values of the song. After plotting the histogram, fixing the interval of each bin where the number of bins is 10 and noting the frequency of each bin, we find the probability of each bin. After finding the probabilities, we cumulatively add them until they reach 0.5 or just cross them for the first time (see sample output Table 4). We note the bin where this is achieved, and the midpoint of that bin will be noted. For CDF, we use the formula,

$$P = \sum P(x_i) \approx 0.5 \qquad (10)$$

where x_i will be noted when this condition is satisfied.

Sample Output

Table 4. Output for CDF

Songs	CDF.5	CDF.10	CDF.15	CDF.30
Adchithooku - Viswasam	1.825	1.842	1.827	1.865
Arabic Kuthu - Beast	1.758	1.733	1.691	1.762
Coldplay - Hymn For The Weekend	1.553	1.539	1.579	1.532
Ed Sheeran - Photograph	1.662	1.680	1.675	1.453
Eminem - So far	1.546	1.708	1.327	1.587
In The End - Linkin Park	1.599	1.604	1.414	1.622
James Arthur - Say You Won't Let Go	1.516	1.560	1.340	1.531
Jolly O Gymkhana - Beast	1.422	1.440	1.327	1.533
Linkin Park - In The End	1.726	1.771	1.705	1.716
Master - Kutti Story	1.888	1.860	1.742	1.878
One Direction - Night Changes	1.661	1.743	1.734	1.732

5.3 Finding Threshold for Classification

After finding all the statistical and information theoretical values, we are required to find the threshold values for each to classify the songs. To do that, we plot a number line with entropy values of the songs of training data set (See Table 5). We then try to find the cluster of each genre and note the range of entropy values. We then define the threshold of each genre based on this observation. This threshold values are then applied to songs of testing data set to find the accuracy of each metric.

Classification of Song Using Threshold Values

After finding out all the entropy values and determining the threshold values for all types, we need to use them on the testing data set. First, we calculate the entropy and their statistical and information theoretical values. Then compare the values obtained with the corresponding type of threshold values.

When a given song has lower entropy than th_{low}, then that song is a melody song. If the song has higher entropy than th_{high}, then that song is a rock song. If it has more than th_{low} but less than th_{high}, then the song is neutral. See Fig. 6 for the flow.

Table 5. Training Dataset

Songs	Estimated Song type	By Mean Entropy.5	By Mode.5	By Expectation .10	By CDF .10
Alizée - J'en ai marre!	Medium	High	Medium	Medium	High
Live is Life - Opus	High	Low	Medium	High	High
Vaseegara - Bombay Jayashri	Low	High	High	Medium	Medium
Stromae - ta fête	High	High	Medium	Medium	Medium
The Weeknd - Blinding Lights	High	High	High	High	High
Ed Sheeran - Shivers	High	High	High	Medium	Medium
Malare	Medium	High	High	Medium	Medium
Priyathama	Low	High	High	Medium	Medium
Bigil - Verithanam	Medium	High	High	Medium	High
Master - Vaathi Coming	High	High	High	High	High
Teri Meri	Low	High	High	Medium	High
Nadaan Parinde	High	High	High	Medium	Medium
Arya - You Rock My World	Medium	High	High	Low	Low
Thirumali - Malayali Da	High	High	High	Medium	Medium

Minimum Intersection Algorithm with Entropy

Instead of attempting to find the threshold for each genre, we have also proposed to find the type of song by checking its similarity with melody and rock songs. For this, we are proposing to use the minimum intersection algorithm, which is primarily used in image processing to find the similarity between two images by finding the minimum area under their histograms.

Original Algorithm

1. Given model song set = M_1, M_2, M_3 ..., M_k
2. Given test song = I
3. For n=1: k
4. Read test song (I)
5. Read model song (M_k)
6. Generate corresponding histograms (h_1 & h_2)
7. Find intersection
8. Store intersection similarity s_{I-M_k}
9. End

Choose the Song Which has Highest s

First, we need to find a set of songs that best represent their genre properly. Next, we select a test song. Then, we plot their corresponding sample histograms. We then find their intersection value by the formula, intersection = $\Sigma min(I_i, M_i)$ i.e., we find the minimum value from each bin of their histogram and add them to find their intersection value. This process is applied to melody and rock song types, and their final values are compared. The one with a higher value would determine the type of song. For example, if the intersection value is higher in a rock song than in a melody song, then it is a rock song and vice versa.

Fig. 6. Flow Chart for Classification of Songs Using Thresholding

Our Proposed Algorithm

Since we are dealing with entropy to classify the song, we have proposed a change(Refer Fig. 7) in the algorithm used. Instead of using the sample histogram, we plot the entropy histograms and use them to find the minimum intersection value for classification. So, the new algorithm will be,

1. Given model song set $= M_1, M_2, M_3 ..., M_k$
2. Given test song $= I$
3. For n $= 1$: k
4. Read test song (I)
5. Read model song (M_k)
6. Split both I and M_k into frames
7. Generate corresponding histograms (h_1 & h_2)
8. Compute entropy values for all the frames
9. Generate entropy histograms of I and M_k

10. Find intersection
11. Store intersection similarity s_{I-M_k}
12. End

Algorithm 1: Minimum Intersection Algorithm

$model\_songs = [M_1, M_2, M_3, ...]$
$test\_song = I$
$total\_similarity = 0$
audio_read(I) // **read test song**
split_into_frames(I) // **split into frames**
for $k \leftarrow 1$ *to* $no\_of\_model\_songs$ **do**
    audio_read(M_k) // **read model song**
    split_into_frames(M_k)
    for $frame\_index \leftarrow 1$ *to* num_frames **do**
        $hist1 = \text{hist}(I, bins = 10)$ // **generate histogram**
        $hist2 = \text{hist}(M_k, bins = 10)$
        $PDF1 = \text{pdf}(hist1)$ // **calculate PDF**
        $PDF2 = \text{pdf}(hist2)$
        $ent1 = \text{entropy}(pdf1)$ // **compute entropy**
        $ent2 = \text{entropy}(pdf2)$
        $ent\_hist1 = \text{hist}(ent1)$ // **generate entropy of histogram**
        $ent\_hist2 = \text{hist}(ent2)$
        $similarity = \text{linear\_interpolation}(ent\_hist1, ent\_hist2)$ // **calculate similarity between test and model song**
        $total\_similarity = total\_similarity + similarity$
        $s \leftarrow total\_similarity$ // **Store the intersection similarity**
        if $s > best\_similarity$ **then**
            $max\_similarity = s$
    return max_similarity // **Return the max similarity between the two songs**

Choose the Song Which has Highest s

Like the original algorithm, we find the intersection value and compare their results to classify the songs. The genre where the intersection value is the maximum is determined as the genre of the song.

Application of Our Proposed Algorithm

In this algorithm, we select only one representational song for each genre. The representational songs are selected based on their mean entropies. Then for the histogram, the range will be the minimum value of the melody genre and the maximum value of the rock genre. This is to mitigate the overlap problem that would occur since different songs would have different entropy ranges. The number of bins for the histogram would be 10. In order to improve accuracy, we would employ correlation on our algorithm with a shift of 5 s. This would provide 3

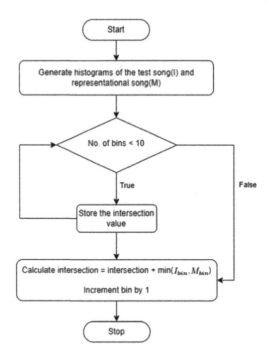

Fig. 7. Flow Chart for Minimum Intersection

values after which we would find the mean to find the minimum intersection value of the song.

Using KL Divergence and Earth Mover's Distance to Find Similarity
After calculating the entropies of each frame, we are calculating KL divergence for high entropy song and any input song. The output from this calculation will act as a metric for similarities between two songs. One main factor to consider KL divergence as a metric is comparing to cross entropy output of KL divergence will show how much first value differs from second value on a relative scale but cross entropy will tell how much two inputs vary on absolute scale. We'll also find KL divergence with a low entropy song. We can compare the relative dissimilarities in both cases and determine if the song has high or low entropy. The same method can be followed with the Earth Mover's Distance calculations.

6   Results

We have compiled the results of various computations and shown their model accuracies in Table 6.

Training Dataset - 310 songs, about 20 h
Test Dataset - 50 songs, about 3 h

Benchmark Songs for KLD and Intersection- 6 songs, about 23 min (3 high, 3 low)

Table 6. Table showing the model accuracies of various methods

Parameters .frame duration (secs)	Gradient Boosted Tree model accuracy	Random Forest model accuracy	Decision Tree model accuracy
Mean .5	0.62	0.62	0.66
Mean .10	0.58	0.6	0.64
Mean .15	0.68	0.64	0.68
Mean .30	0.6	0.6	0.6
Mode .5	0.72	0.74	0.72
Mode .10	0.7	0.7	0.7
Mode .15	0.7	0.7	0.7
Mode .30	0.7	0.7	0.7
Cumulative Distribution Function(CDF .10)	0.56	0.52	0.68
Expectation.10	0.72	0.66	0.74
Min Intersection	0.66	0.64	0.66
Earth Mover's Distance (EMD).10	0.58	0.56	0.58
KL Divergence (KLD).10	0.27	0.72	0.58
Beats per minute (BPM).10	0.5	0.48	0.56
Mean (All frame sizes) + CDF + Expectation + KLD + BPM	0.78	**0.82**	0.68

When we tried to predict the song type using various parameters like mean, mode, expectation, cumulative distribution, KL Divergence, EMD, beats per minute separately with manually estimated thresholds(which we arrived from analysis of the training dataset), the accuracy ranged between 60 s and 70 s. Then, when we used all parameters with machine learning models like Gradient Boosted Trees, Random Forest, Decision Tree, we were able to see a substantial 10% improvement in the overall accuracy implying that it's not just one music parameter that decides the energy of the music.

So, we get the highest accuracy 82% with Random Forest model with the mean, CDF, Expectation, KLD, and beats per minute as parameters.

7 Conclusion and Future Prospects

The project aimed to check whether the entropy of the song can be used to classify the type of the song. For this purpose, we have analyzed statistical data such as mean and mode and information theoretical data such as expectation, Cumulative Distribution Function and minimum intersection algorithm. It has been observed that splitting the songs into frames of size 10 sec gives us the maximum accuracy that is achieved in minimum intersection with correlation while mean metric gives us the lowest of the accuracy and to find out how entropy is use full KL divergence between high entropy song and input song is calculated, this calculation is considered as a metric to figure out how similar two songs are. We are considering KL divergence more in this study rather than cross entropy loss because it gives us the dissimilarity/similarity between the representational and the target songs on a relative scale.

The final findings of this study are:

- There is a much simpler system to classify the songs as opposed to the CNN models that require more high-end specifications.
- It is physically representable i.e., it tells us the background analysis of the signal that is not available in other algorithms.
- It can be applied to songs of all languages mixed with or without vocals.

To improve accuracy, we can add more no of songs both training and testing to

- Determine the threshold values and better set of representational songs.
- Can increase the number of songs in representational songs to improve minimum intersection accuracy.
- Can make use of frequency series and have a multi-nodal system for classification.

References

1. Jiang, W., Sun, D.: Music signal recognition based on the mathematical and physical equation inversion method. Adv. Math. Phys. **2021**, 1–12 (2021). https://doi.org/10.1155/2021/3148747
2. Zhang, W.: Music genre classification based on deep learning. Mob. Inf. Syst. **1–11**, 2022 (2022). https://doi.org/10.1155/2022/2376888. Article ID 2376888
3. Tzanetakis, G., Cook, P.: Musical genre classification of audio signals. IEEE Trans. Speech Audio Process. **10**(5), 293–302 (2002)
4. Foote, J.: Visualizing music and audio using self-similarity. In: Proceedings of the International Symposium on Music Information Retrieval (ISMIR), pp. 67–74 (1999)
5. Faller, C.: Signal processing methods for music transcription. IEEE J. Sel. Top. Signal Process. **4**(5), 786–798 (2010)
6. Muller, M., Kurth, F., Clausen, M.: Music structure analysis for ethnic music styles. In: Proceedings of the International Conference on Music Information Retrieval (ISMIR), pp. 227–230 (2003)

7. Slaney, M., Lucey, P.: Auditory Toolbox Version 2 (2013). http://engineering.purdue.edu/malcolm/interval/1997010/auditoryToolbox

8. Essid, S., Richard, G.: Instrument-specific harmonic atoms for mid-level music representation. IEEE Trans. Speech Audio Process. **10**(2), 108–121 (2002)

9. Dowling, W.J., Harwood, D.L.: Music Cognition. Academic Press, Cambridge (1986)

10. Witten, I.H., Frank, E., Hall, M.A.: Data Mining: Practical Machine Learning Tools and Techniques. Morgan Kaufmann, Burlington (2016)

11. Alghoniemy, M., Mayyas, K.: Nonlinear time-frequency signal processing methods for audio and speech applications. IEEE Signal Process. Mag. **28**(3), 94–103 (2011)

12. Dixon, S.: Automatic extraction of tempo and beat from expressive performances. J. New Music Res. **30**(1), 39–58 (2001)

13. McKinney, M., Breebaart, J.: Features for music audio classification: mel frequency cepstral coefficients and delta MFCCs. In: Proceedings of the International Symposium on Music Information Retrieval (ISMIR), pp. 199–205 (2003)

14. Li, T., Ogihara, M.: Using Kullback-Leibler divergence for music data mining. In: Proceedings of the International Conference on Data Mining (ICDM), pp. 446–453 (2002)

15. Kim, Y.E., Smaragdis, P.: Convolutional neural networks for music classification. In: Proceedings of the International Conference on Acoustics, Speech, and Signal Processing (ICASSP), pp. 859–863 (2013)

16. Brown, J.C.: Calculation of a constant Q spectral transform. J. Acoust. Soc. Am. **92**(5), 2698–2701 (1993)

17. Ellis, D.: Beat tracking by dynamic programming. J. New Music Res. Spec. Issue Beat Tempo Extract. **36**(1), 51–60 (2007)

18. Cox, G.E.: On the relationship between entropy and meaning in music: an exploration with recurrent neural networks (2010)

19. Minculete, N., Furuichi, S.: Types of entropies and divergences with their applications (2023)

20. Jeon, G., Chehri, A.: Entropy-based algorithms for signal processing. Entropy (Basel) **22**(6), 621 (2020). https://doi.org/10.3390/e22060621. PMID: 33286393; PMCID: PMC7517156

Spectral Features Based Spoken Dialect Identification for Punjabi Language

Manjot Kaur Gill[1,3]([✉]) [ID], Simpel Rani[2] [ID], and Parminder Singh[3] [ID]

[1] Department of Computer Science and Engineering, University College of Engineering, Punjabi University, Patiala, Punjab, India
manjotgill@gndec.ac.in
[2] Yadavindra Department of Engineering, Punjabi University Guru Kashi Campus, Talwandi Sabo, Punjab, India
simpel_ycoe@pbi.ac.in
[3] Department of Computer Science and Engineering, Guru Nanak Dev Engineering College, Ludhiana, Punjab, India
parmindersingh@gndec.ac.in

Abstract. Dialect identification for speech based applications has a very bright future in a multi-lingual country like India. But due to the lack of resources like standard dialectal speech databases, it has not gained much importance. This paper focuses on identification of four dialects of eastern Punjab by utilizing the spectral features of speech. The dialectal speech corpus is also created for these four dialectal regions. For training and testing of the system KNN and MLP classifiers are implemented with different training and testing sets in the ratio of 70:30. The results showed that MLP clearly outperformed the KNN for different values of 'K' with the accuracy of 82.25% for MLP and 76.01%, 77.12% and 76.84% for KNN with K = 3, K = 5 and K = 7 respectively.

Keywords: Dialects · Spectral Features · MFCC · KNN · MLP

1 Introduction

In today's digital era, the need of speech based applications has gained a lot of importance due to their ease of use and flexibility. Speech Processing has many fascinating applications like speech recognition, speech enhancement, speech synthesis, speaker recognition, accent recognition etc. In a multilingual and multi-cultural country like India, which is rich in its language diversity, has to excel a lot on these application areas of speech processing. The way of pronunciation of any language is termed as the accent of that language and in contrast the regional accent followed by group of people of any region is termed as dialect of that region. Accent and dialect differs in a way that a dialect uses words or phrases that are characteristics of that region (Najafian et al., 2016). Every language has its own dialects which are spoken prominently by people of belonging to that dialectal region. From the way of pronunciation and the selection of words by speakers of any region can help in detection of the dialectal region of that person.

© The Author(s), under exclusive license to Springer Nature Switzerland AG 2024
B. R. Chakravarthi et al. (Eds.): SPELLL 2023, CCIS 2046, pp. 344–358, 2024.
https://doi.org/10.1007/978-3-031-58495-4_25

In terms of work done on dialect or accent recognition fields, the Indian languages are lagging far behind, and the main reason is the non-availability of standard dialectal speech corpus for these local languages. Very few speech databases on local Indian languages can be found and that too are specific to speech recognition, language identification, speaker identification etc. Mother tongue, aging and recording environment also plays major contributing role in speech quality of the recorded speech datasets. The native dialect of the speaker also acts as influencing factor in dialect pronunciation and identification process which will also affect the performance of automatic speech recognition (Sinha et al., 2015). As dialects are sensitive to linguistic changes and regional restrictions, so the dialect identification becomes a more challenging task. The process of identification of dialect becomes complex if the dialects under consideration share common features or phoneme set (Koolagudi et al., 2017).

Most of the research work published, is done on languages spoken worldwide like English (Hegde et al., 2019), Arabic (Shon et al., 2020), Chinese (Ma et al., 2006), etc. Few traces of work done on Indian languages like Hindi (Agrawal et al., 2016), Kannada (Chittaragi et al., 2019), Assamese (Das and Bhattacharjee, 2022), Ao (Tzudir et al., 2021) etc. are found in some of the published works. Punjabi is the local language or mother tongue of the people residing in the state of Punjab. Due to lack of resources available for the research work on local languages, very less research work has been done on Punjabi language.

1.1 Features of Speech

Speech is non-stationary signal and to study the characteristics of speech signal it has to be divided into very short frames of few milliseconds. Speech signal has information regarding the accent and dialect, and it is based on the region or the area to which the speaker belongs. Age, gender, race and accent of the speaker plays valuable role in the dialect identification process (Mannepalli et al., 2016). The quality of voice or speech signal varies as per the mental and physical state of the speaker (Krishna and Krishnan, 2014).

The information relevant to dialect is present in speech signal at different levels i.e. segment level, suprasegmental level and subsegment level. Segment level is mainly concerned with the shape of vocal tract. Supersegmental level basically means above the level of segments i.e. it uses acoustic features like duration patterns of syllable sequence, pitch and energy contours. Subsegment level is concerned with the shape of glottis i.e. open and closed folds of vocal cords (Rao and Koolagudi, 2011).

The information in speech signal can be extracted in both time and frequency domains. In temporal domain features, the processing is done in the time domain for enhancing the speech components. These features are easy to extract and have simple physical representation. In spectral domain methods, the speech is processed in the transform/frequency domain. By applying the Fourier Transform to transform the time domain signal into the frequency domain signal, spectral characteristics can be obtained (Rabiner and Juang, 2003; Rabiner and Schafer, 2009).

In most of the systems implemented on speech processing applications, Mel Cepstral Frequency Coefficients (MFCC) and Linear Predictive Coefficients (LPC) are mostly used. Due to their comprehensive understanding of human hearing principles and the characteristics of cepstrum, they have been proven to be the most effective spectral feature representatives in speech-related tasks (Sinha et al., 2015).

1.2 Punjabi Language and Its Dialects

The official language of Indian state of Punjab is 'Punjabi', also spelled as 'Panjabi' and it is recognized by the Indian constitution. Punjabi is the mother tongue of the people residing in western Punjab (Pakistan) and eastern Punjab (India). Punjabi is categorized under Indo-Aryan languages and is spoken by more than 150 million people throughout the world. It is ranked 10th most widely spoken language in the world (Mittal and Singh, 2018). After partition of India, eastern and western Punjab was formed along with princely states under the name of The Patiala and East Punjab States Union (PEPSU). Later in 1966, under Punjab Reorganization Act, eastern Punjab was partitioned into three states namely, Punjab, Haryana and Himachal Pradesh.

Punjabi language is spoken in variety of dialects which is due to its vocabulary, grammar and pronunciation in different geographical locations. According to (Sangha, 2012), Punjabi dialects can be classified into two categories: Tonal dialects and Toneless dialects. Tonal dialects are mostly spoken in eastern Punjab or more specifically Indian Punjab and major dialects under this category are Majhi, Doabi, Malwai and Powadhi. The variation of tone changes the complete meaning of the word. Toneless dialects are spoken in western Punjab or Punjab state of Pakistan.

As dialect acts as an identification characteristic for a particular community belonging to distinct geographical location and based on the region there is variation in speech of people belonging to different regions (Singh and Singh, 2015). Standard Punjabi language has 38 consonants, 10 nasal vowels and 10 non-nasal vowels which plays major role in pronunciation of Punjabi dialects. Majhi dialect uses 10 vowels, 20 consonants and 2 half vowels; Malwai dialect uses 28 consonants and 10 vowels; Doabi dialect uses 25 consonants and 10 vowels; Powadhi dialect uses 24 consonants and 10 vowels (Singh, 2017). Due to these dialectal variations very less research work is done on dialects of Punjabi language and non-availability of dialectal Punjabi speech database is also the reason behind it.

As this paper focus on dialects of Punjabi language spoken in Indian Punjab and the major challenges to Punjabi dialect processing are: mergence with other major languages, one to many word mapping, lack of linguistic resources, and presence of sub dialects. As some of the dialect specific words are confined to a limited region, which sometimes leads to non-understanding of those words in other Punjabi dialects. This problem arises mainly due to different meanings of a particular Punjabi word in different dialects. These multiple meanings can act as a communication barrier during interaction of two or more persons belonging to different dialectal regions of Punjab. Thus, dialect acts as an identification characteristic for a particular community belonging to distinct geographical location (Singh and Singh, 2015).

The rest of the paper is arranged as follows: Sect. 2 describes the related work done, Sect. 3 explains the creation of Speech corpus, feature extraction of speech signal and the classifiers implemented in identifying dialects. Results are illustrated in Sect. 4 and at last, Sect. 5 concludes the proposed work and then Bibliography follows.

2 Related Work

The task of identifying the area or region of a speaker from its speech falls under the category of dialect identification. For south Indian language, Kannada, the speech dataset was created by recordings from five dialectal regions of Karnataka i.e. Central, Coastal, Hyderabad, Mumbai and Southern Kannada (Choudhury et al., 2018). (Choudhury et al., 2018) conducted classification experiments using Support Vector Machines designed with Sequential Minimal Optimization (SMO-SVM) function for classification studies, and they found that combining features enhanced performance by 82.75%. As spectral and prosodic features have dialectal information so (Chittaragi et al., 2019) used four different variations of these features for implementation of automatic dialect identification system in which, SVM trained with feature vectors comprising of MFCC features and their variations was implemented.

For Hindi language, (Sinha et al., 2015) worked on four major dialects of Hindi, namely, Khariboli, Bhojpuri, Haryanvi and Bagheli dialect and on the other hand (Rao et al., 2010; Rao and Koolagudi, 2011), worked on five dialects of Hindi, namely, Chattisgharhi, Bengali, Marathi, Telugu and general Hindi dialects. For the speech corpus specific to Hindi dialects they have created the corpus by recordings from the speakers of these dialectal regions. Segmental and suprasegmental features of speech were utilized by (Rao et al., 2010; Rao and Koolagudi, 2011; Sinha et al., 2015) to extract the speech features. The classifiers implemented for recognizing Hindi dialects were Support Vector Machines (SVM) and Auto-Associative Neural Networks (AANN) by (Rao et al., 2010), (Rao and Koolagudi, 2011) and they concluded that SVM performs better than AANN with better recognition accuracy score. Similarly, (Sinha et al., 2017) worked with SVM and Gaussian Mixture Model (GMM) and predicted that by changing the type of features or applying combination of features using human and system perceptions, the accuracies vary.

Telugu language mainly has three accents namely Coastal Andhra, Rayalaseema and Telangana. Speech corpus for these dialects was constructed by (Mannepalli et al., 2016) and analyzed using Praat and Colea tools for identifying the role of prosodic and formant features in accent detection task. As, MFCC features are playing important role in feature extraction and these were extracted for both training and test samples and then fed to GMM for accent base classification of the speech with the overall accuracy of 91% in accent recognition task (Mannepalli et al., 2016). (Satla and Manchala 2021), make use of Deep Neural Network (DNN) based Multi-Layer Perceptron (MLP) model to identify the regional dialects of Telugu by using enhanced MFCC features.

For Tamil language, again no standard dialectal speech corpus is found and (Nanmalar et al., 2019) recorded a speech database from the text collected in both Literary and Colloquial Tamil dialects with sentence duration of approximately 5 s for each sentence. Decent accuracy score of 88% was obtained with the help of MFCC coefficients with GMM model.

With three tones—high, mid, and low—Ao is a low-resource, tonal language spoken by Naga community in Nagaland state. As already discussed, that for Indian languages no standard datasets are available for dialect identification purpose. So every researcher creates their own dataset for their respective tasks. Similarly, for Ao language the dataset was also prepared for three dialects namely Changki, Mongsen and Chungli by (Tzudir et al., 2021). In the initial works reported by (Tzudir et al., 2017) the database was recorded for only two dialects for trisyllabic words. But as the research progressed it was extended to three dialects and that too was recorded with two options, one for the trisyllabic words and another one at passage level in which translated passages from Bible were recorded for all three dialects (Tzudir et al., 2021). Using MFCC features, Shifted Delta Cepstral (SDC) coefficients and F0 to find the spectral changes between the dialects and then for the dialect identification process, GMM was implemented. For dialect identification, they experimented with various combinations of features and achieved maximum accuracy of 87.8% with combination of MFCC, SDC, F0 and delta F0 features (Tzudir et al., 2021).

In the work implemented by (Humayun et al., 2023b), the social backgrounds of the speakers were identified from their speech in English using 'Indian-English' dataset, which contains speakers from five different states of India speaking in English but their native mother tongue is Hindi, Telugu, Malayalam Tamil and Kannada. The acoustic features of speech were utilized using CNN, DNN-LSTM and SVM and achieved accuracy of 85% for predicting the social background of speakers. (G and Rao, 2023) implemented accent classification from emotional speech dataset 'CREMA-D', using low-level and high-level speech features for seven different types of classifiers and performed three different sets of experiments and concluded that Mel scale based spectral sub-band centroid features performed better for two different experiments out of three.

Arabic language is spoken as a first language in Gulf countries and it has many regional varieties of dialects. The Modern Standard Arabic (MSA) is the language used mostly in communication throughout whole Gulf community but the Dialectal Arabic (DA) is the native language of Arab people with regional variations (Elnagar et al., 2021). The Massive Arabic Speech Corpus (MASC) containing almost 1,000 h of speech is a multi-dialect dataset that is of prime importance in the research and development of Arabic speech. The Arabic Dialect Identification 17 country (ADI17) large scale dataset, consisting of audios from 17 Arabic countries, available for research and development purposes has been explored and discussed by (Shon et al., 2020). Similarly, (Nahar et al., 2022) utilized the ADI17 dataset and using MFCC features and Triangular Filter Bank Cepstral Coefficients, it was implemented for dialect identification task with classifiers such as KNN, MLP, Random Forest and Artificial Neural Networks. Another dataset having five Arabic dialects (MGB-3) was implemented by (Humayun et al., 2023a) using fusion of acoustic and linguistic features with DNN and CNN and obtained accuracy of 82.44%. In another work by (Azim et al., 2022), Multi-dialect Arabic speech parallel corpora was used and they implemented for three Arabic dialects using Gaussian Naive Bayes, SVM and CNN for MFCC features extracted from the dataset. Here also, CNN outperformed its counterparts with good accuracy and F1 score.

Chinese language has many dialects and for identification of dialects in Chinese many speech databases are available. (Zhang et al., 2019) utilized IFLYTEK dataset for dialect identification task and implemented for ten Chinese dialects using CNN-BiGRU classifier and concluded that better results were obtained using CNN-BiGRU as compared to i-vector or Long Short Term Memory (LSTM) implementation for same dataset. AP20-OLR dataset was implemented for the three Chinese dialects and the dialect identification system was implemented using transfer learning and equal error rate was decreased by 25.2% (Wang et al., 2021).

For North Sami language with three dialects, (Kakouros and Hiovain-Asikainen, 2023) worked with acoustic features and implemented using feed forward DNN for four different standard datasets and compared their performances in terms of various acoustic features. For Algerian dialects, the research was performed by (Lounnas et al., 2022) based on acoustic and spectral features. They utilized the dataset created from YouTube videos and used CNN for classification and obtained an average F1 score of nearly 97%.

From the review of literature, it is very much clear that Indian languages are far lagging behind Arabic, English and Chinese in terms of availability of dialectal speech corpus and for Indian languages every researcher has created their own dataset for their specific task.

3   Methodology

3.1   Preparation of Punjabi Dialectal Speech Corpus

As already discussed in literature, due to lack of availability of dialectal speech corpus for Punjabi, negligible research work has been done on spoken dialects of Punjabi. As eastern Punjab has mainly four dialectal regions, so for this work the dialects considered for creation of database are Malwai, Doabi, Majhi and Powadhi. The speech corpus is created in two parts. In first part, the dialect specific words are collected and using these words sentences are formed. Then these sentences are recorded by native speakers in controlled environment that is free of noise and external disturbances and the length of recording varies between 3 s to 7 s. In second part, YouTube and other podcasts that contain conversations in various dialects of Punjabi under consideration are used. These recordings are edited using Audacity software, where each sentence is cropped from the original speech and then converted into.wav format with 1411 kbps bit rate and stereo channels. The number of speakers belong to age group of 18 years to 70 years, both male and female for both categories of dataset. For all four Punjabi dialects, the speech dataset has a total duration of more than three hours and number of speech samples are variable (due to variable recording length) in all four dialects but overall duration of each dialect is approximately same. So, final speech dataset is a combination of manual recordings and You Tube conversations which is much closer to real environment.

3.2 Extraction of Spectral Features

In this work, we have utilized the spectral features of speech i.e. MFCC features, due to the reason that they describe the complete shape of the spectral envelope. The complete process of feature extraction is shown in Fig. 1.

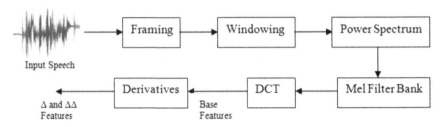

Fig. 1. MFCC Process

Speech signal captured from real environment has noise and other external disturbances and to cope with these factors zero crossing rate method is implemented to remove these artifacts before further processing to extract features. By observing the characteristics of the speech signal, it becomes clear that the signal properties slowly change with time and for studying the properties, the speech signal has to be divided into smaller parts (that are assumed to be stationary). For this purpose, framing of speech signal is done with frame size of 25 ms and overlap of 15 ms and is shown in Fig. 2. This overlapping helps to prevent the loss of information between adjacent frames.

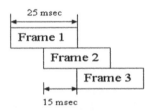

Fig. 2. Framing of speech signal

To minimize the signal discontinuities that occur due to framing, at beginning and end of frame boundary, windowing of speech signal is done with the help of Hamming window. The way of human hearing in different frequency bands is completely different from the way the machine understands. Due to this reason, the Mel scale comes into picture and it is used to map the actual frequency to the frequency that human beings will perceive. The frequency mapping formula used is given in Eq. 1:

$$\text{Mel(m)} = 1125 \ln (1 + f/700) \tag{1}$$

where 'f' is frequency in Hertz, 'ln' is natural logarithm and 'm' is frequency in mels.

In order to detect the frequencies in the frames, the power spectrum is calculated since the human cochlea, which is located inside the ear, vibrates at various locations based on the frequency of the incoming noises. The Mel filter bank computes the filter bank energies in various frequency regions and to compute MFCC features, finally Discrete Cosine Transform (DCT) is computed due to the reason that overlapping filter banks are correlated and DCT de-correlates the energies that can be used to model the features. The MFCC values obtained for all the *.wav files are shown in the form of an array as depicted in Fig. 3. Here, each value is for each frame of speech sample file.

To compute the variations between the frames per filter band, the derivatives of MFCC are calculated, namely Delta MFCC i.e. the first order derivative of MFCC and Delta-Delta or Double Delta MFCC, which is the second order derivative of MFCC. These derivatives are better representation of the speech and they present the trajectories of MFCC over the time.

```
In [55]:  mfcc

Out[55]:  array([[-80.07839337, -52.25051936, -52.88955133, ..., -35.18616201,
            -9.72967021,  -5.51194177],
          [-21.99588274,  -2.1885068 ,   0.80282735, ...,  13.75592012,
            23.180341  ,  21.44814746],
          [-22.3705403 ,  -9.27626398,  -2.54736114, ...,  -6.43454144,
             9.62863904,   2.24934719],
          ...,
          [ -2.86587986,   9.23421005,   8.88297397, ...,  -1.05242783,
            -2.91413951,  -0.30875273],
          [  1.53102683,   5.87777067,  -1.96955067, ...,   2.70778737,
             4.06293145,   5.2859333 ],
          [  4.89696118,  11.04052371,   3.42791144, ...,  12.16883842,
             4.44312009,   4.31808677]]])
```

Fig. 3. MFCC extracted from speech signal

After completion of spectral feature extraction, then comes the classification phase.

3.3 Classification

For any problem related to classification, various statistical approaches are found in literature and this classification entity plays major role in training and testing phases of the system. For obtaining the results that are closer to real picture, the training and testing datasets should not overlap. For this work, 70:30 is chosen as training and testing datasets. Two classification techniques are implemented for this work, namely, K-Nearest Neighbor (KNN) model, and Multilayer Perceptron (MLP) model. The reason for implementing KNN is because it is supervised learning algorithm which makes highly accurate predictions as compared to other algorithms like SVM, LR etc. Also, MLP works well on complex classifications tasks and it is fully connected neural network which gives decent performance.

K-Nearest Neighbor Model
The KNN algorithm is a highly effective supervised learning approach for problem solving in classification. The goal of this algorithm is to identify the closest neighbors from a given query point and the method for computing distance is the Euclidean distance.

The class labels are assigned based on the computed closest distance from a given point and Eq. 2 is used to compute Euclidean distance.

$$d(x, y) = \sqrt{\sum_{i=1}^{n} (y_i - x_i)^2} \tag{2}$$

where 'x' and 'y' are two instances to be computed, their distance, 'n' is the number of dimensions for each instance (Nahar et al., 2022). The value of 'K' in KNN algorithm is defined as how many neighbors will be checked to determine the classification of a specific query point. Deciding the value of 'K' is a crucial factor as it is dependent on input data and also wrong decision can lead to overfitting or underfitting.

For this work, three values of 'K' are considered as K = 3, K = 5 and K = 7, to check the variation in results and the confusion matrix obtained for these values of K are depicted in Fig. 4, Fig. 5 and Fig. 6 respectively.

For K = 3, the classification score obtained is: 76.01%.

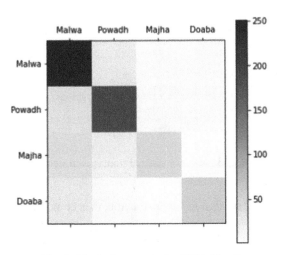

Fig. 4. Confusion matrix for KNN, K = 3

The dataset split is 7:3 where 7 parts are used for training and 3 parts for testing the accuracy of the model. This task is repeated multiple times and each time the testing and the training datasets are shuffled. Each model is then fed the same training data and the accuracy of each of the models is tested on the same test data. The accuracy score for all tested values of 'K' are shown one by one along with the confusion matrices. The accuracy obtained with K = 5 is better as compared with K = 3 and K = 7; and hence it is concluded that with K = 5, the system performed better and it is considered as the optimum value.

For K = 5, the classification score obtained is: 77.12%.

For K = 7, the classification score obtained is: 76.84%.

The choice of 'K' and distance metric has a significant impact on the performance of KNN.

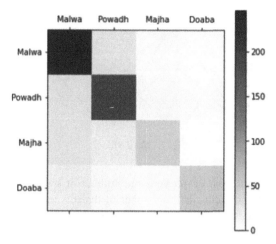

Fig. 5. Confusion matrix for KNN, K = 5

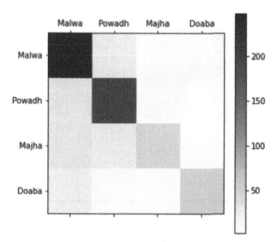

Fig. 6. Confusion matrix for KNN, K = 7

Multi-layer Perceptron Model

A kind of artificial neural network called MLP is employed mostly in machine learning applications. Its application areas are pattern recognition, prediction and forecasting, process modeling, speech emotion recognition, accent recognition and many more. As shown in Fig. 7, the input layer, hidden layer(s), output layer, nodes, activation functions, weights, and biases are the main components of the MLP model. These units are organized in layers where each unit in the current layer is connected to each unit in the next layer i.e. the output of the current layer is an input to the next one. To reduce the error between its predictions and actual outputs, MLP is trained utilizing supervised learning algorithms and optimization techniques like as back propagation and gradient descent.

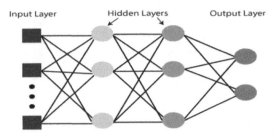

Fig. 7. MLP Model

The number of input nodes represents the number of spectral features i.e. MFCC and the number of output nodes is the number of dialects to be trained and classified (Nahar et al., 2022). In this implementation, the number of output nodes are 4, i.e. same as the number of dialects under consideration. The accuracy obtained using this model is 82.25% and the confusion matrix for the same is shown in Fig. 8.

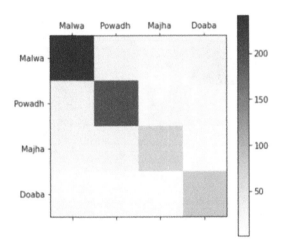

Fig. 8. Confusion matrix for MLP

The goal of the MLP training procedure is to identify the weights and biases with the lowest error between the network's prediction and the actual outputs. The difference between the predicted output and the actual one is the network's total output error and it is then used to adjust network connection weights. For this purpose, supervised learning algorithm, such as back propagation is used and also for optimization, gradient descent method is utilized.

4   Results and Discussion

The performance of spectral features based dialect identification system was tested with two classifiers, KNN and MLP. The performance of the system with both classifiers is shown in Table 1 and Table 2.

Table 1. Comparison of Overall Accuracy of KNN and MLP.

Classifier	KNN, K = 3	KNN, K = 5	KNN, K = 7	MLP
Overall Accuracy	76.01%	77.12%	76.84%	82.25%

It is clear from the comparison that in terms of overall accuracy, MLP outperformed KNN for all the tested values of 'K'. From the results it is also evident that using KNN the system performed best for K = 5 and by increasing or decreasing the values of 'K', the accuracy drops. The prime reason behind it is that when value of 'K' is increased so as the distance computed increases which is against the norms of KNN. Similarly, for very less values of 'K', the distance computed will be lesser thereby making it more sensitive to training data. That is why multiple values of 'K' are tested to find the optimum value for which the results are accurate. Therefore, for this particular dataset the K = 5 (optimum value), achieved the best score as compared to its counterparts.

Table 2. Classification based on F1 Score.

| Region | Classifier | | | |
	KNN, K = 3	KNN, K = 5	KNN, K = 7	MLP
Malwa	0.79	0.80	0.80	0.84
Powadh	0.80	0.80	0.81	0.84
Majha	0.56	0.61	0.58	0.69
Doaba	0.71	0.75	0.71	0.80

F1 score is another metric which gives promising results other than accuracy. F1 score is the harmonic mean of Precision and Recall metrics. So, to compute F1 score, precision and recall must be computed first. The precision and recall are computed from the confusion matrix using true positives, false positives and false negatives. After computation the results are presented in Table 2 in which it is clear that, in terms of F1 score, MLP performed best with decent score of 0.84 as compared to KNN for its different 'K' values. Also, for K = 5 the results are best as compared to K = 3 or K = 7. In region wise comparison, the best performance is seen with Powadh region and least with Majha region. The main reason behind it is that way of pronunciation used in Powadh region is having large variation as compared with other three dialectal regions under consideration. Due to this variation, the system works much more efficiently for Powadhi dialect. Malwa dialect covers the biggest area of Punjab and the data collected for this dialect has many sub-dialectal variations. This is also the reason for its performance as wide range of speakers and sub-dialectal variations are covered in dataset. Therefore, the results of Malwa region are very close to best performer Powadh region. Majha and Doaba regions have lesser variations and use similar kind of vocabulary and pronunciation styles so inaccurate classifications do occur and that become the reason for their lesser performance in comparison to Powadhi and Malwai dialects.

5 Conclusion

This paper presented the dialect identification system for four dialects of Punjabi language. The spectral features - MFCC of speech are utilized for the implementation and for classification purpose, two classifiers namely, MLP and KNN are implemented. The experimental results showed that MLP performed better both in terms of overall accuracy and F1 score as compared to KNN. Also, for all four dialectal regions, the F1 score shows the variations and best outcome is seen in Powadh region. So, both accuracy and F1 score gave similar outcome which means that our system is consistent using different evaluation criteria's and it does not favor any one matric.

References

Agrawal, S.S., Jain, A., Sinha, S.: Analysis and modeling of acoustic information for automatic dialect classification. Int. J. Speech Technol. **19**(3), 593–609 (2016). https://doi.org/10.1007/s10772-016-9351-7

Azim, M.A., Hussein, W., Badr, N.L.: Automatic Dialect identification of Spoken Arabic Speech using Deep Neural Networks. Int. J. Intell. Comput. Inf. Sci. **22**(4), 25–34 (2022). https://doi.org/10.21608/ijicis.2022.152368.1207

Chittaragi, N.B., Limaye, A., Chandana, N.T., Annappa, B., Koolagudi, S.G.: Automatic text-independent Kannada dialect identification system. In: Satapathy, S.C., Bhateja, V., Somanah, R., Yang, X.-S., Senkerik, R. (eds.) Information Systems Design and Intelligent Applications. AISC, vol. 863, pp. 79–87. Springer, Singapore (2019). https://doi.org/10.1007/978-981-13-3338-5_8

Choudhury, A.R., Chittaragi, N.B., Koolagudi, S.G.: Dialect recognition system using excitation source features. In: 15th IEEE India Council International Conference (INDICON), Coimbatore, India, pp. 1–6 (2018). https://doi.org/10.1109/INDICON45594.2018.8987055

Das, H., Bhattacharjee, U.: Assamese dialect identification system using deep learning. Preprint (version 2) available at research square (2022). https://doi.org/10.21203/rs.3.rs-1733629/v2

Elnagar, A., Yagi, S.M., Nassif, A.B., Shahin, I., Salloum, S.A.: Systematic literature review of dialectal Arabic: identification and detection. IEEE Access **9**, 31010–31042 (2021). https://doi.org/10.1109/ACCESS.2021.3059504

Priya Dharshini, G., Sreenivasa Rao, K.: Accent classification from an emotional speech in clean and noisy environments. Multimedia Tools Appl. **82**, 3485–3508 (2023). https://doi.org/10.1007/s11042-022-13236-w

Hegde, P., Chittaragi, N.B., Mothkuri, S.K.P., Koolagudi, S.G.: Kannada dialect classification using CNN. In: Purushothama, B.R., Thenkanidiyoor, V., Prasath, R., Vanga, O. (eds.) MIKE 2019, vol. 11987, pp. 254–259. Springer, Heidelberg (2019). https://doi.org/10.1007/978-3-030-66187-8_24

Humayun, M.A., Yassin, H., Abas, P.E.: Dialect classification using acoustic and linguistic features in Arabic speech. IAES Int. J. Artif. Intell. **12**(2), 739–746 (2023a). https://doi.org/10.11591/ijai.v12.i2.pp739-746

Humayun, M.A., Yassin, H., Abas, P.E.: Estimating social background profiling of Indian speakers by acoustic speech features. J. Sci. Ind. Res. **82**, 851–860 (2023b). https://doi.org/10.56042/jsir.v82i08.3122

Kakouros, S., Hiovain-Asikainen, K.: North Sámi dialect identification with self-supervised speech models. arXiv preprint (2023). https://doi.org/10.48550/arXiv.2305.11864

Koolagudi, S.G., Bharadwaj, A., Srinivasa Murthy, Y.V., Reddy, N., Rao, P.: Dravidian language classification from speech signal using spectral and prosodic features. Int. J. Speech Technol. **20**(4), 1005–1016 (2017). https://doi.org/10.1007/s10772-017-9466-5

Krishna, G.R., Krishnan, R.: Native language identification based on English accent, pp. 63–67 (2014)

Lounnas, K., Lichouri, M., Abbas, M., Chahboub, T., Salmi, S.: Towards an automatic dialect identification system for Algerian dialects using YouTube videos. In: Proceedings of the 5th International Conference on Natural Language and Speech Processing (ICNLSP 2022), Trento, Italy, pp. 258–264. Association for Computational Linguistics (2022)

Ma, B., Zhu, D., Tong, R.: Chinese dialect identification using tone features based on pitch flux. In: 2006 IEEE International Conference on Acoustics Speech and Signal Processing Proceedings, Toulouse, France, pp. 1029–1032 (2006). https://doi.org/10.1109/ICASSP.2006.1660199

Mannepalli, K., Sastry, P.N., Suman, M.: MFCC-GMM based accent recognition system for Telugu speech signals. Int. J. Speech Technol. **19**(1), 87–93 (2016). https://doi.org/10.1007/s10772-015-9328-y

Mittal, P., Singh, N.: Speaker-independent automatic speech recognition system for mobile phone applications in Punjabi. In: Thampi, S.M., Krishnan, S., Corchado Rodriguez, J.M., Das, S., Wozniak, M., Al-Jumeily, D. (eds.) SIRS 2017. AISC, vol. 678, pp. 369–382. Springer, Cham (2018). https://doi.org/10.1007/978-3-319-67934-1_33

Nahar, K.M.O., Al-Hazaimeh, O.M., Abu-Ein, A., Al-Betar, M.A.: Arabic dialect identification using different machine learning methods. Preprint (version 1) available at research square (2022). https://doi.org/10.21203/rs.3.rs-1726491/v1

Najafian, M., Safavi, S., Weber, P., Russell, M.: Identification of British English regional accents using fusion of i-vector and multi-accent phonotactic systems. In: Proceedings of the Speaker and Language Recognition Workshop (Odyssey 2016), Bilbao, Spain, pp. 132–139 (2016). https://doi.org/10.21437/Odyssey.2016-19

Nanmalar, M., Vijayalakshmi, P., Nagarajan, T.: Literary and colloquial dialect identification for Tamil using acoustic features. In: TENCON 2019 - 2019 IEEE Region 10 Conference (TENCON), Kochi, India, pp. 1303–1306 (2019). https://doi.org/10.1109/TENCON.2019.8929499

Rabiner, L., Juang, B.H.: Fundamentals of Speech Recognition. Pearson Education (2003)

Rabiner, L., Schafer, R.: Digital Processing of Speech Signals. Pearson Education (2009)

Rao, K.S., Koolagudi, S.G.: Identification of Hindi dialects and emotions using spectral and prosodic features of speech. J. Syst. Cybern. Inform. **9**(4), 24–33 (2011)

Rao, K.S., Nandy, S., Koolagudi, S.G.: Identification of Hindi dialects using speech. In: Proceedings of WMSCI 2010-The 14th World Multi-Conference on Systemics, Cybernetics and Informatics, Orlando, Florida, USA, pp. 124–128 (2010)

Sangha, S.S.: Punjabi Bhasha Vigyaan, 8th edn. Punjabi Bhasha Academy, Jalandhar (2012)

Satla, S., Manchala, S.: Dialect identification in Telugu language speech utterance using modified features with deep neural network. Traitement Du Sig. **38**(6), 1793–1799 (2021). https://doi.org/10.18280/ts.380623

Shon, S., Ali, A., Samih, Y., Mubarak, H., Glass, J.: ADI17: a fine-grained Arabic dialect identification dataset. In: ICASSP 2020 - 2020 IEEE International Conference on Acoustics, Speech and Signal Processing (ICASSP), Barcelona, Spain, pp. 8244–8248 (2020). https://doi.org/10.1109/ICASSP40776.2020.9052982

Singh, A., Singh, P.: Punjabi dialects conversion system for Malwai and Doabi dialects. Indian J. Sci. Technol. **8**(27), 1–6 (2015). https://doi.org/10.17485/ijst/2015/v8i27/81667

Singh, P.: Punjabi Bhasha da Janam te Vikas. Madaan Publishing House, Patiala (2017)

Sinha, S., Jain, A., Agrawal, S.S.: Spectral and prosodic features-based speech pattern classification. Int. J. Appl. Pattern Recogn. **2**(1), 96 (2015). https://doi.org/10.1504/IJAPR.2015.068947

Sinha, S., Jain, A., Agrawal, S.S.: Empirical analysis of linguistic and paralinguistic information for automatic dialect classification. Artif. Intell. Rev. **51**(4), 647–672 (2017). https://doi.org/10.1007/s10462-017-9573-3

Tzudir, M., Sarmah, P., Prasanna, S.R.M.: Tonal feature based dialect discrimination in two dialects in Ao. In: TENCON 2017 - 2017 IEEE Region 10 Conference, Penang, Malaysia, pp. 1795–1799 (2017). https://doi.org/10.1109/TENCON.2017.8228149

Tzudir, M., Sarmah, P., Prasanna, S.R.M.: Analysis and modeling of dialect information in Ao, a low resource language. J. Acoust. Soc. Am. **149**(5), 2976–2987 (2021). https://doi.org/10.1121/10.0004822

Wang, D., Ye, S., Hu, X., Li, S., Xu, X.: An end-to-end dialect identification system with transfer learning from a multilingual automatic speech recognition model. In: Proceedings of INTERSPEECH 2021, pp. 3266–3270 (2021). https://doi.org/10.21437/Interspeech.2021-374

Zhang, Q., et al.: End-to-end Chinese dialects identification in short utterances using CNN-BiGRU. In: 2019 IEEE 8th Joint International Information Technology and Artificial Intelligence Conference (ITAIC), Chongqing, China, pp. 340–344 (2019). https://doi.org/10.1109/ITAIC.2019.8785614

Hate Speech Detection Using Audio in Portuguese Language

Lucia Americo Tembe[✉] and M. Anand Kumar

Department of Information Technology, National Institute of Technology Karnataka, Surathkal, India
{luciaamerico201it169,m_anandkumar}@nitk.edu.in

Abstract. This study focuses on hate speech in Portuguese language using audio and introduces a novel methodology that integrates audio-to-text and self-image technologies to effectively tackle this problem. We utilize Machine Learning and Deep Learning models to differentiate between hate speech and normal speech. The research utilized a total of 200 datasets, which were categorized into hate speech and normal speech. These datasets were collected by me personally for this project. Four distinct models are presented in the analysis: LSTM, SVM, CNN, and Random Forest. The findings highlight the superior performance of the CNN model when applied to spectrogram data, achieving an accuracy rate of 90%. Conversely, the Random Forest model outperforms others when dealing with text data, achieving an impressive accuracy rate of 73.1%.

Keywords: Deep Learning · CNN · LSTM · Machine Learning · Random Forest · SVM

1 Introduction

In today's globally networked society, hate speech poses serious threats to social inclusion and cohesiveness. The growth of social media and digital platforms in recent years has accelerated the spread of hate speech in a number of languages, including Portuguese. Such bad speech can undermine social cohesion and individual well-being by encouraging prejudice, discrimination, and violence. Therefore, it is essential to have thorough plans for locating, examining, and containing hate speech [9]. This project makes use of cutting-edge language processing methods and cutting-edge picture recognition technologies to counter hate speech in Portuguese. Utilizing methods for converting spoken content into written text, or vice versa, allows for effective study and monitoring of hate speech on numerous digital platforms. Auto-to-image algorithms are also used to identify and extract contextual visual components linked to hate speech, such as insensitive pictures or symbols. The suggested method not only makes it easier to identify hate speech, but also offers insightful information on its prevalence, trends, and dynamics. Researchers and decision-makers can better understand

B. R. Chakravarthi et al. (Eds.): SPELLL 2023, CCIS 2046, pp. 359–367, 2024.
https://doi.org/10.1007/978-3-031-58495-4_26

the features and underlying causes of hate speech in the Portuguese language by examining the transcribed text and visual clues. This information can help with the creation of focused interventions, educational programs, and legislative frameworks to effectively combat and stop the spread of hate speech. By utilizing these technologies, it is feasible to recognize, examine, and effectively oppose hate speech, promoting a safer and more welcoming online community for Portuguese-speaking people.

2   Problem Description

Being a fresh evaluation that was done to completely comprehend the phenomenon of hate speech. The adoption of audio-to-text and self-image technologies facilitated the rapid spread of hate speech, making it more accessible and challenging to mitigate. Researching various hate speeches was one step towards a better understanding and discovery with which people try to share their frustrations. With the help of this technology, people can turn spoken words, audio, or audio clips into written text or even automatically create Images from the audio content.

3   Literature Review

Because the research in this piece focuses on identifying hate speech, we will analyze the same publications in the following sections: Allocation and description. The core concepts and rules against hate speech are highlighted in the introductory phase, which also includes social media sites. During the discovery stage of the process, the usage of several supervised learning algorithms to recognize hate speech is examined. Regarding [2], the text-analysis-based methods for detecting hate speech described in the article make use of models based on both predictive and non-predictive text features. They used the Random Forest Classifier from [10] to recognize hate speech from multiple sources, [7] with an accuracy rate of 71.01% utilized ML formulas [1,6] and attempted to spot bogus news via social websites that used Random Forest Classifier, yet the findings were false for unreliable sources [11]. In Kaggle, retrieve data using the binary technique [8]. This used Logistic Regression, Decision Tree Classifier, and Random Forest Classifier in its search. They were the more accurate Decision Tree classifiers in 72, 71 [4]. With an emphasis on the semantic and systematic origin of the text, computational linguistics was used to the genesis of text in a variety of tasks utilizing SVM (Support Virtual Machine) and Nave Bayes. In this resource, an annotated corpus of hate speech is provided, with a strong emphasis on preserving context information. Two distinct hate speech detection models are introduced, both effectively integrating contextual details. The first model employs a logistic regression approach with contextual features, while the second utilizes a neural network architecture, incorporating elements for context-based learning. The evaluation demonstrates the superior performance of both models, revealing a substantial enhancement of approximately 3% to 4% in F1 score when compared to a robust baseline. Notably, the combination of these two models yields a remarkable 7% increase in F1 score, highlighting the potential for enhanced hate speech detection [5]. We go through To comprehensively assess the performance of the developed model, one can utilize the F-score evaluation metric. This allows [3] for the rigorous testing of the model's capabilities by incorporating the test set and subjecting it to the evaluation process. With this, It is evident that much of the research is directed toward text analysis, With that in mind, the emphasis will be placed on spectrogram images and text.

4 Dataset

The audio dataset was carefully selected from YouTube, including some recordings with human interactions. This collection consists of various audio samples, with durations ranging from one to one and a half minutes. A manual curation approach was employed, involving the selection and concatenation of these audio samples to construct the dataset. Both YouTube and Facebook were used to identify and extract the essential audio content. To streamline the video download process from YouTube, the 4k Video Downloader software tool was utilized. To prepare the dataset for our analysis, several critical steps were taken. These steps included audio segmentation, cleaning, noise reduction, voice duplication for improved audio quality, and conversion of all audio files into WAV format. This entire process was carried out manually, utilizing Audacity, a versatile software tool designed to facilitate noise reduction and audio transformation into the desired WAV file format. Subsequently, the audio was converted into a spectrogram using various tools, resulting in two classes: one for hate speech and the other for normal speech, as illustrated in Fig. 1 and 2. The audio was also transformed into text using Whisper, a tool that assists in the audio-to-text conversion process. This led to two subclasses: one classified as normal (1) and the other as hate (0), as presented in Table 1.

Fig. 1. Normal Spectrogram image

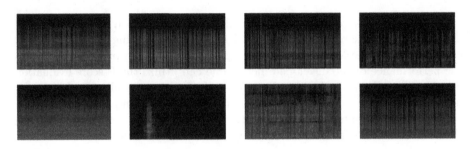

Fig. 2. Hate Spectrogram image

Table 1. Dataset samples

categories	Examples
Normal	Você sabe que nós somos aquele tipo de pessoa que podemos ficar um mês, um mês, dois meses sem nos falar, mas onde vamos começar a falar, Vamos falar como se nada tivesse acontecido, tu já percebeu
Hate	Sua vacabunda de merda! Desde ontem eu tentei te ligar, tu não estás a me atender, achas o que? Achas o que? Achas que és importante mais que quem? Fiseka! Sua vacabunda! Achas que és o que na vida pra fazer isso

5   Preprocessing and Feature Engineering

5.1   Spectrogram Preprocess

This section focuses on preprocessing the images or spectrogram image specifically dividing them into two categories: hate images and normal images. To train the model, we employed Keras' ImageDataGenerator from the preprocessing image module. This allowed us to partition the dataset into training and validation sets. Therefore, it is of utmost importance to standardize the data utilized, as this will greatly enhance the overall performance of the CNN. To achieve this, we will rescale the pixel values of our images from the range [0, 255] to [0, 1], employing the rescale parameter. Furthermore, we will provide the classes, input image size, batch size, input image directory, and class mode for each generator.

5.2   Text Preprocess

The dataset consists of two columns: 'Text' and 'Label'. To prepare the data, we perform several processes. First, we remove all punctuation marks. Next, we convert all the letters to lowercase. Additionally, we utilize NLTK for removing all stopwords.

Engineering resources play a vital role in improving machine learning models by assisting in the process of accurate tuning. The TFIDF Vectorizer package was employed to determine the frequency of each word in the text document. TFIDF stands for "inverse frequency document frequency". While term frequency represents the total number of words used in the text document, inverse document frequencies are often computed for each word in the text. When utilizing TF-IDF, the input is typically tokenized to create a vocabulary that is subsequently used to encode subsequent texts.

6   Implementation

A paradigm for assessing hate speech is proposed in this study, and it focuses on audiovisual content on digital platforms and news organizations. Understanding the issue, defining the job, choosing a dataset, preprocessing, choosing text- and image-based features, and classifying the data using various machine learning algorithms are the procedures used to create the structure. Figure 3 and 4 below depicts the suggested structure's detailed model layout.

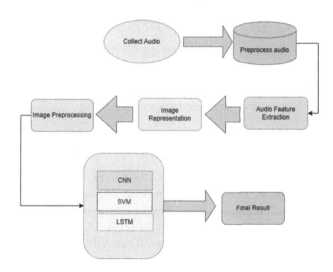

Fig. 3. Framework audio-to-image

7   Classification Models

Based on the conducted systematic literature review, it is evident that machine learning techniques have been employed for hate speech detection. This study examined several classifiers, namely CNN, which was specifically employed for image analysis. Additionally, Random Forest and SVM were utilized to analyze audio-to-text. These particular models were chosen due to their versatility in handling various classification tasks and their distinct attributes and performance across different datasets.

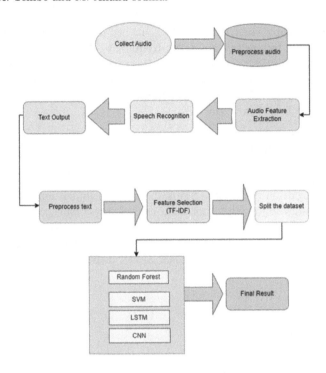

Fig. 4. Framework audio-to-text

7.1 Audio to Image

Convolutional Neural Network and Long Short-Term Memory. A convolutional neural network (CNN) specific type of neural network model designed to handle images and videos. It takes raw pixel data as input, undergoes training, and automatically extracts features to improve categorization. In addition, CNNs simplify image-related tasks very well. Also, Long Short-Term Memory (LSTM) neural networks are a particular kind of neural network made for managing data sequences. It is useful for applications like time series prediction and natural language processing because it is particularly good at capturing long-term dependencies. LSTMs are renowned for their capacity to retain and apply knowledge from earlier stages of a sequence. They are therefore useful in applications like sentiment analysis and language translation.

To build this model, we introduced a flattened layer to convert the input image into a flattened format. The flattened output is then passed to a dense layer, also known as the fully connected layer, which consists of 128 hidden units. For our specific purpose of binary classification, the final layer of the network is a sigmoid function. This ensures that the network output is a single scalar value ranging from 0 to 1, representing the probability that the current image belongs to class 1 (where class 1 represents "Normal" and class 0 represents "Hate"). Moving on to model training specifications, we use the binary crossentropy loss function. The Adam optimizer is employed as it is a reliable optimization algorithm that automates learning rate tuning. Alternatively, RMSProp or Adagrad can be used for similar results. Additionally, accuracy is included as one of the metrics, allowing the model to monitor accuracy during the training process.

7.2   Audio to Text

Random Forest. A random forest classifier uses machine learning to address classification and regression issues. It makes use of collaborative learning, a method for combining classifiers that offer solutions to complicated issues a decision tree-based method known as a random forest. The algorithm's advantages include a Significantly reduced danger of overfitting, flexibility, and simplicity in assessing feature relevance.

Support Vector Machine. When categorizing data points into two distinct classes, SVM is an algorithm that excels at addressing binary classification issues. It has many benefits, including as the ability to handle large amounts of data, resistance to overfitting, and adaptability in both linear and non-linear classification tasks. SVM has consequently been widely applied in a variety of fields, including image recognition, text categorization, bioinformatics, and financial analysis.

8   Results and Discussions

In this section, the experimental setting, evaluation metric, and outcomes will be discussed following the training and testing of several machine learning algorithms. To classify the dataset accurately, separate tests are conducted on each machine learning classifier.

8.1   Experimental Setup

During the experiments, several libraries were utilized, including Numpy, Librosa, PIL, OpenCV, Scikit-Learn, Keras, matplotlib, and pandas. These libraries were chosen because the data used in the experiments was in image and CSV format. The dataset was divided into a training set and a test set, with an 80:20 split, where 80% of the data was used for training and 20% for testing. The classification algorithms employed in the experiments were CNN, Random Forest, and SVM. These classifiers were selected based on a thorough literature review, which highlighted their exceptional performance in binary classification problems, particularly in Hate Speech detection. Hyperparameters for each classification model were adjusted through a series of experiments.

8.2   Evaluation Metrics

Several evaluation criteria, including as accuracy, recall, F1 score, and precision, were used to assess the effectiveness of the various classification models used in this study. The ratio of accurately predicted data samples to all of the dataset's data samples is used to calculate accuracy. Recall gauges how well a classifier can anticipate how many positive examples there will be from the total number of positive examples in the dataset. For a certain dataset, the F1 score offers a measurement of accuracy and recall. Out of all the expected positive examples, precision measures how accurately the classifier predicted the number of positive examples.

Table 2. Result Auto To Text

SI. NO	Models	Accuracy(%)	F1 Score	Precision	Recall
1	RF	73.1	0.74	0.76	0.73
2	SVM	87.8	0.89	0.87	0.91
3	LSTM	57.0	0.50	0.50	0.50
4	CNN	50.0	0.45	0.49	0.47

Table 3. Result Auto To Spectrogram Image

SI. NO	Models	Accuracy(%)	F1 Score	Precision	Recall
1	CNN	0.90	0.49	0.50	0.48
2	SVM	0.49	0.46	0.46	0.45
3	LSTM	0.51	0.47	0.45	0.49

9   Conclusion and Future Work

In conclusion, a viable strategy to address this issue in the Portuguese language is the employment of audio-to-text and audio-to-image conversion in the detection of hate speech. With the use of this cutting-edge technology, audio content can be recognized, examined, and converted into text and images, making it easier to detect hate speech and comprehend its context. It is feasible to analyze spoken language and spot inappropriate words, phrases, and expressions by using audio-to-text conversion. This strategy aids in the development of effective content moderation systems that enable the prompt and precise removal of hate speech from internet venues. The process of converting audio to images also offers a visual examination of the content. It can assist in spotting violent details in videos, such as hate speech, inappropriate imagery, or even hostile body language. The incorporation of this visual analysis to hate speech detection offers new perspectives for a more thorough comprehension of harmful content, It is crucial to emphasize that these technologies are still undergoing ongoing evolution and advancement in order to increase their precision and detection power. The cultural background and peculiarities of the Portuguese language must also be taken into account when creating these tools in order to prevent false positives and guarantee that detection is reliable in a variety of situations. We can also see that the performance of audio-to-spectrogram Table 3 is better than audio-to-text Table 2, with 90% accuracy. In general, using audio-to-text and audio-to-image conversion offers a crucial instrument in the fight against hate speech in the Portuguese language. With the use of these tools, bad information may be quickly identified and moderated, making online spaces for all users safer, more welcoming, and respectful.

Future work will revolve around the exploration of the extensive potential within our results and the extension of the proposed algorithms to a larger, more diverse sample drawn from various sources. Additionally, research endeavors will be directed towards the application of alternative machine learning approaches to leverage the wealth of data in this real-world dataset.

References

1. Breiman, L., Friedman, J.H., Olshen, R.A., Stone, C.J.: Classification and Regression Trees (1984)
2. Castellanos, M., et al.: Hate speech in adolescents: a binational study on prevalence and demographic differences. Front. Educ. **8**, 1076249 (2023)
3. Defersha, N.B., Tune, K.K.: Detection of hate speech text in Afan Oromo social media using machine learning approach. Indian J. Sci. Technol. **14**(31), 2567–2578 (2021)
4. Dolega, L., Rowe, F., Branagan, E.: Going digital? The impact of social media marketing on retail website traffic, orders and sales. J. Retail. Consum. Serv. **60**, 102501 (2021)
5. Gao, L., Huang, R.: Detecting online hate speech using context aware models. arXiv preprint arXiv:1710.07395 (2017)
6. Jahan, Md.S., Oussalah, M.: A systematic review of hate speech automatic detection using natural language processing. Neurocomputing 126232 (2023)
7. Josey, C.S.: Hate speech and identity: an analysis of neo racism and the indexing of identity. Discourse Soc. **21**(1), 27–39 (2010)
8. Silva, A., Roman, N.: Hate speech detection in Portuguese with Naïve Bayes, SVM, MLP and logistic regression. In: Anais do XVII Encontro Nacional de Inteligência Artificial e Computacional, pp. 1–12. SBC (2020)
9. Sutejo, T.L., Lestari, D.P.: Indonesia hate speech detection using deep learning. In: 2018 International Conference on Asian Language Processing (IALP), pp. 39–43. IEEE (2018)
10. Whillock, R.K., Slayden, D.: Hate speech. ERIC (1995)
11. Zhang, J., Dong, B., Philip, S.Y.: Fakedetector: effective fake news detection with deep diffusive neural network. In: 2020 IEEE 36th International Conference on Data Engineering (ICDE), pp. 1826–1829. IEEE (2020)

An Empirical Analysis of the Consonantal Phonemic Patterns and Characteristics of English Spoken in India

Pooja Gambhir(⊠), Amita Dev, and Poonam Bansal

Indira Gandhi Delhi Technical University for Women, Kashmere Gate, Delhi 110006, India
pooja001phd19@igdtuw.ac.in

Abstract. In India, there are a large number of native languages spoken with multiple dialects, allowing the speakers to share various common and distinct pronunciation characteristics. These characteristics are derived from region to region and are highly influenced by their native languages. 'Indian English' is a widespread and well-known language for its many eccentricities. It is widely spoken as a second language comprising 6.8% out of 12% of the Indian population. It influences the quality of pronunciation based on their native speaking style, accents and learning environment. In this paper, we focus on the accent variations in Indian English, emphasising consonant analysis. The present investigation has been performed on the PRAAT tool that signifies notable and observable occurrences of similarities and dissimilarities in the phonetic and phonological aspects of spoken English in India with that of few prominently spoken native languages of India. These inferences in future will lead to the demand for an extensive experimental study on Indian English due to the influence of the native language in the realistic environment.

Keywords: Indian English · Phonetics · Phonology · consonantal phones · grammatical aspects

1 Introduction

English has become a common lingua franca spoken by many Indian Speakers as a second language with a regional native accent. English was one of the Judiciary of India for various diaspora in the 20th century. Since then, the Indian Government has been using it as a supplement to Hindi and a medium of communication in many fields such as Education, Entertainment, Business, Law and Administration. Most seminars, books, magazines, reports and newspapers etc., directed to a nationwide audience are brought out in this language [1]. 11.6% of the Indian population speaks English as one of their official languages, mainly in the Northern and North-Eastern states. Out of 11.6%, 0.02% of people speak English as their first language, 6.8% of the population speak it as their second language, and 3.8% constitute to speak English as their third language. In the South region of India, many of the Indian population speaks English as an official communicative language in the Educational and Professional sectors. Due to the influence of

B. R. Chakravarthi et al. (Eds.): SPELLL 2023, CCIS 2046, pp. 368–383, 2024.
https://doi.org/10.1007/978-3-031-58495-4_27

the native accent, English (expressed as a second language) has developed distinct sound patterns in terms of acoustic, segmental, and prosodic characteristics, which change in unusual spelling-to-sound rules and show divergence with the phonemic orthographic variations with Indian regional languages. India is a linguistically diverse nation with a multitude of native languages and dialects. This diversity has led to the emergence of distinct pronunciation characteristics. Understanding and documenting these linguistic variations is crucial for preserving India's rich linguistic heritage. And therefore, Indian English is considered one of the influential languages for study to investigate the effect of a phonetic and acoustic assessment in the acquisition of English with Indian regional languages. Indian and American English develop distinct pronunciation variations, such as the phrase: How is it going? For Indian Speakers, the expression will be pronounced in separation as individual words. How is it going? But the American speakers usually merge the terms and speak it as Howz it goin?. Similarly, for the phrase How are you? In American English, it is expressed as Hower you?. However, Indian Speakers are gradually gaining the influence of North American English in their speaking styles with similarity in rhoticity and r-coloured vowels while indulging in the educational, cultural, and economic ties between the countries.

Many researchers have worked towards the impact of L1 language influence and accent variations on English spoken as L2 language. Wiltshire and Harnsberger explored the influence of Gujarati and Telugu L1s on Indian English. The authors acoustically analysed and revealed that the native Gujarati and Telugu accents influence both phonetic and phonological characteristics of the consonants, vowels and intonation patterns from five Gujarati English and five Tamil English speakers of Indian English with transfer effects in Gujarati English back vowels, proportion of rising and falling pitch accents and TE rhotic [2]. Hema Sirsa and A. Redford studied the effect of native languages on Indian English sound and timing patterns. They found that Indian English has target phonemics distinct from the phonemics of native Indian languages [3]. Researchers are majorly exploring the phonetic and phonological comparison of English with Indian languages like English and Punjabi, linguistics of Hindi and English speech sounds [4] (Chohan, M. N., & García, M. I. M., 2019); [5] (Mishra, S., & Mishra, A., 2016); [6] (Barman, B., 2009). Samantha explored the linguistic background of Indian English by discussing the phonology of Standard Indian English and its corpus analysis through contrastive study with other Indian languages [7] (Ona Masoko, S. T., 2017). This paper extensively focused on the consonantal assessment of accented phonological and phonetic features or patterns of the English language spoken in India and also discussed the phonetic variations of consonantal phone characteristics of Indian English with a few Indian regional languages spoken in India.

Phonemic Categories of Consonants of Indian English in Comparison with American English

Considered a syllable-timed linguista, English is spoken with a syllabic rhythm and appears to put the stress accents in different forms influenced by native languages. Linguists observed considerable variations in the phonetic characteristics of English spoken in India with the influence of pronunciation connections and variations such as grammar, linguistic variations, and discourse features of speakers of English from various regions of India. A hierarchical variation of phonemes of consonants of Indian English is represented in Table 2. Indian English consists of 34 consonants depicted along its few sound phones in Table 1 followed by the manner and place of articulation in Table 3.

Table 1. Phone sounds of Indian English consonants

Consonants	Phonemic sounds	Example Words
f	[p̈],[b]	five
v	/w/	never
t (th: थ)	/θ/	thumb
d (द)	/ð/	weather
/z/ (ज्ञ)	/dʒ/ or /dz/	prize
/s/	/ʃ/	ship
t	/t̪/	certificate
d (ड)	/ɖ/	london
h	à	house
/h/	/j/ or /w/ (euphonic)	every
n	ŋ	aunty
/r/	/aːr/	cart, car

In the view of consonantal characteristics of Indian English, Indian speakers often perceive two distinct sets of coronal plosives: Dental and Retroflex; in which alveolar plosives sound reflex more than dental consonants. For example-English alveolar /t/ is often articulated **as retroflex /t/ or a dental /t/** in Indian English with different phonological environments [9]. Indian English speakers also shows morphological differences in speaking cousin-sister, cousin-brother in place of cousin and are mostly non-rhotic.

Sound Segments and Variations of Spoken English in India as Second Language
Sound segments refers to time-varying sequence of the vocal tract gestures of the speaker which forms a sequence of speech signal corresponding to the message to be conveyed. These sound segments have distinct articulatory configurations known as phonemes that postulates different articulations of speaking a language. As each language has small set of phonemes, humans have tendency to produce large number of distinctive sounds. On other hand, Phonology is described as the study of the sounds in particular language which elucidates on the similarity or differences in sounds of different words. In the phonemic study, sounds found in a language are explained and described with the

Table 2. Hierarchical representation of the Phonemic characteristics of Indian English consonants (Comprehensive part of Hinglish)

Consonantal Phonemic Characteristics

Affricates	Nasals	Plosives		Fricatives		Liquids
tʃ, tʃʰ	ŋ	**voiced**	**unvoiced**	**Voiced**	**unvoiced**	l
dʒ, dʒʰ	ɳ	b	k	h	f-> pʰ	l
	ɲ	d	p	ð	v->/ʋ/	r
	ɱ	g	t	f	th->θ	
	m	ɟ	c	/zh/->ʝ	sh->ʃ	
	N	ɖ	ʈ	z	S	
			ʔ	ʒ		
			q			

Table 3. Manner and Place of Articulation of American English Consonant sounds

		Place of Articulation								
		Bilabial	Labio-Dental	Dental	Alveolar	Post-Alveolar	Palatal	Retroflex	Velar	Glottal
Manner of Articulation	Stops	p pʰ b		t t̪ d				ʈ ʈ ɖ	k (kʰ) g	
	Affricate					ʃ dʒ				
	Fricative		f (v)		s z	ʃ ʒ				h
	Nasal	m			n				ŋ	
	Approximant	w/ʋ			r		j			
	Lateral Approximant				l			(l)		

Front ──→ Back

manner of articulation and cognitive learning environment (formal and informal learning) which influences the phonetic production of the language. In India, people especially children acquire their mother tongue at home and absorb second language in school in which English language mostly gets an exposure through communication outside home or through media such as telephone, television, reading newspaper etc. Because of the intricacies of the linguistics situation in India, the phonology of Indian English has undoubtedly exhibited a substantial degree of variations with Indian languages. [1] stated that these variations are due to certain factors which affects the pronunciation variability of speaking English. These factors majorly connect to regional and cultural variations of the Speaker, educational environment, influence of first (native) language and proficiency in speaking etc.

Any language undergoes changes in the society which works at syntax and word level. English which is spoken as a second language in India is accompanied by multi-lingualism and has developed versatile and distinct sound patterns in terms of acoustic-phonetics, prosodic and segmental characteristic variations. Due to the influence of first language over the second spoken language, English is often varied with new vocabulary affecting the word formation process and also affecting its syntax significantly. The distinct evolution of regional variations in contemporary usage of English has also led to the creation of macaronic hybrid such as BENGLISH (Bengali + English), HINGLISH (Hindi + English), TANGLISH (Tamil + English) and MINGLISH (Marathi + English) etc. [10]. These languages form phonological amalgamation based on the influence of sociolinguistic aspects such as first language culture, learning environment, Speaker's accent and speaking style etc. There are various other factors as well such as age of the speaker which influences the early acquisition of second language that improves its pronunciation, increases its adaptability, and minimizes the influence of L1 language (native). On the other hand, learning English lately in some period of age allows more influence of phonetics and emphasis of pronunciation variations between L1 language and L2 language in terms of insertion, omission and substitution.

The present study focuses on the empirical study and discussion on phonetic, and consonantal phone sounds of English spoken in India. Single word utterances were recorded and collected from a selected list of words, spoken by 18 female subjects of University for Women under their Centre of Excellence-Artificial Intelligence (COE-AI). There were three utterances per subject for each word, recorded on PRAAT tool at a frequency of 16 kHz and a mono channel. The female participants belonged to their native birth place having native spoken languages such - Hindi, Odia, Bengali, Tamil, Bhojpuri (Uttar-Pradesh district), Marathi, Telugu, Malayalam and Punjabi respectively.(two female participants in common). The use of tools like PRAAT for consonant analysis offers valuable insights into the phonetic and phonological aspects of spoken English in India. This knowledge can aid in language teaching, speech therapy, and enhancing communication skills. Examples from previous and related studies are also reviewed and presented to reach a view about the consonant phonemic characteristics of Indian English language. The results from the tool were compared with the existing work to conclude the effectiveness of this study.

The remaining paper is structured as follows:- Sect. 2 demonstrates the consonantal phonemic variations of English spoken in India with the phonetic and phonemic connections and influence of Indian native language considerably Hindi, Gujarati, Tamil, Odia, Marathi, Telugu, Malayalam, Punjabi and Bengali with English. Section 3 discusses the paper and concludes the paper in Sect. 4.

2 Methodology and Outcome Based on the Visualisation of Word Utterances

2.1 Data Corpus

Audio (.wav files) data was collected and recorded on PRAAT toolkit, for 18 female participants. The reason for selecting only female participants is limited resources. For this study relatively, a required number of female participants were more readily available in the Women based university where this experiment has been conducted. The recording was done in the Centre-of-Excellence: Artificial Intelligence audio studio of the University. Three utterances of each word was recorded per participants, where two participants have same native language. Total 9 languages were selected to compare the consonantal pronunciation of English spoken by the participants as their second language. Table 4 presents the words selected corresponding to the languages chosen for comparison. The words are selected on the basis which are highly affected by its pronunciation when spoken with native languages of India. These words were given in suggestion by the participants of this work. In linguistic studies, using distinct word sets for each experimental language is common to maintain comparability and address language-specific phonological and phonetic traits. Distinct languages possess unique phonological systems, featuring specific phonemes and structures. Using the same word set for all languages may introduce biases or overlook language-specific phonetic and phonological features. Employing language-specific word sets has enabled the authors to study the phonological variations and pronunciation distinctions across languages. Additionally, Sociolinguistic variations in pronunciation, such as regional accents or sociocultural influences, are frequently observed in languages. These variations can be accounted for and analyzed in their impact by using language-specific word sets. It is due to these reasons, this experiment has selected different set of words for all the experimental languages.

Table 4. Languages based words selected for visualisation of spoken utterances

Language	Words selected
Hindi	Advise, Advise, डंॊडा, टापूₒ , ि᷃फ़न् , ि᷃फश , फै᷈ ट, pizza, Straight, Fly, Film, Crow, They, Thing,Pleasure
Gujarati	Favourite, Pen, બરાબર
Marathi	Canal, Carriage, Preside, Relative, Diamond, Gentlemen, immoral, many, sour, tomato,
Punjabi	Connect, bomb, company, America, Class,Paper, Lieutinent, Command, Amritsar, Stamp, Pension
Tamil	Fan, Driver, Help
Bhojpuri	Shame, Sheep, Shoe, लड़का, बड़ा
Telugu	Roxy, Fridge, can, thin
Bengali	Vote, English, Various, Approve, Vice, View,Sale, So what, Separated, Rasagulla, Pizza, were, Forever, Facto
Malayalam	Venice, Every, English

2.2 Methodology

The corpus collected was recorded on PRAAT toolkit. PRAAT is an open-source tool designed for speech analysis and phonetic research. It provides a range of features and functionalities for analysing speech and conducting empirical experiments related to phonetics and phonology of the language spoken. Since the tool helps to understand the complexities of human speech production and perception, the tool was a perfect selection for conducting this experiment and perform analysis.

2.3 Outcome Based on the Visualisation of Corpus Data on Tool

2.3.1 Hindi-English (Hinglish)

Hindi is the first official languages of India which is spoken in highest proportion by the Indian speakers as their first language. Hindi belongs to the family of Indo-Aryan languages and has a large phonemic inventory. Hema Sirsa and A. Redford explored the acoustic measurement to investigate the differences in the production of Indian English with Hindi and Telugu considering the segmental and suprasegmental features of vowels and consonants [3]. Variation in Rhythms, pitch, articulatory sounds and intonation strongly interfere into English language with spoken Hindi accent. These differences occur due to some sounds /ŋ/ and /ʒ/ which are absent in Hindi [5]. Some notable features of Indian English and Hindi consonants sound variations are:-

1. The aspirated voiceless dental plosive /th/ in words such as (months, things, this) is often substituted with the un-aspirated voiced dental plosive ' ð' and aspirated voiceless dental plosive 'θ' for Hindi speakers learning English as their second language. Example:

> *they* → (en) ð eɪ (hi) th is substituted with ð
> *thing* → (en) θ ɪ ŋ (hi) th is substituted with θ,

2. The letter /s/ is exemplified as phoneme /ʒ/in word such as-

pleasure -> pleʒər, pronounced as plejur

3. For Hindi native language speakers, consonant clusters often lead to errors in pronunciation. Few of the words in this context are:-

> Straight → istraight
> Fly→ faly
> film→filam

4. Hindi has feeble but foreseeable word stress compared to spoken English as a second language. Therefore, it is intricate with lop-sided stress pattern of words such as **photograph/photographer**
5. Hindi speakers often call some words (below), causing the problem in the articulation of English sounds in the English manner [5].

crow → Krow
pizza→Pijja/ Pizja

6. Speakers with Hindi as their native language try to clearly articulate short, common words such as: has, and, was, to, etc. that are usually weakly stressed in English but disincline to 'swallow' unstressed syllables such as the first syllables in the words **tomorrow, remember, intelligent etc.**,
7. In Hindi (devanagari) the loaned /f/ from Arabic and Persian dialect is written by tapping a dot beneath the grapheme for native /ph/ < फ >: < फ़ >.

फ़िन →phə००० ́ f̃०००००n (fin)

फ़िश →phiɛə (fish)

फ़ै ००े ट→pha:itə

8. Interference from Hindi also gives way for the voiceless and voiced retroflex plosives /ʈ/and /ɖ/respectively replacing the alveolar plosive of Standard English /t/ and /d/. Example-

English	*Hindi*	*Phoneme*	*meaning*
Danda	डंडा	*ɖ ə nɖa:*	*Stick*
Taapu	टापू	*ʈ a:pu*	*Island*

9. Due to comparative counts of vowels and consonants between Hindi and English, there are several pronunciation problems in words such as said/sad; par/paw; vet/wet; later/letter; advise/aadvise etc. Figure 1 demonstrate the visualisation of pronunciation difference for word aadvise and advise.

advise→ ɐ dv aɪ z
aadvise→ ɑ: dv aɪ z

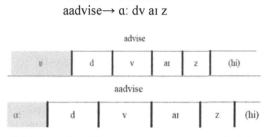

Fig. 1. Text Grid view of the Phoneme characters for word advise and aadvise

2.3.2 Gujarati-English

Gujarati is one of the major Indian Languages which shares common features with the phonology of general Indian English. Gujarati and English language have contrastive difference in terms of manner and place of articulation as regards to consonants phonemes of both the language and also shows variations at suprasegmental level i.e., stress, rhythm and intonation [11]. A thorough study on influence of Gujarati and Tamil language as first language on Indian English is done in [12] representing distinguished features in vowels, consonants and intonational behaviour. Some of the contrastive features of distinct phoneme characteristics of English spoken by Gujaratis are:-

1. Guajarati speakers with less exposure to English often articulate /f/ as aspirated voiceless bilabial plosive **/ph/.**

Favourite → ph eɪ v ɹ ɪ t

2. The voiceless plosive sounds /p/, /t/, /k/ is always unaspirated in Gujarati and Gujarati Indian English. Example:

pen → /pen/ instead of **/phen/**

3. The Gujarati accent of speaking certain words spoken in Hindi but written in English shows variation in its pronunciation. For example, Fig. 2 represents visualisation of pronunciation of word barobar on praat:-

barobar

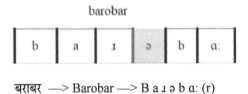

बराबर —> Barobar —> B a ɹ ə b ɑː (r)

Fig. 2. Phone character view of Gujarati word

2.3.3 Tamil-English (Tanglish)

Tamil English is mostly spoken similar to Gujarati's English and thus observe consonantal and intonational differences with general English mostly noted in the production of rhotic across the speakers. While English is a stressed-timed language, Tamil is a syllable-timed language and due to this fact, the Tamil speakers complete every syllable in English with emphasis **/r/,** which is silent and hardly uttered in English by a Tamil speaker. Tamil speakers' English has retroflex stops [13]. Some of the L1(Tamil)-L2 (English) phonological effect and influence is stated below:

1. One or more English segmental are lost in a phonemic realisation where a particular sound is not articulated while speaking and leads to the omission of certain pronunciation variables. For example, *"driver*, **dr** is a consonant cluster occurring in English

and not in Tamil. Therefore /r/ is omitted when the speaker utters it. Another example is word **HELP** in which /h/ is omitted by a Tamil speaker."

2. Tamil does not have the phoneme /f/ and therefore Tamil-English bilinguals uses /f/ with the Tamil /p/.

word : *fan*→/pæn/ **instead of /fæn/**

2.3.4 Telugu-English (Tenglish)

In contrast with Indian English, Telugu is an Indian language belonging to the Dravidian family of languages, spoken by at least 7% of the total population in India [14]. Telugu speakers often speak with a rhotic accent. [15] investigated on the effect of tense lax contrast in Indian English vowels and found that phonological length on tenses-laxness in Telugu does not have much effect on Indian English language. However, there are certain words which shows short-long vowel contrast between Telugu and Telugu-English. B. A. Prabhakar Babu have exhaustively presented a phonetic and phonological features study of Telugu English describing all the consonantal, intonations and vowels characteristics of Telugu and Telugu English [15]. For an instance, In Telugu, /z/ and /dʒ/are allophones, so words such as-

rosy /ˈɹəʊzi/ / **'roːdʒi** / fridge /fɹɪdʒ/ / **friz** /

In certain instances, in languages borrowing words from English[16], the voiceless dental fricative /θ/ may be replaced with the voiceless aspirated dental plosive /tʰ/ referred to as a "reflex. For example a word "thin," pronounced as /θɪn/ in English, may be borrowed into Telugu language with the /θ/ sound being replaced by /tʰ/. Other example is word 'can' in which letter 'c' referring kh is replaced with 'kʰ'. The replacement of /θ/ to /tʰ/ for word 'thin' in Telugu is visualised on Praat in Fig. 3.

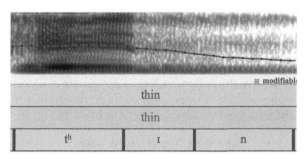

Fig. 3. Replacement of voiceless dental fricative /θ/ to /tʰ/ in Telugu for word 'thin' taken from English language

2.3.5 Bengali-English (Benglish) and Odia English

Bengali and Odia are the classical languages of India. Bengali English refers majorly to the varieties of the west Bengal state and bordering countries of Bangladesh. As per the phonetic table of English and Bengali language, Bangla constitutes more consonants as compared to that of English [6]. There has been less study done on the comparative consonant's phonetic variations between spoken English and Bengali language in India as compared to that of its vowel phonetic study. In addition to Bengali, Odia language spoken as a first language behave similar to Bangla accent of speaking English. Some of the distinctive features of Bengali's and Odia speaking English are-

1. /v/ is pronounced as /β/ and /bɦ/in Bengali. The variation takes place due to different place of articulation depending upon the spoken regional Bengali dialect. For example, Fig. 4 represents phonetic instances and articulation of word bharious (various), bhaice (vice) and bhiew (view) visualised on praat:-

English word	Spoken Bengali/Odia Accent	Phoneme characteristic
vote	Bh-ote	/ bʰʊt/
english	Inglis	/ iŋlis/ (Mahanta, 2012)
various	Bh-arious	/ bʰ eə ɹ iə s/
approve	Approo-bh	/ ɐ p ɹ u: bʰ/
vice	Bha-ice	/ bʰ eɪ s/
view	Bh-iew	/ bʰ j u:/

Fig. 4. Phone Instances of Bengali/Odia words spoken

2. Bengali speakers frequently substitute 's' for 'sh'. Example:-

Sale → shale
So, what...→ Sho, what...
Separated→ Sh e parateds
Rasagulla→ Raw-sho-gol-la

3. Bengali language Speakers (from both Bangladesh and India) and Biharis habitually substitute 'J' for 'Z'. Example:- *'jero'* instead of *'zero'*, *'pijja'* instead of *'pizza'*
4. Regional accent of Bengali speakers varies in their manner of articulation of speech. They often substitute and add 'h' with 'w' placed at the first position of work. Example word forever and facto been visualised on praat as below in Fig. 5:

were w eə r (perceived as where)
substitution of **'f' as 'ph'**: forever ph ə ɹ ɛ v ə , facto ph a k t əʊ

forever

| pʰ | ə | ɪ | ɛ | v | ə |

facto

| pʰ | a | k | t | əʊ |

Fig. 5. Phonemic characteristics of Bengali and Odia accent based English words

2.3.6 Malayalam English (Manglish)

Malayalam and English language are the most widely spoken languages in Kerela and with the exposure to high-level education and learning, English is mostly used there in schools and colleges for communication. English and Malayalam shows higher acoustic variances with each other in Harmonic-to-Noise Ratio (HNR) than did the voiceless stimulus pairs [17], For example, English /v/ and Malayalam /b/, whereas English /f/ and Malayalam /p/ have smaller HNR.

Some distinguished features between Malayalam and English phonemes:-

1. Malayalam speakers represents /v/ as /bh/ in the pronunciation of some English words. For example: 'venice [vɛnɪs] as [bh enis].
2. The response of /p/ to [**pata**] and of /b/ to [**bata**] is often intruded as a response of /ph/ to [**pata**] and of /bh/ to [**bata**] for Malayalam Speakers due to the intrusion of manner of articulated voice segments having distinctive features [17].
3. Some euphonic consonants /j/ and /w/ are occasionally comprehended in place of /h/ for South Indians. Example: every ye-very, english ye-nglish.
4. Closest phonological match between English and Malayalam with reference to the HNR hierarchy are: English HNRs: /v/ > /b/ > /p/ > /f/ Malayalam HNRs: /bh/ > /p/ > /ph/ > /b/.

2.3.7 Punjabi-English (Punglish)

Punjabi and English languages have its place in different families of languages where Punjabi language belongs to Indo-Aryan family and English belongs to West Germanic language. Punjabi is a highly tonal language and carries rich linguistics with English language. Having 20 consonant sounds in common both the language share quality tip of tongue places and manner of articulation and thus allows Punjabi speakers to easily learn English as their second language. More often both Punjabi and English manifest themselves through various dialects based on diversified geographical areas yet they represent phonemic similarities between them. The authors in [18] presented a phonemic comparison of Punjabi and English. A well-distinguished consonants inventory of both Punjabi and English language is represented in their work. In Punjabi and English inventory. Some distinguished linguistic features between English and Punjabi are:-

1. Since Punjabi is a tonal language, it carries major tonal variation while uttering English words. For example, utterance of word:-

$$\text{connect} \longrightarrow \text{kʊ'nekt+tone}$$
$$\text{bomb} \longrightarrow \text{bʌmb}$$
$$\text{company} \longrightarrow \text{koʊmpni:}$$
$$\text{america} \longrightarrow \text{əmrika:}$$

2. Some words lose their English characteristics when introduced into Punjabi, leading to pluralisation by adopting rules of English morphology [18].

Words	English plural	Punjabi plural	Punjabi pronunciation
Class	Classes	Classan	klasã:
Paper	Papers	Paperan	Peɪprã:

3. Punjabi language is influenced by borrowing its lexicon from English language which were gradually accepted in the Punjabi language [18]. For example:-

English words	Punjabi words	Punjabi pronunciation
Lieutinent	laftain	lʌftæn
Command	Kamaan	kʌma:n
Amritsar	Ambarsar	ʌmbarān

4. While pronouncing English with Punjabi accent some words get corrupted from their original pronunciation and demonstrate change in spelling and pronunciation [18].

English words	Punjabi words	Punjabi pronunciation
Stamp	Ashtaam	stʃta:m
Pension	Pinshun	pintʃʌn

2.3.8   Marathi-English (Menglish)

Marathi is an Indo-European language with more than 42 identified dialects and English belongs to the origin of Anglo-Frisian Dialects of the Netherlands and the North-West Germany [19]. Botsh English and Marathi shares a distinguished differences in their linguistic study such as nouns, adverbs, articles, syllables etc., due to rich variation in peoples speaking style influenced from linguistic background. Marathi speakers often duplicate the syllables to convey an adverb. For example: **PATPAT → पटपट.** Marathi language depicts no change in its word order or intonation unlike English language. For example: **tula phooga aavadto तुलुॢ ००T फुॢ गा आवडतो Vs tula phooga aavadto? तुलुॢ ०T फुॢ गा आवडतो?.** Herein, the intonation gives us a clue about the nature of the sentence.

Some of the illustrations followed by "Marathi English" speakers in the phonemic transcriptions with English is shown below in Table 5 [20]:

Table 5. Marathi-english word pronunciation and consonantal characteristics

English words	Marathi-English transcription	English words	Marathi-English transcription
canal	/kæn ɔl/	gentlemen	jɔnl̠temen
carriage	/kær ej/	immoral	immɔrəl
preside	/prisɑy d/	many	/me:ni:/
relative	/rile:ṭi: v/	sour	so:ər
diamond	/ḍay-mənḍ/	tomato	ṭomæṭo

2.3.9 Bhojpuri English

Bhojpuri is an Indo-Aryan language chiefly spoken in western Bihar, north-western Jharkhand and eastern Uttarakhand. It is considered as one of the dialects of Hindi language. The language consists of 31 consonant phonemes and 34 contoids majorly 7 retroflexes, 6 bilabial and alveo-palatal and 1 glottal etc. The people speaking English with Bhojpuri as their native dialect language shows distinct features in pronunciation of words with more release of Swash (Air). For an instance, Bhojpuri language speakers substitute /sh/ as 's' omitting the pronunciation of /h/ in words in a sentence such as "Shame on you" pronounced as "same on you". The tongue tip pointing towards front teeth for consonant cluster /sh/ sitting behind the two front teeth with rounded lips and air blow over tongue is placed against the ridge behind the upper teeth without touching it and squeeze the air between the tip pf tongue and top of the mouth with resistance releasing more air. Odia, Bengali and Assamese is also closely related to Bhojpuri phonetic characteristics. Some more similar example words are:-

English accent word	Phoneme	Bhojpuri accent for English word	Phoneme
shame	ʃ eɪ m	same	s eɪ m
sheep	ʃ iː p	seep	s iː p
Shoe	ʃ uː	soo	s uː

Bhojpuri language speakers often substitute plain retroflex flap ɽ (X-SAMPA-r') with /r/ ɽ when they write spoken Hindi word with Bhojpuri dialect in English. For example:-

Hindi word	Spoken Bhojpuri	Written English
लड़का	Larka	Ladka
बड़ा	Bara	Bada

There has been no significant study done on analysing spoken English with Bhojpuri as a native language and accent in India, which can be extensively explored to determine distinct variations and similarities in phonetic and phonology characteristics in spoken English.

3 Discussion and Challenges

The current study investigated phonetic and phonological study of Indian English and the influence of different languages on English spoken in India. Indian English diverges from Indian native dialects exposed to speaking English as their second language. Due to variations and common findings in the phonetic pronunciation and other phonological aspects such as the influence on English spoken by Indians due to mother tongue (native language pronunciation), Regional & Culture, Educational environment, Indian English observes both deviations and similarities in the accent of speaking English with different Indian language background due to the influence of distinct culture & regional variations such as creation of macaronic hybrid - TANGLISH (Tamil + English), Bhojpuri-English, HINGLISH (Hindi + English), BENGLISH (Bengali + English), and MENGLISH

(Marathi + English) etc., socio-linguistic aspects, age of the speaker (Early acquisition of language), learning environment, accent, speaking style & emphasis on pronunciation variation. Native speakers of Indian languages may exhibit grammatical transfer, where the grammar of their first language influences their English sentence structure, word order, and tense usage. Due to this reason, Indian English exhibits less common similarities in the utterance of English by native speakers of a diverse range of languages. The paper majorly reviews the previous findings and discusses new findings on the manner and place of articulation while learning consonantal pronunciation of English with the mixed variation and influence observed through languages like Hindi, Punjabi, Bhojpuri, Odia, Bengali, Tamil etc. One significant observation is like Hindi, South Indian speaking belt voiceless labio-dental 'f' is realised as [pʰ] and voiced 'vʰ' often overlaps with weakly rounded labio-velar semi-vowel /w/, also realised as [b]. Many Alveolar sounds becomes retroflexed in Indian English. Aspiration for [pʰ], [tʰ], [kʰ] stops at the beginning of accented syllables and un-aspirated for voiceless plosives /p/, /t/, /k/. We have observed spectrographic view of the consonant pronunciation variation through spectrum diagram of words Harder and Partner which illustrated their rhotic accent. The paper realised that an extensive study is required to study the intonational patterns of Indian English. The paper's findings indicate the need for extensive experimental studies on Indian English that highlights the potential for future research that can delve deeper into the influence of native languages on English pronunciation in real-world contexts.Complementary research would be to investigate inclusive variations on phonetic characterisation of English language in Indian regions. For example, we are interested in the possible distinct pronunciation efficacies of the English language spoken by population with Hindi and Punjabi as their native language residing at different states of India. This study in future would disambiguate sociolinguistic and psycholinguistic factors to some degree.

4 Conclusion

Precisely, this paper explored and presented several analytical facts based on the impact of linguistic consonantal variations that an Indian English speaker can have. Even though we follow British English at the dictionary/vocabulary level a great deal of regional and educational differentiation exists among the Indian English speakers. Indian English is generally spoken in syllabic rhythm and seems to put stress accents at incorrect syllables or accentuates all the syllables of English long word. Acoustic phonetic variations of these sounds is studied and mentioned while focusing on the deviation or influence of native languages on Indian English that shows notable and observable phonetic and phonological variations such as the impact of L1 languages and pronunciation contact with English (L2 language). For example: Jungle/ जगंॅ ल, Nirvana/ फनववाण. These inferences lead to the demand for an extensive study on Indian English, having captured the inherent variability in the realistic environment.

References

1. Gargesh, R.: Indian English: Phonology (2016)
2. Wiltshire, C.R., Harnsberger, J.D.: The influence of Gujarati and Tamil L1s on Indian English: a preliminary study. World Englishes **25**(1), 91–104 (2006)
3. Sirsa, H., Redford, M.A.: The effects of native language on Indian English sounds and timing patterns. J. Phon. **41**(6), 393–406 (2013)
4. Chohan, M.N., García, M.I.M.: Phonemic comparison of English and punjabi. Int. J. Engl. Linguist. **9**(4), 347–357 (2019)
5. Mishra, S., Mishra, A.: Linguistic Interference from Hindi in Indian English. Int. J. Stud. Engl. Lang. Lit. **4**(1), 29–38 (2016)
6. Barman, B.: A contrastive analysis of English and Bangla phonemics. Dhaka Univ. J. Linguist. **2**(4), 19–42 (2011). https://doi.org/10.3329/dujl.v2i4.6898
7. Ona Masoko, S.T.: A synchronic analysis of Indian English (2017)
8. Ryan, S.: Indian & American English 3 differences (2014). https://www.confidentvoice.com/blog/indian-american-english-3-differences/. Accessed 3 May 2022
9. Agrawal, S.S.: Second official language of India: the Indian English (2017)
10. Sinha, S., Agrawal, S.S., Jain, A.: Influence of regional dialects on acoustic characteristics of Hindi vowels. In: 2015 International Conference Oriental COCOSDA held jointly with 2015 Conference on Asian Spoken Language Research and Evaluation (O-COCOSDA/CASLRE), pp.166–171. IEEE (2015)
11. Fox, A.: A comparative study of English and German intonation (1984)
12. Joshi, P.: Phonological contrastive analysis of consonant and vowel phonemes of RP and GIE with special focus on Gujarati phonology. ELT Voices **4**(6), 11–19 (2014)
13. Kanthimathi, D.K.: Tamilized English: a study of the phonological features of English spoken by Tamils (n.d.)
14. Bhaskararao, P., Ray, A.: Illustrations of the IPA: Telugu. J. Int. Phon. Assoc. **47**(2), 231–241 (2017). https://doi.org/10.1017/S0025100316000207
15. Babu, B.P.: A phonetic and phonological study of some characteristic features of Telugu English including reference to the source and target languages. University of London, School of Oriental and African Studies, United Kingdom (1976)
16. Bhaskararao, P., Ray, A.: Telugu. J. Int. Phon. Assoc. **47**(2), 231–241 (2017)
17. Mandal, S.K.D., Gupta, B., Datta, A.K.: Word boundary detection based on suprasegmental features: a case study on Bangla speech. Int. J. Speech Technol. **9**(1–2), 17–28 (2007). https://doi.org/10.1007/s10772-006-9001-6
18. Studies, T., & Vol, I. International Journal of English Language, Literature Impact Of English On Punjabi Lexicon : An Analytical Stu (2015)
19. Panshikar, A.: Linguistic differences between Marathi and English (2015)
20. Kelkar, A.R.: "Marathi English": a study in foreign accent. Word **13**(2), 268–282 (1957)

Workshops - Regional Fake, MMLOW, LC4

Multilingual Fake News Detection in Low-Resource Languages: A Comparative Study Using BERT and GPT-3.5

K. Anirudh, Meghana Srikanth$^{(\boxtimes)}$, and A. Shahina

Department of Information Technology, Sri Sivasubramaniya Nadar College of Engineering, Chennai, Tamil Nadu 603110, India
meghana2010694@ssn.edu.in

Abstract. This paper presents a novel attempt at evaluating the authenticity of Tamil news headlines using large language models (LLMs) and evaluating it besides transformer models and existing machine learning results. To tackle this classification task, two potent models—the transformer-based BERT and the LLM, gpt-3.5-turbo—are deployed and fine-tuned to distinguish genuine from fabricated news headlines. Through careful fine-tuning and training of BERT, m-BERT, and GPT-3.5-Turbo, we assess their effectiveness, contrasting a bidirectional transformer with a generative transformer for fake news classification. Careful selection leads us to training based on three types of inputs: (1) Tamil news with English translations and author information; (2) Tamil news with author information only; and (3) English news with author information only. Our evaluation yields intriguing insights, showing that models trained on inputs with English versions consistently outperform those relying solely on Tamil text. Performance metrics, including accuracy, precision, recall, and F1-score, imply the superiority of the LLM -based gpt-3.5-turbo, achieving an accuracy of 0.92, precision of 0.902, recall of 0.949, and F1-score of 0.925. This highlights the effectiveness of LLMs in Tamil fake news classification. Moreover, these findings stress the significance of multilingual data processing for bolstering the accuracy of news headline classification systems. They also provide valuable insights for enhancing the reliability and precision of fake news detection systems in multilingual environments.

Keywords: Low-resource languages · BERT · GPT-3.5 · Fake news detection · Classification · Multilingual · Fine-tuning

1 Introduction

False information presented as news, commonly known as "fake news" [5], is a growing concern due to its potential to undermine trust, distort perceptions, and influence political outcomes. This challenge is particularly pronounced in low-resource languages like Tamil, where limited language resources make fake news detection challenging. Mitigating the impact of misinformation within the Tamil-speaking community is crucial. This research focuses on classifying Tamil news headlines as real or fake, utilizing state-of-the-art language models like BERT and gpt-3.5-turbo.

© The Author(s), under exclusive license to Springer Nature Switzerland AG 2024
B. R. Charkravarthi et al. (Eds.): SPELLL 2023, CCIS 2046, pp. 387–397, 2024.
https://doi.org/10.1007/978-3-031-58495-4_28

The classification task itself presents a formidable challenge, especially considering the limitations of existing machine learning models, especially before the widespread adoption of transformer models [2]. Despite extensive research in high-resource languages, low-resource languages like Tamil have been largely overlooked in this context. This paper aims to address this gap by investigating the performance of advanced language models, highlighting the pressing need for reliable fake news detection in multilingual settings.

Our research involves fine-tuning BERT and gpt-3.5-turbo models for classifying Tamil news headlines. We hypothesize that models trained on inputs with English translations will outperform those relying solely on Tamil text. This assumption is based on the belief that including English versions provides additional linguistic context and features that enhance the models' ability to discern the authenticity of news headlines, leading to improved classification results. We consider three input types: (a) Tamil news with English translations and author information; (b) Tamil news with author information only; and (c) English news with author information.

Additionally, our research aims to assess the effectiveness of BERT and gpt-3.5-turbo models in classifying Tamil news headlines as real or fake across different input types. We also seek to provide insights into the impact of input configurations on fake news detection in multilingual settings, emphasizing the significance of including English translations. Furthermore, we compare and analyze the performance of these models in multilingual settings, particularly when dealing with news headlines presented in both Tamil and English.

The contributions of this paper include innovative techniques for transferring transformer-based methodologies and LLMs across the English and Tamil domains to achieve optimal performance. We also investigate the impact of fine-tuning approaches on the newly introduced transferring methodologies to substantiate our hypothesis that fine-tuning approaches hold significant potential for enhancing overall performance. Finally, we conduct a comprehensive evaluation using both the transformer and fine-tuned LLM results as well as compare them with the performance of existing baseline models, rigorously analyzing the performance disparities.

Our study begins with an overview of the fake news challenge in previous research, emphasizing the importance of detecting fake news in low-resource languages. We then detail our approach and methodology, including model fine-tuning. The paper concludes with results from our experiments and their implications for multilingual fake news detection systems.

2   Related Work

In this section, we provide an overview of pertinent prior research, concentrating on approaches relevant to our study of fake news detection. We emphasize the significance of transformer-based methodologies, while also highlighting classical and advanced machine learning techniques employed in this context.

In our work, we have focused on making use of the dataset curated by Mirnalinee et al. in their work "A Novel Dataset for Fake News Detection in Tamil Regional Language" [1] - a huge corpus having 5,273 Tamil news (2949 fake, 2324 real) which was collected from scraping data from various verified sources. Since a major aspect of our work involves experimenting with the translated version of the fake news of low-resource languages, this dataset, which has both Tamil and English versions, was an ideal choice for testing.

They had additionally provided us with baseline ML models with their accuracy rate for different ML models, with SVMs proving to be the most accurate in that study at 87.85%, closely followed by Logistic Regression at 86.80%, and the least performing of them being RNN with two LSTM layers at 75.04%.

Raja et al. [3] also developed a similar collection but for Dravidian languages - Tamil, Kannada, Telugu, Malayalam [3] provides us with three approaches for a transfer-learning based fine-tuning approach that is also adopted here. This paper explores the effectiveness of mBERT and XLM-R pretrained transformer models in addressing sentence-level fake news classification in a resource-poor setting. The study evaluates the performance of these models, both fine-tuned, in comparison to zero-shot, cross-lingual, and multilingual models using mBERT and XLM-R. The models are trained on a mix of English and Dravidian language datasets, and their performance is assessed on fine-tuned Dravidian language datasets. XLM-R emerges as the superior model, achieving an impressive average accuracy of 93.31%, surpassing mBERT models in multilingual learning.

A BERT model to identify fake news across different languages is developed by Chu et al. [6] in their work. The outcomes showcased the viability of monitoring fake news in both English and Chinese using cross-language datasets, with notably high Recall scores. Moreover, the models achieved an impressive accuracy range of 97% to 99% within the language-specific datasets, underscoring the potential efficacy of advanced NLP models. These promising results inspired us to delve deeper into this approach.

Molina et al. [5] suggests a comprehensive framework for understanding false information, irrespective of its genre or intent, by analysing its message, structure, sources, and network. As a result, this paper strictly relies on the news headline in Tamil, its English translation, and authorship for assessment.

For Alghamidhi et al. [7] the fine-tuning approach is emphasized, crucial element highlighted in our research. It showcases the potential of Pre-trained Language Models (PLMs) for detecting COVID-19-related fake news, bearing crucial implications for the advancement of more accurate detection models.

3 Methodology

In this section, we discuss the problem, models utilized in detail and how they are fine-tuned to solve the problem in hand and the results obtained.

3.1 Problem Statement

Suppose we have a set of news $N = \{N_1, N_2...N_m\}$ with 'm' number of samples, the task is to classify $f(N) \rightarrow \hat{y}$ where $\hat{y} = 0$ for fake and $\hat{y} = 1$ for real for transformer models BERT base and m-BERT. In the language model approach with gpt-3.5-turbo, we choose to classify $\hat{y}$ = "Fake" for fake and $\hat{y}$ = "Real" for real.

Our study explores the intricacies of fake news classification by systematically examining various hyper parameter configurations across three distinct cases. These cases encompass information combinations of English headlines, Tamil headlines and author information. This study aims to fine-tune prominent models, including BERT base, multilingual BERT (m-BERT), and the gpt-3.5-turbo, to discern their performance disparities in the domain of fake news detection.

3.2   Proposed Models

BERT Base- BERT (Bidirectional Encoder Representations from Transformers), a formidable creation by Google AI, has proven to be a powerful tool for text classification [x], [y]. BERT is a multi-layer bidirectional transformer encoder trained on a massive corpus containing 2500M and 800M tokens from English Wikipedia and Book Corpus, respectively featuring 24 layers, 16 attention heads, and 340 million parameters. Our work utilizes the uncased version of BERT, which serves as a baseline model for BERT-based models. Input sequences with a maximum length of 128 tokens are processed, resulting in 768-dimensional vector representations for each token encoding contextual information. We have also experimented with an ensemble of BERT base to compare the accuracy.

m-BERT Base- Multilingual BERT, or m-BERT, extends the capabilities of BERT to a wide range of languages. Similar to BERT, it utilizes a multi-layer bidirectional transformer encoder architecture consisting of 12 layers (Fig. 1) and 12 self-attention heads, making it adaptable for various NLP tasks. m-BERT is pretrained on a diverse multilingual corpus, allowing it to capture linguistic nuances across multiple languages [x]. We leverage m-BERT to enhance the model's multilingual understanding, enabling effective handling of text in different languages. This multilingual model demonstrates its robustness and serves as a significant tool for addressing cross-lingual false news detection difficulties.

GPT-3.5-Turbo - GPT, or Generative Pre-trained Transformers, are neural network models using the transformer architecture, a significant advancement in AI. They power generative AI applications like ChatGPT, enabling them to create human-like text, images, music, and more, and hold conversational interactions. The GPT-3.5 model, a refined version of GPT3, emerged in January 2022, with three variants: 1.3B, 6B, and 175B parameters. Its key improvement was reducing toxic output to some degree. Our work tries to capture the capability of this model, by fine-tuning it to perform fake news classification. In Fig. 1, its transformation sequence is presented with 12 complete layers and one partial layer (hence x12.5) to perform prediction and classification.

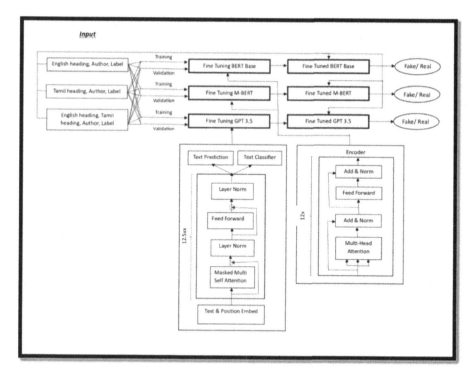

Fig. 1. Workflow of implemented process.

3.3 Experimental Setup

For GPT-3.5, the experiment was carried out leveraging the T4 GPU runtime in Google Colab. We created three fine-tuned GPT-3.5 models by creating fine-tuning jobs for each aforementioned training inputs. For BERT and m-BERT, the experiments were conducted using Google Colab with the T4 GPU runtime. We fine-tuned three separate models for each of the training input scenarios as previously mentioned, specifically leveraging the Transformers and Pytorch libraries.

Evaluation of these models employed standard performance metrics, including confusion matrices, accuracy, precision, recall, and F1 score. This approach allows comprehensive assessment of the models across input configurations.

To create a fine-tuning job for gpt-3.5-turbo, it is required that we provide at least 10 examples, and advised that one should go for 50 to 100 training examples [12]. Being a paid service [13], constrained with price for training, input usage, output usage to fine-tune gpt-3.5-turbo model, BERT results are evaluated with gpt-3.5-turbo tuned with 50 training samples initially.

3.4 Input Selection

Initial appeal of the dataset is based on the fact that both the Tamil headline and English version are readily available. Prior to training the number of anonymous entries in the dataset are tracked to be 78 out of 5,273 – most of the available entries in the dataset has information regarding author. S Rathod's [9] and Sitaula, Niraj, et al. [10] findings suggest that author's history of association of fake news can play a significant role in detecting fake news. We extend the assumption that those generating fake news consistently produce only deceptive articles, particularly over brief intervals. Fake news creators exhibit a unique writing style distinct from genuine news authors, who strive to uphold credibility.

3.5   Dataset Preprocessing

BERT Base. We initiate the process by splitting our dataset into training, validation, and test sets, maintaining a ratio of 70:15:15. These subsets are derived from the 'News', 'Author', and 'English Version' features and the target variable 'Authenticity'. This strategic splitting ensures a well-balanced distribution of data across the subsets, to encourage robust model training and evaluation.

To facilitate effective tokenization and encoding, we employ the BERT model and tokenizer from the HuggingFace Transformers library. The 'bert-base-uncased' model and its corresponding 'BertTokenizerFast' tokenizer are utilized in this context. The text data is converted into string format to ensure seamless tokenization. We set the maximum token length to 15, since majority headlines have a word length under 15.

Tokenization and encoding are performed on the training, validation, and test sets, with tokens subsequently converted into tensors for efficient data processing. To optimize data management during model training, we employ PyTorch data loaders to help in handling batch-wise processing and ensure that the model receives the data efficiently during training and evaluation.

m-BERT. Our methodology centres on harnessing the capabilities of BERT-based model "bert-base-multilingual-cased" while extracting pertinent data similar to the BERT base model to serve as the primary input features to increase the effectiveness of this model. We then tokenize the input data, ensuring adherence to the required format. The tokenized data are subsequently split into training and validation sets, setting the stage for effective model training.

The architectural design encompasses an input layer that adeptly accommodates tokenized text input. This is integrated with a BERT layer responsible for extracting relevant features. For classification, we chose an output layer that employs a softmax activation function, effective for binary classification tasks. The model's compilation is done by tuning of hyperparameters, encompassing the optimizer and loss function, tailored to our requirements.

To facilitate efficient model training, we employ a label encoder to encode the labels effectively spanning a predefined number of 5 epochs. During the training phase, our primary focuses are optimizing accuracy and guarding against overfitting.

GPT-3.5. The Chat completions API from OpenAI necessitates a list of messages, with each message having a designated role and content, serving as the AI framework. Specifically, the user role engages in interactions, and the assistant generates text-based responses to assist the user.

The system role is initialized with three distinct behaviours, corresponding to the three different models with the following prompts:

- "You are a Tamil language fake news classifier; you assess the given Tamil news and author to classify the Tamil news as Fake or Real" – Pure Tamil-headline model
- "You are a fake news classifier; you assess the given English news and author to classify the English news as Fake or Real" - Pure English-headline model
- "You are a Tamil language fake news classifier; you assess the given Tamil news, its English version, and author to classify the Tamil news as Fake or Real" - Tamil and English-headline model.

The training input takes the form of a JSON object, with each conversation within the JSON containing a headline and its authenticity. For example:

{'messages': [{'role': 'system', 'content': "You are a Tamil language fake news classifier; you assess the given Tamil news, its English version, and author to classify the Tamil news as Fake or Real"}, {'role': 'user', 'content': "Tamil_news: மர் இந்திரா காந்தி காலில் விழுந்தாரா கருணாநிதி - உண்மை என்ன?, English_version:Did Karunanidhi fall on Indira Gandhi's feet - what is the truth?, Author: Mageshbabu Jayaram"},{'role': 'assistant', 'content': 'Fake'}]}.

Three fine-tuning jobs are created, each comprising 50 training samples and 20 validation samples, with the number of epochs set to 3.

4 Results

4.1 Fake News Detection Performance

To explain our findings in the context of comparison of these results, the performance measures are calculated under three different scenarios, which to involve configurations of features English and Tamil news headings and author. The performance metrics – accuracy, precision, sensitivity-recall, and f1-score are used.

The results of all 3 types of models used can be compared using their performance metrics as follows:

Table 1. Comparison of metrics on English, Tamil, Author configuration.

Performance measure	GPT-3.5-Turbo	BERT base	m-BERT
Accuracy	0.92	0.80	0.72
Precision	0.93	0.78	0.72
Recall	0.87	0.78	0.73
F1-Score	0.90	0.76	0.72

Table 2. Comparison of metrics on English, Author configuration.

Performance measure	GPT-3.5-Turbo	BERT base	m-BERT
Accuracy	0.92	0.81	0.94
Precision	0.90	0.82	0.95
Recall	0.95	0.82	0.94
F1-Score	0.93	0.81	0.94

Table 3. Comparison of metrics on Tamil, Author configuration.

Performance measure	GPT-3.5-Turbo	BERT base	m-BERT
Accuracy	0.90	0.76	0.79
Precision	0.83	0.80	0.81
Recall	1.00	0.75	0.77
F1-Score	0.90	0.72	0.77

Both BERT and m-BERT models showcase peak performance when it is trained on the English version of news and author input [Table 2]. BERT base is weakest when the configuration is Tamil news, Author [Table 3]. m-BERT performs as well as BERT base in such a case, with a higher recall of 0.77. It is important to note that gpt-3.5-turbo though performing.

Noticeably, including English headlines to Tamil headlines and Author input, results in increase in performance metrics across the board.

In fake news classification, the most undesirable classification would be classifying fake news as true. The BERT base model has performed eloquently in this regard.

Additionally, an ensemble of 5 BERT base models was tested for Tamil headlines and Author configuration alone in order to gauge accuracy compared to the other models tested in this experiment, demonstrating an 86% accuracy signifying a substantial 10% improvement compared to other configurations.

GPT-3.5's results [Table 1, 2 and 3] perform considerably better than the other two models consistently. While it is expected for Tamil to not do exceptionally well, due to the amount of training in that language for gpt-3.5, it still fares considerably well than all combinations tested in BERT-base and all except the English, Author combination in m-BERT.

It is important to note that the overall best performance is obtained when only the English version is supplied along with the author, a little bit more than the model with English as well as Tamil.

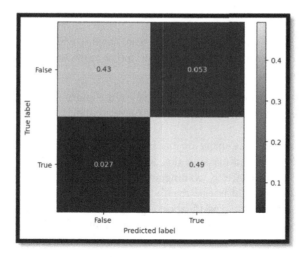

Fig. 2. Best Confusion Matrix of GPT-3.5 [INPUT: English version with author]

4.2   Discussion

The results of this research offer some insights into the classification of Tamil news headlines as real or fake across various input types. Expectedly, the performance of the models, BERT and GPT-3.5, varied significantly depending on the input configuration. Below mentioned are the key findings:

- Models trained on input with English translations [Table 1–2] exhibited better performance in the task of fake news detection compared to those relying solely on Tamil text
- [Table 3]. This suggests that incorporating multilingual data appropriately where available enhances the accuracy of classification.
- Both models demonstrated adaptability and effectiveness in handling the Tamil language classification, affirming their robustness in multilingual settings. [Table 2]
- While the models' overall performance was promising, there were cases where misclassification occurred, indicating the need for further refinement and more extensive training data.
- Fine-tuned GPT-3.5 performs well when instructed to be a fake news classifier prior to sending training.
- Fine-tuned GPT-3.5 performs well with limited training inputs for all combination of training inputs as observed from the best confusion matrix. (see Fig. 2)
- The prompt size can be significantly reduced for fake news classification task in GPT-3.5 as the results of passing the English version along with author is close to the result we obtain with passing both versions of the news – Tamil and English.

Overall, m-BERT with English, Author beats the performance of the fine-tuned GPT-3.5 and BERT base. However, it is worth noting that this performance metric is obtained by training only with 50 examples from 5,273 examples available due to cost constraints, thus reinforcing the idea "Language models are few-shot learners" [8].

4.3   Limitations

Acknowledging limitations will aid future researchers to identify areas for further refinement and generalization, ultimately contributing to the advancement of fake news detection techniques.

- The dataset, although carefully curated, may not capture the full spectrum of fake news diversity in the Tamil language, potentially leading to biased model performance.
- The Tamil language has many distinctive features, which can pose a number of difficulties for automated classification.
- The models' performance is contingent on the availability of accurate English translations, which might not be readily accessible for all Tamil news headlines.
- The study focuses on the classification aspect of fake news detection and does not delve into the broader context of misinformation propagation or its societal implications.
- The experiments with GPT-3.5 are carried out to observe the differences obtained when model is fine-tuned with different input combinations, it would benefit more from increasing training size and test size but due to cost constraints, the results of those are not the focus of this study.

5   Conclusions and Future Research

In conclusion, this research sheds light on the intricacies of fake news detection in the Tamil language domain and the multilingual implications thereof. The study highlights the advantages of incorporating English translations when available, affirming the adaptability and effectiveness of BERT and GPT-3.5 models in this context.

While the models exhibit promising performance, there is room for improvement and further exploration. This research contributes to the ongoing efforts [4–7] to combat misinformation and paves the way for more robust fake news detection systems in diverse linguistic landscapes.

Based on the findings of this research, several areas for future researchers to work emerge:

- Expanding the dataset to include a more extensive and diverse collection of Tamil news headlines to improve model robustness and accuracy.
- Investigating methods to combat biases that may affect model performance, especially in cases where the source of information plays a significant role.
- Exploring additional features or linguistic cues that could potentially enhance the models' ability to differentiate between real and fake news.
- Extending the research to other South Asian or low resource languages to assess the generalizability of the models across different linguistic contexts, starting with other Dravidian languages [3].
- Steadily testing the performance of different fine-tuned models of GPT-3.5 with increasing training size.

- Exploring different prompts made to fine-tune and test the fake-news classifier in order to improve the performance of the LLM as a classifier.
- Comparing and evaluating the performance of different large language models for the same task.
- Closely related to the work of Rangel, Francisco, et al. [11], profiling fake news in Tamil in twitter.
- Delving into the realm of explainable classifiers by curating a new training dataset by prompting LLM to reason out why a particular news headline in fake or real. This would be ground breaking, as it would provide an insight to how the model reasons and give support to any classification.

References

1. Mirnalinee, T. T., et al.: A novel dataset for fake news detection in tamil regional language. In: International Conference on Speech and Language Technologies for Low-resource Languages, vol. 1802, pp. 311–323. Springer, Cham (2022). https://doi.org/10.1007/978-3-031-33231-9_22
2. Ashish, V., et al.: Attention is all you need. In: Advances in Neural Information Processing Systems, vol. 30 (2017)
3. Raja, E., Soni, B., Borgohain, S.K.: Fake news detection in Dravidian languages using transfer learning with adaptive finetuning. Eng. Appl. Artif. Intell. **126**, 106877 (2023)
4. Jacob, D., et al.: Bert: Pre-training of deep bidirectional transformers for language understanding. arXiv preprint arXiv:1810.04805 (2018)
5. Molina, M.D., et al.: "Fake news" is not simply false information: A concept explication and taxonomy of online content. Am. Behav. Sci. **65**(2), 180–212 (2021)
6. Chu, S.K., Wah, R.X., Wang, Y.: Cross-language fake news detection. Data and Inf. Manage. **5**(1), 100–109 (2021)
7. Alghamdi, J., Lin, Y., Luo, S.: Towards COVID-19 fake news detection using transformer-based models. Knowl.-Based Syst. **274**, 110642 (2023)
8. Brown, T., et al.: Language models are few-shot learners. In: Advances in Neural Information Processing Systems, vol. 33, pp. 1877–1901 (2020)
9. Rathod, S.: Exploring author profiling for fake news detection. In: 2022 IEEE 46th Annual Computers, Software, and Applications Conference (COMPSAC), pp. 1614–1619. Los Alamitos, CA, USA (2022). https://doi.org/10.1109/COMPSAC54236.2022.00256
10. Sitaula, N., et al.: Credibility-based fake news detection. Disinf. Misinf. Fake News Soc. Media: Emerg. Res. Challenges Opportunities, 163–182 (2020)
11. Rangel, F., et al.: Overview of the 8th author profiling task at pan 2020: profiling fake news spreaders on twitter. In: CEUR Workshop Proceedings. vol. 2696. Sun SITE Central Europe (2020)
12. OpenAI Documentation. https://platform.openai.com/docs/guides/fine-tuning/use-a-fine-tuned-model. Accessed 17 Nov 2023
13. OpenAI API Pricing. https://openai.com/pricing. Accessed 17 Nov 2023

Bridging the Language Gap: Transformer-Based BERT for Fake News Detection in Low-Resource Settings

Rajalakshmi Sivanaiah[1]([✉]), Subhankar Suresh[1], Sushmithaa Pandian[2], and Angel Deborah Suseelan[1]

[1] Department of Computer Science and Engineering, Sri Sivasubramaniya Nadar College of Engineering, Chennai, Tamil Nadu, India
`{rajalakshmis,subhankar2110120,angeldeborahs}@ssn.edu.in`
[2] Department of Electronics and Communication Engineering, Sri Sivasubramaniya Nadar College of Engineering, Chennai, Tamil Nadu, India
`sushmithaa2110427@ssn.edu.in`

Abstract. Global rise in internet usage and access has caused fake news to become an ever spreading phenomenon. Since fake news is intended to influence public opinion, it has a significant impact on the world. False information spreading has the potential to be extremely harmful and can manipulate the public in many ways. Numerous methods for spotting fake news have been developed to stop its spread. However, it should be noted that this challenge is not only confined to widely spoken languages. Low resource languages face challenges in combating the spread of fake news due to limited semantic and computational constraints. This study demonstrates the use of various BERT models which are considered to be state-of-the-art to classify news as real or fake for a low resource language like Malay, closing the knowledge gap in fake news detection of languages with insufficient linguistics and computational resources. With the help of these experiments, we achieve maximum F1 scores of 86% for mBERT, 80% for XLnet, 87% for IndoBert, 88% for MalayBERT and 84% for mT5 respectively, suggesting their potential in addressing the challenges posed by fake news in Malay. The results of these models are compared with each other to study and draw inferences on their performances. These findings hold significant implications for the development of more robust and language-specific fake news detection systems, contributing to the overall effort to curb the spread of misinformation.

Keywords: Fake news classification · MalayBERT · Natural Language Processing · Low resource languages

1 Introduction

In an era of unprecedented global connectivity and widespread internet usage, the spread of fake news has emerged as a pressing and pervasive challenge [1].

B. R. Chakravarthi et al. (Eds.): SPELLL 2023, CCIS 2046, pp. 398–411, 2024.
https://doi.org/10.1007/978-3-031-58495-4_29

Fake news, characterized by intentionally misleading or falsified information presented as genuine news, has become a potent tool for influencing public opinion and behavior. This trend has far-reaching impacts, particularly as it undermines the public's trust in reliable sources of information and can lead to harmful actions or beliefs.

Low-resource languages, which often lack robust linguistic and computational support, are particularly vulnerable to the spread of fake news. The challenges in detecting and countering fake news in such languages are exacerbated by the scarcity of linguistic resources and computational tools [2]. Despite the gravity of the issue, there has been a notable gap in research addressing fake news detection, especially focusing on languages with limited linguistic and computational resources. Effective fake news detection presents special difficulties due to the Malay language's complexity, rich vocabulary, and nuanced contextual meanings. A trustworthy information environment is greatly aided by the ongoing study and improvements in the field of classifying fake news for the Malay language. The data shown in the findings of a survey conducted in Malaysia in February 2019 regarding the perceived frequency of "fake news" from sources the respondents knew primarily online revealed that, 68 % of Malaysian respondents claimed that the news that they got online from friends and acquaintances consisted of a fair amount of "fake news".

Efforts to combat fake news have encompassed a range of methods, from manual fact-checking to advanced computational techniques [3]. Machine learning algorithms, particularly those employing advanced natural language processing techniques, have showcased remarkable potential in fake news detection. These algorithms utilize sophisticated models, such as BERT (Bidirectional Encoder Representations from Transformers) to analyze linguistic patterns and discern authenticity in news articles. They show promise in distinguishing authentic news from fake content [19].

This research contributes to the ongoing efforts to combat fake news, placing a specific emphasis on languages with limited linguistic and computational resources. In order to contribute to the growing body of knowledge about reducing the spread of false information and improving the integrity of information dissemination in low-resource languages, this work provides a thorough analysis of our experiments and findings.

2   Related Works

Due to the spread of false information in today's digitally connected society, research on fake news detection has gathered significant traction. Work on low resource languages on fake news detection has been relatively scarce compared to the high resource languages. A study involving Indonesian news classification using IndoBert, showcasing the effectiveness of advanced language processing techniques for precise categorization in natural language processing applications for a low resource language has been portrayed in [5]. Szczepański et al. in 2021, introduced a novel explainability method tailored to BERT-based models, enhancing transparency in fake news detection. This approach improves comprehension of model decisions [6]. In their 2021 work, Kaliyar et al. introduced "FakeBERT", employing BERT-based deep learning for robust fake news detection on social media. The research underscores the effectiveness of deep learning in combating misinformation [7]. In addition to BERT, other prominent models have also been utilized in natural language processing. In their research presented at ICCICA 2021, Kumar et al. proposed a method employing XLNet fine-tuning for accurate fake news detection. The study showcases advancements in combating misinformation using advanced language models [8]. In [9], Mahajan proposed news classification utilizing machine learning methods. The study explores effective algorithms for categorizing news, contributing to advancements in automated information analysis. A diverse array of deep learning approaches has substantially propelled the domain of fake news classification. These methods, characterized by different training and architecture strategies, collectively contribute to improved accuracy and efficiency in detecting misinformation.

The scarcity of annotated data and language-specific tools hinders the development of robust fake news detection systems. Tailoring approaches to suit the linguistic nuances of low resource languages is essential, paving the way for effective identification and mitigation of fake news in diverse linguistic contexts. A thorough analysis is conducted in exploring diverse methodologies ranging from linguistic approaches to machine learning techniques in [10] and the review comprehensively addresses notable challenges such as evolving disinformation tactics and the rapid spread of misleading content. In [11], we look at a study where Rahim and Basri present "MalCov", a significant Covid-19 fake news dataset curated in the Malay language. This resource holds immense importance in driving research to counter misinformation during the pandemic effectively. The dataset is a valuable contribution to the field, aiding advancements in fake news detection and mitigation in the context of Covid-19. Nordin et al. employ deep learning to classify Malay fake news in [12]. This pioneering approach contributes to the ongoing fight against misinformation, addressing the specific linguistic nuances of the Malay language. Such studies on online fake news detection have been emphasized by researchers and have been on the verge on increase. Published in 2019, Zhang and Ghorbani present a comprehensive survey on online fake news. The study delves into its characterization, detection techniques, and insightful discussions, providing vital guidance for researchers and practitioners combating misinformation [13]. Maslej Krešňáková, Sarnovsky, and Butka delve into the realm of deep learning methods for detecting fake news in [14]. Their innovative approaches are instrumental in combating misinformation in today's digital landscape, highlighting the ongoing efforts to enhance credibility in online information. Efficient fake news detection in low resource languages remains a critical challenge. Utilizing advanced BERT models offers promise. However, further research and advancements are necessary to bridge the existing gap in linguistic and computational resources for accurate fake news detection in diverse linguistic contexts.

3   Methodology

3.1   Dataset

The motivation of a fake news detection task is to identify and distinguish fake news from real and genuine news with high correctness and accuracy. The dataset used in this work is a secondary dataset obtained from Github by Asyraf Azlan. The dataset originally contains 37,592 rows of Malay news headlines. The modified dataset taken into consideration contains 10056 rows of evenly distributed data, with 5028 rows of fake news and an equal number of 5028 rows of real news. The dataset was split into two parts, training set and testing set. 80 % of the dataset was used for training and 20% for testing respectively. The distribution of the data is shown in Table 1 and the samples of data are shown in Fig. 1.

Table 1. Dataset distribution for training and testing.

Subset	No of rows	Percentage of data (%)
Training data	8044	80
Testing data	2012	20

3.2   Model Architecture

The proposed model focuses on leveraging BERT contextual text understanding, thereby distinguishing fake news from real news. The steps involve tokenizing the input sentence and processing the tokenized sequences by a pre-trained BERT model such as mBERT or XL-Net to capture contextual data. Overfitting is reduced by using dropout layers and dense layers are added for feature extraction and pattern recognition. The output layer predicts the likelihood of the input sentence being real or fake news. Figure 2 shows the architecture of the BERT model.

Tokenization. The BERT model accepts input in the form of input IDs and attention masks derived from the input sentence [4]. To accomplish this, the BERT tokenizer is employed, which involves prepending [CLS] at the start and appending [SEP] at the end of the input sequence, resulting in the generation of input IDs and attention masks.

BERT Embeddings. BERT embeddings are created using the input IDs and input masks. The input IDs are used to look up the corresponding word embeddings from the BERT model's pretrained embeddings table. These embeddings represent the specific words or subwords in the input. The input masks help mask out irrelevant tokens so that the model doesn't waste computation on them. When an input mask is set to 0 for a particular token, BERT effectively

	news	label
0	dalam wawancara siaran pertama sejak berangkat...	1
1	1 closetspaceclosetspace adalah aplikasi mudah...	1
2	washington donald j berturut turut bertemu pad...	1
3	tidak begitu cepat mirada membuka kehamilannya...	1
4	pengiring pengantin yang paling terkenal di du...	1
...	...	...
10051	rasmi israeli diam diam melawat dubai laporan ...	0
10052	yang diposkan pada oktober 28 , 2016 oleh dmit...	0
10053	dapatkan kisah harian terbesar melalui melangg...	0
10054	kesihatan amerika semakin berkurangan di bawah...	0
10055	buletin berita iranian anak anak muda kalah ke...	0

Fig. 1. Sample image of dataset

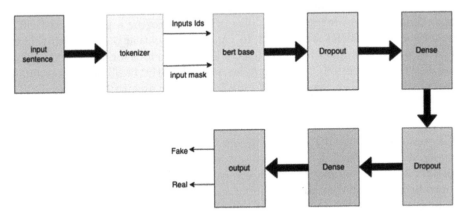

Fig. 2. Block diagram of model architecture [4]

ignores that token during processing. The input ids and attention masks are then fed into a pre-trained BERT model. The model extracts embeddings and features from BERT's output, particularly focusing on the pooler output which provides a pooled representation of the entire input sequence. These features capture the semantic and contextual information in the text, making them suitable for classification.

Dropout Layers. To mitigate overfitting, dropout layers are applied to the extracted features, randomly setting a fraction of input units to zero during training. The proposed model has a dropout rate of 0.2.

Dense Layers. The model includes dense (fully connected) layers, with ReLU activation, for further processing of the features. In the proposed architecture, there is a dense layer with 64 units, which can help the model learn complex patterns in the data.

Output Layer. The final dense layer consists of a single neuron with a sigmoid activation function for binary classification tasks. This output layer produces a classification score that indicates the likelihood of the input text belonging to one of the two classes, such as real or fake news.

3.3   Bert-Base Models

The Bidirectional Encoder Representations from Transformers (BERT) model, has drastically transformed the landscape of natural language processing (NLP). BERT, a transformer-based deep learning model with multiple transformer layers, captures comprehensive contextual information from text through intricate self-attention mechanisms [1]. The two important steps involved in building a BERT model are pertaining and fine-tuning. BERT is initially pretrained on an extensive corpus of English text, employing millions of parameters. Through transfer learning, BERT, with its substantial parameter count, is fine-tuned using labeled data specific to the language in question. This fine-tuning equips the model to discern distinct linguistic patterns and features associated with fake news within that language. Consequently, BERT's adaptability in low resource language fake news classification, thanks to its extensive parameterization, proves instrumental, contributing significantly to the ongoing global efforts to combat misinformation effectively.

This study employs the use of BERT base models, a variant of BERT which is composed of 110 million parameters. It encompasses 12 million transformer encoder layers, where each layer has a dimension of 768. The self attention mechanism of the model is distributed across 12 attention heads. Figure 3 depicts the architecture of BERT.

BERT comprises two pre-training objectives, MLM(Masked Language Model) and NSP(Next Sequence Prediction). The Masked Language Model (MLM) is a technique that revolutionized natural language processing by enabling bidirectional training. Unlike traditional models that can only operate in a left-to-right or right-to-left fashion, MLM predicts masked tokens in a text, allowing it to capture contextual information from both directions. During

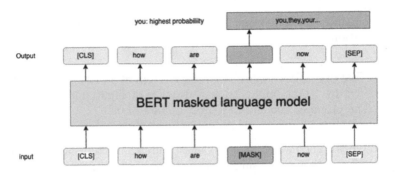

Fig. 3. BERT architecture [20]

pre-training, a portion (15%) of the input tokens is randomly masked, and the model is trained to predict these masked tokens, enhancing the model's ability to understand the meanings of words in various contexts.

Next Sentence Prediction (NSP) is a crucial component in understanding relationships between sentences, a necessity for various tasks like question answering and natural language inference. NSP involves predicting whether a pair of sentences in a text follow one another in a coherent order or not. BERT innovatively employs pre-training on a binarized NSP task, enhancing the model's grasp of these relationships.

4   Implementation

The proposed model was implemented by splitting the dataset into testing and training data. X represents the news sequences, and y denotes the output binary labels, 0 for fake news and 1 for real news. The input data is split into X_train and X_test and output labels into Y_train and Y_test for training and testing respectively. The input data is tokenized for processing. After tokenization, the tokenized input sequences and attention masks are fit as inputs for training the model. The model is then trained over 7 epochs with a batch size of 32, monitored for early stopping based on validation accuracy. Parallel processing with ten workers is employed to enhance data loading efficiency during training

This work provides a comparison between the performance of the different BERT models capable of processing and understanding the Malay news dataset. In this study, the transformer based models that have been used are:

1. mBERT (multilingual BERT)
2. XL-Net
3. IndoBERT
4. MalayBERT
5. mT5

mBERT: Multilingual BERT is a transformer based model which is pre-trained on a vast array of monolingual corpora across 104 languages [17].

mBERT's architecture embodies a revolutionary approach, showcasing its proficiency in understanding and representing a multitude of languages. What sets mBERT apart is its unique capability for zero-shot cross-lingual transfer learning, where annotations from one language guide its fine-tuning for evaluation in another. This transferability extends even to languages utilizing different scripts, underlining its versatility and potential for seamless cross-lingual understanding. Additionally, mBERT exhibits a remarkable ability to handle code-switching scenarios, a testament to its adaptability and robustness in capturing linguistic nuances, making it a suitable model to train Malay data.

XL-Net: It is an expansion of the Transformer-XL model, which is pretrained using an autoregressive approach to acquire bidirectional context understanding by optimizing the expected likelihood across all permutations of the input sequence's factorization order, proving to be highly effective in tackling fake news in the Malay language [18]. By capturing intricate dependencies and relationships between words in Malay sentences, XLNet enhances the accuracy of fake news detection. Its versatility in understanding the context of the Malay language contributes significantly to combating misinformation.

IndoBert: One of the advanced tools for using Indonesian to analyze texts is IndoBert. The architecture that has been created makes use of the English-speaking transformer model on BERT in general. Similar to BERT, this technique uses 12 attention heads and 12 hidden layers, each with a maximum dimension of 786 [5]. Although specifically designed for the Indonesian language, IndoBERT showcases promising potential for fake news detection in Malay. Given the linguistic similarities between Indonesian and Malay, IndoBERT's understanding of the Indonesian language can be transferred and adapted to Malay. This provides valuable insights into identifying fake news within the Malay linguistic context.

MalayBERT: MalayBERT is a specialized BERT model tailored to the Malay language. Pre-trained on a vast corpus of Malay text, it excels in understanding the unique linguistic nuances and context of Malay [15]. In the realm of fake news classification, MalayBERT provides a strong foundation by effectively capturing the language intricacies, aiding in precise identification and categorization of misinformation within the Malay language.

mT5: with its multilingual text-to-text framework, offers a powerful approach to fake news classification in Malay [16]. Its ability to handle diverse NLP tasks, including summarization and translation, positions mT5 as a versatile model for identifying and understanding fake news. Its adaptability to Malay allows for effective processing and analysis of misinformation in the Malay language.

5 Result and Analysis

In this section, the performance of the BERT models such as mBERT, XL-Net, IndoBERT, MalayBERT and mT5, all of which can process and comprehend the Malay language are compared and evaluated on the basis of accuracy, precision, recall and F1 score. Confusion matrix plots, accuracy graphs and loss graphs are plotted to understand the behavior and performance of the model.

Table 2. Comparison of evaluation metrics.

Model (%)	Accuracy (%)	Precision (%)	Recall (%)	F1 Score (%)
mBERT	86.48	86.48	86.48	86.48
XL-Net	78.87	76.14	84.09	79.92
IndoBERT	88.07	92.46	82.90	87.42
MalayBERT	88.07	85.07	92.34	88.56
mT5	84.39	82.76	86.87	84.77

Table 2 shows the comparison of evaluation metrics of the BERT models. It is observed that MalayBERT has the highest accuracy value of 88.07 and F1 score of 88.56 due to its specialized pre-training and fine-tuning on Malay language data which enables it to capture language intricacies and context. This is followed by IndoBERT which has an accuracy of 88.07 and F1 score of 87.42. This can be attributed to the fact that since IndoBERT is a transformer based model primarily designed for Indonesian language, it can effectively process closely related languages such as Malay.

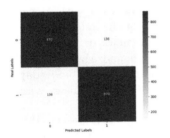

Fig. 4. Confusion matrix of mBERT   **Fig. 5.** Confusion matrix of XL-Net

A confusion matrix is used to depict the exactness of the predictions made by the model while testing the model on the testing data. It can evaluate the performance of the model by depicting true positives, true negatives, false positives and false negatives. Figure 4, Fig. 5, Fig. 6, Fig. 7 and Fig. 8 show the confusion matrix plots of mBERT, XL-Net, IndoBERT, MalayBERT and mT5 respectively. It can be observed that the sum of the true positives and true negatives is the same for MalayBERT and IndoBERT and higher compared to the other models, but MalayBERT results in more number of false positives, i.e. more number of fake news are predicted to be real and IndoBERT results in more number of false negatives, i.e. more number of real news are predicted to be false.

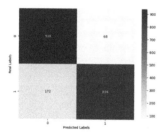

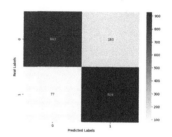

Fig. 6. Confusion matrix of IndoBERT

Fig. 7. Confusion matrix of Malay-BERT

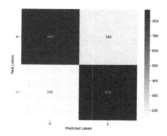

Fig. 8. Confusion matrix of mT5

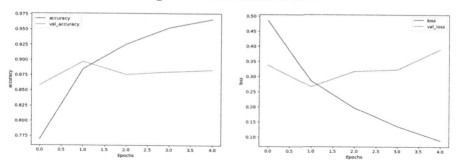

Fig. 9. Accuracy vs Epoch and Loss vs Epoch graphs of mBERT

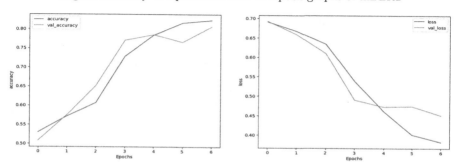

Fig. 10. Accuracy vs Epoch and Loss vs Epoch graphs of XL-Net

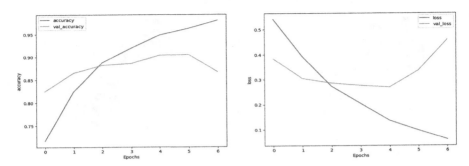

Fig. 11. Accuracy vs Epoch and Loss vs Epoch graphs of IndoBERT

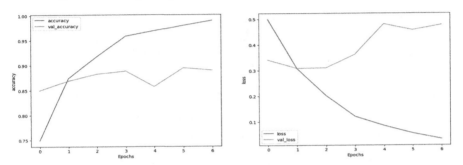

Fig. 12. Accuracy vs Epoch and Loss vs Epoch graphs of MalayBERT

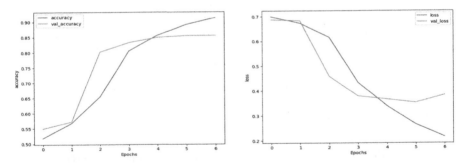

Fig. 13. Accuracy vs Epoch and Loss vs Epoch graphs of mT5

Accuracy vs Epoch and Loss vs Epoch graphs are used for understanding a model's learning progress during training and performance evaluation for detecting overfitting, tracking prediction error reduction and to prevent unnecessary model convergence. Figure 9, Fig. 10, Fig. 11, Fig. 12 and Fig. 13 show the Accuracy vs Epoch and Loss vs Epoch graphs of mBERT, XL-Net, IndoBERT, Malay-BERT and mT5 respectively.

6   Inferences

In the utilization of predefined models such as MalayBERT, IndoBert, XLNet, mT5, and mBERT for fake news detection, few limitations have been identified. These include potential biases in training data, the computational intensity associated with training and fine-tuning, and challenges in accommodating diverse linguistic structures. Moreover, issues regarding the interpretability of these models and their effectiveness across different languages have been noted. To address these shortcomings, an exploration into the integration of advanced models like GPT (Generative Pre-trained Transformer) for fake news classification is in progress. GPT's capabilities, including contextual understanding, transfer learning, and fine-tuning on domain-specific data, offer potential solutions to mitigate biases, enhance interpretability, and elevate overall performance. Our ongoing research endeavors aim to leverage the strengths of GPT to develop a more resilient and versatile solution for fake news detection, transcending the limitations posed by the aforementioned predefined models.

7   Conclusion

This study provides a comparative analysis of the performance of the different transformer based models on Malay news data. The results show that MalayBERT and IndoBERT produce the same accuracy of 88.07%, with MalayBERT having higher values of recall and F1 score of 88.56% and IndoBERT having higher precision but an F1 score of 87.42%. mBERT gives the next best results with an F1 score of 86.48% followed by mT5 with an F1 score of 84.77%. XL-Net has the least performance with an F1 score of 79.92%. This could result from the intricate model complexity of XL-Net or due to the requirement of more data. It can be concluded that MalayBERT has a better performance and produces better results compared to IndoBERT, mBERT, mT5 and XL-Net due to its Malay language specific design, enabling it to capture contextual intricacies more effectively than other transformer based models. It can be observed from the loss vs epoch graphs that all the transformer based models under consideration have less training loss but the drawback of MalayBERT is that the validation loss seems to be high compared to the other models. As a future work, the model can be extended to include more low resource languages, making it more versatile in diverse linguistic contexts.

References

1. Devlin, J., Chang, M.W., Lee, K., Toutanova, K.: BERT: pre-training of deep bidirectional transformers for language understanding. In: Proceedings of the 2019 Conference of the North American Chapter of the Association for Computational Linguistics: Human Language Technologies, Minneapolis, Minnesota, vol. 1, pp. 4171–4186. Association for Computational Linguistics (2019)

2. Gereme, F., Zhu, W., Ayall, T., Alemu, D.: Combating fake news in "low-resource" languages: Amharic fake news detection accompanied by resource crafting. Information **12**(1), 20 (2021). https://doi.org/10.3390/info12010020
3. Shu, K., Sliva, A., Wang, S., Tang, J., Liu, H.: Fake news detection on social media: a data mining perspective. ACM SIGKDD Explor. Newsl. **19** (2017). https://doi.org/10.1145/3137597.3137600
4. Rai, N., Kumar, D., Kaushik, N., Raj, C., Ali, A.: Fake news classification using transformer-based enhanced LSTM and BERT. Int. J. Cogn. Comput. Eng. **3**, 98–105 (2022)
5. Juarto, B., Yulianto: Indonesian news classification using IndoBert. Int. J. Intell. Syst. Appl. Eng. **11**(2), 454–460 (2023)
6. Sczepański, M., Pawlicki, M., Kozik, R., et al.: New explainability method for BERT-based model in fake news detection. Sci. Rep. **11**, 23705 (2021)
7. Kaliyar, R.K., Goswami, A., Narang, P.: FakeBERT: fake news detection in social media with a BERT-based deep learning approach. Multimed. Tools Appl. **80**, 11765–11788 (2021). https://doi.org/10.1007/s11042-020-10183-2
8. Kumar, J.A., Trueman, T.E., Cambria, E.: Fake news detection using XLNet fine-tuning model. In: 2021 International Conference on Computational Intelligence and Computing Applications (ICCICA), Nagpur, India, pp. 1–4 (2021). https://doi.org/10.1109/ICCICA52458.2021.9697269
9. Mahajan, S.: News classification using machine learning. Int. J. Recent Innov. Trends Comput. Commun. **9**(5), 23–27 (2021). https://doi.org/10.17762/ijritcc.v9i5.5464
10. Rani, M., Virmani, C.: Detection of fake news on social media: a review. In: Proceedings of the International Conference on Innovative Computing and Communication (ICICC) (2022). https://doi.org/10.2139/ssrn.4143832
11. Rahim, N.H.A., Basri, M.S.H.: MalCov: Covid-19 fake news dataset in the Malay language. In: 2022 International Visualization, Informatics and Technology Conference (IVIT), Kuala Lumpur, Malaysia, pp. 239–244 (2022). https://doi.org/10.1109/IVIT55443.2022.10033374
12. Nordin, W.A.F.B., Alfred, R., Yee, C.P., Tanalol, S.H., Loudin, R.V., Iswandono, Z.: Malay fake news classification using a deep learning approach. In: Kang, D.K., Alfred, R., Ismail, Z.I.B.A., Baharum, A., Thiruchelvam, V. (eds.) ICCST 2022. LNCS, vol. 983, pp. 17–32. Springer, Singapore (2023). https://doi.org/10.1007/978-981-19-8406-8_2
13. Zhang, X., Ghorbani, A.: An overview of online fake news: characterization, detection, and discussion. Information Processing and Management (2019). https://doi.org/10.1016/j.ipm.2019.03.004
14. Maslej Krešňáková, V., Sarnovsky, M., Butka, P.: Deep learning methods for fake news detection (2019). https://doi.org/10.1109/CINTI-MACRo49179.2019.9105317
15. Mohd Amin, A.F., Kamal, N.A., Shamsuddin, S., Maarof, M.A.: MalayBERT: a pre-trained language model for Malay text. arXiv preprint arXiv:2007.16060 (2020)
16. Xue, M., Ji, Y., Wei, H., Liu, X., Gao, Y., Shao, Y.: MT5: a massively multilingual pre-trained text-to-text transformer. arXiv preprint arXiv:2010.11934 (2020)
17. Pires, T., Schlinger, E., Garrette, D.: How multilingual is multilingual BERT? In: Proceedings of the 57th Annual Meeting of the Association for Computational Linguistics, Florence, Italy, pp. 4996–5001 (2019)
18. Yang, Z., Dai, Z., Yang, Y., Carbonell, J., Salakhutdinov, R., Le, Q.V.: XLNet: generalized autoregressive pre training for language understanding. arXiv preprint arXiv:1906.08237 (2019)

19. Sivanaiah, R., Ramanathan, N., Hameed, S., Rajagopalan, R., Suseelan, A.D., Thanagathai, M.T.N.: Fake news detection in low-resource languages. In: Anand Kumar, M., et al. (eds.) SPELLL 2022. CCIS, vol. 1802, pp. 324–331. Springer, Cham (2023). https://doi.org/10.1007/978-3-031-33231-9_23
20. Turing.com. https://www.turing.com/kb/how-bert-nlp-optimization-model-works. Accessed 15 Oct 2023

Optimized Latent-Dirichlet-Allocation Based Topic Modeling–An Empirical Study

P. Haritha and P. Shanmugavadivu[✉]

Department of Computer Science and Applications, Gandhigram Rural Institute (Deemed to Be University), Dindigul, India
psvadivu67@gmail.com

Abstract. Topic modeling is an unsupervised learning based mechanism used to uncover hidden topics from the voluminous corpus generated out of social media, environment, medicine and all other viable domain. It can be accomplished using a variety of topic modeling techniques based on the types of data, such as complex and short text data. In this article an improved version of LDA named as Optimized LDA (OLDA) is proposed using hyperparameter tuning in order to extract the hidden topics from the huge volume of corpus. The OLDA was trained and tested on three datasets; viz.., Newsgroup, Top Reddit Data and Upvote Data. The performance of OLDA was analyzed and validated by comparing with the existing standard methodologies namely Latent Semantic Analysis (LSA) and Probabilistic Latent Semantic Analysis (PLSA). The improved coherence score of OLDA confirms on its merits and potential in accurate and contextual topic modeling.

Keywords: Topic Modeling · Optimized Latent Dirichlet Allocation · Perplexity · Coherence Score

1 Introduction

Social media serves as a major source of text data, which have ample scope for data analytics. The data generated by the social media are made up of unstructured format on varied topics. The extraction of hidden textual patterns in such data assumes enormous importance for strategic planning, decision making and research. Topic modeling describes the process of extracting hidden topics and clustering of text data on many application domains [1, 2]. This approach plays a significant role in content analysis, despite its shortfalls such as noise sensitivity and poor optimization. It is apparent that the selection of optimal values for the hyperparameters also contribute to the degree of correctness of the models. The Latent-Dirichlet-Allocation, Correlated Topic Model and Pachinko Allocation Model have exhibited their ability on text analytics [3, 4]. It is important to note that the selection of a model should align with the scope for learning from the dataset. The approaches to be used must be chosen in accordance with the datasets available in order to extract the features from the text data. Long-term sequential data, short texts, complex structural relationship data, and other types of data can be explored by using topic modeling methodologies [5–7].

B. R. Chakravarthi et al. (Eds.): SPELLL 2023, CCIS 2046, pp. 412–419, 2024.
https://doi.org/10.1007/978-3-031-58495-4_30

2 Literature Review

Topic modeling [8], combining probabilistic latent semantic indexing and Latent-Dirichlet-Allocation [9], is confirmed to reduce the dimension of co-occurrence patterns found in the corpus, during topic extraction. LDA is typically a graphical model that is unsupervised [10] though developed as a partial supervision model for extracting topic in set knowledge. In comparison to previous approaches, it retrieves more relevant topics. [11] employed the LDA approach to analyze a huge datasets, in particular the tweets. Compared to Latent Semantic Indexing, the LDA model performs better with the accuracy of 98%. In order to mitigate the challenges of topic modeling from data collected from social networks [12–14], a data-driven OLDA model was devised.

3 Latent-Dirichlet-Allocation

It is evident that LDA is a widely used unsupervised probabilistic model for topic modeling is called Latent-Dirichlet-Allocation (LDA). In order to articulate the topics using words with a higher probabilities, Blei, Ng proposed LDA in 2003. The applications of LDA include speech recognition, face recognition, text mining, multimedia information retrieval, and many more. The fundamental purpose of LDA model is to handle the massive text documents as corpora and extract latent topics from them. The latent topic is a representation of a probabilistic distribution over words [15–19]. The inferences and generative processes are two of the processes included in LDA models. The model makes inferences based on corpus data and obtains the latent variables theta (θ) and phi (φ), which represent the word dissemination throughout the topic and the topic proportion of each document, respectively. As a generative process the model describes corpus D of M documents, k topics, and with document d consisting of N_d (d $\in$ {1,....,M}) [20–22]. The model's behavior is explained in the following generative process.

1. The symmetric Dirichlet priors on $\theta^{(d)}$ and $\varphi^{(k)}$ are fixed

$$\theta^{(d)} \sim \text{Dirichlet}(\alpha) \text{ and } \varphi^{(k)} \sim \text{Dirichlet}(\beta)$$

   where α and β are the LDA's hyperparameter
2. Extract the following
   a) Z_n from $\theta^{(d)}$
   b) w_n from φz_n

where z_n and w_n where(n $\in$ {1,...,N_d}) represents topic and word in the document.
   As per the aforementioned expressions and notations words are considered as observable factors whereas the other terms are the hidden factors (φ and θ) and the hyperparameters are (α and β). Equation (1) describes the computation of probability of observed data D for a given corpus.

$$p(D|\alpha, \beta) = \prod_{d=1}^{M} \int p(\theta_d|\alpha) \left(\prod_{n=1}^{N_d} \sum_{Z_{dn}} p(z_{dn}|\theta_d)p(w_{dn}|z_{dn}, \beta) \right) d\theta_d \quad (1)$$

The pair of Dirichlet-Multinomials for the topic distributions at the corpus level is denoted as (α,). The topic-word distributions namely Dirichlet-multinomial pair is denoted by (β, φ). The factors namely θ_d, z_{dn} and w_{dn} are sampled based on the document and word. It perform the probability based computation. Figure 1 depicts the LDA model along with related details.

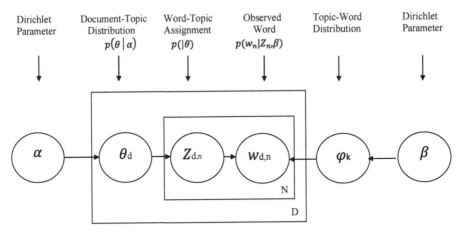

| Dirichlet Parameter | Document-Topic Distribution $p(\theta \mid \alpha)$ | Word-Topic Assignment $p(\mid\theta)$ | Observed Word $p(w_n \mid Z_n,\beta)$ | Topic-Word Distribution | Dirichlet Parameter |

Fig. 1. Latent-Dirichlet-Allocation Model

LDA is a prominent model for the distribution of latent topics throughout a large corpus. To find the hidden topics, LDA gathers words from the documents to build a dictionary and then the hidden topics are extracted based on probabilistic distribution of words in the documents. After the completion of computation by Eq. (1), the words are viewed as a probabilistic occurrence of topics.

4 Preprocessing

Initially, the document was preprocessed separately in order to make the dataset free from outliers, abnormalities and irrelevant values. The following preprocessing approaches are performed on the datasets:

- Removal of Emails
- Elimination of Quotes
- Removal of Newline characters
- Generation of Bigram, Trigram and Lemmatization
- Pass the document to the Python's spacy library to remove unwanted tags
- Stop words are removed

5 Experimental Study

This research work aims to improving the performance of LDA through optimized hyper-parameter tuning. The resultant proposed method is termed as Optimized LDA (OLDA). The proposed work was designed to appraise the performance of OLDA model on three different datasets, newsgroups (https://raw.githubusercontent.com/selva86/datasets/mas

ter/newsgroups), top Reddit data (https://github.com/melaniewalsh/Intro-Cultural-Ana lytics/tree/master/book), and most popular Upvote data in Kaggle dataset (https://www. kaggle.com). The datasets are in the json format and comma separated file types arranged in rows and columns. Table 1 lists the outcomes after fine-tuning the hyperparameters α *and* β. The datasets are evaluated with the performance metrics namely perplexity and coherence [23–26] with the Eq. (2) and (3).

$$perplexity(D_{test}) = exp\left\{ \frac{-\sum_{d=1}^{M} logp(w_d)}{\sum_{d=1}^{M} N_d} \right\} \qquad (2)$$

where N_d is the number of words in document d, w_d is the order of observable words in document d, and D is the test set. Perplexity is a loglikelihood-based generative probability of unseen documents. The lower perplexity value leads to better performance of topic extraction.

The coherence score computes a paired score for each of the chosen words as well as the frequency of terms in each topic. The analysis uses both the coherence measure as CV, an automatic coherence measure that rates topics and computes the pointwise mutual information by Eq. (3).

$$PMIw_i, w_j = log \frac{Pw_i, w_j + \varepsilon}{Pw_i Pw_j} \qquad (3)$$

where Pw_i is the probability of word w_i in the sliding window and $Pw_i \, w_j$ is the probability of words in the sliding window. The coherence score is obtained by integrating it with pointwise mutual information.

Table 1. Fine-Tuning of Hyperparameters

α	β	Perplexity	Coherence
0.25	0.25	−8.46066213178327	0.4719265757002939
12.5	0.01	−76.9435367572183	0.4033711139640432
1.5	1.0	−8.45187294801185	0.5198371176838652
Symmetric	**1.0**	**−8.42505465995855**	**0.5370120751993218**
Symmetric	0.01	−76.7941639137765	0.3750580413390802
Symmetric	0.25	−8.46066213178327	0.4719265757002939
Symmetric	None	−8.46066213178327	0.4719265757002939
None	1.0	−8.42505465995855	0.5370120751993218
Auto	1.0	−8.41387191317805	0.5370120751993218
Auto	0.01	−76.7871974895529	0.3800360196760847
Auto	0.25	−8.46100172429196	0.4707071513064357

(*continued*)

Table 1. *(continued)*

α	β	Perplexity	Coherence
Dataset: Top Reddit data			
0.25	0.25	−7.72667677356965	0.3154029558301849
12.5	0.01	−50.7542009278595	0.3555048496146046
1.5	1.0	−7.68945199537930	0.4060907077646541
Symmetric	**1.0**	**−7.64742879078736**	**0.4385852909591938**
Symmetric	0.01	−50.5179677860246	0.3639139596073719
Symmetric	0.25	−7.72667677356965	0.3154029558301849
Symmetric	None	−7.72667677356965	0.3154029558301849
None	1.0	−7.64742879078736	0.4385852909591938
Auto	1.0	−7.62368029545074	0.4434305302772894
Auto	0.01	−50.4589020437189	0.3554216309420765
Auto	0.25	−7.71489916704533	0.3179038917271452
Dataset: Upvote Data			
0.25	0.25	−8.73001903738737	0.4318834162117086
12.5	0.01	−59.1669714899185	0.3794743899273327
1.5	1.0	−8.46741347922796	0.448665690135691
Symmetric	**1.0**	**−8.41178789832425**	**0.4606418720654208**
Symmetric	0.01	−59.1075540422146	0.3530206111111194
Symmetric	0.25	−8.73001903738737	0.4318834162117086
Symmetric	None	−8.73001903738737	0.4318834162117086
None	1.0	−8.41178789832425	0.4606418720654208
Auto	1.0	−8.37216016813814	0.4469010536656387
Auto	0.01	−59.0800026110892	0.3468964479901687
Auto	0.25	−8.72916906959182	0.4460275826495719

As reported in the literature, experimentation on fixation of optimal values of the hyperparameters of LDA is a worthy exercise in fine-tuning the performance of OLDA. Accordingly, based on the numbers of designated number of topics (k), the α and β values are computed as a fractional value, computed as (1/k). For, k = 4, the α and β assume their values as 0.25. Besides, as per the inferences of the literature, the α and β values were given as (50/k) and 0.01, respectively [27, 28]. Further the default values of LDA model as prescribed in the Python gensim package are symmetric and auto.For the values of (α,β) as (1.5,1.0) the OLDA produces undesirable results.It is observed that the least values of perplexity and maximum values of coherence measure was obtained for the (α,β) as (Symmetric,1.0).

6 Comparative Analysis of Topic Modelling Techniques

Latent Semantic Analysis (LSA), Probabilistic Latent Semantic Analysis (PLSA), and Latent Dirichlet Allocation (LDA) are the most often used approaches used for topic modelling. The texts are transformed into vector representation, and the less significant parts are removed using Singular Value Decomposition (SVD). The LSA procedure demands more computation time and exhibits poor dimensionality reduction. PLSA addresses the shortcomings of LSA by identifying the latent themes using conditional probability, instead of SVD. The PLSA groups words with similar topics based on the statistical principle and also resolves the contextual ambiguity among the words with same semantics. OLDA aims to increase the models' accuracy in capturing the versatility of documents and words. The documents are analyzed with regard to the subjects, and the topics are recommended using the probabilistic distribution of words that are similar [29, 30].The article examined the OLDA procedure and contrasted it with conventional methods, namely LSA and PLSA. It is apparent that, the coherence score of the OLDA model is observed to be higher, compared to its competitive models. Table 2 shows a crispy comparison of those methods chosen for analysis.

Table 2. Comparative Analysis of Chosen Techniques

Topic Modelling Techniques	Coherence Score
Dataset: Newsgroup	
Latent Semantic Analysis (LSA)	0.4765321625859511
Probabilistic Latent Semantic Analysis (PLSA)	0.4155688892293221
Optimized Latent Dirichlet Allocation (OLDA)	**0.5370120751993218**
Dataset: Top Reddit	
Latent Semantic Analysis (LSA)	0.3029230988993531
Probabilistic Latent Semantic Analysis (PLSA)	0.2989471442941068
Optimized Latent Dirichlet Allocation (OLDA)	**0.4385852909591938**
Dataset: Upvote	
Latent Semantic Analysis (LSA)	0.48325240042138945
Probabilistic Latent Semantic Analysis (PLSA)	0.3851639789835011
Optimized Latent Dirichlet Allocation (OLDA)	0.4606418720654208

This Table indicates that OLDA provides a higher score than the other approaches for the Newsgroup and Top Reddit datasets. Moreover, LDA can locate latent subjects in voluminous documents. Nevertheless, the approach is not promising on the identification of topic correlations.

7 Conclusion

This article reports on the evaluation of the influences on the hyperparameters of OLDA and its outcomes. The hyperparameters α and β are the key factors that determine the performance of OLDA. During the experimentation, various confirmations of α and βvalues were, chosen in the process of assessment. It was confirmed that, as per the results obtained for the performance metrics namely perplexity and coherence, the optimal values of α and β are concluded as symmetric and 1.0 respectively. This research work possess ample of scope to improve the performance of OLDA with respect to the additional parameters namely number of topics, random state, passes and iterations. The incorporation of optimal values of these parameters is expected to improve the performance precision of topic modeling using OLDA. The inferences drawn from this study suggest that the exploration and optimization of alternative topic modelling techniques such as the Pachinko Allocation Model and the Correlated Topic Model. On the real-time datasets may provide newer insights into this research domain.

Acknowledgement. This research work was supported by UGC-National Fellowship for Other Backward Classes and the authors thank DST-FIST for the computing lab facility.

References

1. Blei, D.M.: Probabilistic topic models. Commun. ACM. ACM **55**(4), 77–84 (2012)
2. Liu, L., Tang, L., Dong, W., Yao, S., Zhou, W.: An overview of topic modeling and its current applications in bioinformatics. Springerplus **5**(1), 1–22 (2016)
3. Hong, L., Davison, B.D.: Empirical study of topic modeling in Twitter. In: Proceedings of the First Workshop on Social Media Analytics (2010)
4. Girdhar, Y., Giguère, P., Dudek, G.: Autonomous adaptive underwater exploration using online topic modeling. In: Desai, J., Dudek, G., Khatib, O., Kumar, V. (eds.) Experimental Robotics. Springer Tracts in Advanced Robotics, vol. 88, pp. 789–802. Springer, Heidelberg (2013). https://doi.org/10.1007/978-3-319-00065-7_53
5. Agrawal, A., Fu, W., Menzies, T.: What is wrong with topic modeling? And how to fix it using search-based software engineering. Inf. Softw. Technol.Softw. Technol. **98**, 74–88 (2018)
6. Blei, D., Lafferty, J.: Correlated topic models. Adv. Neural. Inf. Process. Syst. **18**, 147 (2006)
7. Yan, X., Guo, J., Lan, Y., Cheng, X.: A biterm topic model for short texts. In: Proceedings of the 22nd International Conference on World Wide Web (2013)
8. Crain, S.P., Zhou, K., Yang, S.-H., Zha, H.: Dimensionality reduction and topic modeling: From latent semantic indexing to Latent-Dirichlet-Allocation and beyond. In: Aggarwal, C., Zhai, C. (eds.) Mining Text Data, pp. 129–161. Springer, Boston (2012). https://doi.org/10.1007/978-1-4614-3223-4_5
9. Schwarz, C.: Ldagibbs: a command for topic modeling in Stata using latent-Dirichlet-allocation. Stata J. **18**(1), 101–117 (2018)
10. Andrzejewski, D., Zhu, X.: Latent-Dirichlet-Allocation with topic-in-set knowledge. In: Proceedings of the NAACL HLT 2009 Workshop on Semi-Supervised Learning for Natural Language Processing - SemiSupLearn 2009 (2009)
11. Negara, E.S., Triadi, D., Andryani, R.: Topic modelling twitter data with Latent-Dirichlet-Allocation method. In: 2019 International Conference on Electrical Engineering and Computer Science (ICECOS) (2019)

12. Ostrowski, D.A.: Using Latent-Dirichlet-allocation for topic modelling in twitter. In: Proceedings of the 2015 IEEE 9th International Conference on Semantic Computing (IEEE ICSC 2015) (2015)
13. Hidayatullah, A.F., Ma'arif, M.R.: Road traffic topic modeling on Twitter using Latent-Dirichlet-allocation. In: 2017 International Conference on Sustainable Information Engineering and Technology (SIET) (2017)
14. Wang, Y., Taylor, J.E.: DUET: data-driven approach based on Latent-Dirichlet-allocation topic modeling. J. Comput. Civ. Eng.Comput. Civ. Eng. 33(3), 04019023 (2019)
15. Blei, D.M., Ng, A.Y., Jordan, M.I.: Latent dirichlet allocation. J. Mach. Learn. Res. 3, 993–1022 (2003)
16. Yu, H., Yang, J.: A direct LDA algorithm for high-dimensional data — with application to face recognition. Pattern Recogn.Recogn. 34(10), 2067–2070 (2001)
17. Ponweiser, M.: LatentDirichlet allocation in R (2012)
18. Hasan, M., Rahman, A., Karim, M.R., Khan, M.S.I., Islam, M.J.: Normalized approach to find optimal number of topics in latent Dirichlet allocation (LDA). In: Kaiser, M.S., Bandyopadhyay, A., Mahmud, M., Ray, K. (eds.) Proceedings of International Conference on Trends in Computational and Cognitive Engineering. AISC, vol. 1309, pp. 341–354. Springer, Singapore (2021). https://doi.org/10.1007/978-981-33-4673-4_27
19. Jelodar, H., et al.: Latent-Dirichlet-allocation (LDA) and topic modeling: models, applications, a survey. Multimedia. Tools Appl. 78(11), 15169–15211 (2019)
20. Putri, I.R., Kusumaningrum, R.: Latent-Dirichlet-allocation (LDA) for sentiment analysis toward tourism review in Indonesia. J. Phys. Conf. Ser. 801, 012073 (2017)
21. Canini, K., Shi, L., Griffiths, T.: Online inference of topics with latent-Dirichlet-allocation. In: Proceedings of the Twelth International Conference on Artificial Intelligence and Statistics, 16--18 Apr 2009, vol. 5, pp. 65–72 (2009)
22. Wei, X., Croft, W.B.: LDA-based document models for ad-hoc retrieval. In: Proceedings of the 29th Annual International ACM SIGIR Conference on Research and Development in Information Retrieval (2006)
23. Pinto Gurdiel, L., Morales Mediano, J., Cifuentes Quintero, J.A.: A comparison study between coherence and perplexity for determining the number of topics in practitioners interviews analysis (2021)
24. Ray, S.K., Ahmad, A., Kumar, C.A.: Review and implementation of topic modeling in Hindi. Appl. Artif. Intell.Artif. Intell. 33(11), 979–1007 (2019)
25. Gan, J., Qi, Y.: Selection of the optimal number of topics for LDA topic model—taking patent policy analysis as an example. Entropy (Basel) 23(10), 1301 (2021)
26. Wang, H., Wang, J., Zhang, Y., Wang, M., Mao, C.: Optimization of topic recognition model for news texts based on LDA. J. Digit. Inf. Manag. 17(5), 257 (2019)
27. Porter, K.: Analyzing the DarkNetMarketssubreddit for evolutions of tools and trends using LDA topic modeling. Digit. Investig.Investig. 26, S87–S97 (2018)
28. Vayansky, I., Kumar, S.A.P.: A review of topic modeling methods. Inf. Syst. 94(101582), 101582 (2020)
29. Alghamdi, R., Alfalqi, K.: A survey of topic modeling in text mining. Int. J. Adv. Comput. Sci. Appl. IJACSA, 6(1) (2015). https://doi.org/10.14569/ijacsa.2015.060121
30. Miller, T.: Essay assessment with latent semantic analysis. J. Educ. Comput. Res. 29(4), 495–512 (2003). https://doi.org/10.2190/w5ar-dypw-40kx-fl99

Gender Recognition Using ANN and Forward Rajan Transform Inclusive of Transgender Identity

K. Priya[1]([✉]), S. Mohamed Mansoor Roomi[1], P. Uma Maheswari[2], and Faazelah Mohamed Farook[1]

[1] ECE, Thiagarajar College of Engineering, Madurai, India
priya5586@gmail.com, smmroomi@tce.edu,
faazelah@student.tce.edu
[2] ECE, Velammal College of Engineering and Technology, Madurai, India

Abstract. Low-resource languages are at risk of extinction due to factors like globalization and the dominance of widely spoken languages. Creating a comprehensive low-resource language dataset for gender recognition from marginalized communities is imperative to ensure fairness, equality, and unbiased representation in gender recognition technology. It also aids equitable representation of gender identities and linguistic diversity. The proposed work addresses the low-resource language dataset collected from the transgender community. This work comprises dataset creation of three classes such as male, female, and transgender, pre-processing, Forward Rajan Transform (FRT) feature extraction, and ANN classification for gender recognition. The performance of the proposed model compared with other ANN models and the proposed model provided a superior accuracy of 96.4%. The experimental results show the efficacy of the proposed model compared with SOTA approaches.

Keywords: Low Resource Language · Gender Recognition · Transgender · Forward Rajan Transform · Artificial Neural Network

1 Introduction

Low-resource languages, commonly referred to as minority or under-resourced languages, are those that have few linguistic resources, such as dictionaries, grammatical analyses, and text databases and are spoken by comparatively small populations. Due to several circumstances, including globalization, growing population, and the dominance of more commonly spoken languages, these languages are in imminent danger of becoming extinct or being endangered. Due to their scarcity in digital and written formats, languages with limited resources encounter difficulties concerning documentation, preservation, and access to education and technology. Through different initiatives, including the creation of linguistic resources, the development of language learning materials, and the use of digital tools for language preservation, linguists and language lovers are attempting to document and preserve these languages. Low-resource languages can provide valuable insights and contribute to more accurate and inclusive gender recognition systems. These languages, often overlooked in technology development, offer a unique perspective due to their distinct linguistic characteristics and cultural nuances. Incorporating low-resource languages into gender recognition technology development not only improves the accuracy and inclusivity of these technologies but also promotes a more equitable representation of gender identities and linguistic diversity.

2 Literature Survey

The existing image-dependent gender recognition research mainly focuses on machine and deep learning paradigms. In machine learning approaches, the features are considered geometric and appearance-based features. In the geometric-based approaches, the features of the whole face or face parts such as eyes, nose, mouth, etc., have been extracted for the classification. Brunell et al. presented a gender recognition model by estimating the distance between the two eyes, eyes to nose tip, nose tip width, and their ratio [1]. M. V. M. Cirne et al. proposed a system using geometric descriptors from predefined face shapes [2]. In appearance-based approaches, some operations or transformations are applied to the pixels in an image. Zhiguang Yang et al. developed a gender recognition model by extracting the LBP features and classifying them by the Adaboost algorithm [3]. Caifeng Shan et al. [4] developed a model by using boosted LBP for the detection of the facial region and classified them by SVM to determine the gender on the Labelled Faces in the Wild (LFW) Database. Bhagyalaxmi Jena et al. [5] presented a model using acoustic features such as Mean and Std of frequency and classified these fused features by SVM. The set of acoustic features is classified by stacked model SVM, Random Forest, and XGBoost in [6]. The same set of acoustic features was used in the gradient-boosting model for gender recognition by Sivasankar et al. [7].

There are many pre-trained deep learning architectures such as VGG19, ResNet, etc., employed in image-based gender recognition systems. The merits of using deep-learned features are they automatically generate features and classify these features themselves. Also, it is capable of providing significant features to avoid the static nature of other feature extraction. Amit Dhomne et al. [8] proposed a transfer learning approach for gender recognition using the VGG pre-trained model. Serna et al. presented a pre-trained model VGG and Resnet and investigated how biasing affected the recognition accuracy [9]. Sumi T.R [10] presented their own Convolutional Neural Network (CNN) model for gender recognition using different optimizers and k-fold validation. Gender Recognition based on voice can be achieved through extracting either acoustic or deep learning features. For a robust gender detection system, researchers are trying to find the most significant features. The important acoustic features that are employed in gender recognition systems are fundamental frequency f0 (pitch), resonance, intensity, etc.,

Archana et al. [11] developed a model by ANN using a real-time gender database. This work used acoustic features such as MFCC, Entropy, and Frame Energy for classification. MFCC with the combination of other cepstral features like Delta MFCC, formant, and pitch were used in [12] for the gender recognition algorithm. Nowadays DNN is used for gender recognition algorithms to improve recognition accuracy.

Deep learning classifiers like CNN, Multi-Layer Perceptron (MLP), Recurrent Neural Networks (RNN), and Long Short-Term Memory (LSTM) were frequently used in gender recognition. D. Kwasny et al. [13] presented x vector-based DNN. This system predicted the age and gender of the speech. In the work [14], a set of acoustic features was extracted and fed to the CNN model for gender recognition. To ensure adequate representation in the technology of gender recognition, it is extremely important to create a comprehensive, in-depth dataset for gender identification across marginalized regions. The proposed technology creates a gender recognition model that prioritizes fair representation and inclusivity by incorporating low-resource languages from marginalized communities (Transgender). By integrating languages that are frequently ignored, this model attempts to address the biases and inequities that currently exist in gender recognition technology. Achieving accurate results in this research using low-resource language has profound implications for social and cultural studies, language documentation, data collection, and linguistic analysis in the context of gender recognition. The development of such a dataset aims to address the existing biases and limitations that often result from using high-resource languages for gender recognition models. A diverse dataset encompassing low-resource languages offers a balanced view of gender expression across various linguistic and cultural contexts.

The significant contributions of the proposed works are

- Proposal of a gender recognition model with fair representation and inclusion of low-resource language from a marginalized community.
- Proposal of the gender recognition system based on Rajan Transform and Artificial Neural Network (ANN).
- Empirical verification of the proposed method with other training functions of ANN models and state-of-the-art methods.

3   Proposed Methodology

The process flow of the proposed methodology is shown in Fig. 1. The preprocessing steps in the proposed method are intended to improve the quality and applicability of audio data for further analysis in gender recognition. The process begins with silence removal, where periods of inactive audio below a certain threshold are identified and removed as represented in Eqs. 1 and 2. It helps to eliminate irrelevant background noise and enhances the accuracy of subsequent processing.

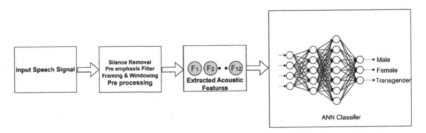

Fig. 1. Flow of proposed methodology

Following silence removal, a pre-emphasis filter is applied to the audio signal as represented in Eq. 3. This filter serves to boost higher-frequency components, effectively compensating for the attenuation that occurs during recording and transmission. By emphasizing these higher frequencies, the overall signal clarity is improved, leading to better performance in downstream tasks.

$$E = \frac{1}{N} \sum_{n=1}^{N} |I(n)|^2 \tag{1}$$

$$C_S = \frac{\sum_{k=1}^{K} (k+1)I(k)}{\sum_{k=1}^{K} I(k)} \tag{2}$$

$$p(n) = \widehat{I}(n) - \alpha \widehat{I}(n-1) \; 0 < \alpha < 1 \tag{3}$$

Subsequently, the audio stream is divided into smaller segments called frames, typically spanning around 20 to 30 ms as represented in Eq. 4. This framing step allows for the analysis of short-time variations in the signal, which is essential for capturing the dynamic nature of sound, especially in speech. Each frame is then multiplied with a Hamming window function as represented in Eq. 5. This windowing process reduces the discontinuities at the frame edges, reducing spectral leakage and enhancing the accuracy of subsequent frequency domain analysis through techniques like the Forward Rajan Transform (FRT).

$$s(n) = \{s_1|s_2|s_3....s_n\} \tag{4}$$

$$S_w(n) = s(n) * w(n) \; where \; n = 1, 2.....N_f \tag{5}$$

$$w(n) = \begin{cases} 0.54 - 0.46\cos\left(\frac{2\pi n}{N-1}\right), & 0 \leq n \leq N-1 \\ 0 & otherwise \end{cases} \tag{6}$$

The feature extracted by FRT from the windowed signal provided a compact representation. Decimation in Time Fast Fourier Transform (DIF-FFT) was employed in FRT and it creates an output sequence with key values as represented in Eq. 7. The first value of FRT is called as Cumulative Point Index (CPI) and it is taken as a feature vector as represented in Eq. 8.

$$FRT = R_D \times (S_w)_{D \times 1} \tag{7}$$

$$\text{Where } R_D = \begin{bmatrix} I_{\frac{D}{2}} & I_{\frac{D}{2}} \\ -e_k I_{\frac{D}{2}} & e_k I_{\frac{D}{2}} \end{bmatrix}_{D \times D} and$$

$$e_k = \begin{cases} -1; where \; k = 1 \; for \; S_w\left(n + \frac{D}{2}\right) & < S_w(n) \\ 0; & otherwise \end{cases}$$

ID/2 the identity matrix. e_k is the key matrix of the Rajan transform.

$$FRT = \{C_1, C_2, \ldots .. C_D\} \tag{8}$$

Then the extracted FRT feature vectors are classified by ANN. A complex machine learning classifier tool uses ANN as one of its components to find extensive non-linear connections between fused FRT information. Different Multilayer Perceptron (MLP) NN models are available for classification problems. The proposed gender recognition model used multilayer feed-forward NN with Bayesian regularisation (BR) training function. The number of hidden layers and neurons in each layer must be chosen through a process of trial and error to increase classification accuracy. The number of hidden layers and particular neurons are chosen, and then the fused spectral features are applied to the NN as represented in Eq. 9.

$$net_j^h = \sum_{i=1}^{N} W_{ji}^h FRT_i + b_j^h \tag{9}$$

Where W and b are the weightage matrix and bias respectively. The network is trained until each input vector's E p (Eq. 10) error becomes minimized.

$$E_p = \frac{1}{2} \sum_{k=1}^{M} \delta_k^2 \tag{10}$$

4   Results and Discussions

The experimental results of the proposed work have been discussed in this section. A total of 70% of the collected speech data is utilized for training, 15% for validation, and the remaining portion for testing. The speech signal is pre-processed for the RT feature extraction. In the pre-processing stage, the speech signal is silence removed and pre-emphasized. Then the signal is applied for the framing and windowing process. After the pre-processing stage, the RT features are extracted and classified these features by ANN with the BR function as listed in Table 1. The MLP NN was trained using the training function for 1000 epochs, taking 1.25 s, for 20 hidden layers, as illustrated in Fig. 2 and stated in Table 2.

Table 1. Network Modelling Parameters

Training Algorithm	Transfer Function	Network Structure	Training Data	Verifying Data	Testing Data
MLP	Bayesian Regularization	147 - 20 – 2	3616*147	1552*147	1552*147

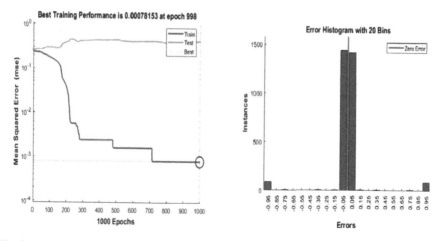

Fig. 2. Training performance of MLP-NN-BR **Fig. 3.** Error histogram of proposed MLP-NN-BR

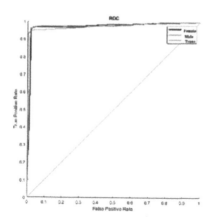

Fig. 4. ROC of MLP-NN-BR

Table 2. Training Parameters

Training Algorithm	No. of hidden layers	Epoch	Performance	Training Time(s)	Accuracy (%)
MLP-BR	20	100	0.000781	300	99

The analysis of the histogram provided the error distributions based on the final ANN predictions. Errors gradually start to disappear as one moves away from the zeroth position, where they are most common. As shown in Fig. 3, this illustrates that the ANN completes the forecast with acceptable error distributions.

The efficacy of the ANN's classification is evaluated using the Receiver Operating Characteristics (ROC) curve. The proposed method's AUC is 99%, as shown in Fig. 4. The performance of the proposed ANN classifier can be evaluated using performance metrics such as precision, recall, F1 score, and accuracy. The precision of the proposed model is highest for the male class and recall for the female class. The overall accuracy of the model is 96.4% as listed in Table 3.

Table 3. Performance classification of the proposed model

Database	Class	Precision %	Recall %	F1 Score (%)	Accuracy (%)
Local Data	Female	97	96.8	96.8	96.4
	Male	97.5	95.5	96.4	
	Transgender	94.8	96.4	95.6	

The performance of the proposed model was evaluated by various MLP ANN models such as cascade net, feed-forward net, and pattern net as listed in Table 4. Pattern Net with BR training function provided better classification compared to other ANN models. Table 5 displays the comparison outcomes for gender recognition when using various ANN training functions of the proposed pattern Net. Among these training functions the proposed BR training function achieved the highest training and testing accuracy.

Table 4. Performance evaluation of the proposed model in comparison with various ANN Models

Database	ANN Models	Training Function	Training Accuracy	Testing Accuracy
Local Data	Cascade	Levenberg Marquardit	75.52	73.5
	Feed ForwardNet	Levenberg Marquardit	76.2	74.2
	Pattern Net	Levenberg Marquardit	79.2	77.5

Table 5. Performance comparison of the proposed model with various training functions

Pattern Net-Training Function	Testing Accuracy	Testing Accuracy
Levenberg Marquardit	79.2	77.5
Scaled Conjugate Gradient	80.9	78.5
Polak-Ribiere Conjugate	82.4	78.23
Conjugate Gradient with Powell/Beale Restarts	81.7	80.9
BFGS Quasi-Newton	82.3	85.4
Fletcher Powell Conjugate Gradient	85.4	89.2
Proposed BR	93.2	96.4

The performance of the proposed gender recognition model compared with existing gender recognition algorithms is listed in Table 6. The existing algorithms provided gender recognition accuracy up to 91.6%. Among these algorithms, the proposed model provided better recognition accuracy of 96.4%.

Table 6. Performance of the proposed method against state of art methods

Reference	Database /class	Features	Classifier	Accuracy (%)
Archana et al. (2015) [15]	Real-Time Audio Dataset/ 2	MFCC + Entropy + Frame Energy	ANN	80.40
Bhagyalaxmi Jena et al. (2021) [16]	Local data (300M and 300F)/2	Mean and Std of frequency	SVM	87.5
Shivangee Kushwah et al. (2019) [17]	Data-3000 voice samples/2	Set of 20 acoustic features	Stacked mode-SVM, Random Forest, and XGBoost	88
R.Shiva Shankar et al. (2020) [18]	Voice Dataset (3000 samples)/ 2	Set of 20 acoustic features	Gradient boosting	90
Assim Ara Abdulsatar et al. (2019) [19]	Local data (40 Speech Samples)/ 2	MFCC + Formant	KNN	91.6
Proposed	Local dataset /3	RT	ANN	96.4

5   Conclusions

The proposed methodology encompasses a comprehensive workflow involving dataset creation, pre-processing, FRT feature extraction, and classification by ANN for gender recognition. Through performance comparison with other ANN models and existing methods, the proposed model emerges as the superior choice, achieving a better gender accuracy of 96.4%. This compellingly suggests that the proposed model holds promise in tackling the challenges stemming from low-resource languages, while simultaneously advancing the domain of gender recognition technology with heightened precision and inclusiveness.

References

1. Brunelli, R., Poggio, T.: Hybrid networks for gender classification. In: Proceedings of the DARPA Image Understanding Workshop, pp. 311–314 (1992)
2. Cirne, M.V.M., Pedrini, H.: Gender recognition from face images using a geometric descriptor. In: 2017 IEEE International Conference on Systems, Man, and Cybernetics (SMC), Banff, AB, Canada, pp. 2006–2011 (2017). https://doi.org/10.1109/SMC.2017.8122913
3. Yang, Z., Ai, H.: Demographic classification with local binary patterns. In: Lee, S.-W., Li, S.Z. (eds.) ICB 2007. LNCS, vol. 4642, pp. 464–473. Springer, Heidelberg (2007). https://doi.org/10.1007/978-3-540-74549-5_49
4. Shan, C.: Gender classification on real-life faces. In: Blanc-Talon, J., Bone, D., Philips, W., Popescu, D., Scheunders, P. (eds.) ACIVS 2010. LNCS, vol. 6475, pp. 323–331. Springer, Heidelberg (2010). https://doi.org/10.1007/978-3-642-17691-3_30
5. Jena, B., Mohanty, A., Mohanty, S.K.: Gender recognition and classification of speech signal. In: International Conference on Smart Data Intelligence (2021). https://ssrn.com/abstract=3852607
6. Kushwah, S., Singh, S., Vats, K., Nemade, V.: Gender identification via voice analysis. Int. J. Sci. Res. Comput. Sci. Eng. Inf. Technol. 5(2) (2019). © 2019 IJSRCSEIT ISSN : 2456–3307, https://doi.org/10.32628/CSEIT1952188
7. Shiva Shankar, R., Raghaveni, J., Rudraraju, P., Vineela Sravya, Y.: Classification of gender by voice recognition using machine learning algorithm. Int. J. Adv. Sci. Technol **29**(6), 8083–8098 (2020)
8. Dhomne, A., Kumar, R., Bhan, V.: Gender recognition through face using deep learning. Procedia Comput. Sci.. **132**, 2–10 (2018). https://doi.org/10.1016/j.procs.2018.05.053
9. Serna, I., Pe˜na, A., Morales, A., Fierrez, J.: InsideBias: measuring bias in deep networks and application to face gender biometrics. In: 2020 25th International Conference on Pattern Recognition (ICPR), pp. 3720–3727. IEEE (2021)
10. Sumi, T.A., Hossain, M.S., Islam, R.U., Andersson, K.: Human gender detection from facial images using convolution neural network. In: Mahmud, M., Kaiser, M.S., Kasabov, N., Iftekharuddin, K., Zhong, N. (eds.) AII 2021. CCIS, vol. 1435, pp. 188–203. Springer, Cham (2021). https://doi.org/10.1007/978-3-030-82269-9_15
11. Archana, G.S. Malleshwari, M.: Gender identification and performance analysis of speech signals. In: 2015 Global Conference on Communication Technologies (GCCT), pp. 483–489 (2015). https://doi.org/10.1109/GCCT.2015.7342709
12. Abdulsatar, A.A., Davydov, V.V., Yushkova, V.V., Glinushkin, A.P., Rud, V.Y.: Age and gender recognition from speech signals. In: SPbOPEN 2019, Journal of Physics: Conference Series, IOP Publishing, vol. 1410, no. 1, p. 012073 (2019). https://doi.org/10.1088/1742-6596/1410/1/012073
13. Kwasny, D., Hemmerling, D.: Joint Gender And Age Estimation Based On Speech Signals Using X-Vectors And Transfer Learning. arXiv:2012.01551v1 [eess.AS] Accessed 2 Dec 2020
14. Jasuja, L., Rasool, A., Hajela, G.: Voice gender recognizer, recognition of gender from voice using deep neural networks. In: Proceedings of the International Conference on Smart Electronics and Communication (ICOSEC 2020) IEEE Xplore Part Number: CFP20V90-ART;. 978-1-7281-5461-9/20/$31.00 ©2020 IEEE (2020)
15. Archana, G.S., Malleshwari, M.: Gender identification and performance analysis of speech signals. In: 2015 Global Conference on Communication Technologies (GCCT), pp. 483–489 (2015). https://doi.org/10.1109/GCCT.2015.7342709

16. Jena, B., Anita, M., Subrat Kumar, M.: Gender recognition and classification of speech signal. In: Proceedings of the International Conference on Smart Data Intelligence (ICSMDI 2021) (2021). Available at SSRN: https://ssrn.com/abstract=3852607
17. Kushwah, S., Singh, S., Vats, K., Nemade, V.: Gender identification via voice analysis. Int. J. Sci. Res. Comput. Sci. Eng. Inf. Technol. (2019). https://doi.org/10.32628/CSEIT1952188
18. Shiva Shankar, R., Raghaveni, J., Rudraraju, P., Sravya, Y.V.: Classification of gender by voice recognition using machine learning algorithms. Int. J. Adv. Sci. Technol. **29**(06), 8083–8098 (2020). http://sersc.org/journals/index.php/IJAST/article/view/25200
19. Abdulsatar, A.A., Davydov, V.V., Yushkova, V.V., Glinushkin, A.P., Rud, V.Y.: Age and gender recognition from speech signals. J. Phys. Conf. Ser. **1410**, 012073 (2019). SPbOPEN 2019, IOP Publishing

Sarcasm Detection in Tamil Code-Mixed Data Using Transformers

Rajalakshmi Ratnavel[1(✉)], R. Gabriel Joshua[1], S. R. Varsini[1],
and M. Anand Kumar[2]

[1] School of Computer Science and Engineering, Vellore Institute of Technology,
Chennai, Tamil Nadu, India
rajalakshmi.r@vit.ac.in
[2] Department of Information Technology, National Institute of Technology
Karnataka, Surathkal, India

Abstract. Social media analytics has been increasingly gaining popularity due to the extensive amount of customer data it offers, benefiting businesses of all sizes, from local ventures to global brands. Analysing textual contents aids context understanding and also enables content moderation to maintain a positive user experience. Sarcasm detection in social media is essential to maintain constructive and respectful online communication, preventing misunderstandings, minimizing conflicts, and fostering a positive and inclusive digital environment. We propose a Transformer based model for sarcasm detection in Tamil code-mixed text. The model consists of two custom-designed layers: Encoder and Embedding layer. It incorporates multi-head self-attention layer and feed-forward neural networks, followed by normalisation and dropout layers. The proposed model has outperformed compared to other state-of-art models for sarcasm detection by achieving an impressive weighted F_1 score of 0.77. This proposed model effectively addressed the unique challenges posed by the Tamil code-mixed text.

Keywords: Sarcasm · Text Classification · Transformer-based Models · Tamil code-mix

1 Introduction

Today, the internet is primarily used by people for retrieving information, expressing their opinions, sharing their life experiences and communicating and connecting with people related to their personal and professional life. The majority of people use social media to deepen their relationships and enhance communication globally with the increased access to the internet. Social media platforms like Facebook, YouTube, Threads and X have made it possible for the people to express their opinion and emotions on any happenings in the world irrespective of their profession, language or location [1]. Even though these platforms allow its users to post content reflecting their emotions without any restrictions, few

B. R. Chakravarthi et al. (Eds.): SPELLL 2023, CCIS 2046, pp. 430–442, 2024.
https://doi.org/10.1007/978-3-031-58495-4_32

people take this opportunity to post biased and offensive comments on target groups intentionally or unintentionally. Due to the threat of abuse or harassment, this hostile environment prevents others from expressing themselves freely [2]. Therefore, the well-being of our society is threatened due to inappropriate information on the internet. Unfortunately there is no mechanism set up to prevent the spread of unnecessary hate speeches, especially for native and code-mix languages due to insufficient resources. In recent days, active research has been conducted in both academia and business.

Social Media platforms strive to regulate and restrict the flow of hatred in order to maintain harmony among the user's community. Although they have laid policies and procedures to regulate offensive content and objectionable behaviour to stop its negative impact on society, with evolving social media languages it is a necessity to build language models suitable for current trends [3]. Most of the existing Natural Language Processing (NLP) models are trained on monolingual datasets which are not sufficient enough to handle low resourced native texts. With increasing code-mix text on the internet it imposes challenges in analysing the user's emotions [4]. Proper methods are essential for English, native languages and code-mix text analysis to better interpret the user's sentiment. Any wrong conclusions might severely affect the business's performance and may end in profitability and reputation loss. Traditional machine learning algorithms fall short in capturing the semantic nuances present in multilingual text. Consequently, researchers focus on Sequence Models, specifically Transformers, which has demonstrated remarkable proficiency in extracting semantic information from diverse datasets [5].

Sarcasm detection is one of the most difficult and important in social media text analysis. This may be either targeted or un-targeted. This is a very challenging task as understanding the emotion of the text is more important than the context. There are many other text categorizations which need to be incorporated to social media platforms. Although single task learning models help to detect and classify the comments, it is crucial to improve its efficiency and reducing the computational time and resources required. Advanced research is being currently carried out in employing these aspects to the model for low resourced code-mix text classifications. This research work is focused on detection sarcasm in Tamil code-mixed text by applying transformer models. The organization of this paper is as follows: Sect. 2 describes the related works in this field. The proposed methodology is detailed in Sect. 3. The discussion on experimental results is presented in Sect. 4. A comparative study is detailed in Sect. 5 followed by the concluding remarks in Sect. 6.

2 Related Works

In recent days, research has been conducted on code-mix dataset, especially in Dravidian languages like Tamil, Malayalam, Kannada, etc. in addition to code-borrowing methods [6] and code-mixing in Hindi and Marathi languages [7,8]. With exponential growth in social media texts, comments, tweets, etc., the amount of code-mix data is also increasing. Developing large language models capable of comprehending, deciphering, and identifying the characteristics of code-mix language is crucial. Various machine learning and deep learning models, notably those based on Bidirectional Encoder Representations from Transformers(BERT), are finely tuned for these specific tasks. For sarcasm detection, study examined five hyperbolic features - interjections, intensifiers, capitalization, punctuation marks, and elongated words - using three well-known machine learning algorithms: Support Vector Machine(SVM), Random Forest, and Bagged Random Forest. Models performed exceptionally well when trained with elongated word features and achieved an accuracy and F-score of 78.74% and 71%, respectively [9]. As text inter-dependencies were not captured using machine learning techniques, Long Short-Term Memory(LSTM) models consisting of recurrent neural network units, specifically designed for capture long-range dependencies in sequential data started to be utilised for text classification tasks. Earlier, different machine learning techniques have been employed for the analysis of documents and short texts [10,11]. For Sentiment analysis of Hindi-English code-mix dataset, a new sub-word level representations were used in LSTM instead of word-level representations to capture sentiments emphasised by morphemes. The techniques performed 18% better than already existing methods [12].

To address the challenge of Multilingual NLP, as in case of Tamil code-mix text, an novel approach of Selective Translation and Transliteration (STT). This method allowed training of BERT models to ensure proper representation of text in the native script rather than in romanized script [13]. Leveraging the STT techniques, along with Word2Vec and FastText word embedding, up-sampling and hyper-parameter optimization of transformer based models achieved F1-scores 0.76 in Malayalam-English code-mix dataset in Sentiment analysis and Offensive Language Identification tasks [14]. An ensemble approach for sarcasm detection that combines embedding from Word2Vec, GloVe, and BERT models and applies fuzzy logic to these embedding in the top layer for final classification has attained an average accuracy of 87.6% on multiple corpus [15]. Sarcasm detection and humor classification in code-mixed conversations relies on contextual and non-verbal cues respectively were classified using A MSH-COMICS, a neural architecture employing hierarchical attention mechanism focuses on small segments of input sentences has comparatively achieved better F1-score for sarcasm detection and a significant 10-point increase in humor classification [16].

Pre-trained BERT models have been applied to both sentiment analysis and offensive language identification tasks due to their shared discourse properties. Multilingual BERT (mBERT), trained with cross-entropy loss, excels in Kannada and Malayalam, whereas Distilled BERT (DistilBERT), trained with cross-entropy loss and soft parameter sharing, performs impressively in Tamil [1,17]. To address these research gaps, we have developed a custom model for sarcasm detection. This model specifically analyses low-resource code-mix Tamil language text from social media comments and tweets, efficiently categorising them. The ultimate goal is to foster an online community that respects and values everyone's opinions and identities.

3   Proposed Methodology

3.1   Dataset Description

Tamil code-mix data set used in this work is focused on sarcasm identification of Tamil and Malayalam (FIRE 2023) [18–20]. The data contains Tamil code-mix YouTube comments annotated to view the comments with sarcasm or not sarcasm tags. The sarcasm - FIRE 2023 contains 41888 rows respectively for Tamil code-mix. The dataset is highly imbalanced as it is taken from real-time situations, primarily consisting of non-sarcastic content commonly found on YouTube. This dataset serves as a valuable resource for natural language processing tasks and research on code-mix data in low resourced Dravidian languages. The statistics of sarcasm data set is shown in Table 1

Table 1. Statistics of sarcasm data in Tamil code-mixed dataset

Task	Labels	Count
Sarcasm - FIRE 2023	Non-sarcastic	30705
	Sarcastic	11183

3.2   Data Preprocessing

Various preprocessing steps have been applied to the dataset in order to attain maximum performance. Handling code-mixed data is challenging due to variability in language switches and multilingual nature of the content. Developing a robust pre-processing pipelines is intricate, requiring careful consideration of linguistic nuances for accurate representation and analysis. Firstly, non-Tamil comments were removed from the dataset, ensuring that only entries containing native Tamil characters or code-mix text with English remained. Secondly, the crucial tokenization step is performed using BERT-based-uncased, an pre-trained BERT tokenizer. A pre-trained BERT-based-uncased tokenizer is better for a code-mix Tamil dataset because it has learned contextual information from a vast amount of text data, enabling it to handle the diverse linguistic characteristics of code-mix text. Their contextual embedding capture the multilingual nature of code-mixing, enabling better performance in code-mix language processing tasks. The final vocabulary size for the dataset after tokenization is 30522 which indicates the high diversity of the text. Thirdly, a sequence padding step is performed to restrict the variable length of tokenized text to 128. After completing the preprocessing the comments the labels were label encoded and then one-hot encoded. Finally, the data was split into training, validation and testing data in a ratio of 6:2:2. The segregation of the categories after data splitting is shown in Table 2. In total the training data contains 25132 rows and both validation and test data contains around 8378 rows.

Table 2. Distribution of data in the dataset

Labels	Non-sarcastic	Sarcastic	Total
Training Data	18422	6710	25132
Validation Data	6142	2236	8378
Testing Data	6141	2237	8378

3.3   Model Architecture

Transformer-based models excel in text classification because of their self-attention mechanism, which captures long-range dependencies in text. They process entire sequences in parallel, making them highly efficient. The proposed model is built with the Transformer-encoder layers as its primary unit. The model basically contains 2 custom layers namely encoder layer and embedder layer. The embedder is used to form an effective representation(embedding) of the sentence vector obtained from the BERT-based tokenizer. These embeddings are passed to the encoder to capture the contextual information through self attention mechanism feed forward neural networks. The model's architecture is illustrated in Fig. 1. Building blocks within model are describe below:

3.3.1   Input Layer After performing all the preprocessing, the text sentence vectors of length 128 are passed into the input layers along with its Y labels.

3.3.2   Embedder This layer contains the fundamental component of the proposed transformer model namely Token Embedding and Position Embedding layers. It is responsible for creating embeddings to the input sentence vectors and additionally incorporating positional information to it. The output embedding dimension of the model is defined to be 50. First, the token embedding layer transforms the integer token from the pre-trained tokenizers into continuous and dense vectors. Second, the positional embedding layer adds positional encoding, enabling the model architecture to understand the relative position of the tokens within the sequence, facilitating its ability to capture complex relationships and dependency in the data. The output is the final input representation with positional information.

3.3.3   Encoder

a. **Multi-head Attention:**
   Multihead attention layer captures dependencies between the embedding from the embedder using multiple layers of self-attention and cross attention mechanisms. As the number of heads is taken to be 2, the built model simultaneously focuses on 2 different parts of the input sequence, thereby enhancing the model's capability in capturing various aspects of the input. The output

of each head is concatenated or linearly transformed (weighted sum) to produce the final multi-head attention result which captures different levels of contextual information from local patterns to global associations.

b. **Feed Forward Neural Network(FFNN)**

It is located after the attention layer, and is responsible for processing the output from the attention mechanism. The first dense layer with Rectified Linear Unit(RELU) as its activation function introduces non linearity into the model. This non-linearity enables the model to transform and refine the weighted attention representation, capturing complex patterns and nonlinear patterns. In total the FFNN contains 32 neurons to extract higher-level features and relationships in the data.

c. **Normalisation layers:**

The normalisation layer stabilises the training of the model to enable faster convergence. It normalises the activation of the layer and mitigates the risk of vanishing or exploding gradient during back propagation. Two normalisation layers are used to standardise the variation in the scale and distribution of the features introduced by the multi-head attention layer and mitigate internal covariate shifts.

d. **Dropout Layers**

Dropout is an effective regularisation technique which randomly deactivates the fraction of neurons. In this model 50% of the neurons are deactivated. Similar to the normalisation layers, dropouts enhance training stability, prevent overfitting, promote robust feature learning, and address issues related to vanishing and exploding gradients.

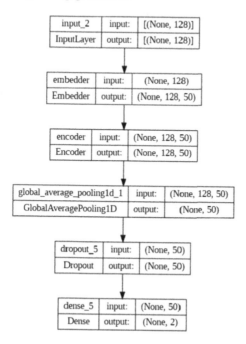

Fig. 1. Model Architecture of the proposed Model.

3.3.4 Global Average Pooling (GAP) The output from encoder is 20 X 50, 2 dimensional in shape. GAP is used after the encoder module before passing the data to the final fully connected layers. By applying GAP, dimensionality of the data is reduced, makes it more computationally efficient and reduces the risk of overfitting. GAP retains the most important semantic information by computing the average across all positions in the sequence.

3.3.5 Dropout Layers 1-Dimension output of length 50 from GAP is forwarded to a dropout layer with a dropout rate of 0.35, before fully connected layers. As mentioned above Dropout acts as a regularization technique by randomly deactivating a portion of neurons during training. This helps prevent overfitting, and forces the network to learn more independent and robust features, which can lead to better generalisation. To handle noisy data or data with irrelevant information, dropout can help the network focus on the most informative features by randomly deactivating less informative neurons.

3.3.6 Dense Layers The final layers of the model are 2 fully connected dense layers which have 64 and 32 units, respectively, and both use the ReLU activation function. These layers are responsible for learning complex patterns and representations from the data, helping to extract high-level features from the output of the previous layers. The output layer uses softmax activation function which is a common choice for multi-class classification problems.

4 Experiments and Results

The proposed architecture incorporates two custom layers that have proven effective in accurately interpreting and classifying texts. The training, validation and test results, as summarized in Table 3. It reveal impressive metrics with an training accuracy of 88% and a low training loss value of 0.28. These outcomes, characterized by higher accuracy and lower cross-entropy values, indicate the model's commendable performance. Validation is essential for assessing model generalization, detecting over-fitting, tuning hyper-parameters, and boosting confidence in results. The outcomes shows a notable 76% validation accuracy and a validation loss of 0.68. These results underscore the model's proficiency in handling the intricacies of mixed-language data, instilling confidence in its robustness and applicability to real-world challenges.

Table 3. Performance Metrics of the Proposed Model

Measures	Accuracy	Loss
Training	0.88	0.28
Validation	0.76	0.68
Testing	0.77	8.22

The classification results shown in Table 4 suggest that the model performs well in identifying non-sarcastic instances with a high precision of 84% and recall of 86%, yielding an F_1-score of 85%. However, its performance on sarcastic instances is comparatively lower, with a precision of 58%, recall of 54%, and F_1-score of 56%, due to the highly imbalanced nature of the data. The weighted averages indicate an overall accuracy of 77%. These metrics highlight a trade-off between precision and recall, with the model excelling in non-sarcastic cases but showing room for improvement in identifying sarcastic instances.

Table 4. Performance Analysis

Class	Precision	Recall	F_1 Score
Non-sarcastic	0.84	0.86	0.85
Sarcastic	0.58	0.54	0.56
Weighted Avg	0.77	0.77	0.77

Figure 2 presents the confusion matrices for the sarcasm detection. The data imbalance has resulted in a bias toward the class with the majority of data, leading to a higher number of accurate predictions.5269 comments in the non-sarcastic class are correctly classified by proposed model. However, correct predictions for the other class are also present, with comparatively lower accuracy. This discrepancy is mainly due to the dominance of the highest frequency class, as it is sourced from real-time situations. The elevated misclassification rate of minority classes significantly impacts various evaluation metrics, including test accuracy, underscoring the challenges posed by imbalanced datasets in sarcasm detection.

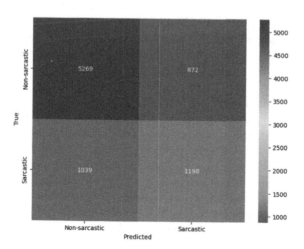

Fig. 2. Sarcasm Classification Confusion Matrix

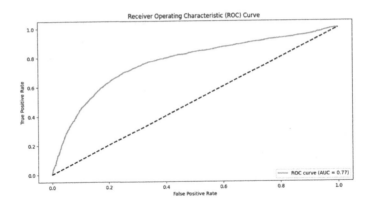

Fig. 3. ROC Curve of Sarcastic Class

The ROC-AUC score and ROC curve shown in Fig. 3 crucial metrics for evaluating binary and multiclass classification models. They assess a model's ability to discriminate between classes, offering a comprehensive view of sensitivity and specificity. As the curve hugs the upper-left corner of the plot indicates that the proposed model is a better classifier. A ROC-AUC score of 0.77 indicates a moderate ability for the model to distinguish between positive and negative instances, suggesting reasonable discriminative performance in the sarcasm classification task. Observing the loss and accuracy curve of a model can help in understanding how well the model is able to learn the hidden patterns in input data and helps to improve its performance over the epochs. Further, using these graphs we can identify if the model is over-fitting or under fitting. The accuracy and loss curves of model is in Fig. 4 and 5 respectively. We can clearly see, initially the validation loss steady increase form 75% to 79% and then even before second epoch the accuracy starts to fluctuate within a certain range. Similar pattern is observed in validation loss graph too, the loss value drops from 0.50 to 0.45 and then increase rapidly. This pattern might attribute to the complexity of analysing code-mix languages. The model's major objective to obtain optimal weights for each layers by maintaining a fair classification accuracy among both classes is achieved.

In real time social media text analytic, it is important to train or fine-tune models as quickly as possible to ensure comments violating the community guidelines are promptly identified and removed. For handling the huge amount of data that flows in rapidly, it is essential to build a computationally efficient model that maximises resource utilisation. The proposed model effectively achieves these objectives while simultaneously delivering robust results. To enhance the model's performance and interpret-ability, we have introduced two sets of normalization and dropout layers, one after the multi-head attention layer and another following the feed-forward neural network layers. Moreover, these additions play a key role in significantly reducing the computational time needed for model training, all without compromising on the results. From the above results, it is evident the

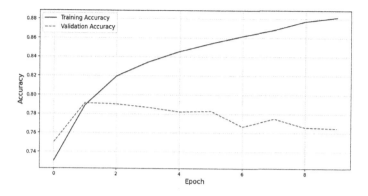

Fig. 4. Training vs Validation Accuracy

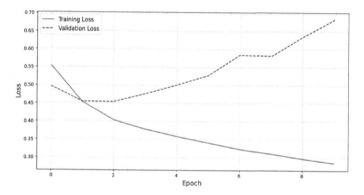

Fig. 5. Training vs Validation Loss

proposed model can achieve exceptional performance despite having significantly fewer trainable parameters of 1,558,327. Overall, the proposed model has been meticulously constructed at each stage to strike a balance between computational requirements and the classification accuracy of the 2 labels.

5   Comparative Study

In recent times, social media text analysis has gained momentum due to the wide range of tasks and varying levels of difficulty they present. With the evolving trends, code-mix language is predominantly used by the majority of social media users. An integrated system that can customize content based on individual preferences and demographics is crucial. It is important to safeguard individuals' emotions by altering the content based on their preferences. Low-resource Dravidian languages like Tamil, Telugu, Malayalam, and Kannada pose unique challenges due to the limited availability of annotated datasets. Various competitions are being conducted focusing on text classification for various low-resource Dravidian languages.

Table 5. Comparative Study

Models	F_1
Proposed model	**0.77**
hatealert_Tamil Rank 1 [20]	0.74
ABC_tamil Rank 2 [20]	0.73
SSNCSE1_Tamill Rank 3 [20]	0.73
IRLabIITBHU_tam Rank 4 [20]	0.72
ramyasiva_tamil Rank 5 [20]	0.71

Sarcasm detection is notably more intricate than other text classification, as sarcasm is a form of verbal irony in which someone says something but means the opposite of what they are saying. Tamil code-mix Sarcasm detection dataset was introduced in the FIRE-2023 competition. The results of the proposed models are compared with top preformed models of the codalab competition - Sarcasm Identification of Dravidian Languages (Malayalam and Tamil) in Dravidian code-mix, Organized by DravidianLangTech. The comparison Table 5, provides a comprehensive overview of sarcasm detection research conducted in competition and in various other languages. The results indicate that the performance of the proposed sarcasm detection model surpasses that of the top 5 ranked models in the Codalab competition, demonstrating a 3% higher accuracy. Even in language-rich contexts like English, where data abundance is common, sarcasm detection attains an approximately 85% weighted F1 score. Our model has achieved a remarkable weighted F1 score of 0.77 in this challenging task. Notably, our model achieves an remarkable weighted F1 score of 0.77 in this demanding task, signifying its effectiveness in addressing the complexities of this specific task challenge.

From all the above comparisons and results, we see that proposed model is exceptionally good when it comes to balancing accuracy across the classes while being less time-consuming and resource-intensive, making it particularly valuable for real-time big data handling. Although there is slight trade-off in performance compared to other prior state-of-art models, it is yet able to capture robust and long range dependencies between the code-mix Tamil comments. The proposed model holds vast potential for further development, offering opportunities to enhance its performance by incorporating various stages of data preprocessing. Moreover, it has the capacity to address specific areas of other text classification, such as offensive language identification, sentiment analysis, community-based discrimination, issues related to minority groups, and concerns within the LGBTQ community. As future enhancements, multi-modal data like text with emojis or images can be integrated, which could provide valuable insights, enhancing the versatility and richness of the analysis. Incorporating diverse modalities can offer a more comprehensive understanding of communication nuances and capture not only linguistic but also visual and emotive elements, enhancing the overall depth and accuracy of information interpretation. Improvising the model can demonstrate the efficacy in identifying and effectively mitigating harmful content, thereby contributing to the creation of a safe and secure social media environment for everyone.

6   Conclusion

Regulations are undeniably vital in today's digital landscape, where individuals can freely post comments on social media platforms without any discernible restraints. An automated monitoring and analysis system to swiftly detect and remove comments that infringe upon community guidelines is indispensable, as manual moderation becomes an impractical task due to the overwhelming volume of data which flows into social media channels. The proposed model achieves the best F_1 score of 0.77 in assessing content based on sarcasm. The model incorporates two custom layers, the Embedder and Encoder to identify the sarcasm in code-mixed Tamil text. The proposed Model holds great potential for addressing the growing challenges posed by the ever-expanding digital landscape in our contemporary era.

References

1. Hande, A., Hegde, S.U., Chakravarthi, B.R.: Multi-task learning in under-resourced Dravidian languages. J. Data Inf. Manag. 4(2), 137–165 (2022). https://doi.org/10.1007/s42488-022-00070-w
2. Rajalakshmi, R., Selvaraj, S., Vasudevan, P.: Hottest: hate and offensive content identification in Tamil using transformers and enhanced stemming. Comput. Speech Lang. 78, 101464 (2023a). https://doi.org/10.1016/j.csl.2022.101464
3. Rajalakshmi , R., Yashwant Reddy, B.: DLRG@HASOC 2019: an enhanced ensemble classifier for hate and offensive content identification. Working Notes of FIRE 2019 - Forum for Information Retrieval Evaluation, vol. 2517, pp. 370–379 (2019). https://ceur-ws.org/Vol-2517/T3-26.pdf
4. Chakravarthi, B.R., et al.: Overview of the HASOC-DravidianCodeMix shared task on offensive language detection in Tamil and Malayalam. In: CEUR Workshop Proceedings, vol. 3159 (2021). https://ceur-ws.org/Vol-3159/T3-1.pdf
5. Rajalakshmi, R., Reddy, Y., Kumar, L.: DLRG@DravidianLangTech-EACL2021: transformer based approach for offensive language identification on code-mixed Tamil. In: Chakravarthi, B.R., Priyadharshini, R., Anand Kumar, M., Krishnamurthy, P., Sherly, E. (eds.), Proceedings of the First Workshop on Speech and Language Technologies for Dravidian Languages, pp. 357–362. Association for Computational Linguistics, Kyiv (2021). https://aclanthology.org/2021.dravidianlangtech-1.53
6. Rajalakshmi, R., Agrawal, R.: Borrowing likeliness ranking based on relevance factor. In: Proceedings of the 4th ACM IKDD Conferences on Data Sciences, pp. 1–2, March 2017. https://doi.org/10.1145/3041823.3067694
7. Rajalakshmi, R., Reddy, P., Khare, S., Ganganwar, V.: Sentimental analysis of code-mixed Hindi language. In: Congress on Intelligent Systems: Proceedings of CIS 2021, vol. 2, pp. 739–751, July 2022. https://doi.org/10.1007/978-981-16-9113-3_54
8. Rajalakshmi, R., Mattins, F., Srivarshan, S., Reddy, L.P.: Hate speech and offensive content identification in Hindi and Marathi language tweets using ensemble techniques. In: CEUR Workshop Proceedings, pp. 1–11 (2021)

9. Govindan, V., Balakrishnan, V.: A machine learning approach in analyzing the effect of hyperboles using negative sentiment tweets for sarcasm detection. J. King Saud Univ. Comput. Inf. Sci. **34**(8), 5110–5120 (2022). https://doi.org/10.1016/j.jksuci.2022.01.008

10. Rajalakshmi, R., Aravindan, C.: An effective and discriminative feature learning for URL based web page classification. In: 2018 IEEE International Conference on Systems, Man, and Cybernetics (SMC), Miyazaki, Japan, pp. 1374–1379 (2018). https://doi.org/10.1109/SMC.2018.00240

11. Rajalakshmi, R.: Supervised term weighting methods for URL classification. J. Comput. Sci. **10**(10), 1969–1976 (2014)

12. Joshi, A., Prabhu, A., Shrivastava, M., Varma, V.: Towards sub-word level compositions for sentiment analysis of Hindi-English code mixed text. In: Proceedings of COLING 2016, the 26th International Conference on Computational Linguistics: Technical Papers, pp. 2482–2491 (2016)

13. Vasantharajan, C., Thayasivam, U.: Towards offensive language identification for Tamil code-mixed YouTube comments and posts. SN Comput. Sci. **3**(1) (2021). https://doi.org/10.1007/s42979-021-00977-y

14. Thara, S., Poornachandran, P.: Social media text analytics of Malayalam-English code-mixed using deep learning. J. Big Data **9**(1) (2022). https://doi.org/10.1186/s40537-022-00594-3

15. Sharma, D.K., Singh, B., Agarwal, S., Pachauri, N., Alhussan, A.A., Abdallah, H.A.: SARCASM detection over social media platforms using hybrid ensemble model with fuzzy logic. Electronics **12**(4) (2023). https://doi.org/10.3390/electronics12040937

16. Bedi, M., Kumar, S., Akhtar, M.S., Chakraborty, T.: Multi-modal sarcasm detection and humor classification in code-mixed conversations. IEEE Trans. Affect. Comput. **14**(2), 1363–1375 (2023). https://doi.org/10.1109/taffc.2021.3083522

17. Rajalakshmi, R., Duraphe, A., Shibani, A.: DLRG@DravidianLangTech-ACL2022: abusive comment detection in tamil using multilingual transformer models. In: Proceedings of the Second Workshop on Speech and Language Technologies for Dravidian Languages, pp. 207–213, Dublin, Ireland. Association for Computational Linguistics (2022)

18. Chakravarthi, B.R.: Hope speech detection in YouTube comments. Soc. Netw. Anal. Min. **12**(1) (2022). https://doi.org/10.1007/s13278-022-00901-z

19. Chakravarthi, B.R., Hande, A., Ponnusamy, R., Kumaresan, P.K., Priyadharshini, R.: How can we detect homophobia and transphobia? Experiments in a multilingual code-mixed setting for social media governance. Int. J. Inf. Manag. Data Insights **2**(2), 100119 (2022). https://doi.org/10.1016/j.jjimei.2022.100119

20. Chakravarthi, B.R., et al.: Overview of the shared task on sarcasm identification of Dravidian languages (Malayalam and Tamil) in Dravidian code-mix. In: Forum of Information Retrieval and Evaluation FIRE - 2023 (2023)

21. Bharti, S., Naidu, R., Babu, K.: Hyperbolic feature-based sarcasm detection in Telugu conversation sentences. J. Intell. Syst. **30**(1), 73–89 (2021). https://doi.org/10.1515/jisys-2018-0475

22. Bharti, S.K., Babu, K.S., Raman, R.: Context-based sarcasm detection in Hindi tweets. In: 2017 Ninth International Conference on Advances in Pattern Recognition (ICAPR) (2017a). https://doi.org/10.1109/icapr.2017.8593198

23. Potamias, R.A., Siolas, G., Stafylopatis, A.: A transformer-based approach to irony and sarcasm detection. Neural Comput. Appl. **32**(23), 17309–17320 (2020). https://doi.org/10.1007/s00521-020-05102-3

Automatic Identification of Meimayakkam in Tamil Words Using Rule Based and Transfer Learning Approaches

A. Vinoth[1(✉)] ⓘ, Sathiyaraj Thangasamy[1] ⓘ, R. Nithya[2] ⓘ,
G. Poovandran[1], V. Mounash[1], C. N. Subalalitha[3] ⓘ,
R. Ariharasuthan[4] ⓘ, Parameshwar Arunachalam[5], and K. Syed Jafer[6]

[1] Sri Krishna Adithya College of Arts and Science, Coimbatore 641042, India
vino.asstprof@gmail.com
[2] Government Arts and Science College (Co-Ed), Avinashi 641654, India
[3] SRM College of Engineering & Technology, Kattankulathur, Chennai, India
[4] DJ Academy of Design, Othakkalmandapam, Coimbatore 641032, India
[5] Infosys, Kanchipuram, India
[6] 3X Kaggle Expert, Chennai, India

Abstract. Over 50 traditional Tamil grammar books are in existence, with Tholkappiyam standing out as the most significant. Written in 14 BC, it comprises three chapters: Ezhuththathikaaram (எழுத்ததிகாரம்), Chollathikaaram (சொல்லதிகாரம்), and Porulathikaaram (பொருளதிகாரம்). These chapters delve into the structures of the Tamil language, encompassing the concept of Meimayakkam (மெய்ம்மயக்கம்), which elucidates the correct spelling usage of Tamil words—an imperative facet for grasping the intricacies of the language. Tholkappiyar expounds on this concept in two sub-chapters, Nuunmarapu (நூன்மரபு) and Mozhimarapu (மொழிமரபு), which encompass 82 rules, including 12 specifically dedicated to Meimayakkam. This paper introduces two methods for automatically detecting spelling mistakes, utilizing the Meimayakkam Rules Multilingual BERT Model, a Large Language Model. These approaches are then compared in the context of the spell-checking task. Additionally, a mobile application has been developed based on the Meimayakkam rules, serving as an educational tool for students learning Tamil. This study is groundbreaking as it marks the first examination of Tholkaappiyar rules from a linguistic perspective, upholding the purity of Tamil words and distinguishing them from vernacular words.

Keywords: Tholkaappiyam · Machined Rules · Learning Techniques · Classification · ML · Algorithm · mBERT

1 Introduction

Tholkappiyam is a work attributed to Tholkappiyar and is believed to have been written in the 14th century BC [1, 2]. Comprising three chapters, the book explores Phonology, Morphology, and material authority. The initial chapter, dedicated to writings, meticulously details the writing systems of the Tamil language through 483 rules. It delves

B. R. Chakravarthi et al. (Eds.): SPELLL 2023, CCIS 2046, pp. 443–458, 2024.
https://doi.org/10.1007/978-3-031-58495-4_33

into the intricacies of the writing system, including sandhi rules and the alterations that occur when combining two words.

Within Tholkappiyam, Tholkappiyar provides rules governing the correct usage of the Tamil language, encompassing aspects such as spelling and grammar. These regulations find application in the concept of consonant clusters and are expounded in the chapters titled Nuunmarapu (நூன்மரபு) and Mozhimarapu (மொழிமரபு). Building upon these rules, this paper introduces two algorithms: the Meimayakkam Rule-based algorithm and a Transformer-based learning algorithm named Multilingual BERT. These algorithms are proposed for detecting spelling mistakes in Tamil words.

In Tamil, when letters or phonemes combine to create a word, they initially organize into syllables, and subsequently, these syllables come together to form the word (morphemes). In essence, there exists a syllabic structure between the individual letters and the complete word. It's important to note that this is not a prosodic syllable but rather a linguistic syllable [30].

The peak (உச்சம்) of a syllable is represented by the vowel sound within it. Consonants மெய்கள் may appear before (Onset) or after (Coda) the peak. A syllable can be constituted solely by a vowel, without any accompanying consonants, and can stand as a complete word. However, consonants cannot occur in isolation [30].

There are restrictions on the occurrence of consonants before and after vowels in Tamil. At the beginning of a syllable, only one consonant is allowed before the vowel. Typically, at the end of a syllable in Tamil, only one consonant is permitted. If two consonants appear, the first consonant must be one of the following: ய், ர், ழ் (as in words like வாய்க்கால்-va:ikKa:l, பார்க்கிறேன்-pa:rkkiren, வாழ்த்து-va:zhttU) [30].

What is Meimayakkam?

In Tamil, specific rules dictate which consonants can initiate the next syllable when a particular consonant concludes the previous one. Tamil grammarians refer to this phenomenon as Meimayakkam மெய்ம்மயக்கம், which encompasses Udanilai Meimayakkam (உடன்நிலை மெய்ம்மயக்கம் - the rule for consecutive consonants within a word) and VettRRunilai Meimayakkam (வேற்றுநிலை மெய்ம்மயக்கம் - Phonotactics, governing the occurrence of consonants at syllable boundaries) [30].

When two consonants appear consecutively within a single word, it is referred to as 'Meimayakkam.' There are two types of 'Meimayakkam.' When the two consonants are from the same family, they are called 'Udanilai Meimayakkam.' (consonants of the same type). Upon careful examination of the samples, you will observe that the consonants are succeeded by others from the same family, known as 'uyirmei letters (Table 1).'

Table 1. Udanilai Meimayyakkam sample words [5, 6]

S.No.	Tamil	Romanized	English
1.	செந்நீர்	Sennīr	Frost
2	தண்ணீர்	Taṇṇīr	Water
3.	கன்னம்	Kaṉṉam	Cheek
4.	பத்து	Pathu	Ten
5.	தாத்தா	Tāttā	Grandfather
6.	எச்சம்	Eccam	Dropping
7.	குப்பம்	Kuppam	Group/Community

When two consonants belong to two different letter families, it is referred to as 'VettRRunilai Meimayakkam', denoting two different consonant types. Upon examining the samples, it becomes evident that the consonants are not followed by letters from the same family. It is notable that the consonants form pairs, showcasing the distinct characteristics of 'VettRRunilai Meimayakkam' in Tamil linguistic structure (Table 2).

Table 2. VettRRunilai Meimayakkam sample words [5, 6]

S.No.	Tamil	Romanized	English
1.	தாழ்ப்பாள்	Tāḻppāḷ	Latch
2	கல்வி	Kalvi	Education
3.	சந்தை	Sandai	Market
4.	ஐம்பது	Aimpatu	Fifty
5.	திங்கள்	Tiṅkaḷ	Monday
6.	தூண்டில்	Tūṇṭil	Bait
7.	ஒன்று	Oṉṟu	One

Why This Product?

The introduction of this product addresses a contemporary challenge faced by students in typing or writing Tamil. With the increasing reliance on technology, students often encounter difficulties in expressing themselves in their native language. This product aims to provide computer-based assistance, offering a solution to enhance Tamil learning for students. By leveraging technology, it seeks to bridge the gap and facilitate a smoother and more accessible approach to typing or writing in Tamil, thereby supporting and improving the learning experience.

In the contemporary world, the pervasive use of the internet and smartphones has spurred the development of Android applications for Tolkappiyar's "Meimayakkam" rule. These applications hold significant potential in facilitating the teaching and learning process, offering a modern and accessible approach to engage with the linguistic intricacies outlined in Tolkappiyam.

In summary, this paper boasts a dual contribution. Firstly, it introduces a Tolkappiyam rules-based algorithm for detecting spelling errors in Tamil words. Additionally, it leverages multilingual BERT to further enhance the accuracy and efficiency of spelling detection in Tamil words.

To the best of our knowledge, this paper is pioneering in proposing the aforementioned algorithm for spelling correction in Tamil words.

The structure of this research paper is as follows: In Sect. 2, we conduct a comprehensive literature review, exploring relevant studies and research that have shaped the context for our work. Section 3 introduces and elaborates on our proposed work, outlining the methodology, objectives, and the rationale behind our research. Section 4 focuses on "Meimayakkam" classification, a pivotal aspect of our study, detailing our approach, findings, and any insights gained from this classification. Finally, in Sect. 5, we conclude the paper, summarizing key findings, discussing their applications, and laying out potential directions for future research and work in this field.

The algorithms were implemented in Python 3 for rule-based analysis, and supervised data underwent machine learning. This research highlights the distinctions between norm analysis and machine language learning analysis. Furthermore, based on these insights, the culmination of this research involves the development of an app.

A dataset consisting of 2724 words was utilized for this study, sourced from the Vadamoli Tamil Alphabetical Dictionary [31]. It is noteworthy that the instructions were standardized for both norm analysis and machine learning approaches.

The purpose of undertaking this work is to conduct a preliminary study aimed at gaining a profound understanding of how to create new Tamil words and determining whether an existing word adheres to the Tamil language system. This knowledge is crucial as it enables us to write in the Tamil language without making spelling mistakes. This endeavor will be immensely helpful in ensuring error-free written content in Tamil.

However, this is a preliminary study. For instance, while the algorithm identifies words like "கற்க", "கேட்க", "செல்க", and "கொள்க" as correct, it may also erroneously label incorrect words such as "கெட்க", "சேல்க", and "கோள்க" as correct. This discrepancy arises because the algorithm relies solely on a spelling-based approach. To provide accurate assessments, it is essential to consider factors like the initial letters, final letters, Tamil dictionary, Tamil grammar suffixes, morpheme arrival rules, and combination rules. This preliminary study aims to comprehensively explore these elements. While a rule-based approach might seem sufficient, the inclusion of machine learning methods is also being explored to discern the distinctions between rule-based and machine learning studies in this context.

2 Literature Review

A consistent methodological approach has been employed in Tholkappiyam, with a significant focus on linguistic research. Specifically, there has been relatively limited exploration in the field of linguistics, particularly in the study of consonant clusters. Surprisingly, there is a noticeable absence of studies that delve into the language's consonant clusters as elucidated by Tholkappiyar. According to Tamizhannal [32], Tholkappiyar dedicated efforts to codifying rules for consonant clusters to decipher specific Tamil words. Notably, the observations of poets Ilamuranar (11th century AD) and Nachinarkiniyar (14th century AD), who provided commentary on the esteemed work Tholkappiyam, do not make any reference to consonant clusters [7–12].

S. Agathialingam [3] linguistically supported the account of consonant clusters in the Tamil language system, a topic that was also addressed by Tholkappiyar (2011, pp. 56–67).

R. Aravendan [4] conducted research on the first grammar of Dravidian languages, in which he highlighted the concept of clusters expounded upon in Tholkappiyam. He not only delved into enumerating the methods of clusters within the Tamil language but also asserted that the same concept is articulated in other traditional grammatical sections such as Sanskrit, Pali, and Prakrit. Upon comparison with Tamil grammatical works, he emphasized a central concept that equally highlights the importance of not allowing the intermixture of languages.

V. Jaya [3] explicates that consonant clusters occur in the middle and end of words, as stated by Tholkaappiyar, as discussed in the paper "The Collections of Clusters by P. Bharathi." The commentator Ilampuranar notes that consonant clusters are prevalent in both individual words and sandhi. Furthermore, Jaya adds that Bharathiar, who prominently utilizes consonant recurrence in both individual and combined words, maintains a consistent ordering in the usage similar to Indo-Aryan languages without discrimination.

M. Ayyaswamy [3], in his paramount article "New Cluster," highlights examples of 16 consonant clusters, each with itself, and 70 consonant clusters, each with the other, in Sangam literature. However, there is a lack of illustration for the purported 30 nonexistent clusters, and some of them remain mysterious. In the article, he explicitly mentions these 30 clusters, some of which Tholkaappiyar did not reference, while others are found in today's colloquial speech.

C. Narayanasamy [3] asserted in his article "Cluster" that it appears that when the word undergoes changes, Sandhi occurs with the influence of Indo-Aryans. The consonants ka, sa, tha, and pa form clusters by themselves and not with others. Additionally, the vowels ra and la cluster with other consonants and not by themselves. There is no defined pattern for the clustering of vowels and consonants interchangeably. These clusters can occur between individual and successive words in a language. Furthermore, Nachinarkiniyar generalizes Tholkaappiyar's view, stating that internal clusters present themselves between individual words, constituting a cluster. However, he raises a question about whether this happens within a sentence. Thus, he distinctly remarks on the various stages of clusters.

In the article on consonant clusters, Suyambu [33] observes that investigations into consonant clusters in Tamil have been conducted based on chapter structures, methods of illustration, and the structures and methods of sutras as outlined by Tholkaappiayar. In accordance with these findings, two results have been exhibited as follows:

- Consonant clusters are common in both single words and Sandhi words.
- They are particularly prevalent in single words.

In the article "Consonant Clusters at the Final Stage," Iyyasamy [3] affirms that there are no words in Tamil that begin with consonants but end with them. Furthermore, there are no instances of double consonant words in the Tamil language. Notably, Tholkaappiyar concentrates on discussing the middle consonant cluster rather than other configurations.

'செய்யுள் இறுதிப் போலி மொழிவயின்
னகார மகாரம் ஈரொற் றாகும்' (தொல். எழுத்.52) [5, 6].

At the final position in | polum | in verse | n | and | m | occur together as a double consonant cluster.

Shorter | m |

In the above sutra, he points out the double consonant (ன்-ம்). The present article contributes to the research on consonant clusters.

In the article on double clusters, A. Adithan [3] states that the commentator highlights Tholkaappiyar's conception of consonant clusters involving letters of the same and different clusters. The translator observes that the same letters cluster as double clusters, specifically in consecutive double consonant clusters. The present article aims to gather perspectives on consecutive triple consonant clusters.

Thus, Tholkaappiyar presented the traceability of consonant clusters in Tamil language word formations and assisted in discerning the rules for error-free language writing. Subsequently, I realized that these laws have been analyzed through computational language technology.

2.1   Tholkappiyam Related Linguistic Works

Several linguistic studies have been conducted based on Tholkaappiyam, approaching the concepts expressed in the Tholkappi book from a linguistic perspective. However, it is worth noting that the technical linguistic foundation associated with this process has not been established [13–21].

2.2   Tholkappiyam + Tamil Ilakkanam Related Computational Works

ThamizhiMorph: A Morphological Parser for the Tamil Language [24], WHITE PAPER ON TECHNOLOGICAL DEVELOPMENT OF TAMIL [25], Morphological Parsing on Tholkappiyam's Perspective [26], VERB IDENTIFICATION USING MORPHOPHONEMIC RULES IN TAMIL LANGUAGE [27], Computational Challenges with Tamil Complex Predicates [28], Tamil Santhi Checker App for Android Phone Thendral [22], and A Rule-Based Grammar and Spell Checking [23] have been previous studies utilizing Tholkaappiyar rule-based data and technological developments in the Tamil language. These articles were not written in accordance with the hypothesis proposed in the present research.

2.3   Literature Gap

In the realm of linguistic analysis, prior studies have focused on morphological-based classifications, with notable attention to Tholkāppiyam. In our proposed work, we adopt a unique approach by integrating both morphological and phonological classification methods. To achieve this integration, we employ two distinct techniques: a rule-based approach and the utilization of machine learning algorithms.

By combining these two methodologies, our proposed method demonstrates a significant improvement in accuracy levels. This approach not only builds upon the traditional morphological foundation but also harnesses the power of phonological analysis and the adaptability of modern machine learning algorithms. The result is a robust classification system that achieves noteworthy levels of accuracy, marking a substantial step forward in the field of linguistic analysis.

3   Proposed Work

3.1   Open Tamil Python Package

The "Open Tamil" Python module, offering a diverse range of capabilities for processing and modifying Tamil language text, has been employed in this study. We utilize the Open Tamil Library to dissect the provided Tamil words into their constituent letters. This process is invaluable for our proposed algorithms based on Tholkaappiyar's Meimayakkam rule.

3.2   Tholkaappiyar Rule Based Algorithm

According to the realm of computing language, it is tasked with formalizing the algorithm aimed at modifying the rules of consonant clusters. Subsequently, as affirmed by, it becomes achievable to pave the way for research. In this context, an attempt was made to formulate specific algorithms for the rules of consonant clusters mentioned by Tholkaappiyar and organize them into 9 rules. The first of these is explained below:

To point out, ட் ற் ல் ள் + க ச ப is the first rule of Meimayakkam by Tholkaap-piyar, which is as follows:

ட ற ல ள என்னும் புள்ளி முன்னர்க்
க ச ப என்னும் மூவெழுத் துரிய. (தொல்.எழுத்து.நூற்.23). [5]

The consonants | Ṭ |, | ṛ |, | ḷ |, and | ḷ | are followed by | k |, | c |, and | p |.

This Tholkaappiyar rule states that after the letters ட், ற், ல், ள் in a word, the letters
க, ச, ப become faint. According to this rule, words such as கேட்க, கற்க, செல்க,
கொள்க are examples of error-free Tamil language words. The primary objective of
this article is to analyze this rule using linguistic technology. Here, we explain one of
the algorithms developed for this purpose step by step.

Step 1: At first, we need to follow the instructions below to obtain the Open-Tamil
Python library. The input from this library will enable us to import the Tamil
language system accordingly.
import tamil.
Step 2: The variable is named 'word' to receive the input word.
word= input("Enter the sentence to check:")
Step 3: 'letters' is the variable that separates the word 'க + ற் + க' to be analyzed
using a Tamil package.
letters=tamil.utf8.get_letters(word)
Step 4: The next variable 'Mei' is designated for consonant analysis.
Mei = tamil.utf8.mei_letters
Step 5: Ensure that the letter 'ட்' in the 'letters' variable is present and is not the last
letter of the received word. Then, the variable 'ind' takes the position of the character
'ட்' (e.g., கற்க-012). After retaining it, if there are letters in the 'Mei' variable after the
position of the letter 'ட்', it will return False. Otherwise, the 'root_words' variable specifies that the next letter may be a vowel or some other type. If it's a string, it splits it
into a tuple. It creates a variable called 'root_last' and checks if it doesn't exist. After
checking, it verifies if one of the letters 'க, ச, ப' comes after the letter 'ட்'. If so, it
returns True. If not, it returns False. This algorithm is as follows:

```
if "ட்" in letters and letters.index("ட்")!=len(letters)-
1:
  ind=letters.index("ட்")
  if letters[ind+1] in Mei:
    print (False)
  else:
    root_words=tamil.utf8.splitMeiUyir(letters[ind+1])
    if type(root_words)==tuple:
      root_last=root_words[0]
    else:
      root_last=root_words #
    if root_last=="க்" or  root_last=="ச்" or
root_last=="ப்":
      print(True)
    else:
      print(False)
```

The corresponding results can be tabulated as follows (Table 3):

Table 3. Tholkappiyar rule based Meimayakkam

S.No.	Tholkaappiyar Rules	Input Word Sample	True/False
1.	ட்ற்ல்ள்+கசப	கேட்க, கற்க, செல்க, கொள்க	True
2	ல்ள்+யவ	கொல்யானை, வெள்வளை	True
3.	ங்ஞ்ண்ந்ம்ன்+இனவொலி (கசடதபற)	மாங்காய், பிஞ்சு, மண்டை, வந்து, வம்பு, சென்ற	True
4.	ண்ன்+கசசுூபமயவ	வெண்களம், வெண்சட்டை	True
5.	ஞ்ந்ம்வ்+ய	உரிஞ்யாது, தெவ்யாது	True
6.	ம்+வ	நிலம்வலிது	True
7.	ய்ர்ழ்+க ச த ப ஞ ந ம ய வ ங	பாய்ச்சு, வாய்த்தது, வேய்ங்குழல், நாய்க்கடி	True
8.	ர்ழ் தவிர -> க்...ன் + க...ன	வாக்கு, அட்டை, அண்ணன்	True
9.	ர்ழ் குற்றொற்றாகா	வேர், நேர், வார், ஆர்	True

3.3   Machine Learning Algorithm

3.3.1   Data Preprocessing

The book "Vadasottramizh Akaravarisai" [31] was downloaded as a PDF from the Internet Archives website. The downloaded book was converted into image files, and subsequently, data was generated using Google Document Optical Character Recognition (OCR). In this dataset, non-text elements such as page numbers, headings, footnotes, and special characters have been excluded. Additionally, issues related to line breaks, formatting, and extra spaces have been addressed to ensure that the text maintains consistency and readability. These preprocessing steps are crucial for preparing the text data from the Tamil book for various natural language processing (NLP) tasks, including sentiment analysis, text classification, topic modeling, and language understanding.

3.3.2   Text Classification

Text classification relies on clean and well-structured text for accurate categorization. To achieve this, preprocessing steps are applied, including tokenization (which involves splitting text into words or tokens), stopword removal, lemmatization, and addressing special characters and formatting issues. Text classification typically employs supervised machine learning techniques, where models are trained on labeled examples associating each text document with a known category or label. It's important to note that while text classification is valuable for organizing and categorizing text documents, it is not directly suitable for evaluating the correctness of Tamil words according to Tholkappiar's Meimayakkam rule. For this linguistic task, specialized Tamil grammar analysis and rule-based methods would be more appropriate.

3.3.3   Multilingual BERT (mBERT)

mBERT, a transfer learning model pre-trained on Wikipedia text in 104 languages, possesses the ability to capture context, understand syntax, and process syntactic information. It can be fine-tuned for various language-specific tasks. In this paper, we fine-tune mBERT specifically for the task of classifying correct Tamil words according to Tholkaappiyar's Meimayakkam rule in the Tamil language.

The transformer component within BERT operates like an attention mechanism, enabling it to grasp the contextual relationships between terms within a sentence. BERT utilizes the [CLS] token, also referred to as the classification token, to signify the start of a sentence. The final hidden state of this token is employed for sentence classification. The base model's embeddings comprise 768 hidden units. BERT's configuration model processes a sequence of words or tokens, up to a maximum length of 512, and generates an encoded representation with a dimensionality of 768. We have utilized the 'bert-base-multilingual-cased' version of BERT. Additionally, we employed the Adam optimizer with a learning rate of 0.00002 and trained the model for 5 epochs.

4   Meimayakkam_Classification Using_mBERT Models

There are nine types of Meimayakkam rules available, and we aim to classify them using mBERT. mBERT, short for Multilingual BERT, is a pre-trained language model suitable for a wide range of natural language processing tasks.

After applying mBERT for classification on the Meimayakkam rules, we obtained the following results: a classification accuracy of 97% for 'true' and 93% for 'false.' This indicates that our classification model correctly identified 97% of the rules as true and 93% as false, showcasing its effectiveness in distinguishing between the two categories.

This version provides a clearer and more detailed explanation of the context and results of the Meimayakkam rule classification using mBERT (Fig. 1 and Table 4).

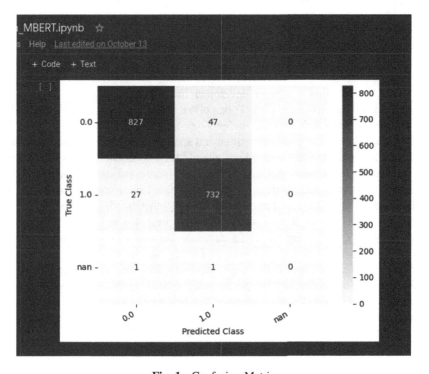

Fig. 1. Confusion Matrix

Table 4. mBERT Classification Report

	Precision	Recall	F1-Score	Support
False	0.97	0.95	0.96	874
True	0.94	0.96	0.95	759
NaN	0.00	0.00	0.00	2
Accuracy	-	-	0.95	1635
Macro Avg.	0.64	0.64	0.64	1635
Weighted Avg.	0.95	0.95	0.95	1635

In the initial stage of the experiment, both the rule-based and mBERT models produced similar accuracy levels. This suggests that they perform comparably when applied to the given task or dataset. However, the significant finding of the experiment is that, after subjecting the rule-based algorithm to a fine-tuning process, its performance improves significantly.

4.1   Tholkaappiyar Rule Set Android App Development

An Android application has been developed based on the linguistic principles of "Meimayakkam" as articulated by Tolkappiyar. This application aims to facilitate learning and teaching activities for students, specifically focusing on improving their Tamil language proficiency in both written and spoken forms. By inputting a word into the application, users can discover which rule of "Meimayakkam" the word adheres to.

For instance, if the word 'கற்க' ("kaRka") is entered, the application will indicate that it is a "correct word" ('சரியான சொல்') based on a specific rule outlined in "Meimayakkam" (as illustrated in Fig. 2). On the other hand, if the word 'கற்க்க' (kaRkka) is input instead, deviating from the rule presented in Fig. 2, the application will highlight it as a "wrong word" ('தவறான சொல்'). This innovative approach empowers students to grasp the nuances of Tamil grammar effectively.

While this creation represents a significant step forward, it is acknowledged that further research is needed to incorporate rules related to the language's syntactical structure. The inclusion of rules governing the beginnings and endings of words will enhance the application's ability to identify and rectify linguistic errors, thereby providing a more comprehensive learning experience for students.

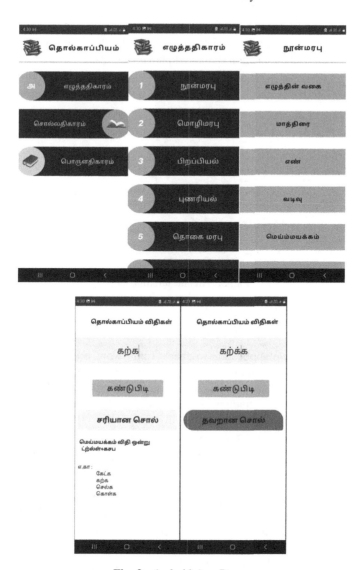

Fig. 2. Android App Pages

4.1.1 Architecture of the Application

The diagram below provides a clear illustration of the development process for the Tolkappiyam Android application described above (Fig. 3).

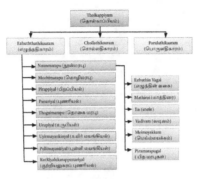

Fig. 3. Architecture diagram

5 Conclusion and Future Work

The creation of a mobile application to check Tamil word accuracy with the help of Tholkaappiyar's Meimayakkam principles is a worthwhile research endeavor that may assist users in ensuring proper linguistic usage. A multidimensional strategy is employed in this project, including language proficiency, adherence to grammatical standards, context awareness, and user-friendly design. This application should not be seen as a static project but rather as one that is continuously evolving. Maintaining its relevance and correctness in the constantly changing Tamil language environment requires ongoing development, frequent updates, and receptivity to user feedback.

Furthermore, by integrating this research on Tamil word accuracy into an Android app, you can enhance accessibility and mobile learning, providing users on the go with valuable tools. The app serves as a beneficial teaching tool with long-term effects due to its offline functionality possibilities and excellent user experience. Its relevance and reach within the Tamil-speaking community can be further increased through community involvement, localization, and strategic promotion.

This study is undertaken using the concepts of Tamil grammar mentioned in Tholkaappiyar's book. In the future, this study will be utilized to identify the proper Tamil grammatical sequence in which to write words. The Tholkaappiyar Meimayakkam guidelines will help us understand what comes before and after each letter in a word. This will be very helpful in ensuring that a Tamil word is spelled correctly and will allow us to determine if a word is spelled correctly or not.

References

1. Nedunchezhiyan, K.: Tholkappiyar period. https://newindian.activeboard.com/t59991225/topic-59991225/. Accessed 14 Oct 2023
2. Ttamil Oneindia Homepage. https://tamil.oneindia.com/art-culture/essays/2010/0429-tolkappiyar-tamil-literature.html. Accessed 14 Oct 2023
3. Durai, P.: Ilakkana Ayvadangal Ezhuthum Chollum (1). Annamalai University, Annamalai Nagar (1992)
4. Aravendan, R.: Tholkappiya Sirappugal, pp. 53–63. Kavya, Chennai (2013)
5. அட்டவணை:தொல்காப்பியம் நன்னூல்-எழுத்ததிகாரம்.pdf. (2023). செப்டம்பர் 6). விக்கிமூலம். Retrieved 04:06, அக்டோபர் 16, 2023. https://tinyurl.com/2kssf2kv. Accessed 14 Oct 2023
6. மெய்ம்மயக்கம். (2023, அக்டோபர் 9). விக்கிப்பீடியா. Retrieved 04:00, அக்டோபர் 16, 2023. https://tinyurl.com/4bupy49d. Accessed 14 Oct 2023
7. அட்டவணை:1941 AD-தொல்காப்பியம்-எழுத்ததிகாரம், இளம்பூரணம்-வ. உ. சிதம்பரம் பிள்ளை.pdf. (2023, செப்டம்பர் 7). விக்கிமூலம். Retrieved 04:12, 04:12, அக்டோபர் 16, 2023. https://tinyurl.com/bdh6mxc8. Accessed 14 Oct 2023
8. அட்டவணை:1847 AD-தொல்காப்பியம், எழுத்ததிகாரம்-நச்சினார்க்கினி-மகாலிங்கையர்-வீரபத்திரை.pdf. (2023, செப்டம்பர் 7). விக்கிமூலம். Retrieved 04:13, அக்டோபர் 16, 2023. https://tinyurl.com/5chw7wev. Accessed 14 Oct 2023
9. "அட்டவணை:1847 AD-தொல்காப்பியம், எழுத்ததிகாரம்-நச்சினார்க்கினி-மகாலிங்கையர்-வீரபத்திரை.pdf." விக்கிமூலம். 7. செப் 2023, 02:28 UTC. 16 அக் 2023, 04:13. https://tinyurl.com/3b49rhat. Accessed 14 Oct 2023
10. அட்டவணை:தொல்காப்பியம் எழுத்ததிகாரம்.pdf. (2023, மார்ச் 21). விக்கிமூலம். Retrieved 04:14, அக்டோபர் 16, 2023. https://tinyurl.com/3hf7h2wd. Accessed 14 Oct 2023
11. அட்டவணை:1928 AD-தொல்காப்பியம்-எழுத்ததிகாரம், இளம்பூரணம்-வ. உ. சிதம்பரம் பிள்ளை-வேலாயுதம்பிரஸ்.pdf. (2023, செப்டம்பர் 7). விக்கிமூலம். Retrieved 04:15, அக்டோபர் 16, 2023. https://tinyurl.com/57emjjwe. Accessed 14 Oct 2023
12. அட்டவணை:1928 AD-தொல்காப்பியம்-எழுத்ததிகாரம், இளம்பூரணம்-வ. உ. சி-அகஸ்தியர்பிரஸ்.pdf. (2023, செப்டம்பர் 7). விக்கிமூலம். Retrieved 04:15, அக்டோபர் 16, 2023. https://tinyurl.com/59dv6nhe. Accessed 14 Oct 2023
13. Agesthialingom, S.: Tholkappiyar's treatment of Syntax, paper read at the Seminar on Grammatical Theories in Tamil. Annamalai University, Annamalainagar (1966)
14. Agesthialingom, S.: Tholkappiyar's concept of Syntax. In: Agesthialingom, S., Kumaraswami Raja, N. (eds.) pp. 1–22 (1978)
15. Agesthialingom, S., Balasubramanian, K. (eds.): ilakkana a:yvu-k-atturaikal-1, Annamalai University, Annamalainagar (1974a)
16. Agesthialingom, S., Balasubramanian, K.: tamil ilakkana marapu (Tamil grammatical tradition) in ilakkana a:yvu-k-atturaikal - 1. Annamalai Univer sity, Annamalainagar (1974b)
17. Agesthialingom, S., Murugaiyan, K. (eds.): Tholka:ppiya moliyiyal. Annamalai University, Annamalainagar (1972)
18. Agesthialingom, S., Kumaraswami Raja N. (eds.): Studies in Early Dravidian Grammars. Annamalai University, Annamalainagar (1978)

19. Ananthanarayana, H.S.: The Karaka theory and case grammar. Indian Linguist. **31**, 14–27 (1970)
20. Ananthanarayana, H.S.: Four lectures on Panini's Asta:dhya:yi.. Annamalai University, Annamalainagar, Tholka:ppiyam, Collatika:ram. Part 1. Arul Accakam, Palayamkottai (1976)
21. Arunachalam, P.: Tholkappiyar. Tamilputtaka:layam, Madras (1975)
22. Tamil Santhi Checker App for Android Phone Thendral, S., Subhashni, R., Madhan Karky, V., Rajaraman, S. https://www.ijitee.org/wp-content/uploads/papers/v8i6s/F60250486S19. pdf. Accessed 14 Oct 2023
23. A Rule-Based Grammar and Spell Checking. https://papers.ssrn.com/sol3/papers.cfm?abstract_id=4139315. Accessed 14 Oct 2023
24. Sarves Github Homepage. https://sarves.github.io/thamizhi-morph/. Accessed 14 Oct 2023
25. acaemiahttps. www.academia.edu/38021834/WHITE_PAPER_ON_TECHNOLOGICAL_DEVELOPMENT_OF_TAMIL. Accessed 14 Oct 2023
26. ResearchGate Homepage. https://www.researchgate.net/publication/326415993_Morphological_parsing_on_Tolkappiyam%27s_perspective. Accessed 14 Oct 2023
27. ICTACTjournals Homepage. https://ictactjournals.in/paper/IJSC_Vol_11_Iss_1_Paper_9_2237_2243.pdf. Accessed 14 Oct 2023
28. Sarveswaran, K.: Computational Challenges with Tamil Complex Predicates (2020)
29. ResearchGate Homepage. https://www.researchgate.net/publication/333563281_Tamil_Santhi_checker_app_for_android_phone. Accessed 14 Oct 2023
30. Deivasundaram, N.: Mozhiyum Thamizh Ilakkanamum. Amutha Nilaiyam, Chennai (2021)
31. Internet Archive Homepage. https://archive.org/details/vvv_20200723. Accessed 14 Oct 2023
32. Thamizhannal, Tholkappiyam Mulamum Karutthuraiyam. Meenachi Puthaga Nilaiyam, Madurai (2008)
33. Suyambu, P.: Ilakkana Nuulkalil Karuttun Valarcci. International Institute of Tamil Studies, Chennai (2004)
34. Agesthialingom, S.: Tholkappiyar's treatment of syntax. In: A:ra:ycci, vol. 1, pp. 238–248 (1969)

Author Index

Printed in the United States
by Baker & Taylor Publisher Services